PRINCIPLES
AND METHODS
OF SECONDARY
EDUCATION

PRINCIPLES AND METHODS OF SECONDARY EDUCATION

JAMES MICHAEL LEE

Graduate Department of Education
University of Notre Dame

McGRAW-HILL BOOK COMPANY, INC.
New York   San Francisco   Toronto   London

PRINCIPLES AND METHODS OF SECONDARY EDUCATION

TO MY MOTHER
ESTEEMED BY HER COLLEAGUES AND STUDENTS
AS AN OUTSTANDING SECONDARY SCHOOL TEACHER

PREFACE

Principles and Methods of Secondary Education is intended primarily for use in Catholic colleges preparing students for teaching in both public and Catholic secondary schools and in Religious houses of study preparing sisters and brothers for teaching in Catholic high schools. It should also prove to be of considerable value to in-service teachers, both lay and Religious.

It would seem that there is a great need for this textbook. To date there is none in its field which offers the Catholic dimension. Indeed most textbooks from which Catholic college students have studied embody a Materialistic philosophy, and thus have not only failed to present them with the Catholic dimension but actually have attacked it. This book attempts to provide a thorough integration of Catholic doctrine with sound pedagogical theory and practice. Catholic teaching is shot through every phase of it. The best of Catholic sources, classic as well as contemporary, are used not only in separate treatments of public and Catholic high schools but also in a consideration of the common problems confronting both. Proper attention is devoted to the problems and issues in Catholic secondary schools, since a portion of the students using this book (especially the Religious) will teach in Catholic institutions. Also it is hoped that such a treatment will motivate more of the students in our Catholic colleges to teach in Catholic high schools. The need for lay teachers in Catholic high schools will increase sharply in the next decade.

However, this book is not narrowly Catholic. To provide maximum breadth and depth it also includes contributions from non-Catholic educational theory and practice. All truth is from the Holy Spirit, and no book can be Catholic if it is not catholic. The student, if he is to become a superior teacher, must possess the total view. Furthermore, this textbook offers the student more than a superficial analysis of the problems, issues, and practices in secondary education. It endeavors constantly to relate both principles and methods to their philosophical, theological, psychological, and sociological bases. The documentation of statements aims to be thorough so that the student will be able to probe even more deeply what he is studying.

Whenever possible the comparative approach to problems is utilized, e.g., the three contrasting positions on the proximate purpose of the Catholic high school, the three chief counseling theories, the four major views on curricular design. Only through a comparative analysis can the student adequately grasp why a problem or controversy exists. Besides, this approach leads to a more meaningful solution to the problem. Nevertheless a comparative analysis does not preclude the author from preferring one theory or viewpoint over others. When I do express a preference I attempt to support my position with theoretical and empirical evidence. However, the other viewpoints are also thoroughly documented in order that the student or in-service teacher may examine these theories as presented by the best of their proponents.

This textbook endeavors to raise to even higher levels the quality of secondary school teaching. Therefore the strengths and weaknesses of both public and Catholic secondary schools are treated in a forthright manner. To this are added proposed solutions for increasing the strengths and eradicating the weaknesses. Recognition of the need for improvement is crucial to progress.

Stylistically, *Principles and Methods of Secondary Education* combines the thought-provoking essay style with the enumeration style found in review books. The enumeration style enables the book to pack a great deal of information within its covers, but even more importantly, it provides the student with a pedagogically sound and simple method of retaining the information.

A definite effort was made to provide more information in this book than can be found in any other comparable work in its field. It presents features not covered in other books on principles and methods, viz., principles of teacher counseling, extended treatment of motivational theory and technique, pedagogical procedures such as the case method and cell technique. It also includes more empirical evidence and other research data than do existing works.

The decision to combine two separate but integrally related books, "Principles of Secondary Education" and "Methods of Secondary Education," into one, *Principles and Methods of Secondary Education*, was made because many Catholic colleges themselves combine the "Principles" and "Methods" courses into a single, one-semester offering. Those colleges whose teacher-training programs provide for two distinct courses will find the unified approach, which this single, combination-type textbook affords, to be of significant help in enabling the student to see the two courses as an integrated whole.

While it is impossible for the author to thank everyone who helped him in one way or another to write this textbook, certain persons must be mentioned for their significant assistance. The administration of St.

Joseph College (Connecticut) made schedule modifications which facilitated research and writing. Sister Marie Celine, the St. Joseph College Librarian, was of great help in locating books, allocating a research study, and providing all sorts of help. Mention must also be made of the "architect's chair" in this research study. Miss Patricia Berberich of the St. Joseph College Library Staff, and Mr. Norman Wadham of the Teachers College Library, Columbia University, were of invaluable assistance in locating research materials. Professor Robert W. Strickler, Head of the Department of Education at the University of Notre Dame, provided encouragement at a time when it was most needed. Professor Edward P. Mahoney, my dear friend, was always on hand to express confidence and provide continual encouragement. Professor Frances Kinsellar of the St. Joseph College faculty read the manuscript and made many helpful suggestions. Fr. Charles A. Curran of the Graduate Department of Psychology at Loyola University (Chicago) examined the chapter on Guidance and Discipline. Professor Frances F. Kline of the Graduate Department of Education, Fordham University, offered constructive comments on several chapters. Mr. Richard DuFour was of great help during the final stages of production. Carol, my very dear wife, made many sacrifices during the period of writing. Finally, I must acknowledge my greatest debt of all to Professor Bernard J. Kohlbrenner, CSE Consulting Editor, for his patience, good humor, scholarship, and invaluable revisional suggestions.

James Michael Lee

CONTENTS

PART 1 PRINCIPLES OF
SECONDARY
EDUCATION

CHAPTER I A SHORT HISTORY OF AMERICAN SECONDARY EDUCATION

Secondary education existed in America almost from its founding. But because secondary schools, like all other educational institutions, are established to satisfy certain needs and aspirations of society, their forms and goals have shifted as society has shifted. America of 1690, overwhelmingly agricultural, needed adolescents on the farms rather than in high schools. Coming from continental nations which possessed little or none of the democratic spirit, the colonists considered postelementary schooling fit only for those who would eventually assume posts in the theological or magisterial aristocracy. America of today is quite different from the America of 1690, and this difference is reflected in modern secondary schools. Our advanced technological society needs highly literate workers, men and women who will score scientific and cultural breakthroughs. America's expanding concept of democracy carries with it the responsibility of education for all as far as their intellectual abilities can take them, for only in this way can there eventuate that type of intelligent citizenry necessary both for the continuation of this country's progress and for greater personal development. The latter is, of course, the more important and more basic task of secondary education.

To condemn early American secondary schools because they were not similar to those of today is both to miss the point and to be guilty of historical anachronism. Civilization is a cultural organism, and like any organism, it grows slowly. In any growth, the succeeding stage is an advance over the preceding one, else there is no growth. Indeed without the first stage there would be no second, without the first and second, no third, and so forth. To condemn early American schools for being early American and not modern is equivalent to condemning an adolescent for being an adolescent and not an adult. Nevertheless one can and indeed should be critical of those modern schools which are still colonial, just as one may rightly criticize an adult who is still adolescent. A mature approach to the history of American secondary education is thus imperative. Contemporary high school education can be ever so much more appreciated and improved if one realizes the centuries of growth and development which took place before it finally evolved into what it is today. Such growth and development were a necessary condition for its very existence. Every stage of this growth made positive contributions which must be neither forgotten nor neglected.

A GENERAL VIEW

The changes in American secondary education during the past 350 years can be placed in five broad groupings. (1) *More utilitarian.* From the early New England emphasis on preparation for college via the classical curriculum, there gradually evolved, first by means of popular demand and then by professional investigation, the modern American high school with its goal of preparation for life activities via a broad plan of general and specialized education. (2) *Less religious.* From the early colonial conception of the secondary school as an institution to deepen religious faith and prepare divinity students, there gradually evolved by means of the spread of secular thought and national exigencies the notion of the role of the modern American high school as an institution which educates citizens for deep personal living in a democratic society. (3) *More humane.* From the harsh discipline and difficult physical conditions to which students in colonial New England secondary schools were subjected, there gradually evolved by means of psychological investigations and philosophical considerations a methodology and physical plant based on a humane conception of pupil nature and needs. (4) *More democratic.* From the excessive authoritarianism in administrator-teacher and teacher-pupil relationship which characterized early American secondary schools, there gradually evolved by means of agitation by educational theorists a greater and freer participation by teachers and students in the planning and management of classroom affairs. (5) *More professional.* From the role of the teacher in early American secondary schools as schoolkeeper, and of education as an instinctive process, there gradually evolved by means of the prodding of teachers' associations an awareness of the teacher as a dynamic educational motivator–leader and of education as an art–science.

SECONDARY EDUCATION IN COLONIAL AMERICA (1635–1789)

The Latin Grammar School

History. The Latin Grammar School was the first type of American secondary school. It was not a colonial invention, but rather was borrowed directly from the contemporary English educational system. Indeed there was an extensive network of Latin Grammar Schools in England by the beginning of the seventeenth century. The vastness of this network can be grasped when it is realized that at this time there was a total of 361 such schools in England, that is to say, 1 school for every 12,500 of the population.[1] While the Latin Grammar Schools in England were primarily for the sons of the wealthy, nonetheless, promising young "scholars" from the lower and middle classes were afforded admittance and even subsidized. The immediate impetus to the establishment of similar schools in the Colonies came from the Massachusetts Education Law of 1647, which required all towns of 100 or more families to establish and maintain a Latin Grammar School. This law, however, was often evaded and breached by various towns. A further stimulus to the founding of Latin Grammar Schools came from the entrance requirements of Harvard College and the English universities, all of which were open only to pupils who were proficient in Latin, Greek, and other subjects taught in the Latin Grammar School. Nevertheless, there can be no question that the Latin Grammar School was far less popular than the elementary schools.

Purpose. The immediate purpose of the Latin Grammar School was preparation for college. Hence, it was regarded as an important stage in the preparation of ministers and public officials. Since the church was closely allied to the state in the Europe and America of that era, it may be said that the overarching purpose of the Latin Grammar School was religious. It was intended to perpetuate and further the City of God and the City of Man.

[1] J. Howard Brown, *Elizabethan Schooldays: An Account of the English Grammar School in the Second Half of the Sixteenth Century.* (Oxford: Blackwell, 1933), p. 7.

Curriculum. The course of studies in the Latin Grammar Schools was classicoreligious, and followed very closely the curricula of their sister institutions in England. There was a seven-year curriculum, with pupils being admitted at an age several years younger than high school freshmen of today. The first three years were spent memorizing a beginning Latin book. This was supplemented with exercise in Latin grammar. The following three years were occupied with the study of Latin literature, close attention being given to careful examination of the works of Ovid, Cicero, and Vergil. In the concluding year, the young "scholars" began to study Greek and to read the New Testament in Latin and Greek. The students also constructed Latin verse and even dialogues.[2] The curriculum was quite inflexible, since it was designed for college preparation, and the college curriculum did not change or alter.

Students. The pupils in a Latin Grammar School came predominantly but not exclusively from the wealthier classes. The Calvinistic conception of the depravity of man meant severe classroom control and discipline. Whippings were not uncommon. The students sat on uncomfortable benches called "forms" in postures of strict attention. The interests of the pupils were regarded as of no importance. Very little opportunity was afforded for relaxation or recreation. School hours were long, lasting roughly from dawn to dusk.

Teachers. Latin Grammar School masters were usually not the most skillful or enthusiastic. Frequently the schoolmaster taught while awaiting appointment as a minister. Until some Colonies eventually outlawed the practice, local ministers also served as the teachers in many town Grammar Schools. In any event, it was the local minister who granted the license to teach. He was also responsible for school supervision, especially to see that sound doctrine was being taught. Town officials usually made periodic inspection tours of the school. No emphasis was placed on educational methods or on understanding education as a process; knowledge of subject matter was deemed sufficient. Notwithstanding, some colonial teachers were men of great learning and considerable pedagogical skill, e.g., Ezekiel Cheever.[3]

Support. The Latin Grammar Schools received less public support than did the elementary schools. They were supported and maintained through a combination of public funds and private contributions. However, many towns which should have maintained these schools failed to do so.

----

[2] This was the curriculum of the Boston Latin School; other colonial Latin Grammar Schools did not always come up to these high standards. Cf. Samuel Eliot Morison, *The Puritan Pronoas.* (New York: New York University Press, 1936), pp. 101–103.

[3] See Elizabeth Gould, *Ezekiel Cheever, Schoolmaster.* (Boston: Palmer, 1904).

The English Grammar School

History. In the first half of the eighteenth century, the American Colonies started to become increasingly active in commerce. As a result there arose a demand for knowledge of practical subjects, such as bookkeeping and foreign languages. Growth in commerce also gave impetus to new intellectual interests in areas such as the history and geography of foreign lands. Commerce provided the colonists with greater wealth, and wealth afforded people the leisure to pursue cultural interests. The demand grew for secondary schools which could provide instruction in practical as well as cultural subjects. The Latin Grammar Schools, with their rigid classical curricula, could not rise to this demand. Consequently, private educational entrepreneurs opened their own schools to meet this need. These private secondary schools became known as English Grammar Schools.[4]

Purpose. The English Grammar School was intended to provide capable and interested citizens with the type of education they wanted, to help them occupationally and personally. Its purpose was entirely secular and in no way religious.

Curriculum. The curriculum was flexible, and based on the needs and wants of the pupils. Since the students were more heterogeneous than were those in the Latin Grammar School, so was the curriculum. The curriculum of the English Grammar School was two-edged, viz., practical, learning how to make a living, and liberal, learning how to live. Commercial subjects, such as bookkeeping, accounting, and business letter writing, were popular. Geometry and trigonometry were taught as aids to a better knowledge of civil engineering. Instruction in foreign languages was given to those who needed it for their overseas commercial ventures. Music, dancing, fencing, and painting were taught to persons interested in assuming roles among the more educated and cultured members of society. English grammar was taught to nearly all students. Spelling word lists, grammar rules, and reading exercises, all found in textbooks such as Dilworth's *A New Guide to the English Tongue* were incorporated into the course in English grammar.

Students. Girls as well as boys were welcomed to the English Grammar Schools. Sometimes they were grouped in the same classroom; at other times, they were separated. Often the classes consisted of older people as well as youths. Classes were scheduled at times convenient for the students, e.g., in the early morning or late afternoon to accommodate those who worked. Discipline was not very severe for two reasons: First, the teachers were not too Calvinistic; second (and more important), the

---

[4] R. Freeman Butts and Lawrence A. Cremin, *A History of Education in American Culture.* (New York: Holt, 1953), pp. 124–126.

pupils would desert the school and go to another if harsh discipline were enforced. It must be remembered that these schools were private and, hence, competitive, with the "customer" being wooed rather than whipped.

Teachers. English Grammar School masters were relatively skilled in the subjects they taught. Sometimes college graduates gave instruction in these schools. Because they worked in a private school, teachers were not obliged to be licensed, a practice which now and then accounted for poor teaching. No emphasis was placed on educational methods or education as a process. Nonetheless, the teachers constantly endeavored to stress the practical application of the material they taught. A negative check on instruction was also present in that students were free to desert the classes of a poor teacher.

Support. English Grammar Schools were financed entirely by the tuition of the students. To this end, schools and teachers alike placed advertisements on behalf of their educational offerings in the local newspapers. Judging from the frequency and claims of these advertisements, English Grammar Schools were probably both popular and numerous.

The Academy

History. The Academy came into existence as a result of concrete proposals made by Benjamin Franklin in the middle of the eighteenth century. These proposals were not altogether new, since in the first half of the century, New York, Charleston, and a few other cities had established schools which resembled the later Academy. Franklin's ideas for an Academy included the following: (1) A new type of public secondary school should be established, the purpose of which should be strictly utilitarian, viz., vocational training and preparation for real life. (2) This school should be called "Academy." (3) The curriculum should be secular, not religious. (4) Good manners and ethical conduct should be cardinal goals of the Academy. Knowledge was not its own end but was important in that it helped people to live a more fruitful life. (5) The school program should be based on the teachings of the philosophers of the French Enlightenment and the British Empirical School. Thus school life should be pleasant and attractive, with a large garden, a library full of books and scientific apparatus, cheerful classrooms, and so forth. (6) The most important single subject in the Academy should be the English language, its appreciation, and use. (7) Creative expression should be fostered by the arts classes. (8) The natural sciences should be included in the curriculum, supplemented with practical apparatus for experimentation. (9) History and geography should be

included to acquaint the students with the cultures of other lands. (10)
The classics should be offered for those who wished to study them.[5]

Franklin's Academy in Philadelphia was a pioneer institution, but it
was not long before Academies mushroomed all over the Colonies. These
Academies were in the main based on Franklin's proposals with, however,
two notable exceptions: First, they included religious as well as secular
elements; and second, the classical department dominated the Academy
through the close of the colonial period. English Grammar Schools tended
to disappear in favor of the Academies, which were founded on a more
permanent basis. Being more democratic, more humane, and less exclusive than the Latin Grammar School, the Academy was a significant
advance in the evolving history of the modern comprehensive high
school.

Purpose. The intention of the Academy was to combine the practi-
cal-cultural approach of the English Grammar School with the classical
emphasis of the Latin Grammar School, all in one institution. In this
way post-elementary school education would easily be provided for all
who were willing and competent. The Academy was to be a terminal
institution, although the graduates from its classical school could go on
to college.

Curriculum. The course of studies in the Academy followed the
lines of Franklin's proposals, with the exceptions previously noted.

Students. The students at the Academy were primarily drawn from
the middle classes, since children of the upper classes went to the Latin
Grammar Schools. Later some Academies were developed exclusively for
girls. Discipline was more relaxed than in the Latin Grammar School, but
not so relaxed as in the English Grammar School. Classes were held
during the day, as they were intended for youths.

Teachers. The instructors in the classical department were generally
college graduates; however, the opposite was true in the English and
mathematics departments. As in the other colonial secondary schools,
the teaching was frequently inferior in quality.

Support. The Academy was intended to be a publicly supported institution, but in fact it was not completely so. State, county, and town
governments encouraged and often chartered Academies, and at times
even gave financial or land grants to them. These grants had to be supplemented by private tuition, endowments, and fund-raising activities.
Some Academies were founded and supported by religious denominations.

[5] Benjamin Franklin, "Observations Relative to the Intentions of the Original
Founders of the Academy in Philadelphia," in Jared Sparks (ed.), *The Works of
Benjamin Franklin.* (Boston: Hilliard, Gray, 1836), vol. II, pp. 133–142; cf. also
Thomas Woody, *Educational Views of Benjamin Franklin.* (New York: McGraw-Hill,
1931).

Apprenticeship

One of the most common forms of secondary education in colonial America, particularly for poor boys and orphans, was apprenticeship. Under this system a formal contract was signed between the youth and the master. Apprenticeship often continued for boys and girls up to twenty-one and eighteen years of age, respectively. Apprenticeship consisted in both learning the trade of the master, e.g., coopering, weaving, and acquiring some intellectual skills, notably reading, writing, and religion. Laws in some Colonies increasingly provided for vocational as well as intellectual schooling. While the intellectual education the apprentices received from their masters was on the elementary school level, the vocational training was of secondary school calibre, and indeed not too dissimilar from the education in our modern vocational high schools.[6]

Catholic Secondary Schools

History. In the colonial period, Catholics numbered 1 per cent or less of the total population of the Colonies. Furthermore, they were directly or indirectly persecuted in practically every Colony, with the exception of Pennsylvania and, for a short time, Maryland and Rhode Island. Not until the adoption of the Federal Constitution in 1789 did Catholics acquire any widespread civil and religious freedom. Because of these difficulties, only two Catholic secondary schools were established during this period.[7] Both were founded by the English Jesuits, who more than any other single group may be said to have laid the foundation of Catholic education in America. Both schools were small, and neither was long-lived. The first Catholic secondary school in the English-speaking Colonies was established at Newton, Maryland, in 1677. About twenty-five years later the school was closed owing to renewed persecutions of the Catholics in Maryland. The second such school was opened in 1744 at Bohemia, Maryland, near friendly Pennsylvania. By reason of the intolerance of the colonial government, it was begun clandestinely. It persevered under difficult conditions until 1765 when it closed its doors. Others, including zealous laymen, tried to open up more Catholic secondary schools, but their efforts failed.

[6] See M. W. Jernegan, *Laboring and Dependent Classes in Colonial America, 1607–1783.* (Chicago: University of Chicago Press, 1931); also Robert F. Seybolt, *Apprenticeship and Apprenticeship Education in Colonial New England and New York.* (New York: Teachers College, Columbia University, 1916).

[7] This treatment refers only to Catholic secondary schools in English-speaking Colonies. The first secondary school established in what is now the United States was founded by Catholics in St. Augustine, Fla., in 1606, twenty-nine years before the Boston Latin School opened its doors. Cf. J. A. Burns, C.S.C., *The Principles, Origin and Establishment of the Catholic School System in the United States.* (New York: Benziger, 1912), p. 145.

Purpose. The immediate end of these two schools was preparation for college, with the pupils intended for higher education in European Catholic colleges, particularly St. Omer's. The alert Jesuits hoped also that these schools would be stepping-stones to a system of Catholic secondary education in America. Education in the humanities and classics, in which the Jesuits have always excelled, was also a cardinal purpose. Naturally the principal and overarching purpose of these schools was religiously oriented education.

Curriculum. The curriculum of these schools was classicoreligious. However, history and algebra were also included.

Students. Not much is known of the discipline, learning conditions, etc., in these institutions, because they did not wish to attract the attention of their hostile neighbors. In all probability, learning conditions resembled those of their European counterparts. Inasmuch as the two schools were primarily for boarders, the class hours were presumably long. These schools were patronized by some of the leading Catholic families in Maryland. Charles Carroll of Carrollton, a signer of the Declaration of Independence, and Daniel Carroll, father of the first American archbishop, were among the students at Bohemia. The teachers felt that the scholastic attainments of the students were high, everything considered.

Teachers. The faculty was very small, consisting of two teachers each at Newton and Bohemia. All four were Jesuits. The faculty was quite learned; probably they were the most learned group of secondary school teachers in all the Colonies.

Support. The schools were supported solely by the students' tuitions, occasional grants from Catholic laymen, and, of course, the Jesuits' own efforts.

SECONDARY EDUCATION IN THE YOUNG REPUBLIC (1789–1865)

History. The Latin Grammar School, chief institution for secondary education in colonial America, faded fast during this period, and by the Civil War had almost disappeared. Its place was taken by the Academy —so much so, in fact, that this period has often been referred to as the "age of the Academy." To be sure, Academies were being established as rapidly as the ever-increasing demand for them. By 1850 there were probably over six thousand such schools with a total enrollment of a quarter million pupils.[8] Most college students were Academy graduates.

It was, however, during this period that the free public high school

[8] Butts and Cremin, *op. cit.*, p. 239.

was born in America. Perhaps its earliest beginnings can be found in the "Bill for the More General Diffusion of Knowledge" introduced into the Virginia Legislature in 1779. Jefferson, the author of this bill, proposed a state-operated network of secondary schools in Virginia. The financially able pupils would pay tuition, while the state would completely subsidize the needy students, provided they were academically promising. The schools would be supervised by a public board of examiners who would periodically visit the schools, appoint teachers, and in general, direct school policy. The curriculum would be college preparatory and thoroughly secular. Jefferson's purpose in introducing this bill was to develop a better citizenry through education. The bill was defeated by the Legislature; however, it laid the intellectual groundwork for a new system of American secondary education.

The inception of the free public secondary school in America occurred in 1821 with the founding of the Boston English Classical High School for Boys. This institution, the first of its kind in America, was founded because of popular demand for a secondary school which was at once free, public, and practically oriented. Boston was becoming increasingly commercial, and workers possessing commercial skills were sorely needed in the area. Neither the Latin Grammar School nor the Academy could satisfy these demands, particularly for the poorer youths. Thus the public high school was born. But the real impetus to this type of school came in 1827 when Massachusetts enacted a law requiring all towns with more than five hundred families to erect a free public high school in their community.

During this period, an increasing number of educational and political thinkers began to feel that the free, public elementary schools which were coming into widespread existence were wedded to a system of private, not public, secondary schools, viz., the Academies. These thinkers believed that America required leaders from all classes and that the contemporary dual educational system neglected schooling of the needy, no matter how promising these young people might be. Thus, in 1839 Henry Barnard's First Annual Report to the Connecticut Board of Education recommended the establishment of free public secondary schools for the "common benefit of society." Correlative to these thoughts and writings of educational leaders, there began to appear about 1830 mounting pressure by the citizenry, particularly the city dwellers, for free public secondary schools. Slowly but surely these demands were heeded, so that by 1860 the Census reported the existence of about three hundred free public high schools in America.[9]

[9] Merle Curti, *The Social Ideas of American Educators.* (Paterson, N.J.: Littlefield, Adams, 1959), pp. 139–168.

Arguments raged pro and con concerning the advisability of establishing free public high schools. The three chief arguments for their founding were: (1) Public support of high schools would also mean public control, and this control would perforce make the secondary schools directly responsive to public and local needs and wants. (2) A lack of free public secondary schools would deprive America of the future leadership of promising youths whose parents were unable to afford the expense of a private high school. (3) Democracy means equality of opportunity, and this implies that every youth should be provided with as much education as his abilities will allow, irrespective of ability to pay. The three principal objections voiced by opponents of free public high schools were: (1) Education is basically a private, not a public, function. (2) Only a comparatively few pupils were really fit for postelementary education. (3) Secondary education at public expense would impose too high a tax burden and hence would be injurious to the American economy. As it happened, there were four chief factors which *de facto* hindered the expansion of the free public high school, namely, competition from the Academy, opposition from taxpayer groups, lack of sufficient funds in most localities, and lack of public interest.

Informal secondary education became quite popular among youths at this time, particularly among youths who were not obtaining a formal secondary school education. The Lyceum Movement, inaugurated in 1826 in Massachusetts, sponsored lectures and forum discussions on a wide variety of social, cultural, and agricultural topics. Lyceums, as well as the many public libraries started during this period, were widely patronized by both young people and adults. Apprenticeship was still quite common for the poorer youth. In general, nonschool educative agencies began to assume considerable importance during this period. Their role was not one to be overlooked.

Purpose. The aim of the Latin Grammar School did not change. The cardinal goals of the Academy remained the same as during the preceding age, namely, first to inculcate in the pupils the principles and practices of ethical doctrine (i.e., those elements of piety and morality common to all religious denominations), and second, to afford the pupils a wide range of practical and cultural knowledge. The purpose of the free public high school was to afford to *every* competent youth the opportunity of a comprehensive education, studying whatever subjects or skills both he and the community chose. The overarching purpose of this school was education for more effective citizenship. The emphasis was both practical and secular.

Curriculum. While the curriculum of the Latin Grammar School continued substantially unchanged, it did broaden somewhat, with the inclusion in the curriculum of several new subjects, including English grammar, geography, and mathematical studies. The Academy curriculum remained as wide as student demand. It made considerable growth in natural science offerings. Experimentation with laboratory apparatus began to come into use. The curricular flexibility of the Academy can be seen from the fact that, between 1826 and 1840, 100 new subjects were introduced into the Academies of New York. Indeed the standard number of subjects offered in New York Academies in 1828 was 50.[10] Military Academies grew and flourished during this period, indicating a new curricular direction. Between 1830 and 1850, under the influence of the Swiss educator Fellenberg and his American disciples, such as Neef, there arose a strong movement to include manual training in the Academy curriculum. The benefits of manual training, as advanced by its promoters, were that it helped to form character, foster good health, and inculcate desirable habits of work. This type of curriculum, advocated as early as the fifth century by St. Benedict and even earlier by certain educators of antiquity, fell out of favor after 1850, and the strict academic tradition prevailed.

The curriculum of the free public high schools aped that of the Academy, and this was natural since these new schools were intended to provide Academy education free of charge. It is interesting to note that the curriculum of the Boston English Classical High School, which was quite typical, included not only history, speech, mathematics, English, and science but also courses in Christian apologetics, natural theology, and moral philosophy. This indicates that the public high schools of this period were more overtly mindful at least in the formal sense of the moral and ethical role of the school than are many of their modern counterparts.

The curricula of the Academy and free public high school, while oriented toward the practical, nevertheless, did not provide direct practical or vocational experiences such as are offered in the commercial and vocational departments in modern high schools. The pupils generally learned *about* these things, i.e., they studied about them from books rather than doing them in the classroom.

Students. Pupil life in the Latin Grammar School and the Academy was much the same as it had been in the preceding period. However, some of the more severe conditions in the Latin Grammar School were relaxed somewhat. In the free public high schools which imitated their Boston exemplar, the average age for admission was twelve. At first the normal curriculum was of three years' duration, but later in the period

---

[10] Newton Edwards and Herman G. Richey, *The School in the American Social Order.* (Boston: Houghton Mifflin, 1947), pp. 275–278.

this was increased to four. In other matters, student life was generally in a similar situation to that of the Academy.

Teachers. Departments in most Academies and high schools consisted of one teacher; still this was an advance over the colonial period when a single teacher would give all the instruction in several departments. The school officials as well as the public felt that the prime requisites for a teacher were morality and religious orthodoxy in preference to scholarship and teaching skill, and instructors were hired accordingly. Textbooks increased as the years passed. Teaching was largely a direct teacher-pupil confrontation, with very little recourse to materials in workbooks, libraries, and other ancillary resources. The use of the monitorial or Lancastrian system of teaching (whereby one teacher instructed a group of monitors, usually the brighter pupils, who in turn instructed groups of students in the class) was characteristic more of elementary than secondary education. The most important advance came in the areas of teacher training and professionalization. These began slowly, but by the end of the period there were some normal schools, professional journals, and even a National Teachers Association. These three developments were originally confined to the elementary school level, but by the end of the period, they were beginning to influence secondary education. There were two chief reasons for this. First, Academies had in effect become primarily private schools and as such did not have to account to the public; hence there was little interest in licensing or standardizing teaching. Second, advocates of the free public high schools were too concerned about getting the idea accepted by the populace to worry about teaching standards.

Support. The chief difference between the Academy and the free public high school was that of support and control, i.e., private and public. By the end of this period, the free public high school was definitely established as an integral part of the common school system supported by public funds. Hence a definite dual system of secondary education, the private and the public high school, arose. This system remains today.

The Catholic Secondary School

History. In general, the growth of Catholic secondary education in this period paralleled the development of the Church, i.e., where the Church flourished so did Catholic education, and where the Church was persecuted from without or rent by dissensions from within, Catholic education did not prosper. The first Catholic secondary school in this period was established at Georgetown, Maryland, in 1789 by the Jesuits. Indeed, most of the earliest Catholic secondary schools in this period were combined secondary schools and colleges. By the Civil War there were about sixty Catholic colleges in America, all offering secondary education. These sixty were fairly scattered throughout the country and formed the nucleus of Catholic secondary education in this age. Aiding the cause of American Catholic education was the political turmoil in Europe, notably around 1848, which caused many teaching Religious to emigrate to the United States. These Religious opened up Catholic elementary and secondary schools in almost every part of the country. Often strong prejudice from unsympathetic non-Catholic neighbors had to be overcome in the founding of these schools. Catholics were pioneers in girls academies; there were at least five in existence before the first such secular institution was founded in America.

Purpose. The proximate goals of Catholic secondary education were to provide the pupils with a liberal education (as European Catholic humanists of that age conceived it) and to prepare them for college. The close relationships between Catholic secondary schools and colleges of the day clearly demonstrate this. The aim of the girls academies was to fit the students to take their places in society. This society was most often conceived of as the society of pre-Revolutionary France, a vanished era; hence, this education was not completely adequate in terms of contemporary American life. Running throughout all Catholic secondary education was, of course, the primary religious purpose and orientation.

Curriculum. In the Catholic secondary schools for boys, the curriculum was usually transplanted from that of a European secondary school, particularly from the French *lycée,* a fact due to the predominance of French Religious Orders in America. The course of studies lasted six years and was classical in character, with some practical subjects added. Some schools, however, broadened their concept of "classical." Georgetown's curriculum at the end of the War of 1812 shows such an expansion, with the inclusion of mathematics (including bookkeeping), the natural sciences, the social sciences, and English and French. Catholic girls academies, on the other hand, did not offer classical subjects but instead concentrated their curricular efforts around the teaching of proper manners and decorum, the domestic arts, and a variety of cultural subjects consonant with education for young ladies. They were finishing schools.

Students. Each class contained students of a wide age range, since the admission age to the freshman year was usually between eight and fourteen. Discipline was quite strict and was stressed as a value in itself, without being tethered to sound psychological principles. Burns and Kohlbrenner note that "in all of [these schools] discipline was emphasized quite as much as, if not more than, the intellectual activities in-

volved in class work," [11] and "in some schools the atmosphere was that of the seminary of the time, rather than what might be expected for lay students." [12] The supervision was extremely close, and the pupils were literally under the eyes of the teachers and ubiquitous prefects continually. Extracurricular activities, mostly of a purely intellectual sort, flourished and were embellished with such names as the Phileleutherian Club and the Philoherminian Club. The school year usually lasted for ten months, but in some girls academies, eleven months. Many Catholic secondary schools accepted non-Catholic students.

Teachers. The instructors in Catholic secondary schools during this period were almost always priests, brothers, or nuns. Catholic secondary education was regarded by Religious as an ecclesiastical function; hence, there was no room for the layman, except in dire emergency and then only as a temporary measure. The doctrine of the Mystical Body was still dormant. Nonetheless, in some localities conditions forced the Religious to employ a goodly number of lay people as high school teachers. Little if any attention was given to the teaching process as such. In some cases, anyone was regarded as capable of teaching, even if he were incapable of anything else, but among many high school teachers, the level of scholarship was quite high.

Support. Catholic elementary schools received financial support from the government in some localities, but Catholic secondary schools did not share in this good fortune. Thus these schools were supported solely by the tuition of the students and the gifts of generous benefactors.

SECONDARY EDUCATION IN THE SOVEREIGN INDUSTRIALIZED UNION (1865–1918)

History. The Civil War bequeathed a legacy of a rapidly growing and increasingly complex industrial life, a life in which all Americans would soon participate. Concomitant education was needed by all citizens if they were to share fully in this new society. Both educators and alert civic leaders became aware of this need. From 1880 onward into the early 1900s the meetings of the National Education Association (NEA) rang with speeches from educators saying that the elementary school did not and could not provide a satisfactory education for all Americans. Business leaders asked for young people with greater training and education.

Meanwhile the Academies began to disappear, so that by the end of

[11] J. A. Burns, C.S.C. and Bernard J. Kohlbrenner, *A History of Catholic Education in the United States.* (New York: Benziger, 1937), p. 241. Much of the information on the history of American Catholic secondary education used in this chapter is based on this important work.

[12] *Ibid.,* p. 238.

the period few were left. The survivors were primarily of three types: denominational, military, and independent. As a result of the growing demand for more widespread secondary education coupled with the decline of the Academy, this period witnessed the establishment of the free public high school as the basic institution for secondary education in America. By the end of the period, the public high school was firmly entrenched in this position, despite opposition from many quarters. Regrettably, one of the loudest voices of this opposition came from the Catholic clergy, who wrote numerous articles in the 1880s and 1890s arguing that education belonged to the home and to the Church, and therefore should not be sponsored by the state.[13] Occasional dissenters like Fr. Thomas Bouquillon of Catholic University were silenced.[14] Happily the Church itself never *officially* committed itself on this issue, and so the opposition, while potent and prestige-laden, nevertheless remained ecclesiastically private. Despite the voices of opposition and despite the increasing enrollments in private secondary schools, public high schools grew at such a rapid pace that by the end of this period 87 per cent of all American secondary schools were public. By 1918 the majority of young people were attending high schools, both public and private, for some part of their lives. However, it must be remembered that less than 10 per cent of the American youths who attended public high schools graduated. As the student body widened in scope, so did the curriculum. Demands arose on all sides that public secondary education became more life-directed. Diverse groups, including the National Education Association, the National Association of Manufacturers, and the American Federation of Labor, asked the high school to provide a practical education. Classicists hastened to offer rebuttals to these arguments, but it was soon apparent that they were losing out. Many schools were becoming comprehensive high schools, i.e., institutions containing under one roof all secondary school programs whether college preparatory, general academic, commercial, or vocational. Some large cities were establishing specialized public high schools for training in various vocational subjects and the arts.

Several important developments occurred which were to decisively shape American secondary education down to the present day. The first was the Kalamazoo decision rendered in 1874 by the Michigan Supreme Court. This decision affirmed the legal right of a local school board to levy taxes for the support of the public high school. The verdict was

[13] Typical examples include Edmund F. Dunne, *Our Public Schools: Are They Free or Are They Not?* (New York: Egan, 1875); and "The School Grievance and Its Remedy," *The Catholic World*, XXXVI (February, 1883), pp. 713–718.

[14] For Fr. Bouquillon's views, see his pamphlet, *Education: To Whom Does It Belong?* (Baltimore: Murphy, 1891).

based on the history of Michigan, which clearly showed that from its beginning the state intended that equal opportunity be provided for all youths who wished to pursue post-elementary school education. Hence the Kalamazoo case legally recognized the public high school as an integral part of the American common school system. Although the decision applied solely to Michigan, it served, nevertheless, as a precedent and guide to other states. The second important development occurred in 1893 with the report of the NEA's Committee of Ten on Secondary School Studies.[15] This report urged that (1) the secondary school be recognized as the terminal educational institution for most youths; (2) there be no differentiation between the program of studies for the college-bound and non-college-bound students, since the traditional subjects are at once the most practical preparation for college and for life; (3) the high school be integrated into the total educational system. This report was taken to heart by the nation's schools, and it did much both to broaden the role and standardize the basic offerings of the public high school.

The third important development occurred in 1899 with the report of the NEA's Committee of Thirteen on College Entrance Requirements.[16] This report urged that a certain number of secondary school subjects be fixed as required for admission to college and that a 6-6 common school system be substituted for the then existing 8-4 plan for both academic and psychological reasons. The fourth development occurred in 1906 when the Carnegie Foundation for the Advancement of Teaching proposed that five periods of classwork per week throughout the entire school year should constitute 1 unit. This recommendation was upheld in 1911 by the Committee of Nine on the Articulation of High School and College which recommended that a high school program have a minimum of 15 units, of which at least 3 were to be in English, 1 in social science, and 1 in the natural sciences. Successful completion of these units, commonly called "Carnegie units," would serve not only as a basis for high school graduation but also for admission to college.

The fifth important development was the formal accreditation of high schools. At the outset it was exclusively a university enterprise, beginning in Michigan in 1870 when the state university there recommended the admission without an entrance examination of graduates from high schools which it had previously certified. This idea spread, and in 1885 the first accrediting agency, the New England Association of Colleges and Preparatory Schools, was formed, to be followed later in

[15] *Report of the Committee on Secondary School Studies.* (Washington: Government Printing Office, 1893).

[16] "Report of the Committee on College Entrance Requirements," National Educational Association *Proceedings* (Washington: NEA, 1899), pp. 632–817.

the period by other regional accrediting agencies. The sixth important development occurred in 1909 in Columbus, Ohio, when a new form of secondary institution, the junior high school, was begun. It comprised the seventh and eighth grades of elementary school plus the first year of high school. The purpose of the junior high school was not only physical reorganization, but even more importantly, program and curricular reorganization based on the results of psychological investigation of the growth patterns and developmental stages of youths. The movement spread quite rapidly, and by 1918 there were over 550 junior high schools in America.

Secondary education as such got on a scientific footing around the turn of the century. It was then that the revealing light of experimental psychology began to be focused on adolescent behavior. The testing movement also came into prominence at this time, with intelligence testing pioneered by Binet and developed by Terman and with achievement testing initiated by Rice and Thorndike. The applications of scientific procedures to secondary education, while perforce limited in their disclosures, nonetheless were significant in that they demonstrated that education was more than a hit-or-miss affair. The professionalization of education was further advanced by two other developments. The first was the formation of the National Education Association in 1857. Growing out of the previously established National Teachers Association, the NEA became increasingly powerful during this period. The second development was the creation of the Federal Department of Education in 1867 to stimulate educational growth in all the states and territories. Unlike its counterparts in European countries, its role was strictly that of stimulator, and not of controller, of education.

Purpose. Throughout this period the general overall purpose of the free public high school was fourfold, viz., citizenship, moral development, mental discipline, and learning a specific body of subject matter, in their order of importance. The twofold immediate purpose was college preparation and practical education for living, with the "bread-and-butter" goal becoming increasingly stressed as the period went on.

Curriculum. Most public high schools continued to offer the two basic types of curricula, namely, classical and practical. But the curricular tracks within the practical expanded to include vocational, commercial, and industrial offerings on a wide scale. Both Census reports and individual studies show the number of subjects offered in public high schools greatly multiplied as this period progressed. This was only natural, since the public high school was slowly transforming itself into an agency which was responsive to the many diverse needs of its pupils. Also the practical outcomes of the subjects were being increasingly stressed; science courses, for example, tried consciously to relate their curricula to the events of everyday life. In the practical curricula, the pupils began to learn directly from experiences rather than learning *about* these experiences from books; they learned to take shorthand by actually taking dictation in shorthand, for example. This also was a definite advance. In the early 1900s Dewey began publishing his thoughts on curriculum and educational philosophy, stressing the child-centered over the subject-centered approach. However, the impact of these ideas on the public secondary school was not felt until the next period. By 1918, the curriculum of public secondary schools as it exists today had definitely taken its basic form in most of the public high schools across the country. The two principal causes of the relative standardization of curricula were the Carnegie unit and the work of the accrediting agencies.

Students. While the public high schools began serving an increasingly diverse clientele, they were not truly representative of all socio-economic classes. The very wealthy and often the wealthy students attended private secondary schools, and the poor pupils were working at jobs. In 1918 the majority of youths from sixteen to eighteen were working, and 25 per cent of the children from ten to fifteen were employed. Child labor laws were not yet in widespread existence. Hence the pupils in public high schools tended to be predominantly middle-class.

The length of the school term kept increasing during this period. Regular times for recreation began to be provided within the school day. Plant conditions improved noticeably over the preceding period. By 1918 most students, except in certain rural areas, had individual seats with attached desks. This furniture was stationary and customarily arranged in rows for easier teacher supervision. The buildings tended to be formal in appearance. The interests of the pupil began to be heeded, although not to any marked degree. The learning outcomes supposedly achieved by the application of the psychological doctrine of formal discipline were still regarded as crucially important in the development of a student, with the result that he had to acquire a great deal of useless information encased in rather rigid formulas. Segregated high schools began to appear in the South. These were, however, comparatively few in number, as there were not many colored youths who had the opportunity of obtaining a secondary school education.

Teachers. The educational ferment in Europe as exemplified in the work of Froebel and Pestalozzi stimulated American educational thought on the role of the teacher, the methods of teaching, and the profession-alization of education in general. In particular, the ideas of the German educator, Herbart, exercised strong influence on American secondary education in this period. The five Herbartian steps of teaching and learning, based on a psychology of association and interest, provided the core of method for pedagogically educated teachers. This period saw a recognition of education as a separate discipline worthy of study. This important breakthrough impelled the NEA to press for the establishment of schools of education at major universities and for departments of education at colleges; both were established all over the nation by 1918. The rapid development of the science of secondary school administration also resulted in increased professionalization. While methodology and professionalization were the chief teacher issues of the day, some advances were made in the increase of salaries, adoption of pension and retirement plans, and establishment of tenure. These advances were on the whole small, scattered, and not commonly adopted, and combined with the new influx of pupils into the high school, they created a situation where the demand for competent teachers far exceeded the supply. The result was that much of the high school teaching was inadequate. In general, secondary school teaching still resembled college teaching, with the lecture method and formal recitation dominant.

Support. By virtue of the Tenth Amendment, support of free public high schools was in the hands of the state and local governments. This led to gross inequalities in support, with high schools situated in Northern states and urban localities receiving far more money per pupil than those in Southern states and rural localities. However, some Federal support of secondary schools was granted in this period, most notably under the Smith-Hughes Act of 1917 by which the national government cooperated with the states in paying the salaries of teachers of home economics, agricultural and vocational subjects, as well as providing certain equipment needed in teaching these subjects. In return for its support, the Federal government imposed specific curricular controls on the beneficiary schools. The Catholic clergy were vehement in denouncing state and Federal support of public high schools on the grounds that (1) the public high schools were in reality sectarian and therefore Catholics should not be compelled to support them, and (2) the government had no business sponsoring education, much less secondary education.[17]

The Catholic Secondary School

History. At least five developments in this period contributed to making Catholic secondary education distinctive qua secondary education. The first was that Catholic colleges gradually effected a clear-cut separation between their college and secondary departments, so that the secondary school (and its program) became a definite entity in itself.

[17] Butts and Cremin, *op. cit.*, pp. 377–378.

This was most beneficial, as it tended both to widen the scope and heighten the definiteness of the Catholic high school.[18] The second development was the reorganization of many Catholic Girls Academies. Spurred on by a new interest in Catholic college education for women, this reorganization began to emphasize four-year academic programs as against the former almost exclusive stress on the finishing school approach. The third development was the influence of the accrediting agencies. These agencies did much to break down the insular posture, to broaden the program, to improve the quality, and to standardize the curricular offerings of Catholic high schools. Without the liberating effect of these agencies, Catholic secondary education might have withered because of narrowness.

The fourth development was the relatively widespread establishment of non-Order high schools. Before the Civil War, it was the Religious Orders who were primarily responsible for the creation of Catholic secondary schools. It was they who laid the foundations for the Catholic high school in America. In this period the diocesan clergy became increasingly aware of the need for more Catholic high schools. The earliest non-Order, Catholic high schools were parochial high schools. Their establishment was due to the desire of the local pastors to keep the youths in a parochial school as long as possible. These parochial high schools grew in popularity. The report of the Committee on High Schools of the National Catholic Educational Association issued in 1911 showed that of the 311 Catholic high schools of which it had knowledge, 85 per cent were parochial high schools. Meanwhile a new type of non-Order secondary school, the central high school, had been created. In 1890, through the foresight of a Catholic layman named Thomas E. Cahill, the first such institution, The Roman Catholic Central High School, was erected in Philadelphia. The difference between the central high school and the parochial high school is that the former is controlled, supported, and patronized by the entire diocese, while the parochial high school is generally controlled, supported, and patronized exclusively by the parish. The central high school was (and still is) favored over the parochial high school by most Catholic educators because the parochial high school was charged with the following disadvantages: (1) difficulty in support; (2) likely to be too small; (3) usually unable to provide adequate laboratory and library facilities; (4) tends to promote civic and intellectual insularism; (5) likely to have a narrow curriculum because of its small size.[19] The fifth development was the recognition in

[18] See John T. Murphy, "Catholic Secondary Education in the United States," *American Catholic Quarterly Review*, XXII (July, 1897), pp. 449–464.

[19] See Paul E. Campbell, "The Central Catholic High School," *Homiletic and Pastoral Review*, XXIX (September, 1929), pp. 1294–1300.

1884 by the Third Plenary Council of Baltimore of the value and importance of Catholic secondary education. The Council expressed the hope that eventually all Catholic youths would be able to receive not only a Catholic elementary but also a Catholic secondary school education.

Stimulated by the Council, many dioceses soon began establishing diocesan school boards. The purpose of these boards was to prescribe the curriculum, select the textbooks, determine teacher qualifications, and make educational recommendations for those elementary and secondary institutions under their jurisdiction. These boards, whose establishment marked a definite advance in American Catholic education, had many problems to face, all of which impaired their effectiveness, sometimes seriously. The establishment of the National Catholic Educational Association (NCEA) in 1904 marked another forward step. This body is basically a deliberation and discussion group.

Purpose. The primary immediate goal of Catholic high schools for boys continued to be college preparation, but gradually and often grudgingly their terminal role was recognized. Those which did recognize the terminal role tended more often to be the parochial and central high schools, since the others were run by Religious Orders who usually conducted colleges fed principally by their own secondary schools. In the Catholic girls high schools the goal was that of preparing the students both for Christian motherhood and for a suitable place in polite society. By the end of the period, however, greater stress was placed on college preparation. In the Catholic central high schools for girls, a functional, terminal role was recognized. Of course, the chief purpose behind all Catholic secondary education was religious, particularly that of conserving the Faith.

Curriculum. Knowledge expanded greatly in the nineteenth century, with the flowering of new fields and the taking on of new dimensions in old fields. In the beginning of this period the curricula of the Catholic high schools in the main did not keep abreast of the times, and the classical languages, mathematics, and natural theology still occupied most of the stage. Some curricula reluctantly included a little of the new learning, but only by way of concession. However, the rise of the parochial and later the central high school, together with the influence of the accrediting agencies did much to broaden the curriculum. Indeed by the end of the period the percentage of students in Catholic and public high schools taking the major subjects was about the same. Only in vocational and commercial subjects were the course offerings of the average Catholic high school weak. The curricula in Catholic secondary schools were beginning to mature and come of age.[20]

[20] Burns and Kohlbrenner, *op. cit.*, pp. 249–252.

Students. The vast bulk of the students did not come from the poorer classes, because of the tuition. The parochial high schools tried, in some measure, to effect a change in this regard. Discipline was likely to be stricter than in the public high schools. The school hours tended to become shorter than in the preceding period. Extracurricular activities were still limited to the intellectual and religious variety, e.g., forensic clubs and vocation clubs. Physical exercise and activities were not common, because it was felt that the students' main goals were in the purely religiointellectual realm. College-bound students were often motivated by the fact that they would almost automatically be accepted by a Catholic college. However, abuses sometimes arose from this practice. The central Catholic high school tended to deinsularize pupil attitudes.

Teachers. New teaching Orders continued to emigrate to America, and indeed in even greater numbers than during the preceding period. This helped increase the supply of teachers. In general, the level of scholarship and educational interest was high, except in those schools which happened to be staffed by Orders which felt that a teaching position was the last refuge for those Religious who failed at other, more important tasks. According to the Third Plenary Council, the Diocesan Board of Examination was supposed to examine all teachers in diocesan high schools (as well as elementary schools) and then certify them. In practice this became a mere formality because the boards, made up of priests who were not professionally trained, held this neither interesting nor important. Also, the boards felt the teaching process was automatic and hence everyone could teach. Moreover, all Religious were not under direct diocesan canonical jurisdiction and consequently could not be examined.[21]

Some interest in professional teacher preparation was discernible in this period. A few Religious Orders such as the School Sisters of Notre Dame included a little professional study in their preparation of teachers. Occasionally summer institutes in teaching were held, and demonstration lessons conducted. In 1895 the Paulists conducted a summer teachers institute which is noteworthy because it was the first of its kind to be attended by sisters of different communities. All these movements were intended chiefly for preparing elementary school teachers; however, some of their graduates did eventually teach in the Catholic secondary schools. A great stride forward was taken by Catholic University in 1911 with the establishment of its Sisters College to prepare teachers professionally from various Religious communities. Some forward-looking dioceses and Catholic universities opened up summer schools in Education for the benefit of Religious desiring to improve themselves professionally. A few

[21] *Ibid.*, p. 190.

Religious communities did conduct Education courses for their own members, but only occasionally were these courses designed for secondary school teachers. The tradition of a Religious rather than a lay person as the teacher in a Catholic high school was reinforced during this period. However, emergencies forced some schools to "take in" lay teachers. There was little or no interest in professionalizing Catholic educational administration during this period. Appointment by a Religious superior, sometimes without regard for ability or background, was the method of selecting Catholic school administrative personnel.

Support. As in prior periods, Catholic high schools were supported chiefly by four sources: student tuition, donations from generous lay people, self-sacrifice of the devoted and hard-working Religious, and volunteer lay teachers who worked gratis or for a mere pittance.

SECONDARY EDUCATION IN MODERN TIMES (1918–PRESENT)

History. This was the period in which the secondary schools were solidified as an essential part of the common school. At present, almost all youths eighteen years of age have attended secondary school at some time or other. Successful completion of high school has become increasingly mandatory for many occupations. Most young people affirm the value and importance of a high school education. Yet today only slightly more than half of our young people are graduating from high school, indicating that it still is not completely a common school. This high dropout rate underscores the necessity for a reappraisal both of current educational goals and contemporary high school programs.

During this period several different psychologies came into prevalence, and they deeply affected the orientation of American public secondary schools. The three most important were Behaviorism, Connectionism, and the Gestalt. All of them explained the mind and its operations (such as learning) in completely materialistic, physical terms. Behaviorism, given its greatest impetus by Watson, held that the basis for learning is the conditioned reflex. Pavlovian in tone, it maintained that learning is entirely the result of controllable physical stimuli. Connectionism, given its greatest impetus by Thorndike, held that the basis for learning is the type and strength of the bond between stimulus(i) and response(s). Learning takes place when this bond is heightened or altered. The Gestalt, originally a German theory associated with Köhler, claimed that the basis for learning is the entire field or background of the thing to be learned. This organismic theory held that learning takes place by a flash of insight in which the learner perceives how and why the particular element fits into the overall field. High school education in this period was based successively on each of these theories, with the latest, i.e., Gestalt, being the one in vogue today. A condemnation of faculty psychology (which is usually confused with the theory of formal discipline) and a stressing of learning as appropriate behavior are two keystones of contemporary educational psychology.

Reports and recommendations by educational organizations have had a strong impact on secondary education during this period. The first, and in many ways the keystone, was the formulation of the famous *Cardinal Principles of Secondary Education,* issued in 1918 by the Commission on the Reorganization of Secondary Education.[22] The chief significance of these principles was that they declared the main purpose of the high school to be life preparation rather than college preparation. Life preparation was not only the best type of education for the terminal students but for the college-bound as well. Thus the Seven Cardinal Principles not only became the war cry of public secondary school educators in the 1920s and 1930s but also formed the wellspring for subsequent refinements and elaborations of the doctrine of life preparation.

In 1935 the American Youth Commission was organized by the American Council on Education. This Commission devoted its attention to studying the problems of young people in modern society. Its investigations and subsequent reports revealed the necessity for increasing the flexibility of the secondary school program so that the needs of every youth currently enrolled in these schools could be adequately met. In 1938 the Educational Policies Commission (EPC) published its famous report *The Purposes of Education in American Democracy.* This extremely influential document did much to shape the broad goals of American education in the decades which followed.[23] The report of the North Central Association's Commission on Secondary School Curriculum, published in 1942, reiterated the necessity for a broad program of general education on the secondary level.[24] In 1944 the Educational Policies Commission published its report *Education for All American Youth,* which stressed the idea that every American youth must have a sound and broad secondary school education if he is to fulfill himself both as a person and a citizen.[25] The Commission on Life Adjustment Education, formed in 1945 by the U.S. Office of Education, strove for a secondary school program based primarily on helping youth adjust to

[22] *Cardinal Principles of Secondary Education,* Bulletin no. 35. (Washington: Government Printing Office, 1918).

[23] Educational Policies Commission, *The Purposes of Education in American Democracy.* (Washington: NEA, 1938).

[24] North Central Association of Colleges and Secondary Schools, *General Education in the American High School.* (Chicago: Scott, Foresman, 1942).

[25] Educational Policies Commission, *Education for All American Youth.* (Washington: NEA and AASA, 1944).

"real life." This type of program, whose name has since become a by-word, was intended chiefly for non-college-bound youth. In 1947, the National Association of Secondary-School Principals (NASSP) identified the "ten imperative needs of youth" around which the Association recommended the secondary school program should be built.[26] In 1949, this Association's Committee on Curriculum Planning and Development made available a plan or "check list" by which high school faculties could evaluate their school programs on the basis of the "ten imperative needs." [27] In 1959, James B. Conant, sponsored by the Carnegie Corporation, published his report on representative American comprehensive high schools. Entitled *The American High School Today*, this report made 21 recommendations for improving high school programs, together with suggestions connected with school size and type. In 1960, the National Study of Secondary School Evaluation (formerly the Cooperative Study of Secondary School Standards) published the third edition of its *Evaluative Criteria* which was of great assistance in both self- and outside evaluation of high school programs.[28] Ever since the first edition in 1940, the influence of this rather complete and detailed instrument has been considerable. In 1961, the National Association of Secondary-School Principals published *Guide to Better Schools*, usually referred to as the Trump Report. This significant report made specific recommendations for improving secondary education in the decades ahead.[29]

The decline in morality, the tremendous increase in juvenile delinquency, and the neglect of religion in the public schools began to be of great concern to many responsible educators during the second half of this period. In 1947 the Committee on Religion and Education of the American Council on Education stated that a common core of religious creed should be taught in the public schools. The Council declared that public elementary and secondary schools had become too secularized.[30] In 1951 the Educational Policies Commission of the NEA published its report, *Moral and Spiritual Values in Public Schools*, which urged the home, school, and community to cooperate in instilling moral and

---

[26] "The Imperative Needs of Youth of Secondary-School Age," *Bulletin of the National Association of Secondary-School Principals*, CVL (March, 1947).

[27] William L. Ransom, "How Well Does Your School Rate on the Ten Imperative Needs of Youth?" *Bulletin of the National Association of Secondary-School Principals*, CLXIV (October, 1949).

[28] National Study of Secondary School Evaluation, *Evaluative Criteria*, 3d ed. (Washington: American Council on Education, 1960).

[29] J. Lloyd Trump and Dorsey Baynham, *Guide to Better Schools*. (Chicago: Rand McNally, 1961).

[30] American Council on Education, Committee on Religion and Education, *The Relation of Religion to Education: The Basic Principles*. (Washington: The Council, 1947).

spiritual values into the pupils.[31] Many states have passed laws permitting Bible reading in public elementary and secondary schools. In 1952 in the case of *Doremus v. Board of Education,* an attempt was made to have the Supreme Court declare Bible reading unconstitutional. However, the Court declined to hear the case, leaving the matter entirely in the hands of the states.[32] In 1962 the United States Supreme Court ruled that no state could compose an official prayer for use in the public schools.

Other developments have furthered the cause of public secondary education during this period. Every state established a state department of education. The Department of Health, Education and Welfare was created as a cabinet office in 1953. A Federal department of education had been opposed in the early part of the century by the National Catholic Welfare Conference (NCWC), Catholic educational leaders, and almost all the clergy on both constitutional and pedagogical grounds. In 1954 the Supreme Court, in *Brown v. Board of Education of Topeka,* ruled that segregation by race in the public schools is unconstitutional.[33]

Beginning in the late 1940s there arose an ever-increasing wave of criticism of America's public secondary schools. This wave reached its crest in 1957 with the launching of the Russian space satellite Sputnik. "Soft pedagogy" and "life-adjustment educational goals" were the chief targets for attack. Defenders of the progressive system pointed to the Eight Year Study begun by the Progressive Education Association in 1933. This study showed that those college students who had graduated from the "progressive" high schools under investigation did slightly better on the whole in intellectual subjects and considerably better in both creative subjects and social matters than did equivalent college students who had graduated from comparable "traditional" high schools. Thus the traditional college preparatory program was shown to be not so necessary or so unique as was believed.[34] In any event, the traditionalist-progressive dispute still rages.

Purpose. The principal goal of the American public secondary school during this period has been fairly consistent, viz., to meet adequately the needs of every American youth. These needs are not conceived solely as intellectual, but physical, social, emotional, and spiritual as well. Thus the chief purpose of the secondary school varies with the

[31] Educational Policies Commission, *Moral and Spiritual Values in the Public Schools.* (Washington: The Commission, 1951).

[32] 342 U.S. 429, 72 Sup. Ct. 394.

[33] 347 U.S. 483, 74 Sup. Ct. 686. For a succinct but meaty commentary on this and four related decisions, see Clark Spurlock, *Education and the Supreme Court.* (Urbana, Ill.: University of Illinois Press, 1955), pp. 206–221.

[34] Wilford M. Aiken, *The Story of the Eight Year Study.* (New York: Harper, 1942).

pupils enrolled therein. Other important purposes include citizenship, social living, group activities, and so forth. Some ultraprogressive educators argue that the purpose of the high school is to serve the needs, not only of the students, but of the entire community.[35] In a number of instances the school has become an octopus.

Curriculum. The influence of John Dewey, and particularly of his followers, such as Kilpatrick, Counts, and Childs, caused a curricular revolution in American public secondary schools. The five most important changes were: (1) Both methods and total curriculum became experimental. (2) Experience became both basis and procedure of the curriculum. (3) The curriculum became student-centered. (4) Problem solving became the vehicle for implementing the curriculum in concrete classroom situations. (5) The total curriculum was viewed as life itself rather than a preparation for life. These changes led to an era of curriculum building, i.e., erection of curricular systems based on the new ideas. The four most important of the new secondary school curricula were the Core, the persistent life situations, the total student-centered, and the social functions. The 1920s and 1930s saw the curricular emphasis placed squarely on the student; in the later decades the direction became more social. While many public schools adopted the new curricular emphasis, others resisted and clung to the traditional approach.

During this period the curriculum broadened vastly due primarily to three causes. First, electives, ranging from driver education to coed cooking, mushroomed. Second, there was a huge increase in the activities program (sometimes referred to as "extracurricular activities"), with some secondary schools scheduling these activities during the regular school day. Third, the nation became totally committed to the ideal that every youth should receive a high school education. The modern public high school now has two curricular tracks, the college preparatory and the terminal. The latter consists of two subarrangements, the vocational, and the modern or applied academic. Regrettably, the applied academic has all too often become a dumping ground for pupils who cannot seem to fit into the college-preparatory or vocational track. A thoroughgoing "needs-meeting curriculum" is still more a verbalism than a reality in the majority of secondary school programs. An interesting curricular development arising in the 1950s was the community-school concept.

Amid the intellectual excitement of the new curricula, the traditionalists stood firm on content, method, and pupil selection. They believed that the curriculum should include only the basics, the traditionally accepted subjects with no "fads or frills." The methods should be the "old standbys" of drill, memorization, and book learning. The

[35] See The National Society for the Study of Education, *The Community School,* Fifty-Second Yearbook, Part II. (Chicago: University of Chicago Press, 1953).

pupils should be only those who could "handle the work." The resultant conflict between the progressives and the traditionalists led to the establishment of several curricular plans based on individual differences. Of these, the three most famous were the Morrison Plan, the Dalton Plan, and the Winnetka Plan. Eventually a three-track system emerged, and this is the one used in many secondary schools today. As far as school organization is concerned, by mid-century nearly 60 per cent of the nation's schools had a 6-6 or 6-3-3 organization, while 40 per cent retained the traditional 8-4 pattern. A few school systems had a 6-2-4 or 7-2-3 arrangement.

Students. The number of youths attending high school mounted. At the beginning of the period there were two million; by 1960 the number had swelled to almost ten million. School terms were extended in the first half of the period, but since 1940 they have remained fairly steady, lengthening only a very little. By 1960 secondary school pupils were representative of all socioeconomic classes. However, of the youths who drop out of high school, a heavy majority come from the economically underprivileged. After World War II school buildings became increasingly flexible; for example, movable furniture, folding wall partitions, and so forth were used more and more. With the burgeoning of extracurricular activities and the promotion of the community-school concept, the students tended to spend longer hours in the secondary school. Some educators began to propose "all-year schools" for increased acceleration through school and more efficient use of the school building.[36] Some schools had previously used this system with varying success. Discipline in the high schools began to shift from punitive to democratic. The "100 per cent promotion plan" was very popular in the 1930s and 1940s, but its popularity has since been on the wane. In the late 1950s and early 1960s the high school program began to tighten considerably because of the mad rush of students to get into college combined with the fear of nonacceptance by the college(s) of their choice.

Teachers. During the fifteen years following the Depression of 1929 there was no dearth of competent, devoted teachers. By 1960, however, the situation had drastically changed. A severe shortage of competent, trained teachers had arisen for several reasons, one being the spectacular increase in the post–World War II birthrate. The Eighty-third Congress's Committee for the White House Conference reported to the President that teachers' salaries were too low and should be raised. In 1956 a prominent American historian remarked that "teachers are the only occupational group whose earnings have actually fallen since 1940. By comparison, those of industrial workers have gone up almost fifty

[36] Grayson Kirk, Commencement Address. (New York: Columbia University, 1956).

per cent." [37] Per hour, the average secondary school teacher earns less than the average bricklayer. In 1957 the NEA reported that although the proportion of each college graduating class prepared for teaching continues to increase, nonetheless, only two out of three so prepared actually go into teaching.[38] Teaching increasingly has become a part-time job. In 1960 it was estimated that almost 60 per cent of male secondary school teachers in New York City were engaged in additional employment. College students majoring in Education were often of poor quality. Of all college graduates who took the Armed Forces Qualification Tests, Education majors consistently scored the lowest ratings.

On the brighter side, there have been significant advances in this period, although these are not all characterized by undiminished luster. Preservice training of teachers for public secondary schools has improved as state certification requirements have become more demanding. However, the mediocre manner in which many professional Education courses are often taught detracts from the effectiveness of preservice training. In-service courses are offered by some boards of education throughout the country but the quality of these courses is notoriously low. Happily, there is an increasing demand by states for secondary school teachers to possess a master's degree. This has done much to improve the tone and quality of instruction. Merit rating of teachers, tied in with salary increases, has been a device proposed by some educators to further improve the quality of teaching. This is a very controversial issue, with everyone agreeing to the principle, but few concurring on concrete applications. Teacher aides have been used with varying success. These aides perform the routine classroom operations, and thus free the teachers to concentrate on instruction. Educational television has been introduced recently to help improve the calibre of teaching. In the 1960s much attention has been directed toward teaching machines. Meanwhile, democracy in school administration has been proceeding slowly but surely. The administrators are more and more consulting with teachers, students, and parents.

The period after World War II has witnessed a great debate in teacher organizations over the question of hiring Communist teachers in public elementary and secondary schools. In 1949 at its annual convention the NEA stated officially that members of the Communist party should not be employed as teachers. Many delegates, however, did not agree with the majority-approved resolution. In that same year

[37] Oscar Handlin, "The Crisis in Teaching," *Atlantic Monthly*, CXCVIII (September, 1956), p. 35.

[38] For a discussion of this and similar statements, see Roger A. Freeman, *School Needs in the Decade Ahead*. (Washington: Institute for Social Science Research, 1958), pp. 45–72.

New York State passed the Feinberg Law which made membership in a subversive organization prima facie evidence for dismissal from a teaching position in its public schools. This law was later declared constitutional by the Supreme Court in the Adler decision (1952).[39]

Support. There arose a crisis in support which became more acute as the period progressed. Higher construction costs, more schools, and increased teachers' salaries meant that the local property taxes soared to an astounding rate. By far the largest single portion of state and local taxes went for school support. Teacher groups, spearheaded by the NEA, came out militantly for Federal financial assistance as the only solution to adequate support. Other groups, such as the United States Chamber of Commerce, opposed Federal aid because they felt the need for additional classrooms had been exaggerated; that teachers were receiving an adequate salary; and that only professional educators were for it—the state governors did not want it. Many Federal aid-to-education bills have been introduced in Congress, but practically all have been defeated. Negro and Roman Catholic groups came out against any discriminatory Federal aid, e.g., bills which would not forbid school segregation and bills which would bar parochial school children from receiving aid.

The Catholic Secondary School

History. The period commencing with the close of World War I has been one of great growth for Catholic secondary education in America. Catholics in this modern era have become increasingly vocal in their claim that public secondary schools do indeed teach a religion, secularism, and that as a result Catholics must bend every effort to erect a high school system of their own. Early in the period, in 1919, a Department of Education was established in the National Catholic Welfare Conference. This department not only has engaged in educational research but has represented Catholic education at meetings of national and governmental agencies. In 1929 Pope Pius XI issued his important encyclical, *Christian Education of Youth*, which reaffirmed both the importance and goals of Catholic secondary education.[40] This document was carefully studied by American Catholic educators. The tremendous growth in Catholic secondary schools may be seen from the fact that, by 1960, approximately 845,000 youths were enrolled in 2,400 diocesan and private Catholic secondary schools, representing a 26 per cent rise in enrollments over 1950.[41] The decade from 1940 to 1950 saw a 40 per cent

[39] 342 U.S. 485, 72 Sup. Ct. 380. See Spurlock, *op. cit.*, pp. 134–143.
[40] Pope Pius XI, *Christian Education of Youth*. (Washington: NCWC, 1936).
[41] "General Summary," *The Official Catholic Directory, 1960*. (New York: Kenedy, 1960), p. 1 (insert); Msgr. Frederick G. Hochwalt, "Catholic Statement on Separate School Loans," *The New York Times*, Mar. 15, 1961, p. 26.

rise in Catholic secondary school enrollments. Enrollments in Catholic secondary schools have been expanding at a much higher rate than those of public secondary schools. Despite these significant advances, much remains to be done. The enormousness of the task can be realized when it is remembered that in 1960 Catholic elementary schools had a total enrollment of approximately 4,385,000 pupils.[42] This means that at best only one out of every five graduates from Catholic elementary schools goes to a Catholic secondary school. Catholic educators have opened a two-pronged offensive to help solve the problem. The first prong was the drive begun on a large scale in the mid-fifties by the bishops of America to raise money to build many more central diocesan high schools. The second prong consisted in requesting the public schools to provide more released time religious instruction for Catholic pupils in those schools. "Released time" means that the public schools will dismiss their pupils from school early on a designated day so that these pupils can receive religious instruction from their respective clergymen. In 1948 in the case of *Illinois ex. rel. McCollum v. Board of Education*, the Supreme Court ruled that it was unconstitutional to have released-time instruction on public school premises. Henceforward pupils had to go to their respective churches to receive released-time instruction.[43] This practice was ruled constitutional in the case of *Zorach v. Clauson*.[44] Catholic educational leaders view released time as a temporary stopgap measure. The goal is "a place in a Catholic school for every Catholic child." [45]

There have been during this period powerful forces at work trying to destroy the Catholic school system in America. Aware that the overwhelming majority of all private schools are Catholic, they centered their attack on the abolition of all private schools. The first effort was made in the courts, but to no avail. In the case of *Pierce v. Society of Sisters of the Holy Names* (1925), the Supreme Court declared unconstitutional an Oregon law which forbade parents to send their children to nonpublic schools. The "Oregon decision," as it is often called, became the charter of rights for the private and parochial schools in America.[46] The second effort started in the late forties and early fifties in magazine articles and books by such prominent educators as Childs and Conant, who charged that private schools were divisive and un-

---

[42] "General Summary," *loc. cit.*

[43] 333 U.S. 203, 68 Sup. Ct. 461. See Spurlock, *op. cit.*, pp. 116–124.

[44] 343 U.S. 306, 72 Sup. Ct. 679.

[45] Msgr. Frederick G. Hochwalt quoted in Butts and Cremin, *op. cit.*, p. 571.

[46] 268 U.S. 510, 45 Sup. Ct. 571.

democratic.[47] These accusations were effectively answered by both Catholic leaders and private independent school educators.

Beginning in the mid-1950s a few of the more mature Catholic educators began reexamining their own schools with a critical eye. Prominent figures like Msgr. Ellis and Thomas O'Dea have charged Catholic schools, particularly Catholic colleges, with being overdefensive, overprotective, and indeed anti-intellectual.[48] While some Catholics rose to defend the Catholic schools and proclaim that everything was wonderful, the intellectual and cultural achievements of American Catholics clearly showed that the critics were in the right. Indeed, it is not too much to say that a lack of searching self-criticism is one of the weakest elements in the Catholic school system today. Fortunately, there have been some recent signs, however faint, of improvement in this direction. For most of this period, owing to the stress and pressures of Dewey's educational ideas, Catholic educators became increasingly negative and defensive in their educational philosophy and curriculum changes. However, in the 1950s, when a new wave of Catholic reappraisal slowly appeared on the scene and opened the eyes of Catholic educators to the relative stagnation of their system, they commenced seeking beneficial changes.

Purpose. The ultimate goal of the Catholic secondary school is to assist the student in attaining salvation. This goal is realized by assisting the pupils to learn and live truth. Recently in some Catholic secondary schools, the purposes have been widened to include social, emotional, and physical needs. In 1944 the Policies Committee of the NCEA's Secondary School Department, after careful study, issued the "Seven Objectives of Catholic Secondary Education in the United States." These objectives have since become the guiding principles of the more alert Catholic secondary schools. Regrettably, the "Seven Objectives" have not been sufficiently publicized or emphasized, with the result that far too many Catholic secondary schools are not aware of their existence.

Curriculum. The course of studies in most Catholic high schools remained pretty much as it was at the end of the preceding period. College preparatory courses were the standard fare, even for those who did not intend to pursue higher education. Usually there were few electives. The basic curricular program revolved around the required

[47] John L. Childs, "American Democracy and the Common School System," *Jewish Education*, XXI (January, 1949), pp. 32–37; also his *Education and Morals*. (New York: Appleton-Century-Crofts, 1950), pp. 244–257; James Bryant Conant, *Education and Liberty*. (Cambridge, Mass.: Harvard University Press, 1958), pp. 79–87.

[48] Msgr. John Tracy Ellis, "The American Catholic and the Intellectual Life," *Thought*, XXX (Autumn, 1955), pp. 351–388; Thomas F. O'Dea, *American Catholic Dilemma: An Inquiry into the Intellectual Life*. (New York: Sheed and Ward, 1958).

Carnegie units. Compared with what was done in many public secondary schools, little was done, as far as the curriculum was concerned, to integrate the subjects. Recently, however, some of the large Catholic secondary schools have been employing a three-track system, thus tailoring the curriculum, to some extent at least, to the pupils' varying abilities. The predominant school organization remains 8-4. One important development occurred in Catholic girls secondary schools, where the curriculum was often adapted to meet the needs of those girls who wished to pursue a practical, job-oriented vocational program. In addition, specialized Catholic commercial high schools for girls sprang up in quite a few dioceses throughout the country. In general, however, Catholic secondary schools still demanded that the pupil adjust to the curriculum rather than vice versa.

Students. By the 1960s the pupils in Catholic secondary schools still were not broadly representative of the Catholic population. This was due primarily to three factors. First, a large percentage of the schools charged a tuition which kept out many economically underprivileged Catholic youths. Second, a large percentage of the schools had scholastic entrance requirements which eliminated many intellectually underprivileged Catholic youths. With the demand for Catholic secondary education greatly exceeding the supply, there is little immediate hope of rectifying this situation. Third, the very wealthy Catholic students all too often go to private, independent "prep schools," chiefly for social and "prestige" reasons. Catholic secondary schools are noted for their adherence to strict, indeed sometimes overly strict, discipline. The 100 per cent promotion plan never gained acceptance in Catholic secondary schools. Extracurricular activities have burgeoned, particularly in sports, where the local Catholic high school often has the best team in town. Some critics have maintained that if the pupils in these schools were encouraged to pursue the intellectual life as eagerly as the athletic, the Catholic high school would be doing more good for both the pupils and the Church. Some, but only a few, plants were constructed flexibly and functionally, with movable room partitions and the like. Guidance services for students were still pitifully inadequate in most Catholic secondary schools.[49]

Teachers. Catholic interest in a professional approach to secondary education began to develop seriously during this period. Several dioceses established diocesan normal schools. Many Communities began to require secondary schoolteachers to take professional course work. However, this was effected slowly at first, as is seen by a 1932 questionnaire which disclosed that of 66 teaching Communities replying, only 5 had a

---

[49] Philip L. Stack, *A National Study of the Guidance Services in Catholic Secondary Schools.* (Washington, D.C.: Catholic University of America Press, 1958).

rule prescribing full-service preparation from which no exception could be made.[50] Today the situation is improving; nevertheless, on the whole, Catholic secondary schoolteachers are not so well prepared, particularly in professional course work, as are public schoolteachers. This is a crucial matter which alert Catholic educators are endeavoring to rectify. In this connection, one of the biggest steps forward ever made by Catholic education was taken in 1954 with the establishment of the Sister Formation Movement. This movement hoped to upgrade the training of women Religious both spiritually and intellectually. One of its most crucial tasks is to assure adequate training for teachers; it also seeks to develop a theology of the work of the teacher.

Other important steps taken in this period were the increase in supervisory personnel sent out by diocese and Order. More and more these supervisors are being sent on for professional courses in Education. Most dioceses and Orders now have curriculum-coordinating committees. Unfortunately many members of these committees have little or no professional training, thus limiting the effectiveness of their work. A further lack of professionalization can be seen by the fact that many of the Religious teaching in Catholic secondary schools were originally elementary school instructors. The teaching in secondary schools thus tends to follow along the lines of elementary instruction. These and other problems are dealt with at the periodic Workshops in Catholic Secondary Education. Sponsored by The Catholic University, they were begun in 1947 and represent a significant advance in professionalization.

Lay teachers in American Catholic secondary schools have been increasing at a tremendous rate in this period. It is estimated that within a generation they will outnumber Religious teachers. The degree to which they have been fully accepted by the Religious has not always been most conducive to the vigorous growth of Catholic education in America.

Democracy in Catholic secondary schools has been slow in coming. Many Catholic educators seem to feel that democracy may be suitable to the political arena but is out of place in an educational context. Students and teachers are supposed to do exactly as they are told by the administration without prior consultation. Parents normally play no role other than to conduct fund-raising activities. Occasionally, a speaker at an NCEA convention criticizes such practices, but he is usually ignored. Nevertheless, there are some signs, however distant, that Catholic education is beginning to mature in this regard and that the second half of the twentieth century will witness a change for the better.

[50] John R. Hagan, *The Diocesan Teachers College.* (Washington, D.C.: Catholic University of America Press, 1932), p. 19.

Support. Catholics in this period became progressively more vocal in demanding Federal and state financial assistance for their schools, both elementary and secondary. The clergy took the lead in pressing forward these demands. The Catholic laity lagged behind, perhaps because of an ingrained tradition of the laity as a silent, passive element in the Church. The essential argument for financial aid was voiced in 1929 by Pope Pius XI in his encyclical on education which stated that distributive justice demands that governments aid pupils in church-related as well as state schools. In America there have been two phases in government financial assistance, viz., auxiliary services and outright aid. Auxiliary services are those which indirectly affect instruction. Independent and church-related schools have won important victories in the courts in the matter of auxiliary services. In the case of *Cochran v. Louisiana State Board of Education* (1930), the Supreme Court sustained a Louisiana law which provided free textbooks from public funds to children in private schools.[51] In the case of *Everson v. Board of Education* (1947), the Supreme Court held that public funds may be used to provide free transportation to pupils attending private schools.[52] In 1946 Congress passed the National School Lunch Act which provided that lunches subsidized by the Federal government be made available to all pupils, both in public and private schools. The constitutionality of auxiliary services to church-related schools is based on the "child-benefit principle," which means that these services benefit primarily the child, not the school. Opposed to auxiliary services, as well as any form of direct state aid to independent and parochial schools, were and still are the NEA, the American Federation of Teachers (AFT), almost all Jewish groups, many Protestant groups and the extremist Protestants and Other Americans United for the Separation of Church and State (POAU, founded 1947). These organizations claimed that aid of any kind, whether auxiliary or direct, violates separation of church and state.

Direct aid to students in all schools, regardless of affiliation, began in 1944 with the *Servicemen's Readjustment Act of 1944,* better known as the "GI Bill of Rights." This act provided tuition, books, and living expenses to veterans who wished to continue their education in secondary school or college. The veterans had free choice of school, whether public or private, and the Federal government paid their tuition directly to the school. The battle for increased aid to private schools became tied to bills for aid to public schools, and erupted with full force in the late 1950s and continued during the next decade. In 1960 the Morse bill for loans to private schools was defeated in Congress. In 1961 the Administrative

[51] 281 U.S. 370, 50 Sup. Ct. 335.
[52] 330 U.S. 1, 67 Sup. Ct. 504. See Spurlock, *op. cit.,* pp. 78–93.

Board of the NCWC, composed of the most important members of the Catholic hierarchy in America, officially demanded that Federal low-interest loans be made to Catholic elementary and secondary schools. Other Catholic educational leaders, such as Fr. Blum, S.J., felt that a system of tuition certificates rather than one of loans was the equitable and constitutional solution to the problem.[53] At stake in the whole controversy are two interrelated issues, namely, survival of a strong Catholic school system and freedom of choice in education.

[53] See Virgil C. Blum, S.J., *Freedom of Choice in Education.* (New York: Macmillan, 1958).

CHAPTER II THE GOALS OF AMERICAN SECONDARY EDUCATION

No writer or committee has as yet given a good definition of the nature of secondary education. Indeed most definitions usually say little more than the fact that secondary education comprises the period following elementary school and preceding college or a job. Perhaps the most famous and influential definition of American secondary school education, that of the former Department of Secondary School Principals of the NEA (now the National Association of Secondary-School Principals), illustrates this point. "Secondary education denotes the education provided by schools for the purpose of guiding and promoting the development of normal individuals for whom on the one hand the elementary school no longer constitutes a satisfactory environment, and who on the other hand are either not yet prepared to participate effectively in society unguided by the school, or are not ready for the specialized work of the professional schools or the upper divisions of the liberal arts college." [1] Other definitions include growth and maturity

[1] Committee on the Orientation of Secondary Education, Department of Secondary School Principals, National Education Association, *Issues of Secondary Education*, Bulletin no. 59. (Chicago: NEA, 1936), p. 22.

factors, adolescent needs, and so forth. Some observe that it is that period in one's formal education when the rudiments of the arts, humanities, and sciences are learned on a more advanced level.

The basic reason for the inability to precisely delimit secondary education flows from the very nature of the total educational process itself. The educational process, considered in its entirety, is a seamless robe. The lower and upper ends are clearly visible, but everything in between flows uninterruptedly. The beginning of elementary education and the termination of higher education can easily be seen, but where does secondary education, somewhere in the middle of the seamless robe, begin or end? There is the problem.

This lack of clarity and definiteness about the *nature* of secondary education has direct ramifications on the identification of the *goals* of secondary education. In order to identify distinct and comprehensive goals, one must know clearly the nature of the object for which the goals are intended. If the object (in this case, secondary education) is not clear, the goals of this object will not be very sharp. Therefore the various statements of the goals of secondary education given in this chapter will also apply, with greater or less cogency, to elementary and even higher education. In view of the many basic similarities of all levels of education, this is quite natural and to be expected.

GOALS OF THE AMERICAN PUBLIC SECONDARY SCHOOL

ULTIMATE GOAL

There is general agreement, as well as wholehearted support, by almost all educators on the ultimate goal of the American public secondary school. This goal is that of happy, free citizens fulfilling their personal and public destiny.

PROXIMATE GOALS

During this period of our educational history, there have been numerous statements made by various educational groups on the proximate goals of American public education. Though often differing in emphasis, approach, and sometimes even in basic philosophical orientation, almost all these goals have one broad theme running through them, namely, that these educational objectives cannot be conceived of in solely intellectual terms, but rather must aim at a far broader realization of the many and varied facets of the pupil's personality. The four most important statements of the objectives of American public secondary education during this period have been *Cardinal Principles of Secondary Education* (1918), *The Purposes of Education in American Democracy* (1938), "The Imperative Needs of Youth of Secondary-School Age" (1947), and "The Report of the White House Conference on Education" (1955).

The Seven Cardinal Principles of Secondary Education

These principles, drawn up in 1918 by the Commission on the Reorganization of Secondary Education, were prefaced by the following remark: "Education in a democracy, both within and without the school, should develop in each individual the knowledge, interests, ideals, habits and powers whereby he will find his place and use that place to shape both himself and society toward ever nobler ends." [2] This broad outlook characterized, as well as set the tone of, the *Cardinal Principles*. The Commission noted that these principles "apply to education as a whole —elementary, secondary, and higher," but that it would "consider specifically the role of secondary education in achieving each of these objectives." [3]

> *Principle Number 1. Health.* The secondary school should provide health instruction, inculcate health habits, organize an effective program of physical activities, regard health needs in planning work and play, and cooperate with home and community in safeguarding and promoting health interests.
>
> *Principle Number 2. Command of the Fundamental Processes.* Throughout the secondary school instruction and practice [in the more advanced stages of reading, writing, and arithmetic] must go hand in hand.
>
> *Principle Number 3. Worthy Home-Membership.* Worthy home-membership as an objective calls for the development of those qualities that make the individual a worthy member of a family, both contributing to and deriving benefit from that membership.
>
> *Principle Number 4. Vocation.* Vocational education should equip the individual to secure a livelihood for himself and those dependent on him, to serve society well through his vocation, to maintain the right relationships toward his fellow workers and society, and, as far as possible, to find in that vocation his own best development.
>
> *Principle Number 5. Civic Education.* [This] should develop in the individual those qualities whereby he will act well his part as a member of neighborhood, town or city, State and Nation, and give him a basis for understanding international problems.

[2] Commission on the Reorganization of Secondary Education, *Cardinal Principles of Secondary Education,* Bulletin no. 35. (Washington: Government Printing Office, 1918), p. 9.

[3] *Ibid.,* p. 11.

Principle Number 6. Worthy Use of Leisure. Education should equip the individual to secure from his leisure the re-creation of body, mind and spirit, and the enrichment and enlargement of his personality.

Principle Number 7. Ethical Character. In a democratic society ethical character becomes paramount among the objectives of the secondary school.[4]

The Commission felt that what up to this time had been the proximate goal of the secondary school, viz., intellectual development, should be deemphasized, though by no means neglected. The secondary school program should be reorganized around the twin proximate goals of total, all-around personal development and the needs of society. The keystone in this arch of objectives was that of ethical character.

The realization of the objectives already named is dependent upon ethical character, that is, upon conduct founded upon right principles, clearly perceived and loyally adhered to. Good citizenship, vocational excellence, and the worthy use of leisure go hand in hand with ethical character; they are at once the fruits of sterling character and the channels through which such character is developed and made manifest. On the one hand character is meaningless apart from the will to discharge the duties of life, and on the other hand there is no guarantee that these duties will be rightly discharged unless principles are substituted for impulses, however well intentioned such impulses may be. Consequently ethical character is at once involved in all the other objectives and at the same time requires specific consideration in any program of national education.[5]

These broad proximate goals of secondary education as embodied in the seven *Cardinal Principles* set the stage for future statements on the proximate objectives. As the years passed, stress on the "whole student" became increasingly pronounced. However, moral education, the cornerstone of the seven *Cardinal Principles*, became less and less emphasized as the period progressed. Today moral education in American public secondary schools is, at best, recognized not as the cornerstone but merely as just another phase of the school's total program; at worst it is relegated to a position of one of the school's lesser goals.

The Purposes of Education in American Democracy

This group of principles drawn up by the Educational Policies Commission of the NEA in 1938 remains today probably the most influential set of proximate objectives for American public education as a whole. These objectives are intended to apply with equal relevancy to all levels of schooling; they are thus directly (but not exclusively) aimed at secondary education.

[4] *Ibid.,* pp. 11–15.
[5] *Ibid.,* p. 10.

The Commission noted that this set of proximate educational objectives is based on the "minimum essentials of democracy." These minimum essentials which are taken to be the basic purposes of American democracy consist of five commitments, viz., the general welfare, civil liberty, the consent of the governed, the appeal to reason, and the pursuit of happiness.[6]

The Commission makes a fourfold division of the proximate goals of education, namely, self-realization, human relationships, economic efficiency, and civic responsibility.

The Objectives of Self-realization

The Inquiring Mind. The educated person has an appetite for learning.

Speech. The educated person can speak the mother tongue clearly.

Reading. The educated person reads the mother tongue efficiently.

Writing. The educated person writes the mother tongue efficiently.

Number. The educated person solves problems of counting and calculating.

Sight and Hearing. The educated person is skilled in listening and observing.

Health and Knowledge. The educated person understands the basic facts concerning health and disease.

Health Habits. The educated person protects his own health and that of his dependents.

Public Health. The educated person works to improve the health of the community.

Recreation. The educated person is participant and spectator in many sports and other pastimes.

Intellectual Interests. The educated person has mental resources for the use of leisure.

Esthetic Interests. The educated person appreciates beauty.

Character. The educated person gives responsible direction to his own life.

The Objectives of Human Relationships

Respect for Humanity. The educated person puts human relationships first.

Friendships. The educated person enjoys a rich, sincere and varied social life.

Cooperation. The educated person can work and play with others.

Courtesy. The educated person observes the amenities of social behavior.

Appreciation of the Home. The educated person appreciates the family as a social institution.

[6] Educational Policies Commission, *The Purposes of Education in American Democracy.* (Washington: NEA, 1938), pp. 7–9.

Conservation of the Home. The educated person conserves family ideals.
Homemaking. The educated person is skilled in homemaking.
Democracy in the Home. The educated person maintains democratic family relations.

The Objectives of Economic Efficiency

Work. The educated producer knows the satisfaction of good workmanship.
Occupational Information. The educated producer understands the requirements and opportunities for various jobs.
Occupational Choice. The educated person has selected his occupation.
Occupational Efficiency. The educated producer succeeds in his chosen vocation.
Occupational Adjustment. The educated producer maintains and improves his own efficiency.
Occupational Appreciation. The educated producer appreciates the social value of his work.
Personal Economics. The educated consumer plans the economics of his own life.
Consumer Judgment. The educated consumer develops standards for guiding his expenditures.
Efficiency in Buying. The educated consumer is an informed and skillful buyer.
Consumer Protection. The educated consumer takes appropriate measures to safeguard his interests.

The Objectives of Civic Responsibility

Social Justice. The educated citizen is sensitive to the disparities of human circumstance.
Social Activity. The educated citizen acts to correct unsatisfactory conditions.
Social Understanding. The educated citizen seeks to understand social structures and social processes.
Critical Judgment. The educated citizen has defenses against propaganda.
Tolerance. The educated citizen respects honest differences of opinion.
Conservation. The educated citizen has a regard for the nation's resources.
Social Application of Science. The educated citizen measures scientific advance by its contribution to the general welfare.
World Citizenship. The educated citizen is a cooperating member of the world community.
Law Observance. The educated citizen respects the law.
Economic Literacy. The educated citizen is economically literate.
Political Citizenship. The educated citizen acts upon an unswerving loyalty to democratic ideals.[7]

[7] *Ibid.,* pp. 50, 72, 90, 108.

The Imperative Needs of Youth of Secondary-School Age

While the above statement by the Educational Policies Commission was both highly influential and extremely important, there were many public secondary school educators who thought that it would be advisable to devise a set of proximate objectives intended primarily, and indeed exclusively, for secondary schools in the modern world. Such a set of objectives, in keeping with the current experimentalist philosophy of education, would not be goal-centered, or ideal-centered, but pupil-centered. The "needs" of the student were to be the basis for the proximate goals of public secondary education. Thus in 1947 the National Association of Secondary-School Principals, after considerable study and investigation, published its statement on the ten imperative needs. This statement was revised in 1951.

The Imperative Needs of Youth of Secondary-School Age

Imperative Need Number 1—All youth need to develop saleable skills and those understandings and attitudes that make the worker an intelligent and productive participant in economic life. To this end, most youth need supervised work experience as well as education in the skills and knowledge of their occupations.

Imperative Need Number 2—All youth need to develop and maintain health and physical fitness.

Imperative Need Number 3—All youth need to understand the rights and duties of the citizen of a democratic society, and to be diligent and competent in the performance of their obligations as members of the community and citizens of the state and nation, and to have an understanding of the nations and peoples of the world.

Imperative Need Number 4—All youth need to understand the significance of the family for the individual and society and the conditions conducive to successful family life.

Imperative Need Number 5—All youth need to know how to purchase and use goods and services intelligently, understanding both the values received by the consumer and the economic consequences of their acts.

Imperative Need Number 6—All youth need to understand the methods of science, the influence of science on human life, and the main scientific facts concerning the nature of the world and of man.

Imperative Need Number 7—All youth need opportunities to develop their capacities to appreciate beauty in literature, art, music and nature.

Imperative Need Number 8—All youth need to be able to use their leisure time well and to budget it wisely, balancing activities that yield satisfactions to the individual with those that are socially useful.

Imperative Need Number 9—All youth need to develop respect for other persons, to grow in their insight into ethical values and principles, to be able to live and work co-operatively with others, and to grow in the moral and spiritual values of life.

Imperative Need Number 10—All youth need to grow in their ability to think rationally, to express their thoughts clearly and to read and listen with understanding.[8]

Since the publication of "The Imperative Needs," most of the discussion by educators on the proximate goals of secondary education has centered on meeting adolescent needs. Perhaps the clearest, most compact, and most comprehensive treatment of these needs is to be found in the Fifty-Second Yearbook, Part I of the National Society for the Study of Education (NSSE).[9] Appropriately titled *Adapting the Secondary-School Program to the Needs of Youth,* this yearbook carefully identified, charted, diagramed, examined, and analyzed adolescent needs from almost every conceivable angle and proposed a secondary school program centered completely around these needs. Educators are passionately committed to this approach, and there is scarcely an issue of a professional secondary school journal which does not include at least one article on adolescent needs and their curricular ramifications.

The Report of the White House Conference on Education

This 1955 report which resulted from discussions of over two thousand educators attempted to reformulate and modernize the broad educational goals recommended in 1938 by the Educational Policies Commission, as it itself observes:

During the past two generations [since the EPC statement] the list of school goals has grown with increased speed. [These new goals include safety courses, driver education, health services, leisure-time activities, school-community programs, etc.] This is a phenomenon which has excited both admiration and dismay. After several decades of experimentation, should this broadening of goals be recognized as legitimate?

This Committee answers *Yes.* Nothing was more evident at the White House Conference on Education than the fact that these goals, representing as they do an enormously wide range of purposes, are an answer to genuine public demand. These goals have, after all, been hammered out at countless school board meetings during the past quarter century throughout the land. The basic responsibility of the schools is the development of the skills of the mind, but the overall mission has been enlarged. Schools are now asked to help each child to become as good and as capable in every way as native endowment permits. The schools are asked to help children to acquire any skill or characteristic

[8] National Association of Secondary-School Principals, *Planning for American Youth,* rev. ed. (Washington: The Association, 1951), p. 9.

[9] National Society for the Study of Education, *Adapting the Secondary-School Program to the Needs of Youth,* Fifty-Second Yearbook, Part I. (Chicago: University of Chicago Press, 1953).

which a majority of the community deems worthwhile. The order given by the American people to the schools is grand in its simplicity: in addition to intellectual achievement, foster morality, happiness and any useful ability. The talent of each child is to be sought out and developed to the fullest. Each weakness is to be studied and, in so far as possible, corrected. This is truly a majestic ideal, and an astonishingly new one.[10]

This quotation expresses very succinctly the views not only of the *Report* itself, but of many contemporary educators. The specific enunciated goals of the *Report* are as follows:

What Should the Schools Accomplish?

1. The fundamental skills of communication—reading, writing, spelling as well as other elements of effective oral and written expression; the arithmetical and mathematical skills, including problem solving. While schools are doing the best job in their history in teaching these skills, continuous improvement is desirous and necessary.
2. Appreciation of our democratic heritage.
3. Civic rights and responsibilities and knowledge of American institutions.
4. Respect and appreciation for human values and for the beliefs of others.
5. Ability to think and evaluate constructively and creatively.
6. Effective work habits and self-discipline.
7. Social competency as a contributing member of his family and community.
8. Ethical behavior based on a sense of moral and spiritual values.
9. Intellectual curiosity and eagerness for life-long learning.
10. Esthetic appreciation and self-expression in the arts.
11. Physical and mental health.
12. Wise use of time, including constructive leisure pursuits.
13. Understanding of the physical world and man's relation to it as represented through basic knowledge of the sciences.
14. An awareness of our relationships with the world community.

To achieve these things for every child, the schools must have an effective program of guidance and counseling for the world of work.[11]

Several things should be noted about this White House *Report*. First, like the objectives of the Educational Policies Commission, the goals enunciated therein are conceived of as equally applicable to all levels of public education. This tends to strengthen the idea of formal

---

[10] Committee for the White House Conference on Education, *A Report to the President*. (Washington: Government Printing Office, 1956), p. 9. The report was officially published the year after it was submitted.

[11] *Ibid.*, pp. 91–92.

public education as a single unified process, not as a collection of three or four separate and distinct levels. Second, it broadens considerably the scope and hence the role of the school to a point where the modern secondary school would be virtually unrecognizable to an educator of a century ago. Of this widening function, which is gladly assumed, the *Report* says: "We must never lose sight of the insistent need to increase the excellence of our schools while increasing their scope; the two goals are not incompatible, except under conditions of bad management or inadequate resources." [12] But, by way of warning, the *Report* further observes that while the school should do all in its power to *help* foster all desirable characteristics in youth, it should not consider itself as the only agency which can or does help young people. The school should not become an octopus.[13] Third, the *Report* asserts that the primary but not exclusive proximate aim of the school is "the development of the intellectual powers of young people, each to the limit of his capacity." [14] This represents a shift in the concept of primary aim; for the *Cardinal Principles,* the primary goal was ethical character; for the Educational Policies Commission it was total personality development for democratic living; and for the NASSP, it was meeting the needs of youth. Nonetheless, the White House *Report* does note that the school must help its students to "apply ethical values which will guide their moral judgments and their conduct, and to develop the recognition that these values stem from, among other sources, their spiritual and religious convictions." [15]

Other Proximate Goals

The four statements of proximate goals of public secondary education given in the preceding pages have been the most significant and influential in the modern period. Many more proximate goals have been proposed at different times by various groups and it is manifestly impossible to list them all. However, there is one set of goals which merits attention, chiefly because it seems to represent the thinking of a great many educators; indeed these objectives might well become the proximate goals for American public secondary schools of the future.

These goals are those of the community school, and can be most lucidly and succinctly found in the Fifty-Second Yearbook, Part II, of the National Society for the Study of Education, entitled *The Community School.*[16] The community school idea was conceived in the

---

[12] *Ibid.*, p. 13.

[13] *Ibid.*

[14] *Ibid.*, p. 11.

[15] *Ibid.*, p. 92.

[16] National Society for the Study of Education, *The Community School,* Fifty-Second Yearbook, Part II. (Chicago: University of Chicago Press), 1953.

1930s, but in its present form it is a relatively new development in American education, emerging after World War II. However, it was not until the 1950s that the movement gained significant momentum. The classic definition of the community school is "a school that has two distinct emphases—service to the entire community, not merely to the children of school age; and discovery, development, and use of the resources of the community as part of the educational facilities of the school." [17] In its most advanced stage of development, the school and local community would merge into one entity, i.e., the school would become the local community and the local community would become the school. From this concept of the community school flow its proximate goals which are as wide and as varied as the community and the pupils. The school's goals, as enunciated in the NSSE's Fifty-Second Yearbook, Part II, include such things as a survey of traffic conditions, management of the community dairy, assistance in slum clearance, and serving as the center for the community's radio and television stations.

Criticisms of the Proximate Goals

While most American public secondary school educators in official positions heartily endorse, vocally at least, the proximate goals of the EPC, NASSP, the White House *Report,* and the community school, there are not a few critics of these objectives. Indeed, if certain evidence is believed (and there is substantial proof that it can be believed), a vast segment of both the public and the classroom teachers are among these critics. This has been particularly true since the Russians launched Sputnik on October 4, 1957. These criticisms are directed more at the secondary school than at any other level. The more prominent of the vocal critics usually fall into one of two groups, viz., the extreme and the moderate.

Extreme Critics. Four names stand out among the more vigorous critics of contemporary American public secondary education: Arthur Bestor, Hyman Rickover, Mortimer Smith, and Albert Lynd. Three elements common to the educational criticisms of these men are the emphasis on a strongly intellectual program as the only valid proximate goal for secondary schools, the rejection of the idea that the primary purpose of the secondary school is to educate the "whole pupil," and the great dissatisfaction with the type of professional educator who controls public secondary schools and sets their proximate goals.

Arthur Bestor, the historian and educator, writes:

---

[17] Maurice F. Seay, "The Community-school Emphases in the Postwar Period," in National Society for the Study of Education, *American Education in the Postwar Period: Curriculum Reconstruction*, Forty-Fourth Yearbook, Part I. (Chicago: University of Chicago Press, 1945), p. 209.

An educational philosophy is both anti-intellectual and anti-democratic if it asserts that sound training in the fundamental disciplines is appropriate only for the minority of students who are preparing for college and the professions, and if it proposes to deprive the rest of the children of our people of such training by substituting programs that minimize intellectual aims.[18]. . .

Let no one be lulled into the fatal belief that professional educationists of this ["functional needs"] stamp are merely reopening the old debate concerning the relative value of different intellectual disciplines. We must face the facts. These up-and-coming public-school educationists are *not* talking about substituting one scholarly discipline for another. They stopped talking about that years ago. They are talking—as clearly as their antipathy for grammar and syntax permits them to talk—about the elimination of all scholarly disciplines.[19]

Hyman Rickover, Vice-Admiral in the United States Navy and "father of the atomic submarine," is equally caustic. He notes:

Our schools are the greatest "cultural lag" we have today. When I read official publications put out by the men who run our educational system— booklets such as *Life-adjustment Education for Every Youth* or *Education for All Youth*—I have the strange feeling of reading about another world, a world long since departed if it ever existed at all. I sense the kindly spirit, the desire to make every child happy, the earnest determination to give advice on every problem any young person might ever meet in life. . . . Today's big problems for young people are not how to choose the proper tie, or how to be socially popular—these are minor problems which any mother can teach her children with little difficulty. They are piddling problems; . . . the only way to prepare [youngsters to meet big problems] is to make sure that all our children will be truly "educated." [20]

Mortimer Smith, an acute if not acid observer of the American educational scene, writes:

The Life Adjustment movement is not new, it is but an old acquaintance going under a newly assumed name. It is the latest manifestation of the idea [of progressive education] that the school's task is only incidentally to train the intelligence and impart knowledge, that its real function is to serve as a gigantic bureau of social services where the attempt will be made to adjust the student to all "real life problems." [21]

Albert Lynd, former college professor turned businessman, remarks:

Details of [the school's] program on "Home and Family Life" may be of hair-raising interest to those parents who still think that a school is a school

---

[18] Arthur Bestor, *The Restoration of Learning.* (New York: Knopf, 1955), p. 8.
[19] *Ibid.*, p. 55.
[20] H. G. Rickover, *Education and Freedom.* (New York: Dutton, 1960), pp 23–24.
[21] Mortimer Smith, *The Diminished Mind: A Study of the Planned Mediocrity in Our Public Schools.* (Chicago: Regnery, 1954), p. 22.

and a home is a home. There are sections on how a family may play together, on games, leisure reading, entertaining, courtesy in the family, vacations and outings, and pets. . . . There is a cluster of topics under the heading of "How can my home be made more democratic?" . . . There is no reference to reading, writing or arithmetic as such. The children will presumably get these by osmosis, while they are making their homes democratic.[22]

Moderate Critics. Far more numerous than the extreme critics are the moderate critics. This latter group is often drawn from the ranks of professional educators themselves, such as Isaac Kandel and Paul Woodring. Among the elements common to the educational observations of the moderate critics are emphasis on intellectual development as the primary but not exclusive proximate goal for secondary schools; due recognition of the pupil's physical, social, emotional, and spiritual needs in the school's total program; stress on the difference between schooling and education, and temperateness in tone and statements of the criticism of the goals.

Woodring offers the following criticisms of the proximate goals of education as enunciated by the Educational Policies Commission. Most of what he says can apply with equal relevancy to the other statements of goals:

There is something here for everyone, whether he looks upon the school as a custodial institution, a playground, a hospital, a propaganda agency, or an educational institution; everyone can find justification for his own pet educational hobby. But as a guide in educational planning, such a list is worse than useless, for it seems clearly to justify as an *educational* objective anything which even the most imaginative person would suggest as an appropriate school activity, and so open the door to all kinds of pressures on the schools to accept ever-increasing responsibilities.

Acceptance of this list, and it has been widely accepted, makes it impossible to decide whether a study of mathematics, logic and history are more or less important than courses in fly-fishing, social dancing or tree climbing; for the last makes no suggestion that objectives of "the inquiring mind" or "critical judgment" are one bit more important as educational aims than the objectives of courtesy, cooperation and friendship, all of which could be promoted by letting the children climb trees in groups.

It may be that the majority of Americans would accept this as a list of *social* objectives; it is most unlikely that they would accept it as a list of the responsibilities of the school.[23]

[22] Albert Lynd, *Quackery in the Public Schools.* (New York: Grosset & Dunlap, 1953), p. 34. Copyright 1950, 1953, by Albert Lynd. By permission of Atlantic-Little, Brown and Company.

[23] Paul Woodring, *A Fourth of a Nation.* (New York: McGraw-Hill, 1957), pp. 107–108.

On the list of proximate educational goals given in the White House *Report*, Woodring makes a criticism which may also be relevant to the other statements:

The list fails to discriminate between the true *aims* and such skills as the three R's, which are clearly means towards ends themselves, though it seems unlikely that the majority of the delegates to the conference would accept the pragmatic position that ends and means are indistinguishable.[24]

The 1945 report of the Harvard Committee, entitled *General Education in a Free Society*, remains one of the classics among the moderate criticisms of the proximate goals of public education. Some pertinent texts from this report are:

It is often despairingly said that the modern school, being expected, like Atlas, to carry the world, is thereby prevented from carrying on its own true work. . . . There is no good complaining that the school is Atlas. People will not let it cease to be such until more generally benign influences surround the young.[25]. . .

But as scholasticism ran the danger of becoming a system without vitality, so modernism runs the danger of achieving vitality without pattern.[26]. . .

The objective of education is not just knowledge of values but commitment to them, the embodiment of the ideal in one's actions, feelings and thoughts, no less than an intellectual grasp of the ideal.[27]

Professional educators reacted to these criticisms in either of two ways. Some prominent schoolmen like Spalding and Alexander vehemently denounced the critics, compiled counterarguments and asserted that these criticisms could only have the effect of harming the nation's public schools. A well-known professor and secondary school specialist at Teachers College, Columbia University, made the statement to one of her classes that men like Bestor should not be permitted to publish. However, other educators, including such outstanding figures as Brickman and Hanna, felt that these criticisms, while limited, were valuable in that they served as a useful resource for school self-improvement. Woodring, commenting on the extreme criticism noted that while "in a very real sense it failed in its real purpose" it was nevertheless "highly successful in probing the soft spots in [modern] educational philosophy . . . [and has] called attention to excesses and stupidities." [28]

[24] *Ibid.*, p. 109.
[25] Harvard Committee, *General Education in a Free Society*. (Cambridge, Mass.: Harvard University Press, 1945), p. 33.
[26] *Ibid.*, p. 49.
[27] *Ibid.*, p. 72.
[28] Woodring, *op. cit.*, p. 10.

Conclusion

Throughout this treatment of proximate goals, several points seem to emerge, factors which should be kept in mind when reflecting on this issue. First, a distinction must be made between formal and informal education. It is the secondary school's task to formally educate the pupils committed to its care. But the school should not permit itself to become an octopus and to assume that it is synonymous with total education. The home, church, social agencies, friends—all these and more —have their place in the education of youth. These other agencies or groups should not be conceived of as "auxiliaries" of the school, but as full-fledged partners. To be sure, these other agencies often have a far greater educational impact on young people than does the school.

Second, the secondary school must sometimes temporarily assume functions not intrinsically proper to it because of the abdication of responsibility of these other agencies. However, the school's assumption of these peripheral functions should be as temporary as possible; the school should continue these functions only until the moment when the other agencies have been sufficiently revitalized. In no circumstances and under no conditions should the secondary school attempt to serve as a church or quasi-church agency, a position implied in the writings of some public school educators.

Third, the primary proximate goal of the secondary school should be truth, which is achieved in an atmosphere of personality growth built around the integrative intellect. It is this characteristic which makes the school so unique and indeed so important in society. The cardinal aim of the secondary school is not to aid a pupil to obtain a better job or to meet a member of the opposite sex. However, man's mind is not an island, and these nonintellectual elements are indispensable corollaries to learning. Hence they should find a place in the school precisely to the extent that they affect the pupil's growth in truth.

Fourth, the issue of the breadth of the proximate goals for secondary education is not, as it has often been made out to be, whether the school should undertake to instruct youth in all things, from mathematics to social dancing; rather the issue is whether the nonintellectual subjects will be taught in such a way and at such a time as to exclude, occlude, or abridge the intellectual subjects. The psychology of human learning and the exigencies of modern American society make it impossible and unrealistic for the school to devote itself exclusively to formal intellectual development.

Fifth, moral and spiritual values are so important and pervasive in life that they must be inculcated by every youth-serving agency, including the secondary school. As United States Supreme Court Justice

Douglas remarked in the Zorach decision, "We are a religious people whose *institutions* presuppose a Supreme Being." [29] Denominational instruction and atmosphere are, of course, unconstitutional in American public secondary schools; however, this is no reason for making them secularistic or even godless institutions. Moral and spiritual values, as the Educational Policies Commission of the NEA has remarked, should be actively promoted in a host of ways in the public secondary schools.[30]

Sixth, criticism of the proximate goals of public secondary schools should not be viewed as a sign of enmity toward those schools, but rather as an indication of friendship. The critics, like the defenders, have as their goals the strengthening and purifying of our schools. Responsible criticism should be encouraged because it affords the opportunity of school improvement through a knowledge of, and subsequent correction of, its weaknesses. This criticism should emanate both from inside and outside the ranks of professional educators; from inside because the schoolmen know the situation firsthand, from outside because no acceptable audit is ever an internal one. The public is paying the educational bill, and it should receive in return both what it wants and what it ought to have.

GOALS OF THE AMERICAN CATHOLIC SECONDARY SCHOOL

This subtitle could also have read "Catholic Goals of the American Secondary Schools." However, the neutralist and secularist philosophy of the public secondary schools precludes these Catholic goals from being realized in any but Catholic high schools.

Catholic educators are as imprecise as public school educators on the definition and delimitation of secondary education; hence, similarly, the proximate goals are not too sharp.

ULTIMATE GOAL

Every Catholic educator agrees on what the ultimate goal of the Catholic secondary school should be, viz., that every student should "know, love and serve God on this earth, and be happy with Him forever in the next." The Catholic secondary school should play its *special* role in helping each pupil to attain this end.

[29] 343 U.S. 306, 72 Sup. Ct. 629, p. 313. Italics supplied.
[30] Educational Policies Commission, *Moral and Spiritual Values in the Public Schools.* (Washington: NEA, 1951), p. 80.

PROXIMATE GOALS

There is no "official" Catholic position on the proximate goals of the American Catholic secondary school binding under faith or morals. Catholic educators disagree, often vehemently, among themselves on the proximate goals. Nowhere is such difference of opinion more apparent than in the identification of the primary proximate goal of the Catholic secondary school. In general, two main positions have been enunciated on this question: the moralist and the intellectualist.

The Moralist Position

This view holds that the primary proximate goal of the secondary school is to directly bring the students closer to Christ. This approach has been the traditional one in the United States. Although its heyday was in the century from 1850 to 1950, it is still very strong today; in fact, it is probably the position held by the majority of those currently teaching in American Catholic high schools. Prominent among those espousing the moralist view are Msgr. Kelly, Fathers J. and K. O'Brien, Fr. Hurley, and Professors Redden and Ryan.

Msgr. George A. Kelly states the moralist position very succinctly when he declares that "moral teaching should hold first place in the classroom." [31] Moral teaching here implies not only instruction in religious truths but the active encouragement of living a spiritual life. He maintains that the superior school is not the one with the best overall scholastic achievement but rather the one which best teaches the pupil the Christian position in his "relationship to his Creator, his fellow man and nature." [32]

Fr. Francis T. Hurley in an address to a gathering of Catholic teachers said, "Intellectual development, however, is not the epitome of true education. Above and beyond the intellect is character, and the Catholic school must 'cooperate with divine grace in forming Christ in those regenerated by Baptism.' Not only is this consistent with a philosophy of Christian education, it is demanded by the moral needs of the youth of today." [33]

Fr. John A. O'Brien affirms that the Catholic secondary school "must seek, directly or indirectly, to assist our students in the attainment of their eternal destiny." [34] He further notes that proficiency in

[31] George A. Kelly, *The Catholic Family Handbook.* (New York: Random House, 1959), p. x.

[32] *Ibid.*, p. 62.

[33] Francis T. Hurley, "Sermon at the Annual Teachers Mass at the Cathedral in Washington, D.C.," *Catholic School Journal,* LVIII (October, 1958), p. 34.

[34] John A. O'Brien, "Catholic Secondary Education and the Fulfilment of the Church's Needs," *Bulletin of the National Catholic Educational Association,* LI (August, 1954), p. 335.

educating pupils in secular knowledge can never substitute for the inculcation of Catholic truths and the fostering of Catholic living.

Professors John D. Redden and Francis A. Ryan assert that the proximate goal of the school is to fit the pupil "to conduct himself as a Christian man of character." [35] Secular subjects "must always be taught as means to ends," [36] that is, in such a way that they will harmoniously lead to the development and enrichment of Christian character.

Fr. Kevin J. O'Brien, C.Ss.R., one of the most vigorous defenders of the moralist position, notes that the important objective of the secondary school is that it teach the pupils to "do all for the love of God." [37] Secular knowledge, he holds, is not that important anyway. Indeed "knowledge without moral formation is simply a weapon in the hands of a criminal." [38] Fr. O'Brien maintains that the world should not worry so much about educating a poor, devout, but intellectually backward savage in some distant land, because "he has in his will charity, which is superior to all knowledge in this life." [39] To be sure, even the best natural knowledge ignores reality.[40] The principal proximate goal of the Catholic secondary school is the encouragement and direction of students toward living a deep Christian life. All else counts but for little. In his words, "It is surely an anomaly to see Catholic high school children coming each day to school and seldom if ever making a voluntary visit to the Blessed Sacrament in the church nearby." [41]

The Intellectualist Position

This view holds that the primary proximate goal of the secondary school, both public and parochial, is intellectual development of the pupil. This development is best achieved exclusively through instruction in what Smith terms "the teachable subjects," i.e., those intellectual disciplines which are metaphysically capable of being learned from an instructor. Nonintellectual areas, including Christian perfection, social needs, and so forth, do not really fall under the purview of the secondary school; indeed if the school does engage in certain nonintellectual functions, it does so incidentally rather than as an essential extension of its primary proximate objective. Although it was advocated by certain

[35] John D. Redden and Francis A. Ryan, *A Catholic Philosophy of Education,* rev. ed. (Milwaukee: Bruce, 1956), p. 134.

[36] *Ibid.,* p. 141.

[37] Kevin J. O'Brien, C.Ss.R., *The Proximate Aim of Education.* (Milwaukee: Bruce, 1958), p. 167.

[38] *Ibid.,* p. 53.

[39] *Ibid.,* p. 184.

[40] *Ibid.,* p. 175.

[41] *Ibid.,* p. 202.

nineteenth-century European educators, such as Cardinal Newman, the intellectualist position did not win any appreciable number of American Catholic adherents until the 1950s. While it is still the minority position in Catholic circles, there are definite signs of its increased acceptance. Prominent among its advocates are Fr. Reed, Fr. Donlan, Fr. Cunningham, and Professor Smith.

Fr. William F. Cunningham, C.S.C., in his highly influential textbook remarks:

> The school has one specific function for which it has been brought into being by society and this is the mental development of youth privileged to share in its ministrations. . . . It is an intellectual agency. . . . The Catholic school recognizes that its *specific function* is the preservation and propagation of the intellectual tradition of Catholic culture and that the means to this end is the development in students of intellectual virtues that they may "advance in wisdom." [42]

Fr. Thomas C. Donlan, O.P., vigorously maintains that "the perfection of the mind through the intellectual virtues" [43] is the proximate aim of the secondary schools. Christian perfection is no more the purpose of the school than it is of the hospital. Morality is an important goal of education, to be sure, but education must not be confused with the school. Education refers to all those people, agencies, and objects which lead to man's instruction, while the school is simply an agency dedicated to intellectual development. The inculcation of morality is, therefore, at best, an indirect function of the secondary school.[44]

Fr. Lorenzo Reed, S.J., a leading figure in American Catholic secondary education, declares:

> The [secondary] school has for its primary [proximate] purpose the development of the child's mental powers. It has other purposes, but they are secondary, and many of them can be achieved concomitantly if the primary purpose is achieved well. . . . Let the school use all of its class time for the fulfillment of its primary purpose. Let it seek to achieve its secondary purposes through a carefully planned extracurricular program.[45]

Professor Vincent Edward Smith, an American Catholic philosopher who recently has turned his attention toward education, is one of the staunchest adherents of the intellectualist position. In his 1961 Delta

[42] William F. Cunningham, C.S.C., *The Pivotal Problems of Education.* (New York: Macmillan, 1940), pp. 556, 557, 560.

[43] Thomas C. Donlan, O.P., *Theology and Education.* (Dubuque: Brown, 1952), p. 58.

[44] *Ibid.*, pp. 37–74.

[45] Lorenzo Reed, S.J., "Excellence for Whom?" *Bulletin of the National Catholic Educational Association,* LVII (August, 1960), p. 268.

Epsilon Sigma address, he maintained that the proximate goal of the school is not to "educate the whole person" (a great fallacy, he claimed) but rather to educate solely a part of the pupil, namely, the intellect. Professor Smith asserted that he was grounding his conclusions in metaphysical and psychological soil; the methods of educating the intellect differ *radically* from the procedures of educating the other faculties and constituents of the "whole person," e.g., the will, the emotions, and so forth. Drawing upon what he had said several years earlier,[46] he noted that only the intellectual disciplines can be included in the category of "teachable subjects"; hence, they and they alone really belong in the school. Moral virtue and the arts can, of their nature, be only fostered, not taught; hence, if these are to be found in a secondary school it should only be by way of accommodation.

Some Weaknesses of the Moralist Position

Intellectualists and kindred thinkers believe that there are several serious weaknesses in the moralist position.

The first great weakness is the confusion between "education" and "the school." Moralists, and in particular Fr. Kevin O'Brien, like to claim the support of Pope Pius's Encyclical, *The Christian Education of Youth,* in their assertion that the primary proximate goal of the secondary school is the inculcation of morality. Smith, addressing himself to Fr. O'Brien says in reply: "In our view the distinction must be made between the total education, described by the Holy Father and having its completion the beatific vision, and formal education or education within the school." [47] Fr. McCluskey, S.J., though by no means an intellectualist, remarks in a similar vein, "The saving of souls is too general an explanation of the school's purpose." [48] The primary proximate goal of the school cannot be the same as that of the Church, else they would not be separate, distinct agencies.

The second great weakness of the moralist position is its refusal to accord the intellectual life its due respect. The moralists tend to separate the world into two spheres, direct Catholic morality and utter worthlessness. This dichotomy results from a lack of awareness of the intrinsic values of diverse realities as they are, not in the ideal order, but in the existential order. Of this lack of awareness Fr. Ward, C.S.C., says: "We assert that in schools the main business is not to convert people, to make

---

[46] Vincent Edward Smith, "The Catholic School: A Re-Examination," *Bulletin of the National Catholic Educational Association,* LII (August, 1955), pp. 37–48.

[47] Vincent Edward Smith, *The School Examined: Its Aim and Content.* (Milwaukee: Bruce, 1960), p. 33 footnote.

[48] Neil G. McCluskey, S.J., *Catholic Viewpoint on Education.* (Garden City, N.Y., Hanover House, 1959), p. 74.

them good or save their faith and morals—good ends, all of them. In some circumstances, an inherently lower end must rate highest; for instance it is better to give a starving man some soup than to pray for him; and good as it is to pray for him, we should not let the praying get in the way of the soup." [49] Fr. Cunningham, C.S.C., further notes: "No matter how important they may be in life, e.g., the moral virtues, they cannot be first in the school, for the simple reason that the instructional activities of the school are aimed at the development of the intellectual virtues." [50] Fr. Ward, C.S.C., sadly observes that all too often Catholic schools have based their programs around the moralist position, so that Catholic schools are a cross between a mission, a parish, and a school.[51] Certainly the not uncommon practice of sending students to Confession during class hours bears out his contention. He further remarks ironically, that "the highest 'save the soul' motives tend in such schools to get in the way of simple plebeian intellectual ends." [52]

The third great weakness of the moralist position is a lack of awareness of the value and critical importance of secular or natural knowledge. Pope Pius XI in his encyclical, *The Christian Education of Youth*, stresses the importance of secular knowledge for youth. Fr. Ward, C.S.C., observes that human beings *need* secular learning.[53] Did not St. Augustine hold that "to understand the Scriptures we need to lean on secular learnings"? [54] Do not theologians teach that a person's degree of glory in heaven will be radically affected by the amount and degree of knowledge he possesses? Indeed, the more a person knows, the more he can love God, since as St. Thomas teaches, one cannot love what he does not know. The attitude of the moralists toward secular learning seems akin to the opinion that Eve sinned because she sought more knowledge. The moralist approach to secular learning results in what the eminent Thomist, Gilson, has often called "the disvaluation of pure knowledge." Such a mentality leads to a sterile activism without life-giving roots in the soil of speculative knowledge.

The fourth great weakness of the moralist position is its failure to realize that the Catholic-oriented secondary school should engage its students in a living dialogue with all reality, not just those elements which are thought of as directly building character. As Cardinal Suhard noted, the education of students must "bear on pure truth and disin-

[49] Leo R. Ward, C.S.C., *New Life in Catholic Schools*. (St. Louis: Herder, 1958), p. 15.

[50] Cunningham, *op. cit.*, p. 561.

[51] Ward, *op. cit.*, p. 9.

[52] *Ibid.*, p. 13.

[53] Ward, *op. cit.*, p. 24.

[54] Quoted in *ibid.*

terested science"; no apologetical interest should interfere with this quest
—rather, the student "must seek *only* what is." [55] To be sure, an excessively apologetical interest which is regrettably present in some
American Catholic high schools has, in the opinion of the intellectualists
and others, a narrowing and crippling effect on the students. O'Dea
observes that some view the task of the Catholic schools as "providing a
life-time supply of answers to 'difficulties' to be memorized and 'filed
away' for future reference, and often the role of the laity is conceived
as having in readiness the 'Catholic answer' to give to non-Catholic
friends. There seems to be an implicit notion abroad in some quarters
that the Catholic mind will be the product of the catechism, the
scholastic manual and finally of the pamphlet rack." [56] Intellectualists
would paraphrase St. Ignatius and say that a secondary school which has
an ounce of sanctity with an exceptionally good intellectual program
does more for the saving of souls than one which exhibits striking
sanctity but with an ounce of intellectual program.[57] The problems encountered by St. Teresa of Avila in finding a good spiritual director
would seem further to bear this out.

The fifth great weakness in the moralist position is the unwarranted
creation of a great chasm between the natural and supernatural. The
following statement of Fr. Kevin O'Brien, C.Ss.R., is most illustrative
of the dichotomy of the natural and the supernatural posited by the
moralists: "Parents and teachers should never forget that a boy of twelve
with a knowledge of the essential truths of faith is on a loftier pinnacle
than a Steinmetz, an Edison, an Einstein without faith." [58] But the fact
is that God interpenetrates all reality, all knowledge, so that such divorce
of natural from supernatural is existentially and theologically unsound. Every cause is somehow and some way in its effect; so it is with
God and His creatures. As Fr. Walter Ong, S.J., observed in an address
before the NCEA, "God's presence in [all reality] has been undervalued,
for his presence in reality is proportionate to its actuality." [59] The
temporal and eternal, natural and supernatural, should never be separated in Catholic secondary education. This is particularly true of the
school's intellectual program. Intellectual perfection for man is *directly*
Christian perfection for him, since at the roots of his being, man is rational. God cannot be taken out of reality, a reality which includes man's

[55] Emanuel Cardinal Suhard, *Growth or Decline? The Church Today*, trans. by
Corbett. (Notre Dame, Ind.: Fides, 1948), p. 82. Italics supplied.

[56] Thomas F. O'Dea, *American Catholic Dilemma: An Inquiry into the Intellectual Life*. (New York: © Sheed and Ward, 1958), p. 111.

[57] The original quoted in Cunningham, *op. cit.*, p. 167.

[58] Kevin J. O'Brien, *op. cit.*, p. 35.

[59] Walter J. Ong, S.J., "Academic Excellence and Cosmic Vision," *Bulletin of the
National Catholic Educational Association*, LVIII (August, 1960), p. 41.

intellectual functions. As Maritain remarks, "Intelligence is at the very basis of Christian life." [60] No knowledge, therefore, can be completely secular; all knowledge is God-soaked whether that knowledge be that of an Edison or Fr. O'Brien's hypothetical boy of twelve. Original sin is important in that it created a disjointedness (but *not* a separation) between natural and supernatural; however, the fact of the Redemption with its healing effect must never be forgotten. Catholic educators must not scoff at the development of the "natural man" in secondary school, for by developing the "natural man," the school automatically develops the "supernatural man." As Rt. Rev. Romano Guardini, the distinguished European theologian, has noted, St. John's Gospel is the most human of all the Gospels, which is one of the chief reasons why it is the most divine. This interpenetrability of natural and supernatural is brought out very well by Smith:

To incorporate biology into a theological world view, biology must first be learned as biology and not as theology. The best thing a mathematics teacher can do for the Christian intelligence is to teach mathematics mathematically. The synthesis of theology and biology on the one hand and of mathematics and theology on the other will be more perfect in proportion as each science involved is learned according to its own specificities. This is the way God made our knowing powers; this is the way God made things in their relation to our knowing powers. There may not be any difference in the long run between seeing things the way they are and seeing them in relation to God; but there is a difference of order in our way of seeing.[61]

Some Weaknesses of the Intellectualist Position

Nor is the intellectualist position without its weaknesses, a fact which the moralists and kindred thinkers are not slow to point out.

The first great weakness in the intellectualist position is the almost total neglect of the "whole man." Intellectualists tend to think of a secondary school student more as a disembodied intellect than as a person. The proximate objectives of secondary education must, of necessity, be based on the nature of the pupil. As Gilson observes, teaching can never be separated from learning.[62] Students are persons—persons who have emotions, social needs, growing pains, and so forth. Pope Pius XI recognized a pupil-directed education when he remarked:

It must never be forgotten that the subject of Christian education is man whole and entire, soul united to body in unity of nature, with all his faculties,

[60] Jacques Maritain, "On Some Typical Aspects of Christian Education," in Fuller (ed.), *The Christian Idea of Education.* (New Haven, Conn.: Yale University Press, 1957), p. 181.

[61] Smith, *The School Examined: Its Aim and Content, op. cit.,* p. 277.

[62] Etienne Gilson, "Education and Higher Learning," in Pegis (ed.), *A Gilson Reader.* (Garden City, N.Y.: Image Books, Doubleday, 1957), p. 325, footnote 6.

natural and supernatural, such as right reason and revelation show him to be; man, therefore, fallen from his original state, but redeemed by Christ and restored to the supernatural condition of adopted son of God.[63]

In contrast to this total view of human personality the intellectualists at worst tend to view the school (and the pupils) as being in a hermetically sealed intellectual vacuum, or at best to view them as being in a one-track system ascending ever higher toward a totally intellectual goal, uninfluenced by any other human forces save the intellect. As Msgr. John B. McDowell told a meeting of the NCEA Secondary School Department, "whether it likes it or not, the [secondary] school is *not* developing intellect—it is developing personalities." [64] Overintellectualism is nonhuman. Catholic educators and educational theorists must not view the goals of secondary education narrowly. This narrow vision might well be caused, strangely enough, by insufficient exercise, for is it not true that the majority of the intellectualist educators have hardly if ever taught in a comprehensive public or Catholic secondary school, and certainly not recently. As a result, moralist educators have not without reason accused intellectualists of being "ivory-tower theorists." In the real world, the adolescent comes to school whole and entire. As Fr. William McGucken, S.J., sagely observed: "The Catholic secondary school has the specific function of training for intellectual virtues. Yet as a Catholic institution it must always recognize that since it is concerned with the whole pupil, intellectual training is not enough, nor is it ever the most important thing in the life of the child." [65]

The second great weakness in the intellectualist position is a somewhat outmoded conception of the role of the secondary school in American society. Purely intellectual goals might have been palatable to students in the days when few attended high school. Before the turn of the century, 75 per cent of all high school graduates went to college. The intellectualists feel, at least implicitly, that the proximate goals of the secondary school are the same as those of the college. The terminal role of the secondary school is thus ignored, despite the fact that high school today is accepted as part of the common school. Today's secondary schools serve *all* American youth, not merely the intelligent. The intellectualists may deplore the increased comprehensiveness of the American secondary school, but they cannot ignore it. The comprehensive high

[63] Pope Pius XI, *Christian Education of Youth.* (Washington: NCWC, 1936), p. 23. The emphasis which the Pope places on the Redemption should be noted.

[64] John B. McDowell, "The Encyclicals on Education and the Catholic Secondary Schools," *Bulletin of the National Catholic Educational Association,* LVI (August, 1959), p. 218. Italics supplied.

[65] William J. McGucken, S.J., "Intelligence and Character," *Bulletin of the National Catholic Educational Association,* XXXVI (May, 1940), p. 11.

school is here to stay, and intellectualists must accept reality as it is, rather than attempt to posit goals inappropriate to this kind of education.

The third great weakness in the intellectualist position is the over-valuation of knowledge. Man is composed of more than mere intellect; he has a will, emotions, a physique, all of which may play a far more important role in a person's daily decisions than does the intellect. As Msgr. McDowell humanistically observes: "The fact is that while Catholic education is in the business of giving knowledge and understanding about life as we Catholics accept it, this is simply not enough. There are habits and skills of living that are equally important—attitudes, opinions, values, virtues of living. . . . Knowledge is important, but it is not enough." [66] Thomistic philosophy maintains that knowledge and virtue are not identical; yet the intellectualists seem to feel that once knowledge is learned in school, the students automatically become virtuous, lead "the good life." Typical of this view is that of one Catholic secondary school teacher who felt that a person who performed a deed which he knew was wrong was a "weakling" or simply "lacked respect for authority." [67] Such an attitude fails to understand how once the intellect is presented with truth, the person can do evil. But the intellect is *not* the person; it is only one of his faculties. As Msgr. McDowell observes, "Knowledge is important, but it is not enough." The school must not only teach about virtue, it must also give youth a chance to practice it.

The fourth great weakness in the intellectualist position is the failure to realize that not all education is directly intellectual. The findings of psychologists have shown that a great deal of learning, and indeed the most influential kind, is acquired by other than purely intellectual means. Over and above this, it is well to remember that formal academic instruction is not the sole method of intellectual formation, a fact which many intellectualists lose sight of. Nor is formal academic instruction necessarily the most effective method of intellectual formation. This is particularly true when such instruction is formalistic and rigoristic.

The fifth great weakness in the intellectualist position is a lack of appreciation of the purpose of Catholic education as it exists in America. If the only direct proximate goal of the Catholic secondary school is to educate the mind, then why should a Catholic parent send his child to a Catholic high school? This question is especially pertinent in those locali-

[66] McDowell, *loc. cit.*

[67] See Sister M. Judith Therese, "Realizing Our Philosophy through Literature," *Bulletin of the National Catholic Educational Association*, LII (August, 1955), pp. 290–295.

ties where the public high schools afford a richer intellectual diet than their Catholic counterparts. Indeed, studies seem to indicate that graduates from church-related high schools do not perform so well scholastically in college as do graduates from public high schools—this despite the fact that graduates from church-related high schools had a higher scholastic aptitude.[68]

A Third Position: The Goal of Truth

It is quite apparent that neither the moralist nor the intellectualist position provides a complete and adequate answer to the proximate goal of the Catholic secondary school. What is needed, as Fr. Ward maintains, is a new vision for Catholic schools. Such a vision cannot come by categorically declaring the two aforementioned positions "false," a regrettable, narrow-minded practice employed by some Catholic educators. This new vision can come only from sublimating the best elements of the moralist and intellectualist positions and adding to these some fresh elements.

The primary proximate goal of the Catholic secondary school should be truth, whole and entire. This goal is considerably wider than that of the intellectualist position, and of a different order from the moralist position. Truth comes into the mind by many and varied channels, through intuition, revelation, grace, and abstraction. Truth in the mind and soul is often aroused by objects both intellectual and nonintellectual. Indeed all truth is Christian, since all reality contains something of God, its Creator. Thus there are no strictly secular subjects or secular truths. Neither does all truth flow from formally labeled Catholic sources. St. Thomas said, "Take truth where you find it," anywhere, anywhere at all. He practiced what he preached, for often he used pagans to refute sermons and textbooks written by saints.

Truth is an all-embracing goal. As Maritain remarks: "Truth is the inspiring force needed in the education of youth—truth rather than erudition and self-consciousness—all pervading truth rather than the objectively isolated truth at which each of the diverse sciences aims." [69]

The possession of truth, whole and entire, cannot fail to lead to wisdom. Indeed Christian wisdom can be said to be automatically implied in the concept of truth as the primary proximate goal. Wisdom,

---

[68] Robert E. Hill, Jr., "Scholastic Success of College Freshmen from Parochial and Public Secondary Schools," *School Review*, LXIX (Spring, 1961), pp. 60–66; see also Leonard V. Koos, *Private and Public Secondary Education*. (Chicago: University of Chicago Press, 1931).

[69] Jacques Maritain, *Education at the Crossroads*. (New Haven, Conn.: Yale University Press, 1943), p. 62.

like the month of June, bursts out all over. As Fr. Kevin O'Brien, C.Ss.R., notes: "The development of wisdom increases the potentiality for the development of the other virtues and vice-versa. Here then is the ontological base for unity and harmony in man's intellectual development." [70] Wisdom is not exclusively intellectual; indeed, it is an integrating thing. As Fr. McCluskey, S.J., comments, wisdom is the "supreme integrating principle" which orders "the knowledge, skills and attitudes" that the pupils learn.[71] Pope Pius XI spelled out this concept of Christian wisdom: "The proper and immediate end of Christian education is to cooperate with divine grace in forming the true and perfect Christian. . . . The true Christian, product of Christian education, is the supernatural man who thinks, judges and acts constantly and consistently illumined by the supernatural light of the example and teaching of Christ." [72] Thus true education is guided Christian wisdom, built around the intellect and reaching out to embrace other pertinent and significant areas of the pupil's nature and living. And this can be done only if the school first presents the truth, whole and entire, and then lives that truth. The school can give truth, but only the child, cooperating with Divine grace, can produce wisdom in himself.

This proximate aim of the secondary school perforce includes the production of a richer person who can plumb the depths of reality and see all things, not only in themselves, but also in the light of their ultimate causes, in so far as the pupils' abilities permit.[73] Truth is the aim, and truth is not only an intellectual object but a Person.[74] Catholic secondary education in its fullest sense should enable the student to see Christ as St. Francis of Assisi did, in all people, in all things, and not just in the tabernacle.

Some Catholic educators of the narrow sort seem to delight in poking fun at the noble secondary school goals of non-Catholic educators, e.g., to serve humanity better. These Catholic educators appear to restrict Christ's presence to the altar or to religion classes. Indeed, in word and deed their naturalist neighbors seem to have lived the doctrine of the Divine indwelling in others far better than have some Catholics. The primary proximate goal of the secondary school is truth, and truth is not restricted to edifice or pulpit.

[70] Kevin J. O'Brien, *op. cit.*, p. 150.

[71] McCluskey, *op. cit.*, p. 76.

[72] Pope Pius XI, *op. cit.*, pp. 35–36.

[73] For a more complete analysis of this concept, see James Michael Lee, "The Place of Science in the High School," *Catholic Educational Review*, LVII (May, 1959), pp. 305–306.

[74] "What is truth?" asked Pilate. Christ did not answer verbally but responded by His Presence. *He* was truth, but who was there at that trial perceptive enough to catch this existential communication of Christ's?

Means of Achieving This Proximate Goal. Truth, as has been previously observed, it not implanted in the student in any one exclusive way. It is fostered in a variety of ways in a good secondary school. There are at least five separate but related avenues through which the secondary school can inculcate truth in its students, viz., the intellect, moral formation, habits, attitudes, and skills.

The Intellect. The ultimate goal of the Catholic secondary school is to help its students attain God. The proximate goal, to be adequate, must somehow contribute in its own unique way to the achievement of the ultimate goal. In order to become like Christ, the student must first become himself. The more human he becomes, the more Divine. But we become human primarily (but not solely) through the intellect. Therefore the Catholic secondary school's most important role is intellectual development. It is by *directly* cultivating the intellect that the secondary school performs a great and indispensable task. This concept should replace the idea, all too common, of "Oh well, I suppose intellectual development is necessary for life, but isn't it a pity it's not connected to the spiritual life?" Faith and natural knowledge must interpenetrate each other, lest each wither and die from lack of breadth. As St. Anselm remarked centuries ago, the Christian believes that he may better understand, and understands that he may better believe. Faith seeks knowledge, and knowledge seeks faith. Only in their union can there be truth, whole and entire.

As both McCluskey[75] and Smith[76] have observed, a secondary school conducted according to Catholic principles will direct all that is taught, whether through the intellect, by habits, etc., to the ordering wisdom of theology. Each subject, problem area, and activity will be autonomous, but not completely so; it will be somewhat related both to other subjects, problem areas, and activities, and to Catholic theological principles. Only this type of secondary school can be said to give to its students adequate objective knowledge, for the simple reason that objective reality constitutes, among other things, Revelation, the teachings of the Church, and the relationship of all subjects, problem areas, and activities to theology. Secondary education, to be valid, must in its own special way help each youth achieve his own eternal destiny.

Secondary education must therefore be broadly intellectual. It must be remembered that all knowledge is not factual—certainly neither truth nor wisdom is. Formalism, undue adulation of the past while neglecting the present, exaggerated traditionalism—all these must be avoided. A balance must be struck between a changing presentism and

---

[75] McCluskey, *op. cit.*, p. 93.
[76] Smith, "The Catholic School: A Re-Examination," *op. cit.*, p. 47.

a static eternalism. Secondary education should not be thought of as consisting solely of formal instruction.

Moral Formation. Spiritual living, to paraphrase Ortega y Gasset, is not some sort of ornamental accessory to the life of leisure. It is a necessary and indispensable part of education, as the educational pronouncements of Popes Pius XI and Pius XII attest. Christ must be formed in the minds and hearts of the students. A secondary school assists the students to become more Christlike precisely by performing its unique task, not by transforming itself into a disguised novitiate. Of course the nature of human learning demands that the relations between theology and individual subjects and activities be explicitly and implicitly indicated. However, to indicate relationships between the two is not to substitute one for the other.

The school's desire for moral education should not be corrupted into "molding." God gave every person free will, and any attempts to mold, however high and lofty the motives, are contrary to human nature the way God made it. To be sure, molding is not only a crime against the student, but is also a crime against a reality and against God. Moral education should be *inculcated* in the student; there can never be an excuse for molding.

Habits. It is a universally known fact that man is a creature of habit; he acts for the most part habitually. The aim of the school thus is not merely truth, but truth habitually present in the youth's mind and actions. As Aristotle observed, while knowledge leads to virtue, in itself it is not virtue. Virtue is habitual. Knowledge of facts and theories fade with time, but habits linger tenaciously. Habits of truth in themselves and in their proper relationships should be fostered in the student; and indirectly but powerfully this will lead to habits of prayer as well as habits of the sacraments. Good habits may well be built around Canon Cardijn's Young Christian Students' triple method of observe, judge, act—all in accord with truth, whole and entire. Good habits will carry over into the student's postschool life when he will have considerable leisure. Worthy use of leisure time is no idle goal of secondary education; a person's thoughts are often colored by his use of leisure time. The student must learn to use leisure to continue to perfect himself in truth. Here is where the type of habit previously developed plays its deciding role.

Attitudes. Closely linked with habit is attitude. A person's attitudes are of crucial importance in determining the course of both his future intellectual development and his future concrete actions. As Fr. Cunningham, C.S.C., himself an intellectualist, notes, "The striking difference . . . between a Catholic school informed by the philosophy of supernaturalism, and a school conducting a purely naturalistic program will be in the matter of attitudes." [77] A student in a secondary school operated on Catholic principles acquires a Christian attitude toward reality and life. This attitude conditions all his future knowledge and makes it meaningful. Attitudes largely account for a person's approach and subsequent response to value. It is almost impossible to exaggerate the importance of attitudes in man's life as he actually lives it. The students acquire attitudes from the entire life of the school, not merely from its formal instructional program or from one aspect of the program. This fact was dramatically borne out in a survey by Sister Antonina Quinn of 4,000 Catholic secondary school students. The investigator found that formal religious instruction was not sufficient for shaping Christian attitudes. Her survey disclosed that the courses offered, their presentation, the physical plant, the activities program, and the personalities of the teachers were decidedly more important than formal religious instruction in inculcating Christian attitudes in the students.[78]

Skills. The Greeks regarded physical skills as a necessary ingredient in the schools. Christ who as a young man "grew in age and grace before God and man" acquired the skill of carpentry. Many Religious Orders require their novices to learn manual skills. Thus the entire Christian tradition speaks out loudly and clearly about the necessity of skills not only for vocational education but for general, liberal secondary education also. The secondary school should perfect some previously learned skills, e.g., art, music, as well as teach new skills, e.g., typewriting, woodworking. The skills should not be slighted (as they often are, particularly by Catholic high schools), but integrated into each institution's particular program.

Some Conclusions Flowing from This Proximate End. This goal of truth should lead to action. To be sure, there is a great deal of pragmatism (in the nonphilosophical sense of the word) in the Catholic view of secondary education. The pupil is taught the truth so that he will think and do what is right. The reason for the truth goal of secondary education is not merely truth itself but rather truth guiding the student to more ultimate ends, to "choose good and avoid evil," to make the wise decisions. This is by no means a disvaluation of truth; rather it is truth at its fullest realization. Truth in man is not complete in itself; it is an intellectual virtue which seeks its expression, its fulfillment in moral virtue. In God, intellectual virtue and moral virtue are so united that they are one. God is the Living Truth, pure Truth in perfect act. In man, the intellectual virtue of truth and the moral virtues are closely

[77] Cunningham, *op. cit.*, p. 554.

[78] This study is cited in Edmund J. Goebel, "Making the High School Truly Catholic," in McKeough, O. Praem. (ed.), *The Administration of the Catholic High School.* (Washington, D.C.: Catholic University of America Press, 1948), p. 169.

united, but are not one. Truth is its own complete action in God, but in man it is only part of his action, his intellectual action. Intellectualists propose a proximate goal for secondary education adequate to God's nature but not to human nature. The secondary school tries to educate the whole student, which is another way of saying that it gives his will and his body an opportunity to live the truth, existentially as a human being, which the intellect knows.

Such a proximate goal of truth living in the student implies the necessity of proper guidance. It is the function of guidance to make truth livable in the actual concrete lives of the students. The NCEA took cognizance of this when it made an official resolution to the effect that guidance programs are *essential* in education.[79] A fulfillment of the proximate goal of truth reveals that a guidance program is necessary in a secondary school. The adolescent nature of the pupils in whom this proximate goal is to be realized further demonstrates this. It is folly to think of the goal apart from the students in whom the goal will be realized.

The latter observation is a capital point: The primary proximate goal of the secondary school must be radicated in the student. Each pupil must learn to accept and live this primary proximate goal and the means to its fulfillment; otherwise the goal will not take hold in his life— and then of what value is it? The pupil's view and the school's view of this goal must coincide, else this goal will remain a mere objective datum external to the student rather than a vibrant reality living within him. This goal, adequately realized only in the student himself, must thus be adapted to individual differences.

This goal of truth must also be expansive in time. As Bishop James W. Malone declared at the 1961 annual convention of the Secondary School Department of the NCEA, the high school must educate its students to be reeducable. New knowledge in so many fields is growing with such rapidity that unless students continue their learning after graduation they will become intellectually obsolete. Automation, with its resultant increases in leisure time, makes this growth in learning imperative, he asserted. Thus the secondary school has an obligation to strive so to inculcate the proximate goal of truth seeking in the pupils that they will live this goal for the rest of their lives.

Official NCEA Statement of Catholic Secondary School Goals

In April, 1944, the Secondary School Department of the National Catholic Educational Association issued its official statement entitled "Objectives of the Catholic High School." Prepared by a study group

[79] "Resolutions," *Bulletin of the National Catholic Educational Association,* LVII (August, 1960), p. 33.

under the auspices of the Policies Committee of the Secondary School Department, this statement was the result of long, comprehensive, and careful deliberation. The study group prepared a tentative draft which was superseded by a second tentative draft of the statement, but both were rejected by the Policies Committee as being too heavy and cumbersome, hence not usable. The third draft was mimeographed and submitted to more than one hundred competent principals, administrators, and professors of Education, both Catholic and non-Catholic, for their frank criticisms. The fourth and final draft, which resulted from this evaluative criticism, was officially presented to the Secondary School Department at the NCEA's annual convention in 1939.[80] The following year a rather drastic revision of this statement was proposed.[81] Two years later still further revisions were urged. The fourth and last revision group decided in 1944 that the original 1939 statement should be accepted with certain minor changes. It is this 1944 statement which constitutes the official "Objectives." [82]

Fr. Julian L. Maline, S.J., a member of the Policies Committee, made the following observations about the proximate "Objectives" which must be kept in mind in both the assessment and use of the "Objectives."

The Committee has really had a twofold purpose in preparing this document: first to provide our Catholic high schools with material which will *help* them (not do the work for them) in framing a statement of objectives for submission to examining bodies which may ask for such a statement; second to provide our schools with an instrument for periodic self-examination by means of which they may judge whether or not the actual conduct of their schools corresponds with the Catholic philosophy of life and education which they profess.

In carrying out its task the Committee has at the same time tried to produce a statement which (1) is distinctively Catholic, (2) is general enough to apply to practically all Catholic secondary schools in the country, (3) is yet detailed enough to avoid the charge of pious vagueness.

The Committee has tried to express the objectives of Catholic secondary education in the United States in meaningful, concrete language, in terms of the high school graduate's behavior; that is, in terms of results. Instead of listing its seven major objectives in such abstract terms as intelligence, morality, culture, health and so forth, it states [the goals] in dynamic terms.[83]

[80] See Julian L. Maline, S.J., "Aims and Results of Catholic High Schools: A Tentative Statement of the Objectives of Secondary Education in the United States," *Catholic School Journal*, XL (May, 1940), pp. 146–149.

[81] A. F. Schnepp, S.M., "Objectives of Catholic Secondary Education," *Catholic School Journal*, XL (December, 1940), pp. 325–327.

[82] For the accounts of revision developments, see "Report of the Policies Committee," *Bulletin of the National Catholic Educational Association*, XLI (August, 1944), pp. 234–235.

[83] Maline, *op. cit.*, p. 146.

The official statement is divided into seven divisions, each division dealing with one of the seven proximate goals of Catholic secondary education as identified by the Policies Committee. These objectives, whose overall result is intended "to guide, nourish and stimulate the adolescent mind and heart" [84] are to develop *intelligent* Catholics, to develop *spiritually vigorous* Catholics, to develop *cultured* Catholics, to develop *healthy* Catholics, to develop *vocationally prepared* Catholics, to develop *social-minded* Catholics, to develop *American* Catholics. The entire statement of these proximate goals is as follows:

I. To Develop *Intelligent* Catholics:

1. Who have acquired the common store of secular knowledge which may be expected of pupils of secondary-school age; and have learned to use and to interpret the common sources of information
2. Who have a reasonably thorough understanding of Catholic practice, and can give a reason for the faith that is in them
3. Who realize that Catholicism, as a way of life based upon eternal truths, must affect their attitude and conduct toward every problem of life, whether personal or social in character
4. Who recognize that there are eternal principles; and that there is no incompatibility between the externally true character of such principles and their application to a changing civilization
5. Who have developed a thirst for knowledge, and display initiative and energy in their pursuit of it—qualities which are revealed in a capacity for further formal education if opportunity offers, or for continued self-education if formal schooling ends with their high-school days
6. Who value things of the mind above material wealth and personal comfort; and have accordingly developed the habit of reading what is worthwhile in Catholic and secular literature
7. Who are interested, in a modest way, in intellectual creation (scholarship) as well as in assimilation
8. Who can recognize a problem when faced by one, can formulate it definitely, and can, in the light of available evidence, project a reasonable plan for its solution
9. Who are intellectually humble, honest, and objective, yet discriminating in their judgments—not duped by prejudice, slogans, or propaganda
10. Who have profited, according to capacity, by a training given in season and out, in such fundamental "virtues of intellect" as concentration, accuracy, logicality, clearness, thoroughness, and persistence

[84] Policies Committee, Secondary School Department, National Catholic Educational Association, "The Objectives of Catholic Secondary Education in the United States," *Catholic High School Quarterly Bulletin*, II (April, 1944), p. 21.

II. To Develop *Spiritually Vigorous* Catholics:

1. Who *personalize* truth, especially moral and religious truth, by applying it to their own conduct
2. Who have a vital realization of God as the source and sanction of all moral obligations; have therefore a sense of *personal accountability*, first, to Him, and, second, to self and to others, whether superiors, equals, or inferiors; and have a correct appreciation of the origin of *authority* and of its correlative, the principle of *obedience*
3. Who habitually act on Christian *principle* rather than from mere instinct, feeling, or passion (or from consideration of mere expediency, humanitarianism, or servile compliance with fashion), yet strive to *use* these mighty instruments of self-realization—as reason and Faith direct
4. Who also understand and prudently follow the Christian way of *renunciation* in dealing with these emotional drives
5. Who face with confident Christian *fortitude* the manifold dangers that menace the life of body and soul; and welcome the inevitable trials which toughen human character and prove man's worth during his probation
6. Who strive to advance in *all* the natural and supernatural virtues —not excluding such "passive" Christian virtues as meekness and humility
7. Who have learned to find in the lives of Christ, Our Lady, and the Saints, and in books on ascetical doctrine, inspiration leading to *better than mediocre* Catholic lives
8. Who recognize and meet their Christian obligation to *help others* achieve similar moral and religious self-improvement, either through personal contact or through vigorous Catholic Action in family, parish, school, and other social groups
9. Who have learned to express their devotion to Christ's divine person, principles, and ideals through their devotion to the person, principles, and ideals of Christ's Mystical Body—the Church—under the headship of His Vicar on Earth, aspiring, if their talents warrant, to courageous, dynamic *leadership* in the rich field of *Catholic Action*
10. Who see their absolute need of *supernatural aid* to lift their lives to supernatural levels; seek it through prayer, the Sacraments, and other good works; and cooperate with it generously

III. To Develop *Cultured* Catholics:

1. Who recognize the ennobling force of an intelligent appreciation of beauty, whether that beauty be found in nature, human works of art, human character, the majestic liturgy of the Church, or in the ideally beautiful Christ—all reflections of the infinite beauty of God

2. Whose taste has been refined by instruction—with particular attention given to the rich heritage of Christian art—by the example of cultured teachers, and by a school environment which is itself educative of man's aesthetic nature

3. Who guard against any minimizing of the intellectual or any exaggerating of the physical and sensuous in beautiful things

4. Who contribute, according to their talents, to the creation and diffusion of true beauty in all the arts and particularly in literature

5. Who have learned to select, to support, and to participate in what is good and wholesome in art, music, literature, drama, and other forms of entertainment and recreation

6. Who out of regard for Our Lady do their part to maintain the high traditions of Christian chivalry; if men, by showing a fine respect of all womanhood; if women, by meriting and demanding this chivalrous respect from all men

7. Who show their good taste as well as their Christian charity by painstaking attention to refined manners, careful dress, and cultured speech, and by avoidance of all that is vulgar, boorish, and cheap

8. Who appreciate the role and value of imagination as judged by the inter-relationship with thought, will, and emotions; and have cultivated it by proper exercise

9. Who, aware of the irrational character of the imagination, control it, particularly through control of the avenues that lead to it—the senses

IV. To Develop *Healthy* Catholics:

1. Who have a fine Christian respect for the body as the partner of man's immortal soul, destined to share one day its happiness in heaven

2. Who accordingly are equipped with the necessary knowledge, and exercise due precautions to protect themselves and others against accident and disease

3. Who, likewise, keep the body a physically fit instrument of the soul by the proper amount and kind of exercise and recreation, but refuse to yield to "athleticism" and the modern cult of the body

4. Who out of regard for the body refuse themselves the pagan's ready indulgence of the body's every urge and clamor for satisfaction

5. Who, further, mindful of the Fall and of the consequent "war of the members," practice a positive Christian asceticism, refusing the body at times even lawful indulgence, in order that the proper domination of spirit over matter and of Grace over nature may always be maintained, for the ultimate good of body and soul alike

V. To Develop *Vocationally Prepared* Catholics:

1. Who in their secondary-school days have given serious and prayerful thought to their future life-work, not excluding priestly and religious vocations, and have taken proper counsel regarding it

2. Who are properly equipped either to step at once into a gainful occupation or to profit by further instruction and training designed to lead to a gainful occupation in the future

3. Who have mastered that body of knowledge and those fundamental skills which are indispensable or highly valuable in every vocation

4. Who realize that the universal obligation to labor applies to them, whatever their station or condition in life

5. Who appreciate the Christian dignity of every toiler and of every form of honest toil and see at least the moral beauty in every task well done

6. Who are conscientious in the execution of whatever work they assume and mindful of the worker's obligation to give a fair return in work for a fair wage paid

7. Who have a sound notion of what recompense they may equitably demand or accept for work done

8. Who scorn the idea of amassing great wealth at all costs as the dominant motive of occupational life

9. Who realize that their work affects favorably or adversely the society of which they are members, and particularly in their choice or acceptance of employment carefully weigh the effect of that employment upon their own moral life and that of others

VI. To Develop *Social-minded* Catholics:

1. Who, in preparing for their probable roles as Catholic fathers and mothers, have developed a genuine *love of family life* and a Christian respect for and understanding of, the responsibilities of parenthood

2. Who have cultivated such essential *family virtues* as the spirit of work, of thrift, of hearty cooperation, and of unselfish, affectionate devotion to the happiness of others

3. Who have at least elementary knowledge of these four points:
   a. The multitude and complexity of their social relations and of the importance of these relations for the individual's well-being and growth
   b. The social conditions in their own communities and in larger units of society, and of the social problems which this knowledge reveals
   c. The basic principles of the Christian social doctrine expounded in the Encyclicals of the Popes and Programs of the American Bishops

   d. Effective methods of securing recognition for, and application of, this Christian social doctrine

4. Who are aware of the solidarity of human society and of the effect of their actions on the lives of others for better or for worse
5. Who are mindful of the added strength given to this solidarity by membership in the Mystical Body of Christ—the Church
6. Who are mindful, likewise, of the responsibilities to parish, diocese, and Universal Church which this membership creates
7. Who are alive to their responsibility to God no less for their social than for their personal conduct
8. Who are alert to the need of corporate as well as personal worship of God
9. Who are scrupulously just in their respect for the rights of others, whether individuals or groups
10. Who "love their neighbors as themselves" and so are sensitive to the claims of *charity,* whether to heal or prevent distress, particularly in the case of the exploited and unfortunate
11. Who are averse to the bitterness, envy, and vindictiveness which set class against class, race against race, or nation against nation in unsocial, un-Christian antagonism
12. Who, recognizing the fundamental equality of all men, exercise toward all, regardless of position, race, or nation, a sincere Christian courtesy
13. Who applaud "those who share and sacrifice rather than those who acquire and hold"; and are themselves ready to sacrifice time, money, comfort, convenience, recreation, and prejudices in order to promote the common good, and in order to discover and eliminate, or at least reduce the causes of injustice and suffering

VII. Develop *American* Catholics:

1. Who are loyal and devoted to the government of the United States of America
2. Who insist that the American form of government, like any other, exists for the benefit of the individual citizens, and not the citizens for the benefit of the state
3. Who appreciate the fact that American democracy is based on the sound moral principle that man has received from God inalienable rights, which the state does not give and cannot take away
4. Who know and value these rights and are determined to preserve them against attack, yet distinguish between freedom and license in the exercise of these God-given rights
5. Who respect as God-given the authority inherent in properly constituted officers of government

6. Who recognize the fact that such officers may, with sufficient reason and for the common good, limit the exercise of man's natural rights, but not abrogate them wholly and permanently

7. Who by their conduct express their realization that the well-being of American democracy depends upon the moral integrity of the individual Americans

8. Who are ready to contribute, in due time, to the formation of wise public policies and to the solution of public problems

9. Who are eager and prepared to fulfill their duty as voters, and to elect to public office competent and conscientious men of high moral principles

10. Who will accept public office, if elected to it, as a sacred trust, for which they are morally responsible to God

11. Who see the need, particularly in a democracy, of respect for the opinion of others and of a ready spirit of cooperation which are opposed both to domineering aggressiveness and to selfish aloofness, timidity, or self-sufficiency

12. Who, finally, are patriotically ready for any self-sacrifice necessary to promote the common good of the whole American people[85]

Analysis of the NCEA Goals

These goals are so well stated and so all-embracing that they should be most carefully studied and analyzed in detail, item by item, by every student of American secondary education. Such study is particularly imperative for those Religious and lay people who are preparing to teach or who are now teaching in Catholic high schools. Regrettably, such intensive examination of these objectives has been all too often lacking, so much so that many Catholic high school administrators and staff members are unaware even of the very existence of this official statement of goals for Catholic high schools.

Some High Points of the NCEA Statement on Goals. There are so many excellent elements in the NCEA statement that only a few of the high points can be briefly treated.

First, the statement puts the educational emphasis and direction squarely on the whole student. Thus its goals are broader, richer, and indeed more human than cultivation solely of the intellect (intellectualist position) or solely of the will (moralist position).

Second, it emphasizes both the intellectual and affective powers of the student. Both are to be developed. A narrow rationalism, on the one hand, and a pious pragmatism, on the other, are regarded as educationally and humanly insular.

Third, the comprehensive role of the secondary school is advocated.

[85] *Ibid.,* pp. 22–28.

The Catholic high school should serve *all* Catholic youth; the terminal student is not neglected in favor of an exclusive emphasis on the college-bound.

Fourth, the value of the body as an integral partner in human living is affirmed. The body is regarded neither as an ultra-Montanist entity worthy of chastisement nor as a Platonic prison house of the soul; rather the body is viewed in its true, Christian aspect as a necessary, vital, and integral component of the human person, as significant in its own right as the soul is in its realm.

Fifth, the statement of proximate goals recognizes the importance of both creative intelligence and assimilative intelligence. The student is not considered a glorified sponge whose task it is to soak up as much information as possible; rather he is seen in a wider context, as a person who uses the truth he has learned to create a new vision, perhaps even a *Weltanschauung,* for himself and possibly for the world around him.

Sixth, the emphasis on creativity is viewed as applicable to the arts as well as to the intellect. The school is encouraged to abandon life-killing formalism and to initiate instead a program which will give full expression to *all* the student's artistic powers, particularly when these powers surpass and go beyond the intended lesson outcomes so nicely typewritten in the lesson plan.

Seventh, the statement calls for a thoroughly Catholic high school. Such a school should not be basically a "protest school," erected solely because the Catholic community does not wish its children to attend a secular secondary school. A protest school is founded essentially on a negativistic basis. Rather the program of the Catholic high school should be thoroughly Catholic, and not just a duplication of the nearby public high school. The Catholic high school should be completely soaked with the teachings of Christ and the Church; to paraphrase Sartre, the Catholic high school should ooze Christ.

Eighth, stress is placed on the Catholic high school as an institution where positive truths are given the foremost position; the Catholic high school is not viewed as essentially a miniature society dedicated to the grinding out of "the Catholic answer" to secular "opponents" or to the turning out of students whose mission in life will be to "refute the enemies of the Church" by a well-turned syllogism. Rather, personal development in living the truth is the goal.

Ninth, great emphasis is placed on charity, not just as an abstract doctrine to be studied from euphemistically titled textbooks in religion, but rather as an ever-present living force in the personal and social life of every student. Charity, love, is to pervade the school and fecundate it.

Tenth, the interpenetrability of Catholic teaching and all reality is affirmed. Catholic doctrine, in its deepest positive elements as well as in its negative cautions, is seen applying to all reality, not only to religion class or Sunday Mass. Just as Christ is shot through all reality, so should Catholic doctrine be and the living of it.

Eleventh, the statement rings with a true appreciation of obedience. The pupil is taught to obey because of the inherent value in what is being obeyed. Obedience is not allowed to degenerate into a blind, nonreasoning submission, or into a sterile passivity, or into an excessive docility.

Twelfth, the proper emphasis is placed on citizenship, and a wise course is steered between chauvinism, jingoism, and nationalism, on the one hand, and a disvaluation of the American democratic system, on the other.

Like other human documents, the statement of the Policies Committee is not without its defects. Considering the range and scope of the document, however, these defects are remarkably few. Two of its shortcomings will be mentioned in the hope of stimulating Catholic secondary school educators to refine even further this valuable statement of proximate goals. *First,* there seems to be a lack of proper respect paid to the imagination (III.9). The imagination is crucial to the exercise of creative intelligence. The great and constant emphasis on control of the imagination which has characterized much of American Catholic education is doubtless an important factor in explaining why American Catholics have contributed relatively few new ideas to the world. Imagination is a power to be harnessed, not to be stunted. *Second,* Christian chivalry must be recognized as resting on a broader base than solely that of Our Lady (III.6). The concept of the Mystical Body, the Divine indwelling, and the soul of the Church cannot be neglected in any practicing chivalry. Our Lady would doubtless be the first to give such counsel. Also the notion of chivalry as expressed in III.6 seems to be heavily flavored with the nostalgic medievalism which American Catholic thinkers such as Fr. Ong, S.J., have so eloquently denounced.[86]

One final word of caution: these proximate goals enunciated by the Policies Committee should be used prudently and realistically. As one of its members admonished:

It is neither the desire nor the intention of the Policies Committee that these "Objectives" be copied verbatim and offered by schools as peculiarly their own. They are merely suggestive, and may be drawn upon at will. They are put at the disposal of all Catholic secondary schools as an aid in drawing up a statement of local objectives. Eliminations, additions and adaptations will be found necessary according to variations of locality and type of school.[87]

[86] See Walter J. Ong, S.J., *Frontiers in American Catholicism.* (New York: Macmillan, 1957).

[87] Policies Committee, "The Objectives of Catholic Secondary Education in the United States," *op. cit.,* p. 20. Ed. note.

The Policies Committee which was responsible for drawing up the official statement of objectives was composed entirely of clergy and Religious. No lay person was represented. This was regrettable for several vitally important reasons, some of which are deeply radicated in the heart of Catholic dogma and teaching. (1) Many, if not most, educational advances both inside and outside the Church have been made by laymen. Thus to restrict lay people from participating in the Catholic educational enterprise is to deprive it of valuable human resources. (2) Lay people, because they live in the world, can understand more experientially and more deeply the needs of the high school graduates. (3) As an integral member of the Mystical Body, the layman, ex officio, by this very membership has a right to be represented in Catholic educational matters. He is a unique type of witness, and this witnesship must be recognized; to do otherwise is to make a farce of the doctrine of the Mystical Body. (4) Education is primarily a right of the Christian family, and hence this family should be truly represented in the formulation of Catholic educational goals and policy. (5) Catholic lay people bear the financial burden of supporting the Catholic school, and thus they should have a right to a voice in the determination of their school.[88]

The Effect of the NCEA Statement of Catholic Secondary School Goals

The NCEA statement unfortunately has not received from Catholic high school educators attention commensurate with its worth. Notwithstanding, this statement and the viewpoint it embraces, have had a considerable impact on alert educators and alive schools. Though there are still quite a few Catholic secondary school educators who cling to the intellectualist or moralist positions, their number is dwindling annually. More and more Catholic educators are broadening and deepening their objectives for the secondary school. This attitude is well exemplified by Power, who lists the following proximate goals for Catholic secondary education: mastery of the tools of education, assimilation of the social inheritance, continued development of the moral and theological virtues, satisfaction of individual needs, social integration, exploration of interests and capacities, and guidance.[89] No longer can the statement be made by any serious Catholic secondary school educator that ". . . our Catho-

---

[88] For a further discussion of the layman's role in the Church and in Catholic education, see Yves M. J. Congar, O.P., *Lay People in the Church*, trans. by Donald Attwater. (Westminster, Md.: Newman, 1957); William Ferree, S.M., *Introduction to Catholic Action*. (Washington: NCWC, n.d.); Justus G. Lawler, *Catholic Dimension in Higher Education*. (Westminster, Md.: Newman, 1959); Leo R. Ward, C.S.C., *Catholic Life, U.S.A.: Contemporary Lay Movements*. (St. Louis: Herder, 1959).

[89] Edward J. Power, *Education for American Democracy*. (New York: McGraw-Hill, 1958), pp. 189–190.

lic (secondary) schools are the modern monasteries within which Catholic truth and ancient culture must be preserved in a world where a neopagan barbarism of material values seeks to destroy the beauty of the ages." [90] The NCEA goals do not confuse monastic education in medieval times with secondary school education in modern times. They see the world, not through the eyes of an ultra-Montanist, but with the vision of St. Francis of Assisi in his *Canticle to Brother Sun*. Life, the world, modern times—these are all exciting realities, with much to teach the eager adolescent. The goals of the Catholic high school promote the active encounter of the youth with these realities. A negativistic outlook has been replaced by a positive program.

The Catholic High School Goals for Today

As Sister Mary Emmanuel noted, "The Catholic high school today seems to be outgrowing the juvenile stage of development." [91] How fast this growth is taking place is not too clear. However, the NCEA goals have lucidly and comprehensively suggested the direction in which this growth has been, and hopefully will take place.

In any event, the Catholic secondary school, if it is to fulfill its high mission, must radically affect the life of every student. This is a vast and penetrating task, and in many specific instances necessitates a revision of goals and outlook. Particularly is this true of the school's religious emphasis, which is supposed to soak every aspect of the instructional and noninstructional program. As one Jesuit writer noted, "Only by ceasing to be medieval in manner, ecclesiastical in character and negative in spirit can theology become a vital force for the layman [in the schools] of today." [92]

Leon Bloy once said, "There is only one tragedy in life, and that is not to be a saint." It is the ultimate goal of the Catholic secondary school, in its unique and special way, to lead the student to a vision of God "not darkly, as in a glass, but then face to face." [93]

[90] Joseph G. Cox, "The Curriculum in Post-war Education," *Bulletin of the National Catholic Educational Association*, XLI (August, 1944), p. 239.

[91] Sister Mary Emmanuel, "Continued Excellence in Education," *Bulletin of the National Catholic Educational Association*, LVII (August, 1960), p. 262.

[92] Editor's comment in John L. McKenzie, S.J., "Theology in Jesuit Education," *Thought*, XXXIV (Fall, 1959), p. 347.

[93] I Cor. 13: 12.

CHAPTER III THE NATURE OF AMERICAN SECONDARY EDUCATION

Control

The Tenth Amendment to the United States Constitution leaves to the separate states any power not specifically delegated to the Federal government. Since it was not mentioned in the Constitution, education, by virtue of this amendment became subject to state control. Each state, therefore, independently has set up its own educational standards and has created an organization to implement these standards. Of course the standards in the various states have quite a few similar elements because of several common influences. Nonetheless, in theory, each state is almost the absolute master of educational matters within its borders; in practice, there are both great similarities and wide differences in the educational standards of the various states.

Public Secondary Schools. Control of the state's public schools, elementary and secondary, resides in the state legislature. The legislature delegates its power to the state board of education, which in turn entrusts power to all the various local boards. These boards, state and local, are elected or appointed, and their purpose is to establish educational policy. This policy, once determined, is executed and implemented on the state level by the state school superintendent, and on the local level by the local school superintendent. The latter in turn delegates some of his power to the individual school principals within his district. The following table illustrates in a simplified fashion, the pattern of school control:

Control of Public Secondary Education in the State

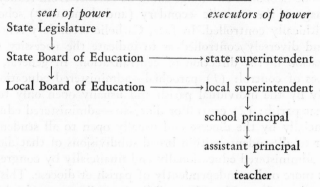

seat of power   *executors of power*
State Legislature
↓
State Board of Education ⟶ state superintendent
↓   ↓
Local Board of Education ⟶ local superintendent
↓
school principal
↓
assistant principal
↓
teacher

N.B. Arrow denotes "delegation of power to"

In short, the state performs several services for secondary schools (as well as for elementary schools). First, it maintains a state system of education. The state normally does not establish schools—individual districts and localities do this. But the state makes certain that every youth has the opportunity to attend a public secondary school. Second, it supports public secondary schools financially, the amount of money allocated to each school being determined on the basis of its average pupil daily attendance (ADA). Third, it exercises control over the secondary schools, both public and private, in the state. Thus the state enacts laws which bind, at least minimally, all secondary schools within its boundaries, e.g., school building codes, a basic curriculum, prescribed examinations or their equivalent (as in New York). However, the tradition of local control, that is, control of education primarily by local districts, ensures that the state will phrase its laws of educational control in a broad and minimal way. Fourth, the state delegates most of its power to local school districts. (Here is the legal basis for local control.) Fifth, it exercises leadership by recommendation, constructive supervision (which is also a form of control), cooperating with pilot programs in selected schools, and so forth.

Federal encouragement and assistance to schools (but *not* Federal control) have been a tradition in America since the days of the Northwest Ordinance. The U.S. Office of Education is the chief Federal agency cooperating with American schools. Alexander and Saylor list five distinct ways in which the U.S. Office maintains this cooperation: "(*1*) providing data and information which will promote education; (2) conducting research studies and investigations of various aspects of education; (3) administering exchange of students and educators with foreign countries; (4) providing consultative services; (5) exercising leadership." [1]

Catholic Schools. Few things could be further from reality than the public image of the Catholic secondary (and elementary) school system as monolithically controlled. In fact, Catholic secondary schools are so loosely and diversely controlled as to indicate the necessity of drastic reorganization in the direction of centralization. In general, there are three types of control: (1) parochial—administered educationally and financially by the individual parish and usually open only to students within that parish; (2) central or diocesan—administered educationally and financially by the diocese and usually open to all students in that diocese or to all students within broad subdivisions of that diocese; (3) private—administered educationally and financially by congregations of Religious more or less independently of parish or diocese. This threefold distinction is, as Sister Mary Janet, S.C., notes, "not completely accurate, since many parochial and private schools really function as central schools, frequently through arrangement with the bishop or through cooperation among several parishes." [2] The trend in locus of control of Catholic secondary schools established since World War II has been a substantial decrease in the number of parochial high schools and a great increase in the number of diocesan high schools. The number of private Catholic high schools has remained fairly constant. In 1956, the percentages were as follows: parochial, 45.1 per cent; diocesan (which includes some interparochial), 18 per cent; private, 36.9 per cent. [3]

In parochial high schools, the seat of power lies with the pastor, who is often the principal, nominally at least, of the school. The control is thus closely knit, subject only to extremely loose and usually vague diocesan control. In diocesan high schools, the bishop is the seat of power. In theory, the bishop normally delegates his power to the diocesan school board, which in almost all cases is composed of clergy and Religious. However, the diocesan board has much less power than its counterpart in the public school system. Most often its actual function is to serve as advisor to the diocesan superintendent of schools. The real delegatee of the bishop's power is the episcopally appointed diocesan superintendent, who is always a priest. The superintendent in turn delegates power to

[1] William M. Alexander and J. Galen Saylor, *Modern Secondary Education.* (New York: Rinehart, 1959), pp. 675–677.

[2] Sister Mary Janet, S.C., *Catholic Secondary Schools, U.S.A.* (Washington: NCWC, 1960), p. 4.

[3] *Ibid.,* p. 5.

the individual high school principal. In private high schools, the Superior General of the Order is the seat of power; this power is in turn delegated to the regional superior, to the local superior, and finally to the high school principal. Sometimes the local superior lives on the high school campus. In general, the administrators of Catholic high schools, superintendents, principals, and pastors, are not nearly as well trained professionally as are their counterparts in the public school system. Some alert dioceses and Orders are endeavoring to correct this deficiency.

The Department of Education of the National Catholic Welfare Conference has much the same relationship to the Catholic school system as the U.S. Office of Education has to the public school system. However, the extensiveness and hence the impact of the NCWC services are far less than those of the U.S. Office of Education because of the disparity in the financial resources available to each agency.

Revenue

Closely connected to secondary school control is the source of the school's revenue. Public school income is classified under two broad categories: revenue receipts and non-revenue receipts. Revenue receipts, which constitute the major portion of school income, are additions to assets which do not increase the school indebtedness and do not represent exchanges of school property for money. They are derived more or less regularly from specific sources, such as general funds of Federal, state, county, and local governments, receipts from taxes levied for school purposes, tuition, gifts, endowments, and so forth. Non-revenue receipts are those which incur either a future obligation or a change in the form of asset from property to cash and therefore decrease the amount and value of school property. Money received from loans, sale of bonds, sale of property purchased from capital funds and proceeds from insurance adjustments constitute most of the non-revenue receipts.[4]

There are, in general, five sources for public school revenue. In order of the percentage of revenue derived therefrom, these sources are local; state; Federal; intermediate; and other miscellaneous.[5] The local district thus makes the greatest financial contribution. Property tax is the chief source of revenue for local districts.

Financial support varies from district to district and from state to state. The extent of support generally bears a direct relationship to the

[4] These definitions, together with their components, were taken directly from U.S. Office of Education, *Biennial Survey of Education in the United States: Statistics of Local School Systems, 1955–1956.* (Washington: Government Printing Office, 1959), pp. 16–18.

[5] *Ibid.*, p. 17; see also National Education Association, "How the States Compare on School Support," *NEA Research Bulletin*, XXXIX (February, 1961), p. 11.

wealth of a state. Thus, for example, in 1960–1961 the estimated total expenditure per pupil in average daily attendance ranged from a high of $585 in New York to a low of $217 in Alabama. The median for all the states was $390.[6]

Like the public schools, Catholic schools get financial support from revenue and non-revenue receipts. In some Catholic high schools the major source of income is revenue receipts, particularly from parish and diocesan funds; in other Catholic high schools, the chief source of income is tuition. This is especially true of many private high schools conducted by Religious Orders and explains why these schools generally charge the highest tuition. Indeed quite a few Orders require every one of their high schools to be self-supporting; some even require each high school to turn a certain percentage of its tuition money over to the general funds of the Order to help finance the Order's charitable and missionary activities. This practice is of questionable validity, not only from a financial, but also from a moral, viewpoint vis-à-vis the parents of the students and vis-à-vis prospective pupils in a low economic bracket.

Secondary Education—for Whom?

The public secondary school is an institution which strives to serve *all* youth, and to a significant degree does. Comprehensive high schools and special purpose high schools (e.g., vocational schools) have programs to meet the needs of almost every type of youth. The Catholic high school, on the other hand, does not serve *all* American youths. It exists primarily for Catholic young people. Not only that, but Catholic high schools serve only a portion of Catholic youths, that is to say, those who meet certain minimum entrance standards of scholastic achievement, those who have the ability to pay tuition, and so on. Catholic educators all over the country are most unhappy over this situation and are earnestly striving to find a place in a Catholic high school for every Catholic youth.

Public secondary schools, particularly of the comprehensive type, are to a large extent inclusive, i.e., nonselective. However, there are certain factors which may force the public high schools to be selective, viz., location, gender, race, special abilities, and so forth. Inclusiveness, or nonselectivity, in admission to secondary schools has several advantages. Every youth is afforded the opportunity to develop himself to the fullest. No student is deprived of a secondary school education because he is intellectually or economically underprivileged. Social distance is reduced and social mobility is increased.

Enrollments in high schools have rocketed during this century, thus

[6] *Ibid.*, p. 13.

reflecting the greater inclusiveness of the secondary school. The U.S. Office of Education reported that "while the population of high school age (14–17 years) increased 71 per cent from 1889–90 to 1955–56, enrollments in grades 9–12 multiplied almost 34 times." [7] Total public high school enrollment (grades 9 through 12) as reported in 1960 was almost 10 million pupils. Enrollments in Catholic high schools have soared at a much higher rate than those of public high schools. Total Catholic high school enrollment as reported in 1960 was 845,000 pupils.

What really determines the degree of a high school's selectivity is not only the percentage of the total number of youths of high school age which it admits, but also the percentage of these youths which it graduates. A U.S. Office of Education study revealed that "public and non-public high schools in the United States graduated 1,400,000 persons in 1955–56, a number equal to 62 of each 100 persons 17 years of age." [8] Because of their lack of selectivity standards, public high schools fail to graduate a greater proportion of entering pupils than do Catholic and other private high schools; slightly more than half of those entering grade 9 in public secondary schools go on to graduate. One of the chief reasons causing pupils to fail to graduate from public high schools is economic. A report of the NEA showed that the number of high school graduates in 1955–1956 in terms of percentage of eighth-grade enrollment in 1951–1952 was in very close (but not perfect) relationship to the per capita wealth of the state, i.e., the poorer the state, the higher the percentage of dropouts.[9] Bloom has further shown that students from wealthier states do far better educationally than students from poorer states.[10] This unhappy condition tends to become a vicious circle, because it has been conclusively shown by investigators such as Harold Clark and by the U.S. Census Reports that, in general, the more formal education a person has, the greater is his wealth.[11]

Nor are Catholic high schools above reproach in this dropout selec-

[7] U.S. Office of Education, *op. cit.*, pp. 10–11.

[8] U.S. Office of Education, *Biennial Survey of Education in the United States: Statistical Summary, 1955–1956.* (Washington: Government Printing Office, 1959), p. 30.

[9] National Education Association, *Research Report: Rankings of the States.* (Washington: NEA, 1959), p. 16. The median for all the states was 64.7 per cent, with the highest ranking state having 93.1 per cent and the lowest having 43.4 per cent.

[10] Benjamin S. Bloom, "The 1955 Normative Study of the Tests of General Educational Development," *School Review,* LXIV (March, 1956), pp. 110–124. This study, based on the GED standardized test in 1943, showed that "the test results indicate that the [public] high schools are doing a significantly better job of education in 1955 than they were doing in 1943" (p. 113).

[11] See any of Harold Clark's numerous articles on this subject; also see U.S. Bureau of the Census, *U.S. Census of Population: 1950,* vol. IV, *Education,* special reports, part V. (Washington: Government Printing Office, 1953), table 12.

tivity. The fact that there are considerably fewer seniors than freshmen in Catholic high schools shows the failure of these schools to serve all their previously screened and selected youths. Thus a Catholic high school is doubly exclusive—selective in entrance and selective in retention.[12]

Types of Secondary Schools

There are, in general, three distinct types of American secondary schools, viz., comprehensive; specialized; and special. Each strives to build its program more or less around one of the three basic forms of education existing in America (and indeed in much of the world).

General education is education for man as man. It teaches man the broad principles of human life so that he may enjoy a richer existence. The humanities, together with the social and natural sciences, form the basic program of general education.[13] *Specialized education* is education for anything less than the "whole man." While general education stresses "being," specialized education emphasizes "doing." Specialized education aims at developing some particular talent, ability, or skill for present and future use. *Special education* is education for adjustment to normal life. It aims at teaching the physically and mentally (and more recently the economically) handicapped how to find happiness and fulfillment in a world in which principles, practices, and goals of living are based on the "normal" persons.

The Comprehensive High School. The comprehensive high school is one "whose programs correspond to the educational needs of *all* the youth of the community." [14] A comprehensive high school attempts to combine under one roof all the various curricula into one unified organization. This type of high school is a unique American product which is now being copied to some extent in Europe and to a large extent in some of the newly emerging nations. In 1918 the Commission on the Reorganization of Secondary Education recommended that the comprehensive high school become the basic and standard American high school. Ever since that time, American public school educators have increasingly come out in favor of this position. Most educators have emphatically endorsed the comprehensive high school as the one most consonant with American ideals of equality and democracy.

The three main objectives of a comprehensive high school are to

[12] See National Catholic Welfare Conference, Department of Education, *Summary of Catholic Education, 1955–1956.* (Washington: NCWC, 1958).

[13] For a fuller treatment of the natural sciences as humanistic disciplines, see James Michael Lee, "The Place of Science in the High School," *Catholic Educational Review,* LVII (May, 1959), pp. 302–307.

[14] James B. Conant, *The American High School Today.* (New York: McGraw-Hill, 1959), p. 12.

provide a general education for all future citizens; to provide good elective programs for terminal students; and to provide a college preparatory program for students intending to pursue higher education.[15] In his report, Conant notes that there are not too many contemporary American high schools which meet his criteria for comprehensiveness.

The Specialized High School. The specialized high school is one which "offers a program adapted to a special group of students and [which] usually requires evidence of certain aptitudes on the part of candidates for admission." [16] Some of the larger urban communities have erected specialized high schools. New York City is the leader in this field, with approximately thirty such institutions, ranging from the least specialized Bronx High School of Science to the highly specialized Schoolship John W. Brown (the Maritime Division of Metropolitan Vocational High School). One state has regional specialized high schools for industrial courses, with all other vocational curricula being given in the community's comprehensive high schools. Specialized high schools are characteristic of the European pattern of secondary education.

The four main types or categories of specialized high schools are based, respectively, on: (1) vocational interest and aptitude, (2) intellectual ability, (3) special interest, (4) gender.

Vocational High Schools. Many pupils feel that the normal academic education given in high school is neither adequate nor appropriate to their needs or abilities. They wish a strong, vocationally oriented program. The vast majority of vocational courses lie in four separate departments, each with its own distinct rationale, curriculum, and resources. These four are industrial arts; agriculture; business education; and home economics (sometimes called homemaking). Most of the pupils enrolled in the first two are boys, in the last two, girls. Despite its strong vocational stress and flavor, the vocational high school always has a rather large core of courses in general education. Some vocational high schools integrate actual work experience into the curriculum; i.e., the pupils work in actual jobs for a few hours during the school day. Of course, specialized vocational high schools are not the only secondary institutions offering vocational curricula; most American students now enrolled in vocational courses are doing so in the vocational department of their community's comprehensive high school.

High Schools for the Intellectually Gifted. Many pupils of superior intellectual ability—often encouraged by their parents and teachers—feel that the ordinary academic course content is insufficient for them. They further feel that only in a school catering exclusively to the men-

---

[15] See *ibid.*, p. 17.
[16] *Ibid.*, p. 12.

tally superior can the proper environment be created for full development of their ability. Some communities have therefore decided to establish specialized schools for the intellectually gifted. The curriculum in such schools is almost always one of exclusively general education, usually with a college preparation emphasis. The courses are taught at a level suited to these students. Electives are often offered to pupils who wish to pursue to a fuller degree some area of general education, e.g., science.

Special Interest High Schools. Many pupils feel that the quantity, diversity, and creative quality of the courses offered in the comprehensive high school are not sufficient to develop adequately their special interests. Most frequently these interests lie in the arts. Schools like New York City's High School of Performing Arts have arisen to give a rich program to pupils with exceptional dramatic, artistic, or musical talent. The curriculum consists of a broad core of general education, with both the electives and the activities program aimed at unfolding the students' talents. A creative atmosphere pervades the entire school. Students are sometimes afforded work experience in experimental and professional theater, concert work, and so forth.

Single-gender High Schools. Some pupils and their parents feel that an all-boys or all-girls high school provides both a better learning situation and a better moral atmosphere than does a coeducational institution. Therefore, some large urban localities have not only retained existing single-gender high schools but in some instances have set up new ones. Theoretically, at least, the pattern of instruction, the manner of teaching, the scope of the activities program, the type of electives, and so forth are supposed to be based on the peculiar nature of either boys or girls. Boys are obviously not the same in nature as girls; hence, they do not think in precisely the same manner, nor have they the same interests. The curriculum, group counseling, and teaching should take these differences into account. General education furnishes the core, and in some cases (e.g., college preparatory students) the program in its entirety. At mid-century, 54 per cent of all Catholic high schools were coeducational.

The Special High School. This type of high school may be defined as one whose program is specially geared to the nature and needs of mentally or physically handicapped youths.[17] The youths enrolled in

[17] Some educational authorities, such as Cain, hold that special education is education for all exceptional children, including the intellectually gifted; other educators, such as French, maintain that the programs for the gifted are a part of specialized education. This text follows the French interpretation. Cf. Leo E. Cain, "Special Education," *Encyclopedia of Educational Research.* (New York: Macmillan, 1960), p. 1325; Will French, J. Dan Hull, and B. L. Dodds, *American High School Administration.* (New York: Rinehart, 1957), p. 190.

this kind of school need special provisions for their care, development, and education; a conventional high school would be unable to care for them adequately. Special high schools vary in range from those for the mentally retarded to sheltered workshops for the cerebral palsied. A study made by Fr. Jenks, C.Ss.R., showed that, compared with their other educational endeavors, Catholic educators have not interested themselves sufficiently in the work of special education.[18] As their name implies, special high schools are special; hence, their curricular, guidance, and administrative principles and practices are almost completely different from those of comprehensive and specialized high schools.

Advantages of the Various Types of High School. Educators are in sharp disagreement whether comprehensive or specialized high schools are superior. Advocates of the comprehensive high school argue that this type of institution has at least three distinct advantages. First, the comprehensive high school is the only type that is truly democratic, for it is the only one that accommodates everyone, regardless of level of talent, ability, or skill. Thus the comprehensive high school is not divisive in any way. Second, the comprehensive high school is the only type in which the programs of general and specialized education, of required and elective courses, can be totally integrated into one overall unified program, thus securing proper curricular balance and emphasis. Third, the comprehensive high school is the only type in which the pupils can develop totally, humanistically; in specialized schools they develop only certain of their talents, skills, or abilities, and thus become narrow specialists. Many advocates of the comprehensive high school would, for these reasons, like to see the specialized high school abolished.

Educators favoring the specialized high school argue that this type of institution has at least three distinct advantages. First, a specialized high school is permeated with a definite directional approach. Such definite direction cannot be found in a comprehensive high school. The curriculum, methods of instruction, guidance activities, activities program, plant—all are designed to heighten and deepen this directional approach. Second, only in a specialized high school can the pupils have at their disposal the means of fully realizing their talents. Specialized instructors, courses, and activities which form the core of these institutions, would not be feasible or practical in most comprehensive high schools. The resources—teachers, materials, and schoolmates—all motivate and are otherwise conducive to a full realization of a pupil's talents. Third, the vastness and costliness of equipment involved in industrial education preclude the possibility of its being supplied to many schools in

[18] See William F. Jenks, C.Ss.R., *Function and Growth of the National Catholic Educational Association in the Field of Special Education.* (Washington, D.C.: Catholic University of America Press, 1961).

the same city or area. Furthermore, industrial education is characterized by extreme vocational orientation. No comprehensive high school can adequately provide so rich a program of industrial education, either from a physical or psychological point of view.[19] Nonetheless, it must be borne in mind that from 75 to 95 per cent of the nonprofessional occupations require little or no training, and that 95 per cent of those workers requiring skilled training are trained on the job.[20] Also, increasing automation is making many machines and techniques obsolete almost before they have a chance to come into the specialized high school. These two factors, viz., on-the-job training and stepped-up automation, must be kept in mind in any assessment of industrial education.

Special high schools are obviously so necessary, important, and distinct that most secondary school educators in the United States vigorously support this type of institution.

Specialization and Catholic High Schools. The vast majority of American Catholic high schools are specialized high schools. Catholic high schools do not cater to *all* Catholic youth, and the *intent* of the curricula is to prepare mentally superior students for college. (Whether the *content* of these curricula is on as high a level as their aim is a matter which is presently being vigorously debated in Catholic educational circles.) But as Sister Mary Janet, S.C., has observed:

It is still true, however, seventy years after the founding of Roman Catholic High School as a school for all types of boys, that [today] Catholic secondary schools for the most part have a curriculum which is primarily college preparatory in content. Business education departments have become quite extensive, but this is the only area in the vocational field of which this is true. Technical and mechanical courses and arts and crafts are taught in comparatively few schools and proportionately few classes. There has been a noticeable increase in education for home and family living in schools for girls. In some dioceses such courses are even obligatory for all girls in at least one year of high school. Music has a certain degree of status, but art has yet to gain a foothold. Financial stress is at least partly responsible for lack of vocational education. . . . There remains the necessity of finding an adequate place for the arts as a vital part of the [Catholic] spiritual and cultural heritage.[21]

It would be natural to presume that this Catholic secondary school emphasis on programs for the mentally superior would result in the production of Catholic graduates of such a high calibre as to make an impact

---

[19] On this point, see Franklin J. Keller, *The Comprehensive High School.* (New York: Harper, 1955), p. 38.

[20] Charles A. Prosser and Thomas A. Quigley, *Vocational Education in a Democracy.* (Chicago: American Technical Society, 1950), pp. 387–388.

[21] Sister Mary Janet, *op. cit.,* p. 12.

on American civilization. But as Msgr. Ellis,[22] Professor O'Dea,[23] and others have observed, American Catholic intellectual achievement in this is most dismal. A reassessment of the purposes of the entire Catholic school system, including the secondary level, is therefore in order. Indeed, curriculum modification is also imperative, both in the quantity and quality of content, as well as in possible reorganization of basic curricular designs in the direction of greater flexibility and increased encouragement of individual student work. Perhaps a diocese-wide reorganization would be profitable, with each diocese maintaining one central specialized school exclusively for the highly intellectually gifted. The other diocesan high schools could then be open on an equitable basis to all Catholic youth, slow, normal, or mentally superior (excluding the gifted). Certainly all Catholic high schools should become more comprehensive in the arts and in cultural subjects, for these are at the very theological root of the Catholic's proper encounter with the world.

The Graded Secondary School

American secondary education, both public and Catholic, is subdivided into formally differentiated levels called "grades." The formally differentiated graded system in American secondary education is a relatively recent phenomenon. Before the mid-nineteenth century, the high school, like other American schools, was ungraded. In those days a teacher taught all subjects to all the pupils in the class and assigned the separate students different levels of work, according to their stage of mastery of the subject being taught at that moment. The graded system, properly so called, was introduced in 1847 by John W. Philbrick in the elementary schools of Boston. Later it was extended to the secondary schools. The graded system in the United States was based on the German system. This imitation was quite natural because a great many prominent American educators of the nineteenth century received much of their education in Germany, and hence were influenced by that country's educational system. Bunker observes that the classic 8-4 American grade pattern (eight years of elementary school, four years of secondary school) was based on the German system requiring compulsory elementary education for eight years, terminating with Confirmation and Communion in the established church.[24] In addition, the system of eight years (rather than five or six) had a physiological significance; viz., by

[22] John Tracy Ellis, "American Catholics and the Intellectual Life," *Thought*, XXX (Autumn, 1955), pp. 351–388.

[23] Thomas F. O'Dea, *American Catholic Dilemma: An Inquiry into the Intellectual Life*. (New York: Sheed and Ward, 1958)

[24] See Frank F. Bunker, *Reorganization of the Public School System*, U.S. Bureau of Education Bulletin 1916, no. 8. (Washington: Government Printing Office, 1918).

that time the pupils usually had attained puberty. Bunker also notes that even if German influences had been nonexistent, the graded system would undoubtedly have developed in America, because recognition of elementary and secondary education as constituents of the common school demanded that the vast numbers of pupils be somehow classified for purposes of learning, teaching, and administration. Indeed there are some modern educators who maintain that the chief and only advantage of a graded secondary school is ease of administration, which should hardly be the chief basis for structuring the pupils' educational development.

The graded system has many disadvantages. The root from which practically all these disadvantages stem is the fact that each youth's mental, physical, social, emotional, creative, and spiritual growth takes place at a different rate—all-around growth does not fall neatly into the administrative lockstep grade framework. Notwithstanding, many educators feel that the school, faced with the necessity of educating great numbers of young people must organize the program into some pattern of learning units for administrative control. However, they realize that the graded system is not realistic in terms of each youth's development. For this dilemma, three types of solutions have been suggested: (1) group within grades by growth, (2) change the basic grade pattern, (3) abolish the grade pattern altogether.

The first solution uses homogeneous grouping, i.e., placing pupils of roughly the same level of growth in appropriate classes of the same grade. Thus arose the multiple-track system, whereby the pupils of various general ability and growth levels proceed through the grades on the "track" best suited to them. The most common multiple-track system is that of the three track—one for the slow, another for the normal, and a third for the bright. Some alert Catholic secondary schools such as Xavierian High School in Brooklyn, New York, have experienced outstanding results with the three-track system. There are, however, two chief disadvantages of homogeneous grouping by tracks: (1) The system is inadequate because it fails to provide properly for each student's *individual* growth level and rate. No group is completely homogeneous. The disadvantages of the graded system have thus been merely minimized, not eliminated. (2) A multiple-track system is only possible in the larger school systems where there is a sufficient number of pupils for such homogeneous grouping. Hence, only in a small minority of American schools can there be a multiple track. Conant, who favors ability grouping, attempts to make the multiple track flexible by recommending that, in all courses, "the students should be grouped subject by subject." [25] Thus a pupil who excels in English but is weak

[25] Conant, *op. cit.*, pp. 49–50.

in mathematics will be placed in a bright English class and a normal (or even slow) mathematics class, all within the same grade level. This proposal, while retaining many of the disadvantages of the graded system, nevertheless has much to recommend it. Indeed this plan is probably the best solution within the context of the graded system.

The second solution consists of reorganization of the grade pattern. Psychologists and others testify that the customary 8-4 grouping is not realistic in terms of the youth's psychological or physical growth. From this there emerged the recognition by most educators that grades 7 and 8 are truly part of secondary education. Since the end of World War I the reorganization movement has become increasingly popular in American schools. At present there are still more 8-4 patterns in public education than any other single type. However, there are more pupils enrolled in reorganized schools than in the older type. This seeming paradox is caused by the fact that most of the 8-4 systems are located in districts having less than 2,500 population. These are the most numerous districts. Their schools have the smallest enrollments. A 1958–1959 NEA survey showed that only 20 per cent of school districts with over 2,500 population retain the 8-4 pattern.[26] Most reorganized systems are either 6-3-3 or 6-6. In general the larger districts have a 6-3-3 system; medium-size districts, 6-6; and the smallest districts, 8-4.[27] Very little reorganization has taken place in Catholic secondary education. Indeed the number of Catholic junior high schools is extremely small. Other systems either proposed for, or in operation in, public education are 7-5, 7-2-3, and 4-4-4. The basic disadvantage of the grade reorganization plan is that it does nothing to break the lockstep graded system—it just reorganizes the lockstep in a different pattern. Nevertheless, reorganization has brought with it certain benefits. Some educators, like Woodring, propose a possible solution to the problem of continuous student growth versus the inflexible graded system by altering the grade pattern to fit the pupils' intellectual ability. Thus the intellectually mature and able will spend two years in an ungraded primary school, five years in the elementary school, and three years in high school, while the slower students will spend five years in an ungraded primary school, four years in elementary school, and two years in high school. This plan has a great deal of merit.[28]

The third solution is the complete abolition of grades. Such a plan has already worked with considerable success in ungraded primary schools

[26] National Education Association, "The Junior High School Today," NEA Research Bulletin, XXXIX (May, 1961), p. 47.

[27] Ibid.

[28] Paul Woodring, A Fourth of a Nation. (New York: McGraw-Hill, 1957), pp. 143–152.

both in public education and alert Catholic school systems.[29] Failures have been reduced and successes heightened. An ungraded school system would involve team teaching, small- and large-group classes, flexible evaluation practices, and so forth. At the present time there seems to be no trend toward an ungraded secondary school. However, it is being discussed more and more by forward-looking educators. Indeed the Trump Report recommends that the secondary school curriculum be "divided into stages or steps not identified as years or grades, and without any fixed number. The rate of progress through the school will be determined by the student's previous achievements and his capacity to take the next step. His readiness to move on, again will be gauged by professional decision and not by a test, a grade or a unit of credit." [30] Grouping will thus be made by ability and performance in each subject, not by grades. In this way the curriculum will be geared to the pupil's actual concrete situation rather than to a grade-structured system which a priori assumes a level of pupil development which may or may not exist. Some "tradition-directed" educators (to paraphrase Riesman's term) may at first balk at the elimination of the graded system. However, the fact that a practice is old does not necessarily testify to its intrinsic worth. Surely these same educators do not use gaslight for illumination because it is more "traditional" than electricity. Catholic educators especially should take the lead in the elimination of the graded system inasmuch as they are members of a Church which has through the centuries shown itself ever ready to abandon outmoded practices in favor of improved forms.

Closely allied to the graded system is the unit system. Determination of a pupil's grade placement in secondary schools is normally made on the basis of the number of units of schoolwork completed. As was noted in Chapter I, the determination of what constitutes a "unit" of schoolwork was made in 1906 by the Carnegie Foundation for the Advancement of Teaching. The "Carnegie unit" consists of a class period of at least forty minutes' duration, meeting five times each week for at least thirty-six weeks. Laboratory classes meet for a slightly longer time, viz., 280 minutes per week. Carnegie units are thus based not on educational objectives, intrinsic worth of the course, or the course's subjective value to the student, but merely on the amount of time spent in class. For administrative purposes some sort of measurement is necessary. Whether the Carnegie unit is the best solution is quite another matter.

[29] See the dynamic article by James E. Hoflich, "The Ungraded Primary," Bulletin of the National Catholic Educational Association, LVII (November, 1960), pp. 8–25.

[30] J. Lloyd Trump and Dorsey Baynham, Guide to Better Schools. (Chicago: Rand McNally, 1961), pp. 55–57.

Courses

At mid-century, there were 270 commonly offered courses and 518 more uncommon courses in the nation's public secondary schools, grades 9 through 12. It is impossible to determine precisely the number of courses offered, because some old courses have new content, and some newly titled courses are just rehashes of the old content. Allowing for similar courses with differing names, the total number of courses is perhaps in the neighborhood of 500. The total number of commonly offered courses has increased since 1933–1934. These courses were grouped by the U.S. Office of Education into 13 broad subject fields: (1) English, (2) Social Studies, (3) Science, (4) Mathematics, (5) Foreign Languages, (6) Industrial Arts (nonvocational), (7) Trade and Industrial Arts (vocational), (8) Business Education, (9) Home Economics, (10) Agriculture, (11) Health, Safety, and Physical Education, (12) Music, (13) Art.[31] Catholic high schools, being selective and more or less specialized, have far fewer specifically different courses. This is particularly true in those high schools operated by Religious Orders, where a widespread curricular similarity tends to be fostered. Catholic high schools offer courses in all these broad subject areas except Trade and Industrial Arts and Agriculture.[32] Of course, Catholic high schools give courses in a broad area noticeably absent from the curricula of their public school counterparts, i.e., religion.

The Conant Report recommended that the graduation requirements for all students include "four years of English; three or four years of social studies—including two years of history (one of which should be American history) . . . one year of mathematics . . . and at least one year of science." [33] For the academically talented, the report recommended "four years of mathematics, four years of one foreign language, three years of science, in addition to the required four years of English and three years of social studies." [34] A study by Alexander and Saylor showed that most college freshmen while in high school took programs quite similar to the Conant recommendations for the academically talented, except in the area of foreign languages.[35]

Since the Soviet scientific successes, increasing attention has been

[31] U.S. Office of Education, *Biennial Survey of Education in the United States: Offerings and Enrollments in High School Subjects, 1948–1949.* (Washington: Government Printing Office, 1951), pp. 109–118. There is a fourteenth category, entitled "Other Instruction or Courses," but this is a collection of unrelated subjects and hence does not comprise a broad subject field, properly speaking.

[32] Sister Mary Janet, *op. cit.,* p. 9.

[33] Conant, *op. cit.,* p. 47.

[34] *Ibid.,* p. 57.

[35] Alexander and Saylor, *op. cit.,* p. 331.

focused on the American secondary school's course offerings in mathematics and the natural sciences. In 1954, 33 per cent of all public high school students pursued chemistry and physics, and 64 per cent took algebra. However, enrollments in these subjects have been increasing. Thus "in 1956 enrollment in Chemistry equalled 34.6 per cent of the number of pupils in the 11th grade; in 1954 the figure was 23.5 per cent." [36] Studies have shown that a higher percentage of Catholic high schools than of public schools offer mathematics and science.[37] This higher percentage is to be expected, since most Catholic high schools are in urban communities, whereas a goodly portion of public high schools are in districts under 2,500 population. These small districts often lack sufficiently trained teachers and proper apparatus. Furthermore, Catholic high schools, being college preparatory and academically selective, naturally offer courses tailored to both college entrance requirements and college entrance desiderata. Secondary schools, both public and Catholic, should offer a rich science and mathematics program, primarily for their values as liberal disciplines rather than simply for a nationalistic, "beat-the-Russians" goal.[38]

Like many educators before him, Conant recommended that "in the twelfth grade a course on American problems or American government should be required," [39] with the class being heterogeneously grouped. Catholic high schools might well take this recommendation to heart. Church-state relations in America, the church and democracy, life in the democratic society of America, the ideal of Christian citizenship—all these and others are crucial problems to Catholic youths, and the Catholic high school should require such a course as one of the culminations of its program. History, particularly European history, can all too often lead a student to believe that the monarchy is a more suitable climate for Catholicism than is democracy. Pope Pius XII, of course, said precisely the opposite. A "Problems of Democracy" course should go a long way toward deepening the understanding and importance of democracy in Catholic youth. Some forward-looking Catholic high schools have made this course compulsory for all seniors.[40]

[36] Kenneth E. Brown and Ellsworth S. Osburn, *Offerings and Enrollments in Science and Mathematics in Public High Schools.* (Washington: Government Printing Office, 1957), p. 2.

[37] John J. Green, O.S.F.S., and Neil C. D'Amour, "Science and Mathematics in Catholic Schools: A Pilot Survey," *Bulletin of the National Catholic Educational Association,* LIV (May, 1958), pp. 16–17. "It is interesting to note that in the advanced fields of Solid Geometry and Trigonometry, the diocesan [central] schools are considerably in advance of the private [Order] and parish schools" (p. 9).

[38] See Lee, *loc. cit.*

[39] See Conant, *op. cit.,* p. 75.

[40] Sister Mary Janet, *Catholic Secondary Education: A National Survey.* (Washington: NCWC, 1949), p. 103.

Types of Courses. There are two basic types of courses, required and elective. Furthermore, there are different kinds of required courses, viz., those required of all students and those required of certain groups of students, e.g., pupils in industrial education. Required courses of the first kind are generally those which give the pupil a broad base of general education. Required courses of the second kind, and also electives, are usually those which are designed to develop the students' specialized interests, abilities, or vocational objectives; these courses are ones which the school judges to go beyond the minimal base of general education appropriate to the average pupil. Hovet estimates that a national "norm" of required courses in public high schools would be something like: "English, 3 units; social studies, 2 units; mathematics, 1 unit; science, 1 unit; health, 1 unit." [41] Public high schools vary greatly in the number of courses they require. In Catholic high schools, the predominant practice is to make two-thirds or three-fourths of the courses required. Many schools, however, make only one-half of the total number of courses required. Some schools permit the student but one or two electives.[42] Sister Mary Janet, S.C., reporting on a nationwide survey of Catholic secondary education, observes:

> The regulation [concerning required courses] is sometimes stated [by Catholic high schools] in terms of the "solid" and "light" subjects. A not uncommon statement is the following: "We require twelve units in the solid subjects, and four in the light ones." The statements are not without provocative features: "We require twelve in solid subjects, and four in light subjects, such as religion and the arts." It seems that there is among some people a great stress on the importance of the heavy, or hard, subjects, so-called, without a clear definition as to just what constitutes the heavy or the hard, except a traditional attitude concerning foreign languages and mathematics. But these subjects are in a sense easy for students endowed with a certain type of natural ability, whereas the same students may lack manual dexterity or be appalled by the difficulty of music or art. The fact is that some will excel in one type of program and others in another. The ease or difficulty arises from native endowment, and not from the inherent difficulty of the particular subject.[43]

Elective courses are those which a student is permitted to choose for himself according to his interests and abilities. Two questions arise in connection with the ratio of required to elective courses in a student's total program: Who should be permitted to take electives? How many

[41] Kenneth Hovet, "What Are the High Schools Teaching?" *What Shall the High Schools Teach?* 1956 Yearbook, Association for Supervision and Curriculum Development. (Washington: ASCD, 1956), p. 72.

[42] Sister Mary Janet, *Catholic Secondary Education: A National Survey, op. cit.,* p. 103.

[43] *Ibid.,* pp. 103–104.

electives should there be in a student's program? To the first question, the Association for Supervision and Curriculum Development (ASCD) answers: "Any elective course should be available to any qualified student regardless of his grade level." [44] The ASCD asserts that only in this way can individual differences be properly handled. To the second question, the ASCD responds: "One-half to two-thirds of each student's secondary school program should be elective" so that each pupil will be free to "develop his talents and further his goals." [45] Whether such freedom should be offered to immature adolescents is, however, open to serious question. Experience has shown that youths not infrequently tend to elect subjects and teachers that in their particular school are less demanding of time and energy. The ASCD recognizes this danger and recommends that, as a safeguard, electives should be chosen after a conference with student, parents, and academic counselor. However, it would seem that once a student has selected a basic curricular objective, e.g., college preparatory or home economics, the subjects necessary for a wide and deep grasp of that objective are so numerous as to preclude the taking of more than a few electives. Only in the so-called "general academic" or "modern academic" streams where the pupils have no clear-cut objectives would a high number of electives be either wise or profitable. As Hovet suggests, the prescription of required courses should be studied carefully to see what is best for the student. As he observes, the research to date on this question has been conflicting.[46] Vocational electives, such as business education and Smith-Hughes subjects, usually comprise five Carnegie units. Yet in one sense these electives can be considered required courses, since they are necessary for certain groups of students.

Old courses, both required and elective, die hard—and new ones pop up too quickly. Despite the fact that Latin is a dead language, it was not until the 1940s that more public high school students enrolled in Spanish than in Latin. On the other hand, some "life-adjustment" courses were adopted without any sort of careful consideration. As Hovet remarks ironically:

In the meantime, courses multiply in the secondary school, and almost anything considered "good" by some group can eventually become part of the program of studies. . . . Any course can be introduced as long as its advocates are able to show how it "contributes" to the achievement of some one or several objectives that have been stated since 1918. If no stated objective is available

---

[44] Association for Supervision and Curriculum Development, *The High School We Need*. (Washington: NEA, 1959), p. 11.

[45] *Ibid.*, p. 10.

[46] Hovet, *op. cit.*, p. 78.

a new one can be formulated and advocated with vigor. There are no readily discernible limits to a process like this.[47]

In the same place Hovet suggests that educational research into the philosophy, goals, and outcomes of the courses should be a major determinant in any decision regarding the addition or retention of a course.

The School Day

Throughout the country the school day for public senior high school students has, on the whole, steadily lengthened since 1948.[48] The median length of the school day (excluding the after-school activities program) was 6 hours and 58 minutes in 1958–1959 for senior high schools. The median school day was consistently longer in the smaller public districts than in the larger ones.[49] In Catholic high schools, the median length of the school day is somewhat shorter. Six was the median number of periods in public senior high schools. The percentage breakdown on school periods for 1958–1959 was as follows: 9 periods—1.5 per cent of the public senior high schools; 8 periods—10.3 per cent; 7 periods—26.7 per cent; 6 periods—56.3 per cent; 5 or fewer—5.2 per cent.[50]

In terms of length, there are three types of periods dominant in American secondary education: short—under 45 minutes in duration (but usually 40 to 45 minutes); medium—50 to 60 minutes; long or extended—over 60 minutes (usually 100 to 120 minutes). Laboratory or Core classes constitute the bulk of the extended periods. The median length of periods in public senior high schools is 56 minutes.[51] In Catholic high schools, the percentage breakdown for period lengths at mid-century was as follows: less than 40 minutes—2 per cent; 40 minutes—15 per cent; 45 minutes—50 per cent; 50 minutes—23 per cent; 60 minutes—10 per cent.[52] In its 1958–1959 study, the NEA reported that "high schools in 86 per cent of the districts regularly scheduled study hall periods, but 1 district in 7 was planning to reduce the number." [53] The median time for the lunch period in public high schools is 45 minutes.[54] Most secondary schools have a homeroom period or periods, lasting from 5 to 15 minutes depending on school and cir-

[47] Ibid.
[48] National Education Association, "How Long Is the School Day?" NEA Research Bulletin, XXXIX (February, 1961), p. 8.
[49] Ibid.
[50] Ibid., p. 9.
[51] Ibid., p. 8.
[52] Sister Mary Janet, Catholic Secondary Education: A National Survey, op. cit., p. 102.
[53] NEA, "How Long Is the School Day?" op. cit., p. 8.
[54] Ibid., p. 10.

cumstances. Some secondary schools, particularly in large metropolitan areas, are on double session; i.e., the school day comprises two distinct sessions with two entirely different sets of pupils. Thus, typically, a first session might last from 7:45 A.M. to 12:45 P.M., and the second session from 1:00 P.M. to 6:00 P.M. Often there is overlapping of the two sessions. The double session is a most undesirable practice from almost every educational viewpoint.

The amount of time a school allots its various subjects is often an indication of how important the school regards these subjects. By this yardstick the status of religion in Catholic high schools, amazing to say, is not high. In a mid-century survey, it was found that 28 per cent of the Catholic high schools studied allotted less than 200 minutes a week to the study of religion.[55] Indeed two schools devoted only 30 minutes per week to religion. The fact that so many Catholic high schools give less than a Carnegie unit of instruction in religion seems to cut the ground from under one of the cardinal principles of the *raison d'être* of a Catholic high school. On the happier side, 65 per cent of the schools surveyed reported that they devoted from 200 to 300 minutes a week to religion. The quality of these courses, however, was not investigated in this study.

Some educators are of the opinion that "the school day should be so organized that there are at least six periods in addition to the required physical education and driver education which in many states occupy at least 1 period a day." The reasoning behind this proposal is that a school day of less than six periods "places electives in a strait jacket," [56] to use Conant's words. The Trump Report makes more sweeping recommendations. It proposes a 30-hour week, or a 6-hour school day. The amount of time spent on required and elective courses, in large-group and small-group classes, and on independent study varies from student to student, depending on age, ability, and progress. An average fourteen-year-old student would spend his time as follows: required basic education, a total of 1,200 minutes per week. This is broken down into 540 minutes in large-group classes, 300 minutes in small-group classes, and 360 minutes in independent study; electives (consisting of a choice among the various courses in the required subject areas to promote depth in these areas), a total of 600 minutes per week, broken down into 240 minutes for group activities and 360 minutes for independent study.[57] The Trump Report also urges elimination of the equal-length periods on the ground that certain subjects and lessons require greater or lesser

[55] Sister Mary Janet, *Catholic Secondary Education: A National Survey, op. cit.*, p. 69.

[56] Conant, *op. cit.*, p. 64.

[57] Trump and Baynham, *op. cit.*, pp. 53–57.

lengths of formal class time than do others. The school day "will be divided into 15- or 20-minute modules of time, instead of equal periods." [58] In this way the length of the classes can be changed constantly to adapt to the dynamics of the particular lesson or subject. This is possible because of the large amount of independent study time a pupil will have. Hence a prolonged class will not conflict with another class, but rather take up some time during which a student is normally occupied in independent study. The Trump Report states that such a school day will adequately provide for individual differences, individual initiative, and accelerated individual growth as a replacement for the stagnant uniformity of teaching which characterizes most secondary schools. The Trump Report, with all its strengths and weaknesses, deserves the careful study and mature reflection of all secondary school educators, foreign and American, public and Catholic.

The School Year

The average school year is of 180 days' duration. It usually begins either the day after Labor Day or the following Monday. School closing varies from the first week of June to the last day of that month. In general the Northeast section of the country has the latest school closing.

More and more public districts are including optional summer school, thus lengthening the school year and increasing plant utilization. A 1959 NEA survey of 302 school districts revealed that nearly 85 per cent of them had summer schools on the secondary level.[59] Two-thirds of all the summer schools are in urban districts of 10,000 or more population. Summer schools exist primarily for two purposes, viz., acceleration and deficiency makeup. Many eager and industrious students wish either to graduate earlier than normal or to take subjects which their busy school schedules will not permit them to take. Other youths failed courses during the regular school year and wish to "make up" the work so that they may continue their school careers at the normal rate. The previously cited NEA survey showed that 80 per cent of these school districts noted that "enrichment is the primary goal of summer school." [60] Forward-looking Catholic high schools have long been operating summer schools. Their scope and intensity should be further widened and deepened. In view of the high mental ability of most students in Catholic high schools, the need for Catholics in the first rank of American intellectual life and for maximum personal ful-

[58] *Ibid.*, p. 41.
[59] National Education Association, "Summer Schools = Opportunity," *NEA Research Bulletin*, XXXVIII (February, 1960), pp. 23–24.
[60] *Ibid.*, p. 23.

fillment, a vigorous summer school program should be instituted by every Catholic high school where this is possible.

The NEA study of summer schools revealed that 65 per cent of the surveyed districts charged tuition for students attending the summer sessions.[61] Conant recommended that these summer schools be made tuition-free.[62] The President's Commission on National Goals urged that within ten years "all but the smallest unified districts should operate tuition-free summer schools (attendance voluntary)." [63]

Class Size

In 1955–1956 the pupil-teacher ratio in American public secondary schools was 20.8:1; in American Catholic high schools it was 20.1:1.[64] These figures are somewhat misleading on at least two counts. First, they lump together the small, middle-sized, urban, and metropolitan high schools. Class size in metropolitan public high schools, for example, is far closer to 30 or 35. Second, pupil-teacher ratio is not the same as class size; indeed class size is always larger than pupil-teacher ratio, since the teachers are not in class for as many periods as are the students. The class size in Catholic high schools is generally not so favorable as in public high schools, and in fact, probably averages about 40. There are many reasons for this, including urban location, lack of enough teachers, overcrowded buildings, and so forth. Some diocesan systems, cognizant of the difficult learning situations which prevail in large classes, have placed limits on class size. In the Hartford (Connecticut) Archdiocese, for example, the ceiling is set at 40 pupils per class. A majority of the secondary school educators hold that under the existing type of instruction, a class size of 25 is the optimum.

A fifteen-year extensive study of class size made by the Institute of Administrative Research of Teachers College, Columbia University, revealed the following general conclusions about the superiority of small classes: "(1) More educational creativity exists when classes are small and promising new procedures are more readily adopted in small classes; (2) children are more likely to receive individual attention in small classes; (3) small classes tend to have more variety in instructional methods

---

[61] Ibid., p. 24.

[62] Conant, op. cit., p. 68.

[63] John W. Gardner, "National Goals in Education," The President's Commission on National Goals, Goals for Americans. (Englewood Cliffs, N.J.: Prentice-Hall, 1960), p. 89.

[64] See U.S. Office of Education, Biennial Survey of Education in the United States: Statistics of State School Systems, 1955–1956. (Washington: Government Printing Office, 1959), pp. 27–57.

than do large classes." [65] This study also noted that three-fourths of the larger classes were "totally textbook classes."

Some individuals and groups connected with or otherwise concerned with Catholic education vehemently assert that large classes are just as good as, if not better than, small classes. Thus, for example, Menniti, in his doctoral dissertation, concluded that no relationship could be proved between class size and achievement.[66] Patrick Scanlon, editor of the Brooklyn *Tablet*, frequently cites the Fund for the Advancement of Education studies which show that the test results of pupils from small and large classes reveal no difference in performance. These results are certainly not surprising since large and small classes usually use the identical lecture-recitation-textbook approach. If the methodology is the same, the results of the studies will obviously be similar, regardless of class size. Class size, then, is no solution in itself. Reduction in class size must be accompanied by a radical change in teaching methodology—use of discussion, small-group work, pupil-teacher interaction, problem-solving techniques and so forth. Regrettably, those Catholics who defend large classes seem to do so more in defense of their oversized classes than as a desire to improve the learning situation.

The Trump Report urges flexibility in class size. It recognizes the value of the lecture-textbook technique as an occasional teaching device and notes that when such a method is used, the quality of learning is not affected by class size. But the report is equally cognizant of the crucial and irreplaceable value of small classes for thought-provoking discussion and individual work for individual initiative. The Trump Report calls for three types of classrooms in a school: (1) large-group instructional areas, seating from 150 to 600 students, used for classes of the lecture or textbook type and for audio-visual lessons (by motion picture, television, tape, or radio); (2) small-group instructional areas, seating about fifteen students, used for discussion classes; (3) individual laboratory spaces or cubicles, in which the students can pursue independent study, science experimentation, or foreign-language work.[67] These Trump recommendations have so many advantages that there seems to be little reason to delay putting them into effect. By making class size flexible, one promotes learning in the best way possible. The new Catholic high schools now being built everywhere would do well to take the Trump recommendations to heart in plant planning.

[65] Bernard H. McKenna, "Greater Learning in Smaller Classes," *NEA Journal*, XLIV (October, 1957), p. 438.

[66] Daniel J. Menniti, *The Relationship between Class Size and Pupil Achievement in the Catholic School Eighth Grade*. (Washington, D.C.: Catholic University of America Press, 1959).

[67] Trump and Baynham, *op. cit.*, pp. 35–40.

School Size

In 1952 there were 23,746 public high schools in the United States. Of these, more than 13,000 had 200 students or less, more than 7,000 had 100 students or less, and more than 2,700 had 50 students or less.[68] Almost 75 per cent of American public high schools offering a diploma in 1956–1957 had a twelfth-grade enrollment of less than 100 students. Nearly 32 per cent of all twelfth-grade pupils attended such schools.[69]

Findings such as these call for an examination of the optimum size of a high school. In 1949 the U.S. Office of Education recommended 300 as the minimum total enrollment in a high school.[70] The Conant Report emphatically urged a minimum total enrollment of 600 students, with a graduating class of at least 100 pupils. Indeed this report remarks that "in many states the number one problem is the elimination of the small high school." [71] This should be given top priority in any consideration of the American public high school. It is believed that with adequate enrollments, the total number of public high schools would be about 9,000.[72]

Of all the disadvantages attributed to the small high school, three are mentioned most frequently. First, course offerings are greatly restricted. The narrow range of course offerings makes it impossible for the high school to adequately serve all the enrolled pupils. The academically gifted can neither be grouped homogeneously nor take those additional courses which would add to the depth of their knowledge and interests, e.g., advanced physics. Students interested in and suited to vocational programs are handicapped even more severely. Because of the huge capital outlay, most vocational courses are impossible in small high schools. Second, the teachers' competencies are not utilized in the most advantageous manner. Properly qualified teachers can put their training and talents only to limited use in a small high school. Thus a trained physics teacher, for example, would at best be compelled to teach general science, at worst some other subject, e.g., English composition. Third, the small high school tends to become insular. A vital part of a pupil's education is meeting people of different backgrounds, interests,

[68] U.S. Office of Education, *Biennial Survey of Education in the United States: Statistics of Public Secondary Day Schools; 1951–1952.* (Washington: Government Printing Office, 1954), p. 14.

[69] Conant, *op. cit.*, pp. 132–133.

[70] Walter H. Gaumnitz and Ellsworth Tompkins, *How Large Are Our Public High Schools?* U.S. Office of Education circular no. 304. (Washington: Government Printing Office, 1949).

[71] Conant, *op. cit.*, p. 38.

[72] *Ibid.*, p. 81.

and abilities. A small high school normally does not have a sufficient number of students to ensure that such a wide range will be adequately represented.

Some educators defend the small high school, chiefly on two grounds. First, in a small high school the students get to know one another better than in a large high school. Thus, a comradely, friendly atmosphere pervades the school. Second, in a small high school the teachers come to know the individual pupils better than in a large high school. This makes for a greater understanding of personal problems, individual differences, and the like.

Both small and large high schools have their commendable features, but there can be little doubt that the advantages of the large school render it far superior to the small one. Indeed in a good, large high school the students can be known to one another and to the teachers fairly intimately. The "school-within-a-school" and the "little-school" concepts in more forward-looking high school building designs are a major step toward combining the advantages of both large and small high schools.[73] It seems doubtful, however, that all small high schools will in the next ten years consolidate into larger units. Therefore small high schools should concentrate on newer ways of improving their comprehensiveness, such as by television teaching. The results of the Nebraska Supervised Study and Small Community Education Programs should give positive direction along this line.[74]

Many Catholic high schools could be profitably combined, thereby enriching learning resources, providing for ability grouping, and reducing insular outlook. Religious Orders should give consideration to whether large inter-Order high schools might not result in superior programs. This will, perhaps, require some selflessness among those Orders which feel that their high school represents the crowning educational work of that Order in the region. Happily, inter-Order cooperation is increasing, as is evidenced by the Marillac College Program. Indeed there are several successful inter-Order Catholic high schools throughout the country. In the larger metropolitan areas, specialized Catholic high schools for the academically and creatively gifted should be established, as was suggested earlier in this chapter.

[73] On this concept, see such articles as W. E. Scott and W. C. Glenwright, "What Are Recent Developments in the Construction of New School Buildings?" *Bulletin of the National Association of Secondary-School Principals*, XLI (April, 1957), pp. 211–215; also "Subject: Designing for a High School's Needs," *The School Executive*, LXXIX (September, 1959), pp. 69–73.

[74] Cf. Teachers College, University of Nebraska, *The Nebraska Community Education Project.* (Lincoln, Nebr.: University of Nebraska Press, 1959); also its *Small School in Action* series.

School Districts

In many states and localities small high schools cannot be consolidated unless school districts are first reorganized. There is a definite trend, particularly noticeable in recent years, toward reorganizing school districts into smaller units, thus giving each unit a larger population. In 1931–1932 there were in the United States 127,530 school districts; in a little over twenty-five years the number had decreased by two-thirds to 48,036.[75] Two years later the number was further reduced to approximately 40,000.[76] The President's Commission on National Goals recommended that by 1970 the school districts be reduced to about 10,000.[77] The NEA is equally vehement about the necessity of redistricting. Educational experts have mentioned 2,000 pupils as the minimum enrollment of an efficient school district. The necessity of drastic redistricting to achieve this goal can be appreciated when it is remembered that in 1957, 76 per cent of all school districts had enrollments of less than 300 pupils.[78] The primary purpose for redistricting is to provide better elementary and secondary programs for all American children and youth, to enable more pupils to have more educational resources at their disposal, to have a wider range of course offerings, and to provide for more efficient grouping.

The problem of redistricting hardly affects Catholic high schools. As Sister Mary Janet, S.C., has observed, "Most Catholic high schools are located in urban centers, and such schools enroll more than 90 per cent of Catholic high school students." [79] The problem confronting Catholic high schools is building and staffing them in nonurban areas. Many Catholic youths in small towns as well as in rural areas have no opportunity to attend a Catholic high school. Such schools must be built in centrally located areas. This situation is serious and should not be neglected very much longer.

Secondary Schools, U.S.A.

American secondary education, both public and Catholic, is certainly the greatest of its kind in the world. There are at least three reasons for the eminence of public secondary education: It is free, universal, and open to all; it provides a complete spectrum of opportunities for all youth to develop themselves to the fullest; it is a professional, not an amateurish, enterprise. Of course there are still a great many defects in

[75] U.S. Office of Education, *Small Schools Are Growing Larger.* (Washington: Government Printing Office, 1959), p. 13.

[76] Gardner, *op. cit.,* p. 95.

[77] *Ibid.*

[78] *Ibid.*

[79] Sister Mary Janet, *Catholic Secondary Schools, U.S.A., op. cit.,* p. 4.

public secondary education but these defects are being erased gradually.

Similarly American Catholic secondary education is the finest Catholic secondary education in the world. True, it is not yet universal or free. Its opportunities are open only on a selective basis.[80] In many instances it is still not conducted on a thoroughly professional basis. Nevertheless, the accomplishments of American Catholic secondary schools have been great, and in future years their shortcomings will be remedied.

Good American secondary schools provide a twofold service—a service to the youth himself and a service to the community. To the youth, the good secondary school renders the following services: (1) raises his level of education, (2) broadens and deepens his intellectual and cultural perspectives, (3) affords him guidance and counseling, (4) prepares him for life in the adult world, (5) gives him specialized education for a job or for college, (6) provides incidental services such as free lunches, medical examinations, and bus transportation. To the community the good secondary school provides these services: (1) raises the educational standards of the community, (2) prepares the pupils for effective citizenship in the community, (3) elevates the intellectual and cultural standards of home life, (4) raises the community's potentiality for wealth.

A good Catholic secondary school, in addition to rendering all these services, also prepares its students both for personal sanctification and effective citizenship in the Church. This twin service, not performed intentionally by the public high school, is the principal reason for the superiority of the Catholic high school as a total educational institution, other things being relatively equal.

As has been evident in this chapter, there are at once many similarities and dissimilarities in American secondary schools. Factors affecting similarity include (1) common commitment to the American ideal of democracy; (2) common commitment to the basic purposes of secondary education in an American democracy as enunciated in many widely publicized reports, e.g., *Cardinal Principles of Secondary Education*; (3) the common influence of the accrediting agencies and college entrance requirements; (4) the common training of the educational leaders (highly influenced by the common fabric woven through textbooks in education and the impact of schools of education, notably Teachers College, Columbia University); (5) the similarity of educational materials (many of the same high school textbooks and audiovisual aids are used all over the country); (6) the similarity in school

[80] On this point see James Michael Lee, "A New Role for the High School," *Bulletin of the National Association of Secondary-School Principals*, XLIII (December, 1959), pp. 102–105.

organization, from state superintendent down to the clerk and bus driver.

Factors affecting the differences in American secondary schools include (1) type of school, whether public, parochial, or independent, whether comprehensive or specialized; (2) size of the school; (3) location of the school (urban or rural, rich or poor section of town); (4) financial support given to the school; (5) degree of curricular and guidance flexibility of the school; (6) the quality of the school's educational leadership.

American secondary education is one of the nation's most important enterprises; hence, cooperation between public and private schools is both necessary and urgent. Neither should view the other with suspicion or look hopefully forward to the day when the other will cease to exist. It is very doubtful whether either will cease to exist. Public secondary education can learn much from Catholic high school education in many respects, such as emphasis on spiritual values; high degree of dedication of the staff; elevated moral tone; and acceptance of an integrating principle. Conversely, Catholic schools have much to learn from public high schools, including commitment to democratic administrative and teaching procedures; willingness to accept and try new educational ideas; dedication to the principle of secondary education for all; and professional training of the entire staff. Catholic educators must bear in mind that it has consistently been the public schoolmen who have pioneered new educational theories and practices. Not very much in the way of fine fresh ideas have emanated from Catholic educational quarters. Nor must it be forgotten that about two-thirds of all Catholic adolescents are in public secondary schools. These youths need the help which cooperation between public and Catholic schools can give. Furthermore, Catholic colleges annually prepare a great many teachers for public high schools. Cooperation is essential if these future public secondary school teachers are to receive adequate professional training.

More and more the recent decades have witnessed the sincere efforts of Catholic and public school educators on every level to cooperate in the common educational enterprise. Catholic educators have often taken the lead in extending the hand of friendship and cooperation. As both groups mature, even greater cooperation can be expected. Insularism and excessive partisanship are giving way to a common desire to provide all American youths with the best secondary education possible.

CHAPTER IV
THE SECONDARY SCHOOL STUDENT: PERSON AND LEARNER

In any book written as a text for teachers and prospective teachers, the preeminent place of the student in the learning process can never receive too much attention. As St. Thomas and indeed most other philosophers have observed, the student is far more important than the teacher in the educational enterprise.[1] Every activity carried on in the school, whether by the teacher, the administration, or other staff members, is done with the student primarily in mind. Hence the school, and particularly the teacher, must be constantly student-directed. To accomplish this end, the teacher must know the ultimate and proximate natures of the pupil both as a person and as a certain type of person, in this case an adolescent. Also the teacher must know each student *en situation*, i.e., as he or she exists as a distinct self in a particular setting. Such knowledge is necessary for the most fruitful type of learning by the student. This has been borne out by Sturgis, who investigated the relationship between teachers' knowledge of the students they taught and the achievement of those students. The findings suggest that students learn more when their teachers possess a great deal of information about

[1] See St. Thomas Aquinas, *De Veritate*, q.11.

them as *individuals*.[2] Teachers must constantly beware of an excessive preoccupation with subject matter, with issues, with intellectual objectives or other abstract matters to the neglect of the cardinal entity, the student as he exists here and now.[3]

The adolescent is not a hermetically sealed essence, totally unaffected by anything except his fundamental nature. Rather he is a self, influenced at every moment of his life by a wide variety of forces, both internal and external. These forces do much to shape his personality and his behavior, and hence must be recognized, understood, and compensated for by the teacher. The internal forces include his native intelligence, his rate of physical and psychological growth, his emotions, his needs, his ability to adjust to external reality, and his moral and religious values. External forces affecting and influencing the adolescent student consist of the basic culture pattern (Western, American, regional) and the particular environmental setting (neighborhood, family, playmates, classmates, church). Thus the adolescent whom the teacher encounters in the secondary school is not a static being, but a person whose personality, at least the accidental manifestations of it, are constantly being impinged on by an unending, swirling series of forces.

Adolescence

Adolescence is like secondary education—it is defined more by its boundaries than by its essence. It is the period lasting from the end of childhood to the beginning of adulthood. Its lower boundary, the onset of puberty, is fairly easy to ascertain. However, just when a person reaches adulthood is impossible to say. Some people seem to remain adolescents all their lives. Moreover, no two children reach adolescence at the same time and under the same conditions. Girls generally attain puberty before boys, and within the same sex there is often as much as a three- to five-year difference in reaching this stage. At any rate, adolescence is a period of transition from childhood to adulthood, and so it is a period of intense biological and psychological goal seeking.

This twin and interrelated goal seeking is directed toward ability to live an independent, relatively self-sufficient existence. The human child, who has lived both for a greater time and in a state of greater helplessness under his parents' care than any other created thing,

[2] See Howard W. Sturgis, *The Relationship of the Students' Background to the Effectiveness of Teaching*, unpublished doctoral dissertation, New York University, N.Y., 1958.

[3] It is interesting to note in this regard that a recent and rather widely hailed analysis of the educational enterprise by a leading contemporary Catholic philosopher failed to devote any considerable attention to the student. Such a non-person-directed, ivory-tower approach is, however, rejected by most Catholic educators in the field. See Vincent Edward Smith, *The School Examined.* (Milwaukee: Bruce, 1960).

progressively seeks to attempt to live on his own. Nowhere is this more evident than in his seeking independence from his parents. Klausmeier has succinctly summed up the stages of this quest for independence from parents:

> (1) as the child approaches puberty he obeys parental commands without much rebellion; (2) early in adolescence he seeks independence in choosing clothing, friends and activities; (3) agemates of the opposite sex replace the parent as the primary objects of affection; (4) this greater freedom and association with agemates make him feel less need for parental affection; (5) plans and decisions are made in discussions with parents but are not dominated by them; (6) economic independence is the final step in gaining full freedom from parental control.[4]

Hence it can be seen that adolescent attempts at independence from parents and teachers (who, after all, actually and legally take the place of the parents) are natural and to be expected. Teachers should not try to block such efforts at independence (unless they become extreme); nor should they regard these efforts as signs of poor behavior, emergent "discipline cases," or evidences of the hostility of youth to authority. Such teacher attitudes display an ignorance of the very nature of adolescence. The real "problem student," therefore, is not the one who seeks independence but the one who does not.

Contrary to popular opinion, adolescence is not "a period of storm and stress." This fact, now accepted by most psychologists (but regrettably by fewer teachers) first received widespread attention in a 1937 article by Reutter. This sociologist observed that the unpredictable and erratic behavior of youth results far more from societal expectations of what an adolescent *should be* than from his own psychophysical maturation. Comparative studies of other cultures bear this out, Reutter maintained.[5] This thesis has far-reaching implications for both the secondary school and its teachers. Neither should promote that type of overly restrictive, excessively negative, and fiercely competitive atmosphere which causes storm and stress in adolescents. To be sure, adolescence for most young people can be a period of harmonious and relatively tranquil development, if the teachers so wish it to be.

Growth. Without a doubt, the overarching characteristic of the adolescent during this period is growth. The adolescent is constantly

[4] Herbert J. Klausmeier, *Teaching in the Secondary School.* (New York: Harper, 1958), p. 44.

[5] E. B. Reutter, "The Sociology of Adolescence," *American Journal of Sociology,* XLIII (November, 1937), pp. 414–427. Furfey, the noted Catholic sociologist, took a similar position three years later. See Paul Hanley Furfey, "The Group Life of an Adolescent," *Journal of Educational Sociology,* XIV (December, 1940), pp. 195–204.

growing. The youth in the ninth grade is quite different from the twelfth grader. This growth is of two types, viz., physical and mental.

Physical growth in many directions is characteristic of adolescents. There are at least ten important areas of physical growth which occur markedly during adolescence: (1) substantial increase in height; (2) substantial increase in weight; (3) great increase in hunger (sometimes causing a wide variety of digestive disturbances); (4) development of primary and secondary sex characteristics (e.g., increase in pelvic size of girls (primary) and voice change in boys (secondary); (5) significant muscular growth; (6) appreciable development of motor skills; (7) increase in glandular secretions, especially from the endocrine and sweat glands; (8) notable expansion in the size of the heart; (9) noticeable facial changes (due to permanent teeth, hairline displacement, and so forth); (10) marked skeletal growth.[6]

The teacher must be cognizant of the growth factors during the course of his instruction. Certainly they provide no basis for similar pedagogical techniques irrespective of the age-grade being taught.[7] Also the teacher should be patient and understanding of pupil difficulties arising from this period of accelerated physical growth, e.g., clumsiness, ill-fitting clothing. Teacher comments, such as "you big gawk," are not only uncharitable but reflect an ignorance of student growth patterns.

Physical growth is important not only in itself but also because of its intimate connection with mental development. Philosophers and psychologists, whether Thomistic or Deweyan, Stimulus-Response or Cognitive, all stress the dependence of the mental processes on sensation. The secondary school, therefore, must set up a program of physical education which will provide optimum conditions for sound physical growth and development. Such a program is essential for a good learning environment. American high schools have been failing in this regard, as the following quotation points up:

A recent study shows that American youth is markedly inferior in health to continental youth despite the best food, airiest schools, and most plentiful civilization adjuncts in the world. . . . Only 8.5 per cent of the European children, but 78.3 per cent of the American children given the Kraus-Weber test

[6] For a fuller treatment of these areas of physical growth, see National Society for the Study of Education, *Adolescence*, Forty-Third Yearbook, Part I. (Chicago: University of Chicago Press, 1944), pp. 8–145; also Alexander A. Schneiders, *The Psychology of Adolescence*. (Milwaukee: Bruce, 1951), pp. 53–94.

[7] On this point, see Arnold Gesell et al., *Youth: The Years from Ten to Sixteen*. (New York: Harper, 1956), pp. 284–287.

for physical fitness failed the test. The percentage of American children failing two steps of the test was more than fifty times the European percentage.[8]

A well-rounded physical education program, rather than mere emphasis on sports, is needed. Catholic high schools, committed to the dictum of a sound mind in a sound body, should take the lead in this direction. The necessity for such a program is further heightened when it is realized that during adolescence, the body, because of intense physical growth, takes on a new and special significance. Indeed the body may often become the symbol of the self.[9] Hence both teacher and school program can help the adolescent student develop an adequate, healthy self-concept by affording him opportunities for purposeful, educative physical growth.

Less externally spectacular, but also of vital importance, is the mental growth which accompanies adolescence. It is during this period of life that the intellect begins to blossom. As Maritain so aptly put it, ". . . Ascending reason, natural reason with its freshness, boldness and sparkling ambitions is the mental heaven of adolescence; it is with reasoning that adolescence happens to be intoxicated." [10] This mental growth is far stronger in the adolescent than most people believe. Moreover, this mental growth is not confined to any one direction, e.g., discursive ratiocination, but rather develops along all lines, including imaginative, intuitional, and even mystical. It behooves the high school teacher to plan his lessons so as to allow for the further growth of all these facets of mental life. Nowhere is this more important than in the ninth grade, when the adolescent is more heady with the wine of the intellect than perhaps at any other time during life. The teacher, and the school too, should foster not only assimilative mental growth, but creative mental growth as well. This is especially important for Catholic high schools. The adolescent wishes to create with his mind, to be an artist in the true sense of the term.[11] The teacher should not stifle this

[8] Reported in the *New York State Journal of Medicine* as quoted in *The New York Times,* Sunday Supplement. (Nov. 6, 1955), p. 17.

[9] Herbert R. Stolz and Lois Meek Stolz, "Adolescent Problems Related to Somatic Variations," in *Adolescence, op. cit.,* pp. 83–84.

[10] Jacques Maritain, *Education at the Crossroads.* (New Haven, Conn.: Yale University Press, 1943), p. 61.

[11] Man is by nature a maker, and art consists in making. Art is the impressing of a person's idea, nay more, one's personality on some external entity. As Ryan observes, before the Fall man was primarily an artist, and only secondarily a scientist. After the Fall, man retained these powers, but in a diminished way. Hence to neglect the inner artistic thrust of the student's personality is to neglect to educate him adequately. See John Julian Ryan, *Beyond Humanism.* (New York: Sheed and Ward, 1950), pp. 57–59.

creativity, this artistry, by reducing learning to mere assimilation of facts. This important concept is recognized by the NCEA statement on the objectives of Catholic secondary schools (see Chapter II) as well as by most responsible educators, both Catholic and non-Catholic.

In the moral and religious development during adolescence, there tends to be a transition from external to internal morality. Belief becomes more important than mere good deeds. Conduct begins to flow from an intellectual grasp of and adherence to principles rather than from the external compulsion of the commands of others or from nonintelligible rules. Hence the teacher, particularly the Religious or clerical teacher, should not attempt to inculcate or enforce morality solely by appeals to authority, whether personal (status) or traditional. Instead, the teacher should strive to show the pupil the basic underlying intellectual and moral reasons for the existence of norms of belief and conduct. Far from destroying the basis of morality, such a procedure reinforces it, thus harmonizing faith and reason. Indeed such an approach flows not only from the spirit of St. Thomas, but also from the nature of the adolescent learner.

Moral and religious development does not take place in a vacuum; rather, it occurs in a social and personal context. Indeed there are at least five separate external influences in the moral and religious development of adolescents: family values, the immediate environment, cultural influences, education, church attendance. The effect of social influences was clearly brought out by Sister Mary Amadeus Dowd in her study of the moral reasoning in high school girls at various age-grade levels. From her investigation Sister Amadeus concluded that "the introduction of social factors seem to complicate some of the situations for the adolescent and therefore to blur the ethical issue, and that the effects of these social factors were shown more by subjects in grade twelve than in grade eight." [12] This clearly shows the necessity for the adolescent to learn in the classroom the interpenetrability of dogma, morality, and real-life situations. A pupil's personality develops in a social setting; hence the school's efforts at inculcating moral and spiritual values in the adolescent student must, to be effective, proceed along similar lines.[13]

Emotional growth also accompanies the adolescent years. Emotions are extremely important in leading a well-balanced life; accordingly, great care should be taken to ensure their proper development during adolescence. Youths must learn to control their emotions, neither sup-

[12] Sister Mary Amadeus Dowd, *Change in Moral Reasoning through the High School Years.* (Washington, D.C.: Catholic University of America Press, 1948), p. 110.

[13] See Educational Policies Commission, *Moral and Spiritual Values in the Public Schools.* (Washington: The Commission, 1951); also Gerard S. Sloyan (ed.), *Shaping the Christian Message.* (New York: Macmillan, 1958).

pressing them completely nor giving them full vent. They must learn that their emotions can be forces for tremendous good, if properly harnessed. The teacher and the guidance specialist should work with the student to ensure proper emotional development.

Social growth is another important adolescent phenomenon. Group acceptance becomes more important than during any other period in life. The desire for group acceptance and the conformity which such acceptance demands lead to the unique adolescent behavior in similarity of clothing (e.g., motorcycle jackets), group values, speech (which almost takes on the qualities of a separate language, e.g., "kook"), social groupings (e.g., a gang), and so forth. Adolescence is also a period of formation of intense friendships, with youths having several close friends from both their own and the opposite sex.[14] Since, as Aristotle affirmed, man is a social animal, social growth in adolescence is normal and natural. Because the classroom situation is really learning in a social context, the teacher should use these phases of adolescent social development as a positive force in his instruction. He should teach with the individual, the individual-in-the-group, and the group-as-a-whole in mind.

During adolescence, youths are growing; they are maturing. Growth brings with it learning, and this kind of learning is often painful. Indeed it may be argued, as Aristotle believed, that there is no learning without some pain. Students should be made aware that pain is a natural concomitant of growth. Athletic coaches have long realized this truth and never fail to inculcate it into students. Thus, although pain is a continual risk involved in life, it is also a source of supernatural merit. The teacher, however, should try to ease the pain of growing, of learning, wherever possible, but he should not try to eliminate it completely for if he does, learning too will be eliminated.

The teacher must similarly recognize that the adolescent's mental growth is most often achieved through a series of conflicts, especially in the clash of old and new ideas. Such conflicts, psychologists maintain, are crucial and vital to real mental development, a *sine qua non* of growth. Thus the perceptive teacher will present such conflicts in a good learning context, rather than allow them first to develop in the student. The teacher, therefore, can do much to relieve unnecessary adolescent anxiety. In presenting conflicts (which is nothing more than the Socratic technique), the skillful teacher should so conduct the learning situation that the student can successfully resolve the conflict or problem. Such a solution reinforces learning. This technique is one of the finest of its kind, not only pedagogically, but psychologically as well. This type of

[14] For a good general treatment of social growth in adolescence, see Luella Cole, *Psychology of Adolescence.* (New York: Rinehart, 1948), pp. 211–273.

procedure is particularly crucial in religion classes where student problems and conflicts have sometimes been flicked off as "heretical," "foolish," "unimportant," or "irrelevant to the topic we are now studying."

Teachers who received their education in Catholic colleges must be especially alert both to the existence of and the importance of adolescent growth. Frequently the emphasis in Catholic colleges, notably in philosophy courses, is on "being" as opposed to its alleged mortal enemy "becoming." There is, as a result, a tendency to look on the world as static. The emergent awareness by contemporary Catholic thinkers of the importance of "becoming," of man in a changing universe, of essences not in themselves but in spatiotemporal beings—this awareness should take hold of every Catholic secondary school teacher and fill him with a new appreciation of his adolescent students as they are in the real order.

Individual Differences. The Harvard Report observes that "students are both united and divided: united as heirs of a common past and agents in a joint future; divided, as varying in gifts, interests and hopes." [15] At a more ultimate level, students are united in being sons of the One God and in being rational, divided in that the substantial form of each has informed varying degrees of matter. Thus adolescence, like humanity, is a general term—and within the category "adolescence" are to be found great variances from person to person. The major areas in which individual differences occur in adolescents have been summed up by Mulrooney:

> (1) in physique and general appearance, the presence or absence of physical handicaps, in status of physical health; (2) in the social and cultural background from which they come or in which they are raised; (3) in the affectional climate, the feeling of security in which they are brought up; (4) in their relations with their peers, the roles and status that is accorded them; (5) in their mental abilities, their aptitudes, ideals, interests and goals; (6) in their ability to adjust to various life situations and their resulting emotions, the satisfying and thwarting of their desires, etc.[16]

All these varying individual differences affect learning and teaching. Indeed they cause one of the great dilemmas of American secondary education, viz., how to meet adequately the educational needs of each learner (who differs in so many respects from his classmates) within

[15] Harvard Committee, *General Education in a Free Society.* (Cambridge, Mass.: Harvard University Press, 1945), p. 103.

[16] Thomas W. Mulrooney, "Curricular Provisions for Individual Differences," in *McKeough* (ed.), *The Curriculum of the Catholic Secondary School.* (Washington, D.C.: Catholic University of America Press, 1949), p. 49.

the context of a group setting such as the classroom presents. As was discussed in Chapter III, the graded system is an attempt, however poor, to solve the dilemma. Ability grouping is another such attempt.

Psychologists like Gesell and his associates realize that, although there are great differences among individual youths, there is also some degree of similarity at each age level. Thus, for example, he compared student-school relationships at selected age levels (called "growth gradients") and found the following common elements:

14 Years. Many more Fourteens (in our group) say they like than that they dislike school. Expansively enthusiastic, energetic, sociable, Fourteen may do well in school. . . . Fourteen thrives on a variety of program. Enjoys participation in extracurricular activities and clubs.

15 Years. Fifteen's attitude toward school is often extreme: enthusiastic and wholehearted or hostile, rebellious and indifferent. . . . Many are extremely critical of the way school is run. . . . Many show a "15 year-old slump"—indifferent, don't work but don't know why not.[17]

An age-characteristics study of this type is valuable to the teacher provided he remembers that it is but a generalization which does not in any way minimize individual differences. Gesell himself reiterates this point through the book. While there are undoubtedly some general growth patterns, it must be remembered that every adolescent develops at a different rate, however slight. Some are early developers, some average, some late. Nor are the late developers necessarily mentally retarded. Both the teacher and the school must conduct the learning situation with individual differences in mind—the school by providing for a flexible (even perhaps ungraded) organizational and curricular framework, the teacher by constantly striving to provide as far as possible individual learning experiences for every youth in his class.

There are, of course, other general laws governing the development and subsequent learning behavior of adolescents. It has been repeatedly proved that there is a significant correlation between intelligence and other growth factors; i.e., the pupils possessing high IQ scores as a group tend to mature faster physically, be more adept at motor skills, and become more emotionally balanced than students having lesser intelligence.[18] Some valid generalizations may also be made on this basis in personality patterns. Neel's investigation of the relationship between an authoritarian personality and learning showed that "the more authoritarian a person is, the more likely he would be to have difficulty (a) in learning material which involves humanitarian philosophy and the need

[17] Gesell et al., op. cit., pp. 457–458.
[18] For a typical discussion of this psychological phenomenon, see Harold W. Bernard, Adolescent Development in American Culture. (Yonkers, N.Y.: World, 1957), pp. 56–57.

for understanding people, (*b*) in mastering ambiguous material which requires him to think on his own, but (*c*) *not* in learning factual subject matter." [19] Riesman's analysis of the three basic personality types, viz., tradition-directed, inner-directed, and other-directed, and their effects on learning constitute another fruitful and valid generalization.[20] As Father Ong, S.J., observes, Catholic education has all too often encouraged a tradition-directed learning, with the result that individualism, self-searching, and creativity have been atrophied in the Catholic student.[21] Alert teachers can profit by generalizations such as those of Neel and Ong, first, by divesting themselves of authoritarianism and exclusive tradition-directedness, and then, by organizing the learning situation so that their students may do the same. The result will be more human, more Christlike, and hence better education. Despite the existence of the above-mentioned generalizations, individual differences are all too real. Never for one instant should they be neglected by the teacher. Indeed the most difficult and challenging task for any teacher is providing for the individual differences of each of his students. Failure to do this relegates a teacher to the level of mere information dispenser in an intellectual supermarket.

A very encouraging sign in this direction in Catholic secondary education is the increasing recognition by Religious Orders and also by the clergy of the value of individual differences. Happily, there is a tendency away from suppression of individuality (formerly viewed as a sign of pride and self-seeking), toward a more wholesome development of each distinct personality. God did not make every student exactly the same; neither should the teacher.[22]

The Nature of Man

How does the adolescent student learn? The answer to this difficult question is radicated in the essential nature of the learner. "Act follows being," St. Thomas said, and therefore, in order to know about the act

[19] Ann Filinger Neel, "The Relationship of Authoritarian Personality to Learning," *Journal of Educational Psychology*, L (October, 1959), p. 199; cf. also the classic work by T. W. Adorno et al., *The Authoritarian Personality*. (New York: Harper, 1949).

[20] David Riesman et al., *The Lonely Crowd*. (New Haven, Conn.: Yale University Press, 1950).

[21] See the penetrating analysis by Walter J. Ong, S.J., *Frontiers in American Catholicism*. (New York: Macmillan, 1957), pp. 39–44.

[22] For two contrasting but concurring approaches to this problem, see Dennis J. Geaney, O.S.A., *Christians in a Changing World*. (Notre Dame, Ind.: Fides, 1959); and Rev. Charles W. Paris, "How Nuns Kill Vocations," *Catholic World*, CXC (February, 1960), pp. 301–305 (also reader reactions in the April issue of the same magazine, pp. 3–4).

of learning, it is necessary first to comprehend the essential nature of the human learner. It is not an overstatement to say that every psychology of learning—indeed every intelligently used method of teaching—is ultimately based on the psychologist's and teacher's philosophic viewpoint of man's essential nature.

In the history of thought, there have been three basic philosophical systems: Idealism, Materialism, and Realism. Within these systems there have been, of course, wide variations. However, each variation within a particular system does agree with the others in basic, general beliefs.

Idealism maintains that the ultimate nature of man is spiritual. Some Idealists deny that the physical body has any existence other than as a purely mental construct; other Idealists, like Berkeley, held that the body, as well as other physical things, had no existence without some mind to know or perceive their existence; other Idealists, like Hegel, viewed the body as an objectivization of the mind; still other Idealists, closer to the Realist position, admit the separate existence of the body but see it as essentially a spiritual entity which can often become a block to pure mental activity.

Materialism stands at the opposite end of the pole from Idealism. This philosophical system maintains that the ultimate nature of man is purely physical, wholy material. Most Materialists hold that man is continuous with nature, that man differs in degree but not in kind from other animals. Materialists, like Heraclitus, on the other hand, held that man is an ever-changing composition of physical opposites, e.g., fire and air; Materialists, like Spencer, believed that man is a composite of creative, evolutionary physical forces; those like Russell see man as a physical entity caught up in the onrolling of that all-encompassing great machine, the universe; while Dewey and his followers view man as the physical sum total of his past experiences, of the interaction between himself and his physical environment.

Realism stands midway between Idealism and Materialism. Realists maintain a position of dualism; i.e., man is composed of two separate principles, material (the body) and spiritual (the soul). The majority in this school believe that while both principles are necessary and indispensable components of man's nature, the spiritual is the more important. Some Realists, such as Descartes, hold that these two principles operate in a parallel fashion and are not intimately interrelated, but others, such as St. Thomas, maintain that in every action of man, both principles operate simultaneously.

Although Idealism held sway in American education in the second half of the nineteenth century, it is today for the most part dormant. Materialism, particularly of the Instrumentalist or Experimentalist type of Dewey and Kilpatrick, is in the ascendancy, nominally at least, in contemporary American secondary schools. Realism of the Thomistic type is dominant in Catholic high schools.[23]

Besides the natural dimension of man, of the student as a person, there is also the supernatural dimension. Both are inextricably interwoven in the student's actual existence as a person. As Mouroux has observed, a solely philosophical analysis of man "fails to touch the human person in his concrete conditions: in point of fact, it is in Christ that the person is called to being. The bond with God is essential to the person." [24]

Each person is made to the image and likeness of God. Original Sin tarnished but did not destroy this image. Since the death of Christ, each person is now a redeemed man. Further, God dwells within the very core of man's being, not merely by His power, but in a deep ontological fashion resulting from the effect-cause relationship man bears to God. God dwells in many people in a further way, by sanctifying grace. This triple relationship of man to God, viz., by image, by redemption, and by indwelling, places man in a radically new dimension, a perspective of which the teacher must ever be mindful. Fr. De Letter, S.J., observed that everyone at all times makes in everything and everywhere a "personal encounter with God." This encounter is made not only through the sacraments, but also through the ontologically derived psychological approach each person makes with reality.[25] Jung realized this when he put over the door of his villa the inscription "Called or not, God is present."

Fr. Congar, O.P., in a classic work states that every Christian, lay and Religious, has three common functions emanating from his membership in the Mystical Body: a priestly function, that of redeeming the world and offering it up to God; a royal function, that of representing on earth God's kingship over all reality; a prophetic function, that of acting as witness of God and the truth to all mankind and to all things.[26] This rich Catholic view of the nature of man raises him to the level of "Christopher," Christ-bearer. Thus a complete vision of the nature of

[23] For a fuller analysis of these comparative philosophies, see such works as J. Donald Butler, *Four Philosophies and Their Practice in Education and Religion*, rev. ed. (New York: Harper, 1957); the admirable multivolume series by Frederick Copleston, S.J., *History of Philosophy*. (Westminster, Md.: Newman, 1946–   ); National Society for the Study of Education, *Modern Philosophies and Education*, Fifty-Fourth Yearbook, Part I. (Chicago: University of Chicago Press, 1955); William K. Wright, *A History of Modern Philosophy*. (New York: Macmillan, 1941).

[24] Jean Mouroux, *The Meaning of Man*. (New York: Sheed and Ward, 1948), p. 134.

[25] P. De Letter, S.J., "The Encounter With God," *Thought*, XXXVI (Spring, 1961), pp. 5–24.

[26] Yves M. J. Congar, O.P., *Lay People in the Church*. (Westminster, Md.: Newman, 1956), pp. 112–308.

man embraces three elements or levels, all of which must be present: the animal, the rational, the Divine.

The Nature of Man's Knowing

For an Idealist, man knows by intuition, i.e., direct, nonsensory, immediate apprehension of the object by the mind without any intermediary.[27] Intuition, of course, can only occur if the mind and external reality are either the same entity or both spiritual entities. On this type of learning, Radhakrishnan remarks, "Intuitive knowledge is not non-rational; it is only non-conceptual." [28]

For the Experimentalism of Dewey and his disciples (and of all forms of Materialism, this is the most influential in American public secondary education), man knows by experimental, reflective experience, i.e., the encounter of the physical mind with the physical environment and the subsequent mental reflection and reconstruction of this encounter into new elements called thoughts. The act of knowing is divided by Dewey into five steps or stages as follows:

> (1) suggestions, in which the mind leaps forward to a possible solution; (2) an intellectualization of the difficulty or perplexity that has been *felt* (directly experienced) into a *problem* to be solved, a question for which the answer must be sought; (3) the use of one suggestion after another as a leading idea, or *hypothesis,* to initiate and guide observation and other operations in collection of factual material; (4) the mental elaboration of the idea or supposition as an idea or supposition (*reasoning,* in the sense in which reasoning is a part, not the whole, of inference); and (5) testing the hypothesis by overt or imaginative action.[29]

Any act of knowing is, therefore, at root, a person's experimental attempts to solve a problem. Knowing and intelligence are of extreme importance to the Experimentalists, because it is by intelligence that new patterns of complex actions are shaped. The mind is not a separate entity but rather man's physical organism in intelligent action. Hence the mind (if this term must be used) is both the complex sum of past experiences plus the operational activity of present thought. On this point Werkmeister observes, "the whole conception of the efficacy of

---

[27] St. Thomas teaches that it is by intuition that God and the angels know reality.

[28] S. Radhakrishnan, *An Idealist View of Life,* rev. ed. (London: G. Allen, 1937), p. 153. Intuition as a mode of knowing must not be confused with so-called "feminine intuition," of which some contemporary women's magazines so often speak.

[29] John Dewey, *How We Think.* (Boston: Heath, 1933), p. 107. The tremendous influence of this five-step analysis can be seen in almost every book on secondary school principles and methods, e.g., Klausmeier, *op. cit.,* pp. 66–69.

intelligence is, for Dewey, an outgrowth of biological considerations." [30]

For the contemporary Thomistic Realist, man knows primarily by discursive ratiocination, i.e., the gathering into the mind of the "intelligible forms" of reality and their subsequent judgment of and reasoning about these forms by means of a successive interplay among the various functions of the mind. Discursive ratiocination takes place in three basic stages. The first stage, abstraction, is that by which the idea is generated. In the abstractive process the external individual impressions are reduced to internal, universal ideas. Ideogenesis, or the birth of an idea, takes place in five successive steps: *Sensation*, i.e., the stimulation of a sense receptor by an external stimulus. This is a crucial step indeed, for as St. Thomas asserts, "There is nothing in the mind that was not first in the senses." In sensation, an external stimulus impinges upon a sense receptor in the human body. This stimulus then becomes a neural impulse which is transmitted via interlinking nerve connections to the cerebral cortex of the brain. *Perception*, i.e., the immediate and automatic cognitive coordination of this and related sensations into a sensorily meaningful whole. Thus, for example, a man instantly perceives a house, a perception which arises from the coordination of many individual sensations about the house, e.g., the color of the roof and siding, the reflection from the windows, and so forth. There is no sensation without perception. *Phantasm*, i.e., the construction by the imagination of the objects perceived. The phantasm retains the individual, concrete attributes of the perception. *Agent intellect*, i.e., the faculty of the mind which abstracts the individual concrete notes of the phantasm and reveals the nonmaterial, universal essence of the object perceived. The essence is the substantial nature of the object, the thing which makes it to be what it is. This essence is universal, i.e., common to all objects of a similar kind. It is with the act of the agent intellect that thought is transformed from the physical to the nonphysical. *Possible intellect*, i.e., the faculty of the mind which, having been fecundated by the active intellect with the essence of the perceived object, forms a concept, an idea. The work of the possible intellect thus gives the person the power to understand. It does this, as Aristotle observed, by becoming the very object it understands.[31]

The concept, together with the properties, accidents, and various

[30] W. H. Werkmeister, *A History of Philosophical Ideas in America.* (New York: Ronald, 1949), p. 556.

[31] For a fuller treatment of the Thomistic stages of knowing, see St. Thomas Aquinas, *Summa Theologica* I, q.12, a.4; q.55, a.2; q.84, a.6–8; q.85, a.5. See also Robert E. Brennan, O.P., *Thomistic Psychology.* (New York: Macmillan, 1941), pp. 169–209; Tad W. Guzie, S.J., *The Analogy of Learning.* (New York: Sheed and Ward, 1960), pp. 48–113.

relations of the essence, forms the basis for ratiocination. The second stage of ratiocination takes place through judgment, i.e., the intellectual discernment by means of composition and division of the identity or diversity between two concepts. In every judgment there are three steps: apprehension of the concepts, comparison of the concepts, and awareness of their agreement or disagreement. Basically every act of thought, at its deepest ontological level, is an act of judgment. Fr. Donceel, S.J., notes that the judgment is the central point of man's intellectual life precisely because his intellect seeks the dynamic, not the static (the concept merely being a static representation of a reality).[32]

The third stage of man's knowing is reason (in the precise sense of the term), i.e., the mental operation in which two judgments are compared through the medium of a third judgment, and a new judgment is derived from this comparison. The normal external expression of the reasoning process is the syllogism. The two most common types of reasoning are induction and deduction. Kelly defines induction as "the method of reasoning which consists in forming judgments about a number of particular cases [or judgments] and then deriving from these cases [or judgments] a general rule or principle by discovering the common qualities presented by these cases [or judgments]." He defines deduction as "the method of reasoning which consists of the application of a general principle or law [or judgment] to particular facts."[33] Induction thus is synthetic reasoning, and deduction is analytic reasoning.

The Thomistic theory of knowing is based on "faculty psychology," i.e., that there are in man several interrelated powers or faculties, each of which makes man capable of a certain type of action. St. Thomas essentially accepted the Aristotelian classification of five basic faculties of man, viz., vegetative, appetitive, sensory, locomotive, and rational.[34] The highest of these faculties, the rational, contains within itself several important powers, the three most significant being the intellect, memory, and understanding. There is scarcely a chapter on learning in any secular textbook on educational psychology or secondary school teaching which does not scoff at "faculty psychology," indicting it as outmoded and disproved. However, the authors of these secular textbooks are themselves usually not conversant with the latest studies and developments. The

[32] J. F. Donceel, S.J., *Philosophical Psychology.* (New York: Sheed and Ward, 1955), p. 235.

[33] William A. Kelly, *Educational Psychology*, 4th ed. (Milwaukee: Bruce, 1956), p. 133.

[34] Technically, these are the powers specifically of the human soul. St. Thomas Aquinas, *op. cit.*, I, q.78, a.1–4 and q.79, a.1–2.

scholarly work of Kolesnik, one of the most recent and exhaustive treatments of this problem, notes that "the relevant empirical data reported thus far seem to be in harmony with Thomistic teachings on the matter [of faculty psychology]. Factorial analysis indicates that there are established differences in the way man's mind operates, that these differences represent general tendencies to act in particular ways; that these tendencies are native, but must be developed. . . ." [35]

Underlying the belief or disbelief in faculty psychology is the more fundamental doctrine of the nature of man. Being materialistic monists who deny the existence of the rational soul as a distinct entity, Experimentalists can hardly be expected to be adherents of faculty psychology. Some Experimentalists, notably authors of many textbooks on secondary education, ignore both the speculative and empirical evidence and make such statements as, "So far as psychology is concerned, this doctrine [of faculty psychology based on the existence of the mind as a separate substance] is dead." [36] Other Experimentalists, more cognizant of the research which has been going on, attempt to explain it in other non-faculty psychology terms. Thus the *Encyclopedia of Educational Research* notes that concepts "are not facts, nor are they generalizations in the form of rules or laws," but nevertheless are "marked by consistency of differential, generalized symbolic responses." [37] Indeed, it is becoming recognized more and more that the Experimentalist notion of "faculty" as an independent, unitary, quasi-physical entity resembling a muscle is not the same notion of "faculty" held by Thomistic and kindred psychologists.[38] Thus the Experimentalists have been attacking a straw man as far as Thomists are concerned. The redirection of current non-Catholic psychological thinking can be readily discerned in the following quotation from the *Encyclopedia of Educational Research*: "Concepts are such an integral part of thinking that it is difficult to find any research in learning which does not include them at least in part." [39]

The Thomistic analysis of the nature of man and how he thinks is crucial to an understanding of the learning process and for that reason

[35] Walter B. Kolesnik, *Mental Discipline in Modern Education.* (Madison, Wis.: University of Wisconsin Press, 1958), p. 102.

[36] Harold Alberty, *Reorganizing the High-School Curriculum,* rev. ed. (New York: Macmillan, 1953), p. 62.

[37] "Concepts," *Encyclopedia of Educational Research,* 3d ed. (New York: Macmillan, 1960), p. 323.

[38] Kolesnik, *op. cit.,* pp. 89–112; cf. also William D. Commins, "What Is Faculty Psychology?" *Thought,* VIII (Fall, 1933), pp. 48–57; Charles A. Hart, *The Thomistic Concept of Mental Faculty.* (Washington, D.C.: Catholic University of America Press, 1930).

[39] "Concepts," *op. cit.,* p. 329.

should form the basis for the pedagogical methods which the teacher uses in every phase of his instruction. Unless the teacher has an ever-present awareness of how the pupil learns, his instructional methods are doomed to ineffectuality, hence to failure.

Teaching must be rooted in learning, never separated from it. From the viewpoint of Thomistic philosophical psychology, the teacher should always keep the following principles in mind: First, the basic type of learning comes through direct experience. A person comes to know himself through knowing things outside himself. The age-old psychological problem of the chasm between the knower and the known can only be completely bridged by direct experience during which, as St. Thomas says, the knower becomes the known (thereby eliminating the chasm). The basic teaching method for a Thomistically oriented teacher must be that of experience. Second, learning is fundamentally an active process, not a passive mode of endurance. Since learning is dynamic self-activity, the teacher's methods should be geared to stimulating the student to mental activity, rather than to treating the pupil as a sponge whose task it is passively to sop up information.[40] Problem solving, the teaching technique used by St. Thomas himself in the *Summa Theologica*, thus becomes the pedagogical practice par excellence, since problem solving requires the greatest pupil self-activity. Third, learning involves the total student, not solely his intellect. The teacher must accommodate his instruction to this fact, giving due weight to the role of the senses, imagination, memory, and so forth, not in a grudging manner, but in full realization of the partnership in learning in which every organ and faculty is deeply involved. Fourth, learning is radicated in the nonmaterial soul; it is therefore impossible for all learning to be expressed in physical behavior patterns. Knowledge, the fruit of the intellect, is not the product solely of physical activity. Consequently, the teacher must realize that he cannot perceive all the learning which is taking place within the student. The pedagogical methods must be directed at both the interiority and exteriority of the pupil. Similarly, the teacher's techniques should aim at producing abstractions, appreciations, understandings, and so forth, all of which are of a spiritual rather than a physical nature. Fifth, learning is a complicated process which is greatly affected by all sorts of circumstances, both internal and external. Teaching methods must therefore be directed to the adolescent as he is in his concrete situation rather than to a disembodied intellect. Thus, for example, the studies have shown at least eight separate factors which affect concept formation: the nature of the problem presented; the goal of the learner; the personality of the learner; other charac-

[40] See the commentary of Mary Helen Mayer, in *The Philosophy of Teaching of St. Thomas Aquinas.* (Milwaukee: Bruce, 1929), pp. 120–127.

teristics of the learner (e.g., age, prior experience); the materials used as examples; the manner and order of presentation; the nature of the validation (by parents or experience); and the use of the concept (e.g., how often practiced).[41]

For additional insights into pupil learning, the Catholic high school teacher can draw on other Christian philosophical and theological wisdom not of the Thomistic tradition. Indeed the role of intuition in human knowing, neglected by classical Thomism, has been developed by other Christian thinkers, particularly of the Augustinian and Phenomenological schools. Not only is intuition of a higher order than discursive ratiocination,[42] but it also is, as Fr. De Letter, S.J., observes, the key to the knowledge of God in man's encounter with Him.[43] In using the insights of non-Scholasticism, the Catholic teacher is not doing violence to the spirit of Thomism, but is indeed following the Angelic Doctor's advice: "Take truth where you find it." The Christian teacher should recall Hirscher's words: "It is to the Gospel, and not to Scholasticism, that God from on high has promised indefectibility." [44]

The Manner of Man's Knowing

The analysis in the preceding section of the nature of man's knowing was made from the viewpoint of philosophical psychology, i.e., the examination of man's thinking in the light of metaphysical principles. There is, however, another fruitful way of looking at man's knowing, and this is from the viewpoint of empirical psychology, i.e., the examination of man's thinking through data obtained from experimentation and measurement.[45] The two most common learning theories currently proposed by empirical psychologists are the Stimulus-Response (S-R) theory and the Cognitive theory. Each theory conflicts with the other on a number of basic points. A knowledge of these theories is important, because the one to which the teacher consciously or unconsciously subscribes will drastically affect his pedagogical techniques.

The Stimulus-Response theory is a general term which includes many diverse but allied theories ranging from Thorndike to Hull.[46]

---

[41] "Concepts," op. cit., p. 325.

[42] Etienne Gilson corroborated this point in a discussion with the author.

[43] De Letter, op. cit., pp. 22–24.

[44] Quoted in F. X. Arnold, Serviteurs de la foi. (Tournai: Desclée, 1957), p. 60. Translation the author's.

[45] Empirical psychology is more frequently known as "experimental psychology." The latter term is avoided in this textbook to eliminate possible confusion with the philosophy of Experimentalism.

[46] This twofold distinction between Stimulus-Response and Cognitive follows the basic division made by Ernest Hilgard, Theories of Learning, 2d ed. (New York: Appleton-Century-Crofts, 1956), p. 8. Other psychologists have used different terms, e.g., Association for Stimulus-Response, and Field or Organismic for Cognitive.

This theory maintains that learning consists in the integrative, complex physical response which results as a reaction to various external stimuli. More clearly, the theory can be called "Stimulus-Connector-Response." The connector or intermediary between the object to be learned and the learned response in the person is a series of interlinking nervous and muscular actions. A person reacts to an object as a bundle of various receptors. What is learned is actually a series of habits in which the various connectors (conductors) have been so formed and strengthened that they operate smoothly and easily as a unity. The connection between the stimulus and the response is at the heart of learning, since once the connection has been made, the response automatically results. Learning takes place by trial and error; i.e., the person makes a number of attempts at solving a problem, learns from the error he made in each attempt, and finally from the wisdom he accumulates as a result of these past errors combined with renewed trials, eventually solves the problem and learns.[47]

The Stimulus-Response theory is atomistic; i.e., it places emphasis on a point-for-point relationship between the individual stimuli and the subsequent individual responses. It is mechanistic in that it maintains that the person acts as a machine which reacts automatically and precisely to any appropriate stimulus.[48] It is materialistic, as it declares that man and his learning are totally physical. This theory has been greatly influenced by experiments on animals, particularly Thorndike's mazes and problem boxes (which gave rise to the trial-and-error theory, among other things).

The most important of the Stimulus-Response psychologists, Thorndike, systematized his learning theory into three primary stages or laws which have been highly influential in American teaching methodology. *Law of Readiness*—an individual receives satisfaction, and hence is ready to learn at such time as the "conduction unit is ready to conduct." On the other hand, an individual is annoyed, hence not ready to learn, when the "conduction unit is ready to conduct" but is not given an opportunity to do so, or when a "conduction unit is forced to conduct." [49] Satisfaction and annoyance are important, because if the learning produces satisfaction to the learner he will retain the learned material and will be motivated to learn more, whereas annoyance will

[47] See Edward L. Thorndike, *Educational Psychology*. (New York: Bureau of Publications, Teachers College, Columbia University, 1913) vol. II; also his *Fundamentals of Learning*. (New York: Bureau of Publications, Teachers College, Columbia University, 1932); Hilgard, *op. cit.*, pp. 1–184.

[48] National Society for the Study of Education, *The Psychology of Learning*, Forty-First Yearbook, Part II. (Chicago: University of Chicago Press, 1942), pp. 3–164.

[49] Thorndike, quoted in Hilgard, *op. cit.*, p. 18.

lead the learner to reject the learning and seek to avoid any more. As can readily be seen, Thorndike's learning theory rests heavily on physical hedonism. *Law of Exercise*—the conductors are weakened by lack of use and practice, are strengthened by continual use and practice. In his later writings, Thorndike substantially reduced the importance of exercise in the laws of learning, observing that other factors, such as reward, punishment, and belongingness, are more important in strengthening the connective bond than is mere recurrence.[50] However, past experience remained of extreme importance in Thorndike's learning theory. *Law of Effect*—the consequences of the learned material strengthen or weaken the connective bond. If the learned material produces satisfaction to the learner, the learning is strengthened; if it produces annoyance, the bond is weakened. In his subsequent works, Thorndike modified the law of effect, since experiments had been made which showed that the effects of reward and punishment were neither equal nor opposite, and hence did not produce the same degree of satisfaction or annoyance.

Thorndike also discovered other secondary laws of learning; e.g., the overall attitude or "set" of the learner does much to facilitate or hamper learning. Later, under pressure from the assaults of the Cognitive psychologists, he introduced the law of "belongingness," which stated that the more readily a stimulus fits in with a total situation, the easier is a connective bond formed and strengthened. Belongingness is more important than mere recurrence.[51]

The Cognitive theory is a general term which includes many diverse but allied theories ranging from those of Koffka to those of Lewin. This theory maintains that learning comprises three steps: (1) the dynamic interaction between the learner as a totality and his environment, (2) the perception by the learner of specific significant related elements in the broad environment field, (3) the present, ongoing restructuring of these elements into new meaningful generalized wholes or concepts. Individual stimuli or objects are meaningless outside of their total field, or context.[52] The intermediary between the object learned and the actual learning in the person is the whole ground and field integrated all at once by a perception of the central brain processes. What is learned is actually a basic mental or cognitive structure, a

---

[50] Thorndike, *Fundamentals of Learning, op. cit.;* also his *Human Learning.* (New York: Appleton-Century-Crofts, 1931); and his *The Psychology of Wants, Interests and Attitudes.* (New York: Appleton-Century-Crofts, 1935).

[51] Thorndike, *Human Learning, op. cit.,* p. 46.

[52] On this point, see the interesting explanatory example given by George W. Hartmann in his article, "The Field Theory of Learning and Its Educational Consequences," *The Psychology of Learning, op. cit.,* p. 169.

general concept into which the person can integrate future singulars. The generalized concept is the heart of learning. Learning takes place by insight in which the elements to be learned are perceptually integrated in a sudden mental flash in which the essential relationships between the elements are immediately understood. Trial and error is only a stage in the development of the insightful solution.

The Cognitive theory is holistic; i.e., it places emphasis on the whole organism as a unit (not a mere collection of individual receptors). A person does not react to individual stimuli, but to the whole situation. It is organismic in that it maintains that a person does not react automatically and precisely as a machine but rather functions as a unified entity in a variety of ways, depending on such factors as individual perception or field. It is materialistic, as it declares that man and his learning are totally physical. This theory has also been greatly influenced by experiments with animals, particularly Köhler's apes.

The most influential of the Cognitive schools, the Gestaltists, have formulated several principles or laws of learning, all of which are very influential in contemporary teaching methodology. The three most important of these principles are: *Principle of External Structure*—the more the material to be learned is itself coordinated, structured in some kind of unity, the easier will be perception and the cognitive structuring involved in learning. *Principle of the Gestalt*—mental operations always tend to move in the direction of structuring, of seeing things whole, of the "good gestalt." [53] External conditions help the learner to move in the direction of the "good gestalt." Koffka gives the four most important of these external factors which help perceptual structuring, namely, similarity of parts, proximity of parts to one another, arrangement of parts in a closed rather than an open figure, and the tendency of parts to seem to continue themselves toward a whole (e.g., a partially closed circle tends to continue itself perceptually toward a closed circle). [54] *Principle of Development*—the degree of intelligence, past experiences, level of maturity, adequate goals, and proper motivation increase the frequency and level of insights. However, present cognitive restructuring is far more important in producing insights than is past experience. Goals and motivation radically affect the continuance and depth of this mental restructuring.

[53] American psychologists have great difficulty finding an adequate English translation for "gestalt," and hence have left the word in the original German. Kelly (*op. cit.*, p. 261) has suggested the following English equivalents: "whole, configuration, pattern, form."

[54] See Kurt Koffka, *Principles of Gestalt Psychology*. (New York: Harcourt, Brace, 1935); also Hilgard, *op. cit.*, pp. 225–229. These principles are not particularly new, but rather formed the core of the "laws of association" propounded by psychologists from Aristotle down to the present.

What empirical learning theories which are in harmony with Catholic doctrine have been developed by Catholic psychologists? Regrettably, none. While Catholic scholars have produced detailed (and sometimes overdetailed) analyses of the learner from the viewpoint of philosophical psychology, they have done little or nothing in the area of empirical psychology except to categorize it as "materialistic" or "false." [55] As Nordberg has observed, "Where we [Catholics] should be joyfully leading, we are often following and even resisting." [56] Until a good Catholic theory of empirical psychology appears, Catholic teachers will, for better or worse, have to cast their lot with the Cognitive theory. More and more the Cognitive schools are approaching a Thomistic concept of man and his learning.[57] This similarity can best be seen in the following Cognitive positions: Man is an "integer"—that is, he acts as a whole unit; the emphasis on the self-concept;[58] the thought process as the acquisition of generalizations (universals); the importance of consciousness.[59] However, there are some tenets of the Cognitive theory unacceptable to Catholics, particularly the belief that man is purely physical. Also, some psychologists have criticized the Gestalt school for advocating a perception theory rather than a learning theory. Notwithstanding, Catholics should also remember that the Stimulus-Response theory has yielded many fruitful psychological data and laws, e.g., the importance of mental "set" or attitude in learning.

Each learning theory has markedly influenced teaching methods, as can be seen below.

STIMULUS-RESPONSE THEORY	COGNITIVE THEORY
1. Heavy emphasis on drill to reinforce habits	1. Emphasis on reflective thinking to help produce generalized concepts (little or no drill)
2. Great use of individualized recitation	2. Almost exclusive use of discussion and group work
3. Overstress on the value of objective tests	3. Stress on evaluation based on many types of formal and informal tests

[55] For an example of this approach, cf. John D. Redden and Francis A. Ryan, *A Catholic Philosophy of Education*, rev. ed. (Milwaukee: Bruce, 1956), pp. 75–83.

[56] Robert B. Nordberg, "Behavioral Science Revisited," *Catholic Educational Review*, LVIII (May, 1960), p. 316.

[57] For a development of this point, see Robert B. Nordberg, "The March to Holism: Where Are We?" *Catholic Educational Review*, LVIII (April, 1960), p. 240.

[58] Compare this with Pope Pius XII, *Address to the Rome Congress of the International Association of Applied Psychology*, trans. by NCWC (Washington: NCWC, 1958), p. 2, cited in Nordberg, "The March to Holism: Where Are We?" *op. cit.*, p. 243.

[59] See Robert E. Brennan, O.P., *History of Psychology*. (New York: Macmillan, 1945), pp. 220–221.

STIMULUS-RESPONSE THEORY	COGNITIVE THEORY
4. Reliance on a unidirectional curriculum (e.g., subject-centered, function-centered)	4. Reliance on an integrative curriculum (e.g., Core)
5. Emphasis on functionalism whenever possible	5. Emphasis on generalization whenever possible
6. Heavy stress on individual differences	6. Heavy stress on individual differences as they exist in the total existential and environmental context
7. Great use of external rewards and punishments in motivation[60]	7. Use of inner drives and personal goals as motivators

The teacher should remember, however, that the newer psychologists in both schools have so modified their theories that the schools are beginning to agree on many points, particularly in applied methodology. Thus, for example, Gates, a Stimulus-Response psychologist, could agree (though for different reasons) with the list of "twenty broader pedagogical implications of the field theory" which were proposed by Hartmann, a Cognitive psychologist.[61]

Transfer of Learning

There are few psychological doctrines which possess as much significance for teaching and learning as does the principle of transfer of learning. Kolesnik defines transfer as "the application of knowledge, skills, habits, attitudes or ideals acquired in one situation to another situation for which they had not been specifically learned." [62] Thus, for example, a student transfers principles which he learned in geometry class to a picture he is painting. During the first three decades of this century when the Stimulus-Response theory held sway, most educators and psychologists denied the existence of transfer of learning. They were forced to do so because of their adherence to the atomistic Stimulus-Response theory, which held that learning was the result of individual S-R bonds. Such a belief in singulars could not be reconciled with a universal, which transfer implies. Today, however, transfer is accepted by almost everyone, because the overwhelming weight of empirical evidence supports the existence of transfer[63] and also because the Cognitive theory, which is based on the mental structuring of whole patterns, of generalized concepts, is currently the psychological theory most widely supported.

---

[60] For a more complete list, see Alberty, op. cit., pp. 65–66.

[61] Arthur I. Gates, "Connectionism: Present Concepts and Interpretations," The Psychology of Learning, op. cit., pp. 163–164; Hartmann, ibid., pp. 206–208.

[62] Kolesnik, op. cit., p. 5.

[63] Ibid., pp. 30–57; Pedro T. Orata, "Recent Research Studies in Transfer of Training with Implications for the Curriculum, Guidance and Personnel Work," Journal of Educational Research, XXXV (October, 1941), pp. 81–101.

What is the basic psychological explanation for transfer of learning? The Stimulus-Response psychologist, Thorndike, forced to take some sort of position, held the theory of identical elements; i.e., transfer takes place when the habitual response (content) of one situation is identical with the habitual response of another situation. This theory implicitly denies transfer; if the elements of the two situations are identical, there obviously is no real transfer, for transfer implies different elements in each situation. The Cognitive school of Gestaltists holds the theory of transposition, or the application of the relationship perceived in one situation to a new situation. The person perceives situations whole, and so by insight can transfer meaningful, related patterns within the two whole situations.[64] This doctrine bears a great resemblance to Judd's theory of generalization.[65] Thomists, who have always believed in transfer of learning, explain it by a theory of universals; i.e., every act of thought, a concept, is by its very nature a universal, and can, therefore, be transferred to any situation falling within the same general class. In many ways the empiricist revolt against transfer had its roots in a concomitant revolt against Scholasticism and Scholastically influenced philosophies.

The ability to transfer learning from one situation to another is one of the most important qualities of an educated person. Therefore, a teacher must order his instruction in such a way as to facilitate transfer. He can best do this by keeping in mind:

1. Pupils do not transfer learning automatically. Transfer must be a deliberate aim of the teacher; in short it must be worked for.

2. Transfer takes place more readily when the pupils want to transfer. Hence the teacher should impress upon the students the necessity of transferring learning and should motivate them by encouragement and skillful transfer-directed questions and assignments.

3. Practice in transfer increases the pupils' facility to transfer. The alert teacher should consequently provide the students with as many opportunities as possible to transfer learning, especially application of the general, transferable principles to other fields.

4. The students will transfer better when they know what learnings can and should be transferred. Accordingly, the teacher should always strive to "bring out the feature to be transferred." [66]

[64] Hilgard (op. cit., pp. 252–253) observes that for a Cognitive psychologist, what is common can be transferred "but what exists in common is not identical piecemeal elements but common patterns, configurations or relationships."

[65] Charles H. Judd, "The Relation of Special Training to General Intelligence," Educational Review, XXXVI (June, 1908), pp. 28–42.

[66] "Transfer of Learning," Encyclopedia of Educational Research, 3d ed. (New York: Macmillan, 1960), pp. 15–42.

5. The ability to transfer has a high correlation with general mental ability.

6. The interval between the learned material and the new transferable situation affects the quality and degree of transfer. Therefore teachers desiring to promote transfer should endeavor to present the two situations as close in time to each other as possible.

7. Transfer is easier between broad principles than between individual facts. A study by Kittel concluded by observing that "evidence from this experiment in conjunction with that of similar experiments indicates that furnishing learners with information in the form of underlying principles promotes transfer and retention of learned principles and may provide the background enabling future discovery of new principles." [67] Hence teachers should avoid stressing only factual content in their instruction and concentrate on theoretical, general principles from which these facts flow. This is particularly important for Catholic high schools.

8. Students transfer better when they understand the relationship between what is to be transferred and the new material. Consequently in their instruction teachers should stress understanding, not just memory.

9. "Independently derived principles are more transferable than those given." [68] Accordingly teachers should not tell the pupils the principles directly, as through the lecture technique, but rather promote maximum mental self-activity on the part of the students, as by problem solving and discussion techniques. The teacher should remember Alberty's dictum, "Transfer of training is most effective when the learning situation is so organized as to facilitate generalization and the recognition of relationships." [69]

Formal Discipline. The theory of formal discipline, widely held by most nineteenth-century educators and by some twentieth-century Catholic educators is somewhat related to transfer of learning. Defined by Kolesnik, "Formal discipline refers to transfer which is supposed to result, not from subject matter or methods of study acquired, but from the strengthening of a particular [mental] power or powers." [70] Thus both transfer and formal discipline deal with the application of what is learned from one situation to another; they differ in that while transfer concerns itself with the application of generalized knowledge, skills, habits, attitudes, and ideals, formal discipline deals with the application of specific mental powers. Transference of mental powers was con-

[67] Jack E. Kittell, "An Experimental Study of the Effect of External Direction during Learning on Transfer and Retention of Principles," *Journal of Educational Psychology*, XLVIII (November, 1957), p. 404.

[68] G. M. Haslerud and Shirley Meyers, "The Transfer Value of Given and Individually Derived Principles," *Journal of Educational Psychology*, XLIX (December, 1958), p. 297.

[69] Alberty, *op. cit.*, p. 80.

[70] Kolesnik, *op. cit.*, p. 6.

ceived of in much the same way as transference of muscular powers; it is the exercise per se and not the nature of the material exercised upon that develops biceps or mental powers.

The distinction between transfer of training and formal discipline might be illustrated as follows: According to the notion of transfer, the study of Latin, for example, might reasonably be expected to improve one's command of English or French; vocabulary or principles of grammar learned in one class could be used in another class or on some occasion outside of school. According to formal discipline, the study of Latin would also be valuable outside the Latin class, but for quite another reason. The study of Latin would improve one's powers of attention, observation or retention so well that he would attend, observe or remember better whenever and wherever he might be called upon to do so at all.[71]

Although there is some small and scattered evidence supporting the existence of a loose kind of formal discipline, nevertheless, the overwhelming weight of the investigations and studies has disproved the theory of formal discipline. From a Catholic viewpoint, this was bound to happen since formal discipline was based on a nineteenth-century version of "faculty psychology" which viewed the faculties of the mind not as spiritual powers or manifestations of the soul as did the Scholastics, but as independent unitary realities, as quasi-muscles.[72] Certainly there cannot be much reason for studying Latin if it is admitted that this subject has not worth in itself but is valuable only as a means to something outside itself, such as training the memory. Notwithstanding, there are some people, usually outside the ranks of professional education, who still cling to this outmoded theory. Unfortunately there are not a few Catholic school people among this number.[73] These educators seem to think that the value of a subject is directly proportionate to its difficulty and disagreeableness to the student. Ironically, as Kolesnik observes, there are also many teachers in both public and Catholic high schools who "reject formal discipline as a theory, yet seem to accept and practice a methodology which stems directly from it." [74]

A Definition of Learning

From the foregoing analysis of the nature and manner of man's knowing, it is possible to arrive at a definition of learning. Learning is that form of self-activity through which, by means of experience, con-

[71] *Ibid.*

[72] Hart, *op. cit.*, p. 36. It was Wolff, an eighteenth-century German philosopher who originally explained "faculty" in physical terms; see also Lee J. Cronbach, *Educational Psychology.* (New York: Harcourt, Brace, 1954), p. 247.

[73] See Sister Mary Xavier, O.S.U., "Value of Studying Latin," *Catholic Educational Review,* LVIII (May, 1960), pp. 323–331.

[74] Kolesnik, *op. cit.*, p. 7.

sciousness or behavior is changed. Since teaching must be rooted in learning and never separated from it, the conscientious teacher should be aware of the nature of learning and the elements which comprise its definition. These elements are four in number. The *first element* is self-activity. Learning—knowing—means that in some way the person becomes the object known, not just by an internal image, but as it were, existentially. Thus learning is the process by which an intimate union is effected between subject and object. Learning is therefore dependent on activity, for only activity (not staticness) can produce union. Learning, as St. Thomas observes, arises fundamentally from the pupil's self-activity rather than by the activity of the teacher.[75] The *second element* is experience. There can be no learning without experiences. A person cannot learn anything about himself or other things without using his senses.[76] The mind, a spiritual principle, can get in touch with physical things or other spiritual things only through the world of matter. Indeed Aristotle's idea of learning was "to have insight into the intelligible through the sensible." [77] Further, as St. Thomas notes, a person can have no knowledge of his self except through its acts.[78] Hence experience is a *sine qua non* of learning. The *third element* in the definition of learning is consciousness or behavior. Contemporary Materialist psychologists tend to link learning exclusively with observable behavior, neglecting consciousness.[79] Such a view results from a denial of the existence of the soul. Consciousness can be changed without an alteration in observable behavior; e.g., a person can have learned that it is wrong to lie and be intellectually convinced of this, yet commit a lie. All external action results from learning, but not all learning results in external action. Learning skills affects behavior; learning knowledge affects consciousness. The *fourth element* is change. Change is crucial to learning, for in learning the learner passes from potency to act; from a lack of knowledge, habits, skills, and so on, to a possession of them. Consequently a pupil's consciousness and/or his behavior are more than in being—they are in a state of dynamic becoming. Every good learning situation is so arranged that the factor of change is heightened, not minimized.

The teacher should always keep in mind the words of Fr. McCormick, S.J., "Learning is the path to the attainment of truth, and the end of

[75] St. Thomas Aquinas, *De Veritate, op. cit.*, q.11, a.1, ad.6.

[76] V. Degl'Innocenti, O.P., "*Omnis nostra cognitio incipit a sensibus*," *Aquinas,* I (1958), pp. 379–391 mentioned by W. Norris Clarke, S.J., in conversation with the author.

[77] Aristotle, *De Anima*, III. 7.43.

[78] St. Thomas Aquinas, *De Veritate, op. cit.*, q.10, a.8.

[79] For example, see Lee J. Cronbach, *op. cit.*, p. 47; or Henry E. Garrett, *General Psychology,* 2d ed. (New York: American Book, 1961), p. 246.

this path is wisdom." [80] The teacher who keeps in mind the basic elements of learning can do much to help his students along this path.

Types of Learning

There are four basic types of learning, viz., intellectual, motor, appetitive, and appreciational. All forms of learning can be grouped under one or more of these generic categories.

Intellectual Learning. Learning of this type refers to that kind of self-activity whereby the mental content and processes of the learner undergo a change. Intellectual learning includes mental habits and knowledge of a mental, social, religious, or attitudinal sort. Intellectual learning is of two orders, the ratiocinational and the intuitional. The first is by far the more common and is distinctly human; the second is less common but not unusual. From another point of view, intellectual learning can be classified into two types, viz., assimilative, i.e., mental absorption and subsequent reflection on the data absorbed, and creative, i.e., the mental invention of new ideas or thought processes which, though based on previously acquired data, are nonetheless significantly different from them. The mind feeds itself by the assimilative process, advances itself through the creative process. Understanding is at the root of intellectual knowledge. Understanding is comprehension of both the inner principles and outward manifestations of a reality, and as Fr. McCarthy, S.J., has noted, means far more than glibly repeating words or phrases, whether they be "transubstantiation" or "civil rights." [81] Good intellectual learning should spill over into the student's personal life to serve as a guide. It should form the core of a person's "working philosophy of life" and not remain solely as a set of mental constructs.

Moral and religious learning is the most important part of intellectual learning since it delineates the clearest and deepest means of attaining the student's ultimate end. Moral and religious learning, naturally considered, must be viewed as a type of intellectual learning, for knowledge of morality and religion is acquired through the use of mental understanding together with a seeing faith (as opposed to a blind faith). Regrettably, all too often moral and religious learning degenerates into motor learning, a series of pious but mechanical practices. Together with understanding, God supplies the grace so necessary for moral and religious learning. However, the teacher must keep in mind that the studies have repeatedly shown that moral knowledge does not ensure moral conduct. Thus one investigator found that penitentiary inmates and college

[80] John F. McCormick, S.J., *St. Thomas and the Life of Learning,* The Aquinas Lecture, 1937. (Milwaukee: Marquette University Press, 1942), p. 13.

[81] Raphael C. McCarthy, S.J., *Training the Adolescent.* (Milwaukee, Bruce, 1934), pp. 188–189.

students, when asked to rank the Ten Commandments in order of importance to themselves, came to a high degree of similarity in their conclusions.[82] Nor do intellectual ability and growth mean concomitant moral development. Boynton's study showed no relationship between intelligence and moral judgment. His investigation did reveal, however, a slight tendency for students of high intellectual ability to be relatively liberal on moral issues while pupils of low intellectual ability were inclined to be fairly rigid and formalistic in their approach to moral issues.[83] This underscores the necessity of putting religious teaching on a firm, deeply intellectual basis.

Motor Learning. This type of learning refers to that kind of self-activity by which the physical processes of the learner undergo a change. Motor learning consists chiefly in gaining skills. Skills may be defined as learned patterns of physical action, e.g., typewriting.[84] Learning a skill involves three stages: (1) intellectual awareness, especially by perception, of what is essential in the skill to be learned; (2) acquiring neuromuscular coordination necessary to integrate the various specific movements into one smooth flowing motor action; (3) making permanent this action pattern, chiefly through practice. It is the total pattern, or welding of the different actions into a unit, which constitutes the skill. However, quick effective learning of the skill must at the outset involve intellectual understanding of the nature and working of the skill. Without such understanding the skill will be a series of meaningless motions to the student and hence will be learned slowly and with difficulty and will be executed clumsily.

In the teaching of skills, three things should be borne in mind. First, "personality factors have an important influence on the [learning and] performance of skills, beyond their effects on motivation and effort expenditure." [85] Second, the younger a person is, the more easily he will be able to learn motor skills, since his muscular structure is still flexible and hence formable. Third, repeated practice is the only way in which a motor skill can be effectively learned and reinforced.

Motor skills are invaluable aids to higher learning processes. Also they are extremely important in themselves because they make possible

[82] Ray Mars Simpson, "Attitudes toward the Ten Commandments," *Journal of Social Psychology,* IV (May, 1933), pp. 223–230.

[83] P. L. Boynton, *A Study of the Relations between the Intelligence and the Moral Judgments of College Students.* (Nashville: George Peabody College for Teachers, 1929).

[84] The "skill" referred to here is a physical, motor pattern and must be distinguished from the mental skills of which so many educators speak, e.g., mathematical skills.

[85] "Skills," *Encyclopedia of Educational Research.* (New York: Macmillan, 1960), p. 1286.

effective, fruitful living, e.g., the skill of walking. Hence no secondary school should omit teaching and improving those skills appropriate to this level of education. To scorn skills, as is sometimes done, is to be guilty of the grossest sort of hyperintellectualism.

Appetitive Learning. This type of learning refers to that kind of self-activity whereby the desires or appetites of the learner undergo a change. The most important type of appetitive learning is to be found in the emotions. To modify Harmon's definition somewhat, an emotion is a complex state of psychophysiological excitement caused by the perception of an exciting object or situation and resulting in certain changes in bodily functions, physical behavior, or both.[86] "In the total pattern, it should be noted, the appetitive experience or excitement is the essential element of emotion, while cognition and behavioral reactions figure as cause and effect, respectively." [87]

St. Thomas classified emotions (which he called "passions") into two types, concupiscible and irascible. The concupiscible emotions include love and hatred, desire and aversion, joy and sorrow, while the irascible emotions are hope and despair, courage, fear, and anger.[88] Contemporary empirical psychologists classify emotions into two categories, mild and emergency, based on the physical reaction which each emotion elicits. In general, the mild and emergency emotions are modern equivalents of the concupiscible and irascible passions, respectively.

Several factors should be considered by the teacher in assessing the nature, value, and processes of emotional learning:

1. Emotions are deeply bound up with both the senses and the intellect. Emotions have a tremendous effect on sensible life (e.g., causing ulcers or hypertension), as well as on the intellectual life (e.g., causing psychological disorders or maladjustments).

2. Emotions are extremely important in every type of learning. They often play a vital role in inclining the student toward or away from the object or material to be learned.

3. A student approaches all reality not only with his intellect and his senses, but with his emotions as well. Therefore any attempt by the teacher to completely eliminate emotions from the learning situation is both intrinsically impossible and harmful to the student.

4. Emotions of the extreme sort, e.g., great fears can block other learning almost entirely.

5. A student's emotional reaction toward an object or situation often has more effect on his judgment of and behavior toward the thing to be learned

[86] Francis L. Harmon, *Principles of Psychology*, rev. ed. (Milwaukee, Bruce, 1951), p. 545.

[87] *Ibid.*

[88] Brennan, *op. cit.*, p. 158.

than mere cognition or intellectual apprehension of it. Teachers should keep this principle uppermost in their minds at all times. Intellectual presentation of material is not enough; the proper emotional climate must first surround this material.

6. Religious and spiritual learning should never degenerate into emotional learning. This is particularly important for women teachers to remember.

7. The real emotional reactions of students are difficult to detect. A study by Landis revealed that there is very little correlation between a person's emotional state and his facial expression.[89] Similarly, personality inventories have thus far been of very limited help in ascertaining accurate pupil emotional response.[90] Consequently teachers must be hesitant to reach the conclusion that they have satisfactorily gauged the emotional learning of a student or group of students.

Appreciational Learning. This type of learning refers to that kind of self-activity whereby the learner's estimation of a value undergoes a change. Appreciational learning involves two elements, viz., knowledge and love. In this type of learning the student first attains to a knowledge of the fullness of being which a reality possesses, and follows this knowledge immediately with a love of that reality precisely because it possesses this fullness of being. It is the degree of the fullness of being which a reality possesses, plus the degree to which this fullness of being relates to himself that determines the value of that reality for the student. Thus the pupil's awareness of and subsequent grasp of value depend on both objective and subjective factors. Regrettably, many teachers forget this subjective element when trying to teach appreciation to their students. Students must be taught to relate objective value to their own selves, to integrate value into their personalities. They can be taught to do so only if these values are made eminently relevant to their lives here and now. Appreciation involves more than merely an awareness of a value; it includes a subsequent personal prizing of this value.

Appreciational learning also involves time. It cannot be learned as a result of a single lesson, much less from a test in appreciation. A long contemplative gaze precedes and accompanies appreciation. With this gaze flow love and prizing.

Appreciational learning might have emotional overtones and concomitant outcomes, but it is not basically a form of motor or emotional learning. Thus Bossing incorrectly states that "appreciation is a matter of emotion," and that it "consists of the emotional disposition to choose those values in life conceived to be of greatest ultimate significance to

[89] Carney Landis, "Studies of Emotional Reactions. I. 'A Preliminary Study of Facial Expression,'" *Journal of Experimental Psychology,* VII (October, 1924), pp. 325–341.

[90] Bernard, *op. cit.,* pp. 328–329.

the individual and society." [91] To reduce appreciation to mere emotion is to rob it of its richness. The emotional pleasure a person receives from an appreciational learning may serve as a wholesome motivation toward more of such learning, but this is a far cry from identifying the two.

The determination of whether appreciational learning has taken place is exceedingly difficult. Thus, for example, tests of aesthetic appreciation have been devised, but the fact is that these tests determine not aesthetic appreciation as such, but whether the pupil agrees with the opinion of the test makers on what is aesthetic and what is not. To be sure, many great modern artists and composers would do poorly on such a test.

Pupils learn appreciation differently from the way they learn intellectual data or skills. Appreciational learning, unlike the other two, cannot be taught directly, e.g., by memorization. Thus memorizing a poem will cause a pupil to know it, but not to appreciate it. Appreciational learning is a deeply personal thing, and the task of the teacher is to set the climate for it. To appreciate, a student must go out of himself, immerse himself completely in the object, and then lovingly bring the object back as fully as he can into himself. As Rolland observed, "After having sunk such a claw into life, how can one let go?" [92] Intuition plays a large role in appreciational learning, as most great artists and poets have testified.

For a Catholic, appreciation is rooted in God's presence in all reality. Every reality reflects in a different way some perfection of its Divine Cause. As Maritain has noted, "There are an infinity of literal meanings in the things made by God." [93] This is the basic reason for the preeminence of appreciational learning, that it catches something of God in a deep, soul-shaking manner as no other type of learning can. It is deplorable that so many textbooks on Education either totally neglect or give insufficient attention to appreciational learning. Regrettably, so do most teachers.

Associational Learning. Many books consider associational learning a distinct type of learning. This distinction seems unwarranted, since association refers to the way a pupil learns, rather than to a separate kind of learning.

Rate of Learning

The rate at which a student learns has been subject to a great deal of careful investigation during this century. Psychologists have discov-

[91] Nelson L. Bossing, *Teaching in Secondary Schools*, 3d ed. (Boston: Houghton Mifflin, 1952), pp. 215–216.

[92] Quoted by Jean Cocteau in *Art and Faith: Letters between Jacques Maritain and Jean Cocteau.* (New York: Philosophical Library, 1948), p. 22.

[93] Jacques Maritain in *ibid.*, p. 90.

ered that learning something, whether it be intellectual content or a motor skill, goes through five successive stages which are often plotted graphically, the resultant line being called a curve of learning. The chief characteristic of this curve is its irregularity; i.e., a person's progress in learning something completely does not proceed smoothly and continuously upward until the material is perfectly learned; rather, progress in learning proceeds in spurts interrupted by periods of little or no apparent progress. These five stages of the learning curve are: *Negligible initial progress.* When the learner first approaches new material, his unfamiliarity with it causes him first to seek ways of properly grasping it. This groping results in little progress. *Rapid progress.* Helped by a low base, high motivation, and interest, the learner quickly masters the simpler elements of the material to be learned. *Decelerated progress.* Once the simpler elements have been mastered, the learner proceeds to the more complicated components of the material and consequently makes less progress. *Plateau,* i.e., a period of no apparent progress, of seeming to stand still. Actually progress might be present, especially by reinforcement, but such progress is not easily seen. *Negative acceleration,* i.e., renewed progress, but with the rate of learning progressively diminishing the more the pupil learns. As the student approaches his own psychological and/or physiological limits, progress becomes negligible.

These stages of learning have important implications for the teacher's methodology. First, the teacher should not expect the student to learn at the same rate all the time. Second, the teacher should help the student realize that irregularities in his rate of learning are normal and to be expected. Such knowledge will go a long way in reducing pupil anxiety. Third, the teacher must realize that at certain stages of a pupil's learning, e.g., the plateau, motivation is crucial and indeed might well be the deciding factor in whether or not he chooses to continue learning that particular material.

It should always be borne in mind that understandings, skills, appetites, and appreciations can be learned more rapidly and retained longer when they are taught and learned not piecemeal, but as a unified whole. This is the testimony of modern empirical psychology. Such testimony is indeed not surprising to Catholics who believe in a unified reality and a unified learner. And on earth, just as in the Beatific Vision, individual experience is the key to rapid, efficient, and meaningful learning.

CHAPTER V THE SECONDARY SCHOOL STUDENT: FACTORS AFFECTING HIS LEARNING

A teacher who wishes to be as effective an instructional leader as possible cannot be content with a knowledge of the learner as a person or even with a comprehension of the various theories which explain the way in which the student learns and transfers. To be sure, these are of utmost importance and should underlie every teacher's pedagogical methods. However, the teacher must also understand the complex factors affecting the student during the actual learning process. These ongoing factors constitute the dynamics of learning and help to explain the manifold modifications and differences in learning which are constantly taking place at every moment in every student or group of students.

There are two broad groups of factors affecting learning, viz., general factors and personality-situation factors. There are also other factors which are combinations of these two basic types. General factors which affect learning are those present in every youth, though in varying degrees, precisely because he is a human being. These factors, e.g., perception, forgetting, and so on, are vital constituents of every person's learning no matter what his age or social setting. Personality-situation factors, e.g., adolescent problems, are those which are in a large measure the result of the particular personality of a particular adolescent in a particular social setting. While this twofold distinction is not completely accurate in that many of the factors of one group overlap the other group, nevertheless it has enough validity to make it sufficiently valuable as a clarification device.

GENERAL FACTORS AFFECTING LEARNING

Sensation

As was emphasized in the previous chapter, sensation is a crucial factor in the Thomistic concept of learning. As the primary means by which the self contacts the world outside it, the importance of sensation can never be overemphasized. Sensations provide the vital raw material of learning. Even more than this, St. Thomas holds that the sensory quality of different peoples' bodies is the prime explanation for the difference in their intelligence.[1] In themselves, all human souls are of equal intellectual power; it is the bodies to which they are joined which determine to what degree this ability can be exercised. Those possessing the keenest physiological and sensory systems are the smartest, and so on down the line. Therefore a rich sensory life for every student, and especially for the intellectually gifted, is crucial. Every teacher must do his utmost to provide experiences in which and by which the youths can make use of their senses. Inspired writers like the author of the Canticle of Canticles and great mystics such as St. Bernard of Clairvaux saw the necessity of feeding the mind with rich sensory experiences as a powerful and indispensable means not only in attaining knowledge but in attaining God. Failure to utilize rich and varied sensory experiences in the learning process will only have the effect of stunting both intellect and imagination. Of course sensory experiences can be overdone, as when they are made an ultimate educative end instead of either an intermediate end or a means to an end. Except for some ultraprogressive institutions, most American secondary schools do not provide their students with enough or the right kind of sensory experiences. This is particularly true of private high schools, both Catholic and independent. In providing sensory experiences, the teacher should see that *all* of the learner's senses are stimulated, not merely his eyes. Furthermore the teacher should see to it that the three properties of sensation, viz., intensity, quality, and duration are properly balanced and effectively utilized for maximum learning.[2]

[1] St. Thomas Aquinas, *Summa Theologica*, I, q.85, a.7.
[2] For a discussion of these three properties, see William A. Kelly, *Educational Psychology*, 4th ed. (Milwaukee: Bruce, 1956), pp. 54–55.

Perception

As was pointed out in Chapter IV, it is through perception that the learner becomes cognitively aware of sensible objects and the physical qualities of these objects. It must always be remembered, however, that perception is not a separate process distinct from sensation but rather is the way in which sensations present themselves to the mind. Perception, then, seeks to bestow upon the mind all the intelligible richness of sensory data by coordinating these data into a meaningful whole. These sensory data exist in the real order as integral, inseparable parts of a whole, e.g., the redness, the hardness, of a house exist not as separate entities, but together as one reality, the house. In the learning process the sense receptors temporarily receive each sense datum as separate from the whole; perception restores the original unity so that the mind perceives the sense object as it actually exists. Perception thus results in a conformity between the sense datum in the mental order and the sensible object in the real order, a conformity necessary if adequate, true knowledge is to exist.[3]

Gage lists seven characteristics of perception, viz., (1) quality and dimension, (2) configuration, (3) constancy, (4) frame of reference, (5) object or event character, (6) set and expectancy or apperceptional effect, (7) intervention.[4] The two most important for the teachers seeking to establish a perceptual situation conducive to effective learning are apperceptive mass (number 6 on the Gage list) and figure ground (somewhat of a combination of numbers 2 and 4).

The apperceptive mass of a learner consists of his mental background, the cognitive residue of his past experiences. Except immediately after birth, no one perceives things completely fresh, as a *tabula rasa;* rather every act of perception involves a unity between the present experience and the complex cognitive totality of past experiences, both conscious and subconscious. It is these past experiences which form the basis for the organization of the present perception, i.e., for the way in which this perception will be interpreted and made meaningful by the mind. These past experiences which the learner psychologically brings with him to his present perception consist of such varied things as particular data, mind-set, attitudes, needs, values and ideals. The significant influence of the apperceptive mass on present perception has been shown in many studies. One of the most celebrated of these investigations, that of Bruner and Goodman, disclosed that poor children overestimate the

[3] For a treatment of the relation of perception to the Scholastic idea of an internal synthetic sense, see Thomas Verner Moore, O.S.B., "The Scholastic Theory of Perception," *The New Scholasticism,* VII (July, 1933), pp. 222–238.

[4] N. L. Gage, "Perception," *Encyclopedia of Educational Research,* 3d ed. (New York: Macmillan, 1960), p. 944.

size of coins to a greater degree than do wealthy children.[5] Here perception was influenced by cultural factors arising from past experiences. Similarly, art students perceive objects somewhat differently from those without such a background, showing the influence of education. The failure of a person to properly perceive a given object or situation, and hence to learn properly, is often the result of past experiences. This can be easily demonstrated in the learning of a language. One psychologist reported that while on an automobile trip through the West, his two children shouted "Howdy oats!" at some passing cowboys. Eventually the psychologist realized that the children were repeating a sound which they thought they had heard on television westerns, namely, "adiós!"[6] When the children heard this new word on television, they had simply imitated it in terms of things familiar to them, in terms of their apperceptive mass. Teachers, particularly of religion, must always be alert to clarify every new word or concept for their students in terms of the pupils' background and past experiences. Similarly, teachers should also realize the great effect of the apperceptive mass for positive and even negative motivation.

The second very important characteristic of perception is figure field. This term refers to the perception of organized wholes or figures as standing out from a general background of a situation. Thus, for example, in the American flag, each star comprises an organized whole or figure which is perceived as standing out from an unorganized whole, the blue field. If for some reason no figure stands out from the general field or ground, the mind will often attempt to "find" an organized whole within the field. This frequently leads a person to construct organized wholes which do not exist. Sometimes the mind is confronted with unclear figures, i.e., situations in which the perceived figure suddenly becomes the ground and the ground suddenly becomes the figure. Thus, for example, what at first looks like a white vase on a black field becomes, after a slightly prolonged gaze, the silhouettes of two men on a white field. This switching of figure and field can be caused by a variety of factors, e.g., focus of vision, past experiences, ambiguous figures. In any case the ground in which a figure is placed will definitely affect the perception of the figure, as any interior decorator knows. A yellow figure in a blue room will be perceived as being of a slightly different hue from the same figure in a green room. As Harmon observes, the field surrounding a figure assumes two functions, viz., "It helps determine the percep-

[5] Jerome Bruner and Cecile Goodman, "Value and Need as Organizing Factors in Perception," *Journal of Abnormal and Social Psychology*, XLI (January, 1947), pp. 33–44.

[6] Lee J. Cronbach, *Educational Psychology*. (New York: Harcourt, Brace, 1954), p. 279.

tual qualities of the figure, and it helps stabilize the organization of the figure." [7]

To teach for effective learning presupposes teaching for effective perception. The nature and determiners of a student's perception suggest that the skillful teacher employ the following pedagogical practices to improve pupil perception:

1. Organize the learning situation in such a way that the material to be learned is placed within a field in which it will most effectively stand out. Choice of the learning background is often as important as the choice of the specific material to be learned.

2. Strive at all times to have the students repeatedly see *for themselves* (rather than merely being told) how and why the material to be learned stands out from the field.

3. Present the material to be learned within the context of the pupils' apperceptive mass. Such a practice will, as Mills and Douglass have noted, entail proceeding from the simple to the complex, from the concrete to the abstract, from the near to the remote, from the psychological to the logical.[8] At base, recognition of the pupils' apperceptive mass by the teacher will eventuate in his proceeding from what the students know to what they do not know.

4. Help the students to develop their powers of cognitive discrimination so that they can quickly make the proper perceptual distinctions without being disproportionately affected by either the ground or the apperceptive mass.

5. Develop the students' attentiveness, since the degree and quality of attention often determine the character of perception.

6. Remove or minimize any physical defects in the student which may impair his perception. Thus, for example, students with poor vision or hearing should be seated in front of the classroom.

7. Attempt to arrange the external elements of the learning situation so that they will best utilize Koffka's four laws of perceptual structuring described in Chapter IV.

Imagination

Imagination has been defined as "the mental power of forming representations of material objects which are not actually present to the senses." [9] The use of the word "representation" instead of "image" in

---

[7] Francis L. Harmon, *Principles of Psychology*, rev. ed. (Milwaukee: Bruce, 1951), p. 164. See also Louis W. Gellermann, "Form Discrimination in Chimpanzees and Two Year Old Children. II. Form Versus Background," *Pedagogical Seminary and Journal of Genetic Psychology*, XLII (March, 1933), pp. 28–49.

[8] Hubert H. Mills and Harl R. Douglass, *Teaching in High School*, 2d ed. (New York: Ronald, 1957), p. 90.

[9] Kelly, *op. cit.*, p. 78.

this definition is more accurate, since the word "image" connotes a visual picture. In actual fact, the fruit of the imaginative power is a representation of any past sensory experience, e.g., the smell of a hot apple pie. Nonetheless it is true that visual and aural imaginal representations tend to be more frequent and more vivid than those from other senses. All imaginal representations depend on prior sensations and perceptions; the imagination cannot reproduce or create any new representations completely afresh. Imaginal representations are voluntary or involuntary, depending upon whether or not the learner intentionally brings them to mind.

Following Aristotle, psychologists assert that there are two basic types or functions of the imagination, viz., the reproductive and the creative. The reproductive imagination consists in the representation of original sensory experiences in more or less the exact form in which they occurred. The creative imagination consists in the mental construction of images which had not been originally perceived in the form in which they are now represented, e.g., the creation of an imaginal centaur from the perceptions of man and horse. The process of creative imagination results from the cognitive separation of elements of previous perceptions and the subsequent reconstitution of these elements into new imaginal wholes. In turn these new imaginal wholes may be separated and reconstituted into even newer wholes.

Imagination provides the learner with two extremely important services. First, it re-creates as present living realities the actual perceptual experiences of the past. Second, it alters the content of these experiences to make exciting new realities. The importance of imagination in the learning process can never be sufficiently stressed. Imagination is a tremendous power; it is a power which brings the learner new freedom, freedom from having to be constantly present to external objects in order to have images of them. While the senses must feed on the present, imagination nourishes itself on the absent. Indeed because of imagination there need be no past; all things can be ever present to the learner. Thus imagination enables a person to share to some degree in a power of God Himself, the power of knowing all things as eternally present.

St. Thomas realized the great importance of imagination. He noted that imagination is a permanent principle of knowledge, precisely because it frees the person from the necessity of having the object immediately before himself.[10] Imagination, like sensation, can be abstracted into a

---

[10] St. Thomas Aquinas, *De Anima*. III, 1.15 and 16, cited in Robert E. Brennan, O.P., *Thomistic Psychology*. (New York: Macmillan, 1941), p. 376. In his *Summa Theologica*. II–II, q.173, a.2, ad.2, St. Thomas further highlights the importance of the imagination when he states that Divine prophecy sometimes has resulted from imaginal representations enlightened by God.

conception, and thus is a valuable source for new knowledge and new understanding.[11] The creative imagination is particularly crucial to the development of new ideas and deeper insights. As Novak remarks, "The key to intelligence is a flexible imagination, or what is called a creative imagination, for men understand nothing except what they capture and arrange there, not as madmen or dreamers, but in line for understanding." [12] The creative imagination is a great power, and teachers should help their students develop their imaginal powers rather than bend every effort to stunt them as is so often done, especially in certain high schools, both public and Catholic.[13]

Despite an awareness of the importance of imagination by many thinkers and writers since Aristotle's time, the role of imagination has often been neglected in education. With the experiments of Galton on imagery and Freud on dreams, educators are now paying more heed to the role of imagination in the learning process. One psychologist investigated the imaginal development in learners by asking them to complete a story which he had begun. The psychologist gave various hints whose aim was to bring out the pupils' imagery. The results of this study show a marked imaginal development of adolescents over children.[14] Thus, stimulating the students' imagination and providing that kind of outlet for it which will be conducive to better learning are even more the task of the secondary school teacher than the elementary school teacher.

Of course excessive use of imagination by students will be harmful to their thinking, as many experimental studies have shown.[15] This is particularly true in the case of problems of a highly abstract nature. Psychologists usually assert that the imagination is helpful in the solution of a problem to the degree to which the problem situation involves concrete elements. Nevertheless, this must remain at best a limited conclusion, for it neither strikes at the root of the problem situation nor accords to the imagination its full power. As Novak states, "Problems arise because not enough data are present; or because the imagination

[11] St. Thomas Aquinas, Summa Theologica. II-II., q.173, a.2; see also Arthur D. Fearon, "The Imagination," The New Scholasticism, XIV (April, 1940), pp. 181–195.

[12] Michael Novak, "St. Thomas in Motion," The Downside Review, CCLIII (Autumn, 1960), p. 294.

[13] See S. J. Parnes (ed.), Compendium No. 2 of Research on Creative Imagination. (Buffalo: Creative Education Foundation, 1960). The creative imagination, of course, must be distinguished from the creative intellect.

[14] T. Valentiner, "Die Phantasie im freien Aufsatze der Kinder und Jugendlichen," Beihefte zur Zeitschrift für Angewandte Psychologie, 1916, cited in Luella Cole, Psychology of Adolescence, 3d ed. (New York: Rinehart, 1948), pp. 453–456.

[15] See John F. Dashiell, Fundamentals of General Psychology, 3d ed. (Boston: Houghton Mifflin, 1949), p. 583.

inclined by habit continues in a too rigid pattern and prevents conception of the one unity that would reconcile all the data." [16]

A second limitation to unrestrained use of the imagination in learning is the progressive unreliability of the sensory representations themselves. Studies have disclosed that imaginal representations deteriorate in vividness, clarity, and detail over a period of time. A third limitation is the possibility of the imaginal representations becoming hallucinations in which the youth somehow deludes himself into thinking that the imaginal representation is in fact an objective reality. A fourth limitation is that imagination can become a substitute for proper adjustment to the world outside the person, as in fantasies.

Daydreaming is often regarded by teachers as one of the worst fruits of the imagination. Psychologists have shown, however, that the daydreaming done by most youths is not only harmless but is sometimes actually a healthy outlet. As Schneiders has noted, "Daydreams are an integral part of childhood experiences as are ordinary sensations and perceptions." [17] Indeed daydreaming on the part of youths, while common and natural, does not occupy as much time as many teachers seem to think. A detailed study by Fleege revealed, for example, that nearly 40 per cent of the adolescent boys studied daydreamed ten minutes or less a day, while only 18 per cent daydreamed a total of more than one-half hour a day.[18]

The alert teacher should use every opportunity to cultivate the pupils' imaginations to improve learning. All too often imagination is regarded as a path toward sin. But so are thoughts, words, and deeds, yet what educator would stunt these? The teacher should present problems to the class in such a way that the pupils will be able to use their imaginations toward solving the problem, e.g., asking pupils the best way to reach the planet Saturn. Moreover, the teacher should himself employ imaginal representations for motivation. Indeed this is one of the best ways to begin a lesson. During the course of the lesson the teacher should illustrate the material taught by use of sensory representations to heighten clarity and facilitate retention. Exercises to develop the imagination along constructive channels are very important, e.g., asking a pupil to give a word picture of the people and places surrounding an event. This type of exercise is doubly valuable, since it also motivates the student to engage in independent research about the people

[16] Novak, *loc. cit.*

[17] Alexander A. Schneiders, *The Psychology of Adolescence.* (Milwaukee: Bruce, 1951), p. 464.

[18] Urban H. Fleege, *Self-Revelations of the Adolescent Boy.* (Milwaukee: Bruce, 1945), p. 227.

and places surrounding that event in order that his word pictures may be accurate.

Every teacher should remember Kelly's statement, "The pupil who is lacking in imagination does not learn; he merely imitates." [19]

Memory

Memory may be defined as the cognitive power by which past experiences are recognized and recalled. Memory is thus a type of retention; it is retention brought above the threshold of consciousness.[20] Memory involves the identification of recalled material as having been part of one's past experience. It is this identification which distinguishes memory from imagination. Memory is of two types, sensory and intellectual. Sensory memory is the cognitive power by which past physical experiences are recognized and recalled, e.g., the pain caused by stubbing one's toe. Intellectual memory is the cognitive power by which past mental experiences are recognized and recalled, e.g., the fact that God is love. Animals have only sense memory to guide their learning; human beings have both sense memory and intellectual memory. They use the two constantly. The seat of sense memory is in the brain; the seat of intellectual memory is in the mind. Viewed from another angle, memory can be classified as rote or logical. Rote memory is the cognitive power to recognize and recall past experiences by means of sheer repetition without being aware of any intellectual elements that may be involved in these experiences, e.g., memorizing the alphabet. Logical memory is the cognitive power to recognize and recall past experiences by means of associating, understanding, and integrating the intellectual elements involved in these experiences, e.g., remembering that John and Peter are brothers because they both have the same last name. Mental association of facts, concepts, attitudes, and the like is characteristic of logical memory. Logical memory is of a higher order than rote memory. It is more distinctively human; animals have been taught to reproduce material by means of rote memory.

Memory is the basis for learning but is not the same thing as learning. Some teachers seem either to divorce the two or merge the two. Woodworth has precisely delimited the relationship between memory and learning by noting that "remembering proves previous *learning;* and it proves also that what was learned has been *retained* in the interval between learning and remembering." [21] McGeoch and Irion have ob-

---

[19] Kelly, *op. cit.*, p. 85.

[20] The person retains all his past experiences. Most of these, however, remain in his subconsciousness, or below the threshold of his consciousness.

[21] Robert S. Woodworth, *Psychology*, 4th ed. (New York: Holt, 1940), p. 329.

served that "by and large, individual differences in learning are reflected in individual differences in memory." [22]

Tests for memory are either one of two types, recognition or recall. Recognition is the ability to relate two or more given materials or happenings as having been somehow joined together in one's past experience; e.g., when given the names Columbus and Hudson and the dates 1492 and 1609, the student matches Columbus with 1492 and Hudson with 1609. Recall is the ability to reproduce fully in part or in total some previously learned material; e.g., when asked what year Columbus discovered America, the student answers by recall, 1492. All educational psychologists agree that recognition is easier than recall for materials learned by rote memory; however, there is a difference of opinion in the case of logical memory. Most psychologists seem to agree with Morgan in holding that "recognition is easier than recall in *all* types of materials." [23] However, other psychologists such as Anastasi have made studies which indicate that "the alleged superiority of recognition over recall does not hold for logical memory." [24]

The teacher must not think that the adolescent's memory is like an inert piece of wax statically waiting to be impressed with learning experiences. The memory is not a disembodied faculty. On the contrary, a student's memory is greatly influenced by a host of dynamic factors which cause it to be selective, i.e., to consciously retain some experiences and to forget others. These dynamic factors include: (*1*) Age. An adolescent's memory, contrary to popular opinion, is more acute than that of a child. Furthermore, a student's memory becomes more acute with each passing adolescent year.[25] (*2*) Sex. Girls seem to be able to memorize more quickly than boys.[26] This may possibly be due to extrinsic factors, such as docility or fear of teacher disapproval, rather than to

[22] John A. McGeoch and Arthur L. Irion, quoted in James B. Stroud and Lowell Schoer, "Individual Differences in Memory," *Journal of Educational Psychology,* L (December, 1959), p. 285.

[23] John J. B. Morgan, *Psychology.* (New York: Farrar & Rinehart, 1941), p. 302; see also Sister Adelbert Matousek, *Reproductive and Retroactive Inhibition as a Function of Similarity in the Recall and Recognition of Paired Associates.* (Washington: Catholic Education Press, 1939).

[24] Anne Anastasi, "Further Studies in the Memory Factor," *Archives of Psychology,* no. 142. (New York: Columbia University Press, 1932), p. 54, cited by Sister Columba Mullaly, *The Retention and Recognition of Information.* (Washington, D.C.: Catholic University of America Press, 1952), p. 33.

[25] James B. Stroud and Ruth Maul, "The Influence of Age upon Learning and Retention of Poetry and Nonsense Syllables," *Pedagogical Seminary and Journal of Genetic Psychology,* XLII (March, 1933), pp. 242–250.

[26] Robert J. Havighurst and Fay H. Breese, "Relation between Ability and Social Status in a Midwestern Community. III. Primary Mental Abilities," *Journal of Educational Psychology,* XXXVIII (April, 1947), pp. 241–247.

intrinsic memory factors, since there is a high correlation between memory and intelligence. (Boys seem to perform better on intelligence tests than do girls.) (3) Life experiences. A student remembers material better when it is related to his life experiences. (4) Meaningfulness. The learner commits to memory faster and for a longer period material which is meaningful and purposeful to *him*. (5) Desire. Retention is greater where students memorize with a determined attempt to remember the material permanently rather than just memorizing the material to pass a test or to "get it over with." (6) Pleasantness. Pleasant material is retained longer than unpleasant material.[27] (7) Vividness. Vivid materials are remembered longer than confused or fuzzy learnings. (8) Rest. "Retention after a rest interval, in terms of both recall and recognition, is superior to retention after work conditions." [28] Teachers should never forget these dynamic factors, whether they are teaching for retention or testing for it.

Nor should the factor of forgetting be overlooked. Just as there is a curve of learning, so is there also a curve of forgetting. Ebbinghaus, in a classic study, showed that 56 per cent of perfectly learned material was forgotten in one hour, 66 per cent at the end of one day.[29] This study is all the more startling when one considers the fact that it dealt with perfectly learned material. There are at least three factors which contribute to forgetting: (1) Disuse. The less the pupil uses or adverts to the material learned, the more likely he will forget it. (2) Rote memory. Materials learned logically, intellectually, associatively, are retained much longer than materials memorized by rote. (3) Retroactive inhibition, i.e., the negative effect on remembering caused by the intervention of some new material between the time the original material was memorized and the time it was reproduced. For example, a student memorizes the word "Deus" in Latin class, then goes to Spanish class and learns "Dios," and the next day is tested for the Latin word for "God" in his Latin class. Fr. Houlahan's study shows that retroactive inhibition occurs in practically every student.[30] The nature of the material greatly affects the degree of retroactive inhibition, i.e., the greater the similarity between the original and interpolated materials, the greater the retroactive inhibition. Fr. Houlahan's investigation revealed that the temporal posi-

[27] Harmon, *op. cit.*, p. 484.

[28] Sister Adelbert Matousek, *op. cit.*, p. 39.

[29] See Hermann Ebbinghaus, *Memory*, trans. by Ruegger and Bussenius. (New York: Teachers College, Columbia University, 1913). It must be remembered, however, that Ebbinghaus was experimenting with the retention of nonsense syllables. The less meaningful the material, the less the retention.

[30] Francis John Houlahan, *Retroactive Inhibition as Affected by the Temporal Position of Interpolated Learning Activities in Elementary School Children.* (Washington, D.C.: Catholic University of America Press, 1937).

tion of the interpolated learning had a significant effect on retention of the material. Retroactive inhibition was greatest, first, when the interpolated materials were introduced immediately after the original materials were memorized, and second, when the interpolated materials were introduced just before a test for the retention of the original materials.[31]

A teacher who wishes to improve learning must endeavor to help every pupil become more retentive. Memory can be strengthened in several ways.

1. The student must be given a chance to use his memory in many different ways and situations. Material learned by rote requires a greater amount of practice than that acquired by logical memory. Easly remarks that the latter becomes "well fixed by a small number of repetitions, and thereby causes the elimination of large numbers of practiced responses to which [logical memory] is so completely antagonistic." [32] It must be remembered that no amount of practice can actually improve a student's mental ability per se, as a study by Fr. Victor Drees, O.F.M., has shown.[33] This is to be expected in view of the invalidity of the theory of formal discipline. Fr. Drees's investigation did reveal, however, that memorizing did help the learners use their memory more effectively and efficiently.[34]

2. The teacher should remember that overlearning is the best antidote for forgetting.[35] This is especially true of materials acquired by rote. Overlearning means that the learner continues his efforts to remember the material even after he can reproduce it perfectly. The teacher can best promote overlearning by conducting careful and thorough reviews.

3. The teacher should use a logical intellectual basis for the data learned. Rote should be employed only as a last resort.

4. The learning material should be associated with other material which is deeply a part of the student. Integration into the apperceptive mass furthers retention.

5. The intrinsic worth of the learned material should be allowed to manifest itself to the pupil.

6. The subjective importance of the material to be retained should be emphasized. The material should be presented in such a way that the learner will see in it an expansion and partial fulfillment of his needs, goals, ideals, and so forth.

7. The teacher should take care to so present the materials that retroactive

[31] *Ibid.*

[32] Howard Easly, "The Curve of Forgetting and the Distribution of Practice," *Journal of Educational Psychology,* XXVIII (September, 1937), p. 477.

[33] Victor Drees, O.F.M., *The Effects of Practice on Memory Performance.* (Washington: Catholic Education Press, 1941), p. 58.

[34] *Ibid.*, p. 61.

[35] William C. F. Krueger, "Further Studies in Overlearning," *Journal of Experimental Psychology,* XIII (April, 1930), pp. 152–163.

inhibition will be minimized. Selecting the optimum time to introduce particular materials is one of the most important and crucial elements of the instructional process.

8. Eliciting "immediate recall by the student is a very effective way of improving retention." [36] Moreover, educing such recall has the further advantage of enabling the teacher to ferret out and correct any mislearnings of facts, impressions, and ideas before the student starts to retain these permanently.

9. The teacher should help plan a type of curriculum which will strengthen and increase retention. This calls for an integrated, e.g., Core, rather than a fragmented, e.g., subject-centered, curricular design.

Teachers who become dejected at the thought that students forget so much of the material they learned should take heart from Ebbinghaus whose investigations have shown that material, once learned though now forgotten, can be relearned much more quickly than material not previously learned.[37] From this point of view, anyhow, no learning is ever in vain.

Association

Association is the mental process by which the contents of present and/or past experiences are connected with each other. Relationship between objects or ideas is the key element in association. Association underlies all types of learning. There would be no learning without association. If a person did not have the power to associate, all the data which he acquired would be isolated, unrelated, and hence not meaningful. Association is, then, one of the most important ways in which a student learns. It is closely linked to recognition and recall inasmuch as it implies relationships involving past experiences. This connection with past experiences reflects itself in the experimentally verified fact that associated materials are recognized and recalled more easily and more accurately than those not associated.

Following Aristotle, psychologists have formulated the so-called "laws of association," i.e., principles which seem to accompany and affect the associative process. The primary laws of association are usually listed as (1) similarity, (2) contiguity, (3) contrast. The secondary laws of association are (1) recency, (2) frequency, (3) vividness.[38] The law of similarity states that the more materials are alike, the more the mind will associate them. The law of contiguity states that the closer materials are

---

[36] Herbert F. Spitzer, "Studies in Retention," *Journal of Educational Psychology*, XXX (December, 1939), pp. 641–656.

[37] Hermann Ebbinghaus, *Grundzüge der Psychologie*. (Leipsig: Veit, 1905), Bd. I, p. 681, cited in Harmon, *op. cit.*, p. 478.

[38] For a more complete treatment of these laws, see J. F. Donceel, S.J., *Philosophical Psychology*. (New York: Sheed and Ward, 1955), pp. 107–108; Kelly, *op. cit.*, pp. 106–109; Morgan, *op. cit.*, p. 295.

to each other in time and space, the more the mind will associate them. The law of contrast states that the more materials are opposed to each other, the more the mind will associate them. The law of recency states that the more recently related materials have been learned, the more the mind will associate them. The law of frequency states that the more often related materials are repeated, the more the mind will associate them. The law of vividness states that the more intense the related materials are, the more the mind will associate them.

These laws are not automatic; they do not operate at the same time and in the same way in all learners. Rather, these laws function with differing force at differing times, depending on the nature and circumstances of the concrete learning situation. The laws of association are even more dependent for their operation on the person of the learner, his attitudes, values, and past experiences; e.g., the word "divorce" will likely be associated with the concept "wrong" by a Catholic high school student, while the son of a movie star might well associate it with the idea "happiness." Hence the teacher must organize the learning situation so as to promote association not only by the class as a whole but by every individual in the class. This means recognizing individual differences.

Association can be classified into two types, viz., free and controlled. Free association is that in which a person forms relationships between objects or ideas at random without intending to form such relationships. Daydreaming utilizes free association. Controlled association is that in which the person makes a deliberate effort either to form or to recall relationships between specific objects or ideas. Students attempting to learn new material make extensive use of controlled association either purposefully or in a contrived manner, e.g., by mnemonic devices.

When viewed from another angle, association can be categorized as meaningful or arbitrary. Meaningful associations are those which are made because of the deep relationship to each other inherent in the nature of the objects or ideas; e.g., God is associated with the concept of love. Arbitrary associations are those which are made for no reason inherent in the nature of the material, e.g., that "Sb" is the chemical symbol for antimony. (Why not "An"?) [39]

A teacher should always attempt to organize the learning situation in such a manner that associative learning will be promoted. This can be accomplished if the teacher does the following:

[39] See William A. Brownell and Gordon Hendrickson, "How Children Learn Information, Concepts and Generalizations," *Learning and Instruction*, National Society for the Study of Education, Forty-Ninth Yearbook, Part I. (Chicago: University of Chicago Press, 1950), pp. 98–104.

1. Afford students the opportunity to associate materials. The teacher should with guidance let the pupils make their own associations rather than make the associations for them.

2. Attempt to make associations meaningful. Arbitrary associations, such as the alphabet, are, of course, crucial to learning; however, all too many autocratic teachers have made associations dependent on their authoritarian statements per se rather than on the relationships inherent in the material. Arbitrary associations, after all, constitute a very low level of learning and are forgotten more readily than meaningful associations.

3. Encourage the students to relate what they learn in class to their own individual life situations out of class; e.g., ask the students to illustrate the effect of air pressure (one answer—in the balloon tires of their bicycles). Association of basic principles learned in class with a pupil's actions outside of class is especially crucial in moral and religious learning. Much of the failure of religious instruction to take hold in the lives of pupils can be traced to poor associative teaching.

4. Set up the learning situation in such a manner as to promote efficient operation of the six basic laws of association.

5. Recognize individual differences in association. It should be remembered that the power and depth of association are determined by each pupil's particular intellectual ability. Standard intelligence (IQ) tests are of course basically association tests.

6. Never teach material as isolated data but always in relation to something else.

The Will

The will may be defined as the mental faculty which exercises control over man's cognitive and physical actions. It is an appetitive faculty which has as its object the good. The will is the necessary complement to the intellect because it provides the external thrust to knowledge, to truth. When a person learns something, he has a natural tendency to put this knowledge into an appropriate form of action, into a behavior pattern. It is the will that provides for this diffusion.

The will is substantially free; i.e., it is capable of free choice among whatever alternative courses of action the intellect presents to it. Thus freedom is at the very center of the will and can never be separated from it. Some philosophers and psychologists have maintained that the will is not free, but is completely determined by certain irresistible forces, such as one's surroundings (environmental determinism) or one's physiological structure (biological determinism). Such a position would either totally wreck education or make it a totalitarian monster. To be sure, determinism can be disproved by common sense, by psychological analysis, and by philosophical demonstration.[40] Thomists agree, however,

[40] See Donceel, *op. cit.*, pp. 238–262.

that the exercise of the will is never completely free. It is limited by many factors, such as past habits, prior experiences, attitudes, and so on. It is harder (but nonetheless possible) for a habitual liar to will to tell the truth than it is for the average person. The greatest limitation to the free exercise of the will is normally lack of knowledge. A person cannot will what he does not know.

Thus despite certain limitations in use, every human being is essentially a *free* person, capable of making free choices. Liberty is at the center of the person; but liberty too has its center—which is love.[41] Love is an act of the will, indeed its highest and most human act. Love is a dynamic act and is constantly seeking unity in the presence of the knower and the known, the lover and the beloved. As Fr. Robert W. Gleason, S.J., observes, the will makes the proper response, the human response to good, to value, by loving it.[42] Love is so great, so transcending, that *to a certain extent* it is unlimited even by knowledge, as St. Thomas himself remarks, "A thing can be loved more than it is known, since it can be loved completely even though it is not known completely."[43] Love reciprocates the directional impetus which knowledge gives to it by in turn urging the lover on to acquire more knowledge. A person in love wishes to know everything he can about his beloved. A student who loves mathematics wants to know more about this subject. Love brings with it a completeness, an abiding character. As Fr. Robert O. Johann, S.J., observes, it is through love that "man is *already* in union with the infinite, unchanging God," and indeed with all reality.[44]

As can easily be seen, the education and use of the will are a very important part of the learning process. The will is vital to every student, for he must exercise it properly to attain beatitude, to reach heaven. The intellect is not enough. A student must not merely know what is good; he must also practice it. Therefore teachers, particularly in Catholic high schools must organize the learning situation with the pupils' wills in mind. However, the teachers must base their instruction on what is real—hence they must never forget that the will is, at bottom, free. Unfortunately many teachers do not respect the freedom of the students' wills; they attempt, usually in the name of good, to force on them facts, theories, and opinions. They attempt to "mold" their students. This is

[41] Jean Mouroux, *The Meaning of Man*. (New York: Sheed and Ward, 1948), p. 196.

[42] Robert W. Gleason, S.J., "Reason and Revelation on the Subject of Charity," in Schwarz (ed.), *The Human Person and the World of Values*. (New York: Fordham University Press, 1960), pp. 132–141.

[43] St. Thomas Aquinas, *Summa Theologica*. I–II, q.27, a.2, ad.2.

[44] Robert O. Johann, S.J., "Charity and Time," *Cross Currents*, IX (Spring, 1960), p. 143.

even true of some teachers seeking to instruct their students in morality and religion. "Molding," forcing—these violate the pupils' God-given power of freedom. God gives people love (grace); he does not "mold" them. Teachers should imitate God, the Perfect Teacher, in this as in all other matters.

The teacher should attempt to instruct the students so that they will choose the right things. Since proper choice is based on sufficient knowledge, education for truth is *directly* education for the will. But the teacher must give his pupils more than truth—he must also give them love. The will without love is barren. Teachers tell their students to obey the Commandments, to choose good and avoid evil. But regrettably these are all too often presented as bare acts, not surrounded by love. The will is a goal-seeking faculty, and the goal it seeks is the good, is love. The will cannot be taught habitually to choose what is right apart from the motive and goal of love.

The will to learn is one of the most important qualities in a student. Differences in achievement among high school students are sometimes due to differences in the will to learn. Somehow, some way, the teacher and the school climate must inculcate this desire in the pupils. This can be accomplished only by the injection of love into the materials and the lesson itself. This will to learn is highly correlated with a love of learning. The relatively sorry state of American Catholic intellectual life is in large measure due to a disvaluation of learning, a lack of love for learning.[45]

Above all the teacher in his instruction and other dealings with pupils should constantly recall Mouroux's observation that love in human beings is both spirit and flesh.[46]

Attention. Attention may be defined as the direction of the cognitive processes toward a particular reality. This direction of the cognitive processes may be either automatic or intentional. Automatic or involuntary attention occurs when the stimulus of the particular reality itself is so forceful that it commands the cognitive processes to be directed toward it, e.g., when a bright flashing light suddenly comes into view or when a very interesting object is perceived. Intentional or voluntary attention occurs when the cognitive processes are consciously directed toward the particular reality, e.g., when the student focuses his attention on a page of a textbook. Intentional attention is dependent on the will. If a student does not will to pay attention, then he won't. Automatic attention is easier and usually more pleasurable than intentional

[45] On this point, see Thomas F. O'Dea, *American Catholic Dilemma: An Inquiry into the Intellectual Life.* (New York: Sheed and Ward, 1958); and Justus George Lawler, *Catholic Dimension in Higher Education.* (Westminster, Md.: Newman, 1959).

[46] Mouroux, *op. cit.*, pp. 196–266.

attention. Therefore the teacher should structure the learning situation so that the instructional methods and materials will *of themselves* produce automatic attention on the part of the pupils.

Attention has the effect of coordinating and unifying into a meaningful whole the various elements of the object or situation being attended to. Attentiveness is thus an important and indispensable aid to retention. Nonetheless it is impossible for a person to pay attention to more than one thing at one time.[47] Teachers should keep this in mind and during the lesson endeavor to avoid presenting a great many attention-getting objects and ideas simultaneously. The teacher should also remember that the capacity for sustained attention grows during adolescence; hence a part of his educative task is to nourish and improve the pupils' utilization of their attentive powers. Like other human powers, attention is dynamic, not static. The degree and manner of its use in any given learning situation are deeply influenced by the adolescent's immediate concrete condition at that time; e.g., he cannot attend readily because of his activities in the preceding class, which was physical education.

The competitor for attention is distraction. A distraction is any reality which causes one's cognitive processes to be diverted from the object or situation being attended to. Distractions cannot be avoided completely, but they can be minimized. The skillful teacher should thwart distractive influences by constantly having recourse to attention-getting practices. These practices are rooted in the intrinsic and extrinsic determiners of attention, i.e., those factors within the learner and those in the object or situation outside him which cause attention to be focused on one particular reality instead of on another. Garrett lists the intrinsic determiners as mind-set and expectation, interest, attitudes, suggestion, needs, and values; the extrinsic determiners as intensity, contrast, change, movement, arrangement, and structural patterns.[48] The importance of proper motivation as a crucial determiner of attention was brought out in a study by Sister Rosa McDonough, R.S.M., which concluded that the purposes of the learner play a large role in determining which particular reality he will attend to.[49]

At the outset of the lesson, the teacher should endeavor to develop a learning situation in which attention will be automatic. Arousing

[47] Attention may rapidly shift among several objects or situations; however, at any given moment a person's attention is limited to only one particular reality.

[48] Henry E. Garrett, *General Psychology*, 2d ed. (New York: American Book, 1961), pp. 137–147.

[49] Sister M. Rosa McDonough, R.S.M., *The Laws of Attention as Illustrated in the Liturgy of the Church*, unpublished master's thesis, Catholic University of America, Washington, D.C., 1917, p. 15.

interest in the material to be learned is the best way to accomplish this. Interest can be stimulated if the teacher demonstrates that the material is *both* worthwhile in itself and valuable to each pupil in his own life. Notwithstanding, the teacher realizes that only in the perfect learning situation will the pupils' attention be continually automatic. Therefore, he must constantly attempt to elicit voluntary attention from the pupils. This can be done in many different ways, including: (1) varying the instructional method, (2) involving the pupil in the situation as an active participant, (3) varying the instructional materials, (4) making the material interesting, (5) using frequent illustrations and examples, (6) stimulating the pupils' will to learn, (7) emphasizing the necessity of healthy self-control as an important avenue toward developing and sustaining attention, (8) being interesting as a person and interested in the pupils.

PERSONALITY-SITUATION FACTORS
AFFECTING LEARNING

"Personality" is concerned with the learner's total self qua his total self. "Situation" has to do with the environment in which every person is constantly enveloped. Neither factor operates in isolation but rather interacts with and so interpenetrates the other in the actual learning process. Hence personality cannot really be considered apart from situation and vice versa. As Davis observes, "Although the private personality is in part a result of organic, genetic and maturational factors, it is in some respects the accumulation of learning and blocks to learning acquired during the individual's socialization." [50]

Personality Factors

Personality, the total human self, is a flowing composite of temperament plus character. Temperament is the sum total of those fundamental tendencies which issue from the physiological constitution of the person. Character is the sum total of those fundamental tendencies which issue from the psychological constitution of the person, based on his temperament, experiences, attitudes, and ideals. Character is limited by temperament, not determined by it. Temperament is inherited at birth; character is shaped more by the will than by any other single factor. The temperament of a person with a well-developed character is not readily detectable because such a person has learned to control the unruly and jagged elements of his temperament. A person with an active or passionate temperament, e.g., a choleric or a sanguine, must exert far more character

[50] Allison Davis, "Socialization and the Adolescent Personality," *Adolescence*, National Society for the Study of Education, Fifty-Third Yearbook, Part I. (Chicago: University of Chicago Press, 1944), p. 207.

discipline on his personality than a person with a passive or mild temperament. Teachers should consider this disproportionateness of requisite effort when they are about to punish one student and reward another because, for example, the first pupil became excited while the second sat calmly in his seat.

Teachers should also keep in mind that knowledge of personality, whether obtained by introspection, speculation, or empirical research, is at best fragmentary and incomplete. Personality can be detected only by perceiving what a person actually does; yet personality is far more than readily observable behavior patterns. The teacher should not delude himself into believing he knows a pupil's personality (and therefore is in a position to pass near-infallible judgments on it) merely by watching the pupil's behavior. The teacher must realize that the personality of each pupil is a private matter and is to a large extent incommunicable. Certainly it behooves every teacher to be very cautious in making personality judgments.

Adolescent Needs. The personality of the high school student is shaped by many forces, one of the most important of which is his needs. A need may be defined as that which a person must have in order to fulfill himself in some way. A need is caused by the failure of a person or society to provide for some essential thrust of a particular existential human personality. The failure to meet a need or needs causes severe personal (and often social) problems, e.g., starvation, feelings of inadequacy, delinquency. Needs differ from wishes (or wants) in that the former are necessary for personality fulfillment, while the latter are merely expressions of some nonessential item which the person would like to have, such as two tickets to a baseball game. Some educators, particularly of the ultraprogressive school, fail at times to distinguish between needs and wants—the two are mingled indiscriminately into a vast and choppy sea of needs.[51]

Needs can be classified in at least three ways, i.e., by source, direction, and perception. First of all, needs either can grow out of one's own personality, e.g., the need for attaining God, or can be imposed by the society in which he lives, e.g., the need to learn how to read.[52] Second, needs are either immediate or ultimate. Immediate needs are those which must be met without delay, e.g., providing rest for a student who is overfatigued from his physical education class. Ultimate needs are those

[51] For an example of this, see Camilla M. Low, "Determining the Nature of the Needs of Youth," *Adapting the Secondary-School Program to the Needs of Youth,* National Society for the Study of Education, Fifty-Second Yearbook, Part I. (Chicago: University of Chicago Press, 1953), pp. 23–24.

[52] See Ralph W. Tyler, "Translating Youth Needs into Teaching Goals," in *ibid.,* p. 218.

which must be continuously met if the person's basic destiny is to be achieved, e.g., providing pupils with the means to spiritual perfection. Third, needs are either felt or perceived. Felt needs are those which arouse one's physical nature and cry out for immediate fulfillment; e.g., a starving student from a tenement area needs food *now*. Perceived needs are those which are known to be such primarily by the mind rather than by the senses; e.g., a juvenile delinquent knows that he needs an object upon which to lavish his affection. Needs and the way in which they are met cause both teachers and students many problems, not the least of which is to integrate and balance pupil needs and societal needs. Thus, for example, pupils need to express themselves creatively and independently while society expects them to "be seen but not heard."

The modern emphasis on the needs of youth has led many secondary school educators, both public and Catholic, to attempt to identify the principal areas of adolescent needs. The three most famous needs lists of public school educators are the National Association of Secondary-School Principals' "The Imperative Needs of Youth of Secondary-School Age" (quoted in Chapter II), Doane's *Needs of Youth*, and Havighurst's *Developmental Tasks*. Doane identifies fifteen major loci of adolescent needs; these loci are of great psychological and educational importance because it is here that youth needs emerge and hence problems arise. Doane's loci of broad adolescent needs are:

> (1) vocational choice and placement; (2) philosophy of life and mental hygiene; (3) getting along with people; (4) morals; (5) plans for marriage and family; (6) leisure time and recreation; (7) finances; (8) relations with the opposite sex; (9) health; (10) sex and reproduction; (11) religion; (12) relationships with family; (13) social competence; (14) conventional subject-matter areas; (15) other areas of interest.[53]

Havighurst's theory of needs, based on what he calls "developmental tasks," has been enthusiastically accepted by almost all public secondary school educators. These developmental tasks of life are simply a series of tasks imposed on the child and the adolescent at each of the various stages of his development. The origin or roots of these tasks are threefold: tasks which arise from physical maturation, e.g., learning to walk; tasks which arise from cultural pressures from society, e.g., learning to read; tasks which arise from his personality or selfhood, e.g., building a philosophy of life. These developmental tasks are of crucial importance, because as the person comes to meet these tasks, with or without outside help, they become the natural motivating power for his

[53] Donald C. Doane, *The Needs of Youth*. (New York: Teachers College, Columbia University, 1942), pp. 43–44.

behavior. Indeed they automatically become urgent biological-personal-social needs which must be met.[54]

The concept of developmental tasks tries to solve the learning dilemma of emphasis on dynamic needs arising from within the person versus emphasis on needs imposed from outside the person by society. Thus it tries to steer a pedagogical course clear of an exclusive need-centered methodology which emphasizes a completely free, uninhibited development of the student (as in the progressivist schools of the 1920s and 1930s) and also clear of an exclusive society-centered methodology which emphasizes restraint of the pupil to force him to conform to societal demands (as in Soviet schools).

Havighurst lists a total of ten developmental tasks:

> (1) achieving new and more mature relations with age-mates of both sexes; (2) achieving a masculine and feminine social role; (3) accepting one's physique and using the body effectively; (4) achieving emotional independence of parents and other adults; (5) achieving assurance of economic independence; (6) selecting and preparing for an occupation; (7) preparing for marriage and family life; (8) developing intellectual skills and concepts necessary for civic competence; (9) desiring and achieving socially responsible behavior; (10) acquiring a set of values and an ethical system as a guide to behavior.[55]

In elaborating on his developmental tasks, Havighurst states, first, the task itself, then successively the nature of the task, the biological basis of the task, the psychological basis of the task, and the cultural basis of the task. The nature of each task is seen as a goal. Thus, the goal of developmental task number 10 is "to form a set of values that are possible of realization; to develop a conscious purpose of realizing these values; to define man's place in the physical world and in relation to other human beings; to keep one's world picture and one's values in harmony with each other." [56]

The chief strength of this theory is its emphasis on the dynamism of needs rooted in the complex interaction of the maturing adolescent with his environment. Its principal weakness is that the spiritual basis of these developmental tasks is neither adequately understood nor appreciated. The adolescent and his environment are more than masses of matter in collision.

The two most significant lists of the needs of youth from a Catholic point of view are those of Schneiders and the Catholic University Workshop on Integration in the Catholic Secondary School Curriculum.

[54] Robert J. Havighurst, *Developmental Tasks in Education*, 2d ed. (New York: Longmans, 1952), pp. 1–4.

[55] *Ibid.*, pp. 33–71. By permission, David McKay Co., Inc.

[56] *Ibid.*, pp. 62–63. By permission, David McKay Co., Inc.

Schneiders' list, based on the thrusts of the adolescent's new, emergent self, is as follows: independence; security; affection; recognition; social approval; conformity; new experiences.[57]

The Catholic University Workshop (CUW) listing of adolescent needs is probably the most important ever enunciated by a group of Catholic educators. The CUW statement declares that students *need:*

> (1) to know their Religion and love it; (2) to learn to live with other human beings; (3) to achieve and maintain sound physical, mental and moral health; (4) to learn to live in their natural and scientific environment; (5) to receive sound guidance; (6) to learn to think logically and express themselves clearly; (7) to prepare for work, for further education, and for family life; (8) to learn to use their leisure well; (9) to learn to live aesthetically in accordance with Christian standards of morality.[58]

This Catholic University Workshop list meshes nicely with the official NCEA statement of Catholic secondary school goals quoted in Chapter II. This is understandable since any good educational program must be rooted in the needs of the youth it attempts to serve. Furthermore, the CUW list is more comprehensive than similar statements by secular educators since it recognizes the primacy and importance of religious needs not only as necessary for living a supernatural life but also for living an adequate natural life as well. As Jung observed in his 1937 Terry Lectures at Yale, a natural religious need exists in every man; if he ignores this urge, he will be in great danger of losing his psychic health.[59]

Like the educational program, the dynamics of learning are also grounded in the pupils' needs. A good learning situation will, among other things, provide educational outlets for student needs. If some of the pupils' basic immediate needs are being frustrated, it is doubtful if they will ever learn or even desire to learn what is presented in class. The skillful teacher organizes the learning situation in such a way that the pupils' needs will serve as both motivator and partial rationale for learning the material which is under consideration by the class. Thus Havighurst, in discussing the function of the theory of developmental tasks, notes that this concept is aimed not at discovering the aims of the

[57] Schneiders, *op. cit.*, p. 22.

[58] James J. McPadden, "College Deans Look at the Needs of Youth, Part I," in Sister Mary Janet, S.C. (ed.), *Building the Integrated Curriculum.* (Washington, D.C.: Catholic University of America Press, 1953), p. 69.

[59] Carl G. Jung, *Psychology and Religion.* (New Haven, Conn.: Yale University Press, 1938); see also Raymond Hostie, S.J., *Religion and the Psychology of Jung.* (New York: Sheed and Ward, 1957).

school but more importantly "in timing educational efforts, in teaching at the teachable moment" for the learner when he is ready, when he has reached a particular task level, a particular stage in the evolution of his needs.[60] Of course, neither the teacher nor the school can be reasonably expected to meet perfectly every pupil need. Nevertheless, the teacher must take these needs into account during the course of his instruction. Teaching is rooted in learning, and learning in the learner. Therefore, unless a teacher wishes to conduct his classes in an ivory-tower intellectual vacuum, he must integrate student needs into his instructional activities.

Adolescent Problems. A problem arises when for some reason a need is not being met; e.g., a youth who needs the understanding of adults is ignored and even ridiculed by his parents and teachers. Many educators and psychologists have attempted to identify the major problem areas of adolescents. Perhaps the most famous of all these is the Mooney Problem Check List, High School Form. This is a psychological test which classifies adolescent problems into 11 broad areas for the purpose of uncovering the particular problems being faced by various youths. These 11 problem areas consist of: "(1) health and physical development; (2) finances—living conditions—employment; (3) social and recreational activities; (4) social—psychological relations; (5) personal—psychological relations; (6) courtship—sex—marriage; (7) home and family; (8) morals and religion; (9) adjustment to school work; (10) the future—vocational and educational; (11) curriculum and teaching procedures." [61]

Schneiders's list of seven categories of adolescent problems is quite familiar to many Catholic secondary school experts: "(1) emotional difficulties; (2) social problems; (3) academic problems; (4) vocational problems; (5) home adjustments; (6) problems arising from leisure-time activities; (7) moral and religious problems." [62]

The problems of young people as they exist in the concrete rarely fall neatly into these specific areas. Rather, the problem structure of any adolescent is complex and interrelated. Thus, Schutz, in his doctoral study on the problems of adolescent girls, observed that the cluster structure of problems "does not correspond closely to any of the theoretical frameworks which have been proposed for studying adolescent problems. . . . The fact that two of the clusters cut across several areas of [one of the leading problem inventory check lists] indicates that the classifying of items in problem check lists into the

[60] Havighurst, *op. cit.*, p. 5.
[61] Oscar K. Buros (ed.), *The Fifth Mental Measurements Yearbook.* (Highland Park, N.J.: Gryphon, 1959), p. 89.
[62] Schneiders, *op. cit.*, p. 20.

traditional functional activity categories is in large part an arbitrary procedure." [63]

Some investigators have discovered that problems increase or decrease in importance depending on the age of the youth. The study made by Sister M. Celine Olegar, O.S.U., of the personal problems of high school students in a Midwestern diocese revealed that sophomore problems centered around social, school, and recreational activities, whereas senior problems indicated difficulties in the personal, financial, and future-life areas.[64] However, whether these problems were caused solely by age, or were greatly affected by the particular grade in which the pupil was placed, is open to question. Certainly it would seem that being a high school senior is a greater causal factor in affecting pupil anxiety about future-life plans than being seventeen years old. Nonetheless, the investigations by Gesell and his associates seem to bear out the hypothesis that age is a prominent factor in determining adolescent problems.[65]

Age-maturation and high school grade level are not the only causes of adolescent problems. The long period of adolescence in American culture, with its delaying of actual independence has been mentioned by sociologists as a cause of a great many adolescent problems. This has been borne out by studies of youth in other cultures in which adolescence is not so prolonged; there the problems of youth are correspondingly less. For an American Catholic adolescent, being a member of a minority group adds even more pressure. This is particularly true since the value system of the majority, especially as expressed in the mass media, is so hostile to his own value system. Teachers in Catholic high schools should be mindful of the latter pressure and never permit religious rigidity or even moral rigorism to replace the love and understanding which should always characterize their relationships with the students. This by no means suggests abandoning principles, but rather seeing both principles and youths in the contextual light of God's redemptive love.

The teacher must realize that every one of his pupils has problems to a greater or lesser degree. Thus a teacher should not organize the learning situation as if these problems did not exist, for such would be delusion. Similarly, a teacher should not deal with these problems as though they existed only because a youth had been bad, for such

[63] Richard E. Schutz, "Patterns of Personal Problems of Adolescent Girls," *Journal of Educational Psychology*, XLIX (February, 1958), p. 5.

[64] Sister M. Celine Olegar, O.S.U., *An Analysis of the Personal Problems of High School Students in the Youngstown Diocese*. (Washington, D.C.: Catholic University of America Press, 1960).

[65] Arnold Gesell et al., *Youth: The Years from Ten to Sixteen*. (New York: Harper, 1956).

would be presumption. Furthermore, an adolescent must be recognized for what he is, viz., an adolescent, and consequently should not be expected to act like a miniature adult. Action follows being; the teacher therefore should not be surprised when an adolescent fails to act like an adult. Accordingly an adolescent has his own problems which, though far removed from adult concerns, are important to *him*. Learning, as St. Thomas so often said, occurs after the manner of the learner. Adolescent learning will thus take place within the context of *the adolescent's* personality, needs, and problems, not the teacher's.

A characteristic of adolescent problems is that they cry out, as far as the youth is concerned, for immediate solution. The teacher, therefore, should not seek to postpone or bury the pupil's problems but rather should organize the learning process in such a way that the material to be learned and the pupil problem will have mutual relevance. This requires a great deal of pedagogic skill, because a balance must be struck between making the entire lesson an extension of the pupil's problems (in which little formal material is learned) and teaching as if these problems did not exist (in which little formal material is learned because of pupil problem blocks). In good teaching, pupil problems and formal material must be related. This is especially true of religious problems, for as Bernard has noted, "Unless [the adolescent] has been cowed into submissiveness he wants to perceive the relation of religion to his personal and social problems *now*." [66]

The teacher should never neglect the invaluable help which a student's classmates can render in constructively solving or at least alleviating his problems. As Tryon has observed, many adolescent problems "can only reach a satisfactory solution for boys and girls through the medium of their peer group." [67] Pupils are not only subjects upon which the teacher exercises his instruction, but joint partners in the common educational quest for truth. Thus the whole class must and should help its members both learn and solve their problems.

Above all, the teacher should endeavor to make the pupil understand that he is not the only one with problems, that it is quite normal for adolescents to be confronted with problems. This awareness will do much to relieve the pupil's anxiety and will enable him to channel his concerns away from an exclusive dwelling on the problem itself and toward its contextual solution.

Finally, the teacher must in due humility realize that he himself

[66] Harold W. Bernard, *Adolescent Development in American Culture.* (Yonkers, N.Y.: World, 1957), p. 383.

[67] Caroline M. Tryon, "The Adolescent Peer Culture," *Adolescence*, National Society for the Study of Education, Fifty-Third Yearbook, Part I. (Chicago: University of Chicago Press, 1944), p. 217.

can be the cause of many of his pupils' problems. If he is autocratic, he can deprive the pupils of the expression their personalities so crave; if he is too permissive, he can deprive them of proper exercise of restraint and self-control. The fact that item 11 on the Mooney Problem Check List concerns itself with teaching methods is a good indication that pedagogical practices do in actual fact frequently result in pupil problems. On the other hand, a balanced class with a minimum of problems is in no small measure due to a balanced teacher whose classroom behavior does not create these problems.

Situation Factors

The influence of the external world upon the manner and direction of learning is considerable. It was not long ago that many psychologists, intoxicated by the importance of situational factors, held that a learner's environment completely determined and shaped not only his learning but even his very nature. Today the organic elements are once again given their proper accord; nevertheless, the role of situational factors in the educative process is still very much appreciated. Formal secondary education takes place in a definite social setting, i.e., in a particular country, region, community, school, and classroom, all of which greatly affect the type of learning which occurs. Indeed the American Catholic school system was founded because bishops, Religious Superiors, and the laity wished Catholic students to learn in a social situation conducive to the integration of Catholic teachings with other intellectual and nonintellectual activities of the school.

Culture and Social Environment. Wayland has remarked that adolescence must be considered "a culture-bound process of maturing. . . . It must be viewed as a cultural phenomenon whose meaning is unique to the special culture in which it occurs. . . . Adolescence is both a universal experience and a pattern of distinctive experiences having special meanings in different cultures." [68] Adolescents are probably more affected by the culture and milieu in which they live than is any other age group. Children are more self-centered and so pay less attention to their environment; adults have learned to compensate for the less-than-good things in their surroundings. Adolescents, however, are just discovering and drinking in the rich and delightful draughts of their newfound environment, and it proves a heady wine indeed. An adolescent's failure is very often the failure of his culture, be it societal, parental, or educational; juvenile delinquency usually has its roots in unfortunate social situations, particularly a broken home.

[68] Sloan Wayland, "Social Context and the Adolescent," *What Shall the High School Teach?* Association for Supervision and Curriculum Development, Fifty-Sixth Yearbook. (Washington, D.C.: ASCD, 1956), p. 28.

Environment affects the pupil's basic use of intelligence and also his behavior. As regards the basic use of intelligence, an investigation by Havighurst and Breese indicates that pupils of higher familial social status tend to do better on tests involving reasoning, memory, space, number, word fluency, and verbal comprehension than do children of lower social position.[69] A study by Loevinger corroborates this finding; however, she takes care to note that other factors such as parental intelligence bore a higher correlation to pupil intelligence than did socioeconomic status.[70] Concerning behavior, Davis has noted that "the middle-class adolescent is punished for physical aggression or for physical sexual relations; the lower-class adolescent is frequently rewarded, both socially and organically, for these same behaviors." [71] Studies have shown that juvenile delinquency varies considerably according to the section of the city.[72]

School life and school performance are also greatly influenced by one's environment and milieu. An investigation by Coster of the students of the three income groups concluded that:

High income pupils were more likely than middle and low income pupils to participate in school and out-of-school activities, hold office in an organization, get high marks in school, be named to the school honor roll, attend Sunday School and Church regularly, successfully complete courses in school and continue education. The number of hours spent studying or working outside of school, during the school year, however, did not differ among the groups.[73]

The particular school milieu also exerts a considerable influence on adolescents. A study by Levinson showed that for Irish and Italian students in Catholic schools and for Jewish pupils in Jewish parochial schools, there is great emphasis by the school on verbal learning and relative neglect of performance arts.[74] As far as Catholic schools go,

[69] Havighurst and Breese, loc. cit.

[70] Jane Loevinger, "Intelligence as Related to Socio-Economic Factors," Intelligence: Its Nature and Nurture, National Society for the Study of Education, Thirty-Ninth Yearbook, Part I. (Chicago: University of Chicago Press, 1940), pp. 159–210.

[71] Davis, op. cit., p. 211.

[72] See M. H. Neumeyer, Juvenile Delinquency in Modern Society. (Princeton, N.J.: Van Nostrand, 1949); also the classic study by Sheldon Glueck and Eleanor Glueck, Predicting Delinquency and Crime. (Cambridge, Mass.: Harvard University Press, 1959).

[73] John K. Coster, "Some Characteristics of High School Pupils from Three Income Groups," Journal of Educational Psychology, L (April, 1959), p. 62.

[74] Boris M. Levinson, "Traditional Jewish Cultural Values and Performance on the Wechsler Tests," Journal of Educational Psychology, L (August, 1959), pp. 177–180.

this finding is most distressing, since it shows that these institutions are failing to develop in the student his natural and supernatural faculty of "maker." [75] It is in his role of maker that the student also imitates Christ, Who was for most of His earthly life a Maker at Nazareth. Also it is through making that the student exercises his creative intelligence and once again renews in the world's history the original Divine creative act. Catholic schools should not exalt the concept of the pupil as assimilator, as sponge, as blotter; rather they should emphasize the dynamic, nature-rooted role of the student as creator, maker, and inventor. An assimilation-laden educational milieu has paralyzing effects on students.

In any assessment of environmental influence on high school students, it is well to bear in mind that studies have shown that community mentality, attitudes, and values are far more influential in shaping the youth's personality and affecting the use of his intelligence than are the physical elements of his environment.[76]

Richardson and Smitter have summed up the various cultural, social, and environmental factors which influence learning: "(1) the social class into which a child was born influences his learning; (2) the ethnic or national background of a child has an effect on the way he learns; (3) the place where a child lives, his neighborhood, the occupations and kinds of people who surround him make a difference in the way he learns; (4) family values affect learning; (5) the kind of life which each family leads affects a child's learning." [77]

Teachers and administrators should remember that it is they who to a considerable extent fashion the school environment and milieu. They should therefore strive to make this environment rich in learning possibilities and productive of a love of learning on the part of the students. Also, every teacher must be mindful of the community, neighborhood, and family background of each pupil and tailor his instruction accordingly. A visit to the home of each pupil is one of the best devices for gaining such a knowledge. In this connection it has been suggested by some Catholic educational writers that Religious Orders of women so amend their constitutions as to permit personal calls at the homes of students, even after dark. If home visitation is for some

[75] On this point, see John Julian Ryan, *Beyond Humanism.* (New York: Sheed and Ward, 1950), pp. 32–47.

[76] C. R. Shaw and H. D. McKay, *Social Factors in Juvenile Delinquency.* National Commission on Law Observance and Enforcement, Report No. 13. (Washington: Government Printing Office, 1931).

[77] Sybil K. Richardson and Faith K. Smitter, "The Learner," *Learning and the Teacher,* 1959 Yearbook, Association for Supervision and Curriculum Development. (Washington: ASCD, 1959), pp. 32–34.

reason impossible, the teacher can at least study each pupil's guidance record for evidences of pertinent environmental influences.

Social Recognition. Social recognition refers to the degree to which a youth is accepted by his peer group and has been shown to have a definite effect upon the amount and kind of pupil learning. Thistle-thwaite's study concluded that social recognition caused a significant degree of motivation in intellectually gifted youths; among the boys such recognition increased the "favorableness of attitudes toward intellectualism, the number of students planning to seek the Ph.D. or M.D. degree, and the number planning to become college teachers or scientific researchers." [78] The desire for social acceptance leads high school youth to be very gregarious, to want to travel around in groups or gangs. These groups or gangs in turn greatly influence the thoughts and actions of those youths who are their members. Thus Shaw and McKay observe that 75 to 89 per cent of the delinquent boys studied committed their crimes in groups, whether large or small.[79] Cannon's study shows that a youth's level of social recognition tends to remain fairly constant throughout his high school years; e.g., a boy who is socially rejected in his freshman year will usually suffer the same group repudiation in senior year.[80]

Despite the overwhelming evidence of the influence of age-mate groups on pupil learning and behavior, most teachers "have a tendency to disregard or minimize the educational significance of a youngster's experiences in his peer group." [81] This is regrettable, and every teacher should endeavor to give the peer group its proper due in the learning situation. All too many teachers cause group social disapproval to fall on brighter youths by the way in which they comment upon or reward the answers these youths give in class. Since the level of social acceptance remains fairly constant in high school, the teacher should review the guidance records at the beginning of the term so as to identify the group rejects and to adjust his instruction toward integrating these students into the group. Above all, the teacher should make learning a group affair rather than merely an exclusive function of a few bright individuals. Such a procedure is not to neglect individual differences, but rather to recognize that in the classroom situation the individual is not only an individual but is also a member of a group.

[78] Donald L. Thistlethwaite, "Effects of Social Recognition upon the Educational Motivation of Talented Youth," *Journal of Educational Psychology*, L (April, 1959), p. 116.

[79] Shaw and McKay, *op. cit.*, pp. 194–199.

[80] Kenneth L. Cannon, "Stability of Sociometric Scores of High School Students," *Journal of Educational Research*, LII (October, 1958), p. 47.

[81] Tryon, *loc. cit.*

School Achievement. Performance in school has a great deal of effect on pupil learning. Success in school has been discovered to be a prime motivator in further learning. Conversely, failure to achieve individual, social, or educational expectations in school has led many pupils to become disinterested in learning and often to leave school. Numerous dropout studies have underscored this point. In an extensive New York study, high school principals gave the following reasons for students leaving school before graduation: (1) low intelligence, (2) retardation, (3) lure of a job, (4) parental attitude, (5) dislike of school, (6) social maladjustment, (7) broken homes, (8) absence.[82] Lack of school achievement is often traceable not only to the students but also to the school's educational program. Inadequate educational goals (e.g., expecting a youth with a 75 IQ to comprehend Shakespeare), failure to gear instruction to individual differences, a faulty curricular design, poor guidance facilities, lack of opportunity for pupils to display their creativity—these and other factors engendered by the school situation are contributory causes to a lessening and perhaps even a deadening of the learning processes within the student.

A Combination of Personality and Situation Factors

While all factors predominantly personal and all factors predominantly situational do interact with one another to a certain extent to produce *some limited degree* of factorial homogenization, there are still other factors whose operations are influenced to a *great degree* by both internal and external forces. The latter factors can best be considered as essentially a combination of factors.

Adjustment. Adjustment may be defined as "the patterning and harmonizing of a person's mentality and behavior with the demands of self and environment in a manner to insure satisfaction and happiness."[83] It consists of the integration of the external world with one's own physical and psychological self to form one person. Adjustment is difficult, because it requires that the various personality and situational elements be delicately balanced in the personal integrative process. Of considerable importance in an adolescent's adjustment is his self-concept. If his self-concept is inadequate or defective in any way, maladjustment will be certain to set in.

Educators and psychologists know what adjustment is, but often they are uncertain whether a particular youth is actually adjusted or not. In the school situation, the judgment of the teachers and guidance personnel is usually considered the most weighty testimony of whether a

[82] See New York State Education Department, *Drop Outs: Their Cause and Cure.* (Albany, N.Y.: NYSED, 1954).

[83] Schneiders, *op. cit.*, p. 30.

certain adolescent is maladjusted. A study by Beilin and Werner showed that, though there was a considerable area of agreement between men and women teachers in characterizing the best and poorest adjusted youth, there were also some differences in emphases.

The criteria which are used significantly more by men teachers are maturity, good judgment, dependability, trustworthiness, lack of self-consciousness and being secure as a person. The criteria employed more characteristically by women teachers are humility and modesty. They also place greater stress in regard to poor adjustment upon negativism, hostility to authority, discipline problems, and getting into trouble at school. In general the "character-control" items are more often mentioned as criteria by women teachers, "emotional-personality" items as a group by men teachers.[84]

Maladjustment can have many causes, both physical and psychological. Lack of sleep, autonomic imbalance, hyperthyroidism, inadequate self-concept, family problems, group rejection—these and a host of other factors can lead to poor adjustment. In adolescents, blooming and heightened emotional and organic factors are a great source of maladjustment. This is particularly true when the youth faces a seeming conflict between his emotions and physical urges and his moral-religious framework. In desperation, adolescents often solve this conflict by compromise or in some other unhealthy manner. It is precisely this defective way of solving a conflict or frustration that causes maladjustment.

The teacher can do several things to promote good adjustment in students. These are quite important, for the maladjusted youth is faced with such problems and anxieties that learning is seriously hampered.

1. The students' personalities must be permitted sufficient self-expression. This is vital for providing for the thrust of every person's inner self.

2. Learning situations must be structured so that adjustment rather than maladjustment is promoted. Thus the teacher should not continually present the student with problems more difficult than he can handle, for repeated failure to solve them may easily lead to self-rejection or rejection of the material to be learned, both of which are unhealthy conflict resolutions.

3. The student's emotions should be used as an aid in his adjustment, and not viewed by the teacher as being always causative of poor adjustment, e.g., shouting an answer out of turn in class may be a particular youth's natural way of using his enthusiasm to adjust to a difficult problem posed by the teacher, yet such a student will most likely be punished by the

[84] Harry Beilin and Emmy Werner, "Sex Differences among Teachers in the Use of the Criteria of Adjustment," *Journal of Educational Psychology,* XLVIII (November, 1957), p. 439.

teacher for disrupting the class. (Is this teacher more concerned with his own classroom control than with the particular pupil's adjustment?) Of course, a balance must be maintained, else bedlam will reign.

4. Problems relating to emotional-organic-religious conflicts must be handled in an understanding and loving manner befitting a member of the Mystical Body. The solution should be sought not so much in the spirit of disciplining a fallen Adam but in cooperating with a redeemed person. The teacher cannot cut off the pupil's supernatural leg and tell him to run. The moral law should be applied to student problems not as a series of negative commands which no circumstance can ever alter one jot or one tittle, but rather as a living, loving, and circumstance-minded guide to natural and supernatural self-fulfillment.[85]

5. Several teachers of both sexes and from different subject fields should cooperate in identifying and assisting in the cure of pupil maladjustment. Such a mixed group would, for example, encourage men teachers to pay more attention to the pupil's character and stimulate women teachers first to look more to the "whole child" rather than merely to abstract character traits, and second, to develop a spirit of give and take among the youths rather than place undue restraints upon student self-expression, which the Beilin and Werner study indicates women teachers often do.[86]

6. Teachers, especially Catholic teachers, must recognize that maladjustment is in itself bad not in the moral sense but in the psychological sense.

Attitudes. An attitude is a relatively permanent disposition or mind-set toward a physical or mental object. It always involves a preconceived judgment about the object together with a preprepared reaction toward it. Thus through attitude the learner is already conditioned on both how to evaluate and how to respond to a particular object before he ever actually encounters that object; e.g., a high school girl will usually respond with interest, pleasure, and affectivity when the term "boy friend" is mentioned.

Learning attitudes toward various realities is probably the most important single work of the school in its goal of inculcating truth. There are at least two reasons for this. *First,* attitudes condition *all* learning. As Allport has observed, "Attitudes will determine for each individual what he will see and hear, what he will think and what he will do." [87] The differences in the rate and amount of learning among the students in a class are often due as much to their individual attitudes as to their intelligence. An investigation by Levine and Murphy in

[85] Theologians assert that every moral act is affected by three factors, viz., object, end, and circumstances. See Adolphe Tanquerey, *Synopsis Theologiae Moralis et Pastoralis,* vol. II, 11th rev. ed. (Tournai: Desclée, 1944), pp. 129–148.

[86] Beilin and Werner, *op. cit.,* pp. 426–439.

[87] Gordon W. Allport, "Attitudes," in Murchison (ed.), *A Handbook of Social Psychology.* (Worcester, Mass.: Clark University Press, 1935), p. 806.

which students of similar intelligence but different attitudes read controversial material showed that if the opinion expressed in the material is in agreement with the opinion of the reader, the reader will remember it better and longer than if the opinion of the material disagrees with that of the reader.[88] Students frequently remember what they are attitudinally conditioned to remember and often forget what they are attitudinally conditioned to forget. *Second*, attitudes are usually more permanent than specific bodies of information. The curve of forgetting as plotted by Ebbinghaus (discussed earlier in this chapter) amply demonstrates that pupils forget in a relatively short period of time most of the facts, data, and theories they learn. The attitudes they acquire, however, are perdurable. When the students graduate from high school they soon forget most of the information they learned there; but the attitudes they acquired during their secondary school years will remain with them for a long, long time. The high school must teach, must exert its influence on the whole lifetime of its students, not just on the years they spend in school.

What is the origin of attitudes? How do students come about acquiring them? Harris, following Allport, discerns four psychological sources of attitudes:

> (1) They may develop through the *integration* of numerous specific responses of a similar type. Thus a number of unfortunate experiences with different members of a cultural group may bring one to the belief that "all such people are unpleasant"; (2) Attitudes may also arise from general approach or withdrawal tendencies. . . . Thus, specific attitudes of distrust or hate may develop gradually out of more general, diffuse patterns of dislike; (3) Attitudes, too, may result from single dramatic experiences. Cruelty received from a child of another ethnic or cultural group may quickly crystallize a strong attitude toward all members of that group; (4) Finally, attitudes may be taken over ready-made from others[89] [e.g., parents, teachers.] Allport considers parents the most important single source of attitudes.

Schneiders find six sociopsychological origins of attitudes: experience and activity; family influence; cultural milieu; psychological factors, such as intelligence, needs, feelings, and beliefs; social facilitation; instruction and propaganda.[90]

Both Harris and Schneiders agree that the teacher and the entire

[88] Jerome M. Levine and Gardner Murphy, "The Learning and Forgetting of Controversial Material," *Journal of Abnormal and Social Psychology*, XXXVIII (October, 1943), pp. 507–517.

[89] Dale B. Harris, "How Children Learn Interests, Motives and Attitudes," *Learning and Instruction, op. cit.*, pp. 140–141.

[90] Schneiders, *op. cit.*, p. 90.

school situation itself are important sources of pupil attitudes. Psychological investigations corroborated these opinions. Indeed, an integral part of learning is change in attitude. Studies have shown that most attitudes which last for life are formed during adolescence.[91] These findings indicate the important role of the high school teachers in inculcating wholesome attitudes in their students. Studies by Kroll and others have demonstrated that teachers can and do effect a change in the attitudes of their students, especially if the teachers desire to do so.[92]

An investigation by Bond on the teacher's use of rational, factual material shows how pupils' attitudes can be changed. A science class was divided into two groups, the experimental and the control. In the experimental section, the students learned the concepts of genetics and were given a few indications by the instructor as to how these concepts might apply to racial problems such as miscegenation. The control group studied genetic concepts without any hint as to their applications. A test administered to both groups after the completion of the instruction revealed that the experimental group was more favorable to Orientals, Jews, and Italians and less favorable to imperialism than was the control group.[93]

The best method to change the attitudes of the pupils is to teach with this type of change as a goal. Such a procedure is not subversive, nor is it "molding." Every teacher changes attitudes whether he intends to or not—the way he dresses, acts, and speaks, the way in which he organizes the learning experiences, the manner in which he faces pupil problems—all these directly affect student attitudes. Furthermore, the teacher and the school have been commissioned by society, whether civic or religious, both to change and raise the attitudinal level of their pupils. Hence both teachers and the school would be remiss in their duty if they did not teach for attitude change. This is particularly true in Catholic high schools. A great many public school educators maintain with Alberty that the actual as well as the ideal growth pattern in religious attitudes should proceed along Positivistic lines, e.g., "*from* religious concern, on the part of some, based on feelings of fear or guilt *to* tending toward a settlement of religious problems based upon a

[91] *Ibid.*, pp. 285–286; also Harold Webster, "Changes in Attitude during College," *Journal of Educational Psychology*, XLIX (June, 1958), pp. 109–116. Webster notes, however, that such studies are limited since they cannot isolate the effects of school on pupil attitudes: "During late adolescence some variations in attitudes undoubtedly have little to do with formal educational experience."

[92] Abraham Kroll, "The Teacher's Influence upon the Social Attitude of Boys in the Twelfth Grade," *Journal of Educational Psychology*, XXV (March, 1934), pp. 274–280.

[93] See Austin de M. Bond, *An Experiment in the Teaching of Genetics*. (New York: Bureau of Publications, Teachers College, Columbia University, 1940).

more abstract concept of God as a disembodied spiritual force, or one based on acceptance of humanitarianism in the place of supernaturalism." [94] One reason Catholic parents send their children to Catholic high schools is to avoid having their attitudes changed in this Positivistic fashion and to ensure that their attitudes will become like those of Christ. Hence, in every phase of his instruction, the teacher should attempt to infuse attitudes as well as material. Dramatic teaching devices, such as anecdotes, illustrations, and audio-visual aids, have been shown to be effective in inculcating attitudes. Facts and theories should not be presented in themselves, but as relevant to some particular attitude. The teacher should always strive for cohesiveness, integration, and contiguity in his instruction, since attitudes are closely interrelated; that is, they often condition one another. Thus, for example, a student's attitude toward the Mystical Body conditions his attitude toward race relations. In Catholic schools, the teacher must demonstrate over and over again that religious attitudes affect one's attitudes toward every reality. This is crucially important, for all too often religious and moral attitudes are inculcated in such a manner that they seem to be somehow relevant only inside church, with no particular application to an interpenetration with the rest of the world. Above all, attitudes must be taught as having rational roots. Nonrational, autocratically based attitudes will soon be perceived by the students as unreasonable, and they will react by either promptly forgetting such attitudes or by adhering to opposite ones.

Values. Closely related to attitudes are values, as it is values in one form or another toward which an attitude is directed. Value is the worth of a reality, and it is at once both objective and subjective. Every reality has value in itself for the fullness of its being, the degree to which it participates in God, gives it an objective worth or value. As von Hildebrand has remarked, "Value is an ultimate datum." [95] However, value also refers to the subjective importance which a person attaches to a particular reality. Thus an ice-cream cone might have less objective value than a Beethoven symphony, but at the moment it has a greater subjective value to a certain youth who is yearning for some ice cream. Dewey and his disciples made all values subjective. For these educators, each pupil at every moment constructs his own set of values. Catholics maintain that there are both objective values (e.g., the goodness of every human being) and subjective values (e.g., one's mother has more value to a pupil than does a schoolmate). Subjective or personal values are both static and dynamic: Some constantly remain of

[94] Harold Alberty, *Reorganizing the High-School Curriculum*, rev. ed. (New York: Macmillan, 1953), p. 118.

[95] Dietrich von Hildebrand, *Christian Ethics*. (New York: McKay, 1953), p. 95.

great importance while others change in importance often or from time to time; e.g., the pupil holds his mother in high regard but in the hour preceding an examination a smart schoolmate might be more immediately valuable than his mother.

The inculcation of proper values is an extremely important task of the public and Catholic secondary schools. Values are products of many forces and influences, both personal and environmental. The Church, school, neighborhood, family, knowledge of the general experience of mankind, one's temperament, character—all these influence a person's value system. Probably the most important determiner of one's values is his attitudes. A youth's attitude toward a particular reality will determine what worth that reality has for him here and now. Conversely, a youth's value system will condition his attitudes.

Secondary school is a vitally important time in the formation of a youth's value system. In fact it is probably the most important single educational level for the inculcation of those values which will last throughout one's life. This does not deny the effect of college education on changing attitudes or values; [96] it merely asserts that during his secondary school experience the youth forms most of his perduring value structure. Thus an investigation by Wilson disclosed that the "differences in values between public and private [high] school graduates persist through four years' experience in a liberal arts college." [97] Of course it is not the school which is totally responsible for such value formation; the changes due to maturation, growth, new experiences, and so forth all play their respective roles; nonetheless, the influence of the secondary school is considerable.

Values which are highly prized by a person are called his ideals. A value may become an ideal because it possesses extraordinary merit in itself (e.g., sanctity) or because it is seen as possessing special worth to the particular person (e.g., the "glamorous" life of an airline stewardess). The school plays an important part in inculcating ideals into the students. A comparative study by Mencotti of Catholic students in non-Catholic schools and Catholic students in Catholic schools showed a far greater preference for religious ideals by the latter group.[98]

There are many ways in which the skillful teacher can so organize the learning situation as to promote effective inculcation of values:

[96] See Webster, *loc. cit.* Jacob's study concluded that, in general, very little change in a person's basic value structure occurs during his college career. Cf. Philip E. Jacob, *Changing Values in College.* (New Haven, Conn.: Hazen Foundation, 1957), pp. 55–56.

[97] W. Cody Wilson, "Value Differences between Public and Private School Graduates," *Journal of Educational Psychology,* L (October, 1959), p. 217.

[98] G. Mencotti, *The Relationship of Children's Ideals to the Degree of Their Formal Religious Education,* unpublished master's thesis, University of Detroit, Detroit, Mich., 1950, cited in Schneiders, *op. cit.,* p. 302.

1. Teach in order to change values. Conscious instruction in value adaptation is the most effective device for producing desirable value learnings. The teacher must be careful, however, not to force his values on the students, for this would be to violate the psychological integrity of the pupil. Similarly, the teacher in a public secondary school cannot constitutionally promulgate overtly a denominational value system.

2. Make the values purposeful and meaningful to the lives of the students here and now. Values denote an element of personal prizing, and such prizing can come about only if the values have a vital relation to the pupils' lives. Telling the students "You will understand the real value of this when you grow up" is no way to inculcate values.

3. Try to enable the students to establish a conforming relationship between their subjective and objective value systems. Too many students are "value schizophrenics" and this causes their great anxiety, which in turn hinders learning.

4. Realize the dynamism of values. Some teachers, particularly religion instructors, convey to the students the impression that all values are static. Certain values such as the intrinsic worth of Charity are indeed unchangeable, but most values are dynamic, e.g., the valuation of various levels of music. Catholic staticness in American cultural and intellectual life results in no small measure from the heavy emphasis in Catholic high schools on the staticness of values.

5. Clarify for the students the relationship between values and faith. Faith is not a blind thing; human beings need faith not because the mysteries are excessive darkness, but because they are excessive light. Faith must be shown as broadening values, not as restricting or narrowing them. Many values are based on faith, but these values must be shown not as irrational but rather as not fully graspable by the mind.

6. Teach for deep values, not superficial values. It is difficult to see how any thinking high school student can possibly want to deeply prize the Church after being exposed to an endless procession of saccharine hymns and marshmallowy holy pictures which are all too often substituted for beautiful chant and the great Christian works of art. These practices are conducive to superficial religious values at best.

7. The teacher should hold up ideals as examplars of value. Ideals are great motivational forces and will easily lead youths to live the values which these ideals represent or embody. Adolescence is a time of great ideals and the burning desire to live and carry out ideals, no matter what the sacrifice. Regrettably, too many teachers do not even attempt to use this great force. Catholic high school teachers quite commonly channel youths' burning ideals into pedestrian tasks, thus extinguishing them quickly. This is not infrequently due to the staleness of the teachers' ideals together with their own age-grown indolence and lethargy.

8. Ideals must be taught so that they conform with reality; e.g., a slow learner should not be encouraged to become a doctor. Similarly the fact that studies consistently show that many more girls than boys hold as ideals members of the opposite sex indicates that teachers should take special care to educate their female students for a feminine role.

9. Emotions should be judiciously used in value inculcation. Values have much too often degenerated into a cheap emotionalism, e.g., church is valuable because a person *feels good* after Mass; on the other hand, emotions have sometimes been eviscerated from values so that the latter are taught in a nonhuman disembodied manner.

Readiness. Readiness consists in sufficient prior preparation of the pupil so that he will react to a new learning situation in a positive manner. A majority of the educational and psychological authorities are in full agreement on the personality-situation factors which promote readiness. They include: mental maturity of the student, physical maturity of the student, needs and goals of the student, skills of the student, past experiences of the student, attitude of the student, emotional frame of the student, relevance of the material to the student, interest in the material by the student.[99] Readiness therefore consists in two elements: first, whether the student is able to learn (based on physical and psychological preparation and limitations) and second, whether he wants to learn (based on attitudes, interest, successful past experiences, and so forth). In Scholastic terminology, readiness is disposition. Hence it is a much broader term than its use in Thorndike's "laws of learning."

Readiness or disposition to learn is of extreme importance since the pupil cannot and/or will not learn if he is not ready to do so. This is because learning experiences must be structured around the nature of the learner, how he actually is in this concrete situation. In any concrete situation the student is either ready to learn or he is not ready. Hence many tests and observations both formal and informal have been devised to test the readiness of the student to learn new material, e.g., intelligence tests, achievement tests, personality tests, case conferences, anecdotal records, casual or systematic observations. The results of these tests are only general signs or indications of pupil readiness; e.g., an intelligence test examines for intelligence, not for readiness—readiness is only an inference from intelligence.

In addition to individual readiness, there is group readiness. The latter consists in the climate of the group as preparation to the new learning. If the atmosphere pervading the group is hostile, indolent, lethargic, indisposed—then the group as a group is not ready to learn. Since the teacher instructs not only individuals but individuals-within-a-group and also the group, he must attune himself to detecting group readiness or the lack of it.

[99] On readiness, see Cronbach, *op. cit.*, pp. 74–220; also "Readiness," *Encyclopedia of Educational Research*, 3d ed. (New York: Macmillan, 1960), p. 1082.

The teacher should bend every effort to promote pupil readiness before initiating the learning situation as such. This can best be done by taking into account and providing for the nine factors which foster readiness, listed above. The teacher who has initiated a learning situation, without first ascertaining the degree of readiness of his pupils, runs the risk of having his instructional efforts and effects seriously impaired. If these efforts do succeed, the success will be attributable to luck, not to pedagogical skill. But teaching should not be merely a matter of luck. Unfortunately, it often is.

CHAPTER VI THE SECONDARY SCHOOL CURRICULUM

The Meaning of Curriculum

In almost all secondary schools before the close of World War I the curriculum was considered to consist entirely of the particular courses of study which the student took, e.g., history, mathematics. In the onrush of progressive education which began to sweep over America in the 1920s and 1930s, schoolmen rejected this notion of curriculum as being excessively narrow since it excluded guidance functions, "cocurricular activities," and the like. In this postwar era, the curriculum was held to be every learning experience in which the learner was involved, wherever and whatever kind it might be, both in the school and out. This concept of the curriculum was criticized by almost all post-World War II secondary school educators as being too wide and all-embracing. Today most educators accept as the definition of the curriculum all areas of learning for which the school has responsibility.[1]

[1] For a fuller treatment of the development of the concept of the curriculum, see Lawrence A. Cremin, "The Curriculum Movement," in Alcorn and Lindley (eds.), *Issues in Curriculum Development.* (Yonkers, N.Y.: World, 1959), pp. 3–6.

There are a few contemporary public school educators, particularly the "community school" advocates, who still champion the progressive education notion of curriculum on the grounds that the school and community should be one and their functions interweave; hence the curriculum should be as wide as life itself. On the opposite side of the fence stand the ultratraditionalists (including many Catholics) who staunchly adhere to the old, restricted concept of the curriculum.[2] This view confuses formal instruction with curriculum. There is one curriculum which is subdivided into instructional (formal) and noninstructional (informal) areas. The formal curriculum consists of specific courses and closely supervised activities or experiences, e.g., history class, certain types of cocurricular activities, and guidance. The informal curriculum consists of unplanned and not closely supervised activities or experiences, e.g., chance teacher-student or student-student discussions in the corridors. Leighbody and Weinrich have succinctly compared the old and modern views of the curriculum from another angle:

> The modern concept of a curriculum is that a series of learning opportunities is planned and carried out by a teacher and pupils working together. This differs from an earlier view which regarded the curriculum [solely] as a body of preserved factual knowledge to be transmitted from the teacher to the pupils and mastered by them (at least temporarily) through memorization, recitation, and drill, and to be reproduced on the demand of the teacher.[3]

Elements of the Curriculum

Every curriculum, no matter what its base or type, has two essential elements, viz., content and structure. The content of the curriculum is the sum total of the learning experiences which it comprises. The structure consists in the form and arrangement of these learning experiences. The quality of both content and structure will profoundly affect the quality of the curriculum. There are three prevalent and contrasting views on the importance of curricular structure. One extreme, which is held by many progressive educators, holds with McNerney that "the curriculum is the central problem in any society that attempts to organize its educational program." [4] This view is based on an Experimentalist philosophy which holds that process generates its own purpose and content.

The opposite extreme, which is advocated by all traditionalists as

---

[2] See Arthur Bestor, *The Restoration of Learning.* (New York: Knopf, 1955).

[3] Gerald B. Leighbody and Ernest P. Weinrich, *Balancing the Roles in Decision Making,* 1961 Yearbook, Association for Supervision and Curriculum Development. (Washington: ASCD, 1961), p. 166.

[4] Chester T. McNerney, *The Curriculum.* (New York: McGraw-Hill, 1953), p. vii.

well as many Catholic educators, maintains that curricular structure is of little or no importance whatsoever in secondary education. Content alone is of value. Thus Smith, a Catholic philosopher who has interested himself in education, holds that the real issues in education are philosophical and theological.[5] He is of the opinion that Education is not a science and that, therefore, to speak of curricular structure as an entity separate from though related to content is to do violence to the curriculum. Smith considers the curriculum as the presentation by the teacher of the six disciplines which he holds are the basic teachable areas of knowledge. Curricular structure will automatically result from the systematic, step-by-step unfolding of the content of these disciplines in the classroom.

The moderates, which number many public school and alert Catholic educators, hold that *both* content and structure are important. Content is essential because it is precisely this which forms much of the material learned by the student. Structure is crucial because it enables the content to be optimally transformed into concrete learning experiences which are meaningful to the students, which take hold in their daily lives. The curriculum, by its very structure and organization, enables the students habitually to relate now, and throughout their lifetimes, all reality to the first principles, both theological and philosophical. The eleventh item on the Mooney Problem Check List, High School Form, viz., "curriculum and teaching procedures," illustrates the importance to the students of the structural elements of the curriculum.[6] Msgr. Gorham has observed that "efficiency of instruction and learning is influenced greatly by [curricular] organization [since] no single isolated learning experience has a very profound influence upon the learner; educational objectives are reached through the cumulative effort of many learning experiences." [7]

Bases of the Curriculum

The curriculum, both content and structure, has its roots sunk deep into theology, philosophy, psychology, and sociology. A particular curriculum is the form into which these four areas of wisdom all come together and fuse into a living reality; it is in the curriculum that theory is transformed into practice.

Theological Base. The curriculum of a secondary school, especially a Catholic secondary school, should be built around the answer to the

[5] Vincent Edward Smith, *The School Examined.* (Milwaukee: Bruce, 1960), p. vii.

[6] Oscar K. Buros (ed.), *The Fifth Mental Measurements Yearbook.* (Highland Park, N.J.: Gryphon, 1959), p. 89.

[7] Joseph A. Gorham, "Curriculum Construction and Organization," in McKeough, O. Praem. (ed.), *The Curriculum of the Catholic Secondary School.* (Washington, D.C.: Catholic University of America Press, 1949), p. 10.

second question in the catechism, viz., "God made me to know, love and serve Him in this world, and be happy with Him forever in the next." In the school situation, the primary emphasis must be placed upon the "know" element, in its widest sense as explained in Chapter II; however, the "love" and "serve" factors must not be forgotten in the curriculum lest the "know" be rendered sterile. The school must educate for use, not mere possession of content. This is crucial. Fr. Sloyan put it nicely when he remarked:

> . . . Since we are engaged in building up the living Body of Christ, "Does this city feel the impact of St. Mary, or Cathedral or De La Salle graduates? Is there a leaven of holiness at work in the inert mass of society in this area that can be attributed to the efforts of our own teaching staff [and curriculum] over the years? Is Christ reproduced in our graduates through the grace of the Holy Spirit so that men encounter His image everywhere they go in this city and county?" If not, or if only doubtfully, then a reexamination of religion [and its relation to the entire curriculum] in the religious school is in order.[8]

The presence of a strong and deep theological base is the chief reason for the potential superiority of the Catholic high school over the public secondary school as an institution transmitting and developing the truth, whole and entire—other aspects of the curriculum being equal of course. Nonetheless, Catholic high schools on the whole fail to fully capitalize on the incomparable advantages flowing from the theological base. This is one of the saddest aspects of Catholic secondary education in America. As Hutchins has remarked: "Catholic education is not Catholic enough."[9] Certainly flaccid doctrines and morals, on the one hand, and neo-Jansenism, on the other, should not be substituted for an integrated, pulsating, spiritualized curriculum.

Philosophical Base. The nature of man and indeed of all reality should be a pillar upon which the curricular edifice is built. Man is an integrated, natural-supernatural being, and hence it is impossible to build a humanistically oriented curriculum without a philosophical base. Educators who disagree on almost everything else at least agree on this point. All would concur with Wingo (an Experimentalist), who asserted that "the source of a unified theory [of the curriculum] will be found in a theory of knowledge."[10] Naturally Wingo would not agree with Catholic educators on the content and directions of epistemology or

---

[8] Gerard Sloyan, "The Function of Religion," in Sister Mary Janet, S.C. (ed.), *The Christian Foundation Program in the Catholic Secondary School.* (Washington, D.C.: Catholic University of America Press, 1952), p. 9.

[9] Quoted in E. J. Baumeister, "Whither High School Latin?" *Catholic Educational Review,* XLI (November, 1943), p. 524.

[10] G. Max Wingo, "A Theoretical Basis for the Activity Program," in Herrick and Tyler (eds.), *Toward Improved Curriculum Theory,* Supplementary Educational Monographs, no. 71. (Chicago: University of Chicago Press, 1950), p. 92.

philosophical psychology; indeed he charges Catholic educational philosophy (perhaps to some extent justifiedly) with having been in the past "a fertile field for uncontrolled speculation, logic chopping, and esoteric doctrine." [11] The significant thing, however, is everyone's awareness of the importance (and therefore necessity of existence) of an all-embracing educational philosophy which will permeate and color every area of the curriculum without exception.

Psychological Base. The curriculum arises out of human needs, wants, and problems. It hopes to meet and solve them in the most rational, educative, human—and also most divine—way possible. Thus the curriculum must be rooted in the particular psychical existences of the students it hopes to serve. It is not enough for the curriculum to be built on the essence "rationality" as philosophers educe it from human behavior; the curriculum must also rest on the concrete individual personalities of the students in whom the essence of rationality inheres. As Kilpatrick has observed, learning builds personality;[12] therefore, the curriculum, to be valid, must directly and meaningfully relate every learning experience to the student's total personality as it exists here and now. The curriculum of itself translates learning into personality development.

Sociological Base. Formal education, i.e., the curriculum in action, takes place in a particular social setting. Therefore, the curriculum must not be insensitive to, but rather built around, individual social settings, e.g., nation, community, classroom. Differences in social settings must reflect themselves in differences in curricula. The curriculum of a high school in a democratic society will be different from one in an autocratic society;[13] also, the curriculum in a public secondary school will be different from one in a Catholic high school. There will be different curricular emphases in all-boys, all-girls, and coeducational schools, since, as Davis remarks, "Girls appear to be influenced by social factors to a greater extent than do boys." [14] Certainly curricular emphasis should be on the contemporary, upon the particular student in a certain sociological framework integrating truth into himself so that he can act as a wise man.

[11] *Ibid.*

[12] William Heard Kilpatrick, "Life, Learning and Individuality," in Rugg (ed.), *Democracy and the Curriculum.* (New York: Appleton-Century, 1939), pp. 346–378. Learning here means the processes and outcomes of *all* learning, not merely intellectual learning. Cf. Chap. V.

[13] See Philip W. L. Cox, "The Community in an Industrial Society," in Douglass (ed.), *The High School Curriculum,* 2d ed. (New York: Ronald, 1956), pp. 72–86.

[14] Robert A. Davis, "Psychological Bases for Curriculum Planning," *ibid.*, p. 59. This point shows the deep relationship between the psychological and sociological bases of the curriculum.

These four bases, theological, philosophical, psychological, and sociological, should not only completely underlie the curriculum but interpenetrate it in every way. The result will be a thoroughly homogenized curriculum.

The Good Curriculum

The good curriculum is one which carries out and implements the school's general and specific aims in a unified manner. In other words, the good curriculum embodies not only the four bases listed above, but also the specific content learning and other outcomes which the school hopes to imbue in its students. The characteristics of a good curriculum are that it:

1. Is unified
2. Is flexible
3. Provides for the effective realization in depth and breadth of all the school's goals
4. Maintains a proper balance among these goals not only in themselves but in relation to each pupil's needs
5. Deepens the pupils in truth and truths
6. Inculcates attitudes based on truth and love
7. Furnishes a continuous stream of learning experiences, both intellectual (e.g., rational skills, specific items of information, transferable generalizations or universals) and nonintellectual (e.g., habits, certain skills)
8. Promotes the integration of the student with the material to be learned and/or the activity to be experienced
9. Synthesizes in its structure both theoretical and practical knowledge together with their applications
10. Facilitates moral and religious growth and development
11. Makes provision for personality development
12. Provides for individual differences
13. Utilizes all available learning resources
14. Develops guidance mindedness among staff and students
15. Incorporates guidance practices and facilities
16. Is planned cooperatively by teachers, pupils, supervisors, administrators, board of education, parents, and lay public

Building the Curriculum

Curriculum building is a composite process whereby the bases, content, and structure are organized and integrated. In the professional literature, curriculum building is often called educational engineering, a term originated by Herbert A. Thelan and popularized by the Progressive Education Association.

In general, curriculum experts, whatever their philosophical viewpoint, agree explicitly or implicitly that the school's educational program should have a functional approach. This functionalism means that the curriculum will promote the acquisition of knowledge, attitudes, and the like, which will aid the pupil in making wise decisions concerning his own life problems, concerning his mode of acting. Therefore the curriculum should operate around an axis of decision making, with the chief areas of wisdom acting as vital tributaries flowing into this mainstream of decision making. This mainstream will in turn irrigate and soak all areas of the curriculum. In this way man's intellectual, cultural, and spiritual resources, far from being lost will be marshaled more effectively and contribute to the pupil's development more than would otherwise be the case. The intellect is greatly stressed in this approach, not for itself, but as an engine for decision making, which is a common core of life. From a Catholic point of view, this is the proper way for the curriculum to put the intellect to use for man's proximate and final ends. Both ends are, of course, intimately related and indeed inseparable.

Because high school education is either preparatory or terminal, the curriculum must be flexibly built with both goals in mind. Nonetheless, as Sister Mary Janet, S.C., has noted, "First consideration in curriculum building should be given to common learnings since high schools are schools of general education." [15] Special terminally oriented parts of the curriculum should by all means be built, but not in isolation. General education must be the unifying and integrating core.

STRUCTURAL ELEMENTS OF THE CURRICULUM

There are six separate but related elements which together as a unit constitute the structure of the curriculum. All must be present in the good curriculum; all must be internally and externally sound, as well as in dynamic equilibrium. The six elements are design, scope, sequence, continuity, balance or range, integration.

Design

Curricular design is "the pattern or framework or structural organization used in selecting, planning, and carrying forward educational experiences in the school. Design is thus the plan that teachers follow in providing learning activities." [16] Thus design is the manner in which the learning experiences are organized and structured as a whole. Design

[15] Sister Mary Janet, S.C., "The Christian Foundation," in Sister Mary Janet (ed.), *op. cit.*, p. 6.

[16] J. Galen Saylor and William M. Alexander, *Curriculum Planning for Better Teaching and Learning.* (New York: Rinehart, 1954), p. 245.

affects not so much the content itself, but rather the way in which the content is presented to the learner.

Saylor and Alexander remark that a curricular design is important because it: "(1) indicates the elements that should receive attention in the matter of planning the curriculum and the interrelationship of these elements in the process of curricular development; (2) serves as a method for determining the selection and organization of the learning experiences provided by the school and; (3) indicates the role of teachers, students and others concerned in the process of curriculum planning." [17] A curricular design is crucial since it implements the goals of the school in a flowing and interwoven form.

The criterion of any curricular design is the degree to which it fulfills the previously enumerated characteristics of a good curriculum.

The two chief types or categories of curricular design are the fragmented pattern and the unified pattern. The characteristics of each design are contrasted in the list below.

FRAGMENTED	UNIFIED
1. Every subject is taught as a separate, distinct unit, in isolation from every other.	1. Subject-matter lines are broken down—the problem under study unifies the subjects, forming an intersubject or interdisciplinary nucleus.
2. Subjects are taught in separate time intervals or periods.	2. Short, rigid periods are eliminated, and large, flexible blocks of time are instituted to facilitate problem solving in depth.
3. Subjects are usually taught in a rigid manner as prescribed by the syllabus, with the teacher and pupil having little voice in planning.	3. There is considerable provision for pupil and teacher planning, modifying, and discussing the specific problem areas; however, there is some conformity in similar grades or achievement levels because the problem areas or situations usually have been broadly determined in the syllabus.
4. Teaching is done completely in a total class group situation.	4. Besides total class groups, small-group work and individual study are utilized in the learning situation.
5. The instructional procedure is relatively inflexible, with recitation the customary method.	5. Instructional procedures are quite flexible, employing not only discussions but panels, seminars, projects, small-group research activities, field trips, and the like.

[17] *Ibid.*, p. 248.

FRAGMENTED	UNIFIED
6. Guidance is almost solely the task of the guidance counselor and homeroom teacher, with subject teachers concerned almost exclusively with teaching their individual subjects.	6. Guidance is an integral and important part of every teacher's work, both inside the classroom and out of it.
7. Content material is brought into the lesson in a machinelike, logically organized fashion, according to a predetermined syllabus rather than according to pupil needs, interests, and abilities.	7. Content material is brought in as the problem areas demand it.

In general, the traditionalists favor the fragmented design, while most modern educators, including some forward-looking Catholic schoolmen, advocate the unified pattern. Traditionalists often criticize the moderns for neglecting content. This charge is unwarranted because, as Bellack remarks, "All shades of educational opinion recognize, implicitly or explicitly, the central importance of content or subject matter in curriculum theory and practice. . . . Instruction is always about 'something,' whether that something be carried in the matrix of first-hand personal experience or whether it be imbedded in the systematically and theoretically organized subject matter of the disciplines." [18] Even John Dewey, who can hardly be numbered among the traditionalists, has said that "experiencing has no existence apart from the subject matter experienced." [19] Flaum, an ultraprogressive, has stated that in a unified curriculum "learning fields are used interchangeably as they are needed in order to bring the civilized learning and concepts of living to bear upon the functional living of our own day." [20] The disagreement, then, is not over content but rather *how* the content should be selected and presented to the learner.

Gardner and his associates list the following guidelines for selection of content:

(1) content cannot be kept in a deep-freeze, [i.e.,] the curriculum can no longer be seen as bodies of subject matter, accumulated from the past, organized, "frozen" into courses of study, to be thawed out and consumed at each grade level; (2) learning is a lifetime process, [i.e.,] no

[18] Arno A. Bellack, "Selection and Organization of Curriculum Content: An Analysis," *What Shall the High Schools Teach?* 1956 Yearbook, Association for Supervision and Curriculum Development. (Washington: ASCD, 1956), p. 97.

[19] John Dewey, *Philosophy and Civilization.* (New York: Putnam, 1931), p. 261.

[20] Laurence S. Flaum, *The Activity High School.* (New York: Harper, 1953), p. 29.

one can learn during . . . the years of his schooling all that he will need to know, for as Margaret Mead says, "No one will live all his life in the world into which he was born; and no one will die in the world in which he worked in his maturity"; (3) both teachers and learners must select curriculum content, [i.e.,] current headlines almost daily point up the fact that youth are more up-to-date and expert in certain fields than are their teachers; (4) all concerned with content selection must be students of the current scene, [i.e., good content selection] requires not only seeing realistically *what is* but also seeing this in the perspective of *what has been.* The past is thus interwoven in the present; (5) decision making concerning changes in content must include "built-in" provisions for preparing teachers, i.e., teachers, whose area of competence should be the learning process, can no longer be regarded as authoritative sources of information—nor should they be made to feel self-consciously ignorant in this day when experts are available at the turn of a switch; (6) all decision making [concerning content selection] is tentative.[21]

From what has been said, the unified curricular design would appear clearly superior to the fragmented pattern. From a Catholic point of view the traditional fragmented approach is inadequate from almost every aspect. Certainly it does violence to the essential Catholic doctrine that the spiritual interpenetrates everything, that all reality is homogenized. As Msgr. Goebel has said concerning the importance of the unified design: "If we are to prepare youth adequately for life in two worlds, then it is necessary that we integrate his life so completely that there will be unity of his school and post-school life in all the essentials of Christian social living. To do this effectively calls for an understanding of the work we have before us, namely that we are educating not solely for academic achievement, but as well for life in society and God's eternal Kingdom." [22] Not only public secondary schools but Catholic high schools should attempt to discard their fragmented designs and introduce a unified pattern. An effort in this direction has been made in Catholic elementary schools which use the syllabus series, *Guiding Growth in Christian Social Living,* prepared by Sister Mary Joan, O.P., and Sister Mary Nona, O.P., under the auspices of the Commission on American Citizenship of Catholic University.[23] The

[21] Gordon Gardner et al., "Balance and the Selection of Content," *Balance in the Curriculum,* 1961 Yearbook, Association for Supervision and Curriculum Development. (Washington: ASCD, 1961), pp. 124–125.

[22] Edmund J. Goebel, "Building the Integrated Curriculum in the Diocese," in Sister Mary Janet, S.C. (ed.), *Building the Integrated Curriculum.* (Washington, D.C.: Catholic University of America Press, 1953), pp. 60–61.

[23] See Sister Mary Joan, O.P., and Sister Mary Nona, O.P., *Guiding Growth in Christian Social Living.* (Washington, D.C.: Catholic University of America Press, 1944–1946), vols. I–III.

same idea, carried through even further, represents a needed break-through in Catholic secondary education.

The most common fragmented design is the traditional subject-centered curriculum while the most popular unified curricula include the total student-centered design, the persistent life situations (PLS) pattern, and the Core approach.

Subject-centered Design. The subject-centered curriculum utilizes bodies of information classified into intrinsically systematic branches of knowledge as both the organizing force in and center of learning, e.g., the subject of English literature is learned in chronological fashion. The subject-centered curriculum is thus a series of individualized intellectual specializations, the sum total of which is supposed to give a picture of the totality of reality. The necessity of mastering the material is given prior consideration over whether it is meaningful to the pupils or whether they wish to learn it. If possible, however, the teacher will use motivational techniques to render this material purposeful to the student.

A subject may be defined as an organized body or field of knowledge, e.g., history, biology, French. The origin of the subject-centered curriculum[24] may be traced back to the trivium and quadrivium of ancient Greek and Roman schools.

It has been often asserted that the subject-centered design has the following advantages:

1. It is hallowed by tradition and use throughout the centuries.

2. It is the type of curriculum upon which the American system of education is based. If it were eliminated a disruption in the present procedures concerning college admissions, units of credit, and so on would ensue.

3. It is the design used by most contemporary high school teachers.

4. Subjects are in themselves an inherently logical and highly systematic way of learning and assimilating new knowledge.

5. It leaves no gaps in learning; e.g., all the facts in history will be known by studying it chronologically rather than in terms of problem areas.

6. It is the most efficient of all the designs, since it does not involve the wasting of time with something outside itself, e.g., wasting valuable class time relating historical events to modern problems.

7. It is the easiest design for the teacher to use since it involves a single discipline and hence does not demand additional knowledge necessary to relate this discipline to the rest of reality.

8. It has proved an excellent vehicle for developing the students' mental abilities.

---

[24] The term "subject-centered curriculum" is preferred to "subject curriculum" because all designs use subjects, but only one makes these subjects its axis.

9. Evaluating, marking, and reporting are much easier in the subject-centered pattern than in any other design. The material is clearly in evidence, and the teacher need just test for it.

The subject-centered design has the following disadvantages:

1. Tradition by itself is no proof of the worth of the subject-centered curriculum. Dead traditions encrust life and smother it. Thus the question is not whether this design is traditional, but whether it is living, vibrant, and doing its job. Evidence, both internal and external, points to the contrary.

2. The present subject-centered curriculum on which American high school education is based is not worth retaining if a better one can be erected. Indications point to the fact that a better curriculum can be built.

3. It has been said that most contemporary high school teachers have their mechanical foot in the airplane, their pedagogical foot in the oxcart. All too many teachers use the easiest form of curriculum design, the subject-centered approach, because it involves less effort than the unified curricula. However, ease of attainment is no solid criterion of worth, else hell would be more valuable than heaven.

4. The subject-centered design does violence to reality by compartmentalizing knowledge. Certainly knowledge is not a series of disconnected subjects or ideas. While it is true that human knowledge involves the abstractive process resulting in isolated elements, nonetheless, human understanding requires that these abstracted isolated elements be placed back into the heart of a unified reality. The subject-centered curriculum fails to do this. The curriculum itself should synthesize reality; it should not place the total burden of integration upon the student. If the curriculum is disintegrated, can the school legitimately expect the students all by themselves to put together the pieces? If the students can achieve integration amidst a disintegrated curriculum, perhaps they should run the schools, and the teachers and curriculum experts should take the courses.[25]

5. The subject-centered curriculum causes greater gaps in retention than do other designs. The pupil may have been taught the material in such a way that few gaps existed, but what he remembers will be islands. Learning can never be divorced from forgetting, and forgetting is selective. There will be greater gaps in the retention of material meaningless or unrelated to the student than in the retention of material learned in a unified, purposeful manner.

6. The subject-centered design is at bottom an inefficient organization of knowledge since it usually fails to present information to the student in such a way that he will use it in his own life.

7. This curricular pattern fosters lopsided teacher training. Teachers are not really competent if they are trained primarily in the particular subject

[25] See John L. McKenzie, S.J., "Theology in Jesuit Education," *Thought*, XXXIV (Fall, 1959), pp. 347–357.

which they are teaching without constant, interpenetrable reference to other disciplines.

8. This design fails to develop critical thinking to any marked degree. Memorization and retention of information are one thing, critical thinking quite another.

9. The subject-centered curriculum has practically made testing a god. It presupposes that content material is the only validly learned experience, neglecting the acquisition of the more important attitudes, generalizations, and process outcomes which thus far have resisted adequate testing.

10. The subject-centered pattern is weak in psychological organization. Students learn not areas of knowledge isolated from reality but rather knowledge intimately related to their concrete condition, whether it is to solve a present problem or to attain heaven.

11. The subject-centered curriculum all too often neglects meaningfulness of material in terms of the pupil's present and future life. As Spaulding has noted, "A major reason for young people's lack of success in meeting out-of-school problems is that secondary schools give them insufficient chance to master important abilities which the out-of-school world will require of them." [26]

12. This type of design demands class periods too short in length to permit any serious probing of problems via discussions or seminars.

13. The subject-centered approach prevents the teacher from fostering certain desired outcomes and by-products, e.g., positively promoting mental health.

14. This design usually fails to put into practice the Thomistic concept of the learner as the primary active agent in the learning process; it transfers this role to the teacher.

Whitehead compared the subject-centered curriculum to a table of contents, with each item existing in isolation from the others, waiting to be put together in a unified whole.[27] The curriculum *of itself* must put the various areas of knowledge into a coherent integrated unit. Certainly the subject-centered design has failed to achieve such unification, with the result that too many pupils, especially in public secondary schools, have been dumped into modern academic or general courses which are so watered down from the original that their existence is a *de facto* admission that the subject-centered approach is not adequate for all the students, but only for the bright or normal students.[28]

Because of the criticisms of the subject-centered curriculum by its

[26] Francis T. Spaulding, *High School and Life.* (New York: McGraw-Hill, 1938), p. 149.

[27] Alfred North Whitehead, *The Aims of Education and Other Essays.* (New York: Macmillan, 1929), p. 11.

[28] See, for example, "General Students Find Jobs Scarce," *The New York Times,* June 30, 1961, p. 29.

opponents and because of the recognition of its limitations by its advocates, serious efforts have been made to improve this type of curricular design. These efforts, which have centered around broadening the exclusive watertight subject compartmentalizations, have resulted in two modified subject-centered curricula, namely, the correlated and the fused designs.

In the correlated form, certain selected subjects are brought into close relation to each other. Each subject, however, retains its own identity. For example, the teaching of American history can be correlated with instruction in American literature. The students are often taught by the same teacher to ensure better correlation. The correlated curriculum, while attempting to compensate to some extent for the lack of integration caused by subject-matter lines, still fails to provide for thorough integration, since it usually ignores a common purpose or problem. Instead it contents itself with horizontal connections between existing subjects.

In the fused (often called "broad fields") form, certain selected subjects are combined into a new whole, built either around a central integrative theme or around some thread of development. For example, a fused or broad fields course entitled "Our American Heritage" would be the central theme for a somewhat meshed, chronological, developmental study of American history, literature, music, art, and ideas. The fused approach, then, is basically what is known as a survey course and is popular not only on the high school level but also in colleges. The integration at which the fused curriculum aims is usually thwarted in actual classroom procedure, because quite commonly the disciplines comprising the fusion are taught as a series of separate subjects rather than as an integrated unit.

Total Student-centered Design. The total student-centered curriculum is one which is completely and wholly rooted in the learner as he is here and now—his changing needs, purposes, emotions. Emphasis, sometimes exclusively so, is placed on the dynamic aspects of the pupil's personality. Subject matter is brought into the lesson when, how, and if the learner himself feels he needs it to solve some problem of immediate urgency to him. The total student-centered design is based on the philosophy of Experimentalism, which in the words of one of its exponents, Flaum, holds that "experiences, like the rest of one's environment are not constant or fixed." [29] This type of design consists not in predetermined subject-matter areas but rather in centers of pupil interests and needs, which, of course, are always in flux.[30] The origin

[29] Flaum, *op. cit.*, p. 14.
[30] On this point, see Lois Coffey Mossman, *The Activity Concept.* (New York: Macmillan, 1938).

of the total student-centered pattern may be traced to John Dewey's Laboratory School at the University of Chicago in the 1890s. In the early 1900s, J. L. Merriam's Laboratory School at the University of Missouri continued this work. The publication of William Heard Kilpatrick's *The Project Method* in 1918, together with a growing interest in Herbert Spencer's educational theories, signaled the great interest in the total student-centered approach which characterized the 1920s and 1930s.[31]

It has often been asserted that the total student-centered approach has the following advantages:

1. It is a unified, not a fragmented design.

2. It places the primacy of school activities where it belongs, in the student.

3. It has a great deal of psychological soundness. The pupil is not regarded as a person to be somehow fitted and squeezed into a watertight subject-matter compartment, but rather as one into whom the subject material will come. This has Thomistic roots, for to the Angelic Doctor learning is according to the mode of the learner, not according to the thing to be learned.

4. It is functional.

5. It makes learning preeminently purposeful to the learners.

6. It places responsibility for learning where it belongs, in the students.

7. It does much to relieve the pupils' stresses and strains.

8. It promotes the attainment of many desired outcomes of the school program, e.g., personality development.

9. It eliminates the necessity for a separate extracurricular or cocurricular structure, since all student interests and needs are taken care of directly in and through the curriculum itself.

The total student-centered design has the following disadvantages:

1. It is based on a defective philosophical appraisal of reality. Not all things change, are in constant flux. There are some absolutes.

2. It places too much emphasis on the student. To give the primary role in the school to the pupil does not imply giving him the total role. Since it is the pupil who is in the state of ignorance, he must give himself over, to some degree at least, to a person (the teacher) who possesses what he does not and what he consciously or subconsciously aspires to, viz., the truth. In stressing the primacy of the student, the importance of the teacher should never be disvalued.

3. It is not completely psychologically sound, since it overstresses process per se while neglecting the directions of this process. A sense of direction-

[31] The term "total student-centered curriculum" is preferred to "activity curriculum" or "experience curriculum" because all designs use, to some extent at least, activities and experiences, while only one makes these its complete basis and method.

lessness on the part of the student results not only in poor learning but often is injurious to mental health.

4. It is not completely functional, since of itself it fails to provide an essential element of functioning, viz., the material to be acted upon in the process of functioning. In the operation of the total student-centered curriculum the student may or may not absorb the material. Too much is left to chance, and chance is not a friend of function.

5. The total student-centered curriculum causes the pupil to become imprisoned by the narrowness of his own purposes. Because he is young and relatively inexperienced, the range of his purposes is limited. He needs the teacher and other pupils to open for him the gates of new purposes so he can behold new vistas.

6. It places excessive responsibility on the learners. The fact that each pupil inherits the stain of Original Sin will often dispose him to shirk work, if he is not properly guided and supervised.

7. It often aggravates pupils' stresses and strains. Overpermissiveness causes greater anxieties in students than is commonly believed. Psychologists recognize the importance of some (but not too much) conflict and thwarting in the learning process.

8. It leaves to chance and often neglects two of the more important outcomes of the school program, namely, a high degree of proficiency in intellectual and attitudinal learnings.

9. The quest for truth should, in an overall way at least, be methodically planned rather than left to fortuitousness or luck. Too little emphasis is placed on positive organization for learning. Pupils are too immature to plan an entire educational program for themselves. It is difficult enough for adolescents to plan things about which they know; but to plan their whole education, which by its nature implies they have no knowledge (but are seeking it), is at the outset putting them into a hopeless, hence frustrating, position.

10. The total student-centered curriculum results in large gaps in pupil knowledge. The pupil will have studied only those problems of interest to him, those he felt he needed to investigate.

11. It can never really attain its purposes, since the school can never provide for all or even for a majority of a pupil's needs or interests. Thus, for example, if a student is interested in Russian culture, the best he can do is to read a book or see a movie, vicarious experiences both. The school cannot send him personally to Kiev or Kazakstan to gratify his interests.

12. It tends to lead to egotism, for undue stress is placed on the individual, too little on the group. It must not be forgotten that every student is a social being.

13. It tends to concentrate solely on the present, the here and now, while neglecting the past and future. Man without a knowledge of his past becomes intellectually crippled. Similarly, the future must be planned for.

14. It fails to enable the teacher to distinguish between pupil expressions of needs, interests, and problems which are genuine and those which are the result of caprice or whims.

15. The total student-centered curriculum makes it almost impossible to have any administration of the school, since no one can predict where the pupils' interests will lead.

16. This type of curriculum design makes it virtually impossible to carry out a unified educational program from elementary school through college, because varying pupil interests and needs cause each student to undergo a different education.

17. It necessitates abandonment of present school buildings, since the pupils' interests and needs will take them all over the community and its hinterlands during school time. This problem is further heightened in those high schools whose students own automobiles.

Persistent Life Situations Design. The persistent life situations curriculum is rooted in those continuing situations in which every individual finds himself in a particular society at every stage of his development. The three major areas of these persistent life situations, together with their chief subareas, are (*1*) growth in individual capacities, having four subareas including health, intellectual power, aesthetic expression and appreciation, and moral choices; (*2*) growth in social participation, having three subareas including person-to-person relationships, group membership, and intergroup relationships; (*3*) growth in ability to deal with environmental factors and forces, having three subareas including natural phenomena, technological resources, and economic-social-political structures and forces. For each of these three major areas and chief subareas, a master list of recurring persistent life situations has been devised as a curricular guide.

The persistent life situations design received its impetus from the book *Developing a Curriculum for Modern Living* by Florence B. Stratemeyer and associates. It was first published in 1947 and revised ten years later.[32] This work was the first to propose this type of curriculum and to provide guidelines for its implementation. However, because it has a very limited number of adherents, the PLS has not been introduced into the nation's secondary schools except in an extremely few isolated instances.

The persistent life situations curriculum is based exclusively on the pupils' immediate concerns and needs as they fall within the purview of the persistent life situations matrix. Thus it is related to the total student-centered approach since it substitutes persistent life situations

[32] Florence B. Stratemeyer et al., *Developing a Curriculum for Modern Living*, rev. ed. (New York: Bureau of Publications, Teachers College, Columbia University, 1957).

for indeterminate centers of needs and interests. The relative advantages and disadvantages of the persistent life situations design are therefore much the same as those of the total student-centered curriculum.

Core Design. The Core curriculum is one which centers around interdisciplinary problems of both eternal and personal concern. Subject material is brought into the learning situation as it is needed to solve the problem under consideration, without respect to precise subject-matter boundaries. Thus, for example, a study of the problem of social injustice might bring in such diverse subject areas as history of the American Negro, music of the slaves, literature on man's inhumanity to man, religious writings on the question, and so forth.

While most writers concur on the interdisciplinary aspect of Core, many disagree as to its basis. Spears mentions that it centers on the "general development of the students";[33] Smith, Stanley, and Shores hold that it focuses on social values and effective social living;[34] Caswell asserts that it is rooted in a student's "significant personal and social problems." [35] Saylor and Alexander even go so far as to declare that at base the Core, strictly speaking, is not a true curricular design but rather an "administrative method for scheduling and offering major aspects of the program of general education." [36] Most authors, however, affirm that Core is a true curricular design.

There is also disagreement as to the exact scope of the Core curriculum. Many educators maintain that it includes only areas of general education, excluding specialized education. However, other schoolmen observe that Core can be used for any subject or group of subjects at any level of education right up to postgraduate university seminars. Faunce and Bossing resolve this conflict neatly by distinguishing between "Core program" and "Core curriculum." The Core program is that area of general education taught as a Core unit, while the Core curriculum consists of the entire curriculum of general and specialized education "utilizing consistently the same basic principles of learning, teaching methods and problem organization." [37]

The Core design stresses the interdisciplinary approach to learning, an approach which is currently in favor in the curricula of certain advanced colleges. This interdisciplinary method serves as a stimulator

[33] Harold Spears, *The High School for Today.* (New York: American Book, 1950), p. 103.

[34] B. Othanel Smith, William O. Stanley, and J. Harlan Shores, *Fundamentals of Curriculum Development*, rev. ed. (Yonkers, N.Y.: 1957), pp. 314–319.

[35] Hollis L. Caswell, "Curriculum Proposals for the Future," *The American High School*, Eighth Yearbook of the John Dewey Society. (New York: JDS, 1946), p. 143.

[36] Saylor and Alexander, *op. cit.*, p. 321.

[37] Roland C. Faunce and Nelson L. Bossing, *Developing the Core Curriculum*, 2d ed. (Englewood Cliffs, N.J.: Prentice-Hall, 1958), p. 58.

which welds the various subjects into a living, meaningful, organic whole. Longer blocks of time are a feature of Core classes. This is especially important for Catholic high schools which might wish to embark on Core, for deep interpenetration of religion with various subjects cannot occur in a single forty-five-minute period.

The Core first began to be seriously considered in the late 1920s and 1930s by American educators who were attempting to combine the advantages of the traditional curricular design with the total student-centered pattern. However, the Core received its concrete impetus during the Eight-Year Study when participating secondary schools were attempting to make the curriculum serve the needs of youth and still provide a rich intellectual education. At first the method consisted in breaking down subject barriers. Then subjects were correlated, e.g., American literature with American history. As the Eight-Year Study progressed, a central theme approach for the unification of subject matter was evolved, using the problem method. Some schools went even further, eliminating subject-matter lines completely.

Wright has identified four various Core curricula in existence in American secondary schools.[38] The first two are called "Core types" because they only represent steps toward Core; the other two are termed "total Core" because they represent a true Core, a total integration of subjects.

"Core type," variety I, is in reality the correlated design, while "Core type," variety II, is the fused or broad fields curriculum, both treated earlier in this chapter. Since the correlated and fused approaches are modifications of the subject-centered design, they cannot be considered true Core curricula. At best, they can be thought of as preludes to a Core design.

In "total Core," variety I, the curriculum consists of a number of broad, preplanned problems relating to some central unifying theme. The problems selected for study represent an integration of the two focal problem areas, viz., those with which the students themselves are concerned and those which society, the school, the teacher (and in Catholic institutions, the Church) think the pupils should deal with. The various subject information and skills are brought into the learning situation to the degree and in the manner which will best facilitate the solution of the problem. This represents a reversal from the traditional curriculum practice of manufacturing problems to fit in with the exist-

[38] Grace S. Wright, Core Curriculum Development: Problems and Practices, Bulletin 1952, no. 5. (Washington: Government Printing Office, 1955), pp. 7–8. Alberty, in his famous classification of Core designs, lists six different types. See Harold Alberty, Reorganizing the High-School Curriculum, rev. ed. (New York: Macmillan, 1953), pp. 169–191.

ing subject matter. For example, the course "Problems of Democracy," when made a Core class, would deal with such pressing concerns as juvenile responsibility in the nation and the community, the history and ethics of American party politics, literary and movie censorship in a democracy, the difficulty of an artist in a democracy, and so forth. In a Catholic high school the moral and religious element which underlies these problems would continuously be interwoven in the entire lesson. Members of the class may or may not have a choice from among the problem areas under study; however, they may choose specific activities within the problem areas.

In "total Core," variety II, the curriculum is much the same as variety I with the large exception that the study problems are not predetermined; i.e., both pupils and teachers are completely free to work on whatever problem they might choose. This involves considerable teacher-pupil planning, since it is this planning which results in the selection of problems to be studied. Sometimes this variety becomes an "on-the-spot curriculum," i.e., one which is planned at the moment the pupil's problems arise, and not before. "Total Core," variety II, cannot be regarded as a genuine Core since it partakes too much of the elements of the total student-centered design. Therefore the only true Core is "total Core," variety I. Henceforward in this book the use of the term "Core" will be synonymous with this variety.

The Core design has the following advantages:

1. It is a unified rather than a fragmented curriculum.

2. It merges logical learning with sound psychological principles; i.e., the students learn material not only logically but in a psychologically desirable manner.

3. It enables students to see the unity of knowledge by appreciating reality in the only true manner, from an interdisciplinary approach. All subjects are really taught today as interrelated; e.g., biology is really a combination of botany, zoology, physiology, etc. However, the Core does not stop with partial integration but achieves total meshing.

4. It links theory with action by showing the inner relevance of what is learned in the classroom to real life. This is crucial, particularly in Catholic high schools.

5. It uses problem-solving techniques, thus promoting a high level of critical thinking.

6. It deals with problems which are meaningful, significant, and purposeful to the learners.

7. It enables the teacher to better provide for the guidance needs of the students. Long blocks of time permit the teacher to obtain a more intimate knowledge of the students and a deeper understanding of their personal

and social problems. Guidance and learning go on hand in hand rather than separately.

8. It allows the pupils to easily attain desired broad educational outcomes, e.g., personality development.

9. It permits the teacher to use flexible methods, thus helping him to make greater provision for individual differences, situations, and exigencies.

10. Evidence from a number of studies has shown that it is the optimum curricular design for all-around general education.

The conclusions of carefully conducted research investigations of the learning outcomes derived from Core as compared with subject-centered classes have almost consistently revealed the superiority of Core. The results of the Eight-Year Study showed that students from schools with a Core curriculum performed better in college than did matched students from schools utilizing the traditional design.[39] Wrightstone's report of the study comparing students in experimental Core classes with matched pupils from the traditional curriculum in New York City high schools discovered that Core pupils were superior to a statistically significant degree in the sciences and mathematics in ability to recall facts and ability to transfer and apply generalizations from science to nonscience fields; Core pupils were superior to a statistically significant degree in recall and interpreting facts in English literature and working skills in English composition; Core pupils were superior to a statistically significant degree in English and science activities requiring personal initiative and social cooperation; Core pupils were superior to a statistically significant degree in a battery of physical fitness tests; Core pupils were superior, but not to a statistically significant degree, in recalling social studies facts; Core pupils were superior, but not to a statistically significant degree, in an art judgment test; Core pupils were superior, but not to a statistically significant degree in Latin prose translation, Latin vocabulary, and in the whole battery of Latin tests; traditional pupils were superior, but not to a statistically significant degree, in Latin grammar tests.[40] Other investigations, most notably that of Capehart and his associates,[41] demonstrate that students in Core classes made significantly greater gains in expression, self-confidence, study skills, critical thinking, and civic attitudes. These, of course, are important outcomes of the curriculum

[39] See Wilford Aiken, *The Story of the Eight-Year Study*. (New York: Harper, 1942).

[40] J. Wayne Wrightstone, *Appraisal of Experimental High School Practices*. (New York: Teachers College, Columbia University, 1936), pp. 186–189.

[41] Bertis E. Capehart et al., "An Objective Evaluation of the Core Program," *School Review*, LX (February, 1952), pp. 84–89.

and should not be neglected. Leonard summed up the situation when he stated that in quite a few school systems a problem-oriented curriculum, well thought out, planned, and evaluated, has resulted not only in meaningful learning but also in a good grasp of subject matter.[42] The various New York City studies of schools in which Core has been introduced show that the experimental teachers overwhelmingly favor retaining the Core design.[43]

The disadvantages of the Core design are:

1. There is a lack of qualified teachers. A Core class necessitates a very intelligent and pedagogically skillful teacher. This is due to the extensive fund of interdisciplinary knowledge which the Core teacher must possess. Furthermore, the highly flexible and dynamic teaching techniques which the Core design requires for its successful implementation demand that the teacher also possess a marked degree of pedagogical proficiency. Owing to economic and related factors, the teaching profession is experiencing great difficulty in recruiting highly intelligent college graduates who also have those personality traits requisite to superior pedagogical skill. This shortage of highly competent teacher personnel is perhaps the most serious obstacle to Core.

2. Few non-Catholic and no Catholic colleges as yet have special professional courses on how to teach Core. As a result, schools wishing to introduce Core must provide some other preservice or in-service training program to prepare their teachers for Core. This problem will be solved only when colleges begin on a broad front to introduce professional course work in Core principles and methods.

3. It takes a great deal of teacher effort to plan and implement a Core class. Many teachers are unwilling or perhaps unable to devote the time and effort necessary.

4. There is an insufficiency in the number and quality of curriculum guides and teaching materials for use in Core.

5. Core is valuable primarily in a program of general education; therefore, it is often not the best design when more specialized learnings are required, such as by those vocationally oriented pupils for whom the high school is a terminal institution.

6. The introduction of Core into a school or school system requires careful planning and implementation on the part of staff, students, and parents— it cannot be introduced all at once. Romine has suggested that before the introduction of a Core design is undertaken, "There should be on the

[42] J. Paul Leonard, *Developing the Secondary School Curriculum*, rev. ed. (New York: Rinehart, 1953), pp. 289–293.

[43] See Joseph Justman, *An Evaluation of the Core Programs in Junior High Schools. II. The Expressed Attitudes of the Teachers toward the Core Curriculum.* (New York: Board of Education of New York City, 1957).

faculty at least several teachers who are interested in the Core and willing to embark upon it." [44]

7. The hostility of many parents and the community in general to Core often serves as an effective block to its introduction. While this hostility is usually based on a lack of knowledge, it represents hostility nonetheless.

8. The present educational organization in America militates against (although certainly does not preclude) Core.

Core is really the most natural and true to life of the curricular designs. In everyday life when a person discusses things with others (in serious conversations, not in idle talk or gossip), he does not confine his dialogue to one single topic selected by some distant and shadowy figure. Rather the topic of conversation is selected by the persons themselves from among problems of mutual concern, and the discussion, while retaining one central theme, cuts across many subject lines in an integrative manner; e.g., a back porch discussion of censorship will draw from religion, history, literature, good taste, government, and so forth. Aristotle has said that art imitates nature; the teaching and curricular arts should take this dictum to heart.

Catholic high schools should be among the strongest exponents of the Core because the adequate learning of religion would seem to demand this type of design. Only by a thoroughly integrated curricular pattern will religion be seen not as a separate discipline (hence occupying a separate compartment in one's life), but rather as the leaven of living, in intimate relation to all human concerns and problems. Despite this, Catholic high schools have clung to the subject-centered curriculum. As Sister Mary Janet, S.C., has so tellingly stated, "Catholic educators have said too often 'Religion is the core' or 'Theology is the core' without examining what it should really mean to have them as the core." [45] Theology and philosophy should contribute to the integration of the high school curriculum not as speculative disciplines but as flowing truths, circulating realities homogenized with individual and social problems of the pupils and the world they live in. Thus Sister Mary Annetta, P.B.V.M., notes that all too often the curricula of Catholic high schools are like Ezechiel's plain of dry bones. She proposes an integrative unit such as Christian Family Living to make these curricular dry bones come alive with the plasma of integration and vitality. Her subdesign represents an excellent example of how a wealth of subject matter can

[44] Stephen A. Romine, *Building the High School Curriculum.* (New York: Ronald, 1954), p. 358.

[45] Sister Mary Janet, S.C., "Christian Principles as Integrating Elements," in Sister Mary Janet, S.C. (ed.), *The Integration of the Catholic Secondary School Curriculum.* (Washington, D.C.: Catholic University of America Press, 1951), p. 8.

be coalesced into one vibrant Core type of design.[46] Such an integrative subdesign could well serve as the precursor to the introduction of a full-blown Core curriculum.

Cooperative planning for effective learning is a feature of Core. As Henry has remarked:

The nature of general education is such that subject matter must be extensively preplanned. . . . A school is a school because here experiences with ideas are ordered, and because the pupil is educated not only because he perceives order but because he can make it his own. The hitch is that this order may be qualitatively low. It can be raised only to the extent that the pupil's intelligence creates this order, and that he be permitted to experience all the kinds of ways men have ordered ideas to live by.[47]

The curriculum, its structure and content, is the school's chief means of helping the pupils' intelligence find and even create this order.

Of course, planning is different at the various grade levels and among the different integrated problem areas. Electives admit of more teacher-pupil planning than do required classes. Planning should not become too lengthy or too detailed else the whole lesson and/or term be consumed with planning, leaving little time for the actual investigation of the problem area.

What is the present balance sheet on Core throughout the schools of the nation? Harmer gives six signs indicating that it is moving toward an untimely demise: (1) the prestigious Conant Reports with emphasis heavily on college preparatory secondary school programs; (2) the fact that 86 per cent of all Core programs in 1958 (according to a U.S. Office of Education study) were simply combinations of English and social studies; (3) the fact that "adolescent-needs" Cores and the unstructured Core programs have decreased in number in the nation's secondary schools; (4) less emphasis on Core discussions in meetings of the NEA, the Association for Supervision and Curriculum Development (ASCD), and the American Association of School Administrators (AASA); (5) the decreasing number of articles in recent years on Core in the *Education Index*; (6) the fact that only a few colleges have established professional courses on how to teach Core classes.

Notwithstanding, Harmer gives the following reasons for concluding that Core is neither dead nor dying: (1) a steadfast group of educational theorists who still advocate Core; (2) accumulation of evidence of the success of Core curricula and subsequent refutations

[46] Sister Mary Annetta, P.B.V.M., "Christian Family Living as the Element of Integration," in *ibid.*, pp. 26–50.

[47] George H. Henry, "Foundations of General Education in the High School," *What Shall the High School Teach? op. cit.*, p. 163.

that it fails to teach sufficient subject matter; (3) growth of publications, such as *Core Teacher*. All in all, Harmer concludes that Core has become a permanent fixture in the American educational edifice.[48]

Despite the superiority of Core, the vast majority of public secondary schools and almost all Catholic high schools still base their curricular framework on a strict, compartmentalized subject-centered design. Some schools use the correlated or fused approach, while a few have total student-centered curricula. However, a considerable number of forward-looking public secondary schools are utilizing Core. This is especially true of the junior high school level, but there are also senior high schools which have a Core design.

Scope

Curricular scope is "the breadth, variety and types of educational experiences that are to be provided pupils as they progress through the school program. Scope represents the latitudinal axis for selecting school experiences." [49] It concerns itself with the problem, "What shall be included in the curriculum?" Should French be taught for two or three years or not at all? Scope tries to solve the dilemma "Art is long and [school] time is short."

In the subject-centered design, the scope of the content is selected beforehand by a group of curriculum experts on the basis of various disciplines to be offered, and this choice is implemented by the teacher. In the total student-centered pattern, the scope of the content is based on the choices dictated by the immediate felt needs of the students. In the persistent life situations approach, the broad scope of the content is decided upon by a group of experts and is based on developmental stages of the pupils, while the limited or classroom scope is determined by the immediate felt needs of the pupils. In the Core, the scope of the content is usually selected beforehand by a cooperative group of experts and is based on a series of important problems which mankind has continuously faced and which are relevant to the students' lives; the scope of these problem areas is modified to a greater or less degree by each class.

The curricular scope should include the presentation of alternative solutions to problems. This is particularly important in Catholic high schools. No problem can really be settled in a student's mind unless he knows the alternative solutions. To present only one solution to a problem, such as lying, freedom, divorce, and so on, does not solve the problem, but rather reinforces ignorance. If only one solution exists,

[48] Earl W. Harmer, "Le Mort de Core," *Education Digest,* XXVI (February, 1961), pp. 40–41.
[49] Saylor and Alexander, *op. cit.,* p. 248.

how can there be a problem? All sides of the question must be presented so that the students may learn not only why a problem exists, but also why one solution is correct and the others incorrect. Teaching by way of alternatives is true education; teaching only one solution is dictatorial indoctrination. St. Thomas taught by way of alternatives, and he has been declared the Patron of Schools. A scope which presents alternatives will do much to foster understanding of the problems, errors, and sins of ourselves and others—surely this is one of the highest aims of education. A student who snappily flicks off problems and solutions of others as "false" without trying to understand the inner dynamics of these solutions is not receiving a true education.

Sequence

Sequence is the order in which educational experiences are developed with and presented to the students. Sequence is the answer to "when" in curriculum development and implementation.

In the subject-centered design, the sequence flows from the inherent logic and organization of the content material itself and/or the decision of the curriculum commission as to the order in which the subjects are to be taught; e.g., in American history, the Revolutionary era would be followed by the Federalist period. In the total student-centered pattern the sequence results from the shifting concerns of the learners rather than from any objective content material; e.g., today the students may be interested in the problem of censorship, tomorrow in religious discrimination, and so forth. In the persistent life situations approach, the sequence resides in the persistent life situations themselves, i.e., the particular developmental stage of the situation in which each pupil finds himself. For example, the persistent life situation of "Using Physical Forces" will in the ninth grade probably be focused on the physics underlying a bicycle, while in senior year the focus will shift to the mechanical principles of the automobile. In the Core, the sequence is determined both by the nature of the problem itself and by the way in which the teacher and pupils choose to investigate this problem; e.g., Catholic students investigating religious discrimination in America might wish first to learn the basic Christian principles involved, then move to a study of the history of religious groups in America, after which they will proceed to an examination of current discriminatory practices in education, the arts, and the like.

Continuity

Msgr. Gorham has defined continuity as "the progressive reiteration of learning situations which demand the exercise of major learning products, such as skills, knowledge and appreciations basically necessary for the attainment of an important [educational] objective." [50] Fr. McKeough, O. Praem., has called it "the vertical reiteration of major curriculum elements." [51] Because it emphasizes the unity and relatedness of the content material, continuity is closely related to sequence.[52] Hence, continuity must reside not only in the content material itself but also in the way in which the student apprehends the material and how he relates it to his own life.

In the subject-centered design, continuity resides in the addition of intrinsically and logically related concepts to one another in accordance with laws inherent in each discipline and/or arbitrarily extrinsic to the material; e.g., the Revolutionary and Jeffersonian periods have successive chronological continuity. In the total student-centered pattern, there is no continuity, since what is studied depends on the direction and course of the pupils' ever-shifting concerns. Certainly there would be no continuity if yesterday the pupils investigated censorship, tomorrow polio. In the persistent life situations approach, overall continuity resides in each recurring developmental situation. The shifting concerns of the students, however, may or may not preclude continuity in the individual lessons; e.g., there would be no continuity if yesterday the pupils studied a situation dealing with aesthetic appreciation, tomorrow a situation dealing with group membership in the United Nations. In the Core, continuity resides in the direction of the problem itself and the manner in which the teachers and pupils go about solving the problem; e.g., the problem of war can proceed from an investigation of the principles of a just war, to a history of American wars, to an investigation of Gandhian principles, to a consideration of the Christian doctrine of charity.

Balance

Balance is the range of educational experiences which the student encounters in the learning situation—experiences designed to help him grow intellectually, spiritually, physically, emotionally, and socially.

In the subject-centered design, balance comes only from the teacher, textbook, and whatever other reading material the students may be required to know. In the total student-centered pattern, balance flows only from the learner's awareness and experience of his own felt needs. In the persistent life situations approach, balance proceeds only from

[50] Gorham, op. cit., p. 11.

[51] McKeough, op. cit., p. 3.

[52] However, as Msgr. Gorham (op. cit., p. 11) has observed, "Though related to continuity, sequence goes beyond it. Sequence emphasizes the importance of having each successive experience not only build upon the preceding one, but also go more deeply into the subject or field studied."

the immediate and persistent life situations themselves as they are erupting in the student's life both every day and at his different developmental stages. In the Core, balance comes from the range of the problem area itself, plus the insights and contributions of both teacher and pupils as the problem is probed.

Integration

"Integration refers to the coordination of learnings resulting from experiences in several separate areas." [53] Msgr. Goebel states that curricular integration is "a process which leads to the perfection of the individual and to social progress through the elimination of conflicts within the individual, within society and between the individual and society." [54] Integration, then, is the synthesizing of curricular structural elements, content material, and teaching methods into a unified learning situation.

There are two kinds of integration, viz., horizontal and vertical. Horizontal integration is the synthesis of the various curricular elements in the school. Vertical integration is the unification of the various school levels into one continuous learning experience, e.g., coordinating ninth and tenth grades, or meshing the curricular gears of elementary, secondary, and higher education. Vertical integration does not eliminate grade achievement or school levels, but rather enables them to work as a unit so that a student's education will be a continuum rather than a series of fragmented and often unrelated learning experiences.

Integration presupposes a principle of integration. As Sister Mary Janet, S.C., has observed, "If integration is really to take place it must depend on an agent outside and above" [55] the content materials themselves. In the public secondary school the principle of integration, if any exists, is useful living in a democracy. However, this principle is regrettably quite often neglected in the actual learning situation. In Catholic high schools the principle of integration is Catholic doctrine, coordinated with philosophical, sociological, and psychological principles which so intertwine that Christian belief, content material, and personality are effectively integrated. This coordination, this intertwining, is imperative for fruitful, vibrant curricular integration because, to paraphrase Melvin, subject matter scatters, life integrates.[56]

Catholic educators hold three shades of opinion on horizontal integration, particularly when such integration concerns the meshing of religion with other subjects. The first position, advocated by educators

[53] Gorham, op. cit., p. 11.

[54] Goebel, op. cit., p. 59.

[55] Sister Mary Janet, "The Christian Foundation," op. cit., p. 6.

[56] A. Gordon Melvin, Activated Curriculum. (New York: John Day, 1939), p. 25.

such as Sister M. Theodore Kelleher, R.S.M., believes that "it is unethical to bring religion into the teaching of any subject other than religion." [57] The second position maintains that while integration should take place, it should be unplanned and incidental rather than consciously worked for by pupils and teachers. The third position, held explicitly or implicitly by most Catholic schoolmen, declares that the more religion is integrated with other subjects, the richer will be both religion and the other disciplines. Religion cannot exist apart from life, and neither can life or any part of it exist apart from religion. Ours is a universe in which the natural and supernatural are forever meshed; the two can never be separated except by artificial mental constructs. Catholic scholars agree that one of the major reasons theology has ceased to be a vibrant discipline in the past two hundred years is that it has been eviscerated from life, particularly from the integrative life with other areas of knowledge in the classroom.[58] Of course, such integration does not mean that all subjects merely become thinly disguised religion courses. This state of affairs, which sometimes happened in Catholic schools of former days, violates the integrity of both religion and the other disciplines. Such a procedure is not integration; it is disintegration into a mass of undigested sameness.

The importance of the integrative principle of moral and spiritual values can be more readily grasped when it is remembered that such integration has characterized American private and public secondary education since the founding of the nation. It is not a curricular "newcomer," as Gwynn erroneously asserts.[59] Interest in such integration by public school educators is evinced by such relatively recent works as the Educational Policies Commission's report, *Moral and Spiritual Values in the Public Schools*,[60] and the American Council on Education's *Religion and Public Education.*[61]

In the Catholic high school, religion must pervade the curriculum as a mixed integrator; i.e., it must be mingled throughout the whole school program. Bishop Noll stressed this point when he observed that all too many Catholic teachers operate on "the false assumption that religious instruction imparted in the school will of itself produce spiritu-

[57] From a detailed conversation on this topic between the author and Sister M. Theodore Kelleher, R.S.M.

[58] On this point, see Msgr. Philip Hughes, *A Popular History of the Catholic Church.* (Garden City, N.Y.: Image Books, Doubleday, 1954), p. 226.

[59] J. Minor Gwynn, *Curricular Principles and Social Trends*, 3d ed. (New York: Macmillan, 1960), p. 393.

[60] Educational Policies Commission, *Moral and Spiritual Values in the Public Schools.* (Washington: NEA, 1951).

[61] American Council on Education, *Religion and Public Education.* (Washington: ACE, 1945).

ality." [62] Bishop Noll went on to note that spirituality must be constantly applied to a youth's life as he lives it here and now. As Fr. Danielou, S.J., has pointed out, the word "today" is of the very essence of Christianity. If the student is to integrate religion into his adult life, he must learn to do it in his adolescent life. The curriculum of itself should be a prime means to promote in the students this integrative facility.

Many and varied curricular focal points for the integration of religion with the other disciplines can be located in the Catholic high school. Mother Emmanuel Athill, C.S.A., has consistently maintained that the liturgical year is a good integrative core around which to build the curriculum, or at least part of it.[63] Dialogue Mass, altar facing the people, and other ancient liturgical practices recently revived can be woven into such a curriculum.[64]

In the subject-centered design, there is no real integration. The pupil rather than the curriculum is supposed to provide the integration. Indeed the absence of an integrative structure is one of the weakest points of the subject-centered curriculum. In the total student-centered pattern, the major centers of pupil interest integrate the subject matter studied. In the persistent life situations approach both the immediate concerns as well as the persistent situations are the integrators, with the further advantage that the latter tend to integrate the former. In the Core, the problem under investigation serves as the integrator for all the subject matter from the diverse disciplines needed to solve the problem. Pupil interest and experience cement this integration. Thus, for example, the problem of censorship in a democracy will integrate religion, literature, art, history, and political science into one unified structural pattern.

IMPROVING THE CURRICULUM

Times change, communities change, teachers change, needs change. If the school is to educate its pupils both for today and tomorrow, its curriculum must change, to some extent at least. Knowledge grows,

[62] John Francis Noll, *From Friend to Friend.* (Huntington, Ind.: Our Sunday Visitor Press, n.d.), quoted in Roland Simonitsch, "Religion and Integration," in Sister Mary Janet, S.C. (ed.), *Building the Integrated Curriculum.* (Washington, D.C.: Catholic University of America Press, 1953), p. 19.

[63] Mother Emmanuel Athill, C.S.A., *Teaching Liturgy in the Schools.* (Notre Dame, Ind.: Fides, 1958); see also Abbé Michonneau, *Revolution in a City Parish.* (Westminster, Md.: Newman, 1950), pp. 25–46.

[64] There is a wealth of literature on this topic, all of which provides the alert Catholic educator with rich curricular opportunities. See, for example, Angelus De Marco, O.F.M., *Rome and the Vernacular.* (Westminster, Md.: Newman, 1961).

techniques improve, and the curriculum must also progress. Only God can create a perfect instrument; the fabrications of finite man can always be improved, made better. Anyone who denies this explicitly or implicitly plays God. Hence secondary school educators, public and Catholic, must always be seeking new ways to perfect the curriculum.

The school's curriculum results from many things, ranging from objectives (e.g., teaching for intelligent decision making rather than molding for blind obedience) to plant (e.g., mobility in the furniture so that group discussions may be facilitated) to class size (e.g., the possibilities for a seminar approach in a class of 50 students). Consequently, a change in the curriculum necessitates a change in some or perhaps even all of the structural or content elements. All too often, the total curricular change resides in a decision to change textbooks. This type of curricular change illustrates that the curriculum in many schools unhappily resides solely in the textbooks and also that the notion of the curriculum and methods for improving it are improperly understood in many educational institutions.

The greatest enemies of curricular improvement are the attitudes of defensiveness and formalism which permeate the educational thinking of the various groups who should be concerned. As O'Dea has pointed out, these unfortunate states of mind seem to be especially characteristic of Catholics;[65] however, public school educators, while paying lip service to the importance of curricular change, in actual practice effect little in the way of progress. A flexible mentality is needed both to see the importance of and to effect a change in the curricular structure. Educators must realize that the curriculum is based on past choice, decisions on what courses to offer, when, how, and so forth. New circumstances, new insights, all cry out for changes in the curricular pattern. The school is not true to itself if it fails to heed these cries. What some great nineteenth-century schoolman did or what Mother Foundress innovated proved excellent in days gone by, but times have changed, and the living waters of tradition have perhaps been allowed to become stagnant. Were that great nineteenth-century educator or Mother Foundress alive today, they would doubtless be among the first to recognize the need for revision.

Procedures in Curricular Revision

Curricular revision does not just happen; it is cooperatively planned and organized for. There are nine steps involved in the undertaking of curricular revision.

[65] Thomas F. O'Dea, *American Catholic Dilemma: An Inquiry into the Intellectual Life.* (New York: Sheed and Ward, 1958), pp. 80–92.

1. The school's philosophical, psychological, sociological, and, in Catholic institutions, theological principles should be formed and enunciated.

2. The broad educational objectives which flow from these principles should be formulated. This step is important since it involves that transposition of basic principles to educational goals so necessary for a rich and deeply rooted curricular program. These objectives must be coupled with suggestions for their implementation in the classroom, for as Sister Mary Janet, S.C., has said, "The objectives of Catholic education are stated well enough, but their implications with respect to curriculum planning and teaching are ignored, at least in part." [66] The same can be said in large measure of public secondary schools.

3. The school's existing curriculum must be examined both in overall structure as well as in detail.

4. The existing curriculum should be evaluated objectively and honestly in the light of steps 1 and 2. As Sister Mary Janet, S.C., has observed, all too often the curricula in Catholic high schools (and also in public secondary schools) are chosen not "in relation to stated objectives, but tend to follow closely whatever has been taught by predecessors or what appears in the catalogues of long established schools." [67] The evaluating procedure should ruthlessly cut away such subjective standards and strive for an objective curricular overview. Evaluation is too often the weakest link in the chain of curriculum revision.

5. The program of revision should be planned both comprehensively and in sufficient detail to render it useful. This planning should be cooperative; it should involve everyone concerned with the curriculum.

6. The teachers who will implement and execute the new curriculum must be trained in the revised principles and methods. Provision must be made sometime during the school day or before the school year for this in-service training.

7. The revised curriculum must be injected into the school program replacing the old curriculum.

8. The new program and its results must be evaluated critically and cooperatively in the light of steps 1 and 2. If the new curriculum is found to be poorer than the old one, then it must be either discarded or substantially revised. Not everything which has replaced the old is superior to it, but the spirit of replacement must be alive, else progress will wither. The formulation of check lists, such as the one devised by Knudsen for evaluating not only the basic philosophy underlying the curriculum change, but also the planning, organization, and development of this curricular change, can prove both helpful and revealing.[68]

[66] Sister Mary Janet, "The Christian Foundation," *op. cit.*, p. 4.
[67] *Ibid.*
[68] See Charles W. Knudsen, "Evaluating Programs of Curriculum Development," in Harap (ed.), *The Changing Curriculum.* (New York: Appleton-Century, 1937), pp. 167–177.

9. The decision must be made cooperatively by all involved whether to retain, alter, or discard the present curriculum.

As Ahrens has stated, "An organization for curriculum development should provide for and encourage experimentation and research." [69] Curricular revision must be accompanied by educational research, both action and traditional. Action research in education is that which is engaged in by the person or group undertaking the activity which the research is investigating, e.g., a twelfth-grade science teacher researching into new methods of physics teaching. Action research attempts to translate the findings immediately into practice.[70] Traditional research is that which is undertaken by a person not engaged in the activity in which he is researching, e.g., a curriculum expert researching educational literature on the methods of teaching Physics. This type of research is not so much concerned with immediacy in the application of its findings. Educational research must go on everywhere—in pilot schools, in curriculum specialists' libraries, in every teacher's classroom. From these sources flow the wellsprings of curricular revision.

Personnel Involved in Curricular Revision

Curricular revision, like curriculum building, is a cooperative group process involving everyone concerned with the curriculum. It should never become the autocratic dictate of one person, be he principal or superintendent or pastor. Every group has a distinct role to play and a special contribution to make. There are at least nine different roles in curricular revision, namely, those of the pupil, teacher, building principal, superintendent, curriculum specialist, subject-matter or problem-area specialist, board of education, outside educational groups, and lay public.

The pupil should have an important role in curriculum revision because, after all, in him reside the object and purpose of the curriculum. The curriculum must not only be rooted in the learner, but be an expression of his aspirations as well.

Teachers should exercise the leading role in curriculum improvement, for it is they more than anyone else who bring the curriculum to life in the school. Curricular revision will come to nought if teachers are not integrally taken into the planning, for they will have neither the knowledge nor the desire to implement the new curriculum in their classrooms. Regrettably, in both public and Catholic high schools, the administration has usually impressed on the teachers that their only job

[69] Maurice R. Ahrens, "Organizing the Curriculum," in Douglass (ed.), *Education for Life Adjustment*. (New York: Ronald, 1950), p. 297.

[70] See Stephen M. Corey, *Action Research to Improve School Practices*. (New York: Bureau of Publications, Teachers College, Columbia University, 1953), pp. 9–16.

is to teach; curriculum planning is outside their province. Such an autocratic atmosphere has led to educational torpor in many schools. Furthermore, a heavy teaching load is an obstacle to curricular revision since such a situation saps the staff's time as well as vitality. Among the ways in which teachers can organize themselves for cooperative study of the curriculum are school department meetings, system-wide department meetings, separate curricular interest groups within the school, separate curricular interest groups within the system, and integrated combined meetings of department and separate curricular interest groups. The community life of Religious who teach in Catholic high schools is a potential engine for fruitful staff discussions centering around curriculum change, if the Religious and their Superior wish it to be so.[71]

The building principal, as instructional leader of the school, should have a vital role in curricular revision. Indeed it has often happened that in actual practice he has been the key figure in initiating curricular improvement. This is less than desirable, since it smacks of autocracy. Nevertheless, as instructional leader, the building principal has the responsibility to be a curricular energizer. In some situations, as Spears has noted, state syllabi and curriculum commissions have "tended to relieve the principal of any feeling he may have had in supplying the initiative for instructional reorganization." [72] Curricular revision is a cooperative thing, and when one group uses its functions excessively the other members suffer, and the whole process thereby becomes the poorer.

The superintendent, the chief school officer, should be concerned not only with administrative detail, but even more important, with providing impetus to and mobilizing resources for curricular improvement on all fronts. As Miel has observed, educational officers have an obligation to generate leadership for curriculum improvement; indeed such generation is one true measure of an administrator's leadership.[73]

The curriculum specialist plays an important role in ascertaining whether the curricular structure itself needs overhauling or repair. He coordinates the work of the various subject-matter specialists.

The subject-matter or problem-area specialist is necessary, because as a scholar in a particular discipline or interdisciplinary field, he will have insights into methods of improving the way in which content is taught to the students. He is thus a prime resource. Curricular and

[71] For an example of how such a program was implemented, see Sister M. Borromeo, O.S.F., "Integration through Cooperative Family Planning," in Sister Mary Janet (ed.), *The Integration of the Catholic Secondary School Curriculum, op. cit.,* pp. 51–64.

[72] Harold Spears, *The Emerging High-School Curriculum.* (New York: American Book, 1940), p. 33.

[73] Alice Miel, *Changing the Curriculum.* (New York: Appleton-Century-Crofts, 1946), pp. 178–180.

subject or problem-area specialists should work closely and harmoniously since every good curriculum demands the smooth meshing of structure and content.

The board of education, as a legal arm of the state and the citizens, has the right and obligation to have a prominent voice in curricular revision. The board should allocate funds both for the periodic study of existing curricula and for the establishment of pilot classes to try out newly proposed curricular changes.

Outside educational groups can be of great assistance in the work of curricular revision. Educational associations like the National Education Association and the National Association of Secondary-School Principals can be used to aid and even initiate programs of curricular revision. To a limited extent the Secondary School Department of the National Catholic Educational Association is willing to help Catholic high schools on curriculum improvement. The NCEA is generally more interested in defending the rights of Catholic education and outlining broad goals for it than in sending out experts to assist schools in curriculum planning.

Parents and citizens have a right to a voice in curricular revision because more than any other single group, theirs is the *prime* responsibility for the education of their children. Besides, it is the parent who is financing the school whether it be public or Catholic. Parents are beginning to play some role in curricular investigation; as Msgr. Goebel remarked, parent participation in curricular planning is "an important step forward in education." [74] Yet unfortunately, in most public secondary schools the administration attempts to render the parents' role to that of an innocuous discussion group about trivial matters. In most Catholic high schools, the parents' role is regarded almost wholly that of raising funds, with complete delegation of curricular responsibility as well as other affairs of importance to the Religious administration. Parents must come to realize their crucial role in planning the education of their offspring. This is no privilege; it is a natural right. The school should use more than Parent-Teacher Association meetings to ascertain the wishes of the parents. Polls, questionnaires, and interviews are three excellent devices for canvassing parental opinion on what *parents* wish the goals and outcomes of the school to be. (Once these broad objectives are learned, the school people can provide the proper structure.) The school can also hold "unmet needs conferences," where parents can systematically discuss with educators those educational objectives which they feel are important and which the school is neglecting.[75] A permanent school-community council should be established to serve as a coordinator

[74] Edmund J. Goebel, *op. cit.*, pp. 63–64.

[75] See Joseph O. Loretan and John W. Polley, *Approach to Public Participation.* (New York: Metropolitan School Study Council, 1951).

for cooperative planning by parents and citizens.[76] Catholic high schools should take the lead in involving parents in the curriculum planning as well as in other school matters, that is, if these schools wish to take seriously Pope Pius XI's words that the family has "priority of nature and therefore of rights" in education.[77] In Catholic high schools the preeminence of the Church in education is also stressed by Pope Pius XI; however, it must never be forgotten that the parents are as much a part of the Church as the Religious and clerical administration.

Curriculum change is simultaneously social change among the participants.[78] As Benne and Muntyan have noted, human relations is usually a neglected factor in curricular change.[79] Anderson feels that some time should be spent in the study of group dynamics and group-process skills before the staff and other persons begin their work of curricular revision.[80] This is especially true in schools where autocratic leadership has held sway, where staff, consultants, and parents have never been previously permitted to participate in decision making.

Curriculum Guides

A curriculum guide is an educational resource, usually printed, which details broad objectives, desired outcomes, and suggested procedures for developing general and specific classroom experiences. These guides are quite important to the teacher, for from them he draws his overall pedagogical approach as well as many of the actual practices he uses in each learning situation. This is especially true for that segment of the teaching profession which is unable or unwilling to exercise sufficient individual instructional leadership.

A good curriculum guide should perform the following services:

1. Carefully implement the school's philosophical-psychological-sociological (and in Catholic institutions, theological) framework in a concrete educational program.

2. Ensure that the learning outcomes are the ones desired in terms of the school's philosophical-psychological-sociological (and theological) base.

3. Keep in constant equilibrium the various curricular factors such as scope and sequence.

[76] See Romine, op. cit., pp. 449–450.

[77] Pope Pius XI, Christian Education of Youth. (Washington: NCWC, 1936), p. 6.

[78] See Smith, Stanley, and Shores, op. cit., pp. 438–440.

[79] Kenneth D. Benne and Bodizar Muntyan, "Human Relations: A Neglected Factor," in Benne and Muntyan (eds.), Human Relations and Curriculum Change. (New York: Dryden, 1951), pp. 2–15.

[80] Vernon E. Anderson, Principles and Procedures of Curriculum Improvement. (New York: Ronald, 1956), pp. 39–61.

4. Stimulate the teacher so that he will want to initiate his own procedures within the curricular framework rather than rely exclusively on the guide.

5. Provide a wide latitude of instructional suggestions so that every teacher's individual personality can find adequate expression in some stated or implied procedure.

6. Afford a wealth of built-in sources and suggestions for methods and materials to arouse pupil interest, excitement, imagination, and intellect. Catholic curricular guides should be shot through with a Christocentric outlook.

There are seven types of curriculum guides commonly in use in American secondary schools:[81] (1) general guides to overall curriculum concepts, e.g., how the curriculum implements the school's educational philosophy; (2) general guides to design, scope, sequence, continuity, balance, and integration, e.g., how to plan a Core curriculum; (3) guides to the development of learning experiences in various areas or at different levels of maturity, e.g., suggestions about what specific learning outcome should be sought day by day in sophomore English class; (4) inclusive guides to the entire secondary school program, e.g., listing together side by side learning experiences and outcomes of all the subject and problem areas of the entire curriculum; (5) guides for different subject areas, e.g., suggestions for desirable learning activities and outcomes for each subject at each different grade level; (6) guides to Core programs, e.g., suggestions for desirable learning activities and outcomes for the various Core problem areas; (7) guides to special instructional areas which of themselves cut across subject-matter lines, e.g., suggestions for desirable learning activities and outcomes in citizenship, safety, aesthetics, and so forth.

THE ACTIVITIES PROGRAM

Student activities is that area of the school's educational program which takes place outside the normal classroom situation. Usually no Carnegie unit credit is given to a student for participation in these activities.

Formerly student activities were called "extracurricular activities," and later, when their true function became clearer, "cocurricular activities." Contemporary educators prefer the designation "student activities" because it does not imply in any way that these experiences are outside the *direct* scope of the school's educational goals or program.

In American secondary schools it was the students who were responsible for the introduction of the activities program into the school's

[81] See Saylor and Alexander, *op. cit.*, pp. 381–383.

work. Since it was the pupils who initiated and often sustained interest in them, the administrations of different schools have accepted student activities with mixed reactions. What Treacy says of Catholic high schools in this regard is also true to some extent of public secondary schools: "In some Catholic high schools, so-called extracurricular activities are merely tolerated; in some they are permitted but limited and supervised carefully; in some they are considered an essential part of the program, definitely related to the objectives of the school." [82]

The cardinal purpose of student activities is to extend the curriculum and, indeed, the school's educational endeavors outside of formal class time, e.g., departmental clubs, musical activities, special interest clubs. As Fretwell has noted, "Wherever possible, extra-curricular activities should grow out of curricular activities and return to enrich them." [83] Despite the clarity of this objective, public and Catholic high schools still fail seriously in properly organizing and evaluating student activities. Trump's study of 901 public high schools showed that there was a need for a more exact formulation of the nature and function of the activities program and for a continuous evaluation of this program.[84] The doctoral dissertation of Fr. Edward F. Riley, C.M., revealed that while Catholic high school administrators agreed that the activities program must contribute to the objectives of Catholic education, "few had seriously thought how this was to be done"; furthermore "in no school had there been attempted any evaluation of the extracurricular program in the light of the specific objectives it was supposed to achieve." [85]

Criteria

The criteria for any student activities are fourfold: worthwhileness, availability of a good sponsor, sufficient time, enough students. If an activity does not possess these four qualifications it should be neither initiated nor retained. Certainly activities should not be scheduled solely because they were offered the previous year. They should grow out of present pupil interests. Indeed it is these pupil interests which should be the core and the *raison d'être* of an activity, especially in the traditional high schools built around a subject-centered curricular design.

[82] John P. Treacy, "Issues in Catholic Secondary Education," *Catholic School Journal*, LX (September, 1960), p. 47.

[83] Elbert K. Fretwell, Extra-Curricular Activities in Secondary Schools. (Boston: Houghton Mifflin, 1931), p. 2.

[84] J. Lloyd Trump, *High School Extracurriculum Activities*. (Chicago: University of Chicago Press, 1944), pp. 171–173.

[85] Edward F. Riley, C.M., *Extracurricular Activities Programs in the Catholic High Schools*. Abstract. (Washington, D.C.: Catholic University of America Press, 1954), p. 2.

To satisfy their interests and special skills is precisely why students elect a particular activity.

To ensure an activities program based on pupil interests, the school should, every spring, poll the students on what activities they would like to join the following fall. Those activities which enough students want should be offered; the others, no matter how hallowed by tradition, discontinued. Provision should be made on the poll sheet for unlisted activities which the students might wish, e.g., an outer space club.

More than any other phase of the school's program, student activities should be characterized by a pervading democratic orientation. No student should be forced to join an activity, even if the teacher thinks he or she has some particular talent. The operations of the activity, built as it is on pupil interests, should feature the sponsor working *with* the students rather than *on* them. Pupils should be able to speak their minds instead of being subjected to the rigid classroom structure characteristic of many high schools. Nothing kills pupil interest more than an autocratic atmosphere.[86] Students should come to know the sponsor not as a totalitarian teacher but as a person. Such a situation permits the realization of a major outcome of the activities program, namely, promoting guidance opportunities. The activities program, properly used, is an excellent channel toward better pupil-teacher relationships, and it is from such relationships and the resultant mutual understanding that good guidance inevitably flows.

Tompkins has noted that student activities, properly organized and developed, tend to furnish a major basis for the students' school spirit.[87] However, as Patty has remarked, this added spirit is often used by the school to "anesthetize students to curriculum defects," [88] especially in subject-centered designs which usually make little provision for pupil interests and hence often fail to generate much enthusiasm.

Developing pupil creativity is an important goal of the school, and the activities program is a valuable medium for nurturing this creativity. Based and organized as it is almost exclusively on student interests, the activities program is a built-in engine for creative experiences. However, creativity can flourish only when the pupils' interests are given relatively free rein and where the sponsor atmosphere is permissive. In education, as in politics, creativity has always withered in a totalitarian climate.

[86] See Frederick C. Gruber and Thomas B. Beatty, *Secondary School Activities*. (New York: McGraw-Hill, 1954), pp. 17–29.

[87] Ellsworth Tompkins, *Extraclass Activities for All Pupils*, U.S. Office of Education. (Washington: Government Printing Office, 1950), p. 4.

[88] W. W. Patty, "What Basis for School Activities?" *School Activities* (January, 1945), p. 163.

Eligibility and Scheduling

For various reasons schools have chosen to restrict membership in student activities. This is done by setting up eligibility requirements. Eligibility systems are generally of two types, scholastic and point. A scholastic system is one which demands that the student maintain a specified school mark or average of marks in order to qualify for an activity. The point system assigns a different number of points to every curricular subject and student activity, with no student being able to take more than a given number of points per semester. The number of points allotted each subject is determined by the hours the average student devotes to this activity; e.g., the student newspaper would normally be assigned more points than participation in the chess club.[89]

Eligibility requirements should be used with the greatest discretion, for often they present an insurmountable obstacle to the very students the activities can help the most. Activities, like other aspects of the school's program, must be for *all* the students. Certainly there can be little justification for scholastic requirements. McKown has cited six separate studies, all of which indicate that there is no evidence to support the assumption that participation in the activities program affects school marks adversely.[90]

Schools normally schedule their activities program in one of three ways. The first, before and after school hours, is the most common. There are many advantages to this system, the chief being that it extends the school day only for those participating. The second, the activity period, is a period set aside during the actual school day for activities participation. This period may be either fixed or rotating each week.[91] The third sets aside one complete day, e.g., Friday, for activities participation. The chief advantage of the activities period and the activities day is that they permit all students to participate, not only those who do not have to work or perform other tasks after school.

Various Student Activities

Student government is not new; it was part of Plato's Academy and Aristotle's Lyceum. Today most American high schools have their Student Councils, whose function theoretically at least, is to participate in the administration of the school. In almost all Catholic high schools and in most public secondary schools the Student Council is a farce. It

[89] See Edgar G. Johnston, *Point Systems and Awards*. (New York: Barnes, 1930).

[90] Harry C. McKown, *Extra-Curricular Activities*, 3d ed. (New York: Macmillan, 1956), pp. 600–602.

[91] Ellsworth Tompkins, *The Activity Period in Public High Schools*. U.S. Office of Education. (Washington: Government Printing Office, 1951), p. 3.

is really a sop thrown the students by the administration to keep them quiet and amused. The Student Council should be given real power so that it may learn firsthand how a democracy operates. Almost all educational theorists, Catholic and secular alike, agree on this; nonetheless, school administrators commonly observe it in the breach.

Both varsity and intramural athletics have long been a thorn in the side of conscientious educators. At base they must constitute first and foremost an *educational* program. As the Educational Policies Commission of the NEA has observed, "False notions are rampant when the notion prevails that school athletics exist primarily for public amusement. A school program of public relations based on athletics provides, in the long run, an ineffective basis for good school-community relations." [92] Athleticism has much too often permeated American high schools, public and Catholic, even to the point where, as Fr. Cox has noted, "At times codes of eligibility and fundamental Christian ethics are ignored in athletic relationships." [93]

Miller, Moyer, and Patrick have stated that it is doubtful whether the assembly period is "fully understood, appreciated and utilized." [94] Assemblies are frequently associated with dullness, particularly when they are vehicles for the seemingly endless speeches of the administration. Assemblies should be basically a learning experience, a curricular variant rather than a mode of expression for the administration. The students should be the chief participants in any assembly program. Forum and panel discussions on issues of pressing concern to the students make interesting and meaningful assemblies. Club productions, e.g., concerts by the music club or dramatic presentations by the Thespians, provide rich educational outcomes for both participants and audience.

The social program, particularly that part which pertains to social life, should be vibrant. Lee has defined social life as consisting of "the opportunities to contact and mix with members of the opposite sex." [95] Since the student is an integer, the quality and quantity of his or her social life have a direct bearing on every other aspect of his or her personality, including the intellect. Catholic high schools should be in the vanguard in sponsoring social life activities, since a lack of such sponsorship all too often leads to mixed marriages or to spinsterhood or

[92] Educational Policies Commission, *School Athletics: Problems and Policies.* (Washington: NEA, 1954), p. 7; see also Charles E. Forsythe, *Administration of High School Athletics.* (Englewood Cliffs, N.J.: Prentice-Hall, 1954), pp. 5–9.

[93] Joseph G. Cox, "Co-Curricular Activities," in McKeough (ed.), *The Curriculum of the Catholic Secondary School, op. cit.,* p. 93.

[94] Franklin A. Miller, James H. Moyer, and Robert B. Patrick, *Planning Student Activities.* (Englewood Cliffs, N.J.: Prentice-Hall, 1956), p. 496.

[95] James Michael Lee, "Catholic Women's Colleges and Social Life," *Catholic Educational Review,* LIX (May, 1961), p. 324.

bachelorhood. The residual Jansenism which exists in some Catholic circles should give way to wholesome Christian humanism.

The school newspaper properly developed can do much to cultivate not only journalistic but literary skills. The editors and assistants of school newspapers in Catholic high schools would do well to heed Bishop Wright's address in 1961 to the Catholic Press Association. Bishop Wright there stated that the Catholic press must counter the popular non-Catholic image of the Church as clerical or domineering by seeing to it that "the place of the laity in the sanctified life of the Church is heightened and made clear."

Dramatic, music, and dance clubs are important in developing pupil creativity and self-assurance, both cardinal educational goals of the NEA and NCEA.[96] Subject-area clubs, e.g., a French club, should integrate their activities as closely as possible into the regular classwork. Fr. Riley's study shows that this is taking place in alert Catholic high schools.[97] The existence of honor societies is a thorny educational problem and must be handled with care. These societies have eligibility qualifications, with a grade or mark required for membership. The assumed advantage of honor societies is that they are an incentive to greater pupil scholarship. Whether this is true is a debated point. In any event, honor societies, if not developed properly, can lead to feelings of intellectual snobbery by their members or to intellectual inadequacy on the part of those who failed to qualify for admission. Most secondary schools, both public and Catholic, have honor societies.[98] There are many books on the market which give the sponsor and the pupil helpful suggestions for improving their club activities.[99]

In Catholic high schools the Sodality should occupy a special place in the activities program. Sadly, the Sodality, despite its importance and the vigor of some of its members, has often drawn to its ranks more than its share of marshmallowy personalities. Constant effort must be made to attract also dynamic, wholesome leaders to the Sodality. One of the best ways of doing this is for the Sodality to be true to its spirit as a branch of Catholic Action.[100] Too often the Sodality has been allowed

[96] See Gruber and Beatty, op. cit., pp. 108–124.

[97] Riley, op. cit., p. 4.

[98] For a brief discussion of the National Honor Society sponsored by the National Association of Secondary-School Principals, see Louis R. Kilzer, Harold H. Stephenson, and H. Orville Nordberg, Allied Activities in the Secondary School. (New York: Harper, 1956), p. 78.

[99] Thompson lists suggestions for 500 different club activities. See Nellie Zetta Thompson, Your School Clubs. (New York: Dutton, 1953).

[100] Pope Pius XI, Apostolic Constitution of the Sodality of Our Lady, Acies Ordinata, nova series. (Rome: Borgo S. Spirito, S., 1948), p. 7, cited in Louis E. Riedel, "Integrating the Extracurriculum with the Curriculum," in Sister Mary Janet (ed.), The Integration of the Catholic Secondary School Curriculum, op. cit., p. 71.

to degenerate into a pious form of Catholic activity rather than remain in its rightful position as an official Catholic Action group characterized by cell meetings and mandate.[101]

Besides the Sodality, other Catholic Action groups should be started not only in Catholic high schools but in public secondary schools as well. The Young Christian Students and the Grail are two groups specializing in pupil Catholic Action.[102] Membership in such groups should do much to produce vibrant Catholics whose religion influences all their actions. Fathers Bouscaren, S.J., and Ellis, S.J., two prominent Canon lawyers, state that "according to repeated declarations of His Holiness, Pius XI, the energetic promotion of Catholic Action is one of the *duties* of pastors" under Canon Law.[103] Pastors of parochial high schools thus have an obligation to establish Catholic Action cells there and, by inference, so do principals of other Catholic secondary schools. Newman Clubs in public secondary schools should similarly be organized along Catholic Action lines.

Sponsors

An activities sponsor is a faculty member who is the educational leader of a particular activity. The characteristics of a good sponsor as stated in the literature are so lofty and multitudinous that their possessor would undoubtedly have to be a paragon of virtue. While the full attainment of these characteristics can never be realized, nonetheless the sponsor should constantly attempt to develop as many of them as possible.

Lee lists ten characteristics of a good sponsor. He should:

> (1) be able to bring out the maximum of the potential values inherent in the activity; (2) be able to make suggestions while at the same time avoiding the subtle pressuring of students to do a certain thing in a prescribed manner; (3) understand the relationship between the activity and the school's total educational program; (4) be a skillful planner, organizer and coordinator; (5) be guidance-minded; (6) be willing to give unselfishly of his time, energies and thought to insure the success of the activity; (7) have a pleasing personality; (8) have a respect for the students' personalities; (9) be well adjusted psychologically; (10) be vitally and acutely interested in the world around him.[104]

[101] For a clarification of the deep difference between Catholic Action and Catholic activities, see William Ferree, S.M., *Introduction to Catholic Action.* (Washington: NCWC, n.d.), pp. 26–66.

[102] Fur further information on these groups, the Chicago, Ill., and Loveland, Ohio, headquarters of the YCS and Grail, respectively, should be contacted.

[103] T. Lincoln Bouscaren, S.J., and Adam C. Ellis, S.J., *Canon Law: A Text and Commentary,* 2d ed. (Milwaukee: Bruce, 1951), p. 216. Italics supplied.

[104] James Michael Lee, *Commencement Activities in Secondary Schools,* unpublished manuscript, 1960.

Activities sponsors should not be autocratically appointed by the administration, for this can easily lead to the selection of a faculty member whose interests, abilities, or personality are unsuited to lead the activity assigned to him. Rather, sponsors should be chosen by a committee composed of representatives of the administration, faculty, and students. This procedure should ensure the selection of the best available sponsor for each activity.

In order that a sponsor may have the time and energy to lead his activity, he should be given a lighter teaching load in accordance with the amount of time the direction of his activity consumes. Failure to do this will result in a tired and dispirited sponsor, with ensuing consequences for the educational outcomes of the activity.[105] An element of social justice is also involved.

It is a sad fact that many activities sponsors are without preparation or knowledge for activity leadership. Johnston observes that teacher-training institutions have not provided adequate professional preparation to prospective teachers for sponsoring student activities.[106] Further, a doctoral dissertation by Nodell revealed that of all the problems of beginning teachers who sponsored activities, the clubs, the dramatic activities, and student council accounted for 60 per cent of the total number of professional problems of the teachers studied.[107]

The administration, staff, and sponsor must always remember that student activities are *student* activities. They should not be dominated by anyone else.

[105] See Paul W. Terry, "Cooperation of Teacher Advisors," *Extra-Curricular Activities,* National Society for the Study of Education, Twenty-Fifth Yearbook, Part II. (Bloomington, Ill.: Public School Publishing Co., 1926), pp. 108–110.

[106] Edgar G. Johnston, "Critical Problems in the Administration of Student Activities," *Bulletin of the National Association of Secondary-School Principals,* XXXVI (February, 1952), pp. 3–12.

[107] Paul Howard Nodell, *Meeting the Problems and Difficulties of Beginning Teachers as Sponsors of Student Activities in the High School,* unpublished doctoral dissertation, Teachers College, Columbia University, New York, 1954, p. 46.

CHAPTER VII THE SECONDARY SCHOOL TEACHER

Nature of the Teacher

The teacher occupies a place second only to the priest and Religious in the objective hierarchy of vocations. Like the priest, the teacher can touch men's souls. The teacher is the minister of God in cooperating with Him in enabling the student to perfect himself by acquiring and increasing truth. This is a divine work. Henry Adams has said: "A teacher affects eternity; he can never tell where his influence stops."[1]

The eminence of the teacher also springs from the fact that he combines in one person the active and contemplative life. The former grows out of the latter, since, as Gilson has noted, teaching "finds its source in the teacher's contemplation, and is, so to speak, its outward manifestation."[2] St. Thomas amplified this point when, commenting

[1] Quoted in B. J. Chandler, *Education and the Teacher.* (New York: Dodd, Mead, 1961), p. 9.
[2] Etienne Gilson, "The Christian Teacher," in Pegis (ed.), *A Gilson Reader.* (Garden City, N.Y.: Image Books, Doubleday, 1957), p. 224.

on the teacher's eminence, he stated that it is better to hand over to others the fruits of one's contemplation than merely to contemplate.

Teaching is rooted in learning; the two can never be separated in the actual educational process. Of this the eminent American lay Catholic philosopher, James Collins, has written: "Although the educational experience constitutes a single social activity of intelligence, it can be viewed as both teaching and learning." [3] Teaching is not an operative art, i.e., one exercised on passive matter as in sculpturing, but rather a cooperative art in which the activity of the student's mind is of primary, not secondary, importance. This notion of the teacher as merely a cooperator is of crucial importance to the proper understanding and exercise of the teacher's role.

St. Thomas's definition of teaching is "to cause knowledge in another in some way." [4] The teacher, then, is the proximate external agent in the effecting of learning in the student. As such, he is not the most important factor in the learning situation; the student is. In this, St. Thomas was fond of comparing the work of the teacher to that of the physician. The teacher causes knowledge in the student much as the physician causes health in the patient. Just as the internal bodily operations of the patient are the most important single element in regaining health, so are the internal mental operations of the pupil the most important single element in learning knowledge, attitudes, skills, and the like.

In learning, then, the student's mental activity is the primary proximate cause, and the teacher's external activity is the secondary proximate cause. This principle is of the utmost importance and can never be overstressed. It will necessitate concentration more on the learning than on the teaching. It will mean that all teaching will be geared to the nature and procedures of student learning. It will demand that the teacher abdicate his position as the dominant element in the learning situation and return it to its rightful owner, the student. It is indeed unfortunate that Catholic high school teachers, committed to a belief in Thomism, sometimes use teaching methods which do violence to St. Thomas's stated principles of teaching. Public secondary school teachers, who are not so fortunate as to be rooted in Thomism, frequently actualize the principles of St. Thomas more than do the Thomists.

St. Thomas further emphasized the primacy of the student in the learning process when he wrote about the ability of the student to come to a knowledge about things by himself.[5] He distinguished between

[3] James Collins, "Introduction," in St. Thomas Aquinas, *The Teacher* (trans.). (Chicago: Gateway, Regnery, 1954), p. viii.

[4] St. Thomas Aquinas, *De Veritate*, XI, a.1, obj. 1.

[5] *Ibid.*, a.1.

learning by discovery, as when the pupil's reason by itself reaches a knowledge of unknown things, and learning by instruction, as when someone else assists the student's natural reason.[6]

As Mayer has noted, the teacher does not transmit truth to the student except in moments of communicative intuition.[7] Rather truth is communicated through symbols, whether gestural, artificial, or linguistic, to use the threefold division of symbols made by Fr. Herbert Musurillo, S.J.[8] Hence the causality which the teacher exercises is indirect. As Gilson has written, "There is no transfusion of learning in the sense that there are transfusions of blood. We [teachers] can give our own blood to others; we cannot give them our own learning." [9]

The teacher, therefore, must realize that learning ultimately can result only from the pupil's mental self-activity. Teaching, while necessary, is still ancillary. Many philosophers and educators have repeatedly stressed this point over the centuries. Boethius wrote that teaching does no more than stimulate the mind to know.[10] Kahlil Gibran noted that the good teacher "gives not of his wisdom, but of his faith and lovingness. If he is indeed wise he does not bid you [the student] enter the house of his wisdom, but rather leads you to the threshold of your own mind." [11] Cardinal Newman remarked that "self education in any shape, or in the most restricted sense is preferable to a system of teaching which, professing so much, really does so little for the mind." [12] Msgr. George Johnson, one of the great figures in American Catholic education of this century, observed that "the temptation of the teacher is to ignore the fact that the temple of life and mind can be built by none other than the inward dweller. The teacher ignores this fact when he puts a premium on pupil passivity and loses sight of the fact that personal experience is the only sound basis for learning." [13]

This in no way minimizes the importance of the teacher; rather it serves to put into clear focus his proper role. The teacher is a necessary

[6] St. Thomas distinguished between teaching oneself and learning by oneself. While he admitted the latter, he denied the former. See De Veritate, a.2.

[7] See Mary Helen Mayer, The Philosophy of Teaching of St. Thomas Aquinas. (Milwaukee: Bruce, 1929), pp. 136–137.

[8] Herbert Musurillo, S.J., "Symbolism and Kerygmatic Theology," Thought, XXXVI (March, 1961), p. 67.

[9] Etienne Gilson, "The Eminence of Teaching," McAuley Lecture, 1953. (West Hartford, Conn.: St. Joseph College, 1954), p. 8.

[10] Boethius, De Consolatione Philosophiae, cited in De Veritate, q.11., a.1, obj.12.

[11] Quoted in "Editor's Note" in Elmo Pack, "Meaningful Teachers," The Clearing House, XXXVI (September, 1961), p. 21.

[12] John Henry Newman, The Idea of a University. (New York: Longmans, 1947), p. 131. By permission, David McKay Co., Inc.

[13] George Johnson, "Progressive Education," Bulletin of the National Catholic Educational Association, XXXVII (August, 1940), p. 562.

part of the educative process. The pupil's mind needs an external mover to help actualize it. The teacher further aids pupil learning by acting as motivator, stimulator, and counselor. But in the last analysis, learning is more rooted in the internal actualization of the student's potency to knowledge than the external presentation of knowledge.

Pope Pius XII warned good teachers to interest themselves in education rather than in mere instruction.[14] Education lasts a lifetime; most of instruction is forgotten at week's end. Barzun has cited the case of the average American adult who gleefully states that he has forgotten everything he ever learned at school and who mentally contrasts "this happy oblivion with the fact that he still knows how to open oysters and ride a bicycle."[15] This man (and regrettably he is the average American adult) undoubtedly received much instruction but little education during his school career. In education, the teacher cooperates in aiding the student to attain truth; in instruction, the teacher presents the pupil with the ready answer. In education, "the energy of the pupils is released so that they apply themselves fully," to use Butler's words;[16] in instruction, the energies of the pupils are prevented from being exercised because they must sit passively and listen to the teacher.

McDonald has commented that good teaching, especially in Catholic high schools, should be neither paternalistic nor protective.[17] Good teaching, as Collins describes it, results in "the steady ability of the disciplined mind of the student to undertake its own rational explanations, make its own assessment of the evidence, and thus to secure its distinctive, wholly inalienable hold on truth."[18]

Teachers should not make their students "fact foolish." Certainly it is a fallacy to think that the teacher who dispenses the greatest amount of information (as in the subject-centered curriculum) is a better teacher than the one who dispenses less but who allows great freedom for the pupils to develop their own thought processes (as in Core). What is important is not how much the teacher teaches but how much the pupil learns. The more a pupil is personally involved in the learning situation, the more he will learn. Such a situation, of course, precludes persistent teacher domination of the lesson.

Many philosophers, theologians, and educators have decried over-

[14] Pope Pius XII, "El especialismo amor," in The Pope Speaks, I (First Quarter, 1954), p. 21.

[15] Jacques Barzun, Teacher in America. (Garden City, N.Y.: Anchor Books, Doubleday, 1955), p. 23.

[16] Frank Butler, The Improvement of Teaching in Secondary Schools, 3d ed. (Chicago: University of Chicago Press, 1954), p. 18.

[17] Gerald E. McDonald, "Some Starting Points in Reforming American Catholic Education," Catholic Educational Review, LVII (November, 1959), p. 528.

[18] Collins, op. cit., p. x.

emphasis on acquiring information, facts, in education. Pegis has noted that a famous teacher in antiquity, Plato, in his *Republic* "conceived of the education of man, not as a pouring into the soul of facts and opinions, but as an opening and an interior turning of the soul to the truth and the good." [19] Bossing has written, "Modern pedagogy recognizes more clearly than ever that in the learning situation the personal influence of the teacher is much more significant than subject matter achievement alone." [20] The teacher should be cognizant of *all* the pupil's needs and problems rather than merely be preoccupied with academic success. Of this Jersild has contended that all too many teachers "in league with the prevailing competitive pressures in our society, attach greater importance to certain school achievements than they merit, and apply pressures which make the child feel he is worthless in all respects because he does not happen to be a top performer in some respects." [21] Fr. Leen, C.S.Sp., has remarked that "a misconception is here to be guarded against. For many, formation of the intellect is thought to consist in the acquisition of knowledge. This is erroneous because the possession of unrelated and unanalyzed items of information encumbers rather than invigorates the mind. Fitting the mind for the reception of truth rather than filling it with knowledge is the proper object of education." [22] Fr. Farrell, S.J., synthesizing the educational direction of St. Ignatius's *Spiritual Exercises* and the *Ratio Studiorum*, has stated that ideal teaching, "while demanding a mastery of subject matter, nevertheless primarily focuses the teaching effort on developing in the student the ability *to form for himself* sound judgments, intellectual, aesthetic, ethical." [23] Sister M. Corita, B.V.M., has observed that "it has been argued with telling effect that the Catholic school in America has followed the false philosophy that the most important thing about education is *information* or the acquisition of knowledge." [24] As a general rule, the same indictment can be leveled at public secondary school teaching, especially since Sputnik.

A good teacher must disconcert his students, set their preconcep-

[19] Anton C. Pegis, "Teaching and the Freedom to Learn," *McAuley Lecture, 1953, op. cit.*, p. 17.

[20] Nelson L. Bossing, *Teaching in Secondary Schools*, 3d ed. (Boston: Houghton Mifflin, 1952), p. 516.

[21] Arthur T. Jersild, *In Search of Self.* (New York: Bureau of Publications, Teachers College, Columbia University, 1952), p. 91.

[22] Edward Leen, C.S.Sp., *What Is Education?* (New York: Sheed and Ward, 1944), p. 35.

[23] Allan P. Farrell, S.J., "St. Ignatius and Education," *Catholic School Journal*, LVI (April, 1956), p. 108.

[24] Sister M. Corita, B.V.M., "Report Cards Based on Christian Social Principles," *Catholic School Journal*, LIV (September, 1954), p. 214.

tions free. Only in this jarring way will he challenge rather than spoon-feed them. Teaching for creative use of the mind is of a much higher order than teaching for mere acquisition of knowledge. All this demands the greatest degree of pupil self-activity and consequently a pedagogical method designed to produce this self-activity.[25] Probably the best such method is that of problem solving. More than any other teaching device, problem solving promotes creative pupil thinking, maximum self-activity. It was the method used by St. Thomas and the other master educators of the Middle Ages. This method requires the teacher to be selfless in that he will be eclipsed as the center of classroom attention. As such, it might prick the balloon of his pomposity. Also, the teacher must possess sufficient patience to permit the students to painfully work through their own solutions to the problem under study. It often may seem far easier for the teacher to simply present the solution, but this procedure will seriously cripple the student's independent thinking processes and mental self-activity. It must also be remembered that creative work occurs not only within a single individual but also among persons acting in collaboration. Hence problem solving should be both an individual and a group activity.

A good teacher must know first what he is teaching, the content, and secondly how to teach, the methodology. The first is obvious, but some people seem to fail to grasp the importance of teaching techniques. These persons think that good teaching procedures flow automatically from either desire to teach or knowledge of the subject matter. Gilson has said, "Piety never dispenses with technique. For technique is that without which even the most lively piety is incapable of using nature for God." [26] Neither is a knowledge of subject matter sufficient; a thorough understanding of physiology does not mean that because of this a person is competent to perform an appendectomy. The teacher must know *both* what he is teaching and how to teach. Eels, in a carefully conducted study of the relationship between academic and professional preparation of secondary school teachers and the quality of their teaching, concluded that "quality of teaching is, generally speaking, more directly related to amount of preparation in Education courses than it is to amount of preparation in subject-matter courses. In fact for most teachers there is little evidence of any significant relationship between quality of teaching

---

[25] See Herbert A. Thelan and Ralph W. Tyler, "Implications for Improving Instruction in the High School," *Learning and Instruction,* National Society for the Study of Education, Forty-Ninth Yearbook, Part I. (Chicago: University of Chicago Press, 1950), pp. 304–333.

[26] Quoted in Leo R. Ward, C.S.C., *New Life in Catholic Schools.* (St. Louis: Herder, 1958), p. 14.

and amount of preparation in subject matter." [27] Other studies have indicated the importance of both subject matter and professional preparation.

Every teacher must be free to adapt his methodology to his own personality, to the particular needs of his students, to the given circumstances. An inflexible methodology, the same for all teachers at all times, quickly loses its life and becomes petrified.

A teacher does not merely instruct; he is the director of learning activities. His responsibilities include: (1) formal instruction, (2) discussion leader in classroom activities, (3) selection of instructional materials, (4) guidance and counseling, (5) sponsoring student activities, (6) curricular revision, (7) sharing in the democratic administration of the school. To discharge these manifold obligations the teacher must be grounded in professional knowledge, be steeped in the principles and practices of education.[28]

The teacher in the Catholic high school should attempt to integrate religion into every facet of his teaching. This is not to remake all subjects into religion but rather to deepen them by meshing them with religious truths. This interweaving is not too difficult, since each subject in its own way and of itself mirrors Divine Reality. As Fr. Shields has noted, "Religion is not a thing apart from life." [29] Thus, for example, in a course on world history, the role of the saints as shapers of history should be properly brought out, i.e., more than their personal holiness should be discussed.

Teaching can be and should be a lesson in humility and patience for the teacher. The real, most important results of one's teaching can never be seen, for not only is education a cumulative process, but also the teacher can never see the most important outcomes of his teachings. To paraphrase St. Paul, one teacher plants, another waters, but it is God Who gives the increase.

Teacher-Pupil Relationship

From the foregoing analysis of the role of the teacher in the learning process, it is evident that the basic relationship between teacher and

[27] Kenneth Walter Eels, *The Relation of Preparation in Subject Matter and in Education to Ratings on the Quality of Teaching of Secondary-School Teachers,* unpublished master's thesis, University of Chicago, Chicago, 1942, quoted in Laurence J. O'Connell, "Outcomes of the Curriculum," in McKeough, O. Praem. (ed.), *The Curriculum of the Catholic Secondary School.* (Washington, D.C.: Catholic University of America Press, 1949), p. 142.

[28] See Hubert H. Mills and Harl R. Douglass, *Teaching in High School,* 2d ed. (New York: Ronald, 1957), pp. 14–18.

[29] Thomas Edward Shields, *Philosophy of Education.* (Washington: Catholic Education Press, 1917), p. 402.

student should be that of joint searchers for truth. The teacher must realize that because every student has a different personality and comes to the classroom with a different set of experiences, every student has a distinct contribution to make. Similarly the secondary school teacher must realize that he is not the repository of all knowledge, that the students have some information about reality as well as fresh insights into it which are unknown to him. This is especially true in this age when knowledge is expanding so rapidly. No one can know all there is to be known.

The teacher is the instructional leader. Two different types of leaders can be identified in any society, viz., status leaders and actual leaders. A status leader is one who has leadership chiefly because of the position he occupies and not for any latent or manifested leadership abilities. An actual leader is one who has his leadership chiefly because people wish to follow him. People are forced to follow status leaders; many would desert these leaders if they could. People want to follow actual leaders; they do not desert these leaders. Many teachers are status leaders, and unless they become actual leaders their leadership will be ineffectual and have only a transitory result. The teacher must remember that an actual leader is a member of a group, not apart from it. Therefore he must function as a group member. He is the most important group member, but a group member nonetheless. Hence a teacher should not be autocratic, since such a posture will inevitably cause the students to feel that the teacher is no longer a member of the learning group and hence not to be actively cooperated with.

Teachers, especially those in Catholic high schools, should be educating their students to be leaders in society.[30] Education for leadership necessitates the pupils' apprenticing for leadership during their school years by actually being leaders in school. A teacher or an administrator who insists that the students have no actual voice in the operation of either classroom or school is directly thwarting the realization of education for leadership. Student opinions and participation, even when they disagree with the convictions of teachers, should be welcomed and encouraged.

A lack of understanding by teachers of the principles of group dynamics, the give and take involved in the activities of social groups, often prevents them from allowing the students to exercise leadership in class activities. A lack of knowledge on the teacher's part induces fear, and fear is soon concretized into autocratic classroom control. A teacher of this sort stresses the importance of developing listening skills in the students; he forgets that one of the best ways to teach the pupils

[30] See Adrian Dupuis, "Training Catholic Leaders," *Catholic School Journal,* LVIII (October, 1958), pp. 21–24.

to be skillful listeners is to be one himself. A student learns by imitation also.

Catholic high schools should be in the vanguard in developing the leadership potential of their students. Often, however, they fail in this regard. On this point, Fr. O'Connell has remarked that Catholic high school pupils have "an unusual respect and reverence for their teachers. It may be that, because of this respect and reverence, they have become too dependent on their teachers, accepting their word as the final authority in all things and looking to them for the solution of every problem." [31] Two characteristics which seemed to impress at least one visiting committeeman evaluating Catholic high schools on the basis of the *Evaluative Criteria* were "the high personal qualities of the pupils on the one hand and their lack of initiative and self-reliance on the other." [32] Some committeemen received the impression that "there exists an ever present danger of imposing such an authoritarian control over the students, and inducing upon them such a reverential blindness to the necessity of thinking for themselves that they may leave school poorly equipped to take their place in the world and stand on their own feet." [33] Thus the Catholic high school, while it is superior and even outstanding in many areas, seems to be lagging in education for leadership. Nor is the public secondary school above reproach in this matter. Happy to say, alert Catholic educators are endeavoring to correct this condition in their schools.

Teachers must not be so preoccupied with values, ideals, or goals that they forget the pupil as a person. After all, it is primarily the person who is being educated. It is in the pupil, not in the values, ideals, and goals, that education has its roots. The teacher must constantly ask himself: "Have I sufficiently respected the personality of my students, developed completely spiritual liberty, exercised individual initiative so that they will be prepared to lead a Christian life?" [34] The teacher should accept the unique individuality of each student. He should not strive to make every pupil an image of his own personality. This is especially important for Religious teachers; respect for the person of the student and religious obedience must not be confused in the teacher-pupil relationship.

Teachers must realize that they know far less about their pupils than they would like to imagine. Fooling the teacher has long been a favorite indoor pastime for students of all ages, particularly during high school.

[31] Laurence J. O'Connell, *op. cit.*, p. 157.

[32] *Ibid.*, p. 145.

[33] *Ibid.*, p. 146.

[34] R. F. Louis-Raoul, "Valeur de notre enseignment religieux," *L'enseignment secondaire*, XL (November–December, 1960), p. 7. Translation the author's.

Besides, the pupil's personality is often hidden from the teacher in many classroom situations. Thus Moreno conducted a study in which students were asked to select two classmates whom they would prefer to have sit on either side of them.[35] At the same time the investigator invited the teachers to judge which students would receive many choices and which would receive few or no choices. At the seventh-grade level the teachers were 25 per cent accurate. Of this Tryon has observed:

> Often a teacher is completely surprised or shocked to learn the facts about the social role of certain individuals. For example, Elliott reports as typical of other teachers the comment of one classroom teacher after she had seen the sociometric test on her group. "At first I couldn't believe that Ray had no friends. I would have said that he is very popular. After observing the class for a while, I discovered the facts shown by the friendship chart are correct. I misjudged Ray because he is always so friendly with me and goes out of his way to do nice things for me. I like him, but the other children don't pay any attention to him." . . .
>
> Teachers and other adults fail so often to grasp the dynamic social patterns of the children's group. The teacher and the research worker, too, are operating on their own value systems, which usually makes it difficult if not next to impossible to move into that objective position which is necessary to recognize and appreciate another value system. Further, the very fact that children's values change as they progress through the growth period may impress the casual observer as evidences that the child's standards and purposes which he derives from the group are not very stable, not very important. It is with regard to these changes that adults often fail the child most seriously.[36]

Sister M. Stephen, O.S.B., holds that every teacher must constantly ask himself the following questions as to whether he *really* respects the unique personality of each of his students:

> (1) Do I sincerely believe in the worth of *all* my students, regardless of low or high mental ability and of all differences among any group of human beings? (2) Do I cater to one student or to a certain group because of economic, social, or academic status? (3) How do I encourage self-confidence and full personal development? Do I, at times, stifle such growth by my tone of voice, facial expression, or by the way I accept a pupil's efforts and contributions? (4) How do I praise and correct youngsters? Am I alert to the needs and sensibilities of all? (5) Do I recognize that I must adjust standards, procedures, materials, etc., to the varying abilities, needs, and rates of growth? (6) Am I, while trying to give everyone a portion of my time and attention, fitting all into one mold? Or am I aware that the children must be allowed and helped

[35] Cited in Caroline M. Tryon, "The Adolescent Peer Culture," *Adolescence*, National Society for the Study of Education, Forty-Third Yearbook, Part I. (Chicago: University of Chicago Press, 1944), p. 225.
[36] *Ibid.*, pp. 225–226.

to develop according to the gifts they have received? (7) Do I realize, at least occasionally, that youngsters' readiness and ability to develop their individual talents is partly my responsibility? [37]

Qualities of the Good Teacher

No one knows precisely what the characteristics of a good teacher are or what causes his effectiveness. Indeed, the literature shows that there is considerable disagreement about the criteria of a good teacher.[38] Criteria of teacher effectiveness are often colored by the philosophy of the evaluator, e.g., an Experimentalist principal rating the performance of a teacher who uses a methodology based on Thomism. Ryans, in his classic study, has noted that "a person's concept of a good teacher seems to depend on (a) his acculturation, his past experience, and the value attitudes he has come to accept, (b) the aspects of teaching which may be foremost in his consideration at a given time, and (c) characteristics of the pupils taught." [39]

This is not to say that it is impossible to have any knowledge of the characteristics, criteria, and effectiveness of a good teacher. The results of a study by Peck show that "there may be some fairly universal standards for judging teacher effectiveness," based on the personality of the teacher.[40] Studies have indicated a higher correlation between success in teaching (as rated by supervisors) and the teacher's scholastic achievement in college than between success in teaching and the teacher's native intelligence.[41]

Fundamentally, there are two kinds of criteria of teaching effectiveness, viz., product criteria and process criteria. Product criteria are based on the quality and quantity of the student's new learnings, while process criteria refer to the value of the educational situation itself, e.g., active

---

[37] Sister M. Stephen, O.S.B., "Accept Individual Differences and Appreciate Them," *Catholic School Journal*, LXI (March, 1961), pp. 25–26.

[38] For a good review of the pre-1957 literature, see Sister M. Brideen Long, "A Synthesis of Recent Research Studies on Predicting Teacher Efficiency," *Catholic Educational Review*, LV (April, 1957), pp. 217–230.

[39] David G. Ryans, *Characteristics of Teachers*. (Washington: American Council on Education, 1960), pp. 370–371. Used by permission.

[40] Robert F. Peck, "Predicting Principals' Ratings of Teacher Performance from Personality Data," *Journal of Educational Psychology*, L (March, 1959), p. 74.

[41] See Leo Lins, "The Prediction of Teacher Efficiency," *Journal of Experimental Education*, XV (September, 1946), pp. 2–60; also Joseph Shen, *The Predictive Value of Various Combinations of Standardized Tests and Subtests for Prognosis of Teaching Efficiency*. (Washington, D.C.: Catholic University of America Press, 1955).

participation by the student in the lesson.[42] A good teacher will possess both product and process skills.

Instruments which are intended to rate or predict teacher effectiveness have never actually told how much a student *really* learned from his teacher. In the late 1950s, the Division of Teacher Education of the municipal colleges of New York City constructed a rating instrument called the Observation Schedule and Record (OScAR). When this instrument was tried out on teachers in various classroom situations, it gave valuable information on the socioemotional climate of the classroom, the relative emphasis on verbal learnings, and the degree to which the social structure centered about the teacher.[43] Thus the instrument really measures certain overt behaviors of the teacher which are very important in the learning process. Nevertheless this is not the same thing as measuring teacher effectiveness.

Much the same can be said for the Minnesota Teacher Attitude Inventory (MTAI). This is a pioneering educational tool which attempts to predict the effectiveness of a prospective teacher. However, the MTAI does not attempt to predict the degree to which the students will learn from the teacher; rather it endeavors to forecast the type of social atmosphere a teacher will maintain in the classroom. Several validation studies of the MTAI indicate the value of this type of prediction.[44] Both MTAI and OScAR deal with process rather than product criteria.

Ryans's exhaustive Teacher Characteristics Study shows that both intrinsic and extrinsic factors are involved in the characteristics of a good teacher, e.g., intrinsic ("men teachers at both the elementary and secondary levels appeared to be markedly more emotionally stable than women teachers") and extrinsic (the superior women teachers on the whole reported more participation in religious activities than the inferior ones).[45] Barr, surveying teacher rating devices, has placed teacher characteristics into five categories: (1) personal qualities (e.g., resourcefulness, intelligence); (2) competencies (e.g., directing discussion, motivating); (3) effects of teacher leadership (e.g., results on examinations, changes in pupil attitudes); (4) behavior controls (e.g., knowl-

---

[42] See Harold E. Mitzel, "Teacher Effectiveness," *Encyclopedia of Educational Research*, 3d ed. (New York: Macmillan, 1960), pp. 1481–1485.

[43] Donald M. Medley and Harold E. Mitzel, "A Technique for Measuring Classroom Behavior," *Journal of Educational Psychology*, XLIX (April, 1958), pp. 86–92.

[44] See W. W. Cook, C. H. Leeds, and R. Callis, *Minnesota Teacher Attitude Inventory*. (New York: The Psychological Corporation, 1951); H. L. Stein and J. Hardy, "A Validation Study of the Minnesota Teacher Attitude Inventory in Manitoba," *Journal of Educational Research*, L (January, 1957), pp. 321–338; Lloyd S. Stanlee and W. James Popham, "The MTAI as a Predictor of Overall Teacher Effectiveness," *Journal of Educational Research*, LII (April, 1959), pp. 319–320.

[45] Ryans, *op. cit.*, pp. 365, 386.

edge of subject matter taught, knowledge of professional techniques);
(5) status (e.g., experience, salary).[46]

Evaluations of a teacher's effectiveness as far as the principal and
superintendent are concerned are usually made on the basis of supervisory
reports, direct classroom observation, pupil achievement records, special
rating devices (e.g., OScAR), anecdotal records of teacher achievement
(kept on file by the principal), student comments about the teacher, and
parent comments about the teacher. These seven sources when taken
together give well-rounded, but by no means infallible, evidence of a
teacher's skill. It must always be remembered that much of what a
student has learned can neither be tested for nor directly observed.

The characteristics of good teachers listed by professional educators
and by students furnish an interesting and fruitful comparison. The 15
characteristics of good teachers most commonly listed by professional
educators (not necessarily in the order of their importance) are (1)
health, (2) knowledge of subject matter, (3) ability to maintain discipline, (4) use of voice, (5) use of English, (6) personal appearance,
(7) attention to individual differences, (8) initiative, (9) leadership,
(10) open-mindedness, (11) enthusiasm, (12) self-control, (13) preparation of classes, (14) classroom management, (15) community-
mindedness.[47]

The 15 characteristics of good teachers commonly listed by pupils
(not necessarily in the order of their importance) are (1) cause students
to learn the material, (2) exercise good but reasonable control of the
class, (3) democratic rather than autocratic, (4) human, friendly, com-
panionable, (5) fair and impartial, play no favorites, (6) honest, keep
their word, (7) sense of humor, (8) cheerful, (9) interested in pupils
and understand them, (10) teach clearly and thoroughly, (11) helpful
with schoolwork, (12) explain assignments well, (13) make work interesting, (14) patient, kind, sympathetic, (15) flexibility of method.[48]

This comparison is quite revealing. While there are several similar
items (e.g., learning subject matter, discipline), there are also other

[46] A. S. Barr, "The Measurement and Prediction of Teaching Efficiency: A
Summary of Investigations," *Journal of Experimental Education*, XVI (June, 1948),
pp. 5–9.

[47] Ryans, *op. cit.*; Commission on Teacher Education, American Council of
Education, *The Improvement of Teacher Education*. (Washington: ACE, 1946), p. 37;
Bossing, *op. cit.*, p. 525; W. W. Charters and Douglas Waples, *The Commonwealth
Teacher-Training Study*. (Chicago: University of Chicago Press, 1929), p. 18.

[48] Ryans, *op. cit.*; Frank J. Drobka, "The Teacher and the Integrated Curriculum,"
in Sister Mary Janet, S.C. (ed.), *Building the Integrated Curriculum*. (Washington,
D.C.: Catholic University of America Press, 1953), pp. 86–87; Carroll H. Leeds,
"Teacher Behavior Liked and Disliked by Pupils," *Education*, LXXV (September,
1954), pp. 29–36.

items which indicate that educators place heavy stress on externals (e.g., use of voice, use of English) while the students emphasize human personality traits of the teacher (e.g., sense of humor, friendliness). Because they represent the two polarities in the learning situation, namely, the teacher and the students, both lists of characteristics should be heeded by all teachers. Indeed studies have shown that the students' viewpoints are on firm foundation. Thus an investigation by Sheldon and his associates bore out the assumption that teachers and teacher candidates who were friendly and had good rapport with students were more intelligent, less authoritarian, and had a higher need for affiliation and a lower need for aggression and succorance than teachers and teacher candidates who were not friendly and whose rapport with students was poor.[49] Hearn, in case studies of 77 teachers, reported that skill in human relations was an important characteristic of a good teacher.[50]

Of course student opinions on what constitutes a good teacher are, like any other opinions, subjective. Chansky's study showed that student ratings of teacher attitudes are influenced to a significant degree by the attitudes which the rating students themselves hold, e.g., a freedom-loving student toward an authoritarian teacher.[51] However, this very pupil subjectivity is what is so important in the learning process, since the teacher is teaching subjective personalities, not objective entities. Hence a pupil's subjective analysis of his teacher's characteristics is always vital and to the point. Good teachers, ever desirous of improving their teaching, often make use of this principle by asking their students to list their good and bad points as teachers. In this way the teacher's skill in directing the lesson will constantly advance. To ensure accurate and forthright pupil ratings the pupils should write their evaluations on paper and hand them in unsigned. Nor should the teacher make any attempt to discover the author of any particular comment.

Gilbert Highet has noted that a good teacher must like his pupils.[52] Conversely it makes learning much easier and more delightful if the teacher is liked by his students. Being popular increases a teacher's effectiveness, but one of the greatest mistakes a teacher can make is constantly to strive to be popular. Endeavoring to improve one's personality is more effective in increasing one's popularity than attempting to gratify every whim of the pupils in an effort to buy their affection. Also it is

[49] M. Stephen Sheldon, Jack M. Coale, and Rockne Copple, "Concurrent Validity of the Warm Teacher Scale," *Journal of Educational Psychology*, L (February, 1959), pp. 37–40.

[50] Arthur C. Hearn, "Case Studies of Successful Teachers," *Educational Administration and Supervision*, XXXVIII (October, 1952), pp. 376–379.

[51] Norman M. Chansky, "The Attitudes Students Assign to Their Teachers," *Journal of Educational Psychology*, XLIX (February, 1958), pp. 13–16.

[52] Gilbert Highet, *The Art of Teaching*. (New York: Vintage, 1954), p. 25.

well to keep in mind that if the teacher's personality is lifeless and unenthusiastic, it will be exceedingly difficult for him to become popular with young people who by age and nature are pulsating with activity and vibrancy.

Personal example is a very potent force in increasing a teacher's effectiveness. As the old saw goes, "Your actions speak so loudly that I can't hear what you are saying." Herein is a capital advantage of the Catholic high school, for the shining example of the devoted lives of many of the Religious and lay teachers cannot but succeed in educating the students in a most important lesson, total consecration to God according to one's state in life. Vocation directors have often testified that the personal example of Religious and clerical teachers induces far more vocations to the religious life than do vocation talks. On the other hand, poor personal example on the part of Catholic Religious and clerical high school teachers has, for this same reason, an increased detrimental effect, since more is expected of them.

From what has been said in this section, a distinction must be made between criteria of teaching effectiveness and predictors of teaching effectiveness. The criteria are the bases from which the predictions can be made. Predictors are less accurate since, unlike criteria, they attempt to forecast the future effectiveness of a teacher. While predictors have not achieved the desired level of accuracy, they are nonetheless necessary in order to sift out unlikely prospects from among teacher candidates.

Some educators and people interested in education, notably Catholics, have maintained that the most important characteristic of a teacher is dedication. Thus Msgr. Kelly has written, "A teacher's most important requirement is that she have a whole-hearted interest in her pupils' complete development." [53] However, as Canon Drinkwater has observed, such a view is oversimplified and naïve.[54] Piety or good will is no substitute for knowledge and technique. Indeed dedication without knowledge and pedagogical techniques is dangerous to the pupils, since it can lead to many errors and actually harm the students. Teaching is a profession; hence competence and the skillful exercising of this competence are the chief requirements of a teacher. A person in the street may have deep dedication to humanity and to medicine, but this does not make him qualified to perform a brain operation. Studies have shown, for example, that the amount of money public schools have spent in hiring good teachers bears a much higher correlation to the quality of education

[53] George A. Kelly, *The Catholic Marriage Manual.* (New York: Random House, 1958), p. 61.

[54] F. H. Drinkwater, "The Use of Words: A Problem of Both Content and Method," in Sloyan (ed.), *Shaping the Christian Message.* (New York: Macmillan, 1959), p. 263.

than having dedicated teachers.[55] Because a teacher is a professional, dedication, while very helpful, is not necessary.

Authority of the Teacher

The authority of a teacher consists in his lawful right to teach. In a public secondary school this authority rests on three foundations, viz., standing *in loco parentis*, duty of the state, and personal expert knowledge. First, parents, in view of their relationship to the child, have the primary authority to educate their offspring. The parents delegate this authority to the teacher who, by virtue of this delegation, stands "in the place of the parents." Second, the state has the authority to ensure that all its citizens are properly educated. The state delegates this authority to the teacher. Third, the teacher's expert knowledge of both his subject field and pedagogical techniques gives him authority for educating the pupils in truth.

In a Catholic high school the teacher's authority rests on four foundations, viz., the three aforementioned and the Church. Because all men are supernatural beings, because theologically no one is outside the Church's purview, and because Christ gave a teaching function to the Church, authority for teaching also resides in the Church. The Church delegates this power to the teachers in its schools, *both* Religious and lay. The Church's authority in education is also the basis for her endeavors to provide adequate religious instruction for her children in non-Catholic schools.

Teacher-Parent Relationship. Because of the parents' deep-rooted rights in the education of their offspring, they must be permitted an important voice in deciding basic issues in their offspring's education. This should be true not only in public secondary schools but in Catholic high schools as well. The parents by nature are full-fledged partners of the Church and state in charting the course of their children's education. Hence, in the basic policy decisions of the school, the parents must of necessity be involved. Otherwise they would be robbed of one of their most important and cherished rights. This is not to imply that the parents should say how the courses of study are to be taught. This is a matter outside their sphere of competence. It remains for the school administration and the teachers to implement the basic decision of the parent, Church, and state.

This crucial role of the parents has definite and pointed implications for both administration and teachers. The basic purpose of the Parent-Teachers Association should not be to have cake sales or card parties in order to raise money for some needed piece of school equip-

[55] See "News from the Field," *Catholic Educational Review*, LVI (April, 1958), p. 272.

ment. Regrettably, this is often the case. PTA general meetings and committee meetings should be characterized by lively discussions of basic educational questions involving the school and its educational program. It frequently happens, however, that the administration in both public and Catholic high schools spends more time trying to repress the PTA than in devising ways to release their creative energy. For more intelligent parent participation in the running of the school, the administration and staff should encourage affiliation with the national organization. For public school parents, the national body is the National Congress of Parents and Teachers (founded in 1897). This organization not only advises local organizations but also publishes a magazine, *National Parent-Teacher*. On the international level, The World Federation of Home and School acts as a worldwide clearing house on home-school relationships. For Catholic parents, the national body is the National Catholic Home and School Association (founded in 1960), operated jointly by the National Council of Catholic Men and the National Council of Catholic Women. Catholic parents should also become affiliated with the National Congress of Parents and Teachers, so that they do not become isolated from the problems and issues confronting their community's public secondary school(s). Such affiliation will also prevent Catholic parents from becoming victims of an educational "ghetto mentality." Furthermore, it might also lead to better relations between the public and Catholic schools.

The teachers too have an obligation to see that the parents' educational wishes are being implemented. Individual parent-teacher conferences are an excellent device for achieving this. These conferences should be held periodically, not just when the parent's offspring has become involved in some sort of difficulty. Nor should the conferences take place only in the school building. Discussions in the students' homes can prove even more profitable to the observant teacher. Pope Pius XII stressed the necessity of mutual cooperation of parent, school, and teachers in getting to know the pupils' home conditions.[56] The absence of time-consuming family obligations on the part of Religious and clerical faculty in Catholic high schools gives them an added advantage over their married counterparts in public secondary schools in the implementation of the Pope's advice. Such implementation would, of course, entail the modification of regulations which might forbid certain women Religious to visit the homes of lay people after dark.

Lay Teachers in Catholic Schools. Sister M. Delrey, S.N.D., has called lay teachers "the displaced persons of the Catholic school sys-

[56] Pope Pius XII, "Aims of an Italian Teachers Union," in *The Pope Speaks,* I (Second Quarter, 1954), pp. 11–15.

tem." [57] Numerous articles by lay teachers bear eloquent testimony to this. Studies often corroborate Fr. Hausmann's investigation of the Catholic schools in Kansas in which lay teachers expressed the feeling that they were not considered on a par with their Religious coworkers.[58]

Such an attitude is based on a misconception of the teacher's authority in a Catholic school. As much authority is vested in a lay teacher as in a Religious or clerical teacher qua teacher. The Church's *magisterium* in no way undercuts this professional authority of the layman. It is necessary to separate in the Religious teacher his religious and/or ecclesiastical authority, deriving from his state as a Religious and/or cleric, and the professional authority, deriving from his possession of knowledge and pedagogical skills. On this point, Fr. Graham, S.J., has observed that many works, formerly thought to be exclusively the priest's apostolate, are now discovered to be performed better, if not exclusively, by laymen.[59] Thus outstanding Catholic educators such as Msgr. Ryan are advocating that laymen teach religion in Catholic schools.[60] A start in this direction was made by the Jesuit-sponsored Institute of Lay Theology, affiliated with the University of San Francisco. Begun in 1960, this Institute is preparing lay people to teach theology to men and women in parishes. The next step will undoubtedly be to prepare laymen to teach religion in Catholic schools.

A balance of Religious and lay teachers is important, if not imperative, for Catholic secondary schools. A complete faculty representation of the different states within the Mystical Body is one of the best ways of enabling the students to see this great, all-embracing doctrine in action. Also, a representative of each state in life can give to the student attitudes and, even to some extent, knowledge which the other cannot give. In this vein, Fr. Sheerin, C.S.P., has remarked that "lay teachers frequently make a deeper impression on students than do Religious teachers because they have a clearer understanding of what it is to live in the world." [61] Religious teachers, because of their vocation, occupy a different social and ecclesiastical status from their lay students and so have the problem of bridging a gap, as the priest-

---

[57] Sister M. Delrey, S.N.D., "Attitudes of Parents toward Lay Teachers," *Catholic Educational Review*, LIV (October, 1956), p. 459.

[58] Henry J. Hausmann, *The Present Status of the Lay Teacher in the Catholic Elementary and Secondary Schools in Kansas*, unpublished master's thesis, The Catholic University of America, Washington, D.C., 1958.

[59] Robert A. Graham, S.J., "The Laity, the Council and the New Apostolate," *America*, CV (May 6, 1961), p. 246.

[60] See Carl J. Ryan, "Shall Lay Teachers Teach Religion?—Yes," *Catholic School Journal*, LVIII (September, 1958), pp. 31–32.

[61] John B. Sheerin, C.S.P., Editorial Comment on Paul M. Donovan, O.SS.T., "Lay Teachers Are a Blessing," *Catholic World*, XIXC (April, 1960), p. 15.

worker movement in France realized. The lay teacher, being of the same status as the student, is not confronted with this problem and hence is in a position to operate with greater effectiveness. Furthermore, for a cleric or Religious, teaching is psychologically as well as canonically his or her secondary vocation, while for the lay person it assumes the role of primary vocation.

It is estimated that within a generation lay teachers will outnumber Religious teachers in Catholic schools two to one. Therefore Catholic colleges should give more emphasis in course work and student teaching to train lay people for work in Catholic secondary schools.[62] A training plan for Catholic college students who wish to work as lay teachers in Catholic schools was pioneered by Mt. St. Agnes College in Baltimore. This is a four-year program which provides a half-tuition scholarship for candidates and features, among other things, student teaching in Catholic schools. College course work includes such subjects as Theology of the Laity as well as other subject-matter and professional courses. This program is intended for elementary teachers but can be adapted for the secondary level.[63]

To attract lay people to Catholic secondary school teaching it is imperative that the Religious faculty of these schools accept the lay teacher as an equal. Written policies spelling out the role and position of the lay teacher are very important. Such written policies will serve not only as a positive guide to Religious administrators, but also as a bulwark against the layman's falling victim to the possible whims of a particular administrator or faculty clique. Since World War II, written policies have been coming into practice more and more, particularly in diocesan systems. As a further inducement to attract lay teachers, it should be possible for them to rise to administrative positions such as principal. A job with little or no promise for advancement will not attract the best candidates. The Religious faculty should make every effort to emphasize to the parents that the lay faculty is fully as competent as the Religious. This task should be relatively easy since, as a study by Sister M. Delrey, S.N.D., showed, the vast majority of the parents she surveyed were favorable to the idea of having lay teachers in the Catholic schools.[64] Unfortunately, this is not true in all communities.[65]

Concerning lay teachers in Catholic secondary schools, the words of Pope Pius XI should constantly be recalled: "Indeed it fills Our soul

[62] See Sister M. Austin Schirmer, O.S.B., "An Evaluation of Teacher Education in Catholic Colleges for Women," *Catholic Educational Review*, LVII (May, 1959), pp. 312–314.

[63] "A Training Plan for Lay Teachers," *Catholic School Journal*, LXI (September, 1961), pp. 101–102.

[64] Sister M. Delrey, *loc. cit.*

[65] Hausmann, *loc. cit.*

with consolation and gratitude to the Divine Goodness to see, side by side with Religious men and women engaged in teaching, such a large number of excellent lay teachers." [66]

Academic Freedom. MacIver has defined academic freedom as "the intellectual freedom within an institution of learning." [67] Academic freedom is usually thought of as pertaining to the university level, but it also has applications to secondary education. The purpose of academic freedom is to protect both students and teachers in "meeting their obligations in the pursuit of truth." [68] Truth is the basic objective of the school; thus a lack of academic freedom will prevent the school from attaining its end. Fr. Bierberg, C.PP.S., has noted that academic freedom means not only the liberty to investigate truth, but to express it as well.[69] Academic freedom must protect both teachers and students, not just the teachers. Academic freedom is a fragile thing and must never be permitted to degenerate into academic license.[70]

The Catholic concept of academic freedom is based on the Thomistic doctrine that truth is not easily attainable by the mind, and consequently in order to discover truth, a free and unhampered search for it must be permitted. Once the truth is found, it must in justice be permitted to be diffused. Except in certain extenuating circumstances, everyone has a right to the truth.

Academic freedom is limited by two factors, namely, positive facts and the moral law. If evidence adduced from positive facts conclusively proves something, a teacher cannot hold the opposite merely because he wishes to exercise his academic freedom. A teacher must realize that personal sincerity or even subjective conviction is not a guarantee against error. However, if this person does have some positive contrary evidence, he should be permitted a hearing. The moral law also restricts academic freedom; e.g., a teacher would be violating academic freedom if he passed obscene or racist remarks during a lesson. To a certain extent academic freedom is also limited by the wishes of the community; e.g., if the community does not want a certain course to be given, then the teachers should not give this course. It should never be forgotten by teachers or students that the school is the agent of the community, whether civic or religious. (The term "religious community" is here

[66] Pope Pius XI, *Christian Education of Youth.* (Washington: NCWC, 1936), p. 34.

[67] Robert M. MacIver, *Academic Freedom in Our Time.* (New York: Columbia University Press, 1955), p. 67.

[68] Russell Kirk, *Academic Freedom.* (Chicago: Regnery, 1955), p. 1.

[69] Rudolf P. Bierberg, C.PP.S., "Basis of Academic Freedom in Catholic Education," *Catholic Educational Review,* LIV (September, 1956), pp. 400–403.

[70] See Aldo J. Tos, *A Critical Study of Modern American Views on Academic Freedom.* (Washington, D.C.: Catholic University of America Press, 1958).

taken in its widest sense, viz., parents, parishioners, and the Church teaching.) Conversely, however, the teachers have a duty to educate and enlighten the community in truths which they have discovered but of which the community is still unaware.

In the nineteenth century, restrictions were placed on teachers both inside and outside the classroom as to dress, manner of deportment, and choice of companions. Clearly these were violations of academic freedom, and happily they no longer exist. However, today in both public and Catholic high schools the academic freedom of teachers and students is sometimes seriously restricted because their beliefs, even though they are based on positive facts and are in accord with the moral law, are at variance with the pet theories of the principal or religious superior. Teachers and students must do all in their power, within the limits of reason and dignity, to ensure that the truth be heard. Often this entails great personal sacrifice. The courageous students and teachers press forward, but many others shrink out of fear of the possible consequences. Thus Riesman has noted that teachers are increasingly avoiding teaching items or issues which may prove controversial or troublesome.[71] To protect and safeguard academic freedom in public schools, the NEA in 1941 established its National Commission for the Defense of Democracy Through Education. The NCEA, or the Department of Education of the NCWC, would do well to establish a commission to protect academic freedom in Catholic schools.

The degree of academic freedom in high school cannot be so great as in the university because of the difference in the students and the teachers. The students are less mature on the high school level and so cannot safely be exposed to things which may prove fruitful experiences on the university level. Also, unlike university professors, secondary school teachers are usually not scholars, and hence their perceptions into the truth are normally not as keen.

The Teacher in the Community

Because of his advanced education and professional commitment to disseminate the truth, the teacher has an obligation to be active in community life. The teacher should be a leaven in society. By sharing with community groups the benefit of his knowledge, he will amplify his mission of bringing the truth to those who do not possess it. In particular, teachers in Catholic schools should make their presence felt in the community. Not only will such participation go a long way toward presenting a correct image of the Catholic high school to the community, but it will also elevate community living because of the

[71] David Riesman, "Thoughts on Teachers and Schools," *Anchor Review No. 1* (Garden City, N.Y.: Anchor Books, Doubleday, 1955), pp. 27–60.

further injection of truth into its life stream. Organizing book discussion clubs, joining service organizations, and even participating actively in the town's or city's political life are ways in which the teacher can discharge his obligations to the community.

The teacher's role in the community also consists of bringing community resources into the school. One of the best devices to achieve this is establishing a human talent file, a library of people. Most communities have specialists whose knowledge would be of great advantage to the pupils during the course of a particular problem unit. The teacher should then invite the specialist into the school to discuss the problem under consideration. The school should establish a systematized talent file of human resources to best achieve this end. Alexander and Halverson suggest that such a file consist of two cards: one, a list of pertinent information about the resource person so that he may be called when needed, the other, an evaluation card of the resource person to be filled in by the teacher and supervisor after the community expert has been utilized. This evaluation card will detail his effectiveness in the learning situation and will serve as a guide as to when and whether a certain resource person will be called in the future.[72] Some public secondary schools and a few alert Catholic high schools, such as Chicago's famed St. Xavier, are using the talent file idea to further enrich their educational program.

A good teacher, then, is also a mediator, a bridge between school and community, bringing the resources of each to the other.

Teacher Aides

Teacher aides are people who assist the teacher in the noninstructional duties of the classroom, e.g., clerical work, certain aspects of classroom management, and so forth. The first teacher-aide plan was adopted in 1952 in the schools of Bay City, Michigan. Financed by a five-year grant from the Fund for the Advancement of Education and carried out in cooperation with Central Michigan College, it was known as the Cooperative Study for the Better Utilization of Teacher Competencies. The plan was undertaken because preliminary studies had shown that from one-fourth to two-thirds of the teacher's time in the classroom was spent on noninstructional duties.[73]

In the Bay City classes using teacher aides, the number of students in each room was deliberately set at from 45 to 57. A study revealed that despite the large number of pupils, each teacher actually had more

[72] William M. Alexander and Paul M. Halverson, *Effective Teaching in Secondary Schools.* (New York: Holt, 1956), p. 146.
[73] See Urban H. Fleege, "Why Not Use Teacher's Aides?" *Catholic School Journal,* LIV (October, 1954), pp. 251–252.

time to devote to each student because he or she had been relieved of noninstructional duties. The net result was that the growth of the students in the experimental teacher-aide classes exceeded that of the students in the control classes established for this experiment.[74]

Teacher aides have thus far been used chiefly on the elementary level. However, with certain limitations (e.g., marking papers), there is little reason why this plan could not be adapted to the secondary level. Not only public but also Catholic high schools would do well to consider hiring teacher aides. The plan would do much to alleviate the over-burdened teacher. Of interest is the Dixon Plan which provides for full-time paid teacher aides in parochial schools. The Dixon Plan has proved especially successful in providing for remedial work.[75] Teacher aides for both public and Catholic high schools are recruited from among interested citizens and parents. Indeed, parents are often excellent teacher aides because being parents they are vitally concerned with young people and are sympathetic to their needs. Certain diocesan school systems have been using Catholic college students as classroom assistants at the elementary level.

The role of classmates should not be overlooked in any consideration of teacher aides. It has been shown that classmates who are good students often make good teachers for poor students, particularly at examination time. One Texas high school has set up a Student Help Program. For an hour each morning before regular classes began during the week preceding examinations, honor society members conducted special classes for slow students. Taking the subject he knew best, each student-teacher consulted with a faculty member and emphasized the areas in which weak students were failing. Teachers urged students needing help to attend. Classes were kept small, about five students to a group. Experience with the program has indicated that students who might have been shy in asking questions of regular teachers were not at all reluctant to reveal their difficulties to student-teachers. The student-teacher, in his turn, viewed the job as a challenge. The program has proved a success in that high school.

Teacher aides should not be regarded as a desirable permanent educational fixture. Rather they must be viewed as only substitutes until the teacher shortage is eliminated.[76] The report by Briggs should be kept

[74] See "News from the Field," *Catholic Educational Review*, LIV (December, 1956), p. 630.

[75] See S. J. Eye, "The Dixon Plan," *Catholic School Journal*, LIX (November, 1960), pp. 72–73; also Sister M. Carola, S.S.N.D., "Working with Teacher's Aides," *Catholic School Journal* (September, 1960), pp. 58–59.

[76] Paul W. Briggs, "The Bay City Experiment," *The Journal of Teacher Education*, VIII (March, 1957), pp. 3–6.

in mind, viz., that "the staff at Bay City Public Schools still feels that it would prefer to have smaller classes with regular teachers than to have larger classes and teacher-aides." [77]

Team Teaching

The present concept of team teaching arose in 1957. Noall has defined team teaching as "a combination of two or more teachers who work with variable sized groups of pupils during an adjustable time period which covers two or more regular sections." [78] The Trump Report noted that "teaching teams fit no one pattern. They are of various sizes and compositions." [79] Organizationally there are two chief types of team teaching, the coordinate and the associate. The coordinate pattern is that in which several classes are combined from time to time; the basic unit remains the regular classroom. The associate approach is that in which the basic organizational unit is a large class under the direction of the team as a whole; this larger unit is periodically subdivided for separate study in depth.[80] The associate approach is true team teaching; the coordinate pattern is a type of teaching team rather than a team in the full sense of the term.

Team teaching involves many different combinations of teachers and other staff personnel. For example, one team may consist of a subject-matter specialist and the guidance counselor. Another team would have a group of teachers comprising such related specializations as zoology, botany, physiology, and bacteriology. In the large combined class they would teach in an interdisciplinary fashion. This large class would then be broken up periodically so that each specialist might meet in small class discussion groups with those students whose interests or course requirements called for probing more deeply the various areas of specialization. Still other types of teams use a master-teacher–regular-teachers combination, with the master teacher conducting the large-group lesson and the regular teachers being the instructional leaders in the subdivided small-group classes. The team-teaching approach in Fairfield County, Connecticut, is a comprehensive plan in which a team of experienced teachers, student-teachers, and college and high school graduate teacher aides all work together to take care of a large group of several hundred students under flexible arrangements.

[77] *Ibid.*, p. 6.

[78] Matthew F. Noall, "What Are Some Promising Practices in Team Teaching?" *Bulletin of the National Association of Secondary-School Principals*, XLIV (April, 1960), p. 4.

[79] J. Lloyd Trump and Dorsey Baynham, *Guide to Better Schools.* (Chicago: Rand McNally, 1961), p. 83.

[80] Will Hemeyer and Jean B. McGrew, "Big Ideas for Big Classes," *School Review*, LXVIII (Autumn, 1960), pp. 308–317.

Team teaching necessitates flexibility. Schedules must be organized in such a way that there are large blocks of time allotted for the combined large-group–small-group lesson. The school building itself must be flexible so that large rooms can be easily transformed by movable yet soundproof partitions into several separate rooms for small class discussions. School organization must be flexible so that pupils get to know one another better. Such fine rapport is necessary for effective group discussion. The famous Newton Plan provides for the subdivision of the school into various "houses," each with its own administration, guidance personnel, and faculty.[81]

There are many advantages of team teaching, the chief of which include: (1) increased learning opportunities for the pupils; (2) flexible program of instruction; (3) greater opportunities for guidance; (4) better utilization of the various abilities of the different teachers and staff members; (5) more efficient teaching methods and procedures; (6) increased opportunities for younger teachers to learn pedagogical techniques from older, more seasoned, master teachers; (7) more effective use of audio-visual materials; (8) improved utilization of plant space.

Cunningham lists seven difficulties which will be attendant upon the introduction of a team-teaching approach into a traditionally oriented school: (1) obtaining faculty support, (2) selecting team members, (3) providing staff relationships, (4) appraisal, (5) providing instructional space, (6) scheduling, (7) providing special facilities.[82]

Team teaching is one of the most exciting concepts to cross the educational scene in many years. Effectively used, it is able not only to revolutionize the traditional concept of teaching, but also to greatly expand the learner's knowledge by providing him with a wealth of new learning opportunities. The nation's secondary schools should not tarry in involving the faculty and staff in the planning and subsequent introduction of team teaching into their programs.

PROFESSIONALIZATION

Teaching has for the most part become a profession. It was not always this way. At one time it was customary to think of teaching as a task any person with disciplinary powers could perform. If such a person existed, then he could automatically teach. However, during this century, first in the public school system and now increasingly in the Catholic school system, teaching has become recognized for what it

[81] See Trump and Baynham, *op. cit.*, pp. 83–87.
[82] Luvern Cunningham, "Keys to Team Teaching," *Overview*, I (October, 1960), pp. 54–55.

is, namely, a profession which requires specialized training and abilities for its proper performance. Professionalization involves two separate but highly related phases, viz., preservice education and in-service education.

Preservice Education

All teachers in American public secondary schools and many teachers in Catholic high schools have undergone two concurrent types of preservice education: (1) academic, consisting of specific subject-matter learnings intended to make them competent to teach that particular subject in high school (e.g., history) and (2) professional, comprising courses in Education intended to make them competent in the process, bases, and multifaceted techniques involved in teaching as teaching (e.g., Philosophy of Education, Guidance, Principles of Secondary School Teaching).

Some persons not fully grasping the concept of teaching as a profession have criticized the amount of required professional preservice education, labeling it as excessive. This charge has been effectively answered in a study by Cogan which showed that only 16 to 21 per cent of the secondary school teacher's entire college education is devoted to professional course work, and 30 per cent of these courses consist in student teaching.[83] Cogan concluded with this inquiry: "Why do so many laymen and teachers deprecate courses in Education, yet look with admiration at the secondary schools of Australia, England, Germany, France and Russia, where teachers almost universally take more courses in Education than the teachers in the United States?"[84] The Eels study cited earlier in this chapter underscores the necessity and importance of professional preservice work in teaching. Academicians are beginning to realize the importance of professional preservice course work. Toward this end a series of annual conferences (commencing with the Bowling Green Conference in 1958) was held in order to enable academic scholars and professional educators to meet together and discuss the interrelated function of the academic disciplines and Education in the preparation of future teachers.

Of the two aspects of preservice education, viz., academic-professional training and the basic potential of the candidate, the latter presents the greater problem. As Lawson has noted, "Too often teaching attracts those of mediocre ability, and those who lack ambition, vision, energy

[83] Morris L. Cogan, "Professional Requirements in Collegiate Programs for the Preparation of High School Teachers," *The Education of Teachers: New Perspectives.* (Washington: National Commission on Teacher Education and Professional Standards, NEA, 1958), pp. 317–321.

[84] *Ibid.*, p. 321.

or self-confidence, and who select teaching as a safe haven of security." [85] Lieberman cites a 1932 study by Learned and Wood "comparing the scholastic achievements of unselected high school seniors and college seniors preparing to teach. These comparisons revealed that a substantial number of high school seniors were scholastically better qualified than large numbers of college seniors preparing to teach, often in the very subject which the prospective teachers had been preparing to teach." [86] Lieberman implies that there is some doubt whether this unfortunate situation has improved. Wolfe made a study based on the IQs of college graduates with bachelor's degrees who took the Army General Classification Examination. Majors in physics ranked the highest while majors in home economics and physical education scored the lowest. Humanities majors placed twelfth out of the twenty subject fields (nursing majors placed higher).[87] An investigation by Traxler showed that the average IQ of freshmen in teachers colleges was consistently lower in the decade 1935–1944 than the average IQ of freshmen in other four-year colleges.[88] However, it must be remembered that less than 25 per cent of all teachers in public secondary schools and a negligible percentage in Catholic high schools are graduated from non-Catholic teachers colleges.

To further professionalize teaching and save it from being a refuge for mediocrity, at least three conditions must exist. First, the prospective teacher must realize his deep moral responsibility to prepare himself adequately, in both his academic and professional courses. His is a deep responsibility to thousands of young souls. A willful neglect of his duty by failure to study to the best of his ability constitutes a sin, perhaps even a mortal sin. Second, the college must do all in its power to elevate standards in both academic and professional departments. Building drives, a desire for increased enrollment, or other reasons should not be permitted to dilute the quality of the institution's course offerings. Third, the accrediting agencies should vigorously see to it that colleges preparing teachers maintain a high standard of excellence. The establishment in 1954 of the National Council for the Accreditation of Teacher Education (NCATE) to coordinate the efforts of the various accrediting agencies constituted a step in the right direction.

[85] Douglas E. Lawson, "Society's Stake in the Merit Rating of Teachers," *School and Society*, LXXXV (April 27, 1957), p. 141.

[86] Myron Lieberman, *Education as a Profession*. (Englewood Cliffs, N.J.: Prentice-Hall, 1956), p. 231.

[87] Dael L. Wolfe, *America's Sources of Specialized Talent*. (New York: Harper, 1954), p. 199.

[88] Arthur E. Traxler, "Are Students in Teachers Colleges Greatly Inferior in Ability?" *School and Society*, LXIII (February 16, 1946), pp. 105–107.

In-service Education

In-service education consists in those learnings, whether organized by the system, the school, or by the individual teacher himself, which are intended to improve the teacher professionally. The primary purpose of in-service education is to continue the content and professional preparation of teachers so that, thus enriched, they can create better learning situations for their students. As Chandler has stated, "Knowledge expands and changes; hence to retain his status as an expert, the teacher must be a student. Continual study is required of the teacher if he is to keep abreast of developments." [89] The teacher who does not continue to grow personally and professionally will wither both as a person and as a teacher.

Teachers need in-service education, particularly in those professional areas which were not covered in their 18 hours or so of college course work in Education. Thus Archer's comprehensive review of the studies has revealed that many teachers feel the need of in-service course work in such areas as audio-visual techniques, motivation procedures, methods of teaching exceptional students, ways of constructively handling disciplinary problems, and human relations skills with colleagues and parents. [90] Teachers in Catholic high schools also require in-service education. A study by Brother Conall A. Cody, F.S.C., concluded that more preservice and in-service courses in professional Education are needed by men Religious and especially by priests teaching in Catholic secondary schools. [91] A vocation survey of 14,000 secondary school students of Religious women made by the Sister Formation Conference disclosed that only 20 per cent of the pupils thought the religious life was broadening, only 22 per cent rated the nuns as professionals, and less than 50 per cent thought that the sisters were cultured. [92] A vigorous in-service program could go far in eliminating some of the basic factors which gave rise to these students' poor impressions.

Provision for a comprehensive program of in-service education, both compulsory and noncompulsory, should be made for all school personnel, especially for teachers, supervisors, and administrators. Re-

[89] Chandler, op. cit., p. 329.

[90] Clifford P. Archer, "In-service Education," Encyclopedia of Educational Research, 3d ed. (New York: Macmillan, 1960), pp. 703–708.

[91] See Brother Conall A. Cody, F.S.C., Education for Secondary-School Teaching in Religious Communities of Men. (Washington, D.C.: Catholic University of America Press, 1960).

[92] Sister M. Judith, "Report on the Sister Formation Conferences' Vocation Survey," Sister Formation Bulletin, III (Autumn, 1956), pp. 1–7, cited in Raymond F. McCoy, American School Administration: Public and Catholic. (New York: McGraw-Hill, 1961), p. 289.

search studies have shown that systematic in-service programs are planned by most public school systems.[93] (Catholic school systems have lagged behind in this matter; however, many of the more alert dioceses are beginning to introduce some in-service work, particularly by way of annual or semiannual teachers' institutes.) Attendance at public school in-service programs is motivated chiefly through compulsion, inducements, or personal interest. Compulsion is the poorest of these as it often creates insurmountable emotional blocks to learning, especially in public school teachers not committed to the spirit of obedience. Inducements, such as additional salary increments or extra pay for attendance at given institutes (such as in science), have proved effective and are customarily employed in public school systems. Personal interest is the most preferable of the three and often serves to motivate conscientious teachers. An interesting device employed by a few public school systems is the hiring of teachers on a year-long basis. The teachers are given one month's vacation with pay and during the other summer months they engage in planned professional activities, e.g., teaching special summer programs, preparing curricular materials, and so forth. A better solution might be to allow each teacher one complete summer free every other year for rest, travel, or other beneficial purposes.

Teachers themselves have testified directly or indirectly to the value of in-service education. Studies such as that by Mork have shown that the students of teachers who have taken in-service courses learn more than students of teachers who have not taken in-service courses.[94] Hence in-service education is fulfilling its primary purpose. Ginther, in a comprehensive investigation of one large child-study program, discovered that the classroom performance of teachers who had participated in in-service programs for three or more years could be differentiated positively from that of teachers who had not participated at all.[95] A study by Sister M. Celine Hynes showed that despite the fact that four-fifths of the Religious teachers in Catholic secondary schools said they felt competent, nevertheless 85 per cent of them thought in-service courses were of definite value to them.[96]

There are many different types of in-service education, the most

[93] Archer, *loc. cit.*

[94] Gordon A. Mork, *Effects of an In-service Teacher Training Program on Pupil Outcomes in Fifth and Sixth Grade Science,* unpublished doctoral dissertation, University of Minnesota, Minneapolis, 1953.

[95] John R. Ginther, *An Evaluation of the Atlanta Area Teacher Education Service.* (Atlanta: Atlanta Area Teacher Education Service, 1955).

[96] Sister M. Celine Hynes, *A Survey of Teacher Opinions Regarding In-Service College Courses Taken by Secondary-School Teachers,* unpublished master's thesis, The Catholic University of America, Washington, D.C., 1956.

common consisting of: (*1*) formal courses, (*2*) faculty meetings, (*3*) professional reading, (*4*) membership in professional associations, (*5*) workshops, (*6*) institutes, (*7*) vigorous spiritual life. Formal course work may be given either under the auspices of the board of education or by the graduate school of a university. Normally the latter is of a higher calibre than the former. Formal courses are an extremely important aspect of in-service education, as they put the teachers in contact with experts in the field and so enable them to be on the growing edge of knowledge and methodology.

A faculty meeting is, or at least should be, a cooperative enterprise whereby teachers and administrators pool their ideas in order to further the educational program of the school. As a part of in-service education, a faculty meeting should be essentially a learning situation rather than a device used by the administration to make its wishes known to the faculty. Sister M. Claire, O.S.B., has written that faculty meetings should be held "in order to stimulate professional growth and give the teacher opportunity *to participate in the formulation of the policies of the school.*" [97] Such growth and active participation cannot take place in a faculty meeting in which the role of the faculty is to sit passively and listen to the principal or one of his assistants for the entire time. The faculty meeting should not be a glorified autocratic classroom as is often the case. Faculty meetings should be held in an atmosphere conducive to the free interchange of ideas between teachers and teachers, between teachers and administrators. Free speech should prevail, with no fear of recriminations or reprisals. As Sister M. Alida, S.S.N.D., has observed, "The faculty meeting belongs to the teacher." [98] To promote increased staff learning growth, the faculty meetings should feature the principal and supervisors in a consultative rather than in a dictatorial role. In Catholic high schools faculty meetings should feature the forthright opinions of all the teachers, Religious and lay. Laymen should not be given the impression that this is not their school, that their participation, except to praise present policies, is unwanted or superfluous.

Sister M. Vernice, S.N.D., has observed that for the in-service teacher the greatest opportunities for professional growth come from professional reading.[99] Professional reading is that reading which is directly related to the improvement of one's skills in two areas—subject-matter and pedagogy. Both types of reading are vital and interrelated.

[97] Sister M. Claire, O.S.B., "A Program of Faculty Meetings," *Catholic School Journal*, LIX (June, 1959), p. 39. Italics supplied.

[98] Sister M. Alida, S.S.N.D., "Let's Improve Our Faculty Meetings," *Catholic School Journal*, LX (October, 1960), p. 20.

[99] Sister M. Vernice, S.N.D., "The Sister in Service and Her Reading," *Catholic Educational Review*, LVII (May, 1959), p. 291.

Indeed it may be said that professional reading provides the most important and pervasive type of in-service growth. Unfortunately, not all teachers fulfill their moral obligations for improved competence through professional reading. The Holy See realized the necessity of continuous professional reading when it stated that "every [religious] house shall have a library containing Catholic books on the entire field of pedagogy." [100] Since many non-Catholic books contain much valuable information and many fresh insights, these too should find their way into the professional libraries of religious houses. Such books will also prove an effective antidote to inbreeding.

Teachers' manuals are published by many public school systems. A manual may serve as a handbook for understanding the system's basic philosophy as well as the exigencies peculiar to that particular system. Some larger Orders of teaching Religious in Catholic schools have compiled teachers' manuals, a practice which the smaller Orders would do well to emulate. These manuals should be made available to the lay and other non-Religious faculty members so they might have a clearer understanding of the teaching beliefs and educational aims of the Order. Teachers' manuals for both public and Catholic school systems should be periodically reexamined and revised in a cooperative manner, involving faculty as well as administration, lay teachers as well as Religious.

Professional reading should include periodical literature. This type of reading is extremely valuable because it gives up-to-the-minute developments in both subject matter and pedagogy in a way which no book can hope to accomplish. In general there are three types of periodical literature which constitute professional reading for the secondary school teacher: (1) strictly professional journals which, in the main, treat of new advances and theories in the process of education; (2) specialized subject-matter journals which explore areas in a certain academic discipline; (3) combined journals which seek to give the reader a knowledge of a certain academic discipline as well as new approaches in the teaching of that subject.

Some of the strictly professional non-Catholic journals of especial interest to secondary school teachers, together with their incidence of publication, intended educational level, and purpose include:

1. *Bulletin of the National Association of Secondary-School Principals*—monthly—secondary—deals comprehensively with problems, issues, and methodology in secondary education, each month treating of one specific topic

[100] Quoted in Sister M. Vernice, *loc. cit.*

2. *Clearing House*—monthly—secondary—concerned chiefly with practical classroom and teaching problems

3. *Education*—monthly—general—devoted to an overview of educational theories and practices

4. *Educational Forum*—quarterly—general—treats chiefly with theoretical and comparative issues involved in education

5. *High School Journal*—monthly—secondary—deals with problems and issues in high school teaching, each month exploring one specific topic

6. *Journal of Educational Psychology*—bimonthly—general psychological—gives a description of recent psychological experiments affecting the learning process

7. *Nation's Schools*—monthly—general—devoted to the practical problems of school administration

8. *Personnel and Guidance Journal*—monthly—general guidance—discussion of problems and research in guidance and the better integration of guidance into the overall curriculum

9. *Review of Educational Research*—five times a year—summarizes research in 15 broad educational areas, each issue being devoted exclusively to one specific area

10. *School Activities*—monthly—secondary—gives practical suggestions on how to improve student activities

11. *School and Society*—biweekly—general—short, brisk articles concerned with topical or controversial issues in education today

12. *School Review*—quarterly—secondary—scholarly treatment of fundamental problems and issues in secondary education

13. *Teachers College Record*—monthly—general—discussions of basic problems in education, each issue concentrating on one topic

Some strictly professional Catholic journals of especial interest to teachers in Catholic high schools or to teachers in public high schools interested in the Catholic approach include:

1. *Bulletin of the National Catholic Education Association*—quarterly—general—deals with problems, issues, and new frontiers in Catholic education

2. *Catholic Counselor*—thrice annually—general guidance—treatment of issues, techniques, and research developments in guidance applicable to Catholic schools

3. *Catholic Educational Review*—monthly—general—scholarly Catholic interpretation of the basic problems and issues in education

4. *Catholic High School Quarterly Bulletin*—quarterly—secondary—deals with problems and techniques of interest to Catholic high school teachers and administrators

5. *Catholic School Journal*—monthly—special high school section in each issue treats of techniques for improving teaching in Catholic secondary schools

6. *Lumen Vitae*—quarterly—general religious education—a scholarly international journal of catechetics devoted to improving Catholic religious instruction on all levels

Specialized subject-matter journals, both non-Catholic and Catholic, abound, and it behooves each teacher to keep up with the latest developments and interpretations in his field by periodically reading these magazines. Thus in history, for example, there are the *American Historical Review*, the *William and Mary Quarterly*, the *American Catholic Historical Review*, and many other outstanding scholarly publications. Combined professional–subject-matter journals such as the *Music Educator* are important, since they are intended primarily as aids to improved teaching rather than reports on scholarly investigations.

In-service teachers wishing to do research on a particular professional topic would do well to consult *The Education Index*. This invaluable research tool lists by author and by subject all books on Education as well as every article published in a professional journal. *The Catholic Periodical Index* provides a similar service for all Catholic books and for all articles in specifically Catholic periodicals of all kinds.

To promote his own continuous and fruitful in-service growth every teacher should be a member of at least one professional association. Basically there are four levels of professional organizations, viz., local, state, national, and international. Some local and state organizations are independent entities, while others may be affiliates or branches of a national association. The three most important national professional associations in America are the National Education Association, the American Federation of Teachers, and the National Society for the Study of Education. The NEA was founded in 1857. The purpose of the NEA, as stated in its charter, is "to elevate the character and advance the interests of the profession of teaching and to promote the cause of popular education in America." Included in the organization are many departments, such as the Department of Classroom Teachers, the Department of Social Studies Teachers, and so forth. Membership in the NEA general is distinct from membership in one of its departments. The NEA is the largest professional education association in the world.

The AFT was founded in 1916. Its purpose is to strive for improved working and salary conditions for teachers through union affiliation and union tactics. A part of the AFL-CIO, it is a bitter rival of the NEA. Like the NEA, it has local affiliates.

The NSSE was established in 1895. Its purpose is to promote mature, scholarly investigation and study of problems relating to education. It has no local affiliates; all membership is solely on an individual basis.

The most important international professional association is the World Confederation of Organizations of the Teaching Profession (WCOTP). Organized in 1952, WCOTP has affiliates in many countries. Its purpose is to work for an upgrading of teaching and of the teaching profession throughout the world and to promote a closer relationship among the teachers of various countries.

Catholic professional organizations are on three levels, viz., national, regional, and diocesan. Cutting across and through these levels are Religious Order associations such as the Jesuit Educational Association and the Franciscan Educational Association. The sole national professional Catholic teachers association is the National Catholic Educational Association, established in 1904. Its purposes are "to unite Catholic educators, create mutual understanding and encourage mutual assistance for safeguarding and promoting Catholic educational interests in the United States." [101] The NCEA has seven departments, including the Secondary School Department, and several sections, such as the Vocation Section. The Secondary School Department has seven regional affiliates whose purpose is to concentrate on problems and issues of more or less local concern.

Diocesan teachers associations are flourishing in the United States. These associations are contributing to increased professionalization of Catholic teachers. While these organizations are not so vigorous as they might be, nevertheless they have been improving steadily over the past decades and there is no reason why they will not come to full flower in the years ahead.[102] The same may be said for Religious Order associations. Both of these organizations represent concrete opportunities for continuous in-service growth of teachers in Catholic schools.

Professional organizations are not without defects. Lieberman has observed that the NEA is in the main controlled by administrators rather than by the classroom teachers it purports to serve.[103] For its part, the NEA has contended that the union affiliation of the AFT and its use of such union tactics as strikes are not in accord with the nature of a profession. From a Catholic point of view, both of these associations stand against freedom of choice in education by their opposition to

[101] "The National Catholic Educational Association," *The National Catholic Almanac.* (Paterson, N.J.: St. Anthony's Guild, 1961), p. 514. Copyright © 1962 by St. Anthony's Guild. Reprinted by permission of St. Anthony's Guild and Doubleday and Co., Inc.

[102] See Sister M. Judine King, I.H.M., "Diocesan Teachers Associations," *Catholic Educational Review,* LVIII (October, 1960), pp. 469–472.

[103] Lieberman, *op. cit.,* pp. 287–295.

Federal aid to Catholic schools. The NCEA is dominated by priest administrators. There has never been, for example, a layman on the executive level of the Secondary School Department, and the number of nuns represented falls far below the proportion of sisters teaching in Catholic high schools.

All the professional associations publish material of professional interest to teachers. The *NEA Journal* and the *Bulletin of the National Catholic Educational Association* are widely known. Of extreme value to every teacher are the *NEA Research Bulletin,* a quarterly which gives the latest research findings in American education, and the two-part annual yearbook of the NSSE which each year treats of two topics of professional importance.

Workshops are important vehicles for in-service growth. A professional workshop is a gathering of teachers, supervisors, and consultants to discuss cooperatively some professional problem, e.g., teaching reading in high school. Workshops usually last several days. They are important because they permit all the participants to pool their ideas so as to better arrive at improved teaching insights and procedures. Workshops are also useful in that they permit a critical probing of the problem area under discussion. In this way the teachers are not lulled into the dangerous attitude of thinking that everything is pedagogically wonderful.

Institutes are a part of the in-service program. They have been defined as periodic lectures by experts given to large groups of teachers in order to provide them with the opportunity "for the review of the subjects taught in the schools, to give suggestions on methods of teaching, and to stimulate self-improvement." [104] Most public school systems have abandoned institutes in favor of regular courses either given under their own sponsorship or conducted by some accredited graduate school. Diocesan institutes are quite common and are usually held twice a year. The students are given the day off so that the teachers may attend. These institutes often attract outstanding speakers. The retention of institutes by Catholic school systems is one of the brighter features of their in-service programs.

A vigorous spiritual life is a necessity for the Catholic teacher in both Catholic and public high schools. A well-rounded spiritual life includes daily Mass, meditation, visit to the Blessed Sacrament, rosary, and spiritual reading. Teaching, in the full sense of the term, is a holy act, and its most complete and most fruitful exercise requires that its ministers be holy. Unless a teacher is soaked in solid spirituality, he runs the danger of becoming blind to the intimate relationship between

[104] "Institutes," in Monroe (ed.), *A Cyclopedia of Education.* (New York: Macmillan, 1912), p. 467.

what he is teaching and God. If all subject matter in some way refracts Divine light, how can a teacher ignorant of this light deeply teach his students? A vibrant, virile spiritual life is no ornamental accessory to the teacher; rather it lies at the crux of profound and meaningful professionalization. A dynamic spiritual life will force the teacher constantly to ask himself such questions as: Am I treating subject matter as the end of the school rather than radicating objectives in the student who is a son of God? Do I offend charity in my relations with my students? Do my relationships with parents coincide with their rights as integral members of the Mystical Body?

Supervision is becoming recognized as a vital part of a teacher's in-service professionalization.[105] The supervisory act and subsequent evaluation are essentially learning situations for the teacher. They should not be permitted to degenerate into an exercise of authoritarianism or into a fear situation for the teacher observed. Supervision should never become "snoopervision." For best in-service results, the role of the supervisor should be, in Wiles's words, "supporting, assisting and sharing rather than directing."[106] Supervision aims at improving the teacher's skill by releasing his creative talent, not repressing it with curt reproofs. Improvement of the learning situation demands that the supervisor endeavor to correct the mistakes or shortcomings which the teacher manifested during the lesson; however, such correction should not be made sharply or autocratically but in a spirit of a *joint* search for better teaching. Simply to tell the teacher that improvement is necessary is neither enough nor effectual; rather the teacher should be gently led to his *own* awareness and sense of need for improvement. Supervision, therefore, involves both knowledge and human relations skills, and the supervisor must be at once a master teacher, an initiator of new projects, and a resource person.

Supervision needs to be upgraded in both public and Catholic high school. In public secondary schools, supervision is often regarded as an unnecessary nuisance which goes along with the job of administrator. Thus supervision has frequently degenerated into occasional perfunctory visits by administrators who check off a few items on a prepared list and then have a clerk typewrite three good points and three weak points of the lesson. In Catholic high schools the concept of religious obedience is often confused with supervision. Unlike religious obedience, good supervision cannot come about by commands or by

---

[105] See Robert S. Gilchrist et al., "Organization of Programs of In-Service Education," *In-Service Education*, National Society for the Study of Education, Fifty-Sixth Yearbook, Part I. (Chicago: University of Chicago Press, 1957), pp. 293–307.

[106] Kimball Wiles, *Supervision for Better Schools.* (Englewood Cliffs, N.J.: Prentice-Hall, 1955), p. 9.

performing acts chiefly because the superior in his or her wisdom so requires. Good supervision aims at good teaching, and good teaching can never result unless supervisor and teacher work as partners (rather than as superior and inferior) and unless the teacher understands for himself or for herself that certain improvements can be made in the lesson.

Load

Lambert and Iwamoto define teaching load as including "all the time and energy a teacher must expend fulfilling duties and responsibilities relating directly or indirectly to the task of teaching." [107] In secondary schools the common measure of teaching load is the Douglass formula developed in 1932 and most recently revised in 1950. The Douglass formula measures teaching load by mathematically computing the following factors: (1) total number of class periods per week, (2) total number of duplicate class periods in which preparation is very similar, (3) total number of pupils in all classes per week, (4) total number of minutes spent in noninstructional duties, e.g., student activities, (5) total length in minutes of the class period, (6) a mathematical coefficient which attempts to equalize the amount of class preparation required by the different subject fields or areas. [108]

Most states have regulations stipulating the maximum teaching load. These regulations are usually stated in terms of the number of periods that can be taught daily and the pupil-teacher ratio. These maxima are always in excess of the *recommended* load. In a majority of the states the teaching load in public high schools usually consists of 5 to 6 periods, the median being 5.4 in 1957. (This excludes noninstructional duties and the one daily preparation period.) [109] In the vast majority of Catholic high schools, the teacher's period load is higher. Maximum teaching load regulations are often ignored in public secondary schools, particularly with regard to pupil-teacher ratio in large urban localities. Only a few dioceses and Orders have regulations stating maximum teaching load, a situation which must be corrected if increased professionalization and upgrading of Catholic high schools are to take place. In some public and Catholic high schools teachers are assigned courses outside their field of specialization. This is due more to

[107] Sam M. Lambert and David Iwamoto, "Teaching Load," *Encyclopedia of Educational Research, op. cit.*, p. 1496.

[108] See Harl R. Douglass, "The 1950 Revision of the Douglass High School Teaching Load Formula," *Bulletin of the National Association of Secondary-School Principals,* XXXV (May, 1951), pp. 13–24. The statistical formula is given here.

[109] National Education Association, "The Status of the American Public School Teacher," *NEA Research Bulletin,* XXXV (February, 1957), pp. 26–29.

the teacher shortage than to the teacher's presumed wide spectrum of knowledge. It is a practice which should be discontinued wherever possible, as it seriously impairs the learning opportunities of the students.

Of all secondary school teachers in advanced countries, the American teacher has to carry by far the heaviest load in both instructional and noninstructional duties.[110] For greater professionalization, all American secondary schools, both public and Catholic, should attempt to put into practice as soon as possible the recommendation on teacher load made by the National Commission on Teacher Education and Professional Standards of the NEA. This recommendation stated that "twenty-five pupils should be the maximum number enrolled in any one class taught by one teacher. Furthermore the total number of pupil-class enrollments taught by a teacher of academic subjects in secondary schools should not exceed one hundred per day." [111] If the pupil is the most important element in the learning process, then the teacher must be given sufficient time to work with him so as to help him actualize his potentialities.

[110] Cited in the *Catholic Educational Review*, LV (September, 1957), p. 411.

[111] National Education Association, "Teaching Load in 1950," *NEA Research Bulletin*, XXIX (February, 1951), p. 47.

PART 2 METHODS OF
SECONDARY
EDUCATION

CHAPTER VIII PLANNING
FOR TEACHING

Formal planning for teaching is important because it focuses specific learnings as well as instructional techniques on the principal aims of the course, the unit, and the lesson. Thus planning ensures cohesion between the different elements of the lesson, between the various components of the unit and the entire course. Without such unity and cohesion a course could well degenerate into an undigested mass of unrelated learnings, productive only of chaos. Formal planning is particularly important for the new teacher who has never before had the experience of structuring and directing an orderly, unified set of learning experiences.

While planning is extremely important for the development of worthwhile learning outcomes in the pupils, the teacher must not be lulled into the false notion that wise planning and its subsequent implementation are of themselves the *only* sure guarantee of good teaching. An experimental study by Stephens showed that besides the deliberate planning and execution of a given lesson by a teacher, spontaneous, automatic, and unplanned activities or statements resulting from the teacher's personality, attitude structure, and so forth are also important factors in a good teaching-learning situation.[1] This emphasizes what will be reiterated throughout this chapter, namely, that planning must be sufficiently flexible so as to allow for expression of the dynamic factors which are necessarily present in any social situation such as education.

Who Should Plan?

The answer to the question "Who should plan?" will be determined by one's conception of the nature and role of the teacher, the nature of the student, and the way in which learning occurs. The Thomistic concept of teaching and learning, as developed in the preceding chapters, clearly necessitates joint teacher-pupil planning, rather than planning by the teacher alone. The teacher, particularly the Catholic teacher, should recall Bishop Mussio's words that the student "is the center of the whole educative process; he is the life of the teacher's effort." [2] The educative process involves planning as well as other activities. Nor should the teacher forget that the pupil's internal mental activity is the primary proximate cause of learning; the teacher is only the secondary proximate cause. Hence formal education is a cooperative act, a joint enterprise between the student and the teacher. Thus, to be effectively and deeply immersed in the entire learning situation, the student should be involved in this situation in its entirety, which includes the planning phase.

Joint teacher-pupil planning is especially important in Catholic high schools, since it shows that the students have worth both as persons and as *active* members of the Mystical Body. As Giles has noted, "Methods teach values." [3] If these schools are to produce active Catholics, then they must educate their students for activity by making them active in the total educational process, including planning. In learning, both processes and ends are important. Traditional high schools tend to assume that only the ends are important and neglect the tremendous educative value of the dynamic process factors.[4] Learning occurs after the manner of the learner, as St. Thomas often stated, and each student is a person rooted both in the absolute and in process.

The educational enterprise must be based on sound psychological principles. In what is learned, two things are simultaneously important, viz., the objective worth of the material and the subjective worth of this material to each individual student. The purpose of joint teacher-pupil

[1] J. M. Stephens, "Nondeliberative Factors in Teaching," *Journal of Educational Psychology*, XLVII (January, 1956), pp. 11–23.

[2] John King Mussio, "The Catholic Teacher," *Bulletin of the National Catholic Educational Association*, LVI (August, 1959), p. 210.

[3] H. H. Giles, *Teacher-Pupil Planning*. (New York: Harper, 1941), p. 169.

[4] See Ray H. Simpson, *Improving Teaching-Learning Processes*. (New York: Longmans, 1953), pp. 20–37.

planning is to mesh these two, for if they are not meshed, no real learning will go on. Planning must therefore be done with both subject matter and student in mind, especially the latter. The same subject matter and the same pedagogical techniques, for example, should not be used for intellectually superior, normal, and slow pupils.

In the final analysis, the teacher's concept of whether education or instruction is his principal function will determine the extent to which he involves the pupils in planning.

The chief practical reason for joint teacher-pupil planning is that such a procedure will cause the students to learn more. They will not only acquire more subject-matter information and concepts, but they will also find out how to plan worthwhile experiences, how to come to wise decisions by themselves, and other important process learnings. Involvement in planning will have a decided effect on the pupil's attitudinal set toward the material. It is not a waste of time for the teacher to make use of joint planning. The curve of forgetting must always be a prime factor in structuring every learning situation, since as was brought out in Chapter V, meaningful material is retained far longer and more clearly than meaningless material. Pupil involvement in planning does much to ensure that the material itself as well as the way in which it is taught will be meaningful to the students.

Joint planning acts as a significant motivational factor to the pupils, thus spurring them on to a greater desire to learn what is being taught. This is only natural, since participation in planning involves the pupil actively, immerses him existentially in the purposes and implementation of the learning situation. As Wiles has brought out, positive group and individual acceptance of learning goals will motivate the pupils to learn more than they would in mere passive acceptance solely on the grounds of the teacher's dictates.[5]

Hence in planning, as in everyday living, the pupil has both an individual and a group role.

Alexander and Halverson have noted that "to the degree that learners are involved in the planning and evaluation of their activities, they will assume responsibility for their activities."[6] The truth of this statement is known to many teachers. In autocratic classroom situations, when the teacher for some reason leaves the room during a lesson, the students usually begin immediately to discuss things unrelated to the lesson. On the other hand, in classes which feature joint teacher-pupil planning, the teacher may unexpectedly leave the room and the pupils

[5] Kimball Wiles, *Teaching for Better Schools*, 2d ed. (Englewood Cliffs, N.J.: Prentice-Hall, 1957), pp. 111–115.

[6] William M. Alexander and Paul M. Halverson, *Effective Teaching in Secondary Schools*. (New York: Holt, 1956), p. 234.

will not infrequently continue to discuss among themselves what they are learning.

Fr. Maline, S.J., the noted Catholic high school expert, has observed that good teaching of religion in Catholic secondary schools must achieve a personal involvement of the student with the content material, so that he is vitally interested in the specific truth under consideration. Fr. Maline further suggests that much religion teaching is planned on the basis of content alone, and not enough attention is given to adolescent needs and interests.[7] This is true not only of religion but often of most other subjects. The findings of a study of dropouts from selected Catholic high schools by Sister M. Assunta Highbaugh, O.S.B., led her to conclude that Catholic high schools should reevaluate their curricular offerings and the subsequent teaching of these offerings with due consideration given to pupil needs.[8] Cooperative teacher-pupil planning could do much to integrate pupil needs and interests into the structuring of the learning situation.

Joint planning is also psychologically important to ascertain whether students have the conceptual and emotional readiness for a particular set of subject-matter learnings, attitudinal learnings, and the like. Thus, for example, a group of students in a Southern high school may or may not possess the readiness for certain learnings on the race question. If they are not ready, a psychological barrier is erected before the unit or lesson begins, and despite the teacher's efforts, the pupils will learn little or nothing.

Bossing has remarked that teacher-pupil preplanning does not mean that the teacher asks the class, "Now boys and girls, what do you wish to do?" [9] This is not planning; it is teacher abdication and extreme pedagogical *laissez faire*. Joint planning is the cooperative selection of subject-matter content and methods of pedagogical attack. The teacher is not a passive participant in cooperative planning. At all times he remains the director of learning activities. This does not mean that he is a dictator or even the sole source of these activities. In joint planning the teacher functions as a guide, resource person, initiator (at times), motivator, recognized authority on the topic or problem being planned, expert in pedagogical techniques, and practitioner of sound adolescent psychology. Often the teacher must make the pupils aware of subject-matter learnings

[7] Julian L. Maline, S.J., "Does Catholic High School Education Make Catholics?" *Bulletin of the National Catholic Educational Association*, LVIII (August, 1961), p. 256.

[8] Sister M. Assunta Highbaugh, O.S.B., *A Study of the Cause of the Drop-Outs in the Catholic Secondary Schools of Indianapolis, Indiana, 1949–1954*, unpublished master's thesis, Catholic University of America, Washington, D.C., 1960.

[9] Nelson L. Bossing, *Teaching in Secondary Schools*, 3d ed. (Boston: Houghton Mifflin, 1952), p. 82.

which, while objectively important, do not seem so to them. Planning should aim at integrating what the school and the teacher think the student ought to know with what the students believe they should learn. Both integrative elements are important. The teacher's greater knowledge helps the student to broaden and deepen himself, while attention to the student's psychological needs and goals are necessary if knowledge is to be learned and retained. Brother Marion Belka, S.M., has written that planning should always be goal-directed and should merge teacher and pupil goals into a learnable, meaningful unity.[10] In good cooperative teacher-pupil planning the teacher must sift out goals which from the point of view of objective content and his own analysis of subjective pupil needs are poor, insignificant, and inappropriate. This is especially true of things which can be learned just as easily out of school as in it. A lack of appreciation by ultraprogressive educators of the importance of teacher goal sifting has regrettably brought ridicule on the whole concept of the students' role in planning. However, an abuse of a procedure does not nullify its correct use, to paraphrase Aristotle.

Teachers encounter two main difficulties in initiating and implementing cooperative planning. First, the oversized classes in most public and Catholic high schools tend to impede balanced and active participation of all the pupils in the planning process. Second, the pupils themselves are often reluctant to participate actively in planning, owing to overdocility which might have been drummed into them during their elementary school years. Overdocility is often more pronounced in students from Catholic schools and, as Fr. O'Connell has observed, is frequently reinforced in Catholic high schools.[11] However, conscientious teachers should not allow these two obstacles to block initiation and implementation of good cooperative planning. Skillful attention to group dynamics should tend to minimize the participation problem resulting from oversized classes, while a reasonably permissive classroom climate will help the students overcome the ill effects of overdocility and encourage them to express their ideas and goals freely. Catholic high schools, which should emphasize the development of leaders, ought thus to be in the vanguard in developing cooperative classroom planning situations.

Cooperative planning might well include the use of community experts and professors from nearby universities, both of whom are in

[10] Brother Marion Belka, S.M., "Excellence in Studies," *Bulletin of the National Catholic Educational Association*, LVII (August, 1960), p. 318.

[11] Laurence J. O'Connell, "Outcomes of the Curriculum," in McKeough, O. Praem. (ed.), *The Curriculum of the Catholic Secondary School*. (Washington, D.C.: Catholic University of America Press, 1949), pp. 144–148.

a position to make significant contributions to the planned approach to a topic or problem. The Catholic high school is in a uniquely favored position to utilize these resource people, since lay Catholic community leaders as well as lay and Religious professors in Catholic colleges are deeply devoted to the cause of Catholic education and, consequently, may reasonably be expected to do all in their power to further good planning in Catholic high schools.

Cooperative planning of units in schools which utilize the team-teaching approach will vary somewhat from the conventional fixed classroom pattern. In the large-group sections there will be little or no joint planning, since these classes are concerned with presenting the minimal subject matter, attitudinal, and other learnings which the school thinks each student should possess. However, in the small-group sections, there will be a great deal of cooperative planning since each section is concerned with relating the large-group learnings to the needs, interests, and abilities of the particular students within that section.

When the teacher asks himself: "Who should plan?" he must remember that every person plans his or her own life. Should school experiences be disjointed from life, or should they rather teach the students processes which will directly assist them in attaining a richer existence in this life and in the next?

UNIT PLANNING

A unit may be defined as a series of related learning experiences built around one central topic or problem area. It is therefore of longer duration than a single lesson; indeed it usually lasts several weeks. A unit is thus the general content-process framework for the learning of the various interrelated facets of the topic or problem. Hence a unit is a pattern of organization, not a method of teaching.

The idea of a unit was discussed in a general way before 1926, but it received concrete and definite impetus in that year when Henry Morrison's *The Practice of Teaching in the Secondary School* was published. Many educational theorists had previously examined the nature and process of learning and had concluded that learning occurs when a succession of psychological steps is mastered and the student finally arrives at a unified picture of reality. Morrison utilized these psychological bases as the *raison d'être* for developing his unit plan. The theories which influenced Morrison most were the famous five Herbartian steps of teaching and learning, the five components of a learning situation as identified by Dewey, and the different successive elements of learning outlined by Kilpatrick.[12] For Catholic educators, the Thomistic analysis of the stages of ideogenesis and the pattern of learning (probably unknown to Morrison) form the psychological basis of the unit plan.

There are two basic types of unit, viz., a resource unit and a teaching unit. A resource unit is one which is intended to be a general guide in assisting the teacher to enrich the teaching unit. Thus the resource unit is far more general and comprehensive than the teaching unit, since it is aimed at raising the level of the teacher's knowledge of content and skill in pedagogy rather than at the presentation of definite learnings and their introduction into the actual classroom situation. Consequently, resource units will include such items as extensive bibliographies, suggested problem areas, methods of analyzing pupil needs, and suggestions for evaluating various educational outcomes. Resource units are usually developed by a group of curricular experts and classroom teachers and are often given to each teacher when he first begins his service at a particular school.[13]

A teaching unit is one which is intended to be actually implemented by the teacher and the pupils in structuring large related segments of a course. For the prospective or in-service teacher, this is the more important type of unit, hence it will be the type treated throughout the remainder of this section of the chapter. Most school systems have printed preplanned teaching units which are readily available to the teacher. Traditional schools have rigid preplanned units, with definite subject-matter learnings stipulated for each day the unit is in progress. Forward-looking schools, on the other hand, have flexible preplanned units so that the teachers and students can have a certain freedom in which to develop and structure the learning situation. Preplanned units of the flexible variety can, of course, utilize cooperative teacher-pupil planning to a goodly extent. However, a skillful teacher operating within the context of a rigid preplanned unit is still able to utilize joint planning to some degree. Thus, for example, a unit on twentieth-century American politics conducted in a Catholic high school can smoothly bring in the underlying conflicts in church-state theory involved in events such as the 1928 and 1960 presidential elections, Federal aid to parochial

---

[12] See William Heard Kilpatrick, "The Project Method," *Teachers College Record*, XIX (September, 1918), p. 333. For a good historical and comparative analysis of the effect of learning theories on the development of the unit plan, see Donald W. Oliver, "The Unit Concept in Social Studies: A Re-examination," *School Review*, LXVI (Summer, 1958), pp. 204–217.

[13] See Harold Alberty, *Reorganizing the High-School Curriculum*, rev. ed. (New York: Macmillan, 1953), p. 446.

schools, rulings of the Supreme Court on obscene literature, and the like. These learnings can be jointly planned even though they might not be specifically listed as required unit content learnings.

The basic purpose of the unit is to bring together various related areas of knowledge, ideals, values, and attitudes into one cohesive whole so that the pupil can understand reality as it actually is, a seamless robe. The unit attempts to show the student the intimate existential relationship of the parts to the whole—indeed more, that the whole is what gives meaning to the separate parts. A unit, then, endeavors to develop a single grand generalization through the learning of associated facts, concepts, and viewpoints.

The unit has the advantage of defining content and process limits so that the student will not be tempted to try to understand all reality all at once. Rather it attempts to see one particular topic or problem at a time—to see that topic or problem as a related whole, to be sure, but nonetheless to concentrate attention solely on this main area of study. This puts the unit on a sound Cognitive and Thomistic psychological basis. In its turn, the unit becomes, in Woodruff's words, "a guide to the formation of individual lessons." [14]

A good unit plan should possess the following characteristics: (1) internal relationship, i.e., the suggested learning experiences should be logically related; (2) psychological relationship, i.e., the suggested learning experiences should be rooted in both the intrinsic nature of and group dynamics structure of the students; (3) personal significance, i.e., the suggested learning experiences, no matter how lofty in themselves, must be meaningful to the pupils; (4) reasonable comprehensiveness, i.e., the suggested learning experiences should leave no content, process, or psychological gaps in the final educational outcomes; (5) built-in mechanisms to afford definite worthwhile learning outcomes; (6) provision for a great deal of pupil self-activity under the guidance of the teacher; (7) ways in which the students can readily transfer classroom learnings to real-life situations; (8) culminating activities through which the unit will attain its climax and thus crystallize, solidify, and unify the learnings acquired during the course of the unit; (9) a procedure for broadly and specifically evaluating the degree of the unit's success in furthering pupil learning.

Burton has observed that every unit (and indeed every lesson as well) should be developmental; that is, it should lead the pupil to "constantly higher levels of achievement." [15] Both teacher and students

[14] Asahel D. Woodruff, *Basic Concepts of Teaching*. (San Francisco: Chandler, 1961), p. 181.

[15] William H. Burton, *The Guidance of Learning Activities*, 2d ed. (New York: Appleton-Century-Crofts, 1952), p. 423.

should always bear this in mind and so structure and implement the unit plan that it will actualize the learner's potential to the fullest.

Unit plans will vary according to the particular curricular design which serves as their frame of operation. In the subject-centered approach, the units will almost always be entirely preplanned by a group of curricular experts and will focus attention on the acquisition of subject-matter outcomes. In the total student-centered pattern, there may or may not be any units, depending on the felt needs of the students on any given day. In modified total student-centered designs, the units are preplanned entirely by the learners, with some teacher guidance, and are built around centers of pupil interest and needs.[16] In the Core, the basic broad educational outcomes and learnings of the units are preplanned by curricular experts and teachers, while leaving a balanced latitude for cooperative teacher-pupil planning of choice, emphasis, scope, sequence, duration, and types of learning activities, as well as specific methods of attacking the problem area. The Core unit plan is built around some broad interdisciplinary problem area of eternal and personal interest, a problem which the school, teachers, and pupils feel should be solved for successful living in this world and in the next; e.g., the students in a Catholic high school might study the broad problem area of social injustice.

Unit planning, whether entirely preplanned by curriculum experts and teachers or cooperatively planned by the teacher and pupils, should involve at least eight steps.

1. The type of unit, e.g., subject-centered, Core, should be determined in accordance with the basic philosophy of the school and the teacher's own pedagogical preferences.

2. The unit, even in a Core program, should to some extent be "planned for" (rather than totally planned) by the teacher, because he must have time to acquire a good knowledge of the basic minimum subject matter, process, skill, and attitudinal learnings which every student should derive from the unit. He also must make sure that the material and activities of the unit are internally integrated. However, this advance teacher planning must not rule out subsequent cooperative teacher-pupil planning.[17]

3. The statement of the unit should be planned with great care since the content and method of its phrasing may well have a directional effect on the way the unit is developed.

4. Integration of the unit with other units of the course should be skillfully planned by teachers and pupils.

[16] For a further discussion of this type of unit, see Freeman Glenn Macomber, *Teaching in the Modern Secondary School.* (New York: McGraw-Hill, 1942), pp. 108–139.

[17] See Thomas M. Risk, *Principles and Practices of Teaching,* 3d ed. (New York: American Book, 1958), pp. 159–162.

5. The primary objectives of the unit should be thoughtfully planned. These primary objectives can be placed into two chief categories, content objectives and process objectives. Content objectives deal with subject-matter learnings, skills, attitudes, and values. Thus, for example, in a Core unit entitled "Problems Facing Latin America in the Twentieth Century," content objectives would include a knowledge of Latin American history, geography, music, art, and religion, the problems caused by political instability together with Communist infiltration into the continent, and in Catholic high schools, religious and lay missionary activities in the Southern Hemisphere, e.g., Papal Volunteers for Latin America. In joint planning of content objectives, the teacher should help the pupils to themselves become aware of the knowledge they will need to solve the problem. Of course, content objectives must always be planned with due consideration to the pupils' abilities, needs, and interests. In this regard the wise teacher will consult the guidance files of his class group so that he will be in an informed position to discuss pupil unit objectives in terms of pupil abilities and past records, both statistical and anecdotal.[18] Process objectives include such valuable learnings as critical thinking, independent judgment making, charitable behavior, and the dynamic aspects of attitude formation.

6. Activities involved in learning the unit, e.g., research, field trips etc., should be planned. The quality of these activities will do much either to motivate or to disinterest the students in mastering the objectives of the unit.

7. There should be joint planning of the materials and resources necessary to implement these activities.

8. Methods and procedures for the evaluation of pupil attainment of the unit objectives should be determined. These procedures should be planned together so that the evaluation itself will become an instrument for learning rather than a mere rating device.

A week's study of English in a traditional high school might consist of English grammar on Monday, literature on Tuesday, composition on Wednesday, library and research work on Thursday, spelling and vocabulary drill on Friday. In unit-oriented schools this same week's unit (which could indeed be actually a subunit) might be the study of a piece of literature, including on Monday its literary and value problems; on Tuesday, library and research work relating to this particular piece of literature, its author, and his times; on Wednesday, grammar rules derived from the structure of the piece; on Thursday, a vocabulary lesson developed from words, phrases, and purple passages found in the piece, followed by a homework assignment of creative writing based on the

[18] See Robert S. Gilchrist, Wilbur H. Dutton, and William L. Wrinkle, *Secondary Education for American Democracy.* (New York: Rinehart, 1957), p. 324.

piece and the problems it presents (the culminating activity); and on Friday, an evaluation of the various learning activities of the week.[19]

Alert Catholic school educators are beginning to formulate problem-centered units whose learnings will be readily transferable to real-life situations. Such a development is only natural since the *Summa Theologica* is, to a large degree, a compilation of problem-centered units (questions) composed of problem-centered lessons (articles). The three-volume series, *Guiding Growth in Christian Social Living,* prepared by Sisters M. Joan, O.P., and M. Nona, O.P., under the auspices of the Commission on American Citizenship of Catholic University of America, represents the most comprehensive effort to date to structure learning experiences within the broad framework of problem-centered units of eternal and personal concern, of objective and subjective importance.[20] However, this series was written for Catholic elementary schools. A major task facing Catholic secondary school educators is to construct a series of problem-centered resource and teaching units which will integrate content and process into an overall Christian world view.

A good cooperative teaching unit plan, to be effective, usable, and readily available, should be set down in written form. This written form should be constructed in such a way that it will be a comprehensive and flexible guide to structuring the learning situations within that unit. This written plan may take on a number of forms, e.g., an outline (most common), a chart, a narrative. Whatever its compositional framework, the written unit plan should include the following data, in order, and in some sort of list form:

> (1) a tentative title which indicates the nature of the problem; (2) a brief explanation of the underlying idea of the problem which shows the relation to pupils' interests; (3) description of the specific needs of the class; (4) a list of objectives, preferably few and realistic; (5) a list of possible activities and experiences showing a close correlation with objectives and subject-matter content; (6) a list of the subject-matter learnings to be achieved and skills to be employed, taught, and emphasized; (7) expected outcomes in subject matter, skills, and attitudes; (8) specific visual and auditory aids; (9) a bibliography for both the teacher and the pupils; (10) materials needed in the solution of the problem; (11) suggestions for a variety of possible culminating activities; (12) provision for specific means of evaluation; (13) space for comments,

[19] See Robert A. Bennett, "Unit Ideas for the New School Year," *The English Journal,* XLIX (September, 1960), pp. 400–408.

[20] Sister M. Joan, O.P., and Sister M. Nona, O.P., *Guiding Growth in Christian Social Living.* (Washington, D.C.: Catholic University of America Press, 1944–1946), vols. 1–3; see especially vol. 1, p. 255.

changes, and additions, including provision for anecdotal record of progress and significant happenings; (14) estimate of the probable duration of the unit.[21]

A unit is no better than the teacher makes it to be. A problem-centered Core unit plan can easily be transformed, perhaps unwittingly, into a subject-centered approach if the teacher uses autocratic devices, does most or all of the talking, gives answers too readily to the problem under consideration, and the like. The unit plan, then, is only an overall guide to teaching; it is not the perfect and automatic guarantor of effective teaching.

LESSON PLANNING

A lesson may be defined as a series of learning experiences which occur in a single block of time on a particular day. The lesson represents the smallest unitary subdivision of the school's total educational program (which consists of grades, courses, units, and lessons). Like a unit, a good lesson is almost always a planned one.

A lesson plan is an organized statement of general and specific educational goals together with the specific means by which these goals are to be attained by the learners under the guidance of the teacher on a given day. The purpose of a lesson plan is to structure the learning activities in such a way that the pupils will achieve the desired educational outcomes in an orderly rather than a haphazard manner. "Structure" here does not imply autocratic teacher domination of the lesson, but rather the overall pattern in which students will pursue their learning activities. Woodruff has observed that individual lessons "make their best contribution to student progress when each one presents one significant concept or skill from a well planned sequence of concepts and skills, and when each lesson is planned so that it follows the natural processes of teaching and learning." [22]

While considerable cooperative teacher-pupil planning is done at the initiation of a unit, relatively little is done at the outset of the lesson. The chief reason for this is the fact that the unit planning includes in a broad way the goals and scope of the various lessons; hence additional extensive cooperative lesson planning would be a needless repetition. The teacher, guided by his own knowledge of necessary minimal educational goals and by the students' needs and interests as expressed in the

[21] Curriculum Development Divisions of the New York City Board of Education, *Social Studies, Grades 7, 8 and 9*. Curriculum Bulletin no. 5, 1951–1952 ser. (New York: Board of Education of New York City, 1951), pp. 34–35.

[22] Woodruff, *op. cit.*, p. 173.

cooperative unit-planning sessions, has the responsibility of drawing up a lesson plan which will realize these meshed objectives. This is no easy task, a fact which can be readily grasped when one realizes the great number of elements involved in the construction of an effective lesson plan.

A good lesson plan has a great many characteristics:

1. It should be integrated into the unit. It should have continuity with the other lessons in the unit, a continuity of both content and process. A lesson must never become an isolated entity; rather it must be a specific furthering of the total development of the entire unit. Hence the ultimate basic aims of each lesson within a unit will remain the same, while the specific aims and outcomes of each separate lesson will be different but related.

2. It should be orderly. It should provide for a group of learning experiences which will be developed in a proper logical and psychological arrangement.

3. It should be flexible. The teacher must have the freedom to depart from the procedures neatly typewritten in the plan if the dynamic teacher-pupil encounter during a lesson is achieving significant educational content and process goals not anticipated when the plan was originally drawn up. A good teacher is above any lesson plan. The plan helps to keep the goals and procedures of the lesson in focus, and the teacher must not expect any more than that from it. A lesson plan guides the teacher; it should not imprison him.

4. It should be reasonably definite in its suggested pedagogical procedures. However, it should not degenerate into formalism, a rigid set of procedures so definite that it cannot be modified during the progress of the lesson should it become apparent that the exigencies of the situation call for its modification or even possible abandonment.

5. It should include just the proper amount of detail. An underdetailed plan will not provide sufficient guidance to the teacher, while an overdetailed plan will reduce the lesson to a hypermethodical, formalistic, or even unhuman situation.

6. It should suggest a variety of teaching and learning procedures. This is essential if the lesson is to move along briskly and thus ensure continuous pupil mental activity and external participation. As Hosmanek has remarked, the teacher should not overestimate the attention span of adolescent learners.[23]

7. The development of the lesson plan, together with the choice of procedures attendant upon this development, should be founded on a sound psychological basis. The whole-part-whole method in which the students see the material first as a related whole, then analyze its component elements, and

[23] John J. Hosmanek, "Planning for Good Learning," *Bulletin of the National Association of Secondary-School Principals,* XLIII (December, 1959), p. 30.

finally synthesize these elements into the original but now more meaningful whole should be the psychological foundation for the learning activities suggested in the plan.

8. It should suggest content and process learnings that are related to real life and which can be subsequently transferred to nonclassroom situations by the learner. The plan should propose learning experiences which will enable the student to form a personal, existential, and therefore meaningful bond between himself and the content-process material learned; e.g., in a lesson plan on poetry, the pupil should be led to actually share and feel the experience and vision of the poet's glimpse of reality.[24]

9. It should have only one main specific aim. It may include some supporting and ancillary aims, but nonetheless, each lesson should have but one principal aim. This aim should not merely be thought of as encompassing solely a subject-matter goal but can, and indeed should, be broader, e.g., an attitudinal aim, a value aim, and the like.

10. The main aim of the lesson plan, together with whatever supporting aims might also be present, should be educationally significant. They should not be objectively or subjectively trivial, but should substantially further the school's overall goal of enabling the pupils to learn the truth.

11. It should provide for continual intrinsic and extrinsic motivation. Motivation should be one of the first activities of the lesson so as to arouse pupil interest and cooperation. Furthermore, it should perdure throughout the lesson so that this interest will grow rather than wither and perhaps even die.

12. It should suggest methods for enabling the pupils to reinforce the learnings of the previous lesson(s). This reinforcement is necessary to ensure the pupils' grasp of the continuity of the various lessons and the place of the present lesson in the overall unit pattern. The activities to reinforce the learnings of the previous lesson(s) should occur in the initiatory phase of the lesson.

13. It should make provision for pupils' use of their apperceptive learning mass in the unfolding of new and unfamiliar learnings. In this way the pupils will more easily and meaningfully learn new material, since it will be presented in the broad context of, and as an extension of, the body of content-process, truths they already possess.

14. It should suggest activities which will take into account the individual differences of the pupils within the class groups. Students should be presented with problems which might be of especial concern to them at this particular moment in their lives; e.g., an act of grave social injustice might have happened to one of their neighbors last week. The level and type of questions and assignments should be geared to the varying abilities and needs of the different students.

[24] See Max Nadel, "Outline of a Lesson Plan in Poetry Appreciation," *High Points,* XLI (October, 1959), pp. 60–63.

15. It should provide for a significant number of pupil activities, not only of the external type but even more importantly of the mental, internal variety. Thus, Struck has noted that lesson plans "should place emphasis on pupil activity and learning rather than on teacher activity." [25] This concept necessarily flows from the Thomistic doctrine of the primary role of the student in the learning process.

16. It should make extensive use of problem solving as the basic developmental procedure. Problem solving is probably the best single pedagogical technique for helping the student through his own activity to actualize his potentialities for the acquisition of truth.

17. It should contain some previously formulated pivotal and leading questions. These questions will aid the teacher in eliciting from the students those key concepts and attitudes upon which the development of the entire lesson hinges.

18. It should detail the appropriate resource and sensory materials, e.g., filmstrip, chalkboard illustrations necessary for the implementation of the lesson, together with the approximate moment at which they will be introduced into the learning situation.

19. It should include medial and final summaries. These two summaries, the one in the middle of the lesson, the other near its conclusion, are of great importance for ascertaining the degree to which the students are learning the material. The teacher should not do the summarizing; it should be the pupils themselves who synthesize the basic learnings they acquired during the course of the lesson.

20. It should list definite and appropriate assignments to be performed by the students at home and/or in individualized study at school after the lesson has been concluded. This will not only extend the lesson beyond the specific classroom situation but will enable the students to broaden, deepen, and reinforce those learnings acquired in class.

21. It should provide suggestions for evaluation of those learnings attained by the students during the lesson. The form of the evaluation can be written or oral, individualized or socialized, but whatever the type, evaluation should be one of the concluding activities of the lesson.

22. It should be so arranged that it will lend itself to subsequent revision after the lesson has been concluded. No lesson plan is perfect, and its use in a classroom situation will immediately reveal its weaknesses, e.g., some poor pivotal questions, insufficient motivation, lack of attention to individual differences, failure of the students to attain the desired educational outcomes.

There should be a section at the bottom of the lesson plan entitled "Remarks" so that the teacher can note the strengths and especially the weaknesses of the plan as it was implemented in the classroom. For

[25] F. Theodore Struck, *Creative Teaching.* (New York: Wiley, 1938), p. 181.

most effective use, these remarks should be written down as soon as possible after the actual lesson has been given. Regrettably, some teachers never revise their lesson plans, with the result that these plans, instead of being guides to richer learning experiences for the pupils, become mere written expressions of fossilized staticness.

From a structural point of view, each lesson plan has three phases: (1) initiatory activities, i.e., those which launch the lesson, for example, the introductory motivation; (2) developmental activities, i.e., those which will lead the student toward attaining the desired educational outcomes, such as use of pivotal questions; (3) culminating activities, i.e., those which in some way climax the lesson and serve to reinforce the learnings gained in the lesson, for example, the final summary or a project assignment.

Lesson plans should be put into written form. By actually writing them, the teacher will achieve a clarity and definiteness not possible if the plan is a mere general outline in the teacher's mind. Writing makes the precise man. A written lesson plan is also valuable for a substitute teacher who might be called on to fill in for the regular teacher in the case of absence.[26]

In such instances the written lesson plan will enable the substitute teacher to continue the unit apace; it will reduce personal confusion caused by not knowing what to teach and will avoid loss of pupil time and effort to attain the total unit objectives. Besvinick has observed that a formal written lesson plan cannot be prepared between classes as some less professional teachers seem to think; rather, a good deal of painstaking preparation and sustained assiduous effort are required to produce a well-ordered written lesson plan.[27]

In writing out the lesson plan, the teacher should draw on many sources. The overall framework should be, of course, the meshed combination of what the school and teacher think the students must learn, together with what the students themselves believe they should learn from the course. The details of the plan should be synthesized from such sources as specialized books on the subject-matter fields covered in the specific phase of the problem area to be learned during the given lesson, the teacher's knowledge of how adolescent learning takes place, general and specialized curriculum guides, resource units, and his own past experience, including previous lesson plans.

[26] See William L. Phinney, "Producing Better Lesson Plans," *Bulletin of the National Association of Secondary-School Principals,* XLII (November, 1958), pp. 103–104.

[27] Sidney L. Besvinick, "An Effective Daily Lesson Plan," *The Clearing House,* XXXIV (March, 1960), p. 431.

SUGGESTED OUTLINE OF DETAILED LESSON PLAN

School .... *Date* ....

Name of Class .... *Type of Class* (e.g., bright, normal, slow)

Problem or Topic ....

Major Aim ....

Supporting Aims: (1) ....

  (2) ....

  (3) ....

Pedagogical Procedures	*Desired Learning Outcomes*
1. Motivational Devices (Time) .... (list the devices)	interest in problem or topic
2. Apperceptive Mass (Time)	(*a*) reinforce related past learnings (list chief past learnings)
	(*b*) prepare base for new learning
3. Resource and Instructional Materials (list specific materials)	attainment of lesson aims
4. Pupil Activities (Time) .... (list major activities)	acquisition of new learnings (list specific learnings)
5. Individual Differences	tailoring activities to each pupil
6. Pivotal Questions (Time) ..... (list questions)	focusing on major lesson learnings (list major learning for each question)
7. Culminating Activities (Time) ... (list questions)	crystallize lesson learnings
8. Medial and Final Summaries ...... (Time)	reinforce major lesson learnings (list learnings to be summarized)
9. Evaluation Procedures (Time) ... (list procedures)	assessment of pupil learning (list learnings to be evaluated)
10. Assignment (Time) .... (give details of assignment)	continue lesson outside classroom (list learnings to be so continued)

Teacher Remarks on the Lesson ....

CHAPTER IX TEACHING THE CLASS

The particular set of methods a teacher employs during the course of class instruction will be rooted in and determined by the overall curricular design. A subject-centered design will normally result in the following teaching procedures: (1) little or no teacher-pupil planning; (2) dominance of the lecture method, with limited opportunity for all-class discussion; (3) great attention to logical organization of materials to be learned, with some attention to psychological factors; (4) meaningfulness found in the materials to be learned; (5) heavy emphasis on the mastery of precisely what is contained in the lecture notes and textbooks; (6) learning experiences and activities carried on almost exclusively within the confines of the classroom; (7) evaluation made solely through examinations which test exact mastery of the material taught.

A total student-centered approach is usually characterized by the following pedagogical methods: (1) total teacher-pupil planning, with the students themselves doing all the planning in terms of their individual needs and interests; (2) completely individualized teaching procedures, with each pupil studying and experiencing whatever his needs call for; (3) great attention to the psychological factors involved in the learning process, with little or no attention to logical organization of the material to be learned; (4) meaningfulness to be found in the need and interest structure of each individual student; (5) heavy emphasis on learning what the pupils feel they need and wish to acquire; (6) learning experiences carried on wherever a pupil's needs or interests lead him; (7) evaluation made solely on the basis of how well each pupil's needs and interests were satisfied, with the major task of evaluation vested in the pupil.

The Core curriculum is typically implemented through the following teaching procedures: (1) cooperative teacher-pupil planning, the teacher being at all times the director and guide in selection; (2) balanced use of individualized and socialized pedagogical methods, with occasional utilization of the lecture; (3) maintenance of a dynamic equilibrium of logical and psychological factors involved in the organization and presentation of learning materials, with the psychological serving as a base for the logical; (4) meaningfulness found in the integration of the material into the learner's personality structure, so that the material can be existentially synthesized and implemented in all aspects of life; (5) emphasis on the acquisition of those materials which the community, school, teacher, pupils (and in Catholic high schools, the Church) cooperatively think the students should learn for successful living in this world (and in the next); (6) learning experiences and activities carried out within the general framework of the classroom, but with extensive utilization of extra classwork (during school time), such as research in the library or field trips; (7) evaluation made on the basis of how well the students achieved the general and specific educational goals of the class, with various formal and informal instruments of evaluation employed.

Sister M. Joachim, I.H.M., has remarked that "the young teacher is usually so intent on subject matter that sometimes he is oblivious to teaching techniques." [1] This is most regrettable, for it results not only in the students learning far less, but also in the ineffectual implementation of the school's curricular objectives. Without good methodology, a teacher is not a teacher but merely (at best) an information dispenser. Subject matter, attitudes, and values do not enter the student's mind through direct Divine illumination; in a classroom situation they must, according to St. Thomas, be actualized by the pedagogic skill of the teacher who causes the students to actualize their learning potential. Subject matter alone is insufficient to do this; if it were, the teacher could easily be eliminated and replaced by a textbook and a teaching machine.

[1] Sister M. Joachim, I.H.M., "Help for Our Lay Teachers," *Catholic School Journal*, LIX (June, 1959), p. 37.

Socialized and Individualized Teaching

A socialized lesson is one which involves all members of the class at all times in every phase of the lesson. An individualized lesson is one which involves only one student and the teacher. In a socialized lesson emphasis is placed on the interaction of a *group* of pupils and the teacher. The students react on one another instead of just to the teacher. In an individualized lesson, stress is placed on the interaction of just one pupil (at a time) and the teacher. In both types of lesson, the task of the teacher is to guide and democratically direct pupil self-activity, rather than to become the center of activity himself. Socialized techniques include all-class discussion, committee work, panels, role-playing situations, group-directed developmental questions, and other methods touched on in this chapter. Individualized techniques include contract procedures, individual projects, private consultations, and the like. Both socialized and individualized approaches stand in opposition to the old type of lecture-recitation technique which was conducted along different lines.

Socialized teaching flows from the concept held by many thinkers and succinctly enunciated by Pius XI that "education is essentially a social and not a mere individual activity";[2] hence, classroom teaching is a social function. Indeed the classroom is a unique social setting because its primary and basic purpose is the conscious and deliberate effort to enable the students to learn. Since it is a social situation (albeit a unique form, but still truly and fully a social situation), the classroom functions according to the rules common to all groups. Hence the teacher must be constantly aware of the multiplicity of psychological forces which are at work in groups generally and in instructional groups particularly.[3] In socialized teaching, procedures will vary as the composition of the group varies, e.g., an intellectually heterogeneous class, a class from low-income families, a college-bound class. Thus Warren and Iannacone conducted a study of a group of underachievers in junior high school. This group was split into two divisions, control and experimental. The control group continued to be taught in the normal classroom manner as prescribed in the syllabus. With the experimental group, teaching and curricular techniques were adapted to group needs and conditions. The results indicated that while the degree of achievement of the control group remained the same, the experimental group showed a

[2] Pope Pius XI, *Christian Education of Youth.* (Washington: NCWC, 1936), p. 6.
[3] See Jacob W. Getzels and Herbert A. Thelan, "The Classroom as a Unique Social System," *The Dynamics of Instructional Groups,* National Society for the Study of Education, Fifty-Ninth Yearbook, Part II. (Chicago: University of Chicago Press, 1960), pp. 53–82.

marked increase in the mastery of tool subjects, evinced a lessening of discipline problems, and improved in their interpersonal relationships.[4]

Concerning the last element of these findings, it behooves the teacher to realize that the classroom constitutes a social group subject to the dynamics of social and personal relationships. Hence in the classroom situation there is an external environment which impinges on the group from the outside, e.g., school regulations, and the internal environment consisting of the interrelationships existing among the members of the group itself. The teacher to be effective must operate as a member of the internal environment because this milieu has a greater impact on learning and retention than does the external environment. If the teacher sociologically belongs exclusively or even primarily to the external environment, he will possess authority, but not the real leadership, actual power, or friendship so necessary for effective teaching.[5]

Personal relationships in instructional groups, then, are no pretty by-product of learning, but an important cause of effective learning. Wingo, summing up the research in the 1950s, states that the studies support "the principle that learning, in both its qualitative and quantative aspects, is related to the kinds of personal relationships which obtain in the classroom." [6] Personal relationships in the classroom are of two types, viz., between the pupil and the teacher and between the pupil and his peer group in the class. It is the teacher who more than anyone else is most responsible for creating a warm, friendly, and co-operative classroom climate which is conducive to good interpersonal relationships and hence to good learning.

Individualized teaching is based on the individual differences of each pupil. Though he is a member of a group, the pupil always remains an individual. No two students in any group, no matter how homogeneous, learn at the same rate. Hence every classroom must provide for individualized teaching.

In the past, some efforts were made to provide for individualized instruction as an organized part of the curriculum. Perhaps the two most celebrated attempts were the Winnetka Plan and the Dalton Plan. Today the Trump Report, which is an endeavor to provide a blueprint for the nation's secondary schools in the decades ahead, places great emphasis on individualized teaching through large blocks of time devoted to

[4] Sue A. Warren and Lawrence Iannacone, "Normal Children Who Just Don't Try," *School Executive*, LXXVIII (July, 1959), pp. 40–41.

[5] See Gale E. Jensen, "The Social Structure of the Classroom Group: An Observational Framework," *Journal of Educational Psychology*, LVI (October, 1955), pp. 362–374.

[6] G. Max Wingo, "Methods of Teaching," *Encyclopedia of Educational Research*, 3d ed. (New York: Macmillan, 1960), p. 848.

what is termed "independent study." The extent of time a particular student will devote to independent study varies with age, achievement level, and professional decision, but in general, "independent study will average 40 per cent of the school's schedule for students." [7] Independent study is not mere busywork, but a program of work undertaken by the student under the general supervision and periodic cooperative activity of the teacher. This program of work is tailored to the abilities, achievement level, needs, and interests of each student.

In a famous passage, Mearns quotes a high school student who was told by her teachers that in order to do well in the College Entrance Examinations, she would have to devote her high school years almost exclusively to learning and cramming the information required for success in these examinations. Reacting to this, the student wrote to one educator:

They tell us these are the formative years; the indecisive years; the years in which we must ponder; the years on which so much of our future life depends. And then they make out a curriculum which we must follow and leave us no time in which to explore those branches which promise a career.

I love to sing, but if I prepare for college, I have no time for singing. I love and long to cover reams of paper with startling and original thought, but —I have no time. . . .

I do not think I am lazy. Please understand. I want to follow the course that will profit me the most in character and happiness in the end.[8]

This pupil wanted the school to give her not mere bookishness, but a total education, an education which was individualized not only in subject matter but in depth and breadth of creative expression. One of the greatest advantages of individualized teaching (and one which demands its inclusion in the school's curriculum) is that it fosters pupil creativity. Creativity may be defined as the production of something new. A human person, sharing the image and likeness of God, also shares with Him the desire to create. By nature, then, man is a maker, an artist in the true sense of the term. A pupil's desire to create, to make, is a God-implanted urge and must never be considered a form of personal rebellion on the part of the student. Creativity is a highly personal thing and can be satisfied and fructified in the school only by individualized learning.

Creative pupil expression considered objectively might not be at the level of a Michaelangelo or a Shakespeare, but for the student it consciously or unconsciously represents *his* sharing, *his* cooperating with

---

[7] J. Lloyd Trump and Dorsey Baynham, *Guide to Better Schools.* (Chicago: Rand McNally, 1961), p. 27.

[8] Hughes Mearns, *Creative Power.* (New York: Doubleday, 1929), p. 184.

the activity of his Creator; therefore, regardless of its objective merit, creative expression is to be prized. Consequently, teachers, especially in Catholic high schools, committed as they are to the deepest possible pupil participation in Divine activity, should do all in their power to foster individualized creative expression in their classes. The school situation provides an opportunity for the orderly development and skillful refinement by the teacher of these creative expressions of the students. Thus a class in English literature should be characterized not only by critically examining the style and beauty in the writings of British authors, but also by the application of these elements of style and beauty to creative literary productions of their own.

Fostering creativity is often a difficult task for the teacher. Students in both public and Catholic high schools on the basis of past school experience have become thoroughly conditioned to the fact that teachers on the whole do not wish their classrooms to be vehicles for pupil creativity. This conditioning has over the years caused a progressively decreased pupil desire to exercise creativity and initiative in the class-room.[9] Teachers must first break down this wall of resistance and inertia if they are to liberate and constructively channel their pupils' creative talents.

To stimulate creativity in the classroom the teacher must himself possess a sense of security, for as Lindsey has remarked, no one quite knows where a pupil's creativity will lead.[10] Insecure teachers need to make sure at all times that they know exactly where their students' activities are leading so that they (the teachers) will be able to exercise complete control over these activities and thus attain security. The secure teacher has no such need to compensate. Hence a teacher's decision to foster creativity will be essentially a decision based on his own personality. This conclusion has important implications for the preservice education and selection of prospective teachers.

Problem Solving

Problem solving is an educational device whereby the teacher and the pupils attempt in a conscious, planned, purposeful effort to arrive at an explanation or solution to some educationally significant difficulty. Problem solving is a general educational method rather than a specific pedagogical technique. It is probably the method most productive of learning. Socrates used it exclusively in the Platonic dialogues, and St. Thomas in the *Summa Theologica*. In our own times, perceptive educa-

[9] Even experimental schools find difficulty in this regard; cf. Trump and Baynham, *loc. cit.*

[10] Margaret Lindsey, "Preservice Preparation for Creativity in Teaching," in Miel (ed.), *Creativity in Teaching.* (Belmont, Calif.: Wadsworth, 1961), pp. 201–207.

tors and thinkers have recognized its indispensability as an educational tool. Msgr. George Johnson, eminent Catholic educator of this century, wrote that "the best way to train the mind is to confront it with real problems and to give it the opportunity and the freedom to solve them." [11]

Problem solving by its very nature causes the pupil to learn things for himself, by use of his own powers. This is the heart of all true and good education, as many authorities recognize. Fr. Cunningham, C.S.C., the important Catholic educational theorist, said that "all true education is self-education." [12] Etienne Gilson, outstanding Catholic philosopher, stated that "the ultimate end of our pedagogy should be to teach children to learn by themselves, because in fact, there is nothing else we [teachers] can teach." [13] These speculative judgments are supported by empirical evidence. A review of the pertinent studies by Kersh concludes that "the hypothesis that learning through independent discovery is superior to learning by rote is well supported by the existing research evidence." [14]

Because problem solving is so richly productive of the highest quality of learning, it should form the basis of every teaching technique, from the lecture to class discussion, to panel, to role playing.

Since the time of Aristotle, two basic types of problems have been identified. The first type arises from a series of related but seemingly conflicting data and for a solution calls for a universal or generalized concept which will adequately explain and harmonize these data. An example of this type of problem would be: "All Catholic young people know it is sinful to lie, yet in certain circumstances many of these boys and girls commit falsehoods. Why?" This kind of problem is called inductive. The second type of problem arises from two or more related but seemingly conflicting generalizations, and for a solution calls for a reconciliation of these generalizations, or a rejection of all but one of the generalizations, or the formulation of a new universal concept. An example of this type of problem would be: "God is All-Merciful. But God punishes evil. How can a God Who is All-Merciful also punish?" This kind of problem is called deductive. Some problems studied in the

[11] George Johnson, "Education for Life," in Sisters M. Joan, O.P., and M. Nona, O.P. (eds.), *Guiding Growth in Christian Social Living.* (Washington, D.C.: Catholic University of America Press, 1944), vol. I, p. 7.

[12] William F. Cunningham, C.S.C., *The Pivotal Problems of Education.* (New York: Macmillan, 1940), p. 301.

[13] Etienne Gilson, "The Eminence of Teaching," *McAuley Lecture, 1953.* (West Hartford, Conn.: St. Joseph College, 1954), p. 13.

[14] Bert Y. Kersh, "The Adequacy of Meaning as an Explanation for the Superiority of Learning by Independent Discovery," *Journal of Educational Psychology,* XLIX (October, 1958), p. 282.

classroom will, of course, be not strictly inductive or deductive, but a combination of both. Such a combination is often beneficial since it forces the student to use both his analytical and synthetic mental powers. However, more often than not, problems will tend to be primarily inductive.

The procedure by which the students will solve a problem under consideration varies with the basic type of problem. It goes without saying that before any method is employed the students must understand the problem and hold it meaningful. The steps by which an inductive problem and a deductive problem are solved are listed below.

INDUCTIVE	DEDUCTIVE
1. The original facts are carefully examined.	1. The conflicting generalizations or universals are carefully examined.
2. New data are gathered and compared with old data.	2. The facts upon which these generalizations are based are inspected.
3. A generalization or universal concept which attempts to solve the problem is proposed.	3. A new universal is proposed which will attempt to resolve the problem, should the particular data be correct.
4. All the facts are reviewed to determine whether the generalization is both true and solves the problem.	4. This new generalization is compared to other known true generalizations and data to determine whether this new generalization is both true and solves the problem.

There are five characteristics of an educationally worthwhile problem. First, it should be a real problem rather than an artificial one contrived by the teacher solely to give the pupil an exercise in mental gymnastics. Second, it should be an educationally significant problem, one productive of important and worthwhile learnings. Third, it should mesh student concerns with the school's ideal of what the student should learn. Fourth, it should be possible of solution; i.e., it should not be too deep for the particular group of students, and the specific information needed for solving the problem should be available. Fifth, the problem should be related to the subunit, the unit, and the course.

Some authors have made problem solving opposed to "conveying subject matter." [15] This is an unwarranted dichotomy. All problem solving, by its very nature, requires that subject matter be learned and integrated, else how could a problem possibly be solved? Problem solving places emphasis on the students' actively acquiring information and critically examining it, rather than on the teacher's presentation of this

[15] See Ray H. Simpson, *Improving Teaching-Learning Processes*. (New York: Longmans, 1953), p. 153.

material. The former is true education; the latter is information dispensing. Cross and Gaier observe that "successful problem-solving involves both the knowledge of fundamental facts and their effective utilization in arriving at a solution." [16] Hence problem solving is one of the best ways to effectively learn subject matter, since it involves not only learning but actual use of what has been learned. This application not only forces the student to integrate the specific materials which he acquired, but by its very nature reinforces retention of these materials. In problem solving, many bodies of knowledge are utilized and integrated to solve a problem. This is an added reason why the Core, discussed in Chapter VI, is the most educationally worthwhile curriculum.

How does a teacher guide and direct a lesson or unit which is built around a problem-solving approach? There are five pedagogical steps which should be part of every problem-solving learning situation. *First*, the teacher and the pupils should cooperatively choose a problem to be studied. This problem should possess the qualifications of an educationally significant problem discussed above. Cooperative decision is important because only if the problem is meaningful to the students and fully accepted by them will the optimum learning result. Struck has noted that "the pupil's attitude toward learning is more important than well-ordered courses of instruction." [17]

Second, the students should be led to see why it is a problem. A problem exists when several conflicting solutions to a difficulty seem plausible. There can be no problem if there is only one completely satisfactory answer. Hence teaching by alternatives, discussed in a previous chapter, is the procedure basic to a problem-solving lesson. Thus in a lesson on social justice, the teacher in a Catholic secondary school should not present the material but rather formulate and work out with the students such problems as: "This alcoholic refuses to work. To help people who refuse to work encourages sloth. But it is not right to let a person starve." Another problem might be formulated in this way: "Christ taught by word and deed that we should turn the other cheek when attacked. But such an attitude will only result in good people being constantly stepped on and will therefore contribute to the supremacy of evil on this earth." It is important for the students to appreciate the worth of each alternative, else how can they understand not only the problem itself but even more importantly, the deep reasons why one solution is superior to all others? Catholic high school teachers in particular should not fear to present problems which offer a variety of

[16] K. Patricia Cross and Eugene L. Gaier, "Technique in Problem-Solving as a Predictor of Educational Achievement," *Journal of Educational Psychology*, XLVI (April, 1955), p. 193.

[17] F. Theodore Struck, *Creative Teaching*. (New York: Wiley, 1938), p. 371.

enticingly plausible solutions. After all, God gave Adam and Eve an alternative even though He knew they would choose the wrong one! Under the guidance and direction of the teacher, the student can be skillfully led to the right solution but at the same time led to appreciate the reasons why other people hold differing solutions. A true teacher does not offer only one solution and at the same time either fail to mention others or present them in such a way that the class must necessarily conclude that no person of minimal good will or intelligence could hold such a solution. "Commanding is not teaching," observed Vincent Edward Smith.[18] This is especially important in religion classes.

Third, the class should work on the problem under the guidance of the teacher. The method of attack will be determined by the type of problem, whether inductive or deductive. Students must do research to discover pertinent facts and principles, their *raisons d'être,* their causes and effects. In working on the problem, the students should receive continual guidance and direction from the teacher. A study by Aronov concluded that when the teacher gave inconsistent direction and guidance to the pupils during a problem-solving situation, the result was a confusing and detrimental influence on learning as compared with the effect of consistent guidance. Even a lack of guidance was found superior to inconsistent guidance.[19] However, teacher guidance and direction of pupil activities should never degenerate into telling the solution. Craig's review of the pertinent research on directed versus independent discovery of the basic principles underlying correct answers in problem-solving situations concluded that "students use and benefit from [teacher] help given them in their search for the bases determining correct responses; but when correct responses are specified in advance of activity, they neither search nor discover. It is probable that they just try to remember specific responses." [20] Since the teacher is working with a group, socialized teaching methods should normally (but not always) be used in problem-solving situations. An interesting study by Lorge and associates of a problem-solving situation concluded that the solutions to problems offered by a group were markedly superior to the solutions given by separate individuals.[21]

[18] Vincent Edward Smith, "The Catholic School: A Re-Examination," *Bulletin of the National Catholic Educational Association,* LII (August, 1955), p. 41.

[19] Bernard M. Aronov, "The Influence of Consistent and Inconsistent Guidance on Human Learning and Transfer," *Journal of Educational Psychology,* XLIX (April, 1958), p. 84.

[20] Robert C. Craig, "Directed versus Independent Discovery of Established Relations," *Journal of Educational Psychology,* XLVII (April, 1956), p. 232.

[21] Irving Lorge and Associates, "Problem-Solving by Teams and by Individuals in a Field Setting," *Journal of Educational Psychology,* XLVI (March, 1955), pp. 160–161.

Fourth, the class should work out a solution to the problem under consideration. The determination of the correct solution must be made in accordance with right principles and the meshing of these principles with the concrete circumstances in which these principles operate, e.g., the principle of the virtue of charity as seen in the context of an atomic war. A pupil adept at problem solving is one who understands the basic principles and data underlying a problem so that he can arrive at an intelligent principle-directed yet data-conscious solution. The poor problem solver is the one who endeavors to apply memorized solutions of previous situations univocally to new problem situations. The first student is a thinker, the second a rote memorizer. A valuable process by-product of the problem-solving activity is serendipity, which Edward A. Fitzpatrick has defined as "the art of making unexpected discoveries, of finding something for which one was not looking." [22] Often these unexpected discoveries prove more educationally significant than the object of one's search.

Fifth, the class as a whole and the pupils as individuals should implement the solution in their own lives. Failure to do this would be to reduce schoolwork to a mere game in which a pupil indulges with no intention of enriching his life. Failure to implement solutions would be equivalent to neglecting to extend the goals and resolutions of a spiritual retreat into one's life. Thus a religion class working on the problem "Should lay people go to Mass daily?" should not only study the nature and effects of the liturgy and the sacraments, but also the religious attitudes of the community, hours of work, minimum wages, and the like; the study should also result in greater participation at daily Mass by the students, their parents, and friends.

Too many public and Catholic secondary school teachers are unwilling to adopt problem-solving procedures in their classrooms. Some of these do not realize the tremendous value of problem solving as an educational tool for promoting optimum learning. A goodly percentage prefer the lecture-recitation method to problem solving because the latter seems new and represents a change in the pedagogical tradition of the last few centuries. This group should heed the words of William H. Conley, prominent contemporary Catholic educator: "Change which leads to a better fulfillment of our [educational] objectives and our mission must not be opposed merely because it is change." [23] Although this statement was directed to teachers in Catholic schools, it is equally applicable to those in public education.

[22] Edward A. Fitzpatrick, "Definitions and Educational Terminology," *Catholic School Journal,* LVIII (April, 1958), p. 36.

[23] William H. Conley, "Focus on Improvement," *Catholic School Journal,* LXI (September, 1961), p. 4.

TECHNIQUES OF THE LESSON

Lecture

The lecture is a pedagogical method whereby the teacher formally delivers a carefully planned expository address on some particular topic or problem. The lecture technique should not be confused with telling. Telling is the supplying by the teacher of pertinent information which the student needs to know in order to achieve some educational goal, e.g., solving a problem, understanding the background of a topic. Telling tends to be brief, but a lecture is usually quite long, often lasting an entire period.

The primary purpose of the lecture is to present salient facts and concepts in an orderly manner and in as brief a time as possible.

The lecture technique has at least four distinct advantages:

1. It presents the material in an orderly, logical fashion so that it can be clearly understood by the pupils.

2. It covers a great deal of material in the shortest possible time, thus promoting instructional efficiency.

3. It ensures that the students will be exposed to a minimum amount of material.

4. It trains the students in the art of listening.[24]

The lecture technique has at least eight disadvantages which to a significant degree offset its advantages:

1. It makes the learner a passive agent in the learning process. To be sure, the learner is not completely passive, but nevertheless his is primarily a passive role. Good learning requires the student to be as fully an active agent as possible.

2. It is almost exclusively a teacher-centered situation. The pupil in whom the learning is supposed to take place should be the hub of classroom activity.

3. It can be mimeographed. By use of a duplicating machine the students can have the entire contents of the lecture in their hands in the few minutes it takes to distribute these sheets of information to the class. This method is more efficient than the lecture technique since it provides the same amount of information in a shorter time and without the possibility of error. (Students often make errors in transcribing class notes.) Indeed lecturing is really a carryover from ancient and medieval times when the students had no textbooks or printed notes for their courses because these materials were extremely expensive—the only alternative was the lecture

[24] For a development of the last point, see Nelson L. Bossing, *Teaching in Secondary Schools*, 3d ed. (Boston: Houghton Mifflin, 1952), pp. 138–139.

method of teaching.[25] Inexpensive text and reference books as well as extensive use of duplicating machines have eliminated most of the need for lectures.

4. It is often a waste of time because, being passive, the students learn little. The lecture seems to be efficient, but this is solely from the viewpoint of how much material the teacher presented rather than how much the student learned and retained. Moreover, the lecture is an inefficient teaching tool in the development of attitude formation and process outcomes. Fitzpatrick's dictum should always be kept in mind: "There is no teaching where there is no learning." [26]

5. It does not guarantee that the pupils will understand its contents. Being almost exclusively teacher-centered, it affords little opportunity during the lesson to evaluate the amount and degree of pupil understandings.

6. It is conducive to pupil inattentiveness. Pupils, like any other human beings, will pay attention when they are the active agents in a process; when they are passive, inattention is bound to occur.

7. Most high school teachers are poor lecturers.

8. The lecture is often plagiarized from a source unknown to the students. It would be far better to direct the students to that source.

Because of the overwhelming disadvantages of the lecture method, practically all modern educators prefer the discussion method to the lecture. Nevertheless there is no conclusive body of research supporting the superiority of the discussion method over the lecture (or vice versa) as a teaching device in terms of measurable pupil learning.[27] The key word here is "measurable," and unless one holds the Connectionist doctrine that everything which has been learned can be measured, the conclusion must be that other indices of pupil learning have to be used to arrive at a valid generalization. Secondly, the "measurable pupil learning" obtained by most of the research is concerned with factual data, neglecting process outcomes as well as certain nonfactual product outcomes. Thirdly, the measuring devices often employed in ascertaining pupil learning are frequently unconsciously formulated in such a way as to screen out all but factual learning. The first point can be amplified by citing a study by Rasmussen which concluded that, in the groups surveyed, pupils in a student-centered (as opposed to an instructor-centered course) felt that they had learned more; that what they had learned would be of more practical use to them; that more attitude change had taken place;

[25] See Edward A. Block, "An Alternative to Classroom Teaching," *Educational Forum,* XVIII (January, 1954), pp. 221–224.

[26] Edward A. Fitzpatrick, "Perfection of Teaching Technique May Be Meaningless," *Catholic School Journal,* LVIII (January, 1958), p. 26.

[27] See Richard J. Hill, *A Comparative Study of Lecture and Study Methods.* (White Plains, N.Y.: Fund for Adult Education, 1960), p. 3.

that more behavioral change had occurred because of the course; and that the class had been more interesting.[28] The testimony of teachers, together with a theoretical analysis of the discussion and lecture techniques, attests to the superiority of discussion over lecture. The conclusions of students, teachers, and theory, while strictly speaking not empirically measured data, are nonetheless valid. The second of the original three points is corroborated by Stovall's review of the pertinent research which showed that the discussion method had a greater impact on forming student attitudes than did the lecture method.[29] This is of great significance since attitude learnings are one of the most important educational goals of the school. Bovard's summary of the studies revealed that there seems to be a significant correlation between the amount of classroom participation by the students and the development of their perceptions, emotions, interpersonal relationships, and possibly even their personalities as a whole.[30] An investigation by Levine and Butler on the effect of the lecture technique versus group discussion on the attempt to change the behavior of supervisors showed that a change in the behavior of supervisors in a group discussion class was effected while the behavior of supervisors in the lecture class remained unchanged.[31] The third of the original three points is strengthened by a study by Nachman and Opochinsky which confirmed the fact that "the different teaching methods have, in fact, produced differential amounts in learning but that these effects have been masked" in the traditional processes of measurement.[32]

Ultraprogressive educators of the 1920s and 1930s condemned the lecture as an educationally worthless teaching procedure. However, contemporary educators seem to agree that the lecture should enjoy *limited* use in the classroom. The Trump Report recommends the periodic use of large class groups of 100 to 150 students in which team teaching utilizing the lecture method will predominate.[33] Regrettably, in its enthusiasm this report seems to overemphasize the value of the lecture while neglecting its overwhelming disadvantages; nevertheless it is an

[28] Glen R. Rasmussen, "An Evaluation of Student-centered and Instructor-centered Methods of Conducting a Graduate Course in Education," *Journal of Educational Psychology*, XLVII (December, 1956), pp. 460–461.

[29] Thomas F. Stovall, "Lecture vs. Discussion," *Phi Delta Kappan*, XXXIX (March, 1958), pp. 255–258.

[30] Everett W. Bovard, "The Psychology of Classroom Interaction," *Journal of Educational Research*, XLV (November, 1951), pp. 215–223.

[31] Jacob Levine and John Butler, "Lecture versus Group Discussion in Changing Behavior," *Journal of Applied Psychology*, XXXVI (February, 1952), pp. 29–33.

[32] Marvin Nachman and Seymour Opochinsky, "The Effect of Different Teaching Methods: A Methodological Study," *Journal of Educational Psychology*, XLIX (October, 1958), pp. 245–249.

[33] Trump and Baynham, *op. cit.*, pp. 29–32.

indication that the lecture is being once more viewed as a valid educational procedure. Bloom's investigation suggests that at base the value of the lecture method depends on the specific objectives of the teacher. If the teacher wishes to communicate information, the lecture method is reasonably efficient, but if the teacher desires to develop the power of critical thinking, problem-solving ability, and attitudinal change, the discussion method is superior.[34] This is not to imply that the lecture method results in the best and most retainable learning, but rather that as a means of communication it is "reasonably efficient."

Techniques of Good Lecturing. A good lecture, one which will result in pupil learning, should be characterized by at least thirteen distinct features.

1. It should be carefully planned. Planning to deliver a lecture involves basically the same criteria and steps as are involved in preparing a developmental lesson plan (see Chapter VIII), except of course, it makes little or no provision for pupil activity.

2. It should be built around one central problem or topic with ancillary subproblems and topics arranged in properly subordinated fashion. This will preserve unity. Perhaps the best pedagogical basis for good lecture formulation is to pose a problem, delineate the difficulties, present a solution, and finally explain why it is the best solution.

3. It should be outlined rather than typewritten in standard prose style. This will eliminate the danger of the teacher reading the lecture, and so preserve whatever spontaneity is possible in this method.

4. It should be delivered by the teacher in such a way that the students will be immediately aware of its chief topical divisions. This will improve both pupil understanding and note taking.

5. It should not consist in continuous teacher talking, but should be interspersed with occasional developmental questions to the students.

6. It should make extensive use of verbal imagery and other oral illustrations. This is especially important in lectures developing abstract ideas. The examples and illustrations should be geared to the cultural background and intellectual level of the class; e.g., an example involving goats would be inappropriate for students in a slum area school. All examples and illustrations are analogous, not univocal, and therefore the teacher must make sure that the students understand the part of the example or illustration which is similar to the concept or fact to be learned rather than the dissimilar part.

7. It should employ anecdotes and stories so that the students' interest will be aroused and sustained. Jokes must be used with caution for they can easily fall flat or become stale.

[34] Benjamin S. Bloom, "Thought Processes in Lectures and Discussions," *Journal of General Education,* VII (April, 1953), pp. 160–169.

8. It should utilize concrete illustrative devices such as chalkboards, models, slides, motion pictures, and other audio-visual materials whenever possible. St. Thomas repeatedly emphasized the necessity for phantasms and sensory images in learning.

9. It should be delivered at the proper rate of speed. Speaking too rapidly causes confusion in student understanding and chaos in note taking.

10. It should be given in a well-modulated conversational tone of voice. Similarly the voice should be frequently inflected at the appropriate places, thus eliminating monotone and attendant pupil boredom.

11. It should never degenerate into dictation. Most schools have duplicating machines.

12. To be effective, it requires that the pupils be held responsible for the content of the lecture. Because they are passive agents in the lecture, the pupils will not normally be internally motivated to absorb the material unless it is required of them. Pupil note taking during the lecture is the standard method by which this requirement is met.

13. It should be followed up by periodic inspections of the students' notebooks to ascertain whether or not the students are transcribing the right information. If they are not, this failure should be corrected.

There are three methods a teacher may use in dealing with the matter of pupil note taking during the lecture. First he can give the students the entire lecture in mimeographed form after class. The principal advantage of this practice is that it ensures that the students will have in their possession all the important material without any omissions or mistakes. The chief disadvantage is that such a procedure might encourage pupil inattentiveness in class. Also, if the contents of the lecture are mimeographed, why have the lecture in the first place? Second, the teacher can distribute a lecture outline to the students. This outline will give the main topical subdivisions of the lecture, with ample spaces underneath each so that the pupils can fill in the details themselves. The principal advantage of this technique is that it guarantees that the students will get the most important points while preserving the necessity of attentiveness and note-taking skill required in properly filling in the factual details. The disadvantage is that the students might be lulled into thinking that only the printed points constitute worthwhile learning. Third, the teacher can give the students no written assistance. The chief advantage of this method is that it will force the students to assess for themselves the hierarchy of importance of what is said in the lecture, thus developing their powers of judgment and critical thinking. The disadvantage is that it allows the possibility of (and may even actually promote) mistakes in transcription and the omission of some of the more important points of the lecture.

Telling

Telling is the pedagogical device whereby the teacher makes a brief oral presentation of some fact or concept of educational significance. The importance of telling is based on both the nature of learning and the nature of the teacher. Learning, whether problem solving or topical, requires conceptual and/or factual knowledge for its completion. The teacher has the responsibility to supply some of this information. After all, a teacher is a teacher not only because of his familiarity with the manner in which learning takes place and with pedagogical techniques, but also because he knows more information about the problem or topic than do the students.

Risk has delineated eight occasions when telling is an especially useful teaching device: "(1) introducing new topics; (2) summarizing work; (3) reviewing work; (4) supplementing information furnished by student and textbooks; (5) giving illustrative talks; (6) giving inspirational talks; (7) developing the work of the class; (8) introducing important incidental information." [35]

Telling should be used only when needed and as the learning situation demands. Before doing the telling himself, the teacher should endeavor to elicit the information from the students. Only if this fails should the teacher resort to telling. For all its worth, telling still reduces the pupil to a passive agent in the learning process. Telling, therefore, should be used only as a last resort—but on many occasions a necessary and even fruitful last resort. Telling should also be brief else it will degenerate into an unplanned, uncoordinated lecture. As a pedagogical device, telling should utilize all those techniques of a good lecture which are applicable to it.

Recitation

The old type of recitation was little more than "lesson hearing," i.e., asking questions almost solely on what was presented in the previous class lecture and/or in the previous night's homework assignment. There was heavy, if not exclusive, emphasis on straight rote memory, of giving back to the teacher precisely what was studied. The new type of recitation is far wider than merely asking questions on the previous work. The teacher poses problems in which the student must do far more than just repeat by rote what has been learned; rather, the student is compelled by this procedure to apply what he has learned to a new set of

[35] Thomas M. Risk, *Principles and Practices of Teaching in Secondary Schools,* 3d ed. (New York: American Book, 1958), pp. 250–251.

circumstances in order to arrive at a solution. The new type of recitation seeks to relate the material learned to real-life situations and difficulties. Further, the socialized recitation has become quite common, whereby the class as a whole participates in the recitation by all-class discussion, panels, role-playing situations, and the like. The students react to each other and not just to the teacher. The modern recitation is planned in a general and overall way by teachers and pupils cooperatively during the initiatory phase of the unit, especially those learnings which are to be emphasized in the recitation.

The old lecture-assignment-recitation method of teaching is basically a note-read-recite procedure, and as such is probably the lowest level of teaching. A class in which the activities of the pupils consist solely in memory, recall, drill, and conformity is, as Wiles has noted, an unsatisfactory teaching situation.[36] Certainly the old type of recitation made the teacher's function degenerate into that of formally hearing lessons and making assignments. His role as instructional leader, of motivator in leading the students to broaden their educational horizons, was lost in a dull, repetitive procedure. Pupils under the old system were required merely to memorize the textbook, to know exactly what the teacher said in class, and to parrot this material intact the following day—in short, to do the minimum. There was no internal impetus given to do additional outside work. Students were not encouraged (and often discouraged) from creative thinking in favor of blind repetition.

A study by Zelany of classes taught by means of group discussion and by the old type of recitation methods concluded that more factual subject matter was learned, more attitudes were changed, and more personalities moved in the direction of leadership and cooperation through the group discussion than through the old type of recitation method.[37] The method of teaching should promote transfer of learning, and certainly the new type of recitation, with its emphasis on interdisciplinary problem solving and application of learnings to real-life situations, is far more productive of transfer than the old type of rote-directed recitation. Fr. Castiello, S.J., reviewing the pertinent research, has concluded: "The intimate connection between method of teaching and transfer has been proved by numerous experiments. In fact, it has been shown that the amount of transfer can be multiplied by five or six if the method is changed. Narrow views and sheer mechanical drill coop up the mind. Breadth of intelligence and capacity for linking up and

[36] Kimball Wiles, *Teaching for Better Schools*, 2d ed. (Englewood Cliffs, N.J.: Prentice-Hall, 1959), p. 182.

[37] Leslie Day Zelany, "Experimental Appraisal of a Group Learning Plan," *Journal of Educational Research*, XXXIV (September, 1940), pp. 37–42.

unifying all knowledge must effect much more transfer from one field to another." [38]

Thayer's classic work attributed the partial abandonment of the old recitation practices which has taken place in many schools to an increased awareness that factual outcomes are only part of the learning process and that broader product outcomes and process outcomes are of vital educational importance both in themselves and as they influence understanding and retention of factual outcomes. [39] Despite the many advantages and overwhelming superiority of the new type of recitation, the old "memorization-of-the-textbook" recitation still seems to be a common form of instruction in the nation's public and Catholic secondary schools. Catholic high schools, which for the realization of their very *raison d'être* necessitate the application of schoolwork, especially religion, to all areas of life, should move vigorously forward in replacing the old type of recitation.

Group Discussion

Discussion is an educational group activity in which the teacher and the students cooperatively talk over some problem or topic. There are two types of discussion used in schools, viz., the informal and the formal. An informal discussion is one which involves the free verbal interchange of the participants without itself being governed by any predetermined set of rules, e.g., an all-class discussion. A formal discussion is one which proceeds in a predetermined manner according to prescribed regulations, e.g., a symposium. The informal discussion is the more commonly used procedure in classroom situations.

The chief advantage of the discussion is that through this method the learner becomes an active participant in the learning process. As both St. Thomas and modern psychologists have repeatedly pointed out, pupil mental self-activity is indispensable to learning. [40] Discussion also emphasizes self-direction. As such, it is in opposition to the conditioned response system which lecturing, the old type of recitation, and other teacher-centered, autocratic systems necessarily require. Moreover, discussion by its very nature involves critical thinking, while the lecture and recitation demand only rote memorization. Thus, for example, in a discussion class in a Catholic high school analyzing anti-Catholic propaganda, the students, in order to clarify their ideas and discover for themselves the basic errors and falsehoods, must not only see the factual

[38] Jaime Castiello, S.J., *A Humane Psychology of Education.* (New York: Sheed and Ward, 1936), p. 172.

[39] See Vivian T. Thayer, *The Passing of the Recitation.* (Boston: Heath, 1928), pp. 44–45.

[40] St. Thomas Aquinas, *De Veritate,* q.11.

mistakes but also critically distinguish all the famous propaganda subtleties such as name calling, ignoring the issue, misuse of statistics, false implications, making unwarranted generalities, hinting that "everybody does it, therefore it is right," and so on. Discussion is particularly effective in analyzing problems of common concern to the group. This further heightens the importance of making the problem or topic studied in class meaningful to each student.

Every expert analysis of group discussion processes has emphasized the necessity of a permissive climate of thought and expression in which the participants feel free to say precisely what they think and believe.[41] Such an atmosphere is essential for the active participation of each member as well as for the preservation of group cohesion. The classroom atmosphere should be such that the pupils will want to speak freely on what they think and why. Unless such an atmosphere prevails, the teacher will never get to know the pupils' attitudes so that he may effect a change, if that is desirable. Pupils will reveal themselves only if they are permitted to make free choices without fear of reprisals should their ideas, attitudes, or even factual data conflict with those of the teacher. A permissive climate of thought expression can exist only if the teacher creates such an atmosphere. The teacher must actively encourage the students to express their ideas and attitudes, always insisting, of course, that they be buttressed with supporting data and concepts. A mistaken notion of religious obedience which sees free expression as a noxious form of pride must be replaced by a healthy, theologically sound realization that self-expression is in reality the outward, dynamic thrust of the student's God-given personality. Disagreement should not be viewed as rebellion but as an honest difference of opinion. Suppression of disagreement will result in the teacher's inability to correct the mistaken idea or attitude (assuming the student's opinion is wrong). A teacher cannot enable the students to rectify their mistaken ideas if he does not know these ideas exist, which is what happens in an autocratic classroom situation. The teacher should also give the students the opportunity of contact with sound ideas of depth and scholarship by encouraging them to read works other than just the textbooks. Too many public and Catholic secondary teachers place almost exclusive emphasis on the textbook while neglecting to actively motivate and otherwise stimulate the pupils to study additional materials in the library or the museum. The more frequent the contact with collateral and supplementary materials, the more fruitful will be the discussion in terms of learning outcomes.

Thistlethwaite's investigation of the opinions of their high school

[41] John W. Keltner, *Group Discussion Practices*. (New York: Longmans, 1957), pp. 185–189.

education, as expressed by National Merit Scholarship winners from both public and Catholic high schools, revealed the following common comments: "teachers regarded as opponents, not friends; unpopular theories not discussed; no emphasis on critical thinking; too much spoon-feeding; high school was too easy." [42] These comments heighten the necessity of more pupil-centeredness, more pupil activity, and more pupil work in the nation's secondary schools. Good discussions are an excellent pedagogical vehicle for achieving these goals. This is particularly important for Catholic high schools whose task it is to produce the leaven of society. The modern awareness of the Mystical Body should do much to center differently the axis of activity in the classroom. Students should be respected by the teacher and be required to carry the major responsibility for learning. This will be no easy task, for it will necessitate that the teacher break down the diseased yet deep tradition of lethargy and inaction which the average Catholic lay person, both parent and student, has come to believe is the best road to sanctity. Of this, Fr. Kilgallon has remarked, "The modern Catholic layman is all too often characterized by over-docility, too much dependence on the Church. He wants the Church to do all his thinking for him." [43] The problem-solving and discussion methods will do a great deal to encourage the pupils to think for themselves. Excessive lecturing and teacher-centeredness, in general, have undoubtedly been important contributory factors to the situation of which Fr. Kilgallon speaks. Fr. Brooks, O. Praem., elaborated on this point when he stated that some perceptive Catholic students thought that "institutional life, with its routine and techniques of surveillance, engenders and perpetuates immaturity by canonizing conformity and by punishing independent thought and action. The conformist is rewarded and the creative student is branded as a deviant. Initiative is not merely not encouraged; it is forcefully discouraged. The *magister dixit* attitude prevails. There is no spirit of free inquiry." [44]

It must be recognized that some subject or problem areas such as social studies, English literature, and religion lend themselves to discussion more readily than do others, e.g., mathematics or English grammar. Even in the skill subjects, however, discussion is valuable for both

[42] Donald L. Thistlethwaite, "How the Talented Student Evaluates His High School," *School Review*, LXVI (Summer, 1958), p. 168.

[43] James J. Kilgallon, "Honors Programs in Religion," *Bulletin of the National Catholic Educational Association*, LVII (August, 1960), p. 333.

[44] Robert M. Brooks, O. Praem., "The Former Major Seminarian," *Bulletin of the National Catholic Educational Association*, LVIII (August, 1961), p. 49. These opinions were expressed by some former major seminarians about their seminary education, but they can be applied more or less for a variety of reasons to Catholic high schools as well.

motivating the students and enabling them to comprehend the meaning of what they are learning.

Should controversial issues be discussed in the high school classrooms? Most educators contend that they should because of the close relationship of education with real-life problems. From the Catholic point of view, controversial issues should be discussed because the school is committed to inculcate the truth, whole and entire, in the students. Sidestepping issues can by no means be thought of as promoting truth; such an attitude actively fosters ignorance. The Junior Town Meeting League has established 10 criteria for determining whether a particular controversial issue should be discussed in the classroom.[45] The most import criterion is probably whether the students will acquire significant and worthwhile learnings from such a discussion or whether the issue will merely generate heated argument.

Informal Discussions. The teacher is normally the leader in informal discussion groups such as the all-class discussion. In this capacity he has the responsibility of seeing that: (*1*) the problem or topic under consideration remains in the forefront continuously, (*2*) optimum pupil participation is secured, (*3*) the development of the discussion proceeds along worthwhile avenues and at the appropriate pace, (*4*) the pupils derive needed learnings during every phase of the discussion, (*5*) the students receive assistance in evaluating what has been learned.

The necessity for the teacher to be the instructional leader in an informal discussion class does not mean that this method is teacher-centered or that the lesson is conducted in an autocratic manner. Rather, informal discussions emphasize pupil activity; the teacher's leadership is neither autocratic nor laissez-faire, but democratic in the best sense of the word. The teacher is the leader of the group, yet he nevertheless remains a member of the group. His function is to guide and direct the group as an accepted insider.

Democratic teacher behavior is characterized by action involving the class group to some extent in decision making; implementation of decision making in accord with democratic procedures; positive promotion of individual and group creativity; conduct which respects the dignity of the individual and of the class group; actions which seek to make him an accepted member of the group; encouragement of the free interchange of ideas between the class and the teacher.[46] Autocratic teacher behavior is in diametric opposition to these characteristics. Democratic teacher behavior considered from the religious level, can be

[45] Junior Town Meeting League, *Teaching Controversial Issues.* (Middletown, Conn.: Junior Town Meeting League, 1948).

[46] Adapted from a description given by Vynce A. Hines, "F Scale, Gamin and Public School Principal Behavior," *Journal of Educational Psychology*, XLVII (October, 1956), p. 325.

thought of as an implementation of the doctrine of the Mystical Body and therefore a pedagogical fulfillment of the deepest and richest in Catholic theology and educational theory. Autocratic teacher behavior, on the other hand, can easily be seen to represent a classroom extension of Jansenism and ultra-Montanism.

In actual practice, the educational effects of an autocratic or teacher-dominated group can be demonstrated by examining what happens when the teacher unexpectedly leaves the room. The students stop their learning activities and devote themselves to things which have meaning and interest for them. The learning activities had not been truly accepted by the students as their own, but instead had been imposed upon them, perhaps unwillingly, from without. "As long as judgment-making remains the function of the teacher, it will be accepted by the students only as it either endangers or advances their personal objectives." [47] The teacher's function is to help the students to make good and correct judgments *on their own* so that they will continue to do so after they terminate their high school careers. Unless they are given the opportunity to do so in school, the chances are lessened that they will do so after they finish their school careers. The informal class discussion is a valuable pedagogical tool in giving the students guided practice in making their own decisions. Autocratic teaching procedures prevent the students from making their own judgments and thus thwart the realization of extremely important educational objectives.

Msgr. George Johnson has observed that "teacher guidance and direction are always in order but they should never degenerate into spoon feeding and telling the answer." [48] Democratic classroom leadership assists the students in finding the answers by themselves; autocratic leadership imposes the solutions ready-made. The first is developmental education; the second is glorified dictation. Everything ranging from participation motivation to choice of words is a vital part of the teacher's directional function in discussion. Rivlin has noted that "in a good discussion it is the topic [or problem] rather than the marking book that furnishes the incentive which leads the students to participate." [49] A study by Carter and associates confirmed the investigations of Smith and Jones which had shown that the learning scores of individuals tend to be highest for positively toned words, next for negatively toned words, and lowest for neutrally toned indifferent words.[50] A study by

[47] Wiles, *op. cit.*, p. 222.

[48] Johnson, *loc. cit.*

[49] Harry N. Rivlin, *Teaching Adolescents in Secondary Schools.* (New York: Appleton-Century-Crofts, 1948), p. 212.

[50] H. D. Carter, H. E. Jones, and N. W. Shock, "An Experimental Study of Affective Factors in Learning," *Journal of Educational Psychology,* XXV (March, 1934), pp. 203–215.

Morsh and associates concluded that the teacher's verbal facility (as measured by supervisors) correlated significantly with subject-matter achievement of the students.[51]

Laissez-faire teacher leadership is no better (and is perhaps worse) than autocratic control in effecting in the pupils worthwhile learning outcomes from discussion. The teacher by metaphysical and functional necessity provides positive guidance and leadership; to abdicate these is to abandon teaching.

The following are some useful suggestions to assist the teacher in leading an informal discussion class:

1. Establish a democratic climate in which the students feel they have the freedom to discuss without reprisal even if they disagree with the teacher.

2. Positively encourage the pupils at all times to state their ideas.

3. Make some provision whereby the students acquire the essential learnings, whether factual, conceptual, or attitudinal—discussion is not a "bull session."

4. Be particularly alert to opportunities for attitude learning.

5. Attempt to have the students clarify their ideas instead of merely stating them.

6. Encourage the pupils to present conflicting points of view on the problem or topic.

7. Make sure the students do not make any broad generalizations without supporting evidence.

8. Press the student who is discussing a point to think out the logical consequences and practical ramifications of his position.

9. Get each pupil to examine critically the ideas which he himself presents in the discussion.

10. Stimulate the students to examine and evaluate critically all the points of view brought up in the discussion, no matter how traditional or controversial these points may be.

11. Attempt to secure the integration of the various aspects of the diverse subject matter explored in the discussion.

12. Encourage the students to cross-discuss among themselves as much as possible, rather than direct their comments exclusively to the teacher.

13. Secure wide participation by every student.

14. Energize a lagging discussion.

15. Redirect the discussion when it wanders from its goals and purposes.

16. Make sure the discussion results in light rather than heat.

17. Encourage students to periodically summarize the main learnings acquired in the discussion.

[51] Joseph E. Morsh et al., "Student Achievement as a Measure of Instructor Effectiveness," *Journal of Educational Psychology*, XLVII (February, 1956), p. 87.

18. See that all mistakes of fact are cleared up before the discussion ends.

19. Provide enough direction to stimulate pupil thinking and to guide pupils to a correct solution of the problem, but do not furnish so much direction that their initiative and mental self-activity will be destroyed.

20. If possible arrange the furniture in a manner conducive to active group participation, e.g., chairs or desks in a circle or rectangle, rather than in the conventional rows.[52]

A teacher guiding an informal discussion must be far better prepared in both subject-matter and pedagogical skills than the teacher using the lecture technique (which is the reason some teachers prefer the lecture). The only material the lecturer need know is what is already in his notes, which are not uncommonly plagiarized from sources he hopes the students will not detect. A discussion leader, on the other hand, must know virtually all the aspects of the problem or topic under consideration so that he can answer any and all pupil questions and assist the students in pursuing more deeply some particular aspect of the discussion. Hence a teacher guiding an informal discussion must necessarily anticipate probable difficulties of the group in solving the problem or developing the topic, likely pupil questions, and the like. Similarly he must anticipate process problems such as how to deal with dead silence, how to cope with the noncontributor, how to keep the discussion on the proper axis, and so forth.[53]

If in the discussion the teachers must be prepared informationally and procedurally, so also must the students. If the pupils are ignorant of the basic conceptual and factual knowledge upon which intelligent discussion of a problem or topic depends, they cannot effectively contribute to the discussion, and the lesson will be a waste of time. Discussion is not a pooling of ignorance, but an interplay of informed ideas. Therefore the discussion should be preceded by assignments which will enable the students to acquire the necessary background material for fruitful discussion. Similarly, before the discussion commences, the teacher must make sure in one way or other that the students have adequately learned this necessary background material. Also, the students must have a knowledge of the mechanics of good discussion, else the whole procedure will become disorderly and lopsided, with only a few active participants and the rest of the group either inactive or inattentive. A few periods at the beginning of the term devoted to the dynamics of informal dis-

[52] For a fuller treatment of group discussion, see Russell H. Wagner and Carroll C. Arnold, *Handbook of Group Discussion.* (Boston: Houghton Mifflin, 1950).
[53] See Stephen M. Corey, Paul M. Halverson, and Elizabeth Lowe, *Teachers Prepare for Discussion Group Leadership.* (New York: Bureau of Publications, Teachers College, Columbia University, 1953), pp. 15–16.

cussion groups, augmented by pertinent mimeographed readings, should suffice to give the students adequate theoretical orientation to their roles in a discussion class. Actual practice during discussion will facilitate improvement of their discussion skills. During these early discussion periods, the teacher's guidance and direction should be especially skillful.

The "six-six" is a pedagogical device which alert teachers like to use sometime during the course of the all-class discussion. At the suggestion of either the teacher or the pupils, the class breaks up into groups of six pupils who discuss for six minutes some aspect of the problem or topic under consideration. At the conclusion of the six minutes the small groups disassemble and one member of each group briefly reports to the class the outcome or conclusion of his group. The "six-six" is a very useful device for promoting increased mental activity, critical thinking, independent judgment, and interest on the part of the students.

Formal Discussions. There are several types of formal discussions which can be used profitably in a classroom situation. These include the panel, the symposium, the forum, the debate, the interview, and role playing.

Panel. A panel is a program in which a small group of students seated in front of the class informally discuss among themselves a problem or topic on which they hold differing viewpoints. Following this interchange the rest of the class is often invited to address questions to the panel members or to engage in brief discussion with them from the floor. Each of the panelists has previously done guided research on the problem or topic so that in comparison with the rest of the class, he is somewhat of an expert. Besides the participants, the panel also includes a chairman whose functions consist in keeping the problem in focus, providing for full participation by all the panelists, handling questions from the floor, and so forth. It has been found that in panel discussions four or five pupils, plus the moderator, constitute an educationally optimum number. Panels can be used effectively in large-class situations such as those found periodically in schools using the team-teaching approach.

The following are some good techniques which the teacher should use to develop and guide a fruitful panel discussion:

1. Cooperatively select a problem which is both meaningful to the class and of educational significance.

2. Prior to the panel discussion, make sure all the students have studied the problem to be mooted so that they can intelligently listen and participate. Hence, the panel is often the culminating activity of a unit.

3. Choose the panel participants cooperatively with the students, preferably on a volunteer basis. See to it, if possible, that the panelists and particularly the chairman are capable.

4. Outside of class, work with the panel participants and especially the chairman so that everyone understands his role and the way to implement it.

5. Assist the panelists in obtaining the generalized and specialized information they will need for effective participation and worthwhile discussion.

6. Have a few practice sessions so that the panelists become habituated to the topic as well as to discussion techniques. A worthwhile discussion demands that the participants easily and competently discharge both their product and process functions.

7. Afford the nonpanelists some preparation (e.g., concrete guidelines) on what educational values and learnings to look for during the panel discussion.

8. Help the nonpanelists to play their roles effectively, e.g., method of asking questions, ways to keep the postpanel discussion moving briskly.

9. Encourage the chairman and also some nonpanelists to summarize the learnings gained from the discussion.

10. Have both participants and nonpanelists evaluate the discussion in terms of product and process learnings, as well as make suggestions for improvement.

A good panel discussion requires the articulate expression of a diversity of opinion by the panelists. Without such diversity the panel becomes a "yes" session, and the educational learnings which should always result from a clash of opposing viewpoints will be lost.

Much of the success of the panel depends on the chairman. He must motivate the panelists, energize a lagging discussion, bring each panelist into active participation, keep the remarks ever focused on the problem, make both periodic and final summaries, stimulate questions from the class, and adeptly handle badly worded, educationally insignificant, and other types of poor questions.

At all times the result of the teacher's democratic leadership and skillful instructional direction must be felt. A study by Back concluded that faculty members exert a distinct influence on the pattern of participation of the members of formal discussion groups.[54] The teacher must continually work with the panelists not as commander, but as one who exercises his leadership in a cooperative manner by helping the students to actualize their potentialities and to engage in mental self-activity.

Symposium. A symposium or forum is a program in which a small group of students, usually with differing viewpoints, formally present in front of the class short prepared speeches on some problem. This is usually followed by an informal discussion among the participants, questions from the nonparticipants directed to one of the symposiasts, or both of the above. Maaske is of the opinion that while the panel discus-

[54] Kurt Back, "Interpersonal Relations in a Discussion Group," *Journal of Social Issues,* IV (Spring, 1948), pp. 61–65.

sion presupposes a controversial topic, a symposium need not feature such a topic (though it often does).[55] He believes that the symposium has as its basic purpose the supplying of definite information which is needed by the class to solve a problem or understand a topic. Most educational writers, however, seem to follow Bossing, who states that a symposium should be characterized by a controversial problem and that the participants should represent differing viewpoints so that not only is information presented, but also ideas are clarified.[56] Nevertheless, both agree that the original, formal speeches by the symposiasts should be carefully planned and should represent a tightly reasoned exposition. These talks, together with the questions and objections from the participants and the floor (as recorded by the secretary), may be mimeographed and distributed later to the students. This can serve either as a review or as a springboard for further discussion.

As in a panel program, the ideal number of pupil participants in a symposium is four or five. And as in a panel, teacher guidance and leadership at every phase are important if optimum educational outcomes are to be derived. This leadership consists in stimulating the students to mental self-activity and informing them where they can find needed information instead of deadening their initiative by spoon-feeding the answers. The techniques for guiding a symposium are much the same as those for leading a panel.

Debate. A debate is a program in which two or more students holding contradictory opinions on a particular problem present formal speeches advocating their position and subsequently have the opportunity to formally rebut the opposite side. Following the rebuttals the rest of the class is often encouraged to ask the debaters questions or engage in a brief discussion with them.[57] A debate has a moderator but not a chairman. As in the symposium, the talks should present a highly logical and carefully knit presentation of the viewpoints of the speakers. The teacher should work with the debaters as well as with the class so that an educationally significant and meaningful program will emerge. He would do well to follow the basic techniques given in the section on panel discussions, adapting them to the exigencies of the debate situation.

Interview. An interview is a program in which a small group of students interrogates an expert in the expectation of drawing facts and opinions out of him or of having him defend some position. This expert may be the teacher, an outside visitor, or a student who has

[55] Roben J. Maaske, "The Symposium Method of High-School Teaching," *School Review,* LVII (April, 1949), p. 218.

[56] Nelson L. Bossing, *Teaching in Secondary Schools,* 3d ed. (Boston: Houghton Mifflin, 1952), pp. 162–163.

[57] See Herbert J. Klausmeier, *Teaching in the Secondary Schools.* (New York: Harper, 1958), p. 269.

thoroughly familiarized himself with a particular topic. Often (particularly if the interviewer is a student) the interview centers around one predetermined problem or topic. Each of the interviewers has previously done research on the problem or topic so that his questions will be intelligent, pointed, and educationally significant. Occasionally the class is afforded the opportunity of directing a question to the person being interviewed. A moderator is usually present to see that the interview proceeds in a meaningful manner. The optimum number of interviewers is four or five. Like the panel and symposium, the interview is effective in both large and small class situations. The interview should of course be preceded and followed by teacher guidance and leadership.

The interview as an educational device originated in medieval universities and is quite a popular procedure on television today. Its familiarity to the students is a distinct advantage, since they know rather clearly the procedures as well as what is expected of them.

Role Playing. Role playing (sometimes called sociodrama) is "an unrehearsed dramatization of a problem in which the members of a class, without scripts, extemporaneously portray how they would react in a given situation." [58] Jacobs's doctoral study on role playing emphasized the fact that a unique contribution of the sociodrama is that it literally brings to life intellectual, emotional, and attitudinal learnings in a concrete real-life situation as no other learning device can.[59] Role playing is especially valuable in enabling a pupil to become aware of and impressed with the thoughts, attitudes, and perspective of someone else, and thus to appreciate the other person's point of view. Role playing is also very helpful in deepening or changing attitudes, particularly toward members of another group. Not only public secondary schools, but Catholic high schools as well, should try to make more extensive use of this pedagogical device. A sociodrama in a Catholic high school class in social studies might, for example, deal with a problem situation involving a Negro family which has moved into a house in an all-white section of the city. Roles might include the Negro mother, the Negro family's teen-age daughter, the local real estate agent, a neighbor who has invested all his money in his house, and the local parish priest. This situation will be conducive to many valuable learnings, such as the nature of social justice and the difficulties of implementing it in concrete situations.

There are many worthwhile techniques which the teacher should use

---

[58] Hubert A. Mills and Harl R. Douglass, *Teaching in High School*, 2d ed. (New York: Ronald, 1957), p. 198.

[59] Arthur J. Jacobs, *Role Playing as an Educational Method*, unpublished doctoral project, Teachers College, Columbia University, New York, 1951, pp. 73–75.

to develop and guide an educationally worthwhile role-playing situation:

1. Cooperatively select a problem situation which is both meaningful and comprehensible to the class.

2. Cooperatively describe the background or contextual setting in which the particular problem situation takes place.

3. Carefully explain and delineate the different roles to the class.

4. Emphasize very strongly that the pupils are playing a role, are empathizing, and are not portraying their own feelings or attitudes.

5. Endeavor to motivate the students to volunteer for the roles; this failing, select the pupils who are the most likely to play the roles most skillfully.

6. Afford preparation and concrete guidelines to the pupil audience as to what educationally significant values and learnings to look for during the enactment of the sociodrama.

7. Do not interfere in the sequence and development of the actual unfolding sociodrama except when a student ceases to portray his role adequately or is unable to carry it through successfully.

8. Ask the participants and also the student observers to summarize the learnings gained from this role situation.

9. Request both players and spectators to evaluate the sociodrama not in terms of acting but with regard to learning, interplay of ideas, clash of values, causes of attitudes, and emergence of basic principles in this concrete situation.

10. Repeat this same sociodramatic situation just once more with the same students reversing their roles.

The problem situation must be selected immediately before the role-playing sequence is to be acted out, else it be turned into a panel or a debate, with each person having prepared himself with material and arguments. Spontaneity is essential for a successful sociodrama.

To be fruitful, a role-playing sequence should involve a real problem which is of concern to the students as well as educationally significant. The more the situation is conducive to the clash of basic values and principles as they manifest themselves in everyday living, the more valuable will be the sociodrama. The pupils should constantly realize that in the sociodrama they must not express their own opinions or attitudes but, instead, the opinions and attitudes of the persons whose roles they are playing. The subsequent reversal of roles in the ensuing sociodrama teaches the participants (and onlookers) that opposing views are often not so ridiculous after all—and neither are the people who hold them.[60]

[60] For additional information on the sociodrama, see Alan Klein, *Role Playing in Leadership Training and Group Problem Solving.* (New York: Association Press, 1956).

Formal Problem-solving Procedures

A formal problem-solving procedure is one which puts problem solving into a defined pedagogical structure. In such a situation, problem solving is not only a pedagogical tool but also the actual framework of the learning situation. It is this framework, this structure, which sets off formal problem solving as a separate and distinct teaching device. The most important problem-solving procedures are the case, the project, the laboratory, and the cell.

The chief advantage of a formal problem-solving procedure is that it encases problem solving in the very essence of the procedure so that per se its very being compels the student to make the most extensive use of problem solving. In this way the maximum amount of pupil mental self-activity is generated, and not so much by the teacher as by the procedure itself. The formal problem-solving procedure, of all pedagogical methods, by its very nature prescribes maximum pupil and minimum teacher effort. It fixes attention and activity at every moment on the student. All teaching methods are extremely dependent on the teacher's skill, but of all the pedagogical procedures none is less dependent than formal problem solving.

Case. The case consists in the description of the facts or events of a concrete situation. These facts or events are such that inherently they present a problem which seemingly admits of no readily satisfactory solution. In order to arrive at a solution, basic principles must be invoked to justify the preference of one solution over another. An example of a case in a Catholic high school class would be: "A man is on the window ledge of the sixth story of a burning building. Flames are licking all around him. If he jumps, he will be leaping to certain death; if he remains, he will be burned. What should he do? Why?"

There are two basic types of cases, viz., the single case and contrary cases. The single case, as its name implies, involves the examination of one problem case only. The method in which the class works on the single case consists of five steps: (1) presentation of the case by either the teacher or a student; (2) analysis and breakdown of the case, with particular emphasis on the principles involved; (3) collection of the various possible solutions to the case; (4) examination and weighing of the merits of each solution in light of the basic principles, together with the possible formulation of new principles or a refinement of the old ones; (5) arrival at a solution. The story of the man in the burning building is an example of the single case.

The contrary case system consists in the presentation of two cases in which the facts seem to be similar but the principles are opposite. The crux of the problem lies in the arrival at an answer which at once solves both cases without sacrificing either basic principle. John Julian Ryan has suggested the following method in which the class can effectively work on contrary cases. The teacher presents a case to the class. He then asks the students questions designed so that they will commit themselves on the basic principle by which the case should be solved. Without himself commenting on the general applicability of this principle, the teacher then gives another case, somewhat similar to the first, but one in which the principle for action seems contradictory to the principle educted from the first case. Confronted with two similar cases whose principles appear opposite, the students are forced to think out a solution which will in some way reconcile both positions. Toward the end of the formal problem-solving situation the teacher attempts, through adroit questioning, to enable the students to clarify for themselves the basic issues involved.[61]

The primary advantage of the case is that it presents a thought-provoking problem in a graphic, easy to understand, story form. Interest is easily generated, and the students are internally propelled to seek a solution. Furthermore, it is valuable because it integrates principles with concrete facts and difficulties of everyday living. It is this integration which has been responsible for the widespread popularity of the case method in Catholic education over the centuries. Cases can be used profitably not only in religion classes, but also in other problem or subject areas such as social studies, English literature, mathematics, and so on.

Project. The project is a learning activity which involves some sort of problem-oriented educative task to be performed by the student.[62] The task usually involves the development of a product of one type or another. This product may be material, intellectual, or a combination of both. Kilpatrick, who originated the project, thought that it should constitute the basic unit form of learning; i.e., the ideal unit would become one grand project.

The project should be a concretized problem situation requiring constructive student thinking and creative student activity for its successful completion. Thus in a public secondary school, a problems in democracy class would build a voting machine with a listing of the proper candidates, or in a Catholic high school a Core class which integrated English, history, and religion might write a letter to the bishop expressing its views on the advantages of the judicious use of the

---

[61] For examples of contrary cases, see John Julian Ryan, *The Idea of a Catholic College.* (New York: Sheed and Ward, 1945), pp. 130–136.

[62] If this definition seems somewhat vague it is because no one seems to know precisely what a project is. Educators know what it involves, but not what it is.

vernacular in the Mass. This letter would involve use of proper and beautiful English expression, supporting evidence drawn from history and theology, and an active realization of the terrestrial workings of the Mystical Body. A project should above all be a worthwhile learning experience; it should never degenerate into what Crawford has termed "an excuse for the lazy teacher to avoid work." [63]

Kilpatrick's project method has as its unifying nucleus "the whole-hearted purposeful activity, the hearty purposeful act." [64] He proposed four types of projects built around problem-solving situations which would involve the energies, creative powers, and synthetic thinking of the students. These four types were (1) projects which carry out some plan or idea, e.g., writing and presenting a play; (2) projects which provide enjoyment of an aesthetic experience, e.g., composing a short piece of music; (3) projects which directly aim at resolving some existing difficulty, e.g., examining racial discrimination in the community and actually implementing the class decision; (4) projects which assist the students in gaining specific knowledge or skills, e.g., writing a letter in Spanish to the Spanish Tourist Office in order to learn Spanish. [65]

The classic four steps by which a project is developed are choosing the project, planning the project, working on the project, and evaluating the project. As can be readily discerned, this fourfold approach is very similar to that followed in any educationally significant unit. [66]

A noteworthy advantage of the project is that of itself it forces the integration of many subject-matter areas into a unified, comprehensible, and meaningful experience for the students. Furthermore, because the project yields a product, it satisfies a basic need of man, the need to make, an urge implanted in him by his Creator by which he shares with God in renewing all things in Him. A project also places great stress on student activity, thus reversing the educationally undesirable axis of teacher-centeredness. In all phases of the project the teacher's function is that of cooperator, guide, and democratic leader, not that of autocratic commander.

Laboratory. The laboratory or workshop is a procedure in which the students work on a particular problem and arrive at its solution by the methods of experimentation and practice. There are many problem and subject areas in which the laboratory procedure can be used,

[63] Claude C. Crawford, *How to Teach*. (Los Angeles: Southern California Book Depository, 1938), p. 416.

[64] See William Heard Kilpatrick, "The Project Method," *Teachers College Record*, XIX (September, 1918), pp. 319–335.

[65] *Ibid.*

[66] See Sister M. Carter, *The Philosophy of the Project Method*, unpublished doctoral dissertation, Fordham University, New York, 1935.

including the natural sciences, industrial arts, physical education, and more recently, foreign languages.

The principal advantage of the laboratory is that it features learning by doing. This type of learning has been popularly associated with Dewey and his disciples; however, many outstanding educators in ancient and medieval times advocated it. From a Thomistic point of view, learning by doing has great educational significance because it brings together in one situation knowledge and action, coordinating the operations of the intellect, the will, and the body. It provides the natural mode of expression of the intellect, satisfying its outward thrust. Dewey, and particularly his disciples, made the mistake of equating knowledge with action; St. Thomas maintained that the two were distinct but inseparable in man's everyday living.

All desirable educational outcomes necessitate this integration of knowledge and action. A knowledge of religion must for its realization be supplemented by an active spiritual life. A knowledge of English grammar must be accompanied by its proper use in speaking and writing. Knowing the principles involved in good swimming will not automatically make the student a good swimmer; he must practice, experiment, and perfect his technique. Knowing the nature and operations of charity will not of itself cause the student to be charitable; he must implement this knowledge by practicing charity in and out of school. The laboratory is a specially organized learning situation whose purpose it is to afford experimentation and practice, to enable the intellect to fulfill itself through voluntary and bodily operations.

Laboratory work should not be aimed merely at slavishly repeating the teacher's demonstration or submissively following a workbook much in the same way as following a recipe in a cookbook; rather laboratory work should be consciously directed at enabling the student *to discover for himself* certain facts and principles, e.g., what happens when certain chemicals are mixed together. Problem solving takes place first in attempting to work out the initial exercise, and secondly in applying the data and principles learned from this to the production of something new; e.g., the chemicals previously mixed can be combined to make fuel for a small experimental rocket.

What is learned in the laboratory must be meaningful and purposeful to the student. Simply assigning the students to generate oxygen results in a meaningless laboratory task; if, however, the pupils first become aware of the significance of oxygen in industry and medicine, and after it has been generated are given the opportunity of using it experimentally on a white rat or a glowing twig, such as they might have at a campfire, then they will achieve the learnings which a laboratory situation is intended to produce. In his synthesis of the pertinent research on the question whether teacher demonstrations or the traditionally assigned individual laboratory procedures resulted in greater science learnings, Crawford states that the studies conclude that in only one area did traditionally assigned laboratory work show superiority, viz., in the skill of performing the experiments again.[67] This indicates the need of properly guided laboratory work which emphasizes meaningfulness and personal discovery.

Some useful suggestions to assist the teacher in successfully guiding and leading a laboratory class are listed below:

1. Cooperatively set up rules governing pupil conduct in the laboratory. (This is very important in science and industrial arts classes.)

2. Plan the experimental and practice sessions cooperatively with the class so they will grasp both the meaning and purpose of that with which they will experiment or practice and be motivated to successfully complete the task.

3. Make sure that the needed materials are accessible. (This usually necessitates setting out the materials before the class begins.)

4. Be constantly mindful of the safety factor.

5. Provide a good balance of individual and small-group work.

6. Prevent wastage of materials.

7. See that the pupils are learning and are not merely busy.

8. Work with individuals and small groups, encouraging and helping them on their path to discovery.

9. Persuade the students to relate what they are experimenting or practicing with to things outside of class.

10. Develop in the pupils the wise use of notebooks.

Cell. The cell is a learning activity in which a tightly knit group works together according to definitely organized procedures to solve a problem and subsequently to implement this solution in everyday living. The basic purpose of the cell is twofold, viz., deep personal, meaningful, significant learning and subsequent utilization of this learning to transform one's milieu. The cell thus effectively coordinates knowledge and action, classroom experiences and real-life situations. The cell usually consists of four to eight members.

The most celebrated cell technique, at least from the Catholic point of view, is that developed by Canon Joseph Cardijn for use by his militant Catholic Action group, *Jeuneusses Ouvrières Chretiennes* (JOC), the Belgian parent of the Young Christian Workers.[68] So highly did Pope Pius XI regard the Jocist method of cell activity that he proposed it as a "model" and "inspired working example" of Catholic

[67] Crawford, *op. cit.*, p. 364.

[68] See Michael de la Bedoyère, *The Cardijn Story.* (Milwaukee: Bruce, 1959).

Action.[69] This technique is also widely referred to as the "inquiry method."

The basic technique of an inquiry cell consists of three successive steps, namely, observe, judge, and act. First, the cell members pool their observations concerning the nature of the problem situation under consideration, its manifestations in the milieu, and the manner in which it is affecting their own lives and those of their neighbors. Second, the students judge the problem situations according to basic principles in an effort to clarify the situation, the principles, and the relation of one to the other. This judgmental procedure necessitates a deep understanding of both the observational data and the underlying principles, and often requires previous research. Third, the students propose concrete plans of action which will assist them in solving the problem situation for themselves and for their neighbors. After the conclusion of the cell meeting the group members implement the agreed-upon plan in their daily lives. At the next cell meeting the various participants report on how the plan was implemented, what difficulties were encountered, and so forth. The group then continues to work on the problem at future cell meetings until a solution is satisfactorily effected. In a Catholic high school the "judge" phase always includes for consideration a pertinent passage from both the Gospel (Divine Word of God) and the Liturgy (the living Church) so that conscious spirituality will permeate the entire judgmental process. Sister M. Davide Dwyer, O.P., in her doctoral study found that there were quite a few applications of the Jocist cell method as a procedure in classroom teaching.[70]

The inquiry cell is one of the finest types of formal problem-solving procedures because its very structure requires the active relating of what was learned to real-life situations. In this way the chasm between knowledge and action, an abyss which has often impeded effective genuine learning, is successfully bridged.

The teacher in the inquiry cell serves as a guide. He should remain in the background as much as possible.[71] Indeed he should concentrate on preparing the group leader. This student leader will serve as the axis of discussion and will be responsible for motivating and eliciting group responses, ideas, and action. He should also assist the group in the discovery of basic principles and their subsequent application to real-life problems.

[69] Stephen Anderl and Sister M. Ruth, F.S.P.A., *The Technique of the Catholic Action Cell*, 3d ed. (La Crosse, Wis.: St. Rose Convent, 1945), p. 16.

[70] Sister Mary Davide Dwyer, O.P., *Historical Survey of the Jocist Inquiry Method as Exemplified in the Young Christian Student Movement in the United States*. (Washington, D.C.: Catholic University of America Press, 1960).

[71] See Gerard P. Weber, *Chaplain's Manual, Christian Family Movement*. (Chicago: Chicago Federation of the Christian Family Movement, 1952), pp. 18–35.

A Catholic Action cell using the inquiry method should be an important and necessary part of the educational program of *every* Catholic high school. A Catholic Action cell system may be either directly integrated into the curriculum or incorporated into the school's activities program. How Catholic is a Catholic high school which fields fine baseball, basketball, and football teams, but which has not a single Catholic Action cell on campus? In such schools, is the true purpose of Catholic education, and indeed of Catholic life, being diverted if not actually thwarted? This takes on added dimension when the Church's position on Catholic Action is recalled. Frs. Bouscaren, S.J., and Ellis, S.J., prominent Canon lawyers, in their commentary on Canon 139, state that "Catholic Action must be promoted actively by *all* priests, religious as well as secular" and "the energetic promotion of Catholic Action is one of the *duties* of pastors." [72] Pope Pius XI in his famous letter on Catholic Action written to Cardinal Bertram stated that "in the Encyclical Letter *Ubi Arcano* We publicly declared that [Catholic Action] could not in the least be separated from the pastoral ministry." [73] In his celebrated Apostolic letter to the Philippine hierarchy, he stated that Catholic Action is "a precious aid and necessary complement to the priestly ministry." [74] In the last Pontifical document before his death, this same Pope stated that "all members of the clergy ought to know the theory and practice of this new form of apostolate." [75] It therefore seems indefensible for Catholic high schools which have the services of priests as chaplains, teachers, and often principals not to have Catholic Action cells on campus.

Pope Pius XI's classic definition of Catholic Action is "the participation of the laity in the apostolate of the hierarchy." It is thus a completely lay group whose basic task is to complement the ministry of the hierarchy by actually sharing in it. This formal sharing is effected through a mandate given to the group by the bishop. Catholic Action bridges the spiritual and temporal orders; hence, cells will emphasize spiritual formation as well as temporal reformation.

Regrettably, most Catholics, both clerical and lay, harbor a misunderstanding about Catholic Action. [76] Catholic Action is a concrete proper term defining a specific organization; it is not a synonym for

[72] T. Lincoln Bouscaren, S.J., and Adam C. Ellis, S.J., *Canon Law: A Text and Commentary*, 2d ed. (Milwaukee: Bruce, 1951), pp. 117, 216. Italics supplied.

[73] Pope Pius XI, "Letter to Adolf Cardinal Bertram," in William Ferree, S.M., *Introduction to Catholic Action*, rev. ed. (Washington: NCWC, n.d.), p. 82.

[74] Pope Pius XI, "Apostolic Letter to the Philippine Hierarchy," in Ferree, *op. cit.*, p. 86.

[75] Quoted in Francis N. Wendell, O.P., *The Formation of a Lay Apostle*. (New York: Third Order of St. Dominic, 1943), p. 14.

[76] On this point, see Ferree, *op. cit.*, pp. 6–21.

any activity carried on by Catholics; hence writing to one's congressman protesting the sale of obscene books is a laudable Catholic activity but it is not Catholic Action. Catholic Action is the highest form of apostolic activity in which a layman can engage. Pius XII termed Catholic activities "providential auxiliaries" of Catholic Action.[77]

Catholic Action is of paramount importance in evangelizing the world and creating a Christian world climate. As Fr. Ferree, S.M., has observed, "Until the Christian laity assumes its own responsibilities, Christianity can have no adequate grip on the world." [78] The Southern bishops in their important 1953 statement said, "It is not the task of the bishops or priests directly to reform the secular institutions of the country. Such tasks rightly belong to lay apostles, who work in industry, education, agriculture and other activities." Catholics, therefore, should organize and work through Catholic Action groups—and the time to begin is during one's education in the Catholic high school. Every school should set up an affiliation with the Young Christian Students, High School Section, whose headquarters are in Chicago. Campus groups, such as the Sodality and the Legion of Mary, are other types of legitimate Catholic Action, provided of course that these groups are properly organized, lay-oriented, apostolic in nature, and possess a mandate.

A Catholic Action cell is the lay arm of the bishop. In the words of Fr. Weber: "to be effective as such it must be a *lay* movement, directed by *lay* people, planned by *lay* people, and carried out by *lay* people. Hence the independent thinking of the lay people must be encouraged. The lay people work out with the priest the principles by which to judge a particular situation. They then apply this judgment to their own lives. In other words they are not merely "yes men" to Father, but *active* collaborators in the apostolate." [79]

Committees

A committee is a small group of students who intensively investigate an educationally significant problem or topic. Its widespread use in the classroom has been strongly advocated by contemporary secondary school experts.

In committee work, the class is usually confronted with a cooperatively selected problem situation. Different committees are formed to explore separate but related phases of the problem. The work proceeds in six distinct stages: (1) Each pupil on the committee engages in independent research on some facet of the specific phase of the whole-class

[77] Eugenio Cardinal Pacelli, "Letter to Commander Augusto Ciriaci," in Ferree, *op. cit.*, p. 94.

[78] Ferree, *op. cit.*, p. 23.

[79] Weber, *op. cit.*, p. 18.

problem which his particular committee has chosen as its area of concentration. (2) The committee as a whole coalesces the research finding of each member and comes to some tentative solution. (3) Each committee presents formal reports, either oral or written, to the entire class.[80] (4) The class discusses the reports and arrives at a solution to the original problem. (5) Some culminating activity is planned and executed. (6) The reports and the culminating activity are cooperatively evaluated by the teacher, the whole class, and each committee.

There are quite a few advantages to the committee approach in the classroom. It permits the pupils to probe some particular problem in depth. It enables the students to get distilled reports on all phases of the problem. This second advantage, combined with the first, forms the ideal learning procedure, i.e., seeing how the parts relate to the whole. It encourages and indeed requires individual initiative, especially in researching the material. It affords the pupils the experience of working productively yet cooperatively with their peers. This is a very valuable process outcome, since many of the activities in which the students will engage in adult life will be in committees and groups. It ensures the centering of the learning processes in the students rather than in the teacher. Finally, it provides opportunities for the pupils to plan and work out their learning activities. The assignments and their execution are made by the group under the guidance of the teacher.

The two possible disadvantages to committee work are that it can easily degenerate into a waste of time and that it may result in the pooling of ignorance. The eradication of these possible disadvantages depends to a great extent on the pedagogical skill which the teacher exercises during the committee-oriented lesson.[81] He must not sit in a corner reading a book; rather, he should move from committee group to committee group, either as asked or because he thinks a particular committee requires assistance. The teacher should not only serve as a resource person to the committee, but if necessary, he should positively guide it in effectively using group dynamics skills and in attaining product outcomes. The teacher has four separate functions to fulfill in working efficiently with a committee so that valuable learning is assured: *stimulator*, i.e., "the raising of issues, questions, alternatives"; *expert*, i.e., a resource person to whom the students can turn for needed information; *developer of a group conscience*, i.e., awakening in the students a desire to fulfill their obligations to the group and to the situation; *coordinator*, i.e., effectively assisting in the integration of the

[80] On this point see Rosalind M. Zapf, *Democratic Processes in the Secondary Classroom.* (Englewood Cliffs, N.J.: Prentice-Hall, 1959), pp. 242–244.

[81] See Freeman Glenn Macomber, *Teaching in the Modern Secondary School.* (New York: McGraw-Hill, 1942), pp. 159–161.

various learnings of the committee into a meaningful whole.[82] The teacher in a committee-oriented classroom is therefore a very active person.

The composition of the various committees can be determined either by the teacher or by the pupils themselves. The chief advantage of the first method is that the teacher can place the different pupils in appropriate groups for optimum learning. Because of his expert knowledge of the pupils' individual needs and abilities, his choice is often salutary. Its principal disadvantage is that the determination of group composition originates from outside the pupil, thus possibly excluding internal motivation. The main advantage of the second method is that the students will tend to cluster in groups of common and complementary interests and intellectual ability, thus causing a good objective as well as a good subjective climate for optimum learning. Its greatest drawback is that the students will usually tend to choose their friends, the result often being horseplay instead of work. This method also creates problems for the unpopular pupils. Perhaps the best method of determining committee composition is by joint teacher-pupil decision. Proper grouping on committees is of great importance if worthwhile learning is to take place. It must always be remembered that, psychologically, committee learning is to a goodly extent a group thing. Each student's relationship to, with, and among the group has a significant influence on his learning. Summing up the pertinent research studies, Morse remarked that "the power of a group to influence a member will be high if the group is cohesive, attractive to the member, and offers the member the possibility of social acceptance." [83]

Everything considered, the studies seem to indicate that four to six persons constitute the ideal number of participants in committee or small-group work. An investigation by Taylor and Faust showed that groups of four solve abstract problems faster than do groups of two.[84] A study by Slater revealed that member satisfaction for groups of five was higher than for larger or smaller groups.[85] Research by Ziller con-

[82] William M. Alexander and Paul M. Halverson, *Effective Teaching in Secondary Schools.* (New York: Holt, 1956), pp. 274–276. The authors list five roles, but numbers 2 and 3 seem to be practically identical.

[83] William C. Morse, "Diagnosing and Guiding Relationships between Group and Individual Members," *The Dynamics of Instructional Groups,* National Society for the Study of Education, Fifty-Ninth Yearbook, Part II. (University of Chicago Press, 1960), p. 233.

[84] D. W. Taylor and W. L. Faust, "Twenty Questions: Efficiency in Problem Solving as a Function of Size of Group," *Journal of Experimental Psychology,* XLIV (November, 1952), pp. 360–363.

[85] Philip Slater, "Contrasting Correlates of Group Size," *Sociometry,* XXI (June, 1958), pp. 129–139.

cluded that "the accuracy in decision making is superior in groups of six than in groups of two or three." [86]

Each member of the group has a duty to the group to propel it to increased learning. A participant fulfills this obligation by assuming certain functions within the committee as the work progresses. Benne and Sheats have identified 12 roles which participants may take when they function in a group: initiator-contributor; information seeker; opinion seeker; information giver; opinion giver; elaborator; coordinator; orienter; evaluator; energizer; procedural technician; recorder.[87] These authors hold that each member must assume most, and sometimes all, of these roles if the group is to function smoothly and efficiently.

In a classroom committee, as in every small group, some members will, for one reason or another, assume destructive roles. Benne and Sheats have identified three of the most common of such roles: the "playboy" who always seeks to draw a laugh or to have a good time in the group, the "blocker" who always tends to be against any sort of group objectives or activities, and the "hair-splitter" who tends to argue over every point on which a remote distinction can be made or with which everyone in the group does not agree.[88]

Every committee in order to operate dynamically and well must have a leader. However, he should not be an authoritarian leader but rather a leader in the sense advocated continuously throughout this book, viz., guide, director, organizer, energizer, and coordinator—never a dictator. If the teacher wishes student leaders to manifest these skills and traits in committee work, he must first set the example in the way he himself conducts the lesson. Students often learn more by imitation than from exhortation.

Committees must at all times realize that, as Wellington and Wellington have remarked, they are not isolated groups but rather part of the total class.[89] Each committee has a responsibility not only to learn, but also to share its learnings with the entire class and then to work cooperatively with the total group in effecting a solution to the original problem.

Teachers should not be surprised if they experience difficulties after the introduction of the committee procedure. Most pupils are untrained

[86] R. C. Ziller, "Group Size: A Determinant of the Quality and Stability of Group Decisions," *Sociometry*, XX (September, 1957), pp. 165–173.

[87] Kenneth Benne and Paul Sheats, "Functional Roles of Group Members," *Journal of Social Issues*, IV (Spring, 1948), pp. 41–49.

[88] *Ibid.*, pp. 45–46. For an analysis of the functions among group members as an example of personality manifestation see Cartwright and Zander (eds.), *Group Dynamics Research and Theory*. (Evanston, Ill.: Row, Peterson, 1953), pp. 543–547.

[89] C. Burleigh Wellington and Jean Wellington, *Teaching for Critical Thinking*. (New York: McGraw-Hill, 1960), p. 205.

in the dynamics of group activity. They must be taught effective group functioning, when and how to assume one or more of the 12 roles of a group member, how to work effectively together for optimum learning. Every beginning is hard, and often the more worthwhile the task, the more difficult is its inception.

Some ultraprogressive secondary school educators urge that the committee be for all intents and purposes the only pedagogical method which a teacher should use.[90] This is to place overemphasis on one procedure. All the pedagogical methods treated in this chapter have considerable educational worth, and the exclusive use of any one practice would deprive the pupils of those learning opportunities and outcomes which can come only from the skillful utilization of a variety of different teaching procedures.

Questions

Questions are perhaps the most crucial part of a lesson because it is in the questioning process that the student is necessarily engaged in that mental self-activity which is the basis for learning. Gilson once said that "the proper effect of the act of teaching is to cause a personal discovery in the mind of the pupil." [91] This is precisely what the question does; consequently, it occupies one of the highest positions, if not the very highest position, in the hierarchy of pedagogical procedures. A question is basically a problem-solving device and thus perforce should evoke a truly hylomorphic and zesty pupil response. The importance of proper questioning cannot be overemphasized.

There are eight distinct types of questions: (1) pivotal or leading questions; (2) judgmental questions (e.g., true or false); (3) associative questions (e.g., "compare one thing with another"); (4) direct problem-solving questions (e.g., "why?"); (5) drill questions; (6) total recall questions; (7) summary questions; (8) evaluative questions. These forms of questions, while separate, are not mutually exclusive. Most lessons should include questions of each of the eight types. Too often the total recall and drill questions are the types used almost completely by high school teachers. This practice grows out of the outmoded concept of the classroom as solely a lecture-assign-recite situation, or in short, the old recitation method. Thought-provoking questions, such as the judgmental, evaluative, or associative types, should constitute the core of a developmental lesson, with the fact-oriented kind of questions reserved chiefly for the introduction and particularly for the conclusion of the lesson. A lesson should be characterized by

---

[90] See, for example, Zapf, *op. cit.*
[91] Gilson, *op. cit.*, p. 11.

the evocation of pupil mental self-activity rather than solely by the regurgitation of facts and data.

A question may have any one of a number of purposes: to stimulate pupil mental self-activity; to motivate the pupil to think; to encourage every pupil to participate in the lesson; to focus pupil attention on the key points of the lesson; to relate the various parts of the lesson to the principal aim of the lesson, unit, and course; to ensure pupil mastery of the basic knowledge and understandings; to evaluate pupil learnings and achievement.

Questions are self-motivators in that they are directed to the causes, explanations, or bases of a thing. These causes, explanations, and bases constitute that for which all persons intrinsically, necessarily, and dynamically grope. Hence a skillful question is not only appropriate at the beginning of a lesson, but at any time during its progress.

Techniques of Good Questioning. The teacher who wishes to ask good questions, ones which will result in optimum pupil learning, should utilize the following suggested techniques:

1. Pose the question in such a way that it will generate within the pupils a desire to think out the answer. This involves concise, clear, nonambiguous phraseology, together with a tone of voice which attaches importance, meaningfulness, and immediacy to the question.

2. Keep the questions flowing in a developmental stream. Each question should be in proper sequence to ensure the furtherance of desired aims and outcomes of the lesson.

3. Revolve each question around only one single idea. Two questions should not be merged into one.

4. Avoid purposeless questions, i.e., those which are not related to or do not advance the aims of the lesson. Every question should be purposeful.

5. Encourage the students to volunteer answers. This practice will develop good pupil motivation, initiative, and critical thinking. However, there will be occasions on which the teacher will direct a question to a nonvolunteer, particularly the inattentive pupil who needs the motivation and stimulus of a directly posed question.

6. Distribute the questions so as to take into account individual differences. Thus a pupil of high ability should be designated to respond to a difficult question.

7. Provide for an equitable distribution of questions to all the members of the class. Do not direct most of the questions to a handful of "star students," giving less gifted students little or no opportunity to respond.

8. Avoid predetermined distribution of questions to the class in terms of row, alphabet, or marks. Every student should at all times think that he will be called on to respond.

9. Use words within the vocabulary range of the pupils. If the pupils do not understand the meaning of key words in the question, they can hardly be expected to give the correct response or to develop it. Indeed a question would be invalid if its meaning could not be understood. There are other more appropriate times during the lesson or unit for vocabulary enrichment.

10. Refrain from tricky, misleading, or "catch" questions. These not only defeat the educational purpose of the question but also will eventually cause the pupils to lose faith in the efficacy and worth of the question as a learning device.

11. Do not frame the question in such a way as to suggest the answer. This defeats the basic purpose of the question which is to stimulate thought.

12. Avoid questions which can be answered by a simple "yes" or "no." Such questions do not evoke deep pupil thought. Moreover, they permit the student an even chance at guessing the correct answer. Questions should require extended responses.

13. Direct the questions to the class as a whole. Then pause for a few moments before either accepting a volunteer answer or designating a particular pupil to respond. If the teacher directs a question at only one individual, there is a strong possibility that the other students will not attempt to reason out the answer because they do not think the question is asked of them. The whole class must feel a responsibility for every question.

14. Do not, in most cases, repeat either the question or the answer; otherwise the students will not be motivated to constant attention during the entire questioning process, since they know the teacher will repeat what they missed during their span of inattention.

15. Allow sufficient time for the whole class to think out the answer. Some questions require more time to think out than others. Also enough time should be permitted so that the slower students can formulate their answers.

16. Do not ask questions exclusively from behind the desk or the front of the room. Walk around the room so that the pupils will be forced to direct their attention to areas other than the front of the class. In small-group work, such as committees, cells, and projects, the teacher should move from one group to another asking participants questions.

Skillful questioning is not a quickly learned art. It often takes a teacher many years of classroom experience, professional reading, and self-evaluation to develop into a proficient questioner. All the while the teacher must make a constant and persistent effort to improve his questioning ability and technique.[92] Many teachers, for a variety of reasons, never develop proper questioning habits. This was demonstrated by Stevens, who after an extensive stenographic study of questions posed by

[92] See Harry N. Rivlin, *Teaching Adolescents in Secondary Schools.* (New York: Appleton-Century-Crofts, 1948), p. 198.

public school teachers in actual classroom situations concluded that in practically all lessons the teachers asked too many questions too rapidly. According to Stevens, this results in: the teacher, not the pupils, engaging in most of the mental activity; excessive teacher domination of the lesson since the teacher does most of the talking; preventing the students from carefully reasoning out their answers because of insufficient time; a tense, taut classroom atmosphere day in and day out; stunting the students' facility in verbal expression, because answers have to be so rapid; little attention to individual differences since some pupils think more slowly than others and hence require more time to express their answers.[93] The questioning procedures studied by Stevens manifested an undue preoccupation by the teacher with total recall and drill questions. More thought-provoking questions should have been introduced into the lesson.

Catholic high school teachers should take the lead in the use of developmental, problem questions. Regrettably, however, many Catholic educators do not seem to appreciate the necessity, significance, and even the philosophical-theological roots of this kind of question. Thus, for example, a prominent American Catholic educator wrote a dialogue which he felt illustrated the ideal question and answer pattern in a Catholic school.[94] This dialogue was consciously rooted in this educator's conception of a Catholic philosophy of education as specifically applied to classroom methodology, since his exposition appeared as an article in a planned collection of writings, each of which advocates a different philosophy of education. In this ideal dialogue in a model Catholic school, the sister teaching the class used 286 words in her questions. The total number of words used by the students in all their responses was 8.

Student Responses to Teacher Questions. Practically all questions which the teacher poses call for one of three basic types of answer, viz., factual, judgmental, or appreciational. These responses are distinct but not isolated, since all judgments involve facts, and all appreciations include judgments. Factual questions are often used in drill or in providing a base for future judgmental and appreciational questions. However, factual questions while valuable and necessary are the lowest level of questions, a level above which some teachers never seem to rise. This type of question reduces the pupil to the status of regurgitator. Judgmental and appreciational questions necessarily evoke rational or aesthetic responses, and so are more in keeping with the student's rational nature, with his *imago Dei.*

[93] Romiett Stevens, *The Question as a Measure of Efficiency in Instruction.* (New York: Columbia University Press, 1912), pp. 12–16.

[94] Robert J. Henle, S.J., "A Roman Catholic View of Education," in Phenix (ed.), *Philosophies of Education.* (New York: Wiley, 1961), pp. 81–82.

The following are some good techniques for the teacher to observe in reacting to pupil responses to his questions:

1. No answer, not even a totally incorrect one, should be flicked off by the teacher. Rather, he should ask the pupil further questions in an attempt to help the pupil to discover for himself why his original response was wrong. Butler has observed that if there is anything in the pupil's answer that can be salvaged, the teacher should use it instead of remarking "You're wrong!" and passing on to the next pupil.[95] The latter type of teacher reaction will only cripple the pupil's critical thinking and deaden his present and future desire to learn.

2. No wrong answer should be allowed to slip by, else the pupils will learn wrong facts and concepts. The totally wrong answer should be completely corrected, and the partially incorrect response should be rectified to the degree of its falsity.

3. Other members of the class should be encouraged and even asked to correct a pupil's totally or partially incorrect response. This fosters continuous student critical thinking and minimizes undue dependence on the teacher.

4. Correct pupil answers should be praised to the degree of their worth.

5. Every student should be held responsible for the correct responses of other pupils. This has a triple effect, viz., attaching importance to pupil answers, minimizing overdependence on the teacher, and increasing class attention to every phase of the lesson.

6. Other students should be encouraged or even asked to comment on a pupil's response. Often it becomes necessary for a teacher to comment on a student's answer.

7. Student responses should be enunciated in a loud, clear voice and expressed grammatically.

8. Responses should not be shouted aloud by the whole class, but rather made by only one student. Failure to adhere to this principle not only will result in classroom chaos, but also will enable the lazy or inattentive student to go unnoticed.

9. Probably the worst way to handle a student's response is to record it in the mark book. Such a procedure paralyzes critical thinking, hampers spontaneity, introduces into the lesson a persistent climate of fear, and reduces the lesson to the level of the old recitation.

Teacher Response to Student Questions. The student, not just the teacher, should ask questions. This is important because pupil questions reflect pupil mental activity. They are also a manifestation of that wonderment and curiosity which Aristotle said is the beginning of wisdom. A pupil will not be likely to ask questions unless the teacher

[95] Frank A. Butler, *The Improvement of Teaching in Secondary Schools,* 3d ed. (Chicago: University of Chicago Press, 1954), p. 233.

first creates that type of classroom climate in which the pupils will of themselves want to ask questions. Therefore the teacher should constantly encourage the students to make inquiries. This includes the freedom of the student to question the teacher's opinion, especially in matters of interpretation. Questioning the teacher's opinion should not be viewed by the teacher as impertinence but as a genuine effort on the part of the student to arrive at the truth in his own mind. This is especially important for Religious teachers in Catholic high schools to remember.

The following are some good techniques which the teacher should use in responding to student questions:

1. Do not immediately answer a pupil question. First encourage or, if necessary, ask another pupil to answer the question. This ensures a pupil-centered, not a teacher-centered, classroom situation. If this fails, the teacher still should not respond but instead direct a question to the inquirer designed to enable him to reason out the answer to his original question. Only as a last resort should a teacher give the solution to the original question.

2. Students should be required to ask their questions politely. Politeness is the social form of the virtue of charity, an implicit recognition of the Divine Indwelling in each person. Catholic students especially should be taught the theological importance of politeness and be encouraged to practice it at all times.

3. Pupils should be required to frame their questions in good English.

4. Indiscriminate student questions should not be permitted. Trivial, tangential, and educationally insignificant questions should be dismissed by the teacher, not summarily or autocratically, but in such a way that the pupil will realize why the question does not merit attention.

5. Students should be encouraged to ask questions that go deeper than mere factual level.

6. Students who ask questions primarily in an attempt to show off their intelligence should be privately counseled by the teacher to refrain from this form of amusement because it is not furthering the educational goals of either himself, the class, or the teacher.

7. If a teacher is unable to answer a pupil's question, as sometimes happens, he should say so forthrightly. This is especially important for Religious teachers who by habit and profession publicly stand for Incarnate Truth. No teacher is omniscient; he should never play God. Paradoxically, an admission of ignorance will gain rather than lose pupil respect. Students often detect an intellectual fraud more quickly than anyone else. If a teacher bluffs an answer, he is not fulfilling the purpose of the educational enterprise, which is truth. When presented with a question which he cannot immediately answer, the teacher should encourage the pupils to look up the answer; after class he himself should search for the solution.

The Review

A review is the reexamination and retrospective survey of previous process and product learnings. Often a review is thought of as being concerned solely with product learnings such as concepts and facts; as a result process outcomes are frequently neglected during the course of a review.

The two basic types of review are the practice or drill review, which emphasizes the reinforcement of past learnings, and the developmental review, which features a fresh look at previous learnings from different angles and perspectives so as to deepen and broaden these learnings. A developmental review therefore results in new learnings. A good classroom review should combine the practice or drill review with the developmental type.

Every review has at least one of four underlying purposes. It can be utilized to make previous learnings more meaningful (by seeing their application, by understanding the relationship between the individual learnings and the whole lesson, unit, or course). It can serve to increase retention. It can be employed to ensure that the basic learnings of the lesson, unit, or course are thoroughly understood by the learner. Finally, it can help to provide the teacher with some approximate evaluation of the quantity and quality of pupil learning.

A review is based on two psychological principles, namely, that renewed contact with previous learnings increases retention and that the whole-part-whole method augments understanding. The renewed contact should be made not just in a rote but rather in a meaningful, purposeful manner, and the situation must be consciously structured so that the pupils will be able to integrate the various individual learnings into a discernible whole.

The duration of a review should be determined in accordance with sound psychological principles. Review duration may be either concentrated or distributed. A concentrated review is one in which all the time allotted for the review is consumed in one continuous session. A distributed review is one in which the time allotted to the review is broken up and separated by intervals of new and different learnings. Therefore if the class has a certain amount of time available for a lesson or unit review, it must cooperatively decide whether to spend all the time in a single, concentrated review or to divide the time up into many smaller reviews during the development of the lesson or unit. Psychologists have found that distributed review is definitely superior to concentrated review in most learning situations.[96] The general rule is that

[96] Francis L. Harmon, *Principles of Psychology*, rev. ed. (Milwaukee: Bruce, 1951), pp. 461–463.

the more complex the intellectual, appreciational, or attitudinal learning, the more concentrated should be the review, since more time is required by the students to grasp the increasingly intricate associations involved in these types of learning. Hence every good lesson should have *at least* three separate reviews, in the beginning, near the middle, and at the conclusion. This is the minimum; a skillful teacher may utilize more. However, it is sometimes profitable to spend an entire period in review, particularly at the end of a subunit, unit, or course.

Reviews, like lessons, may be either individualized or socialized. Individualized reviews can be conducted with separate students while the class is engaged in a project or in independent study. Socialized reviews can similarly proceed in a variety of ways. Small groups can be formed to improve learnings in skill subjects. This is especially valuable in heterogeneously grouped classes in which drill groups, each working at its own level, can work efficiently toward the mastery of a series of skills. Reviews can be carried out through some formal student activity such as a committee report or a panel program. Teachers and pupils can give periodic summaries which may serve as good reviews. The most common form of review is the all-class question review in which the teacher asks the students drill and developmental questions. This procedure can be varied by having some of the brighter students ask questions of the class.

Some additional suggestions to assist the teacher in conducting a review are listed below:

1. Every phase of the review should exemplify sound psychological principles, particularly those relating to meaningfulness, association, and understanding.

2. It should be properly motivated. Too often the teacher simply announces, "Now we're going to review," and so it becomes an arduous chore to the student instead of a challenging new learning experience. Teachers should not lose sight of the importance of mental set or intellectual readiness in learning and retention.

3. The review should attempt to go over and develop integratively the important basic learnings of the lesson, unit, or course. It should not be focused on every single learning previously required lest it lose some of its succinctness and become as long as the original learning experiences.

4. The review, as the "whole" at the end of the whole-part-whole process, should aim at helping the students to relate their past learnings so that the unity, the total pattern, will emerge.

5. It should constantly endeavor to relate the learnings to actual life lest it deteriorate into a mental game played for the moment only.

6. Questions should be tailored to the type of review being conducted, viz., short and snappy in drill reviews, more thought provoking in developmental reviews.

7. The review technique should be kept varied, e.g., from individualized to socialized, from committee reports to teacher questions. Care must be taken that the review never degenerate into a dull, lifeless repetition of past learnings.

8. It should be augmented further by a follow-up procedure, such as homework, or a culminating activity. The teacher should remember the tremendous positive effect which overlearning has on retention, as the studies have repeatedly shown.[97]

Drill and Practice. Drill consists in the repeated reinforcement of intellectual, emotional, and attitudinal learnings. Practice refers to the repeated reinforcement of motor learnings. Together they constitute one type of review.

Woodruff has observed that "drill is the teaching device for symbolic learning." [98] He emphasized that subjects which are heavily symbolic, such as algebra, English grammar, and foreign languages, require for retention the use of meaningful drill. Gilson has stated that the ultimate reason for this is that such learnings are "the least natural things to learn." [99] Learnings which are in some way artificial, i.e., not natural to the human mind, require continual reinforcement if they are to be retained.

Dewey and many of his foremost disciples favored "incidental learning" over drill and practice, hence the necessity of these pedagogical devices was scoffed at by most ultraprogressive educators of the 1920s and 1930s. However, both drill and practice are accepted by practically all modern educators. Risk has observed, "There is sufficient [research] evidence to show the efficacy of properly motivated drill." [100] Drill and practice will not of themselves ensure learning—they must be properly motivated, meaningful, and interesting. Repetition is not the mother of study; rather, *meaningful* repetition is the mother of study.

Drill should include the reinforcement of principles, concepts, attitudes, and appreciations, and not just be restricted to facts. In this regard, Angus is of the opinion that the excessive emphasis on the rote learning of facts in American high schools causes the students to become

[97] *Ibid.*, pp. 477–478.

[98] Asahel D. Woodruff, *Basic Concepts of Teaching.* (San Francisco: Chandler, 1961), p. 148.

[99] Gilson, *op. cit.*, p. 9.

[100] Risk, *op. cit.*, p. 81.

almost "totally uninterested in the intellectual process." [101] Facts should not be taught as naked facts, but as connected with some ideational learning. Because of its heavy and necessary emphasis on factual learning, drill is one of the most widely abused of all pedagogical tools. Abuse, however, does not nullify its right use.

The following are some techniques which the teacher should employ in conducting an educationally worthwhile drill:

1. Before initiating the drill, ascertain whether the pupils have learned, to some degree at least, the nature and meaning of the material to be reviewed. If this is not done, then the drill will not reinforce previous learnings (since it is impossible to reinforce that which has never existed), but will degenerate into a repetition of nonsense syllables.[102]

2. Focus the drill primarily on the pupils' weaknesses and gaps in learning. Drill is basically a remedial device.[103]

3. As a general rule, ask rapid-fire questions.

4. Never sacrifice accuracy of pupil response for speed. Eventually the speed will come.

5. Distribute rather than concentrate the drill periods.

6. Keep the drill session moving briskly.

7. Use natural associations (e.g., contrasts, similarities) whenever possible. These will increase meaningfulness. Artificial associations such as mnemonic devices should be employed sparingly, if at all.

8. Drill must be progressively individualized since more and more of the pupils will have increasingly mastered the bulk of the material to be learned.

9. Keep drilling to the point of overlearning.

10. Do not mark the students on their responses during the drill. Drill is basically a remedial device. Measurement is not drill.

11. Use repetition sparingly and skillfully. Mere repetition of the same words is usually insufficient to produce good, retainable, intellectual, appreciational, or attitudinal learning.

Repetition, when employed in drill, should be varied so that the pupils learn the same thing in a diversity of ways and situations, e.g., learning the meaning of a particular French word by using it in a variety of different sentences rather than just repeating it together with its translation. Another example, set in a Catholic high school, would be

[101] Sylvia Angus, "Are We Educating?" *School Review*, LIX (Summer, 1961), p. 155.

[102] See William H. Burton, *The Guidance of Learning Activities*, 2d ed. (New York: Appleton-Century-Crofts, 1952), p. 556.

[103] See Edward W. Smith, Stanley W. Krouse, Jr., and Mark M. Atkinson, *The Educator's Encyclopedia*. (Englewood Cliffs, N.J.: Prentice-Hall, 1961), pp. 628–629.

drill in the concept that charity is the greatest of the theological virtues. Here the teacher should avoid asking the student to repeat, "Charity is the greatest of all the theological virtues," but instead ask questions and present problems and short cases designed to enable the student to come to this conclusion *for himself*. Continued repetition often becomes boring and reduces interest in learning. Indeed repetition can be performed mechanically without the mind cooperating. In this regard, some educators recount the old classroom anecdote about the drill assignment which a certain teacher gave to a high school boy weak in grammar. The boy was detained after school and told to write 150 times "I have gone." Just before the assignment was completed, the teacher left the room temporarily. Soon after, the boy placed his completed work on the teacher's desk with an explanatory note, "I have went home."

The Assignment

The assignment is that part of the learning situation which extends the goals and learnings of this situation beyond the formal instructional process. The assignment is both an initiatory and a follow-up device, and hence a vital and integral part of the total learning situation. Its importance is underscored by Burton's review of the pertinent research which showed that poor assignments are among the chief causes of pupil failure to learn.[104] The assignment, then, is not a useless, time-consuming, decorative appendage to the lesson or unit. It is not a synonym for "busywork." As Butler has pointed out, an assignment is really directed study.[105]

There are at least eight different types of assignment: *Mastery assignment*—includes answering questions or problems from the textbook chapter or from the workbook. Its primary purpose is to ensure that the basic facts and concepts have been learned. *Drill assignment*—involves the meaningful reinforcement of certain learnings. Its chief goal is to guarantee complete acquisition of these learnings. *Research assignment*—includes the unearthing from various sources of facts and concepts pertinent to a particular topic or problem. Its principal objective is to promote skill in investigation. *Formal problem assignment*—consists in the presentation of a formal problem which the student must solve, e.g., a mathematics problem, conflicting cases. Its main aim is to develop original thinking. *Evaluative assignment*—requires the student to compare two or more facts, concepts, attitudes, or opinions and make a proper estimate of the worth of each. Its primary purpose is to cultivate judgmental thinking. *Appreciational assignment*—involves a direct encounter with some aesthetic experience. Its chief goal is to

[104] Burton, *op. cit.*, p. 337.
[105] Butler, *op. cit.*, p. 185.

awaken and quicken a love of beauty. *Project assignment*—comprises an educational task which the student performs by synthesizing intellectual or physical materials into a new pattern or completed whole, e.g., constructing a model of a seventeenth-century New England village. Its foremost objective is to stimulate the students' creative abilities. *Experimental assignment*—consists in the testing of a hypothesis and subsequent verification or rejection of this hypothesis on the basis of the standard procedures of experimental inquiry. Its main aim is to sharpen the students' proficiency in inductive and deductive reasoning.

In terms of the pupils for whom the assignment is directed, there are three basic kinds of assignment: *Common assignment*—one on which every member of the class works. This kind of assignment is used in the case of basic learnings required of all the students. *Small-group assignment*—differentiated assignment tailored to the needs, interests, and abilities of each small group in the class. Thus, for example, in a heterogeneous class, a basic assignment will be given to the slow readers, the same assignment but expanded will be given to the average readers, and the same assignment still further enriched will be given to the superior readers. In committee work, panel preparation, etc., each separate group will assign itself the work it needs for successful completion of its goals. *Individual assignment*—one which is different and distinct for each pupil. This type, while the most demanding of teacher time and effort, is particularly valuable in that it is expressly designed in accordance with each pupil's achievement level, interests, abilities, and needs. It is therefore the one which best solves the educational problems created by individual differences in a large group of students.

From the standpoint of length, there are two principal forms of assignment. First, there is the short-term assignment, i.e., one on which the student works for a brief period of time, e.g., overnight, during a study period. Most lesson assignments fall into this category; indeed short-term assignments constitute the overwhelming majority of assignments given by teachers. It is favored particularly by those traditional teachers who still cling to the lecture-assign-recite pattern of instruction. Secondly, there is the long-term assignment, i.e., one whose completion requires an extended period of time such as a week, a month, or a term. Unit assignments, project assignments, committee assignments are representative of this type. Teachers who employ discussion and problem-solving techniques in the classroom tend to make extensive use of the long-term as well as the short-term assignment. The long-term assignment places emphasis on deep and complex student mental self-activity and therefore requires persistent teacher guidance.

Assignments can be completed by the students during one or more of three possible times, namely, during class; during that part of the school day not devoted to instructional classes, e.g., periods or blocks of independent study; outside the school day, e.g., homework. The first of these should be used judiciously and only in special situations such as in certain types of committee work. All too often class assignments constitute thinly disguised "busywork" given by the teacher so he can perform certain clerical or other administrative tasks which should be performed after school hours. The second of the three has always been popular since it provides the pupils with the opportunity as well as the school resources necessary for completing a worthwhile assignment. The effect of the Trump Report will undoubtedly be to expand the old study-hall concept into larger blocks of time for independent study, blocks which will permit increased use of in-depth assignments. The third type of assignment is the most common and is a particularly valuable learning device since it extends the work of the school into home and community.

In lessons characterized by the lecture and/or extended telling method, the assignment plays only a follow-up role, i.e., to ensure that the materials presented in the lecture have been mastered. In a discussion or problem-solving class, the assignment will not only play a follow-up function but, as Yoakam has suggested, will also serve as an initiatory point in the direction of future learning, since the pupils require the information and experience gained through the assignment to discuss intelligently a topic and to solve a problem.[106]

The assignment is especially valuable because it is that part of the learning situation which places the greatest emphasis on individual pupil work. During a lesson, the pupils act and work in a group context; in an assignment they are on their own. Of course, some assignments are group assignments, but even in these, individual work is the keynote.

Some technique-laden characteristics of an educationally worthwhile assignment are listed below.

1. It should involve the students to a considerable extent in its solution and formulation. In democratically oriented classrooms, this is usually taken care of in unit cooperative preplanning. Doll's study of the attitudes of over one thousand high school students revealed that in general the pupils preferred to have their assignments devised in a democratic rather than in either an autocratic or a laissez-faire fashion, for in this way their creative energies would be guided and developed rather than frustrated and thwarted.[107] In excessively teacher-centered classrooms, the assignment is usually the least skillfully and most hastily planned part of the entire lesson.

[106] Gerald Alan Yoakam, *The Improvement of the Assignment.* (New York: Macmillan, 1932), pp. 4–5. This is the classic work on the assignment.

[107] Ronald C. Doll, "High School Pupils' Attitudes toward Teaching Procedures," *School Review,* LV (April, 1947), pp. 22–27.

2. It should be meaningful to the student. He must realize its importance both to his personal development and to his successful learning.

3. It should further the major aim of the present or future lesson.

4. It should result in educationally significant learnings. It should not be thinly varnished busywork.

5. It should reinforce past learnings.

6. It should form a bridge between the present lesson or unit and the future lesson or unit.

7. It should be so formulated that it will require the student to relate classroom learnings to his everyday living.

8. It should be motivated. Externally the teacher should stimulate interest in it, and internally the assignment should be challenging in itself.

9. It should be given at the psychologically opportune moment, generally when the pupils are both properly motivated and possess a sufficient background. This is usually toward the end of the lesson. It is a very poor psychological device to have the assignment already written on the blackboard when the pupils enter the room.

10. It should stress the essentials and not be preoccupied with minutiae.

11. It should be stated in terms of a problem or problems which will involve the students' creative as well as assimilative powers. Thought-provoking questions (rather than simple reply questions) or problem-solving situations are especially worthwhile.

12. It should require the student to a certain extent to think for himself in order to complete it, rather than merely to copy information from a textbook.

13. It should be tailored to the type of learning it is intended to produce. Thus an assignment which seeks to cause behavioral learning should involve the students in some sort of activity in which they can act instead of merely write. Alert Catholic religious educators sometimes refer to this as a "conduct assignment."

14. It should consume an equitable proportion of the student's time. This depends not only on internal factors but also on external conditions such as the number of courses the pupil is carrying, the suggested number of extra class study hours recommended by the school, and the like.

15. It should take into account individual differences.

16. It should be definite. Enough details should be supplied.

17. It should be clear so that the students know exactly what is required.

18. It should indicate the sources of information necessary for its completion. These indications need not be in terms of specific page numbers, but rather general or particular suggestions depending on the goals of the assignment. An assignment should positively guide the pupils' learning, neither spoon-feeding them nor leaving them adrift in uncharted waters.

19. It should be varied. It should change in format, e.g., questions, field trips, interviews, scrapbooks, projects.

20. If the assignment has several phases or parts, these phases or parts should be unified.

21. It should be followed up by the teacher. Written assignments should receive written teacher comments. If the teacher neglects to follow up the assignment it indicates to the students that he feels it is not educationally significant; the pupils will thus be led into thinking the same thing. The follow-up should not consist solely in "checking" the work to see that it was done; the teacher should instead evaluate pupil responses and give definite suggestions for pupil improvement and continued learning.

22. The products of the assignments, if they are of high quality, should be displayed in the classroom as models. This is a good motivational device.

Conclusion

The entire effort of the teacher's pedagogy should necessarily be directed at centering the learning process in the only place where it rightly belongs, in the student. The more teacher-centered the class, the less learning takes place in the pupils. This student axis of classroom activity implies a deep faith and commitment by the teacher in the ability and willingness of the pupil to learn. Some teachers have no faith in the value of the students' learning powers and insights into reality. This lack of faith is the first fruit of Puritanism and Jansenism, and for Catholic teachers, it is a deviation from the Thomistic heritage. As Fr. Brennan, O.P., the Thomistic scholar, has observed, "Aquinas was always on the side of simplicity, which means that he was always ready to support the ordinary man's insights into things." [108] This forms one of the most important Catholic bases for democratic rather than autocratic teaching methods. Classroom teaching often fails because it is carried out *for* the student instead of *with* him.

Modern American high schools educate all sorts of boys and girls —bright and slow, saintly and sinful. No longer is the school's mission only to the "elite" as it was in centuries gone by. Today, teachers and schools must think in terms of the masses as well as of the elite, otherwise they will fail in their mission. This is vitally important for Catholic teachers in Catholic schools. These educators should always remember the words which Pope Pius XI exultantly and joyfully spoke to Canon Cardijn, "At last! Here is someone who talks to me of the masses, of saving the masses. Everyone else talks to me of the elite." [109] Teachers must share the faith in the ability of the common student, a faith

[108] Robert Edward Brennan, O.P., "Troubadour of Truth," in Brennan, O.P. (ed.), *Essays in Thomism.* (New York: Sheed and Ward, 1942), p. 17.
[109] Quoted in de la Bedoyère, *op. cit.*, p. 67.

possessed by such towering giants as Pope Pius XI and Canon Cardijn. If they do not, both the Church and America are lost. The greatest tragedy of the nineteenth century, said Pope Pius XI, was the loss of the masses from the Church. History must not be permitted to repeat itself.

Nor should a teacher defend his own inadequacy by saying that the pupils are too dull to learn.

CHAPTER X IMPROVING PUPIL STUDY AND WORK METHODS

Studying consists in the conscious application of oneself in order to learn something. What is learned may be either a product or a process outcome, e.g., a concept or a skill. Study is a vital phase of the formal learning situation, since it is directed toward the understanding and retention of basic facts, concepts, skills, relationships, and appreciations. Studying is not restricted to intensive reading, although this is its most common form. An examination of art works in a museum is just as much a form of study as is intensive reading. Effective study is not only a matter of ability, interest, and good health, but also of efficient technique. If the techniques of studying are acquired, the student will learn more.

Perhaps the best general procedure of studying is the whole-part-whole method. This method is a study technique whereby the student sees the material first as a related whole, then analyzes and assimilates its component elements, and finally synthesizes these elements back into the original but now more meaningful whole. Thus in studying printed materials, the student begins by making a rapid survey of the chapter he must learn, seeing at a glance the principal division headings so that by grasping the idea of what the whole chapter is about, he can intelligently study its component parts as they are organically related to one another. Secondly, he intensively reads every subdivision, learning each part logically and, in the pertinent parts, by rote. He asks questions of himself to test his learning. Finally, he reviews the entire chapter first in parts, then as a whole. He asks himself additional questions on the chapter and its interrelated parts to ensure and reinforce learning.

A variation of the whole-part-whole method is the SQ3R, a mnemonic formula for studying technique frequently mentioned in educational literature.[1] It means study-question-read-recite-review. First, the student makes an overview of the material to be learned, thus obtaining a broad outline. Second, he writes down questions for which he hopes the reading will supply answers. Third, he reads the material in an effort to obtain the answers. After reading he uses the original questions to determine whether he has found the pertinent answers. If not, he rereads the material. Fourth, he intensively studies the answers so that he will learn them permanently. Fifth, he reviews the answers both to integrate and reinforce them.[2]

Types of Study

There are three basic types of study carried out as part of the learning situation, viz., formally supervised study, independent study, and home study.

Formally Supervised Study. Formally supervised study is that which is undertaken in a large-group context under the direct and constant surveillance of a teacher. There are two areas in which formally supervised study commonly occurs, viz., in a study hall and in a classroom. A study hall is usually a large room in which several different classes are placed under the formal guidance of one teacher. The alleged purpose of a study hall is to provide the pupils with guided study opportunities within the framework of the school day. However, as Logasa has pointed out, the study hall is almost always purely an administrative device in which a large group of pupils can be kept under the watchful eye of the teacher so that those students who have no class will have a place to go, thus effecting a reign of peace and quiet in the corridors. As a result, both teachers and pupils usually have a low opinion of the study hall.[3]

Many educators advocate abolition of the study hall in favor of a

---

[1] See Francis P. Robinson, *Effective Study*. (New York: Harper, 1961), pp. 13–47.

[2] See Edward W. Smith, Stanley W. Krouse, Jr., and Mark M. Atkinson, *The Educator's Encyclopedia*. (Englewood Cliffs, N.J.: Prentice-Hall, 1961), pp. 513–514.

[3] Hannah Logasa, *The Study Hall in Junior and Senior High Schools*. (New York: Macmillan, 1938), pp. 3–17.

system of independent study. Any decision on a study hall should be determined by its educational significance. If the study hall is retained, it should preferably serve as an administrative base from which the students, should they desire, can go and engage in independent study or work with certain teachers. A study hall teacher should help the pupils under his supervision to solve whatever problems, both general and particular, they might encounter during the course of their studying, e.g., teaching them the broad techniques of effective study or working with them on specific study difficulties caused by a particular assignment.

The school library should never be used as a formally scheduled study hall. The library is basically a resource room for the exercise of individual pupil initiative, not a place which functions as an administrative expedient. Transforming the library into a study hall will go a long way toward crippling or even killing favorable pupil interest in and attitude toward the library.[4]

Formally supervised study can also be carried on within the confines of the classroom.[5] Occasionally a teacher will devote an entire period to supervised classroom study. This procedure has a decided educational advantage in that the teacher knows the strengths and weaknesses of every pupil and therefore is in a position to give constructive, individual attention and guidance to each pupil as he is in the very act of studying.[6] The use of periodic supervised classroom study can therefore be very beneficial. However, this procedure should never degenerate into busywork for the students, a device to keep them occupied while the teacher formulates his lesson plan for the next period.

Kilzer has observed that an educationally worthwhile program of formally supervised study necessitates a knowledge on the part of every teacher of the techniques and desired outcomes of formally supervised study.[7] Without this knowledge, the purposes of such a program cannot be realized. As Alexander and Halverson have noted, some directed study periods feature the teacher as watchman, checking for noise, disturbance, and movement, but not for efficient study methods.[8] The

[4] See Maxine Nave Woodring and Cecile White Flemming, *Directing Study of High School Pupils*. (New York: Bureau of Publications, Teachers College, Columbia University, 1935), pp. 242–244.

[5] See Harry Lloyd Miller, *Directing Study*. (New York: Scribner, 1922), pp. 59–89.

[6] See Edward Randall Maguire, *The Group-Study Plan*. (New York: Scribner, 1928).

[7] Louis R. Kilzer, *A Guide to Supervised Study*. (Laramie, Wyo.: Bureau of Educational Research and Service, University of Wyoming Press, 1948), p. 6.

[8] William M. Alexander and Paul M. Halverson, *Effective Teaching in Secondary Schools*. (New York: Holt, 1956), p. 366.

basic purpose of formally supervised study is to consciously improve the students' study and work habits. This program should also emphasize that type of reading and studying which will have a continuing value for the pupils in their postschool life. It should be an individualized as well as a group affair. Under no circumstances should directed study make the pupils overdependent on the teacher.[9] This is particularly important for Catholic high schools where individual intellectual independence and initiative should be constantly stressed.

Independent Study. Independent study is that which is undertaken by individual pupils not in one central area, but in many different places throughout the school. The Trump Report, which places great stress on the necessity of independent study for a rich high school program in the decades ahead, stated that "independent study will involve many types of activities: reading, viewing, listening, writing, working on automated devices, and doing a variety of things under supervision in different kinds of laboratories."[10] Independent study will be pursued either in the school's learning-resources center or in various learning laboratories or research areas in the different parts of the school. The Trump Report maintains that the amount of time during the school day spent by pupils in independent study will be determined by professional decision, i.e., cooperatively by the teachers, guidance counselors, and students. It recommends that pupils spend, on the average, twelve hours each week in independent study.[11]

Both formally supervised study and independent study have their own advantages. Summing up the pertinent experimental research investigations, Burton concluded that superior students profited more from independent study, that slow pupils gained more from formally supervised study, and that for the average student both methods were equally effective. These findings, however, were not statistically significant. Furthermore, the experiments usually compared only various administrative schemes and did not evaluate the important aspects of the development of study skills and abilities.[12] The fact that so many contemporary educators praise independent study should motivate schools to incorporate this valuable educational medium into their curricula.

[9] See Hubert H. Mills and Harl R. Douglass, *Teaching in High School,* 2d ed. (New York: Ronald, 1957), p. 151.

[10] J. Lloyd Trump and Dorsey Baynham, *Guide to Better Schools.* (Chicago: Rand McNally, 1961), pp. 27–28.

[11] *Ibid.,* and pp. 40–43.

[12] William H. Burton, "Implications for Organizing Instruction and Instructional Adjuncts," *Learning and Instruction,* National Society for the Study of Education, Forty-Ninth Yearbook, Part I. (Chicago: University of Chicago Press, 1950), pp. 234–235.

Independent study is always carried on under the guidance of the teacher. Nevertheless, this guidance and direction are always of such a latitude that they provide for the greatest possible exercise of pupil initiative, activity, and creativity. It thus differs from formally supervised study in that it is less structured, less teacher-oriented, more individualized, and more flexible.

Home Study. Home study is that which is undertaken outside of the normal school day. It is usually done in the student's home; however, contemporary educators are increasingly emphasizing such learning activities as weekend excursions to places of culture and interest, interviews with prominent community figures, and public-library research as important types of home study.

Strang suggests four purposes and objectives of home study, to which a fifth may be added: "(1) to stimulate voluntary effort, initiative, independence, responsibility and self-direction; (2) to encourage a carry-over of worthwhile school activities into permanent interests; (3) to enrich the school experience through related home activities; (4) to reinforce school learnings by provoking the necessary practice, integration and application";[13] (5) to consciously relate school learnings to real life.

Home study may be either written or nonwritten. The latter may consist of many kinds, e.g., intensive reading, excursions, projects. Nonwritten home study assumes a greater and greater portion of the student's total home study as he advances through his school years. Regrettably many high school students seem to regard only written work as genuine home study, an attitude often acquired in elementary school. Actually, written work is usually given to ensure that each student has completed the assignment. As the pupil grows in years he should also grow in maturity and responsibility and realize that nonwritten home study is actually the more valuable of the two types. The teacher should constantly emphasize this fact in class so that the student will acquire the proper attitude.

Years ago Breslich observed that "the time spent by many pupils in home study is done under such unfavorable conditions as to form bad intellectual and moral habits and to waste an enormous amount of time."[14] This was and still is undoubtedly true. As a result, some ultraprogressive educators urged the abolition of compulsory home

[13] Ruth Strang, *Guided Study and Homework.* (Washington: NEA, Department of Classroom Teachers, 1955), p. 12.

[14] E. R. Breslich, "Supervised Study as a Means of Providing Supplemental Individual Instruction," *Some Aspects of High-School Instruction and Administration,* National Society for the Study of Education, Thirteenth Yearbook, Part I. (Bloomington, Ill.: Public School Publishing Co., 1914), p. 33.

study.[15] However, it is educationally more sound to enrich and increasingly improve the quality of home study than to abolish it. Abuse of home study does not nullify its proper use. Of course, home study should not be so time consuming that the growing youths have no opportunity to exercise, play, recreate, and develop the nonschool aspects of their personalities. School is only part of a pupil's life, not its totality. Home study in high school should increasingly occupy more of the student's time as he progresses. Two hours a night is considered normal for freshman year, gradually advancing to three hours for seniors. Some educators advocate thirty minutes of home study for each major subject. Honors classes will naturally spend more than the normal time in home study. Probably the best time for home study is in the early hours of the evening. The students are often somewhat tired after school (particularly if their classes are challenging) and so need some recreation. All in all, the restrictions created by a properly balanced and intellectually stimulating program of home study are far less damaging to the physical, emotional, and moral health of a student than idle afternoon and evening hours devoted to movies, television, or street-corner activities.

The quality of a student's home study depends on the teacher, curriculum, parents, and the pupil himself. The teacher's pedagogical methods will either motivate or disinterest the student in the performance of home study. The quality of the home study assignment, as appraised by the ideal factors discussed in the previous chapter, has a positive effect on the student's efforts and achievement. To be sure, some types of assignment actually seem to encourage copying. This points up the fact that home study must involve not only the student's assimilative powers, but his creative abilities as well. If the student is actively encouraged and indeed required to think out solutions for himself, mental self-activity will increase and copying wane.

The secondary school teacher should not restrict home study to reading the textbook, as is frequently the case. Emphasis should also be placed on collateral readings and outside activities. Surely no secondary school worthy of the name can restrict the students' learning experiences to a textbook. Home study should take advantage of its inherently mobile aspect. The student can transcribe information from textbook to notebook in the classroom. Collateral readings, which often necessitate use of the community's public library, aim at the probing of a problem in depth. Therefore collateral readings of necessity constitute

[15] Di Napoli sums up much of the testimony and investigations of progressive educators in the 1930s when this movement was at its zenith. See Peter J. Di Napoli, *Homework in the New York City Schools*. (New York: Bureau of Publications, Teachers College, Columbia University, 1937), pp. 1–13.

an extremely important part of any high school learning experience. A textbook can provide only a broad, general, and hence superficial understanding of the problem or topic under discussion. Outside activities such as independent field trips also deepen pupil understanding. Outside activities, notably in the sphere of the lay apostolate, should be a vital part of every course in a Catholic high school. Pope Pius XII, addressing the 1957 Congress of the Lay Apostolate, stated that the lay apostolate encompasses a wide spectrum of activities, viz. ,"the assuming by laymen of the tasks deriving from the mission which Christ confided to His Church." Hence no Church-operated school program is really complete unless it provides opportunities for the pupils to engage in appropriate lay apostolic activities. These tasks should be commensurate with each person's dignity as a member of the communion of saints. Thus Ball has noted that all too many Catholic laymen consider their "highest public function to consist in signing form letters and sending telegrams" to politicians pleading for or against some bill up for consideration.[16] Catholic Action cells, Catholic social militancy, active *cooperation* with the priests in parish affairs (which consists in more than selling chance books) should be incorporated into home study. A Catholic high school should be totally Catholic, not just a pale imitation of the nearby public school.

A rich curriculum is bound to spill over into a pupil's home study just as an impoverished one will. A curriculum centered around the answering of factual questions will reflect itself in the type of home study. So will a fragmented and unintegrated curriculum. However, a problem-centered, integrated, and creative curricular design such as Core (discussed in Chapter VI) will do much to foster fruitful, meaningful, and challenging home study.

The parents' influence on the quality of a pupil's home study is considerable. Lack of parental cooperation can do much to vitiate and even sometimes paralyze a youth's efforts at home study. Parents should be encouraged by the school to cooperate with it in fostering home study. They can do this by affording constant encouragement; arranging the family schedule so that it will be conducive to optimum home study; providing a suitable place for the pursuance of home study; assisting in formal recitation work, drill, and in whatever other ways they are able; working actively and cooperatively with each teacher to increase the youth's strengths and eliminate his weaknesses; and in Catholic homes where the child attends a Catholic high school, by promoting a spiritual climate which will implement the religious educa-

---

[16] William B. Ball, "Emerging Challenges of the School Aid Question," *Catholic World*, CXCIII (September, 1961), p. 351.

tion received at school, e.g., daily Mass, family rosary, morning and evening prayers, Advent wreath, good spiritual reading, and so forth.

The role of the parents in home study, as in every other phase of school life, can hardly be exaggerated. It is axiomatic among experienced teachers that a parent's attitude toward school is almost always reflected in his child's behavior. Hence the teacher should constantly work closely with the parent so that the child will be continually immersed in a learning-directed atmosphere. Thus, for example, the teacher should discuss with parents the possible subscription by the home to appropriate books and magazines; in a Catholic home this would include those Catholic periodicals and books which are of high calibre. The teacher should not try to educate his students all by himself; he needs the active cooperation of the parents. This is equally important in Catholic high schools.

The student's personal attitude toward home study is a significant factor affecting its quality. To a considerable degree his attitude will be influenced by his teachers, curriculum, and parents; however, psychological and social factors are also very important in shaping his attitude toward home study.

The Teacher's Role in Improving Pupil Study Techniques

Every teacher has a responsibility to assist his students in developing efficient study techniques and work habits. There are six definite ways in which the teacher can promote these techniques and habits: Instruct the pupils in both general and specific methods of study; assist them in improving their reading skills; plan challenging and purposeful assignments cooperatively with them; motivate them so that they will want to study; evaluate what was studied so that they will know the extent to which they have attained the desired learnings; cooperate with the home in developing and implementing an overall, continuous, planned study program.

Di Michael's investigation of freshmen in a Catholic high school revealed that most of these students lacked definite information about efficient methods and techniques of studying.[17] The same is undoubtedly true of pupils in most public and Catholic secondary schools. Other investigations have shown that study habits and techniques were acquired by the overwhelming majority of pupils not in a systematic procedure but in an accidental, haphazard manner of trial and error; furthermore, these poor study habits and techniques were learned early in the pupils' school careers and remained relatively fixed from that time on, unless

[17] Salvatore G. Di Michael, "Increase in Knowledge of How-to-Study Resulting from a How-to-Study Course," *School Review*, LI (June, 1943), pp. 353–359.

corrected by a school's remedial how-to-study program, by an alert teacher, or by a guidance counselor.[18]

Numerous other research investigations have shown that pupil study habits and techniques markedly improve as a result of instruction in methods of study. Such instruction has been demonstrated to be particularly effective with students who possess average or above-average ability but poor study habits.[19] Learning how to study is consequently one of the most valuable and perduring educational experiences which the school and the teacher give to each pupil. Such experiences can either result from a special course or be integrated into already existing course work. A separate how-to-study course should stress general study skills required for all types of classes. It should seek to develop in each pupil the six study skills which every student should possess: (1) location; (2) comprehension; (3) organization; (4) integration; (5) interpretation; (6) retention. Kelly lists nine ways in which the teacher of a how-to-study course can develop general study skills in his students: "(1) how to use a textbook; (2) how to take and keep notes; (3) how to use the library; (4) how to use source and reference materials; (5) how to gather materials; (6) how to organize and classify facts and information; (7) how to evaluate facts and data; (8) how to control attention; (9) how to memorize economically." [20] The best time to introduce a special how-to-study course is in the first term of a pupil's secondary school career. Since these courses have been shown to be quite effective, it would be well for every secondary school, both public and Catholic, to offer them annually.

In addition to general study procedures, each content area of the school's program requires specialized study techniques peculiar to it.[21] Thus, for example, the school sciences and the natural sciences cannot be studied in precisely the same fashion. Pupils who attempt to do so are not likely to enjoy success in one or possibly both areas.[22] It is

[18] Noel B. Cuff, "Study Habits in Grades Four to Twelve," *Journal of Educational Psychology*, XXVIII (April, 1937), pp. 300–301; see also Sister St. M. Esther Camden, "An Analysis of the Study Habits of Catholic High School Students," *Catholic Educational Review*, XLIII (November, 1945), pp. 542–549.

[19] See, for example, James G. Shaw, "An Evaluation of a Study Skills Course," *Personnel and Guidance Journal*, XXXIII (April, 1955), pp. 465–468.

[20] William A. Kelly, *Educational Psychology*, 4th ed. (Milwaukee: Bruce, 1956), p. 301.

[21] See Robert W. Frederick, *How to Study Handbook*. (New York: Appleton-Century, 1938).

[22] For a detailed treatment of the specialized study skills required for practically all the broad content areas offered by most secondary schools, see William C. Brink, *Directing Study Activities in Secondary Schools*. (Garden City, N.Y.: Doubleday, 1937).

advisable therefore, that in addition to a school-wide course in general study skills, each teacher should educate his students in the specialized study techniques required in his content and/or problem area. This type of education is particularly valuable because each teacher can observe every student actually engaged in study during formally supervised classroom study; the teacher is thus in a good position to positively ascertain pupil weaknesses *en situation* and so to remedy them effectively. Some investigations have shown that pupil achievement has improved in those classes in which the teachers at the outset taught their pupils specialized study techniques.[23] In this connection Strang has observed that "there is need for more perceptive analysis of the reading-study skills essential in each content [and problem] field, and for further experimentation in the ways of teaching [study] skills." [24]

An investigation by Butterweck concluded that systematic practice by high school pupils in the use of study skills is generally superior to mere knowledge of what these skills are. Furthermore, the lower the pupil's intelligence, the greater the amount of practice he needs.[25] Consequently in order to render instruction in how-to-study techniques effective, the teacher should afford the pupils the opportunity to actually implement these skills under supervision and attentive guidance. As was noted in Chapter IV all skills need practice for proper learning, effective integration, and adequate reinforcement.

Teachers often cannot, will not, or do not inculcate good study habits into their students because of one or a combination of the following factors listed by Woodring and Flemming: "insufficient teacher knowledge and use of the psychology of learning; teacher difficulties in making adequate assignments; insufficient time in the teacher's schedule for pupil diagnosis and remedial work; insufficient information about individual pupils; lack of teacher preparation for diagnostic and remedial instruction; inability of teachers to give training in specific study skills." [26] Therefore, the teacher should constantly strive to eliminate the causes of his failure to develop effective study habits and techniques in his students. He should also utilize all the resources at his command to continually improve these skills in the pupils.

[23] See, for example, Nettie J. McKinnon and William H. Burton, "An Evaluation of Certain Study Procedures in History," *Elementary School Journal*, XL (January, 1940), pp. 371–379.

[24] Ruth Strang, "Homework and Guided Study," *Encyclopedia of Educational Research*, 3d ed. (New York: Macmillan, 1960), p. 677.

[25] Joseph Seibert Butterweck, *The Problem of Teaching High School Pupils How to Study*. (New York: Bureau of Publications, Teachers College, Columbia University, 1926), pp. 77–79.

[26] Woodring and Flemming, *op. cit.*, pp. 4–7.

Helping the students to read and write better constitutes a vital part of every teacher's responsibility in improving pupil study and work methods. Poor reading skills will almost automatically make one an inferior student. In improving the students' reading skills the teacher ought to concentrate on two essential factors, namely, speed and comprehension. Students should be given periodic exercises to improve in both of these, for efficient reading demands both rapidity and understanding. In this regard the teacher should work closely with the school's reading consultant. He should also familiarize himself with the newest and best techniques of reading improvement. This can be done by reading books on the subject,[27] attending pertinent workshops, observing reading clinics, and so forth.

Similarly, every teacher should help the students to improve their writing skills, since these bear an important relation to efficient study. In this effort the teacher would do well to work cooperatively with the English department. In correcting written reports, the teacher should point out not only content errors but also poor written expression. Indicating mistakes is not sufficient in a remedial writing program; rather it should be followed by concrete suggestions to the student as to how his writing might be improved. An important part of writing improvement is educating the students in the effective use of library resources. This includes learning to use optimally such indispensable reference tools as dictionaries, almanacs, encyclopedias, *Reader's Guide to Periodical Literature, International Periodical Index, The New York Times Index, Statistical Abstract,* the various *Who's Who* volumes, and in Catholic high schools, the *Catholic Periodical Index.*

Teachers should also educate students in how to take a test. Inadequate knowledge of test-taking techniques often results in an unfavorable disproportion between the pupil's knowledge and his examination score. Such a situation not only gives an inadequate picture of the pupil's achievement but discourages and even frustrates him, often causing him to lose interest in study. The teacher should carefully explain the different mechanics operating in objective and subjective tests and the methods most productive of accurate, meaningful answers. Of course, such instruction necessitates knowledge on the teacher's part of the inner dynamics of test construction. This will be treated in Chapter XIII.

[27] Typical books on this subject include Mortimer J. Adler, *How to Read a Book.* (New York: Simon and Schuster, 1940); Norman Lewis, *How to Read Better and Faster,* 3d ed. (New York: Crowell, 1958); Ivor A. Richards, *How to Read a Page: A Course in Efficient Reading.* (Boston: Beacon Press, 1960); Ruth M. Strang, *The Improvement of Reading,* 3d ed. (New York: McGraw-Hill, 1961).

Methods of Note Taking

Note taking is an important phase of effective study. Unless the pupil owns his own textbook, he will not be permitted to mark it up in a manner productive of meaningful learning. Collateral readings, educational excursions, and classes in which the lecture technique is used also require the use of student notes for effective organization, learning, and retention. Palest ink is better than a retentive memory. Hence it can be seen that note taking is an indispensable skill for the high school pupil. Unfortunately, the vast majority of students do not seem to know the most efficient techniques of note taking; therefore, the teacher has the responsibility to so educate his pupils, even if these procedures were treated in the school's special how-to-study course.[28]

The following are some suggested techniques of effective note taking: (1) Notes should be put into the student's own words. This will force the student to think rather than merely copy. Further, it will ensure their being understood when they are reread. (2) Notes should be epitomized. (3) Notes should be organized so that they are coordinated and related to one another, otherwise they will constitute a jumbled mass of isolated information. (4) Notes should be of the proper length, neither overdetailed nor underdetailed. Notes represent the student's extractive judgment. Overdetailed notes are usually just paraphrasing; underdetailed notes are commonly too brief to be meaningful. (5) Notes should indicate their source, together with proper citation. (6) Notes should be taken in a consistent, systematic form, employing either the page or card system, or the paragraph or outline system. Use of standard composition or looseleaf paper is good for notes used in conjunction with studying outside readings or regular classwork. However, because of their mobility and flexibility cards are best when the student is preparing a theme or written project.

Barton has stated that "an outline should be an objective symbol of the thought-relationships that have actually been established in the mind of the maker of the outline."[29] This underscores the value of an outline, namely, that it necessitates pupil discovery of associations and relationships which represent a high level of thinking and comprehension.

Outlining grants to the various concepts and facts an appropriate emphasis and hierarchy according to their respective order of importance. This is educationally advantageous since it eliminates possible treatment of all information as being of equal relevance, a process which

[28] See Edward S. Jones, *Improvement of Study Habits,* 5th ed. (Buffalo, N.Y.: Foster and Stewart, 1939), pp. 33–46.

[29] William Alexander Barton, Jr., *Outlining as a Study Procedure.* (New York: Bureau of Publications, Teachers College, Columbia University, 1930), p. 7.

would reduce the material under study to a vast aggregation of independent, coequal entities.

If outlining is helpful when reading, it is also of considerable assistance to the pupil preparing a theme, written report, or project.[30] It enables the pupil to develop his thesis in a logical fashion, thus achieving the proper unity, continuity, and emphasis.

An outline may be either a phrase outline or a sentence outline.[31] The first is normally preferable since it is shorter and more succinct. However, some teachers might urge their students to use a sentence outline to foster good English usage.

Most educators hold that outlining is the best way to learn material which has been read. Strang, in assessing the pertinent research investigations, observed that "there has been no convincing [research] evidence, however, that making notes in outline form is superior to spending the same amount of time in thoughtful reading." [32] In the absence of conclusive empirical research, the opinion of the majority of perceptive teachers and educators tips the balance in favor of outlining.

Notes should be edited after they have been taken. Good editing of notes should include: eliminating nonessential material; clarifying opaque words, phrases, or sentences; reordering items to secure increased understanding; making sure that the notes are legible; adding any important points which may have been omitted.

Each teacher should positively assist his students in note taking. The teacher should go over every pupil's notes individually, making concrete suggestions for their improvement. This takes time, but it is the only way of ensuring good note taking. The teacher should also give the students specific exercises designed to increase their note-taking skill. One such helpful exercise consists in requiring the pupils to condense a chapter into a page, or a paragraph into a sentence.[33]

Techniques of Effective Study

The techniques of effective study involve three constituent phases, viz., preparation for studying, studying, and following up the studying. Efficient study procedures involve all three; i.e., none of these phases can be excluded in a program of fruitful study.

Preparation for Studying. No worthwhile study activity can dispense with effective preparation. One does not just sit down and study;

[30] See Sister M. Carolyn Klinkhamer, O.P., "Outline to Order," *Catholic Educational Review*, LVII (September, 1959), pp. 361–376.

[31] J. Wayne Wrightstone, *How to Be a Better Student.* (Chicago: Science Research Associates, 1956), pp. 74–76.

[32] Strang, "Homework and Guided Study," *op. cit.*, p. 676.

[33] S. S. Seward, *Note-Taking.* (Boston: Allyn and Bacon, 1910), p. 69.

rather one must first make sure that certain conditions exist which will promote, not hinder, efficient studying. The following constitute the minimal preparatory requirements for profitable study:

1. The student's health should be good. Health problems both permanent (e.g., cerebral palsy) or temporary (e.g., fatigue) have a detrimental effect on study. Of course, as Pear has observed, fatigue should not be confused with boredom.[34]

2. The student's mental health should be sound. Thus, for example, students who are anxious individuals tend to devote too much time to thinking and worrying about themselves and not enough time to the assignment at hand.[35]

3. The assignment to be studied should be written down, not chanced to memory. Every pupil should have a special assignment notebook for this purpose.

4. The pupil should develop a favorable attitude toward both the content area in general and what is to be studied in particular. As was discussed in Chapter V, attitudes determine in large measure the quantity, quality, and type of one's learning.

5. The pupil should regard study as an active, not a passive, process. He must encounter books and experiences in a living way and not as an inert blotter.

6. The pupil should make out a weekly schedule, blocking out definite times for classwork, study, and recreation. His schedule or horarium should leave a certain amount of free time for emergencies. Study time should be apportioned efficiently, e.g., distributed study periods for French vocabulary, more concentrated periods for complex learnings such as solving geometry problems.

7. A favorable room atmosphere should exist. This includes a quiet place, preferably a separate room;[36] proper temperature, neither too warm nor too cold (68° is considered optimum); a desk which is not cluttered; a sturdy but not overly comfortable chair; and good illumination (poor lighting soon causes fatigue). These physical conditions also tend to promote psychological readiness.[37] Parental cooperation is necessary for securing these room conditions.

8. Minimal reference materials should be readily available for consultation.

[34] T. H. Pear, *The Art of Study*. (New York: Dutton, 1931), p. 51.

[35] See Eugene L. Gaier, "The Relationship between Selected Personality Variables and the Thinking of Students in Discussion Classes," *School Review*, LX (October, 1952), pp. 404–411.

[36] See George J. Dudycha, *Learn More with Less Effort*. (New York: Harper, 1957), pp. 187–205.

[37] Herbert J. Klausmeier, *Teaching in the Secondary School*. (New York: Harper, 1958), pp. 312–314.

Certainly a dictionary should be close at hand so that unfamiliar words can be looked up.[38]

Studying. Once adequate preparations have been made, the pupil is ready to begin his actual studying. The following techniques should prove to be of invaluable assistance during the study process proper:

1. The pupil should get to work immediately and not start by dawdling.

2. The pupil should begin each study period by motivating himself. Thus, for example, in an assignment involving the *Canterbury Tales*, he should first spend a few minutes imagining that he is on that very pilgrimage to Canterbury, witnessing the sights, sounds, and people as a living experience. This process should be especially easy for Catholic high school students who undoubtedly have been familiarized with the Ignatian method of meditation.

3. The pupil should immerse himself totally in what he is studying.

4. The pupil should constantly seek to develop concentration and eliminate distractions. This requires unflagging effort and determination.[39]

5. High morale and confidence should be retained throughout the entire study period, particularly when difficulties arise. Good mental attitude is often the wedge which cracks open these difficulties.[40]

6. Associative devices should be used as often as possible, since association is indispensable in learning. Whenever possible these devices should be natural, e.g., Gregorian chant with the history of monasticism, not artificial, e.g., "Every *good* *boy* *does* *fine*" with the five lines of the conventional music staff. Contrived or mnemonic associative devices should be employed sparingly, as they are based on rote, not logical relationships.

7. The pupil should continually attempt to integrate what he is studying with previous learnings.

8. The pupil should constantly strive to see the real-life application to what he is studying. This will make the material meaningful, purposeful, and vital, and hence increase comprehension and retention. In a study by Charters, almost one-half of the pupils investigated stated that they did not connect the important points of what they were studying to something in their own experience.[41] This led to inefficient study.

9. The pupil should outline what he is studying so that he will readily grasp the relative importance of its constituent elements as well as the inner logical connections.

[38] See William H. Armstrong, *Study Is Hard Work.* (New York: Harper, 1956), pp. 39–47.

[39] See S. L. Crawley, *Studying Effectively.* (Englewood Cliffs, N.J.: Prentice-Hall, 1945), pp. 45–57.

[40] See Richard L. Sandwick, *Study and Personality.* (Boston: Heath, 1929), pp. 21–29.

[41] Jessie Allen Charters, "How Two Hundred and Fifty-eight Junior College Women Study," *Journal of Educational Research,* XI (January, 1925), pp. 41–48.

10. The whole-part-whole method should be the basic study procedure.

11. In problem-solving studying, the pupil should ascertain what data are given, then see what kind of solution is appropriate or required, and finally, attempt to see how the data suggest a lead. When the problem is solved, the answer should be tested and checked to see that the result is correct.[42]

12. The pupil should constantly judge with his critical intelligence the soundness and worth of the material he is studying, both material he has read and outside experiences. All material is not of equal importance; indeed some may be incorrect or worthless. Critical thinking and questioning are important in all of life, study included.[43] A lack of these can lead to crippling overdocility.

13. The pupil should study with the optimum number of people. This usually means studying by oneself. However, some types of assignment, notably certain types of problem solving and appreciation, can often be more profitably studied in a group. An investigation of college students by Blue indicated that the group study method results in higher achievements (as measured by marks) for all pupils except the intellectually gifted.[44] Many educators observe that while group study is optimal under certain conditions, the distractive dangers inherent in it indicate cautious use.

14. The pupil should overlearn to ensure retention.

Following Up the Studying. Effective study is not completed when the pupil thinks he has mastered all the material. Indeed such an attitude is often the reason why a goodly amount of what is learned during study is so quickly forgotten. The follow-up in studying is just as important as the follow through in a batter's home-run swing. Study follow-up should occur at three separate times, viz., at the end of every study period, at specially designated periodic intervals, and during the course of everyday life. Some suggestions for effective follow-up of study are:

1. The pupil should test himself on his learnings at the end of each study period. This will ensure that the material has been learned to the point of at least one perfect mastery. Frequently pupils have the false impression after studying that they have adequately learned the material; testing will definitely confirm or deny this impression. Many times parents can assist in this testing process.

2. The pupil should make periodic reviews of previously learned material. Such a procedure propitiously incorporated into the study period will relate both past and present learnings and also reinforce them.

[42] Luella Cole, *Students' Guide to Efficient Study*, 4th ed. (New York: Rinehart, 1960), pp. 27–29.

[43] F. M. McMurray, *How to Study and Teaching How to Study.* (Boston: Houghton Mifflin, 1909), pp. 135–160.

[44] John T. Blue, Jr., "The Effect of Group Study on Grade Achievement," *Journal of Educational Psychology*, XLIX (June, 1958), pp. 118–123.

3. The pupil should continually attempt to apply what is learned both at the end of the study period and in his daily life. This will make the learning become a part of his life, thus heightening meaningfulness and retention.

4. The pupil should remember that study habits and techniques are themselves improved by study. Daily studying, rather than mere fitful cramming before examination time, is therefore beneficial.

5. Regular living habits of eating, sleeping, and physical exercise are important for effective study.[45]

[45] See William F. Book, *Learning How to Study and Work Effectively*. (Boston: Ginn, 1926), pp. 72–91.

CHAPTER XI THE MATERIALS OF TEACHING

In the course of educating his pupils, every teacher makes constant use of instructional materials. To be sure, it is the variety and richness of these materials which are a cardinal reason why contemporary secondary education is so far superior to secondary education of centuries ago. However, mere existence of these materials does not automatically mean that they will be used in an optimum pedagogical manner. The teacher must learn how to use instructional materials in a way that will cause the best type of learning in the students. This must be followed up by constant improvement in their utilization throughout his teaching career.

In general, there are two types of instructional materials, printed and audio-visual.

PRINTED MATERIALS

Printed instructional materials fall into two broad classes, viz., the textbook and supplemental materials.

Textbook

A textbook is that printed work which serves as the basic manual for classroom use. It is the one book used by the entire class. In most public secondary schools it is lent to the students free of charge for the duration of the course. In most Catholic high schools, despite the ruling of the United States Supreme Court in the Cochran decision, the pupils must purchase their textbooks.[1]

The textbook has many advantages which make it an invaluable educational tool. First, it compresses into capsulized form most of the basic information about a given problem or topic. Thus it furnishes an excellent overview, and so can be used as a springboard for examining special problems in depth or as a vehicle for efficient review. Second, it provides all the pupils in the class with a common core of learning, and so serves excellently as a basis for intelligent class discussion, problem-solving situations, small-group work, and so forth. Third, it usually gives a reasonably objective account of a problem or topic and shows both sides of a controversial issue. Fourth, it is a compact volume which the student can take with him for home study (collateral readings are scattered in many places and sometimes cannot be taken home). Fifth, it usually coincides with most school system syllabi, thus being a good and practical vehicle for the latter's implementation. Sixth, it usually includes suggested collateral readings, projects, problems, exercises, and other suggestions for its supplementation by both pupils and teacher. Seventh, it usually supplies enough information so that students in any part of the country, even in underprivileged areas, can attain at least a desirable minimum of learning. This tends to equalize educational opportunities for all American youth. Eighth, it is usually accompanied by a specially prepared teacher's guide which offers helpful suggestions on specific teaching techniques and pupil activities appropriate for given problem or content material. In some instances, a textbook is published with accompanying paperback monographs for special supplemental reading by the students; e.g., an American history textbook would have small ancillary paperbacks on the Civil War, the Great Depression.

Cronbach, following Herrick, has identified and charted three levels of teaching, the lowest being exclusive use of the textbook.[2] Certainly a teacher's *exclusive* reliance on a textbook has many crippling effects on the student. First, it gives him only the superficial aspects of a problem or topic, because by its nature, this is all a textbook can

[1] 281 U.S. 370, 50 Sup. Ct. 335 (1930). In this decision the Court upheld the constitutionality of a state law permitting a state to provide free textbooks from public monies to pupils in private schools.

[2] Lee J. Cronbach (ed.), *Text Materials in Modern Education.* (Urbana, Ill.: University of Illinois Press, 1955), pp. 188–216.

offer. Second, its restricted content does not probe a problem or content area in depth. This might lead a student to think that once he has mastered the textbook he knows all there is to be known about a problem or topic. Third, it does not open many new vistas to the student or present radically new or conflicting ideas which comprise the stuff of learning. Modern textbooks are usually objective and impartial, and hence are often overly bland, mollifying the hurly-burly of controversy. Moreover, Catholic high school textbooks sometimes fail to express adequately other points of view, resulting in a lopsided and narrow education for the students. Fourth, it prevents the student from knowing firsthand, diverse, and varied sources of information. Fifth, it often deprives the student of acquiring attitudes, ideals, and broader conceptual learnings because of the heavy factual emphasis on the textbook. Sixth, it actually defeats a cardinal purpose of the textbook, namely, to provide a base and a springboard for other learning activities.

Many explanations account for the overdependence on, and exclusive use of, the textbook by many teachers in both public and Catholic secondary schools. (1) Tradition. This is the way "teaching" has always been done in a particular school. No reference is made to intrinsic or extrinsic values or to the resultant quality of instruction. (2) Past experience. Most teachers when they were students in secondary school (and sometimes in college) used a textbook exclusively. (3) Poor knowledge of subject matter. Research evidence, together with the testimony of many educators, indicates that a high percentage of secondary school teachers do not have a good knowledge of the problem or subject area they are teaching.[3] Hence they need a textbook as a crutch. (4) Inappropriate content preparation in college. Many teachers did not pursue college courses which would adequately fit them to teach in secondary school. Thus a geometry teacher might have had many courses at college in certain types of higher mathematics but few if any in geometry. (5) Lack of knowledge of pedagogical principles. Many teachers during their college careers thought that Education courses were a waste of time. When they did enter teaching they knew few if any pedagogical techniques necessary for superior teaching and, therefore, had to fall back on textbook recitation procedures. (6) Lack of adequate mental ability. Much research evidence indicates that a goodly percentage of secondary school teachers do not possess superior intelligence.[4] These instructors, consequently, do not possess too much imagi-

[3] Myron Lieberman, *Education as a Profession.* (Englewood Cliffs, N.J.: Prentice-Hall, 1956), p. 231; Hubert H. Mills and Harl R. Douglass, *Teaching in High School*, 3d ed. (New York: Ronald, 1957), p. 255.

[4] See, for example, Dael L. Wolfe, *America's Sources of Specialized Talent.* (New York: Harper, 1954), p. 199; Arthur E. Traxler, "Are Students in Teachers Colleges Greatly Inferior in Ability?" *School and Society*, LXIII (Feb. 16, 1946), pp. 105–107.

nation or insight and are often incapable of doing little more than blindly following the textbook. (7) Increased use of standardized tests. Most standardized tests emphasize only what is found in the basic nationwide or diocese-wide textbooks. Hence some teachers feel it is more expedient and occupationally advantageous to drill their pupils on just what is contained in the textbook than to provide them with enriching supplemental readings and activities which will not appear on standardized tests.

Some ultraprogressive educators have suggested abandoning textbooks and instead initiating a project whereby the students compose their own as they grow in learning. This approach neglects the numerous advantages of the textbook and indeed deprives the pupils of receiving wisdom from more learned people in a compact form, logically and psychologically organized.

Because most modern textbooks represent good planning, careful logical and psychological development, as well as comprehensive content, a poorly prepared teacher with little or no experience will find the textbook very useful in helping him to cooperatively plan with the pupils the objectives and learning outcomes of the course. Notwithstanding, the teacher should exercise great care in the selection of the textbook. Some textbooks have desirable and undesirable biases. Sister Marie Lenore Fell's doctoral study showed a marked and definite anti-Catholic slant in textbooks used in public schools from 1783 to 1860.[5] A doctoral dissertation by Sister M. Linus Gleason, C.S.J., which investigated four sets of literature textbooks that are currently most widely used in the teaching of literature in Catholic high schools concluded that all these textbooks are oriented toward the Caucasian and away from the Negroid and Mongoloid races.[6] Careful choice of the textbook is further heightened by the pivotal role it plays in the formal learning situation. For some teachers, especially the inferior ones, it is at once the syllabus, study outline, sole source of pupil learning, and exclusive font for testing the students.

The determination of which textbook is to be used in a particular course should be made by each teacher. The reason for this is that a teacher must adapt his instruction to each particular class; e.g., a different textbook should be used for a bright, average, or slow class, or a group with special needs and problems. Most public school systems have utilized cooperative teacher–supervisor–curriculum-expert committees for the selection of an acceptable group of textbooks from which each

[5] Sister Marie Lenore Fell, *The Foundations of Nativism in American Textbooks, 1783–1860.* (Washington, D.C.: Catholic University of America Press, 1941).

[6] Sister M. Linus Gleason, C.S.J., *A Study of Intergroup Relations as Revealed by Content Analysis of Literature Textbooks Used in Catholic Secondary Schools,* unpublished doctoral dissertation, St. Louis University, St. Louis, Mo., 1960.

teacher can choose the one most suitable. In no case should any school or school system prescribe one particular text, as this neglects individual pupil needs, interests, and abilities, with the results being educationally undesirable.

The following *general* criteria should be utilized by every teacher when determining what specific textbook should be used for a particular course: Which textbook best promotes the educational philosophy of this school and community? Which textbook best coincides with the educational aims and goals of this course? Which textbook is best suited to the needs, interests, and abilities of this particular class? Which textbook gives the most adequate coverage and the most extensive overview of the subject matter to be learned? Which textbook is the most challenging to this particular group of students? Which textbook is the most interesting to the class? Which textbook suggests the richest and most varied classroom experiences and outside activities? Which textbook best relates its content to real life? Which textbook inculcates attitudes, ideals, and broad concepts rather than merely presenting factual data? Which textbook includes the freshest and most stimulating ideas as well as traditional concepts? Which textbook most readily lends itself to problem-solving and discussion situations? In Catholic high schools, which textbook best integrates in a meaningful and natural manner Catholic principles with the problem or content material?

The following *specific* guidelines should be used by the teacher in the selection of the optimum textbook: Is the information accurate and correct? Does the book represent sound scholarship?[7] Are the vocabulary and style suitable for the level of the class? What are the extensiveness and quality of its reference features, e.g., index, footnotes, glossary, bibliography? What are the extensiveness and quality of its illustrative features, e.g., tables, charts, photographs, drawings? What is the quality of its mechanical features, e.g., strength of binding, durability of cover, attractiveness of layout? [8]

The teacher should constantly strive to utilize the textbook in a manner most conducive to effective pupil learning. The following are some suggestions for achieving this result:

1. Use the textbook as the hub, supplementing it with collateral readings, other classroom experiences, and extraschool activities. Do not use the textbook exclusively, but do not fail to use it.

[7] Some Catholic educators have criticized Catholic textbooks on this account. The current dramatic upgrading of the quality of Catholic textbooks in certain fields should be extended to all areas.

[8] See Samuel E. Burr, Jr., "A Rating Scale for Textbooks," *Journal of Education,* CXXXII (May, 1949), pp. 138–139.

2. Insist that the pupils master the material in the textbook. The textbook provides part of the framework in which the learnings take place, and therefore, its content should be known. If the textbook is to serve as a basis for class discussion it is imperative that it be learned.

3. Do not overemphasize the factual material in the textbook. It is even more important that the pupils learn the broad concepts and attitudes contained therein. Facts are only atoms in the tissue of broader generalizations.

4. Do not teach in a manner which will lead the pupils to make exclusive use of the textbook. Thus discussions, cell meetings, problem-solving situations, tests, and so forth should utilize material drawn from collateral readings, field trips, and the like.

5. Do not spend class time paraphrasing the textbook or in creating one grand textbook recitation period. The pupils can read, and certainly they should be encouraged to think. Class discussions, problem solving, and small-group work should be centered on the broader meanings, the inherent attitudes, the resultant values, the issues involved in what was read and experienced.

6. Teach the pupils the best way to study a textbook, e.g., use of index, cross-references, footnotes.

7. Develop an attitude of pupil critical thinking concerning the textbook. For example, does it present both sides of an issue?

8. Make the textbook fit teacher-pupil planning, not vice versa. The course should not be determined by the textbook, as sometimes occurs. Thus, for example, it might happen that because of cooperative teacher-pupil planning, the chapters in the textbooks will not be studied in the order in which they are printed.

9. Skillfully and constantly utilize the teacher's guide to the textbook in order to provide meaningful experiences which are consciously related to the core learnings.

10. If the pupils own their textbooks, teach them the most effective way of marking them for efficient learning. Many outstanding learners never study a textbook without pencil in hand. Not only are underlining and bracketing helpful but marginal cross-reference notes and comments are also aids to fruitful study.

Textbooks are constantly being improved. In Catholic high schools, books which integrate religious principles with problem and content material are being developed and refined. Recognized Catholic scholars are increasingly authoring Catholic high school textbooks. The kerygmatic approach is slowly beginning to appear, particularly in religion textbooks.[9] UNESCO has been attempting to encourage textbook writers to promote international understanding in their works.[10]

Supplemental Materials

Supplemental materials are those necessary pedagogical complements to regular classwork and textbooks. They include collateral readings, workbooks, work-study programs, and audio-visual materials. Supplemental materials are necessary because it is impossible for high school pupils to adequately explore a problem or topic solely on the basis of what they learn in the classroom or from a textbook. Supplemental learnings provide the dimensions of breadth and depth so vital and essential if a narrow education is to be avoided. Indeed the superficial knowledge possessed by many high school students can often be traced to the lack of use of supplemental materials by their teachers.

Collateral Readings. Collateral readings are those which are related to the problem or topic treated in class or in the textbook. Collateral readings are of two types, voluntary and assigned. Voluntary collateral readings are those suggested by the teacher but which are not required of any student. This is the superior type of collateral reading because the pupil engages in it out of interest, desire, need, or just the fun of learning rather than because of any external pressure. As a result learning is facilitated, meaning heightened, and retention increased.

Assigned collateral readings are those which the whole class, certain groups of students, or individual pupils are given as a necessary requirement for fulfilling the objectives outlined in the original teacher-pupil planning of course goals. Assigned collateral readings should constitute an important part of every high school course. The teacher would do well to utilize the following suggestions for making assigned collateral readings conducive to efficient pupil learning:

1. Make sure that the pupils know in advance the basic purpose and importance of each collateral reading.

2. Provide collateral readings which present contrasting viewpoints.

3. Give collateral readings which supply fresh new insights into the problem or topic being studied.

4. Give only worthwhile collateral readings, ones which are educationally significant and well grounded in scholarship.

[9] For an example of the kerygmatic approach in high school religion textbooks, see the *Revised Catholic High School Religion Series*, 4 vols. (New York: Sadlier, 1959). For underlying theory see Johannes Hofinger, S.J. (ed.), *Teaching All Nations.* (New York: Herder and Herder, 1961); also Gerald Emmett Carter and William J. Reedy, *The Modern Challenge to Religious Education.* (New York: Sadlier, 1961).

[10] UNESCO, *A Handbook for the Improvement of Textbooks.* (Paris: UNESCO, 1949).

5. Assign some collateral readings to the entire class but apportion others to groups or individuals on the basis of needs, interests, and abilities.

6. Make the collateral readings of suitable length, neither excessively long nor unduly brief.

7. Make the collateral readings definite in terms of name of the book and page numbers.

8. Require each student to make brief notes on his assigned reading, usually in terms of delineation of the author's thesis, the manner in which the thesis was developed (with supporting factual data), and the pupil's critique of both the thesis and its development.

9. Hold the pupils responsible for the material in the assigned collateral readings.

10. Discuss the readings with each pupil, either during class discussion or at a separate teacher-pupil conference.

Collateral readings should include newspapers, periodicals, pamphlets, and books. Newspapers and periodicals are of especial importance in that they are more current and up to date than books. Furthermore, they are cheaper and usually more accessible. Pamphlets are an often overlooked form of collateral reading. Government publications and Catholic pamphlets of the better type often present good capsulized treatments on general or specialized problems and topics. Books, both general and monograph, are, of course, a basic and vital type of collateral reading.

Every high school course should of necessity incorporate all types of reading. Once the teacher-pupil goals for the course have been agreed upon, the teacher, working with a special student research committee, should draw up and mimeograph an annotated bibliography of books, pamphlets, and periodical articles. This bibliography will constitute one of the most significant learning tools of the class as it provides the direction and incentive which every teacher should give to the class. It is difficult to imagine a worthwhile secondary school class which does not have such a bibliography. Yet in many American public and Catholic high school classes (and, amazingly, in many college classes as well), no bibliography exists.

Workbook. A workbook is that type of book which expressly provides special remedial and reinforcement exercises directly related to or supplemental to the material learned in class or in the textbook. Occasionally a workbook is used for enrichment. Some textbooks are published with an accompanying workbook for easy integration. Most workbooks are paperbound with perforated pages which can be readily detached so that they can be handed in to the teacher.

The following are some suggestions for helping the teacher to effectively use the workbook to promote good learning:

1. It should be used in positive conjunction with class discussion, textbook work, and student experiences, and not as an isolated exercise.

2. The various problems and exercises should be adapted to individual differences.

3. It should be used as a learning procedure rather than as a means of providing the pupils with busywork.

4. It should be used in connection with a program of independent study.

5. It should be used for both prognostic and diagnostic purposes.

6. When necessary, the problems and exercises should be altered so they will mesh with the pupils' real-life situations.

7. It should be used to stimulate creative thinking instead of leading to mere mechanical insertion of answers.

8. It should be used to further the goals of the course and not merely as an end in itself.

9. It should be used as one of a number of supplemental materials rather than the only such material.

10. The answers to the problems and exercises should be carefully checked by the teacher so that pupil strengths can be reinforced and weaknesses eliminated.

11. The teacher should discuss and evaluate the answers with the pupils.

Work-Study Program. A work-study program is that educational experience in which the student spends a certain number of hours per day (usually three) in classes in the school acquiring basic academic learnings and a specific number of hours (usually three or four) working for some company or tradesman, generally on a salary basis. The actual work experience is jointly supervised by the school and the employer. This type of program has proved particularly valuable for youths who do not like school, or who have little academic ability or interest, and who as a result learn little and become misbehavior problems. Usually a work-study program (which by its very nature supplements classroom learning) begins when a pupil is sixteen years old and lasts until state law permits him to leave school permanently. This program affords youths the opportunity to engage in activities which are meaningful to them, to earn money and thus savor some independence, to obtain on-the-job training without any cost to the school and to continue to have the advantage of expert guidance from the school's personnel and counseling services.[11]

[11] For a thorough treatment of the concept of a work-study program, see Henry T. Tyler, *Report of the Study of Work Experience Programs in California High Schools and Junior Colleges.* (Sacramento: California State Department of Education, 1956).

The fact that this supplemental program involves no additional shop expenditures for the school should indicate its great potential for Catholic high schools. Most Catholic youths of low academic ability are deprived of a Catholic high school education. One of the chief reasons for this is a lack of sufficient funds for the equipment necessary in a program of vocational education. Yet these youths could greatly profit from a Catholic high school education; indeed it might result in a reduction of the number of Catholic criminals. Catholic educators should therefore begin to work out the details of a work-study program so that every Catholic youth may receive a Catholic education.

AUDIO–VISUAL MATERIALS

Audio-visual, (A-V) materials are those sensory objects or images which initiate, stimulate, and reinforce learning. From a Thomistic viewpoint, audio-visual materials should constitute a necessary and indispensable part of every classroom situation, since as the Angelic Doctor has stated, nothing comes into the mind which does not first pass through the senses. All learning therefore is rooted in sensation, and hence effective teaching must utilize the sensory experiences which audio-visual materials provide. The outstanding successes of the great Italian Catholic educator, Maria Montessori, can be attributed in large measure to the great stress she placed on sensory experiences in classroom learning.[12]

Pope Pius XII observed that "the isolated life is likely to restrict a larger view of the world." [13] A classroom which confines learning to written and verbal symbols unduly shelters a student and narrows his perspective of reality. Every pupil, because he is partly corporeal, is limited by time and place. Audio-visual materials help break these bonds which impede the mind's natural thrust. The materials can carry the pupil back in time, as by a reproduction of a Michelangelo sculpture, or transport him to another place, as by a television series on Africa. The mind is in potency to become all things, but before this potency can be actualized, it must first experience these things. Supplemental experiences are particularly important in Catholic high schools, since the Catholic world view is that all reality is God-soaked, oozes God. By drenching himself in God's creation a person is experiencing an earthly sort of Beatific Vision, although darkly, as through a glass.

[12] For a general overview of her approach, see E. Standing, *Maria Montessori: Her Life and Work.* (London: Hollis and Carter, 1957); for its concretization in an American school, see Nancy Rambusch McCormick, *Learning How to Learn.* (Baltimore: Helicon, 1962).

[13] Pope Pius XII, *"Nell'Accogliervi,"* in *The Pope Speaks,* III (Winter, 1956–1957), p. 254.

Despite the philosophical, psychological (and in Catholic high schools, the theological) necessity of using audio-visual materials, there are many teachers who neglect to utilize them. One audio-visual specialist relates an experience in which he observed a teacher who was verbally drilling the pupils in fractions. Never once did this teacher make use of the rulers which the students had on their desks.[14]

The educational advantages of audio-visual materials include the following: (1) They provide the necessary concretized sense experiences which underly all thinking; (2) they enrich the pupil's learning by bringing him into contact with experiences which he would normally be unable to encounter, e.g., a filmstrip on Eskimo life; (3) they extend the walls of the classroom so as to encompass the entire world; (4) they are more vivid than abstract verbal symbols which the teacher uses; (5) they readily stimulate the pupil's imaginative and creative thought processes; (6) they tend to make learning more permanent; (7) they are intrinsic motivators and so generate interest and enthusiasm in the pupil; (8) they give vitality and meaning to heretofore lifeless verbal and conceptual abstractions; (9) they stimulate and trigger a whole chain of learning activities; (10) they often provide rich aesthetic experiences for the pupil.

This last point is of capital importance. Too many so-called "educated persons" are intellectual giants but aesthetic dwarfs. Seeing a color motion picture of the dreamlike castles of Germany's Neckar Valley on a misty morning or a filmstrip of an El Greco masterpiece or hearing a disc recording of a thrilling Mozart symphony is as much a part of education as learning the binomial theorem or the fiscal problems of the Van Buren administration. This is particularly important for Catholic high schools, since beauty is so inextricably wound up with every aspect of the Church's life, doctrine, and worship, whether it be the burstingly beautiful *Exultet* of the Easter Vigil liturgy, the haunting etherealness of St. Zeno's Chapel in Rome's ancient St. Prassede Church, or Pope Pius XII's dying request to hear Beethoven's *First Symphony*.[15] Beauty is necessary for the nourishment of the humanity-divinity that is everyone. Yet sometimes Catholic high schools neglect this aspect of education. As the celebrated religious educator, Fr. Robert Hovda, has remarked, "What a contradiction to the liturgy and to Scripture is this careless disregard for the visual, the audible, the tangible." [16]

[14] Edgar Dale, *Audio-Visual Methods in Teaching*, rev. ed. (New York: Holt, 1959), p. 4.

[15] For a discussion of this point, see James Michael Lee, "Notes toward Lay Spirituality," *Review for Religious*, XXI (January, 1962), pp. 42–47.

[16] Robert W. Hovda, "The Arts in the Service of Worship," *Catholic School Journal*, LXII (February, 1962), p. 78.

Too often teachers and educators think of audio-visual materials as pedagogical crutches to problems caused by overcrowded classrooms and poor instruction. The proper attitude is to view these materials as valuable teaching tools in themselves, rather than as some sort of plugs in a dike. What Sister M. Pius, O.M., has said will be reiterated throughout the remainder of this chapter; viz., audio-visual materials must aid in thinking—they can never replace or substitute for thinking.[17]

Before deciding to use a specific audio-visual material, the teacher must determine whether it will contribute to the realization of the basic objectives of the lesson or unit. Dale lists eight criteria for evaluating an audio-visual material as an instructional tool for a particular class at a specific time:

> (1) Does it give a true picture of the ideas it presents, e.g., pictures of Alaska which show only snow-covered land? (2) Does it contribute to the meaningful content of the topic under study? (3) Is it appropriate for the age, intelligence and experience of the learners? (4) Is the physical condition of the material satisfactory [e.g., torn filmstrip]? (5) Is there a teacher's guide available to provide help in effective use of the material? (6) Does it make the students better thinkers, critical-minded [or does its persuasiveness charm away the pupils' critical faculties]? (7) Does it tend to improve human relations [and other basic values]? (8) Is the material worth the time, expense and effort involved? [18]

Most audio-visual materials, such as chalkboard, exhibits, radio, and opaque projectors, are quite simple and can be easily operated by a teacher without specialized training. However, in the case of more intricate and complicated machines, such as motion-picture projectors, the teacher should leave their operation to specially trained pupil members of the audio-visual squad. Attempts by untrained teachers to operate these machines have often led to equipment breakage and resultant loss, not only in money, but even more importantly in valuable pupil learning opportunities.

Teachers should work with their school's audio-visual coordinator. Every secondary school, both public and Catholic, should have such a coordinator. This expert should be thoroughly trained and knowledgeable in audio-visual theory and techniques and should be given a lighter teaching load by his principal so that he can effectively work with each teacher in improving the quality of audio-visual instruction in every classroom. Allen reported that in urban public school systems, three-

[17] Sister M. Pius, O.M., "Audio-Visual Aids in Junior and Senior High Schools," *Catholic School Journal*, LV (May, 1955), p. 143.

[18] Dale, *op. cit.*, pp. 78–83. The plurals in the original quotation have been changed to the singular, and the punctuation has been altered slightly.

fourths of the schools had audio-visual building coordinators.[19] There is no comparable information for Catholic high school building coordinators, but the percentage is probably considerably lower for a number of reasons. This certainly represents an area of needed improvement.

The teacher should work with the coordinator, particularly in obtaining the materials. In general there are four chief sources of audio-visual materials, viz., the school A-V library, the school system A-V materials center, commercial organizations which supply free A-V materials, and commercial organizations which sell or rent A-V materials. The school's own A-V library should contain such things as exhibit and bulletin board materials, filmstrips, tape and disc recordings, and models. The materials should be cataloged and a list of them sent to each teacher at the beginning of the term. There seems to be a definite trend, at least in urban public school systems, toward establishing system-wide A-V centers and departments with materials libraries, directors, and experimental studios. Some alert dioceses have established diocesan A-V centers. These system-wide centers are important because they make available to all the schools materials which might be too expensive or too specialized for any one school to own, e.g., motion pictures. Also, these centers provide A-V research and experimentation which result in improvement in A-V teaching throughout the system. A number of commercial organizations such as Esso and Ford supply excellent educational A-V materials free of charge. However, there are certain irresponsible corporations which produce educational A-V materials whose sole purpose is to keep the company's product ever before the eyes or ears of the public. The teacher must guard against using such excessively commercialized materials. On certain occasions it is necessary to buy or rent audio-visual materials, e.g., models of the human anatomy, filmstrips, and so on. They should be purchased with care and discretion; on the other hand, no school should fail to purchase necessary and helpful A-V material because of a false sense of economy.

Sands has compiled a rather complete list of the sources of A-V materials.[20] *The Educators Guide to Free Materials* and Salisbury and Sheridan's *Catalog of Free Teaching Aids* should be part of every school's audio-visual library. Catholic high school teachers should utilize the *Catholic Film Directory*. The NEA's Department of Audio-Visual Instruction and the NCEA's Department of Audio-Visual Educators can provide much helpful information. The many specialized audio-visual journals provide current information on the latest A-V materials, the-

[19] William H. Allen, "Audio-Visual Communication," *Encyclopedia of Educational Research*, 3d ed. (New York: Macmillan, 1960), p. 129.

[20] Lester B. Sands, *Audio-Visual Procedures in Teaching*. (New York: Ronald, 1956), pp. 602–633.

ories, and techniques. Catholic teachers should also consult the fine A-V section of the *Catholic School Journal* which monthly reviews the latest materials of both general and religious import. Specialized groups, such as the National Association of Educational Broadcasters and the Catholic Broadcasters' Association, are usually ready to assist teachers in whatever way they can. The Catholic Broadcasters' Association is composed of diocesan units of lay people, clergy, and Religious interested in the promotion of religious and educational radio and television programs. Many dioceses now have a director who is usually not a layman. These directors are frequently very willing to cooperate with Catholic high schools.

A good A-V program requires that every room have special shades for room darkening. Furthermore, it is difficult for a worthwhile audio-visual program to function without a specially equipped A-V room, one which is used only for audio-visual presentations. Older schools should remodel their plants so as to establish such a room, while schools of the future should make provision in their architectural plans for at least one A-V room.

The teacher should not utilize audio-visual materials haphazardly, but in a systematic yet flexible fashion which will actively promote pupil learning. The following are some suggestions which will assist the teacher in attaining this goal:

1. Cooperatively determine with the pupils the specific use of the A-V material, e.g., to motivate a lesson, to introduce necessary supplemental experiences, and so forth. If neither teacher nor pupils have any definite educational goal for the material, its employment will not be purposeful in terms of lesson or unit objectives.[21]

2. Preview, prehear, or preexperience the material. Only in this way will the teacher know what points it covers, emphasizes, and omits—knowledge which is necessary for the effective guiding of the lesson.

3. Prepare the class for experiencing the material, particularly in respect to what specifically to watch for and what learnings to expect. This preparation is a prerequisite to optimum pupil learning. Motivation should accompany this preparation.[22]

4. Make sure the equipment or material is in working order. Sometimes a class has been skillfully prepared and whetted for an audio-visual experience, and then made to suffer disappointment because the equipment did not function or some of the material had disappeared.

[21] For an analysis of the theoretical aspects of this step, see Wilbur Schramm, "Procedures and Effects of Mass Communication," *Mass Media and Education,* National Society for the Study of Education, Fifty-Third Yearbook, Part II. (Chicago: University of Chicago Press, 1954), pp. 113–138.

[22] See Ella Callista Clark, "Audio-Visual Aids Deepen Understanding of Religion," *Catholic School Journal,* LIX (January, 1959), pp. 26–28.

5. Introduce the audio-visual material at the optimum pedagogical moment. The teacher should not suddenly and without warning interrupt the lesson with the remark, "And now we'll see a movie about Rome."

6. When possible, have the pupils participate in the audio-visual experience. This will make them active, not passive, sharers in the lesson, thus causing true learning.

7. If the type of audio-visual material permits (and practically all do), periodically stop during its presentation to ask the pupils questions. This will not only generate student involvement but will also help to ensure step-by-step mastery of the product and process learnings which the pupils are supposed to receive from the material.

8. Hold the students responsible for the basic content of the audio-visual material. If this is not done there is great danger that the pupils will regard the experience as entertainment, not learning.

9. Follow up the audio-visual material with a class discussion, a panel, cell meetings, or a role-playing situation. This will help bind the learnings derived from the material to the pupils' basic informational, attitudinal, and value structure.

10. Make an assignment which will require the pupils to integrate their audio-visual learnings with the other learnings gained from the lesson or unit. This procedure will also tend to make the audio-visual learnings more meaningful and permanent.

11. If possible, repeat the audio-visual material to reinforce learning. Research has found this practice to be very effective, especially with films.[23]

In his important encyclical, *Miranda Prorsus,* Pope Pius XII stated that to audio-visual materials which "are in conformity with sound pedagogical principles and right rules of mental development, We not only give Our approval, but also heartily commend them, and thus We *desire* them to be introduced into schools of every level, Catholic Action groups, and parish societies." [24] Pope John XXIII in his address, *Il Nostro Cuore Si Apre,* urged the use of audio-visual materials by teachers.[25] Catholic schools should therefore be in the lead of those constantly utilizing every type of audio-visual material. Alert Catholic educators have enthusiastically responded to the Papal desires; it remains for the classroom teachers to follow suit with the same eagerness.

[23] See, for example, Yale University Motion Picture Research Project, "Do Motivation and Participation Questions Increase Learning?" *Educational Screen,* XXVI (May, 1947), p. 256.

[24] Pope Pius XII, *"Miranda Prorsus,"* in *The Pope Speaks,* IV (Winter, 1957–1958), p. 329. Italics supplied.

[25] Pope John XXIII, *"Il Nostro Cuore Si Apre,"* in *The Pope Speaks,* VI (Winter, 1959–1960), p. 82.

The Motion Picture

There are two types of educational motion pictures, silent and sound. As a general rule, silent motion pictures have almost disappeared except for pupil-produced movies.

Dale lists 12 advantages of the motion picture as an educational tool. It can:

> present certain meanings involving motion; compel attention; heighten reality; speed up or slow down time [by time-lapse and slow-motion photography]; bring the distant past and present into the classroom; provide an easily reproduced record of an event; enlarge or reduce the actual size of objects; present physical processes invisible to the naked eye; build a common denominator of experience; influence or even change attitudes; promote an understanding of abstract relationships; offer a satisfactory esthetic experience.[26]

A study by Anderson and his associates concluded that a combination of motion-picture presentation and classroom work, which stressed the principles underlying the film, resulted in greater learnings than conventional classroom work alone.[27] Wittich and Schuller have noted that animated cartoons and illustrations are very effective in teaching by motion picture, e.g., animation of the principles of a jet engine in the various stages of its operation.[28] Because of the larger screen, color photography, superior audial reproductions, and other special effects, motion pictures are normally more pedagogically effective than television programs in cases where the person, place, or event to be depicted would be the same.

The motion picture has some disadvantages from a pedagogical standpoint: First, it causes the student to be a passive entity in the learning process, although this is modified to the extent to which he empathizes himself in the vicarious experience taking place on the screen. Second, it cannot depict present events since the educational film normally takes some time to be produced and distributed. Third, it is quite expensive and so is available only in limited quantities. Fourth, it does not of itself enable the student to participate actively in the learning experience; e.g., a pupil cannot address questions to a film. Fifth, while enhancing reality in one sense, it diminishes it in another, since a film is by its nature two dimensional. Sixth, it can lead to erroneous

[26] Dale, *op. cit.*, pp. 218–219.
[27] Kenneth E. Anderson et al., "Toward a More Effective Use of Sound Motion Pictures in High School Biology," *Science Education*, XL (February, 1956), pp. 43–54.
[28] Walter Arno Wittich and Charles Francis Schuller, *Audio-Visual Materials*. (New York: Harper, 1953), pp. 359–361.

concepts about the size of objects or the time interval between events. Seventh, it sometimes cannot be utilized by a teacher because there is no one available who is trained in the operation of the projector. Eighth, many films produced expressly for instructional use are often stilted in action, dialogue, and story line.

There are some educational film series which have been designed to provide the pupils with an entire course of instruction. Such series are substitutes for teaching, so should be used cautiously and as a last resort.

As in the case of most other audio-visual materials, the more the instructional motion picture is related to and built on previous pupil knowledge, the more the students will learn from it. The Yale Motion Picture Research Project concluded that previous instruction on the content of the motion picture greatly increased the pupil learning from the film.[29] Also, the more a student can identify himself with the action in the motion picture, the more real it becomes for him and the more he will learn.

Wendt has asserted that films are helpful in reinforcing attitudes.[30] Whether motion pictures can change attitudes and the extent of such change are more complex matters. Allen's review of the pertinent research studies seems to indicate that pupil attitudes can be changed by the film only if the motion picture expressly deals with the attitude in question and if this attitude is in conformity with the deeper values of the student.[31] This conclusion underscores for the teacher the necessity of laying the groundwork for attitude change before the film is viewed by the students so that the motion picture can reinforce and add increased weight to the desired attitude change; e.g., a teacher in a Catholic high school who wished to alter the pupils' attitude in favor of liturgical advances proposed by the Church's experts (such as celebrant facing the people, and increased lay participation at Mass) would first have to discuss the basic issues with the class and expose them to the pertinent literature before showing them a film illustrating these dynamic rediscoveries of the traditional form of worship.

A study by Sister M. Mark Barrett, R.S.M., revealed that for girls in Catholic high schools, films relating to Religious Orders were more important in encouraging vocations to the sisterhoods than vocation lectures, programs, and literature.[32] However, these devices should be

[29] Mark A. May et al., *Learning from Films.* (New Haven, Conn.: Yale University Press, 1958), pp. 115–122.

[30] Paul R. Wendt, *Audio-Visual Instruction.* (Washington: NEA Department of Classroom Teachers, 1957), pp. 13–14.

[31] Allen, *op. cit.*, p. 118.

[32] Sister M. Mark Barrett, R.S.M., *A Study of the Influences of Catholic High School Experiences on Vocational Decisions to the Sisterhoods.* (Washington, D.C.: Catholic University of America Press, 1960).

properly used. Overglamorous movies portraying the religious life must be guarded against. Films should serve as information and guidance vehicles, not as overt lures. The religious vocation problem is not one of enticing a candidate, however unpromising, to enter the seminary or novitiate, but rather of attracting the right type of person who will be likely to remain in the religious life. The high dropout rate experienced by many seminaries and novitiates is perhaps partially attributable to a hyperemotional appeal on the part of certain overeager vocation recruiters.

The Projected Still Picture

The four most important types of projected still picture are the filmstrip, the slide, the opaque projection, and the microprojection.

The Filmstrip. A filmstrip is a series of related still photographs on a single roll of processed film. Taken together, the separate pictures present some product or process learning in a step-by-step fashion. Most filmstrips are 35 millimeter (mm). The average number of single pictures on a filmstrip is thirty-five, although the number can vary from ten to one hundred.[33]

The filmstrip is often regarded by teachers as an inferior type of motion picture. This is a most unfortunate attitude. Indeed Allen's review of the pertinent research concludes that except for learnings involving motion or dynamic interaction, the filmstrip is a more effective instructional device than the motion picture.[34] This is probably due to the greater versatility of the filmstrip: each picture can be left on the screen for the desired length of time, thus promoting visual reinforcement which permits teacher-pupil discussion during its showing.

The educational filmstrip possesses the following advantages: It allows for student participation either during the actual showing or by shutting it off at intervals to engage in discussion; it has most of the values of visual projection; unlike the motion picture, the image can be retained on the screen for as long as desired; it is inexpensive; it is small and compact and so can be stored easily; the filmstrip projector is a very simple machine which can be operated by any teacher; it can be prepared by the students as well as purchased commercially. (However, unless the pupils are reasonably proficient in photography, it is normally unwise to use student-made filmstrips.)

Because of the relative low cost of a filmstrip, every school should have its own collection of these valuable audio-visual devices. Various Catholic educational agencies have produced a goodly number of excel-

[33] For general information on the filmstrip, see UNESCO, *Filmstrips: Use, Evaluation and Production.* (Paris: UNESCO, 1959).

[34] Allen, *op. cit.*, pp. 120–121.

lent filmstrips which should be a part of the educational program of all Catholic high schools.

The Slide. A slide is a photographic transparency which can be projected. Slides are of many different sizes, ranging from the common 35 mm to 2¼-by-3¼ inches. (Some are even larger.) Their uses and advantages are much the same as those of filmstrips. They are frequently used by alert teachers who project slides of their travels or of special educational objects they photographed. Student slides, if well executed, can also be used.

The Opaque Projection. An opaque projection is the throwing on the screen of an enlarged image of any picture, illustration, printed material, or flat object which is not transparent. This is done by a machine called the opaque projector. Unlike a motion picture or filmstrip projector, the opaque projector is a *reflector* by which a strong light is cast on, not through, a surface. The light which this surface reflects is redirected by a series of simple mirrors into a lens which focuses and, by means of an adjustable barrel extension, magnifies the reflected image.[35]

The opaque projector, because of its great scope and utility, is one of the most valuable yet most neglected of all audio-visual devices as far as classroom use is concerned.

Some advantages of the opaque projection include the following: (1) It has a tremendously vast range, since any nontransparent picture, illustration, or flat object can be projected; (2) it possesses most of the values of visual projection except that of motion; (3) it permits active pupil participation and discussion during projection; (4) the image can be retained on the screen as long as desired; (5) it permits all the students to see clearly some picture, illustration, or object which otherwise would have to be passed around from pupil to pupil with resultant distraction; (6) it is a simple machine which any teacher can operate.

The opaque projector has a variety of uses, e.g., projecting images of postcards, newspapers, student illustrations, pictures or maps in a book, pupil reports, and even projecting a map on a chalkboard where it can be traced in chalk by a student. Images of three-dimensional objects having a flat surface (e.g., mounted butterflies, coins, etc.) can be thrown on a screen by the opaque projector.[36] The skillful teacher should capitalize on all the advantages and uses of the opaque projector, especially those which are not present in other audio-visual devices.

The Microprojection. A microprojection is the throwing on a screen of the image of an object which is by nature very small or which has

[35] For a more complete description of this machine, see Sands, *op. cit.*, pp. 270–286.

[36] See Kenneth L. Bowers, *The Opaque Projector.* (Austin, Tex.: University of Texas Press, 1960), p. 15.

been mechanically reduced in size. The most common form of micro-projection is the microfilm. In this process, printed matter, objects, specimens, and the like are photographed on a roll of 35 mm (or smaller) film. This microfilm can be enlarged by a special microfilm projector whenever desired. This process is helpful for libraries in securing copies of out-of-print books and in preserving perishable materials such as newspapers. Students engaged in research projects should be encouraged to use the microfilms which may be available in the school library, the community library, or the microfilm collection of a nearby college. A variant of microfilm is the microcard in which approximately eighty pages of text are reduced to one side of a 3-by-5 card.

Another form of microprojection is the microscope microprojector, which can throw an image on the screen of objects visible only through a microscope. Biology teachers should make extensive use of this device, since with it they can point out to the entire class the various parts and functions of a living organism in its essential livingness, something here-tofore impossible.

Television

There are two basic types of educational television programs (ETV), viz., a formal classroom lecture given by a master teacher, and the viewing of some event, scene, or drama. Guba terms the first "tele-vised instruction," the second "instructional television." [37] The first type is the one receiving the most attention, not only in public educational circles, but also by certain Catholic school experts, because it represents a new approach to mass instruction and because the second type is really a variant of the motion picture.

There are three kinds of ETV broadcasts: *open-circuit television,* i.e., the usual type of telecast by commercial or noncommercial (educa-tional) networks or stations which can normally be tuned in by home receivers; *closed-circuit television,* i.e., selective telecasts which can be tuned in only by specially equipped receivers; and *recordings,* i.e., repro-ductions of an original televised presentation. Recordings may be either videotape or kinescope. Videotape is an audio-visual recording made on distinctively prepared magnetic tape; a kinescope is a sound motion picture photographed in a special manner during the original television broadcast.[38]

ETV is being produced chiefly by three sources, viz., commercial stations, school systems, and universities. The Federal Communications

[37] Egon Guba, "Ten Years of Research in Instructional Television," *North Central Association Quarterly,* XXXV (April, 1961), p. 302.

[38] See John J. Culkin, S. J., "Television in the Teaching Apostolate," *Bulletin of the National Catholic Educational Association,* LVIII (February, 1962), pp. 24–27.

Commission has allocated several hundred channels for the exclusive use of noncommercial educational telecasting. Most of the televised instruction has been directed toward college students. However, some public school systems such as that of Hagerstown, Maryland, have been making extensive use of closed-circuit television on the elementary and secondary level.

The whole field of educational television seems to have been pioneered by a Jesuit priest, Fr. Roswell C. Williams, S.J., in 1945 in teaching biology over TV to young physicians in training. Since that time, and particularly since 1950, ETV has grown tremendously. Alert Catholic educators have utilized ETV as much as, if not more than, their secular counterparts. The work of the University of Detroit and that of St. Louis University are outstanding examples. One of the earliest and most successful efforts of ETV on the Catholic secondary (and elementary) level took place in Pittsburgh under the dynamic leadership of Msgr. John McDowell and Sister M. Rosalie. In recognition of the importance of ETV, the National Catholic Educational Association has formed a Committee on Educational Television.

Public schools have also been utilizing ETV. The Hagerstown, Maryland, public school system was one of the pioneers in this field. A significant breakthrough toward the full utilization of ETV was made by the Midwest Program on Airborne Television which broadcast educational courses on videotape from an airplane flying over Indiana to schools in six Midwestern states. The curricula of these courses were planned by educational experts from the six participating states.[39]

Educational television has many pedagogical advantages. It can present information to large numbers of students at one time. It can utilize a master teacher so that every student can have a superior instructor. During the course of the lesson it can employ materials, equipment, models, diagrams, and the like which are too expensive, too bulky, or otherwise impossible to duplicate in the average classroom. Close-up photography enables students to see small materials, intricate laboratory demonstrations, etc., which would ordinarily be difficult to view from the middle or back of the classroom. It can depict scenes and events which students cannot possibly experience firsthand. It is timely, since it can bring many events into the classroom at the moment they are happening. The television instructor, because he has only one lesson to plan, is able to devote more effort to that lesson than can the normal teacher with the customary heavy secondary school instructional load. Interesting and

[39] Mary Howard Smith (ed.), Midwest Program on Airborne Television Instruction, *Using Television in the Classroom*. (New York: McGraw-Hill, 1961); see also Fund for the Advancement of Education, *Teaching by Television*. (New York: Ford Foundation, 1959).

competent experts can be easily made a part of the televised lesson, something which is not always easy in the regular classroom. Finally, it provides the student who was absent from school the opportunity of watching the lesson at home, thus minimizing the harmful educational effects
of absenteeism.

Notwithstanding, ETV possesses certain disadvantages which cannot
and should not be overlooked when determining the extent of its usefulness in modern secondary schools. First, it involves instruction rather
than education, because it causes the learner to be a passive observer
rather than an active participant in the lesson. This is perhaps its most
serious disadvantage in that it does not allow that mental interplay
between teacher and student which is so crucial to every good learning
situation. Second, the student cannot ask questions of the instructor
about a part of the lesson which he does not understand. Third, unlike models or most other audio-visual materials, the television broadcasts must usually be received when they are transmitted, regardless of
whether they are pedagogically opportune at that time or not. The
teacher must therefore build his lesson around the telecast rather than
utilize this A-V device at the time he and the class deem best. Kinescopes
and videotapes, as well as the machines necessary to transmit them, are
still usually too expensive for classroom use. Fourth, there is no provision
for individual differences. Fifth, the televised experience is in one sense
not lifelike, since it takes place in a black-and-white, two-dimensional
medium instead of a colored, three-dimensional setting. Sixth, it shares
some of the disadvantages of the motion picture.

Holmes's survey of 281 studies of televised instruction revealed that
in almost 90 per cent of the cases there was no significant difference in
product learning between the televised and the regular classes.[40] Tanner
commented that the chief reason for this lack of significant difference is
that in most conventional classrooms, teachers follow rigid instructor-
centered pedagogical patterns, devoting a very large amount of time
to a review of assignments and relying on the textbook as practically the
sole source of pupil experience.[41] If the instruction on television and in
conventional classrooms is similar, it follows that the product learnings
derived from them will be similar. Tanner's view is fortified by a study
of experienced high school teachers of mathematics and science who
received National Science Foundation fellowships. This investigation
revealed that these teachers stressed factual information very heavily in
their instruction rather than critical thinking, problem solving, and other

[40] Presley D. Holmes, Jr., *Televised Research in the Teaching-Learning Process,*
unpublished doctoral dissertation, Wayne State University, Detroit, Mich., 1959, p. 74.

[41] Daniel Tanner, "Needed Research in Instructional Television," *School Review,*
LXIX (Autumn, 1961), p. 313.

vital process learnings.[42] Despite the rigidity and teacher-centeredness of conventional classroom situations, Holmes in his review of the research could still conclude that "there is significantly greater gain in critical thinking and problem-solving under conventional conditions than there is under one-way television, particularly for high intelligence students." [43]

Most of the studies concerned with student reactions to ETV instruction have been carried out on the college and military levels where the lecture technique is the customary instructional procedure. Even on these levels where the similarity in instruction is the most marked, many students preferred a "live" teacher because of the possibility of some sort of teacher-pupil interaction, if only after class. The research investigation of the St. Louis Educational Television Commission concluded that the secondary school students studied did not, as a whole, react favorably to televised instruction and asserted that they would have learned more in a regular classroom than they did in the televised course.[44] Lee's investigation of ETV teaching on the secondary school level concluded that most of the students studied overwhelmingly favored conventional classroom teaching to televised instruction, provided the former incorporated pupil participation and was challenging.[45]

These investigations underscore the necessity for the secondary school teacher to provide education rather than mere instruction. Certainly there is little or no difference between automated ETV and an automated "live" teacher who stresses the lecture method, fails to encourage pupil problem solving and creativity, and neglects the process outcomes of learning. Pupil participation and pupil mental self-activity at every stage of the lesson are the best defense a teacher can make against those who would replace him with a television set.

Formal televised lectures can be used in one of two ways, viz., for an entire course or in conjunction with and supplemental to regular classwork. The first should be employed only as a last resort. The second can provide a good basis for enrichment if utilized according to the general principles of good audio-visual teaching previously detailed. Teachers' manuals and pupil study guides, if provided, should be used. Classroom television receivers should have the largest screens made and should be set on a table or otherwise elevated approximately 5 feet above the floor for optimum student viewing.

[42] Howard E. Gruber, "Science Teachers and the Scientific Attitude: An Appraisal of an Academic Year Institute," *Science*, CXXXII (Aug. 19, 1960), p. 468.

[43] Holmes, *op. cit.*, p. 77.

[44] Earl G. Herminghaus, "Large-Group Instruction by Television: An Experiment," *School Review*, LXV (Summer, 1957), pp. 119–133.

[45] James Michael Lee, "A Study of Student Reactions to Televised Instruction," unpublished manuscript, 1959.

Some Catholic educators have been leaping a bit overzealously on the ETV bandwagon. They see ETV solving many of the problems currently besetting Catholic education, particularly the teacher shortage and low-grade or average instruction in certain areas.[46] Certainly ETV cannot adequately relieve the teacher shortage if teaching is thought to be of a higher order than a mere supermarket type of instruction. An ETV presentation, used in a proper pedagogical fashion, must be followed up by small-group discussions where the material presented is clarified, made meaningful, and integrated into the pupils' lives. These small-group discussions necessitate as many teachers as do ordinary classrooms. This was borne out in a research investigation by the NEA which disclosed that 82 per cent of the teachers and a majority of the principals surveyed stated that classes taught with the assistance of television could not be increased in size without detrimental effects on the quality of education.[47] While it is true that ETV enables a master teacher to present his material, nevertheless, it can never really substitute for personal teacher-student confrontation. It must also be remembered that ETV is not a direct experience for the students; it is a vicarious experience at which they are spectators. Exclusive use of ETV is therefore a stopgap measure, not an educational *desideratum*. Catholic educators should try to use ETV to supplement, not to replace, classroom teaching. They should ever bear in mind the words of Pope Pius XII, who warned that "so called mass education . . . involves less labor to be sure, but runs the risk of helping only a few, whereas all have a right to profit from the instruction given." [48]

Programed Instruction

Programed instruction refers to presenting material to be learned in such a manner that the student is required to go through carefully preplanned specific processes of learning the material, of testing himself on the accuracy with which he has learned the material, and finally of reinforcing these specific learnings more or less immediately. There are two basic types of programed instruction, viz., the teaching machine and the programed textbook.

The teaching machine, sometimes referred to as instrument learning or automated tutor, is a mechanical device which presents specified content material to the pupil, tests him on his mastery of this material, and provides for the immediate rectification of his incorrect responses.

[46] See, for example, the *National Catholic Educational Association Bulletin,* LVIII (February, 1962).

[47] National Education Association, "Teaching by Television," *NEA Research Bulletin,* XL (February, 1962), p. 8.

[48] Pope Pius XII, *"Nell'Accogliervi,"* loc. cit.

Teaching machines were conceived and developed in the 1920s by Sidney L. Pressey, but despite their use in the military during and after World War II, it was not until Skinner popularized the idea in the mid 1950s that these automated devices began to be thought of as having important educational significance. Since that time, a great variety of teaching machines has been commercially developed, with a cost ranging from $20 to $5,000.

In the programed textbook, the essential program steps of (1) presentation, (2) response, and (3) reinforcement are accomplished not by manipulating an automated device, but by reading a specially prepared book. A regular textbook requires the pupil to perform step 1; a workbook compels the pupil to steps 1 and 2; a programed textbook demands that the pupil perform all three steps. Herein lies its uniqueness as a book.

The psychology of B. F. Skinner, who popularized teaching machines, still provides the main theoretical basis for the vast majority of current programed instruction. This psychological theory, which falls under the Stimulus-Response classification (see Chapter IV), views learning as primarily the active response by the human organism to a stimulus and the immediate reinforcement of this response by means of a reward. Learning can best take place when stimuli are presented in small, finely graded steps so that the organism can make no errors. (Error is regarded as nonreward and hence injurious to learning.) In the late 1950s, N. A. Crowder developed a theory and practice of programed instruction which differed from Skinner's in several ways. First, unlike Skinner, Crowder believed that students learn by their mistakes and hence that at many stages of the total sequence the program should lead the pupil into making mistakes. Second, Crowder maintained that large rather than small, finely-graded steps are more productive of learning, particularly of the higher mental processes. Third, Crowder held that no writer can devise a program that will be best for all students; the various levels of learning must be intrinsically programed into the sequence so that each pupil can proceed according to his own personality structure and ability. Skinner, on the other hand, contended that an experienced writer can construct a programed sequence for all students. Thus Crowder's system has been called "branching," while Skinner's has been termed "linear." Fourth, Crowder's programs require the pupil to make a "selected response" (an answer to a multiple-choice question), while Skinner's programs require the pupil to make a "constructed response" (an answer to a completion question). The eventual settlement of this controversy must, of course, await the results of research during the next two decades.

There is a second controversy in programed instruction, viz., the advantages and disadvantages of the teaching machine versus the programed textbook. Textbooks are cheaper, less bulky, do not admit of mechanical breakdown, and even allow the teacher to construct his own framed or learning sequence. Machines, on the other hand, are better motivators because of novelty and pupil fascination with mechanical devices (the so-called "pinball effect"), afford greater control of pupil learning behavior, are cheat-resistant, and can store more stimuli and responses in a smaller space (by use of 8- or 16-mm film). At present, the teaching machine seems to be in the ascendancy, and hence the remainder of this section is devoted to this type of programed instruction.

The teaching machine is far more than an aid to the human teacher; it is a complete substitute for him in the appropriate instructional process. It is therefore a unique type of audio-visual material.

The purpose of the teaching machine is to allow each student to progress as fast as he can. The machine's mechanism and the arrangement of the programed material keep the pupil from proceeding until he has first mastered the material which has been already presented.

Fattu has described six essential successive functions which every teaching machine should perform:[49] (1) Storing the materials (whether content, problems, or tasks) to be learned and mastered. Different types of machines have different storage devices ranging from slides and discs to specially punched cards. The materials selected for storage should all cause specific desired learning outcomes. (2) Controlling the order or sequence in which the materials to be learned are presented to the student. Normally the sequence of content, problems, or tasks is organized in order of ascending difficulty so that each student can proceed at his own rate. Also finely graded steps result in a low error rate.[50] The sequence is further determined by the type of learning sought, e.g., problem solving, rote, manual task. (3) Presenting the content, problem, or tasks to the student in a manner most conducive to efficient learning and retention of the specific kind of outcome desired. Various types of machines have sundry methods of presentation, e.g., a paragraph to be read, multiple-choice items to be sifted, a manual task to be performed. The presentation often has built-in guides, hints, or prompts which serve to direct the pupil not to the correct answer but rather to think along

[49] Nicholas A. Fattu, "Training Devices," *Encyclopedia of Educational Research,* 3d ed. (New York: Macmillan, 1960), pp. 1530–1532.

[50] James G. Holland, "Evaluating Teaching Machines and Programs," *Teachers College Record,* LXIII (October, 1961), pp. 57–58. Some educators, following Crowder, seem to be in favor of inducing a certain number of errors as an incentive device. See Donald E. P. Smith, "Speculations: Characteristics of Successful Programs and Programmers," in Galanter (ed.), *Automatic Teaching: The State of the Art.* (New York: Wiley, 1959), pp. 91–92.

certain desired channels and patterns.[51] (4) Receiving the response which the student is required to make in order to indicate his solution to the problem stimulus. Different machines have different performance acceptors, e.g., writing an answer in a blank space, checking a specific item from among many, pressing a button. (5) Evaluating the correctness or incorrectness of the pupil's response to the problem stimulus. Most teaching machines accomplish this evaluation in a negative fashion, i.e., by retaining the content, problem, or task until the student makes the proper response. The machine will not present the next problem until the prior one has been answered correctly.[52] (6) Recording the total performance record of the student so that when the "lesson" is concluded the pupil may review and reinforce those responses which he originally got wrong.

The teaching machine as a pedagogical device has many advantages. First, it stimulates and necessitates pupil mental self-activity since it is impossible for the student to be passive when he is using the teaching machine. Second, it mechanizes the routinely systematic aspects of instruction, thus freeing the teacher's time for personal work with each student. Third, it permits each pupil to work at his own learning rate thereby approaching the ideal of instruction based completely on individual differences. Fourth, properly programed, it is conducive to various types of learning, namely, rote, problem solving, abstraction (although like a human teacher, it cannot teach these directly). Fifth, it presents the material to be learned in a logical, step-by-step fashion.[53] Sixth, it supplies reasonable assurance that the student has comprehended and mastered each step before he proceeds to the next (unlike the conventional classroom where the human teacher can arrive at no such degree of assurance for all the students). Seventh, it provides immediate reinforcement of learnings (by reward, namely, the machine delivers the next item; or by punishment, namely, the machine retains the item when answered incorrectly).[54] Eighth, it enables the teacher easily, quickly, and concretely to obtain information about pupil weaknesses so that these may be remedied. Ninth, it is reasonably cheat-resistant so that the pupil will normally have to study the programed material

[51] Jacob Beck, "On Some Methods of Programming," in Galanter (ed.), *Automatic Teaching: The State of the Art, op. cit.,* p. 55.

[52] See Abram Amsel, "Error Responses and Reinforcement Schedules in Self-instructional Devices," in Lumsdaine and Glaser (eds.), *Teaching Machines and Programmed Learning.* (Washington: Department of Audio-Visual Instruction, NEA, 1960), pp. 506–516.

[53] Holland, *op. cit.,* p. 56.

[54] As Clark has observed, *immediate* reinforcement results in the best type of learning. See Ella Callista Clark, "The Teaching Machine and Programmed Materials," *Catholic School Journal,* LXI (December, 1961), p. 19.

before responding rather than resort to the old practice of just copying the material.

The teaching machine has quite a few disadvantages which suggest its careful and judicious use. First, it is completely automated and therefore deprives the student of the necessary, indispensable, and irreplaceable values gained in *live* teacher-pupil interaction. Second, it is based on an outdated and materialistically rooted Stimulus-Response psychology rather than on the Cognitive theory (see Chapter IV).[55] Third, while presenting material logically, it nevertheless cannot educate every pupil in the optimum psychological fashion. Fourth, it cannot generate the pupil enthusiasm that a human teacher can. Fifth, it is unable to promote student creativity, and in fact may stunt his creativity.[56] Sixth, there is the danger of overstandardization of the material throughout the country, thus neglecting regional, local, and even individual differences. Seventh, it can indicate correct or incorrect responses, but often not the reasons why, nor can it clear up any interpretative problems which may arise in the pupil's mind from the particular content, problem, or task presented. Eighth, in many instances the pupils may guess the correct responses, thus circumventing the desired problem solving or abstractive thinking. Ninth, it can reinforce the incorrect response as well as the correct one.[57] Tenth, the built-in low error rate may dull the pupil's ability in selective discrimination. Eleventh, it is usually quite expensive to purchase.

Because of the relative newness of teaching machines, there has been little empirical research evaluating them in terms of amount and quality of product and process learnings gained from them. As a result, most of the discussion is still in the exploratory stage.

Teaching machines will never replace human teachers because of the nature of the educative process. However, teachers should make wise use of these automated devices, particularly in five areas, namely, in the systematized procedures of instruction, for individualized drill, in specific kinds of problem-solving situations, for review, and for certain types of testing and evaluation. Such skillful utilization of machines will enable these devices to perform their greatest service, namely, to provide completely for the pupils' individual differences.[58]

[55] Robert B. Nordberg, "What Teaching Machines Can and Cannot Do," *Catholic Educational Review*, LIX (September, 1961), p. 364.

[56] H. F. Silberman, "Teaching Machines," *Junior College Journal*, XXXI (February, 1961), p. 18.

[57] Lawrence M. Stolurow, "Problems in Evaluating Automated Learning," *Teachers College Record*, LXIII (October, 1961), p. 56.

[58] See B. F. Skinner, "Teaching Machines," in Lumsdaine and Glaser (eds.), *op. cit.*, pp. 155–158.

Radio

Before the advent of television, educational radio was an extremely important audio-visual material. But, as Clausse has noted, learning through all the senses has become the dominant type of education today, thus seriously limiting the use of a strictly unisensory medium such as the radio.[59] Nevertheless, commercial radio listening is still very popular among adolescents, especially with regard to "musical" programs. While educational radio is gradually being supplanted by ETV, it still has a definite place in the classroom. This is notably true for on-the-spot news coverage which television often cannot provide. The fact that it is less expensive to produce educational radio broadcasts than ETV programs means that many of the less wealthy school systems will have to wait some years before obtaining their own ETV facilities. Meanwhile, planned educational radio broadcasts can be profitably used, particularly in the FM band. For this same economic reason, Catholic school systems should work with educational radio, a practice which unfortunately has not been very common to date.

Educational radio, however, shares some of the major disadvantages of ETV. It is not flexible in that the teacher cannot bring in the program at the opportune pedagogical moment, but rather must plan his teaching around the time of the broadcast. It maximizes pupil passivity. Also, it does not allow for a living interchange between program and pupil.

However, when properly used in connection with prepared study guides and in conjunction with system-wide planning, educational radio can be a valuable teaching aid.

The Public Address System

The public address (PA) system is often used solely for administrative announcements. Such restricted use of this audial device is a good example of the neglect of the potentialities of a valuable learning tool. The PA system can be hooked up to a radio or a tape recorder, thus providing all the students in the school, or in selected classrooms, with the advantages of educational radio broadcasts or specially taped programs. This is singularly important for news events or programs of particular interest and educational significance for all the students. The PA system can also serve as a vehicle for daily student newscasts, affording the pupils in the English classes valuable compositional learnings. Student newscasts would encourage pupil attentiveness to the important events of in-school and out-of-school life. Student panels and symposia could also utilize the PA system and each classroom could serve as an

[59] Roger Clausse, *Education by Radio*. (Paris: UNESCO, 1949), p. 29.

already established discussion group, thus eliminating audience adjournment from the auditorium to areas conducive to small-group discussion.

The Recording

A recording is an audial transcription of a specially prepared broadcast or a spontaneous, unrehearsed event. The two main types of educational recording are the disc and the tape. They can be produced commercially (most disc and some tape recordings) or by the school system (some tape recordings) or by the individual school (also some tape recordings).

The Disc Recording. Disc recordings are audial transcriptions made on round plastic platters. These are commonly referred to as records. There are many educationally worthwhile disc recordings now being sold by companies. Recordings of poets reading selections of their works, important speeches of prominent twentieth-century political figures, symphonies, operas, and foreign language instruction are typical examples of the disc recordings currently available. The relative inexpensiveness of these discs means that each school can have its own educational disc record library.

There are quite a few educational advantages of disc recordings. Unlike radio broadcasts, they can be brought into the lesson whenever the teacher wishes. Also, unlike radio broadcasts, they can be stopped at any time for pupil discussion or replayed to clarify certain points. They require the pupil to exercise his creative pictorial imagination, an ability often stunted by television and films. Recordings, unlike radio broadcasts, can be preheard so that the teacher can become familiar with the product and process learnings contained therein. Many educational recordings are accompanied by teachers' guides and supplemental resource data. Recordings are inexpensive and so allow the pupils to experience learnings otherwise possible only by use of more expensive and hence often inaccessible media. Finally, recordings are compact and can be stored easily.

The alert teacher should endeavor to make the most of educationally significant disc recordings.[60]

The Tape Recording. Tape recordings are audial transcriptions made on magnetized plastic tape. They possess all the advantages of disc recordings, plus several more. The most important of these is that the students can make their own recordings simply and inexpensively. When a new recording is desired, the same tape can be used again merely by speaking over the prior sound track, a process which erases the latter.

[60] See James W. Brown, Richard B. Lewis, and Fred F. Harcleroad, *Audio-Visual Instruction: Materials and Methods.* (New York: McGraw-Hill, 1959), pp. 189–190.

Tapes of student voices are particularly useful in speech and foreign language classes where enunciation, diction, and other vocal skills are important content and process learnings.[61] Drama classes can rehearse plays by use of the tape recorder; and in the actual production, appropriate sound effects and music previously taped can be turned on at the proper moment. Speeches given at some other place in the community can be taped and later played for the students; e.g., in a Catholic high school a parish talk by a European Catholic Action leader. The tape recorder has an almost infinite variety of uses. Every secondary school, public as well as Catholic, should own a tape recorder and make continuous use of it. The ease by which splicing can be accomplished enables the students to use their creative abilities to produce a recording of great versatility at virtually no cost.[62]

Electronic Teaching

The most common form of electronic teaching is the electronic laboratory, which consists of a series of separate booths in which the student, usually by means of headphones, can listen to recordings or, in some instances, converse electronically with a live teacher. In the first type, the student alone chooses the recording, the parts he will listen to and repeat. In the second type, the teacher's desk is equipped with an electronic panel which broadcasts by tape three or four separate recordings. The pupil in his booth listens to the recording most suitable for his particular learning level. The electronic panel is also equipped with an intercommunication system connected to every booth so that from his desk the teacher can ask each student questions on the recording and can offer suggestions for improvement.

The electronic laboratory possesses the following educational advantages: It provides individualized instruction; it affords the teacher the opportunity of working with some students while the others are engaged in fruitful learning; it gives the teacher automatic teacher-pupil control devices; it can be used after school hours when many teachers have left the building; it gives the pupils privacy with a minimum of distractions; it provides concrete learning facilities for individuals and groups; in the case of language laboratories, it furnishes the pupils with firsthand contact with the language, with an opportunity for both listening and practicing speech.[63]

[61] See Julia Mellenbruch, *The Tape Recorder in the Classroom*. (Austin, Tex.: University of Texas Press, 1959), p. 30.

[62] For helpful suggestions on how to make an educational tape recording, see C. J. Le Bel, *How to Make Good Tape Recordings*. (New York: Audio Devices, 1956).

[63] See Joseph C. Hutchinson, *The Language Laboratory*. (Washington: Department of Health, Education and Welfare, 1961), pp. 8–9.

In some communities, the electronic laboratory has been put on wheels to serve the needs of several schools. This helps to solve one problem for the less wealthy school systems.

Electronic laboratories, especially in the languages, should be a part of all public and Catholic high schools. Teachers should learn their potentialities and make use of this wonderful new pedagogical learning device.

The Demonstration

The demonstration is a pedagogical procedure whereby the teacher shows and illustrates an object or technique to the class. This is usually accompanied by explanatory remarks. The demonstration is most commonly used in science and industrial arts classes, e.g., illustrating the dramatic action produced by pouring a few drops of concentrated sulfuric acid into a beaker containing a spoonful of sugar, or showing safety procedures in the woodworking shop. However, the demonstration is also used in other problem or content areas, especially those in which the teacher is explaining some model, e.g., the social studies teacher illustrating the function of the postern gate in the model of a medieval castle. Therefore, every teacher should be familiar with the techniques of good demonstration teaching since he will use this pedagogical method quite often in most courses.

The following are some suggestions for making demonstration teaching educationally worthwhile:

1. Cooperatively prepare with the pupils an outline of the important things to be learned.

2. Make sure that all the materials, illustrations and the like are on hand when the demonstration begins.

3. Break down the total demonstration into a simple step-by-step pattern so that it can be easily understood by the class.

4. Pace the demonstration slowly so that the explanations are not rushed.

5. Normally defer any student questions until after the demonstration has been completed.

6. Whenever possible, involve students in the demonstration.

7. If the type of demonstration permits, ascertain after each step whether the students have grasped the meaning, content, and explanation. (If they have not, the pertinent parts of the demonstration should be repeated.)

8. Verbally dramatize the demonstration so as to heighten interest and increase learning.

9. Ask the students to summarize the major learnings in the demonstration after it has been concluded.

10. Make an assignment based on the demonstration; e.g., ask the pupils to draw a picture of the demonstration, labeling the important parts and explaining what happened step-by-step and why.

11. Evaluate the pupil learnings from the demonstration.

12. Repeat the demonstration, pausing for student questions.

As was suggested above, it is wise to incorporate the students in the demonstration whenever possible. Failure to do this may reduce the pupils to passive entities and hence thwart a cardinal goal of teaching, viz., to stimulate student mental self-activity. A demonstration involving the Magdeburg hemispheres, for example, could feature a strong student pulling the hemispheres apart when they are under normal atmospheric conditions, and then trying this same procedure again when the air in the hemispheres has been evacuated. (This involves the whole class much more deeply than if the teacher alone attempted to separate the hemispheres.) Subsequently, air can be surreptitiously let into the evacuated hemispheres by the teacher who then gives them to the frailest student in the class. This student separates the hemispheres with ease. The class, mystified, then has to grope for an explanation and so is compelled to problem-solve.

The Exhibit

An exhibit is a public display of objects or materials of educational interest. An exhibit may be of a classroom or a school-wide kind; again it may be pupil-made or on loan. A classroom exhibit is one which is displayed only in the classroom, e.g., a culminating unit on nineteenth-century English literature showing a model of the Lake District, some books printed during that period, and so forth. A school-wide exhibit is one which is shown in a place where the entire school may view it, e.g., in the foyer. School-wide exhibits feature objects or materials of interest to the whole student body rather than one class, e.g., in a Catholic high school a collection of primitive Indian cooking utensils gathered by lay missionaries in South America.

A pupil-made exhibit is one which is constructed by the students themselves, while a loan exhibit is one in which the materials are borrowed for a specified interval from the school system's central exhibit bureau, a museum, a government agency, a commercial agency, and in Catholic high schools from some religious group. Pupil-made exhibits are valuable because, by involving the pupils, they provide valuable learning experiences. They also give concrete evidence of what was learned in class.[64] In addition, they are good outlets for the students'

[64] A. J. Foy Cross and Irene F. Cypher, *Audio-Visual Education.* (New York: Crowell, 1961), p. 154.

creative abilities. Loan exhibits are valuable in that they bring otherwise inaccessible materials of great educational significance to a place where all the students can carefully observe and study them. Loan exhibits broaden the students' knowledge and horizons and so should form a continual part of every school's educational program. There should always be some loan exhibit on display in the school (not to mention numerous pupil-made exhibits). Catholic school systems should do two things in this regard, viz., first, assemble exhibit material for rotation loan to the various high schools, and second, prepare a list of free loan materials available from diverse sources such as museums and corporations.

An exhibit, if it is to achieve its maximum impact on the students, should possess certain minimal characteristics. First, it should be large enough to be easily seen. Second, it should be placed in a location where it will not only be easily seen but will also command attention. Third, it should be well lighted, perhaps even spotlighted, for added attention. Fourth, the objects and materials should be placed at a reasonable distance from one another rather than crowded together. Fifth, it should be built around one central, unitary idea and theme. Sixth, it should be skillfully labeled in short, crisp, legible fashion. Seventh, it should be adequately protected so that it is not manhandled by the students (unless it is the type of exhibit where touching is an asset). Eighth, it should be supported by explanatory or attention-getting ancillary aids, e.g., a Congolese exhibit together with the Missa Luba, the famous African Mass sung in Congolese style with the musical accompaniment of tom-toms and other African instruments.

The bulletin board is perhaps the most common type of exhibit. Like every other audio-visual material, this should be primarily a teaching device. It has a wide variety of uses, e.g., for student-made or commercial posters, pictures, a display of outstanding classroom work, announcements, and so on. The bulletin board should be attractive, aesthetically pleasing, and attention-getting. Few things are less appealing than a drab bulletin board. The materials displayed should be changed frequently, probably every week. Each classroom should have its own bulletin board and each department should be responsible for one or more bulletin boards in the corridors, auditorium, and so forth. Corridors should not serve merely as passageways for the pupils but should provide learning opportunities as well.

Bulletin board materials should be organized and built around one central theme; present a problem-solving situation, e.g., an unfinished series of pictures; relate what is on the bulletin board to the pupils' past experiences and previous knowledge so that learning is facilitated; tell a story; convey their message visually as well as verbally; make use of color; be properly spaced so that the bulletin board is not cluttered up.

The captions on the bulletin board should be large and legible and should sum up the materials contained thereon. These captions should normally be framed in question form rather than as statements, so that the students will be motivated first to think and then to read the bulletin board to find the answer to the question.

Alexander and Halverson note that teachers "generally find their bulletin boards to be of greater variety and creativity" when the teacher intelligently delegates responsibility for the composition and care of the bulletin board to the students.[65] Such a practice is consonant with good teaching theory which places stress on pupil activity. Kinder advocates the use of movable as well as stationary bulletin boards.[66]

One of the most important features of a Catholic high school should be the liturgical bulletin board. Since the life of the Church is centered around liturgical celebration, the students must be given the opportunity to come to a true and deep awareness of the moments of the liturgy. Liturgical symbolism and the recent magnificent Catholic renaissance in liturgical art of the highest calibre should be a part of every liturgical bulletin board.[67] Pictures or plaster "art" statues of simpering saints, senile St. Josephs, and marshmallowy Little Flowers should not be permitted to find their way into Catholic high schools. As the Getleins have noted, this type of art at best "looks to the past and silently teaches that Christianity is dead or at least asleep";[68] it certainly cannot but fail to repel any normal adolescent.

Each department should have its own illustrative materials file in which are kept posters, pictures, illustrations, etc., which can serve as a core resource for historical, geographical, topical, or liturgical events which recur annually.

The Chalkboard

The chalkboard is a medium upon which words or illustrations can be written or drawn in chalk. The word "chalkboard" rather than "blackboard" is used because many modern chalkboards are green to reduce glare. The chalkboard is one of the most common of all audiovisual materials—and one which is rarely utilized to its maximum potential. The skillful use of the chalkboard by Bishop Fulton J. Sheen

[65] William M. Alexander and Paul M. Halverson, *Effective Teaching in Secondary Schools.* (New York: Holt, 1956), p. 147.

[66] James S. Kinder, *Audio-Visual Materials and Techniques,* 2d ed. (New York: American Book, 1959), p. 358.

[67] Every teacher in a Catholic high school should become well acquainted with the magazine *Liturgical Arts,* one of the glories of the American Catholic Church. This magazine, a quarterly, is edited by a layman.

[68] Frank Getlein and Dorothy Getlein, *Christianity in Modern Art.* (Milwaukee: Bruce, 1961), p. 20.

during his celebrated telecasts in the 1950s brought renewed and deserved attention to this audio-visual medium. As Wittich and Schuller have observed, the chalkboard is an essential tool in classroom education.[69]

As a pedagogical device the chalkboard has a number of advantages: It fosters pupils' participation in the lesson, especially during those times when they can write or draw on it. It provides a good medium for pupil practice, particularly when it is beneficial for this practice to be witnessed by the whole class under the guidance of the teacher. It enables the teacher or pupil to write down concise principles, key words, outlines, and summaries during the course of the socialized developmental lesson. It is handy for making a drawing or diagram illustrating some concept or principle. It can be used over and over again by merely erasing the words or illustrations. Lastly, it is inexpensive.

Most properly taught lessons will utilize some chalkboard work. Some suggestions for improving the quality of chalkboard teaching include:

1. If at all possible, the students rather than the teacher should write the words or draw the illustrations on the chalkboard because this will cause the pupils to be increasingly active participants in the learning process.

2. All words and illustrations should be large enough to be seen by the entire class.

3. All words should be legible and all illustrations clear.

4. Graphs, charts, and diagrams should be employed whenever possible and useful, especially during the discussion or explication of an abstract concept.

5. In some cases, e.g., in certain complicated drawings, the illustration should be placed on the chalkboard before class so that the students will be able to copy it at the optimum learning moment. (This will save time which would be unnecessarily consumed if the teacher or student laboriously made the illustration during class time.)

6. When discussing a word or illustration on the chalkboard, the teacher or student should stand to one side and use a pointer so that the material will not be blocked.

7. The chalkboard should be cleaned daily with a wet sponge so that its surface will be clear and previously erased material will not show through.

8. Different colors of chalk should be used in drawings and illustrations.

The Flannel Board

A flannel board, as its name implies, consists of a large piece of flannel or felt permanently attached to a piece of board or other stiff substance. The principle underlying the operation of the flannel board is that when two pieces of flannel are placed on top of one another, the

[69] Wittich and Schuller, *op. cit.*, p. 37.

naps of each piece will engage or catch the other, causing adherence. Hence a teacher can place light pieces of flannel-backed objects, display signs, etc., on a vertical flannel board without fear of their falling. Other rough-surfaced objects such as those backed with sandpaper will work equally well. Flannel- or sandpaper-backed objects can be kept permanently, thus giving them an advantage over chalkboard items which must be erased. Also these objects are concrete, endowing them with a greater sense of reality than chalk drawings, from a pupil's point of view. Furthermore the objects can be of greater variety in type and color than chalk drawings or letterings. In addition the objects can be easily moved around and rearranged, unlike chalk drawings. Flannel boards used in classroom teaching are normally the size of a chalkboard panel so that by use of hooks they can be directly attached to the chalkboard for easy viewing by the students.

The techniques of effective flannel board teaching are much the same as in the demonstration. The skillful teacher will make sure that the principles of good artistic composition are observed in flannel board teaching, viz., that all the objects on the flannel board are unified into a single concept or impact, that the board is not cluttered with too many objects, and that the objects are arranged in an interesting and attractive manner. Lettered signs should be large enough for the entire class to see easily.

Each department should have a flannel board file of pertinent objects, illustrations, and signs which can be used every year in the course of instruction. This file will be a valuable resource and will save considerable teacher time and effort.

Objects

Objects are concrete audio-visual materials. The most important of these objects are specimens, realia, models, and dioramas.

The Specimen. A specimen is a representative example of some reality in the natural world. A specimen may be organic, e.g., a hamster, or inorganic, e.g., a piece of mica. A specimen is of special educational value because it enables the student to come into personal contact with and to study an inaccessible reality firsthand and not merely look at a representation of it in a photograph or model. A living specimen is particularly valuable since it can do what no other audio-visual material can do, namely, enable the pupil to study and observe firsthand the growth, development, and life processes of some aspect of God's creation. Not only science classrooms but indeed every classroom should feature specimens around the room. Thus, for example, a social studies class could display specimens of desert flowers so that the students could further appreciate life in arid climates. The specimen should be displayed in a part of the classroom, corridor, or alcove where it will be high-lighted; also, there should be a small card under or beside it giving its name and a brief explanation. Logs and progress records should be kept by the students in the case of living specimens.

Realia. Realia are real-life objects, e.g., a foreign coin or a sixteenth-century book. They are distinguished from specimens in that the latter are a part of the natural world, not artifacts of man. Realia are of importance because they bring into the classroom objects which are or have been in actual use in the real, out-of-class world, thus enabling the pupils not only to obtain a vivid idea of what they are studying but also to mesh their knowledge with external reality. Each department should have its own collection of realia in order that the teacher may be able to use them at the pedagogically opportune moment. Students should be encouraged to bring into class realia which are pertinent to the lesson or unit. Like specimens, realia should be displayed in a conspicuous place, and a card detailing pertinent information should be placed close to or beside them. As Sands has observed, both realia and specimens are extremely eloquent teachers.[70]

The Model. A model is a concrete reproduction or representation of some real-life object, e.g., a scale model of a space rocket. Some models have the advantage of reducing or enlarging the real-life object to workable size while preserving its constructional or essential features. Thus a pyramid is obviously too large to bring into class, while the eye is too small, too delicate, and indeed inaccessible to classroom study. But scale models of the pyramid and eye enable the pupils to learn about these realities in a concrete way.

There are certain indispensable characteristics of a worthwhile model. All parts of the model should be reasonably to scale so that the pupils will derive correct concepts. The model should be a convincing likeness of the real object, i.e., recognizable for what it is. It should be workable; e.g., each part should be able to be removed from the model for particular study. If appropriate, each part should be of a different color so as to distinguish it from the adjacent parts. It should be made in such a way that it can be handled by the students; i.e., the material from which the model is made should be sturdy. Finally, it should be large enough so that all members of the class can see it clearly from their seats.[71]

Models can be purchased from a commercial firm or made by the pupils. If at all possible, the pupils themselves should construct the models, since this will afford them a valuable learning experience, e.g.,

[70] Sands, *op. cit.*, p. 77.

[71] Martha F. Meeks, *Models for Teaching.* (Austin, Tex.: University of Texas Press, 1956), pp. 16–17.

in a Catholic high school religion class, building a model of a liturgically functional church. Obviously before they can construct a model, the pupils must possess an excellent knowledge of what they are building. Hence a model can serve as an excellent motivational device and so make a good project. Also constructing a model provides the students with the opportunity to become adept at manual craftsmanship, and for this reason has a distinct place in a Catholic high school where manual skills are not normally provided for by shop or related courses. Sloppy or inaccurate models, of course, should not be permitted, e.g., a lopsided, imprecise globe. Many models are quite complicated and are best purchased from a commercial source.

In teaching with models, the teacher must exercise care that the pupils do not acquire misinterpretational learnings caused by the difference in size between the model and the real object.

The Diorama. Cross and Cypher have defined a diorama as "a miniature, three-dimensional group consisting of small modelled and colored figures and specimens, with accessories placed in an appropriate setting," e.g., a Christmas crib.[72] The diorama has all the advantages of the exhibit, plus an added one, the simulation of a real-life situation. Hence it is a very useful audio-visual material, and the teacher should make wise use of it.

The Field Trip

The field trip is an excursion made by pupils to a place outside the school for purposes of learning. It is often not thought of as an audio-visual material; however, reflection on the matter will show that the field trip is a true representative of A-V learning.

Field trips are indispensable elements of the formal educational process, because the classroom and the school contain only a fraction of the learning resources needed by each pupil for an adequate knowledge of the problem or content area under study. It would be manifestly unjust to the student were the teacher to restrict his guided learning to the confines of the classroom. Such a limitation would not only result in stunted learning, but would more widely foster an ivory-tower mentality. The pupil will live most of his life in the community, not in the school. If the knowledge learned in school is to really become the leaven of his actions, then formal learning should constantly mesh in-school and out-of-school life. This is especially important in Catholic high schools where a student's theological learnings are supposed to radically affect every moment of his living. A person's problems arise in a community setting; if the high school wishes to give its students the effective

72 Cross and Cypher, *op. cit.*, p. 197.

intellectual, attitudinal, and spiritual means of solving these problems, then it should actively and actually relate its activities to community life. Too many public and Catholic secondary schools are run as hothouses rather than as integral parts of the civic (and parochial) community. The only time such schools enter community life is when they seek some publicity for themselves.

The unique value of the field trip is that it provides the students with firsthand experiences of what they are studying and investigating. From the point of view of psychology, the social sciences, and Thomistic philosophy, firsthand encounters are superior to vicarious experiences. Certainly the best way to learn something is by direct experience. Which is the better way of truly understanding and appreciating a coal mine and the problems of coal miners—reading about them or actually going down into a mine and personally *experiencing* the men digging coal, feeling the dampness, seeing the sweat of the men mingled with the chilling drafts of the ventilation system, becoming so saturated with coal dust that it seems to clog the nostrils? Whitehead remarked that "the secondhandedness of the learned world is the secret of its mediocrity." [73] For Catholics, the cruciality of personal experience assumes an infinite dimension because of the central and pivotal role of the Incarnation. God, in Christ, knew men not just intuitively but experientially. One of the glories of the Incarnation is that God took on human form to personally experience humanity. This passage from heaven to earth was the ultimate in field trips.

An investigation by Helliwell involving English secondary school children concluded that the field trip produced learnings which were greatly superior to those gained from a filmstrip on the same topic.[74] A study by Collings indicated that churches provide very few field trips and other educational opportunities for direct experience.[75] Catholic high schools should therefore offer increased excursions to compensate for this deficiency. It is important for the Catholic high school to work with and in the community because such activity will deinsularize the parochial attitudes of the student, will foster a favorable image of the Catholic school system in the community, and also will help spread knowledge of and good will toward the Catholic religion. From an

[73] Alfred North Whitehead, *The Aims of Education,* quoted in Alabama Department of Education, *Better Use of Textbooks.* (Montgomery, Ala.: State Board of Education, 1948), p. 17.

[74] S. Helliwell, "An Investigation of the Values of the Filmstrip and the Educational Visits as Methods of Instruction to Modern School Pupils of 14–15 Years," *British Journal of Educational Psychology,* XXIII (June, 1953), pp. 129–131.

[75] Miller R. Collings, "Exploring Your Community: A Direct Experience Study," *Journal of Educational Research,* XLIV (November, 1950), pp. 225–230.

educational standpoint, the first of these is the most important, for it is concerned with broadening and enriching pupil learning.

Atyeo's doctoral study discussed the important place which the school excursion has continually occupied in European countries, particularly in Germany and England.[76] Contemporary Russian schools make extensive use of the field trip. American public and Catholic secondary schools would upgrade their educational programs if they would follow suit.

There are two types of field trip, namely, independent and formal. The independent field trip is one in which a student or group of students proceed without supervision to a designated place in order to learn something. Usually this type of excursion is made after school or on a weekend. The formal field trip is one in which the entire class proceeds under the teacher's supervision to a designated place in order to learn something. Generally, this type of excursion is made during school hours. Both types are extremely productive of learning, and the teacher should utilize each. He should not hesitate to send pupils to museums, places of historical interest, political rallies, etc., on a Saturday afternoon. Students often derive a great deal of enjoyment from an unsupervised excursion. Formal field trips are valuable in that the teacher is present to guide the students' attention to the significant features of the place visited.

A field trip may be undertaken for any one or a combination of purposes. The most important of these are (1) observation, i.e., to scrutinize carefully some person, place, activity, or object, for example, the visit of Catholic high school pupils to a church having Mass in an Oriental Rite; (2) interview, i.e., to obtain information, concepts, or attitudes from certain people, for example, to interrogate opposing candidates for the state legislature; (3) project, i.e., to embark on a constructional educational activity, for example, to build a model rocket in a local aerospace company; (4) survey, i.e., to investigate community conditions involved in a certain problem, for example, the taking of a parish poll by Catholic high school students to ascertain how many families would like to join a Christian Family Movement (CFM) cell; (5) collection, i.e., to gather materials needed to solve a problem or explore a topic, for example, to gather different types of butterflies.

Every problem or content area can utilize excursions as invaluable components of the student's educational experience. The social studies class can investigate the actual workings of democracy by attending a meeting of the town council or state legislature. The English class can work with the local newspaper. The art class can visit museums,

[76] Henry C. Atyeo, *The Excursion as a Teaching Technique.* (New York: Bureau of Publications, Teachers College, Columbia University, 1939), pp. 8–41.

churches, and public buildings to see aesthetic and architectural principles in action. The biology class can assist in tuberculosis X rays in the community. In Catholic high schools, the religion class can work with liturgically minded pastors and curates in helping to establish the Dialogue Mass, Catholic Action cells, and to initiate full lay participation in parish life.

Field trips, if wisely utilized, can result not only in obtaining information and gaining new concepts, but also in broadening and changing attitudes. The teacher should so structure the excursion that it is conducive above all to the acquisition of worthwhile attitudes.

Some teachers seem to be unaware of the rich educational resources which exist in their community. Ignorance of these resources is often a prime reason why teachers do not accord the field trip its proper place in the learning activities of their classes. A committee composed of teachers, curriculum and subject-matter experts, and community leaders should draw up a list of local resources pertinent to each problem and content area. This should be done in both public and Catholic secondary schools.

The following are some suggestions to assist the teacher in making the formal field trip a truly worthwhile and valuable learning experience:

1. Plan the trip cooperatively with the pupils so that they understand, appreciate, and are vitally interested in the excursion.

2. Make sure that the field trip is educationally significant; e.g., an excursion to the local firehouse is not too valuable because the pupils already know what is going on there.

3. Arrange for the field trip to be taken at the optimum teachable time, just when it will be the most meaningful in the development of a unit or the solution of the problem under study.

4. Make careful preparations for the field trip, e.g., place, route, definite activities, and so on.

5. Ensure that the pupils understand well ahead of time the general and specific learnings which they are to gain from the trip, else the excursion may degenerate into a vague outing for the promotion of idle curiosity.

6. Make the proper arrangements with the pupils' parents and the school administration.

7. Give every student a definite task or assignment to accomplish on the excursion.

8. Devise a list of rules which will serve as guides for pupil conduct, e.g., safety procedures.

9. Provide for adequate teacher guidance and supervision on the trip (this does not mean that the teacher must oversee the pupils at every moment or must construct elaborate surveillance procedures).

10. Devise techniques whereby every student will be compelled to exercise mental self-activity and individual initiative while on the excursion.

11. Cooperatively prepare a general mimeographed outline which will serve as a pupil guideline when he is taking notes or is otherwise engaged in learning.

12. Where pertinent, inform the person or group to be visited that the pupils are coming and why, so that the stage will be set for optimum learning.

13. Follow up the field trip with individual and/or group reports and teacher-pupil conferences to pool and reinforce learning.

14. Cooperatively evaluate with the students the educational learnings gained from the excursion.

With the exception of point number 9, all these suggestions can be used by the teacher in guiding students for their independent field trips as well.

Because they are held during the school day and normally extend for more than one period, formal field trips necessitate adjustment of the regular school schedule. This adjustment is the only serious drawback to their extensive use.[77] Independent excursions, of course, are not beset with such a problem.

Sometimes a reactionary school administration is opposed to formal field trips during school time. In such a case, the teacher has no other course than to obey. However, the administration is normally powerless to prevent a teacher from organizing either formal field trips outside of school hours or independent excursions. The teacher should attempt to enlighten such an administration on the capital advantages of the field trip. Some neanderthal-inclined administrators oppose the excursion merely because they think it is new. The teacher might remind such administrators that field trips have been traditional in European schools for centuries. If this type of administrator is in a Catholic high school, the teacher could point out that Christ's school for His Apostles was not conducted in a formal classroom setting but rather as a series of field trips. In any event, the teacher should stress the intrinsic value of the excursion rather than emphasize its alleged modernity.

[77] See Thomas M. Risk, *Principles and Practices of Teaching in Secondary Schools,* 3d ed. (New York: American Book, 1958), p. 376.

CHAPTER XII MOTIVATING
THE PUPILS

Nature of Motivation

Motivation may be defined as the process whereby a person is internally or externally stimulated toward activity. In education, motivation refers to the process which spurs the pupil to engage in some purposeful learning experience. Motivation has to do with the energy which impels a person's activity toward a particular goal. It is thus goal-oriented, i.e., directed toward a specific objective. This goal may be an object or a situation; it may be remote or proximate.[1]

While motivation is not a product outcome of the school experience, it should be a process outcome. Lynch has stated that modern pedagogical theory places great emphasis on motivation as a key objective in the learning process, especially as it relates to the development within the student of self-motivation, thus minimizing an overdependence on the teacher's motivational techniques.[2] Unless self-motivation is learned by every student, there is a great danger that the school

[1] See Francis L. Harmon, *Principles of Psychology*, rev. ed. (Milwaukee: Bruce, 1951), pp. 506–507.

[2] William Lynch, Jr., *An Approach to the Study of Motivational Problems in Education.* (Indianapolis, Ind.: University of Indiana Press, 1955), p. 10.

will be inculcating in him a crippling ultradocility rather than promoting a spirit of healthy independence coupled with the desire and ability for self-energizing.

Motivation is not learning, but it is an indispensable adjunct to it. Motivation has four effects on learning. First, it assists in initiating learning. Second, it helps in directing learning toward a particular, worthwhile educational goal. Third, it aids in the continuance of learning, especially when obstacles or difficulties arise. Fourth, it contributes to the reinforcement of learning.

Motivation impels pupil activity and this constitutes its chief value in the educational situation, since learning is by its very nature an active, not a passive, process. Motivation also has other important pedagogical advantages. It calls forth greater effort on the part of the student. It makes that effort more pleasant and more enjoyable. It stimulates a wide variety of responses and solutions. It results in greater efficiency in learning, since fewer repetitions are required to secure a specified degree of achievement.[3] It makes failure more annoying. It helps to alleviate one of the most serious obstacles to effective learning, i.e., a lack of willingness on the part of the pupil to learn.

Studies and analyses of motivation have passed from the philosophical level of the *"dispositio"* of St. Thomas and the "will to power" of Nietzsche to a highly complex, scientific, empirical approach, as exemplified by the celebrated annual Nebraska Symposium on Motivation begun in 1953.[4] The reviews by Ryans and Marx of educational literature revealed that proportionately little experimental research has been conducted in that type of motivation directly relevant to the school situation.[5] Both reviewers remarked that this is at once strange and regrettable, since almost all educators regard motivation as crucially important in learning and teaching.

Motivation is usually classified as either intrinsic or extrinsic. Intrinsic motivation is that which originates from within a student's own personality structure, while extrinsic motivation is that which is principally activated by some object or stimulus external to the learner. In actual practice, however, intrinsic and extrinsic motivation do not

[3] See Walter S. Monroe and Max D. Englehart, *Stimulating Learning Activity.* (Urbana, Ill.: University of Illinois Press, 1930), p. 9.

[4] This series is entitled *Current Theory and Research in Motivation.* (Lincoln, Nebr.: University of Nebraska Press, 1953–   ).

[5] David G. Ryans, "Educational Psychology," in Farnsworth (ed.), *Annual Review of Psychology,* VI. (Stanford, Calif.: Annual Reviews, 1955), pp. 431–454; Melvin H. Marx, "Motivation," *Encyclopedia of Educational Research,* 3d ed. (New York: Macmillan, 1960), p. 895. Indeed, most American motivational research has been carried out in laboratory conditions quite dissimilar to classroom situations.

function as two separate realities. They are deeply interrelated and so often intertwine. If one is thwarted, this will have a definite effect on the other. If one is cultivated by the teacher, so automatically is the other, to a lesser extent, of course. Both the school administration and the teacher should remember this interrelatedness; e.g., a different type of motivational technique should be employed when on Monday a particular class follows a period of physical education but on Tuesday it comes after a Latin class in which the instructor happens to be autocratic.

Intrinsic determiners of motivation are not essentially rationally rooted; rather they are grounded in the nature of the organism as it exists in a specific environment. This does not mean they are irrational, although they may at times become so, as when a person is motivated toward alcoholic excesses. A person's intellect cooperates with intrinsic motivational determiners, e.g., a pupil seeking ways of gaining social approval from his classmates. However, cooperation is not causality. Extrinsic determiners are rooted essentially in a person's rational response to some external good which is presented to it. The more the object possesses the good (either subjective or objective good), the more it will motivate the person who intellectually recognizes the good and whose will is thus motivated toward its possession. However, man is an integer, and many forces both internal and external are at work in the motivational situation. Hence a young male teacher with an effervescent personality and a great deal of knowledge will motivate a high school girl to study, not only because of the rational good she perceives, i.e., the objective value of knowledge, but also for intrinsic reasons, such as emotion, affection, and perhaps sexual attraction.

Motivation may be brief or it may be sustained. For learning, sustained motivation is usually the more desirable. Motivating factors may vary in their intensity. Warden's classic studies indicated that in experimental rats, the physiological motivating factors in order of strengths were maternal impulse, thirst, hunger, and sex.[6] Psychosocial and extrinsic motivational factors tend to vary in intensity according to the type and characteristics of the different environmental situations.

Motives are both stable and dynamic. Every person is motivated by a desire for food, for participation, for social approval. A person constantly experiences these motivations throughout his life. Their form and intensity, however, change with age. An adolescent is normally more motivated toward food than is a child. The physical changes which a youth's body has undergone motivate him toward a different kind of

[6] C. J. Warden, *Animal Motivation Studies*. (New York: Columbia University Press, 1931).

participation and social approval than is present in a child. Environment also makes motives dynamic. Various societies motivate their members to different kinds of foods; e.g., octopus is a delicacy in some parts of the world. Participation and social approval are of different types in upper-class New England society and in New York City slums. Teachers should always remember both the stable and dynamic character of motivation. In so doing, pupil individual differences will be taken into account.

The cause of motivation is still a much mooted point among psychologists. Some say it is caused completely by environment acting on the organism; others contend that motives are merely the operational forms of instincts. Many contemporary psychologists take an intermediate position, holding that motivation depends on the interaction of a person's inherited drive structure and his environment, with learning either modifying or energizing one's innate biological drives.[7] Most modern experimental psychologists, being philosophical Materialists, would agree, however, that motivation is basically biological. Ryle, a Materialist philosopher, in his eagerness to refute the position that motivations are mental in origin, derisively refers to them as ghostly thrusts.[8] From the Catholic point of view, such a biological position is excessively narrow, for it fails to take into account the impetus given to a person's actions both by his immaterial mind and by Divine grace. The oft-quoted statement, "There but for the grace of God go I," has implications not only for theology but for the psychology of motivation as well. A purely biological explanation of motivation easily leads to determinism and destroys the notion of free will.

Most empirical motivational research, upon which modern materialistically oriented psychologists rely heavily, has been carried out with animals in laboratory conditions. But simple animal drives, as tested in the laboratory, can be said to apply only in a very limited fashion to the complex human organism. Indeed many contemporary psychologists concede that investigations of animal motivations are not especially fruitful for a deep understanding of human motivation.[9] Robbins has stated that in the perspective of psychoanalytic theory,

[7] For a good discussion on leading theories of motivation, see K. B. Madsen, *Theories of Motivation*, 2d ed. (Cleveland, Ohio: Allen, 1961); also W. Edgar Venacke, "The Drive Modification Theory of Human Motivation," *Journal of Genetic Psychology*, XCVI (June, 1960), pp. 245–268.

[8] Gilbert Ryle, *The Concept of Mind*. (New York: Barnes & Noble, 1950), pp. 32–35, 113–114.

[9] Gardner Lindzey (ed.), *Assessment of Human Motives*. (New York: Rinehart, 1958), pp. 30–31; see also Dalbir Bindra, *Motivation*. (New York: Ronald, 1959), *passim*.

motivation is increasingly complex because it involves impelling elements not only in the conscious, but in the preconscious and unconscious, to use Freudian terminology.[10]

Burton has written that students "ordinarily are not motivated to learn anything; rather they are motivated to relieve tension, to remove any disturbing condition or problem, to restore the pleasantness and security of equilibrium." [11] This again is a totally biological explanation of motivation and learning. It is partially true because man is an animal. However, it is an overly narrow view, because it neglects the inner thrust of man's body *and* soul to value. Motivation is deeply connected with value. To be sure, it is value, or a good, which causes a person to become motivated. Man requires value to live; he needs the good. Physiologically, food is a necessary value because one must be nourished. Psychosocially, independence is an imperative value because it is ultimately self-realization. On the extrinsic plane, the degree of objective worth of an extrapersonal reality is a value which motivates. Man, as diverse figures like von Hildebrand and Fromm have observed, is value-oriented.[12] This is the deepest cause and explanation for motivation. The more the teacher satiates the pupils' constant unquenchable thirst for value, the better he will motivate.

A student's value system is an important conditioner of what will motivate him, and to what extent. A youth with burning religious values will resist motivation to food in order to achieve some spiritual goal which requires that he abstain from eating. Hilgard and Russell have remarked: "It is a mistake to think of motivation only in relation to the completion of isolated assignments or tasks. The whole motivational system of the learner is important: how immediate goals are set in relation to remote goals, how successes and failures are reacted to. . . . Motivation cannot be divorced from the whole personality of the child." [13]

Successful motivation by the teacher involves three essential elements, namely, knowledge of the psychological factors underlying motivation, knowledge of teaching procedures most likely to induce motivation, and ability to utilize and implement this knowledge in the

---

[10] Lewis L. Robbins, "Unconscious Motivation," in Stacey and De Martino (eds.), *Understanding Human Motivation.* (Cleveland, Ohio: Allen, 1958), pp. 365–369.

[11] William H. Burton, *The Guidance of Learning Activities,* 2d ed. (New York: Appleton-Century-Crofts, 1952), p. 69.

[12] Dietrich von Hildebrand, *Christian Ethics.* (New York: McKay, 1953), pp. 72–74; Erich Fromm, *Man for Himself.* (New York: Rinehart, 1947), pp. vii–x, 8–14.

[13] Ernest R. Hilgard and David H. Russell, "Motivation in School Learning," *Learning and Instruction,* National Society for the Study of Education, Forty-Ninth Yearbook, Part II. (Chicago: University of Chicago Press, 1950), p. 44.

actual teaching situation. This chapter will attempt to give the first two of these elements. Only the individual teacher himself can do the third.

THE INTRINSIC DETERMINERS OF MOTIVATION

There are two chief types of intrinsic determiners of human motivation, i.e., physiological and psychosocial.

Physiological Determiners

Physiological determiners or causes of motivation are those which arise from the person precisely because he is a biological organism. All men possess these determiners regardless of the environment in which they are situated. Their motivational force may vary according to environment, time, and intensity, but the fact remains that every person, because he is biological, is influenced by these factors. The most important physiological factors are as follows:

1. *The Basic Biological Drives.* The basic biological drives are physically impelling forces which are directed toward the material continuance of normal body functions. These are extremely powerful forces since they are deeply connected with the successful maintenance of life. Hunger and thirst are the two most important of these drives. The drive toward procreation may be said to fall into this category, although it must be noted that the exercise of a person's procreative functions is not necessary for the maintenance of his life. This fact is often forgotten by some ultraprogressive educators.

2. *Age.* As a person advances in age, certain biological drives develop, increase, or are modified; e.g., the drive toward procreation is far more intense after puberty, and frequently diminishes in strength in old age.

3. *Sex.* A person's gender will cause him to be impelled toward certain activities which a member of the opposite sex is not; e.g., an adolescent girl will be motivated toward things pertaining to motherhood. However, the social roles which a particular society accords each sex have a modifying influence.

4. *Physiological Readiness.* This type of readiness is the sum of all one's biological factors which act in concert to strongly dispose him to act in one way or another; e.g., a person who has just eaten a large meal will not be physiologically ready to respond to a situation involving the consumption of food and drink, whereas a man who has not eaten for two days is in an extreme state of physiological readiness to these influences.

Psychosocial Determiners

Psychosocial determiners or causes of motivation are those which arise from the person precisely because he is an organism *in a social setting*. These determiners are not purely biological, but rather represent the eductive force which any social setting, any milieu, exercises on one's physical make-up. The most important psychosocial factors are as follows:

1. *Security*. Security is the feeling of being safe, of being protected against harm. It is a form of self-preservation and so is an extremely important and ever-present motivational factor. In civilized society, this form of self-preservation is almost always psychosocial; e.g., when a teacher publicly ridicules a student, the student will, in order to preserve both his self-concept and his group status image, resort to a defense mechanism such as withdrawing, shouting back at the teacher, or making faces during the ridicule to display that it is having no effect on him.

2. *Anxiety*. Anxiety is a state of nervous worry about some anticipated event which is thought to involve danger. It is a form of fear. The anxious person does not know precisely what is the evil involved in the event or the cause of his anxiety. Anxiety sometimes arises from a repressed emotion or desire. Reed's review of the pertinent research concluded that while both severe and very low levels of anxiety have a negative effect on a pupil's learning, mild anxiety may actually benefit the student in certain types of learning.[14] On the latter point, studies have shown that in a rote learning situation pupil anxiety frequently motivates learning, while in a complex problem-solving situation, anxiety almost consistently results in disorganized performance.[15]

3. *Frustration*. Frustration is the blocking or thwarting of goal achievement. The effects of frustration on a pupil vary, ranging from hostility toward the original goal to a spur toward new solutions for attaining the goal or to a giving up, a drifting into purposelessness.[16] Thus frustration may or may not act as a desirable motivational force.

4. *Independence*. Independence is the achievement of self-sufficiency. The need for independence arises from the individuality of

[14] Howard B. Reed, Jr., "Anxiety: The Ambivalent Variable," *Harvard Educational Review*, XXX (Spring, 1960), pp. 141–153.

[15] D. P. Ausubel et al., "Qualitative Characteristics in the Learning Process Associated with Anxiety," *Journal of Abnormal and Social Psychology*, IV (October, 1953), pp. 537–547.

[16] See J. Dollard et al., *Frustration and Aggression*. (New Haven, Conn.: Yale University Press, 1949); and N. R. F. Maier, *Frustration: The Study of Behavior without a Goal*. (New York: McGraw-Hill, 1949).

each person; i.e., each human being is a separate and distinct reflection of God. Each person is an integer, a self who wishes to achieve his self-hood. Independence—physical, intellectual, emotional, and spiritual—is necessary for successful living. Hence the desire for independence is a strong and positive motivational factor. In adolescence it is linked to peer group conformity. The explanation for this seeming paradox is that the adolescent group as a group is striving for a type of existence distinct from both the childhood and the adult worlds. Adolescents will often manifest this striving for distinctiveness in peculiar overt group behavior.

5. *Actualization.* Actualization is the fulfillment of one's personality potential. Actualization is an important motivational force, since in Maslow's words, "What a man *can* be, he *must* be." [17] The desire to excel is a form of a student's need for actualization. This need varies in intensity from person to person. Maslow's studies have indicated that people who have actualized themselves to a significant degree tend to be more autonomous, more detached, less autocratic, have more of a sense of a mission in life, and are more comfortable with reality than those who have not attained a significant degree of actualization.[18] A teacher should assist the pupils in intensifying their desire for actualization.

6. *Assertion.* Assertion is the overt manifestation of one's personality. It is a powerful motivational force and arises from the basic need to display the uniqueness of one's personality both to oneself and to others. Assertion takes on many forms, and in the classroom may assume desirable or undesirable behavior patterns, depending in large measure on the way the teacher has structured the learning situation and each student's role in it.

7. *Achievement.* Achievement is the attainment of some worthwhile goal. On the theological level, the need for achievement arises from the fact that man is in the image of God. Since God is a Maker, so is man. Everyone therefore needs to achieve, although the intensity varies from person to person and depends also on the subjective and objective worth of whatever a person is called on to achieve.

8. *Level of Aspiration.* Level of aspiration is the degree of goal attainment which an individual expects to achieve or hopes to reach. It is at once the degree of a person's ambition and his expectancy to achieve. A student usually fixes his aspiration level toward a particular learning goal on the basis of his own self-concept, his assessment of his abilities, the amount of effort he is willing to expend in this situa-

[17] A. H. Maslow, *Motivation and Personality.* (New York: Harper, 1954), p. 91.
[18] *Ibid.,* pp. 199–234.

tion, the subjective and objective worth of the goal, and his previous success or failure experiences in similar or related tasks. An investigation by Sears disclosed that those students who had a previous experience in the subject matter studied, tended to be realistic in their level of aspiration or goal setting as regards further learning of this subject matter.[19]

Level of aspiration varies from person to person. Thus, for example, students whose academic performances fall below their level of aspiration usually react in one of two ways—either they become discouraged and set their goals lower or they put forth even greater effort because they regard their poor performance as a challenge. DiVesta's review of the pertinent research concluded that a definite positive relationship exists between level of aspiration and a generalized inner desire to achieve.[20] Notwithstanding, it is necessary for the teacher to create a climate of group acceptance, as this will affect a pupil's level of aspiration. A study by Buswell indicated that, in general, students who were successful in their academic work were also successful in their social relationships with their peers.[21] Kausler's investigation showed that aspiration level not only emanates from one's inner personality structure, but also is an integral part of one's total frame of reference.[22]

A student's method, procedure, and manner of learning are often affected by his level of aspiration. In a study by Tyler, two groups of students confronted with a similar problem-solving situation were identified, viz., those who had little expectancy to solve the problem and those who had high expectancy. "Significantly, more pupils in the low expectancy group than in the high expectancy group attempt to memorize a solution to the problem in contrast to working out a logical solution." [23]

9. *Recognition*. Recognition is the acknowledgment by others of one's worth or of one's achievement in some activity. Ryans's review of the research indicates that recognition is one of the most powerful of all

[19] Pauline S. Sears, "Levels of Aspiration in Academically Successful and Unsuccessful School Children," *Journal of Abnormal and Social Psychology*, XXXV (October, 1940), pp. 498–536.

[20] Francis J. DiVesta, "Meaningful Learning: Motivational, Personality, Interpersonal and Social Variables," *Review of Educational Research*, XXXI (December, 1961), p. 513.

[21] Margaret M. Buswell, "The Relationship between the Social Structure of the Classroom and the Academic Success of the Pupils," *Journal of Experimental Education*, XXII (September, 1953), pp. 37–52.

[22] Donald H. Kausler, "Aspiration Level as a Determinant of Performance," *Journal of Personality*, XXVII (September, 1959), pp. 346–351.

[23] Bonnie B. Tyler, "Expectancy for Eventual Success as a Factor in Problem-solving Behavior," *Journal of Educational Psychology*, XLIX (June, 1958), p. 171.

motivators.[24] The celebrated Hawthorne experiment dramatically demonstrated the importance of recognition as a stimulant to performance. The management of the Western Electric plant in Hawthorne, Illinois, wished to improve production. As an experiment, it isolated a group of workers and began first to improve lighting conditions, and then successively increased the number of rest periods, reduced working hours, and provided certain added economic incentives. As the management did these things, researchers continually asked the workers' opinions and encouraged them to make suggestions. With each successive improvement in working conditions, production increased. To test the validity of the findings, the researchers removed all the newly acquired benefits, leaving the workers with the same conditions that prevailed before the experiment. The result was unexpected—an all-time high in production. After much careful reflection the researchers concluded that it was not the improved physical conditions which motivated the workers to steadily increase production, but rather it was the recognition and attention which management and researchers were according them by asking their opinions, implementing their suggestions, and involving them in the total situation.[25] A study by Ryan and Davie showed that a small, positive correlation exists between social acceptance and marks.[26] The teacher should accord each student the recognition due him as a human being and as a brother in Christ, as well as for whatever academic achievements he may have attained. This is most important in Catholic high schools. A false concept of humility should not blind teachers from giving every student his proper share of recognition.

10. *Participation.* Participation is the sharing in the experiences and activities of others. Man is a social animal; thus he has an inner thrust to be a definite and accepted member of the group and its activities. The need for participation, sometimes referred to as the need for affiliation, is especially strong. Catholic high schools must strive to involve their students in important apostolic endeavors such as Catholic Action rather than channeling their efforts into pedestrian tasks such as making rosaries (machines can do this). Fr. Greeley has stated that every Catholic youth should be given "a chance to participate *vitally*

[24] David G. Ryans, "Motivation in Learning, *The Psychology of Learning*, National Society for the Study of Education, Forty-First Yearbook, Part II. (Chicago: University of Chicago Press, 1942), pp. 318–319.

[25] For a complete account of this experiment, see F. S. Roethlisberger and William J. Dickenson, *Management and the Worker.* (Cambridge, Mass.: Harvard University Press, 1939).

[26] F. J. Ryan and James S. Davie, "Social Acceptance, Academic Achievement, and Academic Aptitude among High School Students," *Journal of Educational Research*, LII (November, 1958), pp. 101–106.

in the most important and significant work in history—the redemption of the human race." [27] Religious and clerical teachers should constantly strive to motivate their lay students to participate in the apostolate, not as menials but in a coequal way reflective of their status in the Mystical Body. As Pope Pius XII observed, "The laity must be conscious not only of belonging to the Church but *being* the Church." [28] Religious and clerical teachers do much either to quicken or to deaden this consciousness. Fr. Levasseur has stated that lay persons, be they high school students or adults, are called to be active collaborators in the pastoral ministry because essentially their unique witnessship is needed. Hence the "motivation must be much deeper than the shortage of priests and Religious. Lay apostles are not 'spare tires.' " [29] Participation is the key.

11. *Curiosity.* Curiosity is an inner eagerness by which a person wishes to learn about some stimulus, often newly presented. Some Materialistic psychologists have explained curiosity totally in terms of man's biological drive pattern.[30] This is an overly narrow view. Curiosity also emanates from man's natural desire to completely understand the world. Man's mind is in potency to become all things; this is a mental inclination he derives from being made in God's image. Curiosity, or exploration, is not an occasion to sin as some Jansenistically influenced educators seem to believe. Rather, it is a healthy motivational force which helps man attain the good, to reach his supernatural destiny.

12. *Religious Need.* A powerful motivator is one's inner requirement for God. Catholic thinkers have long recognized this; thus St. Augustine wrote of this deep need: "My heart was made for You, O Lord, and will not rest until it rests in You." [31] Some modern psychologists like Jung have also testified to the crucial motivational role of man's religious need. Other psychologists deny its existence, substituting ideals in its stead. The Catholic position is that the need for bald ideals is a desupernaturalized and hence an incomplete explanation; i.e., ideals take on their fullness when grafted on the religious dimension.

Religious motivation, especially with respect to adolescents, must be tethered to rational ground. Fr. McCarthy, S.J., has stated that this will simultaneously ensure a firm foundation and demonstrate to the

[27] Andrew M. Greeley, *Strangers in the House.* (New York: Sheed and Ward, 1961), p. 172. Italics supplied.

[28] Pope Pius XII, *Address to the Second World Congress of the Lay Apostolate,* quoted in Collins, S.S. (ed.), *Religious Education through CCD.* (Washington, D.C.: Catholic University of America Press, 1961), p. 84.

[29] Georges A. Levasseur, "Members of Diocesan and Parish Executive Boards: Parish Unit Members," in *ibid.,* p. 132.

[30] K. C. Montgomery, "The Role of Exploratory Drive in Learning," *Journal of Comparative and Physiological Psychology,* XLVII (February, 1954), pp. 60–64.

[31] St. Augustine, *Confessions,* book I.

adolescent that the teacher looks upon him as a rational being.[32] Mere appeals to authority, whether human or ecclesiastical, are insufficient as motivation; rather, youth must be shown the underlying reasons why the authority maintains a particular position or teaches a certain doctrine. Appeals to authority for its own sake may be construed by intellectually curious adolescents as grounding one's belief in an essentially irrational faith. This especially applies to appeals to human authority, as when the teacher states, "You must accept this because I say so."

The religious need in man, although universal, is modified by many circumstances. Hence the religious need in a Religious and in a lay person manifests itself differently. Clerical and Religious teachers must ever bear this in mind. Fr. Geaney, O.S.A., has stated that "if the layman's spirituality is a trickle-down religious spirituality, there can be disastrous consequences." [33] Fr. Wendell, O.P., has noted that "the lay person must be apprised of the fact that it is in the very accomplishing of the ordinary things in life that he becomes holy." Studying, traveling to school, recreating, attending a dance—"all these are the warp and woof out of which lay sanctity is woven." [34] Lawler has remarked that there is a danger in demanding that lay persons, including pupils, "sanctify the [so-called] profane by a purer intention, of superimposing upon it an adventitious religious veneer which inhibits them from seeing the object as it really is, and so prevents it from witnessing in its own way to God's power and beauty." [35] Lee has commented that the layman must let the glory of God's created world pour in and inundate him, rather than despise this world and steel himself against it as neo-Jansenists would maintain.[36]

13. *Psychosocial Readiness.* This type of readiness is the sum of all one's mental factors (as influenced by environment) which act in concert to strongly dispose him to act in one way or another; e.g., a student who has learned about charity and is convinced of its importance is psychosocially ready to act in a charitable manner toward his classmates. Apperceptive mass contributes to psychosocial readiness.

14. *Interest.* An interest is a conscious awareness of and an inner pull toward some object which has concern or importance for the

[32] Raphael C. McCarthy, S.J., *Training the Adolescent.* (Milwaukee: Bruce, 1934), p. 185.

[33] Dennis J. Geaney, O.S.A., *Christians in a Changing World.* (Notre Dame, Ind.: Fides, 1959), p. 143.

[34] Francis N. Wendell, O.P., *Formation of a Lay Apostle.* (New York: Third Order of St. Dominic, 1954), p. 18.

[35] Justus G. Lawler, *Catholic Dimension in Higher Education.* (Westminster, Md.: Newman, 1958), p. 72.

[36] James Michael Lee, "Notes toward Lay Spirituality," *The Review for Religious,* XXI (January, 1962), pp. 42–47.

person. The five principal categories of interest are intellectual, vocational, aesthetic, social, and spiritual or religious. The last is often neglected or underplayed by many contemporary psychologists.

Interests are closely allied to attitudes. Nevertheless they are different in several respects. Interests involve personal identification with the object while attitudes do not. Interests are directed toward a class of objects, while attitudes are oriented toward a specific object. Interests may be native or acquired, while attitudes are acquired.[37] Thus, for example, an interest in the lay apostolate involves identification of self as an actual, possible, or hopeful lay apostle, while an attitude toward the lay apostolate denotes a more detached view as its being likable or distasteful, worthwhile or worthless. Also interest in the lay apostolate extends to the various types of Catholic Action and lay Catholic activities, e.g., Grail, Young Christian Students, while attitude is directed toward the lay apostolate as a single, composite entity. Interest in the lay apostolate may arise from an innate desire or inner psychosocial need to help others, while an attitude toward it may come from reading the University of Dayton's monthly *Catholic Action Reprints* series.

Interests are affected, conditioned, and even determined by many factors, the most important being personality, ability, socioeconomic status, and experience. Inner personality needs of altruism, achievement, etc., affect a student's interests. A person's socioeconomic status has been shown not only to be the initiatory cause of interest but also to promote or inhibit the development and manifestation of interests.[38] Ability as a determinant of interest is sometimes modified, especially in the case of girls, because of social role expectations associated with the two sexes. A person's experience might alter his interests by opening up aspects of reality about which he previously knew little; e.g., by attending a Catholic school one might wish to enter the religious life, join the Grail movement, or teach in a Catholic high school.

Many interests are relatively permanent, while others change. Schneiders has identified four basic causes of shift in interest: (1) change in basic needs due to age, growth, or developing psychosocial factors (e.g., the muscular development in boys causes them to become interested in acquiring and maintaining a good physique); (2) a realization that a particular type of activity is no longer satisfying (e.g.,

[37] Some psychologists such as Schneiders disagree on this point; however, a review of the research by Darley and Hagenah sustains it. See Alexander A. Schneiders, *The Psychology of Adolescence.* (Milwaukee: Bruce, 1951), p. 228; John G. Darley and Theda Hagenah, *Vocational Interest Measurement.* (Minneapolis: University of Minnesota Press, 1955), pp. 134–263.

[38] See J. P. Jordaan, *The Relationship between Socio-Economic Status and the Vocational Interests of Mechanically Gifted Boys,* unpublished doctoral dissertation, Teachers College, Columbia University, New York, 1949.

playing "Blind Man's Bluff" ceases to fulfill the adolescent's recreational requirements); (3) an alteration in one's social constellation (e.g., the adolescent's social group is no longer restricted to his neighbors but encompasses the entire high school district and beyond); (4) growth in physical, mental, and social maturity (e.g., older adolescents are often less interested in recreation for its own sake and more interested in possible vocational choices).[39] Super's review of the pertinent research concludes that *specific* expressed interests change significantly during high school years; however, *general* interests as measured by interest inventories indicate a substantial degree of interest stability during adolescence.[40] Thus a girl with altruistic interests may at fourteen want to become a teacher but at eighteen wish to be a social worker. Changes of interests are outcomes of an adolescent's growth and are therefore normal and to be expected. Hence a high school pupil who changes his interests should not necessarily be considered by the teacher as flighty.

Witty's extensive study of the interests of American high school students, sponsored by the Department of Health, Education and Welfare, made three significant conclusions. First, televiewing is the favorite leisure activity of youth. Boys spend more time televiewing than do girls. Boys prefer adventure programs while girls like programs featuring teen-age dancing and family comedy. Youth spend on the average almost fourteen hours per week televiewing. Second, an extremely high percentage of pupils hope to attend college. Third, youth spend on the average only one hour a day reading—often just what is required for completion of homework. Girls prefer romance stories while boys like tales of adventure. The reading interests of boys are broader than those of girls. Almost one-third of the junior and senior boys had no library cards. Quite a few pupils still read comic books, the boys preferring Superman and Donald Duck, the girls favoring Archie and Little Lulu. Boys and girls of all grades prefer televiewing, movie attendance, and radio listening to reading.[41]

Witty's findings reveal that the school is having insufficient impact on guiding pupil interests into worthwhile channels. Sister M. Amatora, O.S.F., has given a cardinal reason for this. "Curricula are for the most part organized on the basis of adult-determined needs of pupils. In their efforts to provide what they believe best for the child, educators seldom, if ever, give consideration to pupil interests." [42] Until the curriculum

[39] Schneiders, *op. cit.*, p. 232.

[40] Donald E. Super, "Interests," *Encyclopedia of Educational Research*, 3d ed. (New York: Macmillan, 1960), p. 730.

[41] Paul Witty, "A Study of Pupils' Interests, Grades 9, 10, 11, 12," *Education*, LXXXII (September–November, 1961), pp. 39–45, 100–110, 169–174.

[42] Sister M. Amatora, O.S.F., "School Interests of Early Adolescents," *Journal of Genetic Psychology*, XCVIII (March, 1961), p. 133.

meshes pupil interests and concerns with what the school believes he should know, its work will remain ineffectual for a great many youths.

THE EXTRINSIC DETERMINERS OF MOTIVATION

The most important extrinsic determiners of motivation will be treated in this section.

1. Objective Good

Every reality possesses an inherent value, an objective good. The inherent value of any reality is determined by the extent to which it participates in God, shares the being and qualities of the Trinity. Because man shares in God's nature, every reality will be motivational for him to the degree to which it catches God. Thus St. Thomas wrote, "In itself the understanding of truth is to everyone lovable." [43] Truth is the grasping of the realness of a reality.

2. Pleasantness and Unpleasantness

Pleasantness and unpleasantness, as their names imply, are concerned with whether or not the external object or stimulus is pleasing to the person. This is a psychological phenomenon, more or less influenced by the direct physiological effects of the stimulus, should they exist. Pleasure and pain are the purely physiological counterparts of pleasantness and unpleasantness. Pleasantness and unpleasantness sometimes remain stable (e.g., a bitter herb always tastes unpleasant); sometimes they change (e.g., listening to a musical composition of John Cage might be pleasant during music class but unpleasant when a student is studying intensively for an examination). Pleasantness usually motivates a pupil positively, unpleasantness negatively. Freud made an important observation when he emphasized that pleasantness is more natural to a person than unpleasantness. This has significant ramifications for ascetical theology, particularly when developed in Catholic high school religion classes and retreats. Satisfying emotional responses reinforce learning and increase a readiness for new learning, a fact often overlooked by teachers of a puritanical or Jansenistic bent. On the other hand, pleasantness may become a goal in itself rather than a motivational impetus toward, or reinforcement of, some object.

3. Success and Failure

Success is the attainment of goals, while failure refers to their non-attainment. Success has been shown to be a strong motivator, whereas failure is usually an emphatic discourager. Hence a strong possibility of

[43] Thomas Aquinas, *Summa Theologica*, II–II, q.15, a.1, ad.3.

success will impel a student toward the achievement of an educational goal. Moreover, a success experience will motivate him to attain advanced and upward extensions of the same goal or related goals. Conversely, failure to attain a specific goal in school life, e.g., to "flunk" mathematics, will often serve to deaden student eagerness to pursue that goal further and will sometimes be transferred to related goals, e.g., dislike for school in general.

4. Personality of the Teacher

A most important extrinsic motivational factor, and one which is greatly neglected in the literature, is the teacher's personality. A teacher with an interesting, enthusiastic personality, who loves his subject or problem area, is a great motivational force on his students. The moment such a teacher walks into the classroom, the students tend to be automatically motivated. A teacher with a poor personality may employ various sound motivational devices, but once these techniques are concluded, the class will tend to lapse into inattention. A teacher who is very interesting will have pupils who are very interested.

5. Parental and Teacher Goal Expectations

The type and level of goals which both parents and teachers expect youths to attain are a powerful motivational force. A teacher who expects more from his pupils will get more. (This, of course, must be done within the context of individual differences.) A tragedy in public and Catholic secondary schools is that the teachers so frequently impose on their pupils a low academic, conduct, and spiritual goal expectancy, with little regard to the great desire for self-sacrifice to an ideal, a cause, a goal which characterizes high school youth. The exceedingly high percentage of Jews in the professions is due in large measure to the goal expectancy set for them by their parents and cultural milieu. The review by McClelland and his associates of the research studies, together with their own investigations, concluded that the greatest source of achievement motivation is parental emphasis on their child's independence and self-reliance. The more the parents stress independent development and individual self-expression, the greater is the motivation and vice versa. It would seem logical that this same type of atmosphere and its results can be extrapolated to the teacher's relations with the pupils in the classroom situation.[44] It is another evidence that overdocility is one of the greatest threats to learning. This fact must be constantly kept

[44]David C. McClelland et al., *The Achievement Motive.* (New York: Appleton-Century-Crofts, 1953), pp. 275–333.

in mind by teachers in public and, especially, in Catholic high schools, as O'Dea has trenchantly observed.[45]

6. Knowledge of Progress

Knowledge of progress is the information which a student receives at various intervals in the total learning situation (lesson, unit, course, or entire formal education) as to what his achievement level is in terms of the desired educational goal to be attained. Reviews of the research by Harmon[46] and Kelly[47] have concluded that a knowledge of progress during a learning situation is an important extrinsic motivational force. Students who are kept constantly informed of their progress perform significantly better than those not so informed.

7. Knowledge of Goals

Knowledge of goals refers, first, to a clear comprehension of exactly what the goal is, second, to an understanding of the nature of the goal, and third, to a rational appreciation of why this goal is objectively and subjectively worthwhile. Since a person's desire for an object is limited by the degree of his knowledge of that object, a knowledge of goals is an important motivational factor.

8. Socioeconomic Status

A study by Coster revealed that the high school student from a low-income family "is less likely to enjoy strong parental interest and support than other pupils."[48] Furthermore, underprivileged neighborhoods usually center their value systems around purely physical rather than intellectual goals and activities, thus motivating their adolescent inhabitants against most of the school's program. On the other hand, pupils who come from more wealthy neighborhoods are strongly motivated by their milieux toward successful high school work and acceptance in a college of high caliber.

9. Grace

Grace is a free gift of God to man. Sanctifying grace bestows upon man a share in Divine life, while actual grace assists man to perform

---

[45] Thomas F. O'Dea, *American Catholic Dilemma: An Inquiry into the Intellectual Life.* (New York: Sheed and Ward, 1958), *passim.*

[46] Harmon, *op. cit.,* p. 536.

[47] William A. Kelly, *Educational Psychology,* 4th ed. (Milwaukee: Bruce, 1956), pp. 290–292.

[48] John K. Coster, "Attitudes toward School of High School Pupils from Three Income Levels," *Journal of Educational Psychology,* XLIX (April, 1958), p. 65.

certain actions. Sanctifying grace thus provides a person with a continual, residual, positive, motivational force, while actual grace gives initial or added motivational boosts. Only those baptized by water or desire enjoy the positive habitual motivational impetus of sanctifying grace;[49] however, everyone is constantly bombarded with actual graces. Grace, which is the manifestation of God's love, is a tremendously powerful motivational force; e.g., it impelled St. Augustine to change his entire life. Yet, strangely, it is hardly ever discussed in Catholic treatments of educational psychology. As a result, Catholic college students who become high school teachers sometimes fail to consciously promote classroom conditions which will make God's grace more receptive or more influential in their pupils' learning and living. Perhaps the greatest single thing a teacher can do in this regard is to promote a spirit of charity in the classroom group. He should remember that teaching the ignorant is one of the spiritual works of mercy.

10. Incentives

An incentive is some enticement which will motivate a person to a desired action. An incentive presents to the person a value which is not inherent in the activity itself, e.g., the incentive of a prize if a student solves a certain problem. Incentives are used by the teacher in those learning situations the value of which, for one reason or another, may not be sufficiently compelling to cause the student to engage in the desired activity; or again, they might be employed to add a booster motive for the performance of a particularly difficult problem or task. All incentives have as an underlying characteristic reward and punishment in some form or other. Positive incentives are usually superior to negative incentives not only in the acquisition of subject matter, but also for the promotion of moral conduct, sound mental hygiene, and successful interpersonal relationships. This fact should always be kept in mind by teachers. Kelly's dictum should likewise be recalled, viz., "The most satisfactory type of motivation is a desire on the part of the pupil to do his task without outside pressure." [50] In other words, incentives are at best a crutch, and the pupil will never be able to walk until he first eliminates dependence on this crutch and finally discards it.

The most important incentives will now be treated.

1. *Reward and Punishment.* A reward is an object or token of value given to a person because he performed a deed deemed worthwhile. Punishment is the opposite of reward. High school rewards are often not intrinsically valuable but rather are prized because they are a symbol

---

[49] Those baptized by blood are almost always dead and hence not within the purview of the high school.

[50] Kelly, *op. cit.*, p. 294.

of some other good; e.g., excellent marks give the recipient prestige, a certain type of social recognition, and so forth.

The promise of a reward or punishment motivates action; the administering of the reward or punishment reinforces it. In order for reward and punishment to be effective as a motivator or reinforcer, the student must realize that his actions will be or are being rewarded or punished. Also, the more immediately the reward or punishment succeeds the student's deed, the more effective and the more motivational it will be.

To be effective motivators, reward and punishment must be proportional to the deed. Thus a pupil's moral misconduct, e.g., lying, should not be negatively reinforced with a physical punishment since the latter is not adequate to a volitional crime. Therapeutic counseling which attempts to enable the pupil to appreciate the consequences of his misdeed is far more efficacious.

Hilgard and Russell observe that "because rewards are regulated by authority, too much emphasis on rewards encourages docility and deference to authority rather than originality and spontaneous endeavor." [51] The pupils will more readily strive to please the teacher than to seek truth wherever they find it, or to seek solutions other than what the teacher has presented, or to embark on a creative venture which may be valuable in itself but does not fit neatly into the teacher's tightly constructed and perhaps limited view of reality. Rewards, therefore, can often deaden vigorous growth in learning. Also, a reward by its nature is socially competitive, because if everyone were to receive the reward, its value as a unique special prize would be lost. Social competition, as will be seen later, is often deleterious to a person from the point of view of both mental hygiene and the Catholic spirit.

Most of the experimental studies on reward and punishment have been done with animals and have employed physical techniques such as deprivation of food and electric shock. Consequently the results are only partially applicable to the human level. However, both educators and classroom teachers are of the opinion that reward is usually superior to punishment as a worthwhile motivational force. Nonetheless, punishment is at times valuable in that it can redirect learning and behavior to educationally significant channels and goals. If punishment is properly administered and the student knows and accepts its purpose, it may provide effective motivation and reinforcement. Notwithstanding, punishment is negative motivation at best and must be used with caution, since man is positively oriented. As St. Francis de Sales wrote, "Man's

[51] Ernest R. Hilgard and David H. Russell, "Motivation in School Learning," *Learning and Instruction*, National Society for the Study of Education, Forty-Ninth Yearbook, Part I. (Chicago: University of Chicago Press, 1950), p. 48.

spirit is so constituted that he will balk at severity but submit to kindness." [52]

2. *Praise and Reproof.* Praise is a public verbal commendation of another's worthy actions; reproof is a public verbal condemnation of another's unworthy actions. Hurlock's celebrated study concluded that pupil achievement improved most by praise, next under reproof, and least when the student was neither praised nor reproved but ignored. Praise was more effective with girls than boys; the latter achieved more under reproof than did girls.[53] A review of the pertinent research by Stevenson and Snyder confirmed this conclusion.[54] Kelly's review of the studies indicated that, in general, praise is more effective than reproof as a motivational force, although under certain circumstances and when properly used, reproof may also be an effective motivator.[55]

Tyler's review of the studies dealing with the effect on learning of the teacher's administration of praise or reproof showed conflicting evidence. Some studies concluded that praise facilitates learning in some instances and inhibits learning in others; different studies reached the same conclusion with reproof; still other investigations showed that a combination of praise and reproof constitutes the most effective motivational force.[56] This divergence of results can perhaps be partially explained by a study by Thompson and Hunnicutt which concluded that the effect of praise or blame as motivational factors often depends on the personality of the student; e.g., extrovert pupils respond less negatively to blame than do introverts.[57] In Page's doctoral study of the effects of teacher comments on examination papers returned to high school pupils, it was discovered that "when the average high school teacher takes the time and trouble to write comments (believed to be 'encouraging') on student papers, these apparently have a measurable and potent effect upon student effort, or attention, or attitude, or whatever it is which causes learning to improve." [58]

[52] Quoted in Paul Hoffer, S.M., *Guide for Religious Administrators*, trans. by Rus. (Milwaukee: Bruce, 1959), p. 54.

[53] Elizabeth B. Hurlock, "An Evaluation of Certain Incentives Used in School Work," *Journal of Educational Psychology*, XVI (March, 1925), pp. 145–149.

[54] Harold W. Stevenson and Leila C. Snyder, "Performance as a Function of the Interaction of Incentive Conditions," *Journal of Personality*, XXVIII (March, 1960), p. 1.

[55] Kelly, *op. cit.*, pp. 288–290.

[56] Tyler, *op. cit.*, p. 167.

[57] G. G. Thompson and C. W. Hunnicutt, "Effect of Repeated Praise or Blame on the Work Achievement of Introverts and Extroverts," *Journal of Educational Psychology*, XXXV (May, 1944), pp. 257–266.

[58] Ellis Batten Page, "Teacher Comments and Student Performance: A Seventy-four Classroom Experiment in School Motivation," *Journal of Educational Psychology*, XLIX (August, 1958), pp. 180–181.

3. *Models.* A model is an object or person held up for imitation. Pasteur might be portrayed as a model for high school science students in the hope that the life and deeds of this great scientist might provide an incentive for them to exhibit similar hard work and devotion. The lives of saints are often depicted as models for the Catholic faithful to imitate. Models, while often productive of valuable educational outcomes, must be used with discretion. All too often models are unrealistic. They portray a certain limited number of roles with disproportionate frequency. Certain types of leadership roles are most often portrayed, while the factory worker is rarely held up as a model; indeed when he is depicted, it is generally in the form of comic relief or as a victim of tragic circumstances.[59] In Catholic high schools, models given to the students are usually clerical and Religious saints. Since most students will remain in the lay state, these models are not the most suitable, and actually their exclusive depiction teaches the student that sanctity is somehow the special preserve of those who have a religious vocation. Lay saints and holy people of the past, e.g., St. Thomas More, Frederic Ozanam, St. Benedict Joseph Labre, St. Monica, St. Elizabeth of Hungary, and St. Joan of Arc should be held up for imitation.[60] Similarly, holy and apostolic lay Catholics of our own age should be held up as models, e.g., Dorothy Day, Catherine de Hueck, Jacques Maritain, and Ed Willock.

Models presented to students often stress exclusively dramatic achievement, e.g., Jacqueline Kennedy, rather than the mother who bears and rears six happy children who will co-redeem the world with Christ and help their fellow men. Most high school students will never have the opportunity to become conspicuous public personages. They should learn that some of the most worthwhile achievements often go unnoticed. St. Therese of Lisieux is the Patroness of Missions though she never left her convent walls. Models of life should be realistic lest the adolescent gain the impression that life is a continuous series of dashing, heroic events.

Cronbach has observed that all too often the models in school textbooks and readings "seem always to gain rewards when they carry out the ideas of superiors, but when they act independently they are likely to get into some difficulty or other." [61] Such models lead students to prize overdocility and overdependence, the two great barriers to suc-

[59] For a deeply moving account of the problems which such unrealistic model depiction creates in society, see Dorothy Day, *The Long Loneliness.* (New York: Harper, 1952).

[60] See Selden P. Delaney, *Married Saints.* (New York: Longmans, 1935).

[61] Lee J. Cronbach, *Educational Psychology.* (New York: Harcourt, Brace, 1954), p. 324.

cessful learning and living. The teacher must always remember that he is a model as far as the students are concerned—a model to be imitated or rejected by them. In Catholic high schools many religious vocations are gained or lost because of the suitability or unsuitability of the Religious or clerical teacher-model. Lay teachers in Catholic schools are advantageous because, among other things, they provide lay-oriented students with living lay models.

4. *Prefeeding*. Prefeeding is the process in which a person is given a small portion of the incentive or reward before he engages in the desired activity, e.g., giving a person a small sum of money before he performs a task, with the larger balance to be delivered after the task has been successfully completed. Carnivals and circuses have long utilized prefeeding, and some forward-looking Religious Orders are employing it in vocation recruitment. Prefeeding has been found to be an effective extrinsic motivational factor in school situations.

5. *Fear*. Fear is a psychoemotional state of dread caused by an impending evil or harm. It is often used as a motivational incentive by classroom teachers, especially in the form of threats. Marx has observed that direct or indirect use of fear as a motivator may have very undesirable effects on the pupils in terms of both learning and mental hygiene.[62] The use of fear can easily lead the adolescent to associate learning with unpleasantness. Certainly there can be little justification for the use of fear by a Religious or clerical teacher. Love, rather than fear, should be a teacher's source of motivation.

6. *Other-acceptance*. Thorndike has shown that an individual is motivated toward an object if that object is accepted and used by another individual; e.g., if one student sees a fellow student eating something, he will be motivated to seek that type of food so that he may eat some too.[63] The effectiveness of this incentive can easily be seen by observing women in a bargain basement store. The teacher who focuses attention on the achievement of one or more students is attempting to utilize other-acceptance as an incentive to impel the other students to want to attain similar achievements.

7. *Social Competition*. Social competition is the rivalry within a group of individuals, all of whom are seeking to obtain some particular prize or reward. Many contemporary educational psychologists prefer to use the incentive of social competition only as a last resort, and then with caution. Thus, for example, Cronbach cites three disadvantages to competition: "It tends to help only the better performers; it makes

[62] Melvin H. Marx, "Motivation," *Encyclopedia of Educational Research*, 3d ed. (New York: Macmillan, 1960), p. 897.

[63] E. L. Thorndike, *The Psychology of Wants, Interests and Attitudes*. (New York: Appleton-Century, 1935), p. 12.

little or no provision for learning to evaluate one's own performance; it contributes relatively little to the improvement of responses outside of school because it does not make the activity seem worthwhile to the average student for its own sake" but rather for the purpose of a prize.[64]

Social competition can easily cause deleterious educational, mental hygiene, and moral effects, e.g., discouragement in learning by the losers, emotional upset and frustration by both winners and losers, and cheating or lying by the competitors in order to gain the prize. Social competition also presents an added difficulty, viz., that because of ability, work, etc., only one or perhaps a few will win the prize, the rest of the students will not be motivated. Yet if everyone obtains the prize, the goal will not be challenging and the incentive is lost.

Social competition is based on one of the most primitive, most animalistic notions, namely, the survival of the fittest. Contemporary American society, being in a highly developed stage of civilization in which the weak as well as the strong are conceived as possessing human dignity, should have risen above the jungle concept of social competition. From the Catholic point of view, social competition is not highly regarded; indeed it is considered one of the direct seeds of Original Sin. Christ did not urge men to compete with each other so that the winner of the interhuman struggle would attain the Beatific Vision while the losers would be plunged into damnation. Instead, he urged cooperation with one's fellow man to advance His glory on earth. Religious houses, where charity is intended to be the ruling spirit, stress the necessity of mutual cooperation of all their members for the attainment of the common good. Social competition is held to be prideful. And Religious houses since the time of St. Benedict are supposed to serve as exemplars of Christian living, schools for sanctity.

Kelly's review of the research indicated that social competition can often be a fruitful incentive as far as subject-matter achievement is concerned.[65] Most of these studies, however, did not take into account the effects of conditioning, i.e., the degree to which the students were conditioned by home, environment, and school *in favor of* the notion that the only thing which mattered was gaining the prize and *against* the notion that everyone has a responsibility to see that not only himself but every person should be helped to achieve. Nor did the studies deal with other academic and nonacademic results of this competitive situation, e.g., discouragement with school, frustration, emotional upsets, cheating to obtain the prize, and so forth. A more comprehensive review of the studies by Phillips and D'Amico shows that the experimental conclusions are mixed; i.e., some investigations show that classroom

[64] Cronbach, *op. cit.*, p. 478.
[65] Kelly, *op. cit.*, pp. 292–294.

groups performed better under cooperative conditions and vice versa.[66] Burton, reviewing the pertinent research, concluded that creative and imaginative work is generally not affected favorably by competition.[67] Such work is often characterized by nonconformity and disagreement, and so is not rewarded by a competitive situation which by its very nature encourages conformism, conventionality, overdocility, and toadyism.

The best form of competition from every point of view is competition against oneself. It is realistic, since the achievement level is set not by group standards but by individual potentialities. It is healthy because it is an incentive to personal development by self-fulfillment rather than by slashing rivalry. It is Christlike because it at once requires and offers cooperation with others for goal attainment.

TECHNIQUES OF SUCCESSFUL CLASSROOM MOTIVATION

Motivation is not a specific teaching technique but rather is an integral part of every pedagogical procedure. Therefore the many suggestions for successful motivation given below should oscillate and interweave themselves into every aspect of the lesson. Motivation does not apply solely to raising a student from lethargy to activity, but also to elevating lower pupil motivations to a higher plane, e.g., from social competition to cooperation. The Catholic high school, because of the treasury of lofty yet practical ideals from which it should draw its curriculum and methodological capital, is in an especially advantageous position to provide the highest and richest source of motivation.

The following are some techniques of successful classroom motivation:

1. Be aware of the basic biological drives when teaching; e.g., greater motivation and teaching vigor will be necessary in a late afternoon class than during a 10 A.M. period.

2. Use teaching techniques suited to the mental and chronological age of the pupils in the particular class.

3. Tailor teaching to the sex of the learner; e.g., a girl in a history class usually learns better through a biographical analysis than through a direct study of issues.

[66] Beeman N. Phillips and Louis D'Amico, "Effects of Cooperation and Competition on the Cohesiveness of Small Face-to-Face Groups," *Journal of Educational Psychology,* XLVII (February, 1956), p. 65.

[67] Burton, *op. cit.,* p. 71.

4. Help the pupils to become physiologically and psychologically ready to learn the desired facts, concepts, and attitudes. The more disposed a pupil is to learn, the better he will learn.

5. Promote a classroom atmosphere of security in which every pupil will be unafraid to freely respond, disagree, or create.

6. Use anxiety and frustration cautiously, being mindful of their varied effects delineated earlier in this chapter.

7. Actively encourage a spirit of independence in the class as a whole and in each individual pupil. To repress independence is to foster immaturity.

8. Cooperatively formulate learning tasks which will positively enable each pupil to actualize and assert his own personality and concepts.

9. Make sure that learning goals are objectively and subjectively achieve-able; i.e., the student must actually be able to attain the goal, and further, he must know that he can.

10. Help the student raise his level of aspiration, his learning expectancy. A student who aims high will often achieve more than a person of equal ability who aims lower. Do not anesthetize a pupil's level of aspiration by subjecting him to undue routinization or channeling him into pedestrian activities.

11. Accord each pupil recognition. This recognition should be commen-surate first with his dignity as a brother or sister in Christ, and second with his degree of attainment of cooperatively determined educational goals.

12. Structure the learning situation in such a way that every student will participate vitally in the lesson, e.g., discussion, small-group work, role playing.

13. Use teaching techniques which evoke student curiosity. Wonder is the beginning of knowledge and one of its most beneficial companions.

14. Satisfy the pupil's religious need in a rational, nonauthoritarian, and deeply meaningful way. In Catholic high schools, participation in vital lay apostolic tasks is one way of meeting this need, while in public secondary schools the religious desire can be channeled into extradenominational avenues, such as organizing student groups to practice the corporal works of mercy in underprivileged neighborhoods.

15. Awaken pupil interests in what are to him yet undiscovered realities, and expand and elevate existing pupil interests. Of course, this assumes that the teacher himself has these interests, is deeply immersed in reality, a condition sometimes contrary to fact. The teacher should also endeavor to connect what might be mild educational interests with strong personal interests. Techniques like field trips, interviews, and audio-visual materials tend to quicken pupil interests.

16. Assist the pupil in seeing for himself what is objectively valuable in the fact, concept, attitude, or skill to be learned. Telling the student to "learn this because I say so" or because "it is valuable, even though you don't understand its importance now" is irrational, authoritarian motivation of the poorest quality.

17. Make learning pleasant for every student in so far as possible. In the case of decidedly unpleasant but necessary tasks, link these with pleasantly toned activities. The value of asceticism in learning should be understood by each pupil, but the need for student asceticism should never become an excuse for poor motivational procedures on the teacher's part.

18. Keep the student fully apprised of his progress in achieving all the desired educational goals. This is wider than mere academic attainment. Periodic conferences with the student are a valuable vehicle for increasing his knowledge of his overall progress.

19. Give additional motivation to students from low-income families.

20. Pray to the Holy Spirit to make up what is lacking in one's motivational procedures, and to fructify the effects of one's techniques.

21. Use incentives with great caution, being careful that they do not become ends in themselves. Alberty's dictum should be heeded: "Learning is most effective when the learner is motivated by goals which are intrinsic to the activity." [68]

22. Offer rewards more often than punishments. When punishment is used as an incentive, it should not spur academic achievement at the expense of either the pupil's mental health or his growth in charity.

23. Distribute praise with greater frequency than reproof. Praise should aim to encourage the pupil to greater achievements rather than merely to exalt his past efforts. Reproof should be given judiciously and, as a rule, privately instead of in public.

24. Hold up models worthy of student imitation. Models should be realistic.

25. Prefeed the students with rewards, particularly in difficult learning tasks.

26. Divert pupil social competition into competition against himself. Inculcate a spirit of cooperation rather than rivalry. If for some reason social competition in learning is necessary, it should be carried on with equally matched groups or individuals.

27. Provide each student with experiences of success frequently during the whole learning situation, particularly in the early and more difficult phases. However, the teacher should also occasionally insert, in a cautious and judicious manner, conditions conducive to minor failures so that the pupil will have to utilize his ingenuity. This will also give him a more realistic outlook on himself and on life.

28. Have every student come to the realization that failures are not disasters in themselves but rather temporary setbacks in an eventual large, overall, and ultimate success. Failures are guideposts on what to avoid in the future.

[68] Harold Alberty, *Reorganizing the High-School Curriculum,* rev. ed. (New York: Macmillan, 1953), p. 71.

29. Classroom learnings should always be related to out-of-school life. The classroom is an artificial situation and it can be made real and hence meaningful only by constantly meshing it with the world outside its walls.

30. Maintain warm, personal relationships with the students. Authoritarian teachers generate toadyism and undue deference in their pupils, both of which etherize healthy motivation.

31. Structure the problem-solving learning situation so that it is difficult enough to be challenging but at the same time not so difficult as to frustrate most of the class.

32. Utilize suspense; i.e., withhold the key to a problem, concept, factual series, or story until the end.

33. Guide and structure the learning activity so that the educational goals of the lesson are meaningful and purposeful to the pupil, and therefore he will want to attain them. Group-accepted goals and individual-accepted goals are facilitated by teacher-pupil planning and by constantly helping the students to relate the goals of the lesson to their own lives.

34. Clearly delimit every educational goal. This should be done cooperatively by the teacher and pupils. Fuzzy learning goals are not well understood by the students and are therefore poor motivators. Similarly specific directions and assistance on methods of attaining the goal are superior motivators to nonspecific directions, such as "work harder" or "concentrate."

35. Encourage each pupil to manifest initiative instead of being dependent on teacher cues for action. Initiative connotes an active environment, and such an atmosphere directly promotes motivation.

36. Use problem solving as the motivational pedagogical method par excellence. Students faced with a problem tend to be motivated to solve it and, in so doing, to acquire product and process learnings.

37. Activate pupil needs and thereby extend their horizons. As a result of these new horizons, new needs will be created and the cycle will generate itself upward. As Fr. Kiefer observed, "the absence of broad ideas inevitably leads to routine and obstinacy." [69]

38. Urge the students to engage in reflective contemplation not so much in class as out of it, in walks through the fields, in deserted city streets, on a park bench, in a crowded bus. Reflective contemplation is a rest from the hurly-burly of life rather than a negative withdrawal from a task. Its purpose is quietly to meditate on the inner meaning of an activity, to uncap the human wellsprings, and in so doing, to return to the original activity in a deeper, more meaningful way. Much of the modern world has lost the meaning and importance of reflective contemplation; however, the Catholic heritage has always enshrined and nourished this great motivator and source of knowledge. Fr. Sertillanges, O.P., has written, "Rest is a return to our origins: the origins of life, of strength, of inspiration; it is a retempering." [70]

[69] Quoted in Hoffer, *op. cit.*, p. 88.

[70] A. D. Sertillanges, O.P., *The Intellectual Life,* trans. by Ryan. (Westminster, Md.: Newman, 1948), p. 73.

Individual differences in pupils preclude any single magic motivational technique which will at all times and in all situations impel all pupils to desired activity. Rather, the skillful teacher should interweave all the motivational procedures into the lesson and should adapt these procedures to the exigencies of the student, the time, and the situation. It should be remembered that one of the best solutions to misbehavior problems is effective motivation. Indeed, little or no motivation generates misbehavior problems even in the best of students.

The curriculum of the school is of itself a source of positive or negative motivation. A fragmented curriculum such as the subject-centered design makes it somewhat difficult to motivate a pupil since it offers him artificially sliced reality and thus an unreal world. On the other hand, a unified curriculum such as Core presents subject matter in the perspective of a living problem, in a coordinated way typical of real life. Teachers in a school featuring a fragmented curriculum should strive as best they can to overcome the motivational handicap in which their curricular framework encases them, particularly by integrating the material to be learned, utilizing problem solving, and so forth. They should also work for a curricular revision which will discard the fragmented curriculum and replace it with a vibrant unified design.

CHAPTER XIII EVALU-
ATING AND REPORTING
PUPIL PROGRESS

EVALUATION

Evaluation is the appraisal of a pupil's progress in attaining the educational goals set by the school, the class, and himself. The chief purpose of evaluation is to guide and further the student's learning, to assist in his progress toward the truth. Evaluation is thus a positive rather than a negative process. Weaknesses are uncovered for the purpose of eliminating them so that progress will become more rapid. To be proper and complete, evaluation must not only assess the educational goals set by the school but also those decided on by the class and by each student, since it is this interpenetration of goals which should characterize every classroom learning situation.

Evaluation of an accurate and true type is difficult to obtain. Hilgard has stated that "learning always must remain an inference from performance, and only confusion results if performance and learning are identified." [1] Hence evaluation at best is indirect. Therefore evalua-

[1] Ernest R. Hilgard, *Theories of Learning,* 2d ed. (New York: Appleton-Century-Crofts, 1956), p. 5.

tion is judgmental in that it is impossible to determine with certainty direct evidence of learning. Consequently the evaluator(s) must examine the various aspects of the performance to ascertain whether learning has taken place and to what degree. This difficulty is compounded by the fact that the evaluation device(s) upon which the judgment is founded can never really get at the actual learning itself, but only some performance which may or may not have resulted from the learning which is being evaluated.

The evaluative process involves at least eight distinct steps: (1) statement of the purpose of the evaluation; (2) selection of the educational goals or outcomes which are held to be of sufficient importance to be evaluated; (3) definition of these goals or outcomes in specific terms comprehensible to everyone; (4) agreement on a standard by which these goals or outcomes can be judged; (5) development and construction of an evaluative device which will adequately measure the selected goals and outcomes; (6) administration of the evaluative device; (7) synthesis of all the measurements gained from the evaluative device into an overall, valid estimate of worth; (8) evaluation and subsequent improvement of the evaluative device.

Reviewing many specimens of both standardized and teacher-constructed tests, Douglass and Spitzer concluded that most forms of evaluation are giving little attention to understandings and are placing a premium on memorization and the retention of isolated factual data.[2] Often these factual data are memorized without understanding, and as a result the factual data themselves become inaccurate, e.g., the case of the student who wrote "Martin Luther died a painful death because he was excommunicated by a bull." Not only public high schools, but Catholic high schools as well, have fallen victim to the cult of memorization and the neglect of understanding. Of this situation in Catholic schools O'Dea has written: "Correctness of formula often threatens to replace understanding, while rote memorization is held to be the essence of learning."[3]

All the various types of learning outcomes should be assessed if the evaluation of a pupil's educational progress is to be complete or even adequate. Factual knowledge constitutes only one outcome. Other important outcomes include understanding, attitudes, values, appreciations, adjustment, love of learning, good study habits, (in Catholic schools,

---

[2] Harl R. Douglass and Herbert F. Spitzer, "The Importance of Teaching for Understanding," *The Measurement of Understanding*, National Society for the Study of Education, Forty-Fifth Yearbook, Part I (Chicago: University of Chicago Press, 1946), p. 21.

[3] Thomas F. O'Dea, *American Catholic Dilemma: An Inquiry into the Intellectual Life.* (New York: © Sheed and Ward, 1958), p. 110.

deepening one's union with Christ[4]) and the integration of all these outcomes into improved overt behavior.[5] Numerous educators have remarked that these outcomes are being neglected in the evaluative devices used in both public and Catholic secondary schools. Concerning the latter, Sister Mary Janet, S.C., has stated:

> We know that the aim of Christian education is "the supernatural man who thinks, judges and acts constantly and consistently in accordance with right reason illumined by the supernatural light of the example and teaching of Christ." Yet our standards of evaluation are not really geared to this high aim. We are content for the most part with evaluation in terms of knowledge and too little attention is directed toward what our pupils "think" and how they "judge" and "act." [6]

Lawler has observed that "recent surveys have indicated that students in Catholic schools in the South have fundamentally the same attitude on racial questions as other students" in non-Catholic schools.[7] Have these Catholic schools evaluated the pupils' progress on the basis of attitudes and values or only on factual knowledge which obviously has remained isolated from their daily living? Did the evaluative device in religion class in these Catholic schools assess *all* of the following: background information, both factual and conceptual, necessary for understanding and appreciating God's workings in the world; understanding of this information; functionality of this information, i.e., that which helps the pupil to glorify God, save his own soul, and help his neighbor; the integration of religion with reality, especially one's milieu (of great importance in a fragmented curricular design where religion is learned as a separate subject, cut off from the rest of knowledge and life); the practice of what was learned in religion class.

In evaluation, both product and process learnings must be assessed. Product outcomes are more than factual. The student is not a jug to be filled with information and periodically inspected to see if anything has leaked out. Understanding is a crucial product learning. This outcome is receiving increased attention from educators, particularly since the publication by the National Society for the Study of Education of its 1946 Yearbook entitled *The Measurement of Understanding*. Process learnings, such as critical thinking, problem solving, thinking with

[4] See Donald Dietz, O.M.I., "Conscience and Love," *American Ecclesiastical Review*, CXLVI (April, 1962), pp. 228–232.

[5] E. I. Sawin and M. R. Loree, "Broadening the Base in Evaluation," *School Review*, LVII (Spring, 1959), p. 84.

[6] Sister Mary Janet, S.C., "The Christian Foundation," in Sister Mary Janet, S.C. (ed.), *The Christian Foundation in the Catholic Secondary School*. (Washington, D.C.: Catholic University of America Press, 1952), p. 4.

[7] Justus George Lawler, "Federal Aid and Freedom," *Commonweal*, LXXV (March 2, 1962), p. 595.

Christ, are equally crucial in a total estimation of a pupil's growth. Regrettably, most product and almost all process learnings are not being evaluated by any systematic measurement technique. Part of the blame must fall on the emphasis on external tests. Fr. Sloyan has commented: "Externally administered examinations, be they state, community or diocesan can have a paralyzing effect on classroom practice *if* they are seeking only information while the school is trying to inculcate values." [8] Nevertheless most of the blame must fall on the teachers who in their teaching and on their tests stress facts to the almost total exclusion of other outcomes. As Thorndike and Hagen have commented, "What a teacher emphasizes in his evaluation of pupils, and particularly in the more formal evaluation represented by tests, defines to his students what the teacher considers important." [9]

Evaluation must be continuous and continuing. It should not occur only during examination periods. A system of evaluation should also include provision for individual differences. A student must be evaluated not only in terms of objective achievement of educational goals, but also in terms of the level of his achievement as it relates to his abilities. In this way, the results of evaluation will provide the data for further individualized instruction by the teacher. [10] Similarly, the results of evaluation can be used for proper pupil placement, not only in the graded high school, but particularly in the ungraded high school.

Furst has stated that "evaluation is most conducive to learning when it provides for and encourages self-evaluation." [11] Modern educators have been increasingly stressing the importance of involving the pupil in the evaluation of his own progress. However, in their review of the pertinent research, Hagen and Thorndike have concluded that there is little empirical evidence to show that pupil self-evaluation results in improved learning. The reviewers cited four basic reasons for this: The pupil possesses only a hazy knowledge of the objectives of the school program; the pupil has no stable standard or benchmark by which to evaluate his progress; the pupil's evaluation is likely to be subjective and based on impressions rather than supported by objective data; the social pressure of marks may cause the pupil to distort his self-evalua-

[8] Gerard Sloyan, "Vertical Integration: Elementary and Secondary School," in Sister Mary Janet, S.C. (ed.), *The Integration of the Catholic Secondary School Curriculum.* (Washington, D.C.: Catholic University of America Press, 1951), pp. 80–81. Italics supplied.

[9] Robert L. Thorndike and Elizabeth Hagen, *Measurement and Evaluation in Psychology and Education.* (New York: Wiley, 1955), p. 27.

[10] See Georgia S. Adams and Theodore L. Torgerson, *Measurement and Evaluation for the Secondary School Teacher.* (New York: Dryden, 1956), p. 13.

[11] Edward J. Furst, *Constructing Evaluation Instruments.* (New York: Longmans, 1958), p. 4.

tion.[12] These shortcomings are for the most part due to the continued use by the teachers of outmoded pedagogy and can be remedied by a four-pronged effort on the part of both teachers and school. First, cooperative teacher-pupil planning of classroom goals will enable every pupil to see these goals clearly. The pupil's attainment of classroom goals cannot be at a high level if he is ignorant of these goals, as happens in many autocratic classroom situations. Second, the pupil should be educated in objective techniques of self-evaluation. This itself constitutes an important goal of the school, since throughout his adult life, the pupil must constantly evaluate himself if he is to grow personally and socially. This is especially important for Catholic schools which should teach their students to examine their consciences nightly. Third, the teacher can work with each pupil and help him to rely increasingly on objective evidence. This constitutes both good teaching and good guidance. Fourth, the school should transform its atmosphere from social competition to cooperation, from overemphasis on external marks to stress on individual growth in learning.

Evaluation, therefore, should be done *with*, rather than *on*, the student. However, as Troyer has observed, a student should not be asked to evaluate certain evidence about his achievement unless he is psychologically ready to do so and, indeed, wants to do so.[13] The teacher and the school should utilize the four suggestions given above to promote this readiness on the part of the pupil. It is interesting to note that programed instruction, e.g., teaching machines (treated in Chapter XI) provides the pupil with an immediate self-evaluation. Hence a beginning has been made.

The teacher's quest for accurate and comprehensive evaluation may sometimes be thwarted by the school administration. Fr. Sloyan has stated that a major problem in obtaining a good system of evaluation in Catholic high schools is "the setting of policy and pace by a principal who is an arch-traditionalist. Especially is this true in religious communities which identify religious perfection with complete subservience." [14] The situation in public high schools is often equally as bad, and sometimes worse. In such public and Catholic high schools, it is necessary that a teacher fight for the right, for by not fighting he is perpetuating the system. Evaluation must be broadened to include the totality of the pupil's progress in achieving all desirable educational goals, not just in academic subjects.

[12] Elizabeth P. Hagen and Robert L. Thorndike, "Evaluation," *Encyclopedia of Educational Research*, 3d ed. (New York: Macmillan, 1960), pp. 484–485.
[13] Maurice E. Troyer, *Accuracy and Validity in Evaluation Are Not Enough.* (Syracuse, N.Y.: Syracuse University Press, 1947), p. 14.
[14] Sloyan, *op. cit.*, p. 80.

Sources of Evaluation

Evaluation, if it is continuous and representative, must be based on many sources. Achievement tests, both standardized and teacher-constructed, are important sources of data. These should be supplemented by evaluations of daily classroom work. While formal daily recitation periods should have no place in contemporary high schools for reasons stated in Chapter IX, the following can and should be evaluated: reports of individual students or committees, homework assignments, workbook assignments, and collateral or additional work which a student might take on himself, e.g., pictures of his visit to a museum or assisting the pastor in performing corporal works of mercy. Short written quizzes comprising five questions can occasionally be given. It is a good practice for the teacher to note desirable educational attainments of the students, such as cooperation, eagerness in work, and preparation. This should not be done solely or even primarily for the purpose of marking, but rather for guidance based on sound evaluation. These notations should not be made during class time lest they exert an inhibiting effect on the pupils. Instead, these observations should be recorded after class or after school.

The student's objective achievement in attaining specified educational goals must be correlated with knowledge of his abilities, personality factors, and milieu if a true evaluative picture is to be gained. No evaluation is worthwhile unless it is individualized around each student. Evaluation is not the assessment of growth; it is the assessment of a particular individual's growth. An anecdotal record of each pupil should therefore be made by every teacher. Such a record is especially valuable in evaluating change in overt behavior. Knowledge is one thing; overt behavior is another. A pupil might know the rule for the sequence of grammatical tenses yet still make errors when writing sequential clauses. In such a case, is the educational goal of the class being achieved by the pupil? Partially? Totally?

A pupil's cumulative record should be consulted when an overall evaluation of his progress is being made. This should be supplemented with case conferences and interviews with the school's guidance counselor. Parent-teacher interviews are indispensable to a true evaluation. Frequently these interviews shed great light on the home situation and the pupil's out-of-school personality, neither of which the teacher often knows much about, but both of which are crucial to proper evaluation.[15] Home visits by the teacher give him a great deal of information because

[15] See Denis Baron and Harold W. Bernard, *Evaluation Techniques for Classroom Teaching.* (New York: McGraw-Hill, 1958), pp. 233–234; also Marie A. Kastner, "Instructing and Motivating Pupils in the Light of Test Results," *Catholic Educational Review,* LVII (February, 1959), pp. 106–110.

it is in this context that he observes the youth *en situation*. Public schools should compensate teachers financially or in terms of pupil load for home visitation, and those Religious Orders of women in Catholic high schools whose constitutions forbid home visitation should attempt to have their constitutions modified in this regard. Sociometric methods of evaluation and case studies are also of great assistance to the teacher in assessing pupil growth.

Certainly evaluative sources must be broadened beyond the usual device of paper and pencil tests.

MEASUREMENT AND TESTS

Measurement is the more or less exact quantitative determination of a pupil's educational progress in attaining designated educational goals. A test is the evaluative instrument used to obtain this measurement. If measurements and tests are to provide the basis for adequate evaluation, they must afford as complete a picture as possible. Therefore, for valid evaluation, a battery of measurements and tests should be used. The use of only a single measurement or test can lead to serious misappraisal. Thus, for example, a study by Getzels and Jackson concluded that as a rule schools do not recognize and hence neglect some of their most talented youth because they make a high score on an intelligence test the sole basis for identifying the gifted. The investigations of these researchers discovered that a group of creatively gifted pupils scored in the top 20 per cent in standardized tests of creativity but below the top 20 per cent in standardized intelligence tests.[16]

Materialist educators tend to place almost absolute reliance on measurement. Since all reality including man is quantitative, all reality including man can be measured; hence the celebrated adage, "If it exists, it can be measured." Thomistic Realists, on the other hand, hold that while measurement is extremely valuable, it is nonetheless limited; e.g., the nonmaterial mind cannot be measured directly in an empirical fashion. Measurement affords the evaluator a quantitative appraisal only of *externalized* knowledge and behavior. Educational measurement involves other problems as well; e.g., process learnings are much more difficult to measure than product learnings.

Tyler has noted that the complete process of measurement involves four essential steps: (1) defining and ascertaining the educational outcome to be measured, (2) selecting the test situation best designed for measuring this outcome, (3) recording the pupil's responses to this test

[16] Jacob W. Getzels and Philip W. Jackson, *Creativity and Intelligence: Exploration with Gifted Students.* (New York: Wiley, 1962).

in a manner which will yield accurate and meaningful measurements, (4) evaluating the test results.[17]

Purposes of Measurement and Tests

There are four broad purposes of measurement and tests, viz., instructional, guidance, administrative, and curricular.

Instructional Purposes. There are eight principal instructional purposes of measurement and tests: to promote and increase learning, to ascertain the degree of pupil attainment of desired product and process learnings, to serve as a diagnosis of pupil strengths and weaknesses, to provide a basis for reteaching and relearning in those areas in which the student displayed weakness, to determine the degree to which the student has related classroom learnings to life, to discover the degree to which the pupil is implementing his product and process learnings in his conduct and overt behavior, to check on the effectiveness of the teacher's pedagogy, to afford a prognosis of the degree of pupil success in the course or sequence.

Rothney has stated that "the main purpose of testing is not to grade or rank pupils but to assist classroom teachers in getting achievement of growth" so that further learning will result.[18] Yet a teacher will sometimes use a test chiefly for clerical purposes and not to further instruction. Of this Melvin has remarked: ". . . Examinations have become the fetish which teachers worship and around which their complex of dignity and absolutism revolve. Whether the teachers teach or the students learn is beside the point. Examinations atone for all." [19]

Tests serve as directional forces for study. Students have been made pragmatic by a socially competitive marking system, and hence will study primarily and often exclusively only that which will be tested. Obviously, if only factual material is customarily tested, the students will study chiefly factual data. Classroom teaching which emphasizes factual information further reinforces this attitude of the pupils. To be maximally instructional, a test should examine the students on all the desirable educational outcomes of the class, not merely factual data. Classroom discussion which provides for these learnings and outcomes will strengthen this approach.

Every teacher should constantly keep in mind Lee's dictum: "Test-

---

[17] Ralph W. Tyler, "Elements of Diagnosis," *Educational Diagnosis*, National Society for the Study of Education, Thirty-Fourth Yearbook. (Bloomington, Ill.: Public School Publishing Co., 1935), p. 114.

[18] John W. M. Rothney, *Evaluating and Reporting Pupil Progress.* (Washington: NEA, Department of Classroom Teachers, 1955), p. 7.

[19] A. Gordon Melvin, *Activated Curriculum.* (New York: John Day, 1939), p. 59. Tense has been changed in the sentences quoted.

ing does not follow teaching; rather testing is an integral part of teaching." [20]

Guidance Purposes. There are four basic guidance purposes of measurement and tests: to serve as a sound basis for a pupil's personal, academic, vocational (and in Catholic high schools, religious) guidance; to provide the teacher and the guidance counselor with additional information about the pupil; to assist the school in bringing its guidance functions and its curricular structure into greater harmony; to furnish a basis for the realistic direction of the school's guidance functions, i.e., to identify the areas in which guidance activities should concentrate.

Guidance is one of the most important functions of the school, and measurement and tests have done much to reveal hidden pupil difficulties. Tests, particularly those which measured facets of the pupil's growth other than academic achievement, have helped elevate guidance from its former intensely subjective, impressionistic base to one of reasonable clarity and objectivity.

Administrative Purposes. There are at least six administrative purposes of measurement and tests: to obtain data for pupil classification, e.g., grade placement, special grouping arrangement; to get information upon which to base decisions concerning promotion and graduation; to secure data which may be supplied in the immediate future to prospective employers or college admissions officers; to assemble a file of all students who have attended the school; to have on hand information requisite or helpful to obtaining community support for the school, e.g., success in bond issues or fund-raising drives, initiation of citizens' committees against indecent literature, etc.; to determine teaching efficiency.

Curricular Purposes. There are three curricular purposes of measurement and tests: to serve as a basis for periodic school-wide curricular revisions; to modify or alter the curriculum or syllabus for a specific course (e.g., the pupils in a certain class are encountering particular difficulty in learning how to diagram a sentence but are composing poems in iambic pentameter more rapidly than is normally the case); to relate more closely the curriculum with teaching techniques.

Characteristics of a Good Test

There are seven characteristics which every good test or measuring instrument must possess, viz., validity, reliability, utility, administrability, scorability, interpretability, and economy.

Validity. The validity of a test is the degree to which it measures what it is attempting to measure. Ross and Stanley have asserted that

[20] James Michael Lee, *Teaching and Testing*, unpublished manuscript, 1962, p. 3.

"validity means truthfulness." [21] Validity is the most important characteristic of a test. There are two principal types of validity, viz., curricular and statistical.

Curricular validity is the degree to which the test measures all the various outcomes learned by the students in the unit or course. There are seven sources of curricular validity: the educational goals and objectives of both the teacher and pupils as determined in the initial teacher-pupil planning; the teacher's daily lesson plans; the textbook; required collateral readings; supplemental pupil activities, e.g., field trips; the syllabus; content and curriculum coordinators in the school system. To construct a test which has curricular validity, the teacher must utilize *all* the sources in the construction of his test items, unless of course his teaching was of the narrow and restricted sort which only incorporated one or two sources, such as exclusive textbook work with no required collateral readings or supplemental pupil activities.

Statistical validity is the degree to which the test results correlate with data obtained by other measurement devices. There are four principal sources of statistical validity, viz., intelligence quotient, e.g., a pupil of high intelligence should normally rank high on a test; results of aptitude tests, e.g., a pupil with high linguistic aptitude should normally rank high on his French test; other school marks, e.g., a pupil who is failing in other courses should not normally get an A in algebra; differential groups, i.e., the test scores of pupils who have taken a given subject or problem-area course should be significantly higher than the scores of pupils who have not taken this course.

Many teachers seem to overemphasize the relative standing of pupils on teacher-constructed tests and to underemphasize the degree of validity these tests possess. As Lindquist has noted: "Comparability, after all, is not an independent end in itself. Comparability of scores is an *essential* condition to simplicity and meaningfulness of interpretation, but not a *sufficient* condition. Unless the tests measure the right things, it matters little whether the scores are comparable or not." [22] For example, a test which merely demands recall or recognition of factual data does not provide a valid measure of understandings, critical thinking, appreciations, or applications. Nor should the results of such a test be represented to pupils or parents as anything more than a measure of mere factual information. The reasons why many teachers construct tests which call exclusively for factual recall or recognition are, first, they are simpler

[21] C. C. Ross and Julian C. Stanley, *Measurement in Today's Schools,* 3d ed. (Englewood Cliffs, N.J.: Prentice-Hall, 1954), p. 107.

[22] E. F. Lindquist, "Some Criteria of an Effective High School Testing Program," in Traxler (ed.), *Measurement and Evaluation in the Improvement of Education.* (Washington: American Council on Education, 1951), p. 24. Used by permission.

to construct, and second, the course almost exclusively emphasized factual learnings.

The following are a few suggestions which the teacher should use to improve the validity of a test which he constructs:

1. Include items which will measure all the various learning outcomes of a course.

2. Use vocabulary which is understood by all those taking the test.

3. Utilize clear wording in the test, because if the words obscure the meaning of the item, then more than the item will be measured, viz., comprehensibility, which is not the outcome to be measured.

4. Avoid ambiguous, unclear, or unspecific directions. These can render a test invalid, because the pupil might thereby be led to answer other than what was intended, yet scored on the basis of what was intended.

5. Avoid poor or nonuniform mechanical composition of the test.

6. Under no circumstances deduct for spelling mistakes unless, of course, the test is a spelling test. (Such deductions render the test invalid, as they measure something other than what was designated in the item.)

Reliability. The reliability of a test is the degree of accuracy and consistency with which it measures what it does measure. The three most important determiners of a test's reliability are representative sampling, objectivity, and elimination of guessing. Representative sampling is the degree to which the test adequately both includes items and assigns them relative weight, on the basis of the overall learning outcomes to be measured. Representative sampling is necessary if the most precise estimate of the quality being tested is to be obtained. Objectivity is the lack of effect on the test results of the personality or beliefs of the test scorer. The correct responses are always the same no matter who scores the examination. Objective score keys are especially important if tests which measure understandings and appreciations are to be kept reliable. Without such objective frames of reference a true-false item which stated "Peter Maurin had profound Catholic insights on socioeconomic questions of his era" would admit of different scoring by a forward-looking rater and by a rater with reactionary beliefs. Guessing is the selection by the pupil of the correct response on the basis of chance rather than knowledge.

· Reliability cannot be determined by an examination of a test's structure or composition; rather, it must be determined by comparing consistency of performance. Thorndike has identified four chief methods of ascertaining the reliability of a test: "(1) administration of two equivalent tests and the correlation of the resulting scores; (2) repeated administration of the same test form and testing procedure and correlation of the resulting scores; (3) subdivision of a single test into two presumably equivalent groups of items, each scored separately, and correlation of the resulting two scores; (4) analysis of the variance among individual items, and determination of the error variance therefrom." [23] To the degree to which the test results correlate in each of these procedures, to that degree is it reliable. A test should have a coefficient of reliability of at least .80. As a general rule, the longer the test, the more reliable it tends to be.

Greene, Jorgensen, and Gerberich have observed that reliability is a general criterion of a test because a test is reliable solely on the basis of the internal factors of representative sampling, objectivity, and elimination of guessing, with no relation to the specific use to which it will be put. On the other hand, validity is a specific criterion of a test, because a test is valid not because of internal criteria, but rather because of the specific way in which the teacher uses it with a given group of students.[24] Hence a test can be reliable but invalid. This further points up the importance of validity.

Utility. The utility of a test is the degree to which the test serves a specific educational requirement in the particular school and class in which it is administered. Tests have high utility when they are used as positive instruments of instruction or to assist in guidance; they have low utility when they are given merely to consume time or to obtain a number to be inserted in a space of a required school form.

Administrability. The administrability of a test is the degree to which it is easily presented to the students by the teacher or proctor. There are three principal determiners of administrability, viz., simplicity, uniformity, and self-explanatoriness. Administrability is important because it saves the teacher valuable time which may be profitably spent either in reviewing test items with the students or in otherwise further learning.

Scorability. The scorability of a test is the degree to which it is easily and rapidly corrected. Scorability is facilitated by such devices as a separate score sheet, adequate spacing of answers, and letter rather than word responses wherever possible. Scorability is important because it enables the teacher to have more time to devote to the students.

Interpretability. The interpretability of a test is the degree to which its results can be made meaningful in terms of both personal growth and accepted objective standards of achievement. Without interpretability the test results are a mere mass of unintelligible raw scores.

[23] Robert L. Thorndike, "Reliability," in Lindquist (ed.), *Educational Measurement.* (Washington: American Council on Education, 1951), pp. 574–575. Used by permission.

[24] Harry A. Greene, Albert N. Jorgensen, and J. Raymond Gerberich, *Measurement and Evaluation in the Secondary School.* (New York: Longmans, 1954), pp. 66–73.

Economy. The economy of a test refers to the amount of money each test unit costs. School budgets in both public and Catholic high schools preclude the use of any but limited funds for testing. The use of the mimeograph and other types of duplicating machines has fortunately been able to make most teacher-constructed tests economical.

Types of Tests

There are four basic types or classifications into which educational tests fall, viz., oral and written, subjective and objective, speed and power, standardized and teacher-constructed.

Oral and Written Tests. An *oral test* is one in which the questions and responses are made audibly. It commonly assumes the form of a recitation whereby the teacher calls on a student in class to answer a question vocally. An oral test is different from developmental questioning in that the former does not attempt to push the lesson forward, but rather endeavors to provide the basis for the immediate measurement of learning outcomes, usually factual. Oral tests and concomitant marking are quite common in traditional classrooms; often the entire lesson consists of one grand oral test or recitation.

Oral tests or recitations have a number of advantages. First, they render evaluation a continuous process since they measure pupil progress continuously rather than periodically or at intervals, as do formal written examinations. Second, unlike questions on a uniform written examination, oral test questions can be differentiated so that they can be properly and more closely tailored to the individual pupil's abilities, needs, and achievement level. Third, they increase pupil attentiveness, since no student knows when he will be called on to answer and be marked. Fourth, they motivate the pupil to continuous study, the daily recitation marks being the incentive. Fifth, they afford a more comprehensive and just final mark, since the pupils' achievement will not be measured solely on the basis of a few major written examinations. Sixth, they are important and indispensable in such subject or problem areas as speech, modern languages, and parts of a problems-in-democracy course.

Oral tests or recitations have many disadvantages which to a significant degree offset their strong points. First, they convert the class into a recitation period, causing pupils for the sake of a good mark to study only what they think the teacher will ask, to emphasize rote memorization rather than developmental thinking, and to give answers which conform with the teacher's opinion. Second, they tend to be invalid because the questions asked of different students are of varying orders of difficulty. Third, they often lead to emotionalized responses because answering publicly in a social situation tends to lead to emotionalized responses, thus seriously limiting the validity of these tests. Fourth, they work to the advantage of the aggressive, voluble, glib students, and against the shy, introvertive pupils; hence the validity of these tests is impaired. Fifth, they are usually unreliable because each student has at most only a few chances to answer, a factor which seriously restricts the sampling. Sixth, the responses admit of subjective teacher judgment and of pupil favoritism or dislike (sometimes unintentional, sometimes deliberate) which vitiate reliability. Seventh, they are an inefficient use of class time since the product or process learnings to be evaluated can be determined so much more quickly and effectively by short written tests. Eighth, they tend to emphasize almost exclusively factual learnings since economy of time demands that the pupils' answers be rapid and short rather than consume larger amounts of time necessary for problem-solving questions involving higher thought processes. Ninth, they make constant marking the prime incentive for learning and attention and so deemphasize, if not destroy, in the minds of the pupils the inherent worth of the learning activity itself. Tenth, they transform the teacher from a guider of learning activities into a bookkeeper, a recitational policeman with a pencil for a nightstick.

Most contemporary educators urge that, with the exception of certain subject or problem areas such as speech and foreign languages, oral tests in the classroom be abandoned completely. They feel that continuous evaluation can be gained without resorting to daily recitations and marks. They propose instead that developmental questioning, committee work, projects, role playing, and the other pedagogical devices treated in Chapter IX be substituted for oral tests. Evaluation can be made continuous by maintaining a file of appropriate short and descriptive comments of the daily or weekly progress of the pupils. If oral tests are used, they should preferably be given by the teacher to each pupil privately, rather than in a group situation.

A *written test* is one in which questions appear in printed form and responses are made in a manner other than vocal, e.g., writing, circling, punching. Written tests, if constructed properly, possess all the advantages of a good test treated in the previous section. Their chief disadvantage is that occasionally a pupil becomes frightened and emotionally blocked by tests of this type, since his normal medium of communication and response is the spoken word. This disadvantage can be overcome by a cooperative effort of the school and the teacher. The school, in its special "How to Study" course (see Chapter X) can acquaint the pupils with written tests, instruct them on successful methods of studying for these tests, and thereby elevate pupil confidence and assurance in the presence of these instruments. Individual teachers, exercising patience and understanding, can work closely with those students who after this course still experience emotional blocks to written tests.

Essay and Objective Tests. An *essay test* is one in which the pupil both organizes and writes the responses in his own words according to whatever manner and degree of completeness he chooses within the loosely defined limits set by the question. Essay tests generally are answered in paragraph form. A typical essay test comprises only a few questions.

The essay test has seven important advantages. (*1*) It measures the pupil's higher intellectual attainments, e.g., power of analysis, critical thinking, ability to make meaningful comparisons. These achievements are crucial goals of the school and must be measured if evaluation is to be complete, valid, and reliable. Objective tests often fail to measure these attainments. (*2*) It allows the pupil to exhibit more independent and creative thinking than is normally the case with objective tests. (*3*) It gives the pupil great freedom of selection, organization, and response. (*4*) It acts as an impetus to the furtherance of a pupil's skill in written expression. Students who have experienced only objective tests are often stunted in their ability to express themselves well in writing. (*5*) It causes the student to prepare for the examination by reviewing basic, overall relationships and broad concepts. Objective tests induce the pupil to study isolated, factual data. (*6*) It is relatively easy for the teacher to construct. (*7*) It is simple to administer.

The essay test has four major disadvantages. (*1*) It is not adequate for an evaluation of a wide range of information, understandings, and appreciations. Because the questions must necessarily be few in number, a comprehensive sampling of pupil learning achievements is extremely difficult if not impossible to obtain. (*2*). It requires a long time to score. (*3*) It permits pupil bluffing and obfuscation. A skillful student can blur material of which he is ignorant and highlight that which he does know. While a model answer can be of great assistance in the detection of such inadequacies, a clever student can still attain a high score, particularly in those tests in which organization, creative thinking, and broad relationships are stressed. (*4*) It admits of a considerable degree of subjective scoring by the rater. Subjective elements, such as neatness of the paper, handwriting, spelling, underlining of key words, conformity of expressed ideas with those of the rater, have all been found to influence the test score. Two celebrated investigations by Starch and Elliott highlight the amount of subjective scoring of essay responses. In these two studies the researchers gave the same English and mathematics essay answer to a group of over one hundred English teachers and over one hundred mathematics teachers for rating. The resultant scores on the English examination ranged from a high of 98 per cent to a low of 50 per cent, and on the mathematics test from a high of 92 per cent to a low of 28 per cent.[25] Students, of course, have long been aware of this type of scoring discrepancy by their teachers. An investigation by Starch disclosed that college instructors assigned different marks to the same essay responses when they rescored them without knowledge of the marks they had previously assigned.[26] Subjective scoring is by far the most serious disadvantage of an essay examination, since it renders the test invalid and unreliable. Indeed, even with the greatest care and precaution, subjective scoring of an essay cannot be completely overcome.

During the height of the objective testing movement in the 1920s and 1930s, many ultraprogressive educators advocated the elimination of the essay test from classroom use. Today, however, the distinctive values of the essay examination are once again recognized. A well-balanced, comprehensive, teacher-constructed achievement test should be so structured that 20 to 25 per cent of the total score is obtained from essay questions.

An *objective test* is a completely structured series of short questions which admit only of certain and definite nongraduated responses predetermined by its constructor(s). Every response is either correct or incorrect; unlike the essay, the objective question has no varying degrees of completeness or accuracy. There are several types of objective tests, the most common being multiple choice, alternate response, matching and completion. Each test item contains two separate and distinct parts, viz., the stem and the response. The stem delineates the question; the response either offers the student possible designated responses or requires the insertion of a particular response. Objective tests first became popular in the twentieth century, and for this reason are sometimes called "new-type tests."

The objective test has several important advantages. First, it tends to have high validity, since extraneous achievements, such as spelling, writing skill, penmanship, neatness, and ability to organize information, have no effect on the score. Second, it tends to enjoy high reliability, because the large number of questions admit of wide representative sampling and because the score is not influenced by the subjective prejudices of the rater. Third, it does not permit pupil bluffing or obfuscation of the answer. Fourth, it can be administered very easily. Fifth, it can be scored with great rapidity.

[25] Daniel Starch and Edward C. Elliott, "Reliability of Grading High School Work in English," *School Review*, XX (September, 1912), pp. 442–457; also by the same authors, "Reliability of Grading High School Work in Mathematics," *School Review*, XXI (April, 1913), pp. 254–259.

[26] Daniel Starch, "Reliability and Distribution of Grades," *Science*, XXXVIII (October 13, 1913), pp. 630–636.

But the objective test is not without its disadvantages. First, it often fails to test for the pupil's higher intellectual attainments, e.g., power of analysis, critical thinking, ability to make meaningful comparisons. Of course, a well-constructed instrument can do much to reduce this deficiency. Second, it often overemphasizes purely factual information. This is true chiefly of teacher-constructed tests. Third, it admits of guessing the correct response, which renders the test partially invalid. Guessing can be only partially offset by use of a statistical correction formula. Fourth, it admits of fairly easy cheating by copying. This disadvantage can be overcome by installation of a student honor system, or by use of alternate forms of the same test, or by strict policelike vigilance by the proctor. Fifth, it encourages the pupil to study and review atomistically, rather than in a broad relational comprehensive manner. Sixth, it requires a great deal of time and painstaking effort to construct a valid, reliable objective test.

Power and Speed Tests. A *power test*, sometimes referred to as a "scaled test," is one which requires the pupil to answer a series of questions of unequal difficulty in an unrestricted amount of time. Often a power test is modified in that a definite time limit is set. However, the test is so constructed that the time limit provides ample opportunity for most, if not all, students to finish. A power test is the type most frequently used by teachers. A *speed test,* also referred to as a "rate test," is one which requires the pupil to answer a series of questions of approximately uniform difficulty in a specified amount of time. The time limit is so set that no student can complete all the items.

Standardized and Teacher-constructed Tests. A *standardized test* is one which has been composed by a group of experts and has been extensively pretested for a period of years on large groups of students so that all the criteria of a good test are maximally attained. A standardized test is generally intended for wide pupil use on a national or regional level. This type of test is usually sold to schools by commercial publishers such as the Educational Testing Service or Science Research Associates. There is a standardized test available in almost every area in which the teacher desires measurement, ranging from intelligence tests to attitude tests to achievement tests in specific subject-matter areas.[27]

A standardized achievement test has two main advantages. It has been extensively pretested before publication and hence possesses to a very high degree the criteria of a good test. Moreover, it is national or regional, thus enabling a teacher to compare his pupils' scores with those of similar students in different parts of the country. This com-

[27] For a complete listing of standardized tests available for purchase together with information about each, see Oscar K. Buros (ed.), *The Fifth Mental Measurements Yearbook.* (Highland Park, N.J.: Gryphon, 1959).

parison is fruitful in that it provides a good overall, nonparochial view of pupil growth.

A standardized achievement test has two major disadvantages. It is usually completely objective, and therefore does not adequately measure certain learnings best tested through an essay. Moreover, it is geared to national or regional use and, therefore, does not take into account the individual differences generated by specific localities (e.g., in a farming community it is necessary to spend more time in biology class learning about farm problems such as plant killers and poor fertilization than would be required in a biology class in a metropolis); or the particular needs of different pupils of the group which were incorporated into the educational goals of the class as a result of cooperative teacher-pupil planning; or the various instructional procedures employed by different teachers.

A standardized achievement test, consequently, has general rather than specific uses; i.e., it is valuable for comparison of the achievement of basic learnings of pupils within large areas such as the nation or the state. It is not constructed to provide a valid measurement for pupil achievement in a given class, which by its very nature must provide a different learning emphasis from the next class.

A *teacher-constructed test* is one which a teacher composes in order to measure certain desired educational outcomes of a particular class or small group of students. Most teacher-constructed tests are achievement tests. The principal advantage of a teacher-constructed test is that it can be tailored to the specific abilities, needs, educational goals, and instructional emphasis of a specific class. Its chief disadvantage lies in the fact that it is usually poorly constructed and has at best limited validity and reliability.

In general, standardized achievement tests are superior instruments for the measurement of basic learnings, while teacher-constructed tests are better for the measurement of specific desired outcomes and emphases. Both should be used by a teacher to ascertain pupil growth and attainment. In using standardized tests the teacher must be careful that it is not the professional test maker who determines what he will teach. In some schools this is unfortunately the case, for as Traxler has said, "If the schools, and particularly the heads of schools, regard tests as the goals of instruction and judge teachers by their students' success on tests, then teachers will almost inevitably conduct their classes with an eye to the test score." [28]

---

[28] Arthur E. Traxler, "Are the Professional Test-makers Determining What We Teach?" *School Review*, LXVI (Summer, 1958), p. 147.

The School, the Teacher, and Tests

Every school should develop a policy governing the construction, administration, scoring, and especially the interpretation of tests which it and its teachers give the pupils. This policy should be based on attainment and furtherance of pupil growth in all areas which the school feels it should foster. Similarly, every school should periodically reassess its testing and evaluation program to ascertain the degree to which this program is furthering the goals of the school. This is very important in the case of teacher-constructed achievement tests. As Fr. O'Connell has remarked, "Education is a process of growth, and the acquisition of the outcomes of the educational program cannot be measured directly or adequately by testing for the mere acquisition of facts." [29] Understandings, appreciations, and critical thinking must be part of every achievement test.

In addition to achievement tests, there are six other basic types of tests, viz., intelligence or scholastic aptitude tests, personality inventory tests, interest or vocational tests, attitude tests, performance tests, and tests of special abilities. While these vary in validity and reliability, they are all helpful in furnishing information about the pupil's growth and in diagnosing areas in which special instructional and guidance emphasis must be placed. A worthwhile testing and evaluation program should make use of all these measuring instruments in concert.

Both teachers and college students preparing to teach spend a goodly amount of time in learning how to help the pupil learn, but often neglect to acquire the knowledge of how to evaluate properly what the pupil has learned. Not only is this disastrous from the viewpoint of obtaining accurate assessment, but also it represents a serious gap in teaching technique, since evaluation is a vital part of teaching. Teachers who do not know how to construct or score a test vitiate much of their teaching, e.g., a history teacher who deducts 5 points for each spelling mistake. Despite the great emphasis on testing in current educational practice, there are very few states which require a course in testing as a requisite for certification. This is unfortunate, for unless the testing instrument is of excellent quality, its aims will be thwarted. Ross and Stanley have further stated: "Teachers and school administrators must not only understand and appreciate the functions of measurement in education, but they must realize more fully the limitations of present measuring instruments." [30] Therefore the rest of this chapter

[29] Laurence J. O'Connell, "Outcomes of the Curriculum," in McKeough, O. Praem. (ed.), *The Curriculum of the Catholic Secondary School.* (Washington, D.C.: Catholic University of America Press, 1949), p. 138.

[30] Ross and Stanley, *op. cit.,* p. 133.

will be devoted to teacher-constructed achievement tests in the hope that the quality of these important instruments will be improved.

General Principles of Achievement Test Construction

There are 27 principles which the teacher should apply if he wishes to construct a superior testing instrument. This is a formidable number of principles and should serve to alert the teacher that the construction of a good test is no easy task.

1. Examine the course content for educational objectives. A good test should measure all the goals of the course, viz., factual material, understandings, applications, study skills in the particular subject or problem area, broadening of pertinent interests, and so forth.

2. List the principal educational goals to be evaluated. This will ensure that all the desired goals will be included on the test.

3. "Analyze and define each objective in terms of expected student outcomes," [31] so that the goals are translated into concrete, specific learnings.

4. Decide exactly what is to be measured *generally* by this particular test, viz., knowledge, understandings, attitudes, all of these, and also *specifically*, viz., precisely what knowledges, understandings, attitudes.

5. Determine the conditions under which the test is to be given, such as time and place. The type of test, the number of items, must be commensurate with the conditions; e.g., in a power test, the length of the test must be fixed in relation to the time allotted.[32]

6. Construct a blueprint which will depict in graphic form the outcomes and learnings to be tested. Such a blueprint ensures that the test will give proper emphasis to all the outcomes, with none being omitted or understressed. Thorndike and Hagen have proposed a grid for this type of blueprint.[33] The left-hand vertical column of the grid contains in descending boxes the basic educational outcomes which the test is endeavoring to measure, e.g., factual information, understandings, principles, ability to locate data, and so forth. The second vertical column lists the specific learnings which will be tested, e.g., similarities between guilds and labor unions, effect of collective bargaining, nature of the dignity of labor, use of the *Statistical Abstract*. Other vertical columns can be added if the educational goals of the course so demand. The horizontal columns of the grid relate each particular basic educational outcome with a specific learning, e.g., relating ability to locate data with the use of the *Statistical Abstract*.

7. Block out the sources of the test material. Several steps are involved in

[31] William J. Micheels and M. Ray Karnes, *Measuring Educational Achievement.* (New York: McGraw-Hill, 1950), p. 127.

[32] See Alfred Schwartz and Stuart C. Tiedeman, *Evaluating Student Progress.* (New York: Longmans, 1957), pp. 103–104.

[33] Thorndike and Hagen, *op. cit.*, p. 32.

this process. First, assign relative weights, according to their learning importance, to classroom discussions and activities, committee work, the textbook, collateral readings, and supplemental activities. Second, determine the number of test items which will be based on each of the above; e.g., on a test comprising 100 items, 25 might be drawn from collateral readings. Third, make sure that the items are comprehensively representative of all the source material; e.g., if the collateral readings total 100 pages and 25 items are to be drawn from these readings, these normally should be one objective item covering every four pages. This prevents most of the items from being taken from a skewed portion of the readings such as the last 25 pages. Of course such a procedure must be modified according to the nature of the material.

8. Correlate the results of the blueprinting and the blocking out, so that the number of test items will be adequately representative of the basic outcomes, learnings, and sources. The test should give the greatest weight to the most important objectives, e.g., understandings, applications.[34] Stalnaker has observed that "objective tests commonly prepared by the classroom teacher tend to encourage memorization of isolated facts and cramming of minutiae."[35] Understandings, applications, critical thinking, and the other important basic outcomes must be accorded their due role in the number and type of test items.

9. Pyramid the items on a power test according to the degree of difficulty; i.e., one or two items will be extremely difficult, four or five others will be quite difficult, and so on down the pyramid. In this way the test will properly reflect the student's real level of achievement.

10. Compose each item on a separate 3-by-5 or 5-by-8 index card. This allows a great deal of flexibility and permits reshuffling for later ordering of the items.

11. Construct the test so that 75 to 80 percent of the score will be taken from objective items and 20 to 25 per cent from essay items. A review of the pertinent research studies by Stalnaker concluded that the study methods employed by pupils for essay tests are different from those used for objective tests.[36] Therefore a combination objective-essay test would encourage the pupils to use all study methods, rather than just one.

12. Construct the essay questions first. These items cover the greatest range of outcomes and learnings. Hence their construction at the outset will eliminate overlapping of material on the test.

13. Include items representative of all the various types of objective questions, e.g., multiple choice, alternate response, matching, and completion.

[34] R. Murray Thomas, *Judging Student Progress*, 2d ed. (New York: Longmans, 1960), p. 49.
[35] John M. Stalnaker, "The Essay Type of Examination," in Lindquist (ed.), *Educational Measurement*. (Washington: American Council on Education, 1951), p. 514.
[36] *Ibid.*

14. Compose multiple-choice items before making up other types of objective questions. The reason for this is that multiple-choice items usually test for broad ideas, information range, and understandings. Completion questions should be composed last, since they deal with specific isolated facts. The order of test item construction thus proceeds from the most general to the most particular.

15. Sort the items into homogeneous types, i.e., all alternate-response questions together, all matching questions together, and so forth.[37]

16. Determine whether or not the items in each homogeneous type will be arranged according to apparent order of difficulty. Some test experts hold that the items should progressively increase in difficulty, while others contend that the items should not be so assembled.

17. Write simple, clear, concise, yet comprehensive, directions for each set of items of a different homogeneous type.

18. Examine critically every item of the assembled test to see that it possesses all the criteria of a good measurement instrument. Be especially careful about the wording, and eliminate misleading, ambiguous, or catch questions.

19. Ask other teachers and, if possible, curriculum experts to inspect the test in order to further refine it. If possible, teachers of the same subject or problem area should be asked to take the test.

20. Revise the test on the basis of these critical inspections.

21. Construct the score key of correct responses.

22. Determine whether pupil responses are to be made on the question sheet itself or on a separate answer sheet. The latter increases the scorability of a test, especially if a scoring mask is used.

23. Prepare the test for mimeographing or duplication. Adhere to good mechanical format, such as providing plenty of space so that the items will not be crowded, controlling the position of the blanks, and so forth.

24. Check the mimeographed stencil for typographical errors before the test is duplicated.

25. Arrange for the test to be administered under normal conditions, e.g., in the classroom rather than in the cafeteria, library, or study hall.

26. Permit the pupils to correct their own objective responses. An investigation by Curtis and Woods showed that pupils learned best from objective tests when they were allowed to correct their own objective tests and discuss the items with the teacher.[38] Possible pupil cheating can be thwarted by requiring the students to remove everything from their desks except a red pencil supplied by the teacher. Another solution is to furnish each pupil

[37] Hubert H. Mills and Harl R. Douglass, *Teaching in High School,* 2d ed. (New York: Ronald, 1957), p. 357.

[38] Francis D. Curtis and Gerald G. Woods, "A Study of the Relative Teaching Values of Four Common Practices in Correcting Examination Papers," *School Review,* XXXVII (October, 1929), pp. 615–623.

with two answer sheets when they are taking the test. The student is later given one to correct while the teacher retains the second for comparison purposes.[39] Cooperative marking of a test transforms it from something which is merely undergone to a powerful teaching device. Correct responses are reinforced and incorrect ones rectified. As Lee has noted, testing is not the culminating activity of a unit or course.[40] Only the teacher can and therefore should correct the essay; however, he should discuss the model answer with the pupils.

27. Analyze and improve the test on the basis of the student responses. Some items will be discarded, others refined.

General Principles of Item Construction on Achievement Tests

In order to construct a good test item, the teacher must possess six important qualities, namely, a well-developed set of educational values; an understanding of the particular group of students from a psychological, philosophical, and theological viewpoint; a thorough knowledge of the product and process outcomes for which he is testing; competence in verbal communication; a knowledge of the basic principles of test construction; skill in the special techniques of writing the various specific types of test items.[41]

Ebel has stated: "Item writing is essentially creative. Each item being written presents new problems, new opportunities." [42] Therefore the teacher should not regard item construction as a routine chore but rather as a challenging opportunity. Each item should present a new twist to the pupil in order to measure his real learning achievement. Thus Findley and Scates have remarked that "to provide evidence of understanding, evaluation situations must contain an element of novelty, but not too much novelty." [43] Without the introduction of some novelty into the test item, it is very difficult for a measurement instrument to detect whether or not a student is merely parroting what he has memorized. Besides, without some novelty the items would be intolerably dull. On the other hand, excessive novelty creates too much of a chasm between what was learned and the evaluation situation, thus rendering the situation totally unfamiliar and the measurement invalid.

[39] J. Murray Lee, *A Guide to Measurement in Secondary Schools*. (New York: Appleton-Century, 1936), pp. 329–330.

[40] James Michael Lee, *op. cit.*, p. 4.

[41] See Robert L. Ebel, "Writing the Test Item," in *Educational Measurement*, p. 186.

[42] *Ibid.*, p. 185.

[43] Warren G. Findley and Douglas E. Scates, "Obtaining Evidence of Understanding," *The Measurement of Understanding*, p. 46.

The following are some general principles of item construction on achievement tests:

1. Compose each item so that it tests for one specific educational objective. An item which incorporates many objectives makes accurate diagnosis impossible. Thus, for example, an item might test for both analysis and application. If the pupil gives an incorrect response, was it only because of inability to analyze, or to apply, or both? Remedial learning by the pupil is therefore not given its proper direction by the test.

2. Do not include obscure or trivial items in the test.

3. Do not encumber an item with material not necessary for its solution, e.g., "Columbus, sailing in the *Santa Maria* from Palos, discovered the New World in the year ____." The clause beginning with "sailing" is not necessary.

4. When an item comprises theory or opinion, indicate the name of the author from whom the item is drawn. Every good high school class should have studied conflicting theories and opinions, and unless the source is indicated, the pupil will not have sufficient information to respond properly to the item. The author's name can be placed in parentheses after the item stem.

5. Eliminate internal clues within an item, e.g., "The English metaphysical poet who is famous for his conceits is: (*a*) Donne, (*b*) Wordsworth, (*c*) Chaucer, (*d*) Arnold." A student can respond correctly not because he knows Donne's technique, which the item intends to measure, but rather because he is aware that none of the other alternatives were metaphysical poets.

6. Make sure that there is nothing in one item which may provide a clue to the correct response of a different item; e.g., on the same test one alternate-response item might state, "By crossing the Alps, Hannibal surprised the Romans," while a later completion item might ask for the name of the Carthaginian general who crossed the Alps in the Second Punic War.

7. Write the item in such a way that the chance of guessing the correct response is greatly minimized. A skillful item maker can provide false clues of such a type that pupils who do not know the answer will be led astray by the clue, while pupils who do know the material can easily perceive that the clue is a false one. This procedure of item construction must be used with great caution, however, because it can easily degenerate into the composition of trick or catch questions.

8. Avoid interdependent items, i.e., those which require the proper solution of one item as prerequisite information toward the solution of a second item. This practice invalidates the second item.[44]

9. State each item simply and clearly, refining awkward word arrangement or poor grammatical structure.

[44] James M. Bradfield and H. Stewart Moredock, *Measurement and Evaluation in Education.* (New York: Macmillan, 1957), pp. 101–104.

10. Make sure that each word in the item has a precise meaning wherever possible. Ambiguous words should be dropped. Indefinite terms of degree or amount, e.g., "often," "frequently," "many," should not be included in an item unless absolutely necessary.

11. Do not use specific determiners such as the words "always," "only." Because these terms by definition admit of no exception, items which include them are rarely correct and hence admit of pupil guessing.

12. Avoid, if possible, negative words. If a negative word must occur in an item, underline it so that the pupil will immediately see it. Under no circumstances use double or triple negatives.[45]

13. Eliminate tricky or catch words and phrases. These render a test invalid.

14. As a general rule do not take or "lift" items verbatim from the text-book or collateral readings. This procedure tends to encourage and reward the rote learner.

15. Number the items consecutively from the beginning to the end of the entire test. The numeration should not begin anew with every different part of the test.

Specific Principles of Essay Item Construction on Achievement Tests

An essay test attempts to measure certain types of educational outcomes and learnings which objective items either cannot measure or have great difficulty in measuring, e.g., the higher mental achievements. This is the basic reason justifying its use, despite its low validity and reliability as compared with an objective test. Therefore an essay test must test for these higher mental achievements, and not merely be a variant of a completion test in that it asks for many memorized words instead of one.

Most teacher-constructed tests ask the pupils to "discuss." This is a vague word and usually means that the teacher wants the pupil to transcribe information directly from the textbook. There are at least ten different types of essay questions, each designed to measure a specific type of learning: *Comparison,* e.g., "Compare Macbeth's behavior before and after Banquo's death"; *Contrast,* e.g., "Contrast the major differences between the land and sea campaigns of the American Revolutionary War"; *Explanation and explication,* e.g., "Explain what Pius XII meant when he said, 'The laity *are* the Church' "; *Critical evaluation or critique,* e.g., "Evaluate capital punishment in the light of the Sermon on the Mount"; *Analysis,* e.g., "Analyze Rostand's play *Cyrano de Bergerac* on the basis of grammatical structure, literary devices, domi-

[45] Victor H. Noll, *Introduction to Educational Measurement.* (Boston: Houghton Mifflin, 1957), pp. 124–125.

nant theme, and underlying philosophy"; *Synthesis*, e.g., "What specific political and economic steps would it be necessary for Argentina, Bolivia, Brazil, and Chile to take if they wished to form a Common Market among themselves?"; *Cause-effect relationship*, e.g., "Delineate the effects which Jansenism has had on clergy-laity relations, teacher-pupil relations, free will, and one's outlook on the world"; *Application*, e.g., "Write a 500-word fictitious biography of Abraham Lincoln, utilizing the techniques for research writing learned in this class"; *Summary*, e.g., "Summarize the arguments for and against socialized medicine"; *Basic recall*, e.g., "Give the provisions of the Taft-Hartley Law."

When constructing essay items, estimate the time it will take the student to think through and subsequently write the correct responses. An extra margin of time should be included for the slow writers, else the test will be invalid in these cases.

The following are some specific principles of essay item construction on achievement tests:

1. Avoid the basic recall type of essay wherever possible. This is especially important in a mixed essay and objective test. The other nine types of essay items, if properly constructed, should yield the desired factual pupil responses.

2. Structure the item so that the student will be required to give more than mere factual data.

3. Compose the item in such a way that it will force the pupil to integrate in his response what he learned from class discussion and activities, the textbook, collateral readings, and supplemental activities. An item which tests only textbook material is a poor item indeed.

4. Try whenever possible to ask items on broad topics, delineating several specific subtopics to be treated. For example, "Compare Lutheranism and Calvinism on the following points: sacramental system, priesthood, liturgy, nature of the Church, and relationship of Church and state."

5. Make each item direct rather than vague. An essay item which begins "Tell me all you know about . . ." is a very poor item.

6. Stipulate that essay responses be written in paragraph rather than bare outline form. This practice will tend to defeat the rote learner.

7. Do not permit a choice in essay items, e.g., "Answer any three of the following five." Choice of items destroys the common base of evaluation and renders ranking unreliable.[46] Some teachers seem to delight in complicating their essays with such directions as "Answer either the odd- or even-numbered items," or "Answer item number 1 and any other two." Questions of this type are sophisticated only to those ignorant of the principles of test construction.

---

[46] J. Wayne Wrightstone, Joseph Justman, and Irving Robbins, *Evaluation in Modern Education.* (New York: American Book, 1956), p. 105.

Specific Principles of Multiple-Choice Item Construction on Achievement Tests

A multiple-choice item is one which is composed of a single stem and three or more responses, one of which is either correct or the best answer. Most test experts agree that the multiple-choice item is the most flexible and comprehensive of all objective items. It is applicable to all subject or problem areas and to all types of learning, e.g., facts, understanding, application. A skillfully constructed multiple-choice item can cover a wide range and a great amount of material. Selecting the correct response to a multiple-choice item involves refined discrimination by the student. Hence, unless the item is a bald fact question, it will involve judgment and understanding for its solution.

Mosier, Myers, and Price have identified some types of learnings for which a multiple-choice item can test and measure: definition, purpose, cause, effect, association, recognition of type of error, identification of error, evaluation, difference between two facts or concepts, similarity between two facts or concepts, arrangement or order, partial arrangement calling for a particular response to complete it, application, analysis, synthesis, controversial issues.[47] The teacher should make use of all or at least most of these types when constructing his achievement test.

In a multiple-choice item which attempts to test for application, it is wise not to ask for the information or principle directly but rather to present instead alternative concrete situations, one of which represents the correct application of the basic information or principle. Ahmann and Glock suggest that in a multiple-choice item which tries to test for understanding, it is well to present a statement in the stem and construct the responses so that one of them will give the basic reason why the stem statement is true.[48]

The following are some specific principles of multiple-choice item construction on achievement tests:

1. Confine each stem to only one single problem.[49]

2. Include as much of the statement as possible in the stem. This will save needless repetition of words common to each item.

3. Phrase the stem as an incomplete statement rather than as a question.

[47] Charles I. Mosier, M. Claire Myers, and Helen G. Price, "Suggestions for the Construction of Multiple-Choice Items," *Educational and Psychological Measurement*, V. (Autumn, 1945), pp. 264–267.

[48] J. Stanley Ahmann and Marvin D. Glock, *Evaluating Pupil Growth*. (Englewood Cliffs, N.J.: Allyn and Bacon, 1959), p. 254.

[49] See Robert M. W. Travers, *Educational Measurements*. (New York: Macmillan, 1955), p. 182.

4. Structure the item so that the responses occur at the conclusion of the stem rather than in the middle of it.

5. Offer four or five alternative responses in each item. This will minimize guessing and enable the question to have a wider range.

6. Make sure that in each item one response is correct or decidedly better than the others. In factual items, usually one answer alone is correct and all the others are wrong. However, in many items testing understanding, application, and the other higher mental achievements, all the responses are good, but only one is the best. This is, of course, the reason why the item does test for the higher mental achievements.

7. Compose the responses so that they are all plausible, else the student with no knowledge or a hazy understanding can choose the correct response by the process of elimination, thereby rendering the item invalid. Ridiculous statements or those which are obviously incorrect should similarly be avoided.[50]

8. State the alternative responses to each item in parallel grammatical structure whenever possible.

9. Use alternative responses such as "all of the above" or "none of the above" with caution. Among other disadvantages, these tend to provide a clue to the correct response.

10. Require that the correct response be indicated by the letter which denotes that response rather than asking the pupils to write out the entire response.

11. Distribute the correct responses so that no clues are provided by similarity or definite pattern; e.g., half of the correct responses should not be C, nor should the correct responses to consecutive items read A, B, C, D, A, B, and so forth.

It is often a good policy to include an item whose stem begins: "*All but one* of the following statements about. . . ." The advantage of this type of item is that it increases the value of the test as a teaching device because it puts before the pupil correct facts, understandings, applications, and so forth. The test itself thus is instructing the pupil while he is taking it. This type of item also sharpens the pupil's power of discrimination by requiring him to see flaws in an otherwise acceptable pattern, something which he should be able to do in real life.

Specific Principles of Alternate-response Item Construction on Achievement Tests

An alternate-response item is one which is composed of a single statement which is either correct or incorrect. The most common type

[50] Jum C. Nunnally, Jr., *Tests and Measurements*. (New York: McGraw-Hill, 1959), p. 157.

of alternate-response item is the true-false item; the next most frequent is the yes-no item. A variant of the alternate-response item is that which directs the student to cross out in appropriate items the word which renders the item incorrect and replace it with the correct word. Unless such a test is constructed with great skill, it presents formidable scoring difficulties.

The alternate-response type of item is applicable to all subject or problem areas and to all types of learning. Regrettably, most alternate-response items seem to test bald factual information alone. Actually this type of item is particularly effective in testing for judgmental thinking and should be used to measure this type of learning.

A good alternate-response item is not so easy to construct as some teachers seem to believe. Some simple factual alternate-response statements, such as "Samuel Butler wrote *Hudibras*," might admit of easy construction, but such an item can hardly be considered an especially good alternate-response question. Yet even these purely informational items often present formidable compositional difficulties. The statement, "Columbus discovered America," intended by the test constructor to be "true" might be answered "false" by a bright pupil who knows that Columbus never actually set foot on the American mainland. Indeed, alternate-response items, unless constructed with meticulous care, often work against the pupil with more than average knowledge. A judgmental question must be so phrased that it admits of a definite and clear-cut affirmative or negative response, while still adequately testing for judgmental learnings. Guessing presents a particularly acute problem in an alternate-response item, since by sheer luck and with no knowledge whatever the student has a 50-50 chance of guessing the correct answer. The item should be so constructed as to thwart guessing; using the devices suggested in an earlier part of this chapter will be helpful in this respect.

The following are some specific principles of alternate-response item construction on achievement tests:

1. Make the item perfectly clear and in no way ambiguous.

2. Avoid absolute words such as "always" and "never." These usually indicate that the item is false, because an exception can be found to almost every finite absolute.

3. Do not allow the length of the item to provide a clue to the answer. Test experts have noted that true items tend to be longer than false items.

4. Eliminate any discernible pattern of responses, e.g., *T-N-T-N-T* or three correct responses followed by three incorrect ones.

5. Construct the items so that there is not an imbalance of either correct

or incorrect responses. Certainly not less than one-third of the total number of items should be true or false.[51]

6. Specify that true-false responses be designated either T, N, or $+$, 0, but not T, F. This practice will preclude possible cheating by dishonest pupils who will put a T for an item of which they are uncertain, hoping that when the paper is returned and the response is wrong, they can insert the lower crossbar converting the T into an F. The same applies to the $+$, $-$ combination.

7. Simplify scoring by requiring the pupil to place in a specified blank space the letter or sign indicating the correct response. This is better than circling previously typewritten letters or signs. This rule does not hold when a scoring mask is used.

Many test experts insist that the alternate-response item be totally correct or incorrect. However, this rule would appear to make it difficult to construct a test involving critical judgment; indeed, it would seem to encourage factual items. A partially false item would appear to be valuable, but only if the directions specified that an answer was false if any part of the item was incorrect. This type of alternate-response item is difficult to construct well.

Specific Principles of Matching Item Construction on Achievement Tests

A matching item is one which is composed of a series or column of words or short phrases, each one of which must be paired with the correct response listed in another series or column. A matching test is valuable because it causes the students to identify and recognize relationships. Therefore a matching test should not involve facts exclusively (e.g., pairing "van Kersbergen" with "Grail Lay Apostolate Movement") but also concepts and understandings (e.g., linking "integer" with "6" rather than with "½").

A matching exercise can test the pupil's achievement in relating the following: names with events, causes with their effects, terms with their definitions, parts with their derivative wholes, things with their characteristics, principles with concrete situations to which they directly apply.[52]

The following are some specific principles of matching item construction on achievement tests:

1. Compose the test so that each entire set of matching items appears on the same page.

[51] See H. H. Remmers and N. L. Gage, *Measurement and Evaluation*, rev. ed. (New York: Harper, 1955), pp. 87–88.
[52] See Micheels and Karnes, *op. cit.*, p. 233.

2. Put both series of items in vertical columns rather than in horizontal form. The stem column should appear on the left-hand side of the test page.

3. Place twice as many items in the response column as in the stem column. This will tend to exclude the possibility of getting the correct response by process of elimination.

4. Construct the responses so that there will be two plausible responses for every stem question. This too will tend to discourage guessing by process of elimination.

5. Make sure that each stem has only one response with which it can be correctly matched. Nor should one response serve as the answer to more than one stem.

6. Construct the stem and response columns so that each is in some type of systematic form, such as alphabetical order. This will tend to distribute the correct responses randomly and so avoid one form of internal clue.[53]

7. Employ parallel grammatical structure in each column whenever possible.

8. Do not use too many items in a set. Five to ten stems are considered optimum.

9. Structure each set so that if possible only homogeneous items appear, e.g. rivers, types of clauses, founders of Religious Orders, application of oxides.

Specific Principles of Completion Item Construction on Achievement Tests

A completion item is one which is composed of an unfinished statement requiring the addition of a word, words, or a phrase in order to render it complete. A completion test is unique among all types of objective tests because it alone demands total recall. All other objective tests are based on recognition. Hence the completion item is regarded as the most difficult to answer of all objective-type tests. Consequently a completion item should be restricted to the most important information. It is used to test factual learnings exclusively. It asks "who, what, when, where" kind of material.

The following are some specific principles of completion item construction on achievement tests:

1. Leave only one blank to be answered; e.g., "Fr. Cardijn founded the Young Christian Workers in the year _____." The insertion of more than one blank often fails to provide the pupil with sufficient information to answer the item; e.g., "_____ founded the _____ in the year _____."

[53] A. M. Jordan, *Measurement in Education.* (New York: McGraw-Hill, 1953), pp. 52–54.

2. Require a single, definite answer to each item, e.g., a historical date, a particular hydrocarbon.

3. Construct every item so that it must evoke a specific response. Thus the item "The man who won the Battle of Austerlitz was _____" admits not only of the intended response "Napoleon" but also of "French," "short," "clever," and so on. All would have to be scored correct because the item gave rise to an ambiguous response. The item could be improved by phrasing it: "The name of the general who won the Battle of Austerlitz was _____." Even with this precaution, the response "Bonaparte" would be correct. This example highlights the fact that not even completion items are easy to construct. Furthermore, it shows that in a completion test every correct response must be rewarded even if it is not the exact answer intended by the constructor.

4. Make every blank space of uniform length. Failure to do this might provide the pupil with a clue.

5. Word an indefinite article which precedes a blank as "a(n)," so as to eliminate any clue to the response.

6. Place the blank at the end of the item. This facilitates both pupil thinking and teacher scoring.[54]

General Principles of Scoring Essay Items on Achievement Tests

The following are some general principles of scoring essay items on achievement tests:

1. Construct a model answer at the time the item is composed and adhere to this model answer during the scoring of the pupils' responses. This model answer should indicate the essential elements which must be present in each response, together with the mark weight for each of the essential facts, understandings, associations, inferences, and the like. If such a detailed model answer is neither constructed nor followed, the scoring will become highly subjective. However, the model answers must make some allowances for pupil creativity, i.e., for correct answers not foreseen by the test constructor.

2. Make a separate evaluation of each distinct learning incorporated in the item, e.g., factual data, organizational skills, applications, critiques, and so forth, in those cases in which the test will be used for diagnostic purposes.

3. Endeavor to have the item scored by its constructor. In an essay test only the constructor adequately knows the exact nature, quality, and nuances of the learnings asked.

[54] *Teacher's Note:* The author has found that college students taking the course in Principles and Methods learn this chapter best when, as a course requirement (sometimes in lieu of a term paper), they are asked to construct a 100-item test utilizing the principles expounded in this chapter.

4. Attempt to have the item scored by the teacher of the students whose responses are to be scored.

5. Score the responses anonymously. This will eliminate favoritism, whether intentional or unintentional. It will also avoid the halo effect, i.e., teacher expectation of a particular level of response from different students. Prior to the test the pupils should be instructed to place their names on the back of the test or answer sheet. The scorer should not look at the name until he has completed the scoring.

6. In the case of more than one essay answer, mark each item horizontally rather than score the entire test vertically; i.e., the scorer should mark consecutively essay item number 1 on each paper, then proceed to item number 2, instead of correcting the items of a single pupil's test paper all at once. This horizontal procedure facilitates more rapid scoring and also provides the scorer with a better comparative evaluation of the various pupil responses.

General Principles of Scoring Objective Items on Achievement Tests

Scoring an objective test is primarily a mechanical process. There is, however, one large problem, namely, how to treat the element of guessing. Some test experts maintain that guessing should not be penalized; others hold that it should, since correct guesses partially invalidate a test. Test experts have devised a statistical formula which the scorer can utilize to offset the effects of fortunate guessing. This correction formula can be stated as follows: Score $= R - W/n - 1$. R represents the number of items answered correctly, W the number of items answered incorrectly, and n the number of alternative responses for each item, e.g., two in a true-false test. The score obtained by this formula is called the "adjusted score." The pupils should be apprised before the test whether the correction formula will be employed. Completion items, of course, cannot be corrected for guessing, nor really can matching questions, unless they appear in sets of 10 possible responses or less.

On completion items, deductions should not be made for incorrect spelling, as this will invalidate the test.

MARKING AND MARKING SYSTEMS

A mark is a specific indication of the degree to which the pupil is attaining desired educational outcomes. Wrinkle has stated that "the marking and reporting problem ranks close to the top among those about which most schools and teachers are seriously concerned." [55] He

[55] William L. Wrinkle, *Improving Marking and Reporting Practices*. (New York: Rinehart, 1947), p. 30. This is the classic work on the subject.

then immediately adds that since teachers do not know how to improve their marking systems, no change is instituted. The following section of this chapter is an attempt to rectify this situation.

The basic problem in devising a valid marking system is the difficulty of converting measures into marks.[56] The measures might be accurate, but what exactly do they mean in terms of pupil progress? Does a pupil's mark truthfully tell him, his parents, the school, and the community how much he has learned? The problem is further complicated by the fact that a pupil's academic record, on which marks figure most prominently, possesses the fearsome attribute of indelibility. What is written, remains. One's academic record can sometimes make or break one in adult life. And then there are those teachers who regard the marking system primarily as a device to force their pupils to study, a salvage device to make up for what is lacking in their own pedagogical skill.

Specific Disadvantages of the Current Marking System

Most secondary school teachers today give every pupil a single percentage or letter mark for each academic subject or Core problem. In addition, a mark is often given for certain coacademic traits identified as desirable, e.g., effort, cooperation. However, this type of marking system has 12 disadvantages. *First,* a mark does not indicate what it purports to indicate. Wrinkle has stated that "the No. 1 fallacy in the use of a single A B C D F [or percentage] mark or any other single mark in reporting the achievement or progress of a student is that anyone can tell from the mark assigned what the student's level of achievement is or what progress he has made." [57] In other words, a B or an 84 per cent in English does not indicate the level of a pupil's proficiency in grammar as distinct from literature, as distinct from literary appreciation, as distinct from reading comprehension, as distinct from creative writing. *Second,* a single mark in a subject or problem area does not indicate to the pupil, his parents, or his future teachers the weaknesses which he must eradicate. Nor does it suggest to them the next steps the student must take to continue and improve his growth in learning. *Third,* current marking practices have a tendency to encourage an extrinsic, hence superficial, type of learning and scholarship. Wrinkle has noted that "the stress placed on marks in conventional practice tends to cause the student to believe that getting good marks is the aim of education and therefore the end of education." [58] Burton has

[56] See Thomas M. Risk, *Principles and Practices of Teaching in Secondary Schools,* 3d ed. (New York: American Book, 1958), pp. 441–443.

[57] Wrinkle, *op. cit.,* p. 36.

[58] *Ibid.,* p. 12.

observed that when a first-grade child is asked what he got out of school, he will say, "I learned to read a story"; however, when the same question is asked of a secondary school student, the reply is likely to be, "I got a B." Learning is a sufficient reward for the first grader, while to the "more advanced" secondary school pupil it is the mark which matters.[59] Magnuson has decried what he calls the "pay check approach" to current marking, i.e., "overtime pay" for additional projects, "bonuses" for work handed in before the required time, and so forth.[60] The external trappings of scholastic success have replaced the inherent value of learning. This approach also reduces motivation to a jungle principle. *Fourth,* current marking practices intensify undesirable social competition. This attitude of social competition (as contrasted with self-competition) is basically anti-Christian. It encourages "mark-hounds." *Fifth,* in classes grouped heterogeneously by ability, current marking practices are at once unfair and educationally damaging. Slower students do not have even the slightest chance of achieving an A no matter how hard they try, while the brightest pupils can loaf their way to this mark. Intelligence tests, mental aptitude tests, and the growing awareness of the breadth of individual differences have destroyed the erroneous concept that any youth can learn as well and as much as any other youth if he tries hard enough. *Sixth,* current marking practices often produce deleterious psychological effects in students, particularly those who are consciously striving for marks. A study by Sobel of pupils who attained higher marks than their abilities seemed to warrant concluded that there was a greater proportion of neurotic personalities among them than in other groups of pupils. Suggested reasons for this included the result of overstrain caused by undue pressure and the attempt to seek satisfaction in school marks as a method of remedying emotional maladjustments.[61] *Seventh,* current marking practices often result in the partial or complete neglect of creative students. MacKinnon's investigation showed that good marks in high school may be unrelated to, or negatively correlated with, potential for creative performance.[62] *Eighth,* current marking practices are unjustly biased toward girls and away from boys. An investigation by Ryan and Davis exemplified the findings

[59] William H. Burton, *The Guidance of Learning Activities,* 2d ed. (New York: Appleton-Century-Crofts, 1952), pp. 151–157.

[60] Henry W. Magnuson, *Evaluating Pupil Progress,* rev. ed. (Sacramento, Calif.: California State Department of Education, 1960), p. 193.

[61] Frances S. Sobel, *Teachers Marks and Objective Tests as Indices of School Adjustment.* (New York: Bureau of Publications, Teachers College, Columbia University, 1936), p. 58.

[62] D. W. MacKinnon, "What Do We Mean by Talent and How Do We Test for It?" *The Search for Talent.* (New York: College Entrance Examination Board, 1959), pp. 20–29.

of nearly every other study in that "there is a consistent sex difference in favor of the girls with reference to classroom grades." [63] Reviews of the pertinent research studies by Carter, plus his own investigation, concluded that teachers in public high schools consistently tend to assign higher marks to girls than to boys despite the fact that intelligence and standardized achievement tests showed that the boys were equal and sometimes superior to the girls. Women teachers especially were found to discriminate against the boys.[64] Sobel noted that in the group she investigated, three times as many girls as boys received high marks, while two and one-half times as many boys scored higher in standardized achievement tests.[65] Greater docility, overdependence, neatness, and meticulousness have been cited as prime reasons why girls get higher marks. All these, of course, are unrelated to the achievement supposedly evaluated by the mark. Also, marks seem to mean more to girls; boys are often motivated by their interests rather than by external prizes or rewards (which marks have become). *Ninth*, a number of extraneous factors unrelated to achievement often have a significant effect on a pupil's mark. Thus, for example, an investigation by Magoon disclosed that the seating arrangement in a class has a direct and considerable bearing on the mark assigned by the teacher. Pupils in the side seats received lower marks than those in the center.[66] *Tenth*, marks are sometimes deliberately tampered with. Low marks are occasionally given to a student not because of inadequate achievement, but because the teacher thinks this will "challenge" the pupil. This is poor practice from many standpoints. A pupil, in justice, should not be given a lower mark than he has earned. Certainly Catholic high schools should not violate the virtue of justice. The joy of learning, and the curriculum, should constitute the pupil's challenge instead of some external punishment. Sometimes teachers augment the marks of their favorite pupils. Some Catholic high school teachers are inclined to increase a pupil's mark because of membership in the Sodality, or for frequent attendance at Mass. *Eleventh*, marks are unreliable, since some teachers and schools accord higher marks than others in identical courses. The multitrack system further complicates the situation. *Twelfth*, current marking practices admit of a great deal of subjectivity. This appears not only in

[63] F. J. Ryan and James S. Davie, "Social Acceptance, Academic Achievement, and Academic Aptitude among High School Students," *Journal of Educational Research*, LII (November, 1958), p. 102.

[64] Robert Scriven Carter, "How Invalid Are Marks Assigned by Teachers?" *Journal of Educational Psychology*, XLIII (April, 1952), pp. 218–228.

[65] Sobel, *op. cit.*, p. 21.

[66] Mayo M. Magoon, *Relation of Failure to Pupil Seating.* (New York: privately printed, 1932), p. 41.

academic scores but also in teacher ratings on coacademic trait check lists. Rothney has cited as an example a rating scale on which the following statements under the heading of "Responsibility" are supposedly arranged in descending order of excellence: "(a) Finds additional unassigned tasks after completing assignments; (b) Helps others in the class after completing own assignments; (c) Completes only work assigned to him; (d) Needs occasional prodding to get assignments done; (e) Needs unusual prodding to do his assignments." [67] Perhaps a is the best trait, perhaps not. It varies with classroom, pupil, and teacher. The pupil checked for possessing a might be a servile toady or a lopsided bookworm. The student checked for possessing c might have a healthy outlook on life, not neglecting his education for his studies, while the pupil marked d might have a very difficult home situation which often makes it impossible for him to complete his work on time.

Toward a Revised Marking System

Educators and teachers mindful of the great weaknesses in the current marking system, yet also aware of the importance of some sort of valid, concrete evidence of achievement, have been working on possible solutions. They have classified actual or potential marking systems into three distinct categories. The first type is that which is based exclusively on the degree of each pupil's achievement of a specified educational goal, e.g., a mark of 80 per cent supposedly means that he has attained that much of the goal. This is the traditional marking system. Its chief strength is that it provides a somewhat objective evaluation of the degree of pupil achievement; e.g., the student who received 90 per cent in typewriting is a better typist than the pupil who obtained a 65 per cent. Its principal weakness is that it is unrealistic in that it is unrelated to the ability of the individual student; e.g., the pupil who received a 65 per cent in typewriting may have perfectly achieved the learning goals which his intelligence and personality permitted, whereas the student who received the 90 per cent might be underachieving. Supplementary marks in effort, cooperation, and so forth attempt to correct this inequity to some extent. The second type of marking system is that which is based exclusively on the degree to which each pupil achieves that educational goal deemed appropriate for him. Individual ability is here the key. The chief advantage in this system is that it represents education in its highest form, viz., self-realization based on one's own capabilities. Its principal weakness is that it fails to give an accurate indication of objective achievement, e.g., a de facto superior typist who did not actualize her full potential

[67] Rothney, op. cit., p. 16.

received a 75 per cent, while a poorer typist who overachieved would get a 90 per cent. Yet an employer is interested in knowing who can type faster and more accurately.

The third type of marking system combines the first two, viz., objective achievement and achievement in the light of personal ability. This is called the "dual marking system" and is advocated by most forward-looking educators as the best overall method of marking. The recording of such a dual marking system is comparatively simple. The box in which the conventional mark is normally inserted is divided by a diagonal line into an upper and lower section, thus ⊠. The pupil's objective achievement mark is placed in the upper section, and the mark indicating his achievement relative to his abilities is entered in the lower section. Thus at a glance the pupil, parent, teacher, or employer can have a well-rounded, accurate, and overall evaluation of a student's achievement. Strang has suggested that prior to the introduction of the dual marking system, the school should schedule conferences with parents and community leaders explaining its details.[68] Fine has stated that there is a definite trend away from competitive marking and toward a system which takes into account the pupil's ability.[69] Public and Catholic high schools should begin at once to change to a dual marking system.

Meanwhile educators and teachers have been attempting to refine the objective achievement mark so that it will afford a more accurate picture of the pupil's precise level of accomplishment. The specific areas toward which educators and teachers have been focusing their attention include marking base, normal curve of distribution, group ability level, and course difficulty.

Marking Base. The two most common marking bases are the percentage and the letter. The percentage base consists of one of two types, viz., single numbers, e.g., 76, 84, 97, or multiples of 5, e.g., 75, 80, 85. The chief criticism of the single number percentage base is that while the results of specific measuring instruments might be this discriminatingly fine, evaluation is not. Thus some schools annually have a silly and embarrassing situation of declaring that Mary Smith is the valedictorian because she has a scholastic average of 98.24 per cent while Sara Jones is the salutatorian with the second highest average, 98.22 per cent. The use of multiples of 5 eliminates this extremely fine level of discrimination; however, such a system can be replaced by letters. The most common letter marking system is A, B, C, D, F, corresponding roughly

[68] Ruth Strang, *Reporting to Parents.* (New York: Bureau of Publications, Teachers College, Columbia University, 1947), p. 38.

[69] Benjamin Fine, "A,B,C of Grading Puzzles Parents," *The New York Times Magazine* (Nov. 18, 1957), pp. 33ff.

to the percentages of 100–90, 89–80, 79–70, 69–60, and below 60. Plus and minus signs are suffixed to the letters when finer discrimination is sought. Some schools have instituted two letters, viz., either P or F, or S or U, standing respectively for Pass or Fail, Satisfactory or Unsatisfactory. This two-letter marking system is too crude in that it tells little about the level of a pupil's achievement. Even the five-letter system has its disadvantages in that letters of themselves mean very little to parents and often to the pupil and the community.

Some educators proposed eliminating percentage and letter-marking bases and replacing them with appropriate teacher comments. However, it was soon found that these comments were highly subjective. Moreover, they provided no common base for comparing pupils because every comment was its own base. They also proved too time-consuming for the teacher. Bolmeier has advanced a compromise solution. He has advocated elimination of percentage and letter grading because they mean different things to different people and has urged the substitution of a five-point verbal standard which parents, pupils, and community will understand, viz., "Very High, High, Average, Low, Very Low." [70] This system would also solve the problem of those pupils who think a C is a low mark rather than an average mark, which it is.

Normal Curve of Distribution. Psychologists have discovered that human characteristics in a large average or unselected group will cluster around the central or normal performance and will taper off uniformly in the two opposite directions of greater than and less than normal performance. The normal curve is therefore a graphic chart of variability. Pictorially represented, it looks much like a slightly flattened bell. By translating Harmon's extrapolation of the standard deviations from the normal curve into Bolmeier's five-point verbal marking system, the result would be: *Very High*—5 per cent of the total number of students in the class; *High*—20 per cent; *Average*—50 per cent; *Low*—20 per cent; *Very Low*—5 per cent.[71] The students' raw scores are thus ranked in descending order and solely on the basis of percentiles placed in one of the five groups.

There are several disadvantages to a marking system based on the normal curve. It does not allow for skewed performance. Thus, for

[70] E. C. Bolmeier, Principles Pertaining to Marking and Reporting Pupil Progress," *School Review,* LIX (January, 1951), pp. 19–20.

[71] Francis L. Harmon, *Principles of Psychology,* rev. ed. (Milwaukee: Bruce, 1951), p. 22. Traxler, using as his Average the interval plus 0.5 sigma and minus 0.5 sigma, and continuing a 1 sigma interval toward either end, has established the following percentages for the five-point scale (starting with Very High): 7, 24, 38, 24, 7. See Arthur E. Traxler, *Techniques of Guidance,* rev. ed. (New York: Harper, 1957), pp. 233–234. For a clear explanation of standard deviation, see Thorndike and Hagen, *op. cit.,* pp. 95–100.

example, because of high pupil motivation and good pedagogical methods, a disproportionate number of pupils in a certain class might have scored *Very High.* Yet most of these will have to be relegated to a lower category because only 5 per cent of the class can score *Very High.* Also, the normal curve fails to indicate objective achievement, since rank in class rather than actual pupil attainment is the basis of the mark. Furthermore, in a homogeneous class which is skewed by definition, it is unjust to impose a system based on a random or normal sampling of the population. For these and other reasons, it is generally unwise for a marking system to be based on the normal curve of distribution.

Some educators have proposed the allowance of a latitude within each mark interval, e.g., *Very High,* 0 to 15 per cent of the total number of scores. However, this proposal still does not overcome the basic disadvantages of the normal curve's use. The pupil's mark should have reference to the pupil's own achievement per se rather than be made to fit into the predetermined pattern of a statistical curve.

Group Ability Level. Many alert high schools utilize a three-track curricular plan, i.e., the high-ability group, the average, and the low. Some educators have proposed that explanatory, supplementary letters be suffixed to the pupil's achievement mark (the upper box in the dual marking system). Affixed to the achievement mark of the high-ability group would be the letter *H,* and to that of the low-ability group, *L.* The reason for this proposal, which has been implemented by certain forward-looking schools, is that the quality of objective achievement of each of these groups varies considerably. In other words, a *High* or *B* in a low-ability class in terms of objective achievement would be a *Very Low* or *F* in a high-ability class. However, since the teacher must structure his content and methodology to the special needs and ability of each class, the pupils in the low-ability group must be rated according to their achievement of their educational goals. Furthermore, if the pupils in this group knew ahead of time that they would receive only a *Very Low* or *F,* they would naturally fail to be motivated and would quickly become disinterested. On the other hand, the achievement mark should mean something to the pupil's future teacher, to the community, to prospective employers. The letter-suffix plan is a good device for providing such information.

Some educators, such as Moskowitz, who do not favor letter suffixes, yet appreciate the importance of an objective achievement mark, have suggested that floors and ceilings be placed on marks in the classes of varying ability.[72] In such a system the high-ability group would never

[72] Samuel D. Moskowitz, "Guide Lines for Marking Procedures," *High Points,* LXIV (April, 1962), pp. 26–30.

be marked below *Average* or *C,* while the low-ability group would never be rated above *Average* or *C.* This proposal is quite poor since it destroys motivation, and even more importantly, the concept of structuring teaching to meet individual differences.

Course Difficulty. Some educators have suggested that the high school's courses be rated on a five-point scale of descending difficulty, e.g., physics would be a *5* course, home economics a *1* course. These numbers could be placed after the achievement mark to further enlighten the community and prospective employers. However, this solution is inherently unsound from many aspects. Who will decide which are the harder and easier courses? On what basis will this decision be made? What will be the rating of a hard course taught by an easy teacher? A basic issue is whether the ease or difficulty arises from native endowment or from the inherent difficulty of the particular course.[73]

Cooperative Evaluation. Smith and Dobbin, summarizing the pertinent research, have stated that there is a trend toward the involvement of pupils, parents, staff, and community in the development of a marking system.[74] Such a cooperative endeavor not only represents a realization of the parental and community's rights in education, but also produces numerous beneficial results in the practical order.

Marking in Forward-looking Schools. Some alert high schools have introduced team teaching (see Chapter VII). This new pedagogical system introduces certain testing and marking problems since one master teacher gives the large-group instruction, while other teachers conduct the derivative small-group discussions and activities. Therefore it is wise to use two distinct groups of evaluative instruments, one to assess the learning outcomes of the large-group instruction, the other to appraise pupil progress in the small-group discussions and activities. The two sets of results should not be merged into a single mark, but rather recorded separately in the appropriate boxes or spaces.

In communities sufficiently forward looking to make their high schools ungraded, marking and evaluation will still be done on the twin bases of objective achievement and achievement relative to the pupil's ability. The Trump Report has indicated that evaluation in this type of school will be made largely by professional decision of the teacher in consultation with the pupil and his parents.[75]

---

[73] See Sister Mary Janet, S.C., *Catholic Secondary Education: A National Survey.* (Washington: NCWC, 1949), p. 104.

[74] Ann Z. Smith and John E. Dobbin, "Marks and Marking Systems," *Encyclopedia of Educational Research,* 3d ed. (New York: Macmillan, 1960), p. 787.

[75] J. Lloyd Trump and Dorsey Baynham, *Guide to Better Schools.* (Chicago: Rand McNally, 1961), pp. 53–59.

Requisites of Good Marks and a Good Marking System

Every teacher should keep the following principles in mind when deciding a pupil's marks and when working with students, parents, staff, and community in revising and improving the current marking system:

1. The marking system should directly benefit the pupils and further their learning. This is by far its most important function.

2. The marking system should lead to present and future pupil self-evaluation. In other words, the marking system itself should be a teaching device.

3. The percentage, letter, or word symbols of the marking system should be based on an agreed-upon standard that is clear to all the teachers or markers. The school should have a definite written policy concerning the meaning of the percentage, letter, or word symbols. This will tend to reduce the problem, for example, of the autocratic teacher awarding a *Very High* in school citizenship to the pupil who in class is very quiet, overdocile, toadyistic, and who never manifests initiative or questions authority, while a democratic teacher rates this same pupil as *Low*.

4. The meaning of the marks should be immediately apparent to the pupil, his parents, and the community. Eliminating percentage or letter grades and adopting Bolmeier's five-point verbal standard will help to accomplish this.

5. The marking system should include specific evaluations for the more important goals of the school and not merely for scholastic achievement. This is particularly important in Catholic high schools where the pupils should grow in all the facets of age, grace, as well as knowledge.

6. The marking system should be such that it indicates both objective and subjective pupil achievement. Without this the marking system would be of limited validity, since it would not accurately assess *individual* pupil progress. The dual marking system should therefore be adopted.

7. Marks should adequately reflect a pupil's overall progress in the attainment of worthwhile educational goals. A pupil's mark should not be based solely on one test, but rather on weekly and if possible daily evaluations, including teacher-constructed tests. Furthermore, the final marks should not be considered isolated data, but viewed in the total context of other data, such as guidance information, anecdotal records, pupil and parent interviews. Marks in themselves are only partial indices of pupil progress.

8. Marks should truly mirror the pupil's achievement and not be tainted by subjective teacher likes or dislikes. College Board Entrance Examinations are tending somewhat to diminish the effects of prejudicial marks; however, this does not help the pupil who commences work after high school.

9. The marking system should be sufficiently broad in scope and range so that there will be a significant differentiation between the various levels of pupil achievement of the school's goals. This is vital if marks are to make possible meaningful comparisons. Bolmeier's five-point verbal stand affords a significant differentiation.

10. The marking system should directly benefit the pupils and further their learning. This is by far its most important function.

11. The marking system should discourage social competition while encouraging self-competition. The pupil should compete with his own record, not other pupils' marks. Sister M. Corita, B.V.M., has stated that the traditional socially competitive marking system constitutes a violation of Christian social principles, especially in regard to the virtue of justice within the context of individual differences. She maintains that only a revised marking system can bring about a desirable change.[76]

12. The marking system should foster pupil creativity rather than penalize it. The unusual ideas of students must not be suppressed by marks.

13. The marking system should be determined cooperatively by the teachers, administrators, pupils, parents, and community leaders.

REPORTING AND REPORTING SYSTEMS

The reporting system is that method which the school uses to provide parents with a reasonably detailed evaluation of the degree of their offspring's performance in attaining desired school goals. It does not have as its purpose the offering of this evaluation to students, as is regrettably the case in some schools, especially those run along autocratic lines. In those schools, the student is ignorant of his achievement until his parents show him his report card. However, in a school where sound evaluation techniques are used, he not only knows beforehand the degree of his achievement, together with his particular strengths and weaknesses, but also has mapped out with the help of each teacher a program of remedial work and further learning.

The form of the report to parents will vary, depending on the school's philosophy concerning its goal, i.e., intellectual, moral, or truth (see Chapter II). Schools whose goal is truth rather than a narrow, life-truncated intellectualism or moralism will provide evaluations for intellectual, social, attitudinal, spiritual, physical, and emotional progress. Schools whose goal is purely intellectual achievement will provide only for measurements of subject-matter attainment.

Types of Written Report Forms

There are three different types of written report forms, viz., blanks, checks, and anecdotal comments. The first type consists of a list of specific educational outcomes to be evaluated. Alongside each appears

[76] Sister M. Corita, B.V.M., "Report Cards Based on Christian Social Principles," *Catholic School Journal*, LIV (September, 1954), pp. 219–220.

a blank space in which the homeroom teacher enters the marks appropriate to each. Such a form is shown below:

Mathematics	_____
Problems in Democracy	_____
Effort	_____
Growth in Charity	_____

The second type of written report form also consists of a list of specific educational outcomes to be evaluated. However, alongside each is a series of five boxes, each one symbolizing a different level of performance. The homeroom teacher places a check in the box appropriate to each particular outcome. Such a form is illustrated below:

	VERY HIGH	HIGH	AVERAGE	LOW	VERY LOW
Mathematics	☐	☐	☐	☐	☐
Problems in Democracy	☐	☐	☐	☐	☐
Effort	☐	☐	☐	☐	☐
Growth in Charity	☐	☐	☐	☐	☐

The third type of written report form also consists of a list of specific educational outcomes to be evaluated. After each outcome, there is a space for several lines in which the teacher writes in his own words his evaluation of the pupil's progress.

The first two types have the advantage of being brief, clear, and reasonably indicative. Their chief disadvantage is that they are far too impersonal, and hence do not give the parents any more than categorized information about their offspring's progress. The third type has the advantage of providing the parents with tailored, individual, hence pertinent comments about the youth's achievement. Its disadvantages are that it provides no norm for pupil-to-pupil comparison (since teacher comments are subjectively written, hence not based on any standard); it is usually amorphous and does not indicate in a concrete way the pupil's level of achievement; it is often long and tedious for the parent to read; and its preparation consumes an excessive amount of the teacher's time.

Many schools are combining either the first or second type of written report with the third. This system either allows each subject or problem area teacher to write one or two sentences on the report form about the pupil's achievement or provides a larger space for the homeroom teacher to write a paragraph concerning the student's overall achievement. In any event, the teacher's comments, like his marks, should be accurate if for no higher reason than the fact that failure to be so will stir irate parents to visit the school and demand an explanation. Some teachers try to avoid parental confrontations by awarding excessively high marks and writing glowing comments. These are often the poorest teachers, who hope to mask their own instructional ineffectiveness. Forthright but scrupulously accurate marking and reporting should be one of the hallmarks of every teacher, since each pupil's welfare depends on these.

Principles of Effective Written Reports

The following are some principles of effective written reports to parents:

1. The report should be consistent with and indeed an extension of the educational philosophy and practices of the school. The forms used in Catholic high schools, for example, should reflect in all aspects the attainment of truth in its various manifestations, as treated in Chapter II.

2. The report should furnish information on the extent of the pupil's progress in achieving those goal areas which the school deems most important. Therefore it should include data not only about the student's learning of factual material, but also his growth in critical thinking, appreciation, creativity, understanding, effort, cooperation, growth in charity (in Catholic high schools), and so forth. This practice in no way minimizes subject-matter attainments but rather broadens them to include total development of the student in truth and the methods of seeking and applying truth. An uncooperative and uncharitable student might score a good mark on a religion test, but has he achieved the goals of this class? Some aspects of personal development which should be included on the report card are initiative, independence, resourcefulness, growth in charity, moral and spiritual development, courtesy, conduct, wise use of leisure time, pursuit of cultural and aesthetic interests, social adjustment, study and work habits, care and use of learning materials, reading skill, and participation in student activities. Placing these learnings on the report card and evaluating them will do much to focus parental attention on their importance.

3. The report should be comprehensive, definite, and specific. This is true for both personal development and subject-matter achievement. Rothney's investigation of report forms revealed that most of them used such personal-growth terms as "cooperation," "industry," and "citizenship" without ever defining them on the report.[77] Thus they were meaningless to the parents, and probably even to the teachers. Subject-matter achievement evaluations should not be lumped together, because this is poor from a diagnostic and even from a critical evaluative point of view. Rather, the achievements should be subdivided into their constituent parts. Thus, for example, under

[77] Rothney, *op. cit.*, p. 27.

the heading English ———, there should follow breakdown, separate ratings for: Use of Grammar ———, Skill in Composition ———, Understanding of Literature ———, Appreciation of Literature ———, Reading Comprehension ———, Reading Speed ———. Traxler's review of the research concluded that there is a trend toward rating the specific outcomes of a course and away from the assigning of only a single, omnibus mark.[78]

4. The report should be accurate; viz., it should indicate the correct appraisal.

5. The report should include not only objective pupil achievement but also achievement in relation to ability. Report forms must be personalized. A dual rating report form, based on the dual marking system explained earlier in this chapter, will include both levels of achievement. Some educators favor inclusion of rank in class on the report form. It has been found that while teachers' marks as assigned on the basis of current practice are often inaccurate, their ranking of the pupils in order of achievement is far more precise. Barnes and Barnes observed that colleges have discovered that a pupil's high school rank is a better predictor of college success than his high school marks.[79]

6. The report should be diagnostic, pointing to the specific areas of pupil strengths and weaknesses.

7. The report form should be prognostic. The report should not merely pass judgment, but indicate the specific areas where progress can be made and offer definite, concrete suggestions on exactly how the pupil can improve in these areas.

8. The report should provide ample space for appropriate teacher comments. These comments should be personalized, specific, prognostic; in Strang's words, they should "accentuate the positive." [80] Meaningless cliches, such as "Johnny is progressing nicely," should be avoided.

9. The report should be self-explanatory as far as possible, i.e., immediately understood by all the various parents in the community.

10. The reporting method and form should be developed cooperatively by administrators, teachers, parents, and community leaders. Each local school system and often each school will therefore have the same basic report form with individual modifications. This is important if each community is to truly determine the educational goals of its schools.

11. The report should be able to be prepared without placing a great burden on the teacher. Thus the report should not be extremely involved or unduly detailed. Clerical work should be reduced to the minimum so that the teacher will have enough time to teach. Forward-looking school systems not only give the teachers time during each day to prepare reports, but

[78] Traxler, *op. cit.*, pp. 237–238.
[79] Katherine F. Barnes and E. H. Barnes, "A Realistic Approach to Grading," *The Clearing House*, XXXVI (April, 1962), p. 477.
[80] Strang, *op. cit.*, p. 5.

also dismiss the pupils for a half day before the end of each semester to permit the teachers sufficient opportunity to make a good report.

12. The report should be an adequate reflection of the pupil's cumulative record folder.

13. The reporting system should enable the pupils to share to some degree in the writing of the report form. This will involve the pupil and thereby motivate him. Every pupil should be a partner in the educational enterprise.

14. The formal report form should be supplemented with informal written reports to parents both periodically and when the occasion warrants. Nor should these informal reports be made only when the pupil is failing to progress or when he has become a serious misbehavior problem.

15. The report should be followed up by a parent-teacher conference. A study by Sister M. Cyrena Harkins, R.S.M., concluded that a combined approach of parent-teacher conference and report card is more effective than only a report card in reporting pupil progress to parents.[81] This type of conference promotes increased parental understanding and motivates parents to cooperate with the teacher. It also broadens the teacher's understanding of the pupil. Besides, parents have a right to such a conference because of their preeminent role in their offspring's education (the teacher stands only *in loco parentis*), and because in both public and Catholic high schools, the parents are paying the bill. The school should provide time for parent-teacher conferences.

Toward Improvement

Every teacher and prospective teacher must ask himself if he is using or intends to use obsolete and invalid methods of evaluation, testing, marking, and reporting. If the answer is in the affirmative, he must get to work immediately to correct this situation.

[81] Sister M. Cyrena Harkins, R.S.M., *Comparison of the Merits of the Report Card and Parent-Teacher Conference in Reporting Pupil Progress to Parents,* unpublished master's thesis, Catholic University of America, Washington, D.C., 1961.

CHAPTER XIV GUIDING AND COUNSELING THE SECONDARY SCHOOL STUDENT

Nature and Importance of Guidance

Guidance is that assistance which the school gives the pupil to help him solve his special problems and to aid him in fulfilling his potential. It enables the pupil to discover his inner needs, to overcome his weaknesses, and to recognize his abilities and interests so that he may understand himself better and thereby intelligently formulate and plan both immediate and lifetime goals. Guidance endeavors to help the student achieve a healthy integration first among the various elements of his own personality, and then between this adjusted personality and his environment.

Guidance, therefore, is an integral and necessary component of the total educative process. It consists in more than merely a series of specialized services such as counseling, case conferences, or referral to the child guidance clinic. Guidance is also a point of view which underlies every relationship which any of the school personnel have with the student, whether it be in teaching, counseling, or even chance meetings in the corridor. Teachers must be always guidance-minded. There was a theory quite popular in the late 1930s and 1940s that teaching *is* guidance. Contemporary educators no longer hold this theory because guidance is now recognized to be more specialized than teaching. Nevertheless, there is still much truth in the old theory, since a guidance-minded teacher during every phase of instruction will give his teaching a guidance thrust; e.g., an English teacher will individualize an assignment for a student who wishes to become a journalist.

Guidance, like every other aspect of the school's program, is rooted in the educational philosophy of the school. Catholic and non-Catholic educators who hold to the intellectualist goal of the school (see Chapter II) maintain that no priority should be given to guidance in the school's program, since intellectual goals constitute the primary and all-embracing end of the school.[1] What guidance there is will be almost exclusively scholastic guidance. Those educators who advocate the moralist position hold that spiritual and religious guidance should be the principal and, to a large extent, the only necessary form of guidance. This explains why most Catholic high schools which are chiefly based on and organized around the moralist position have concentrated whatever guidance activities they may have on religious guidance while neglecting the other areas of guidance.[2] Educators who hold that truth is the goal of the school emphasize all types of guidance.

Guidance is important because it assists the pupil in making wise decisions regarding his personal life. Inasmuch as it affects his whole life in such a deep way, guidance can be considered one of the most vital and, in some respects, the most important part of the entire school program. Thus, for example, the religiovocational guidance which a boy receives in a Catholic high school that is instrumental in causing him to enter the Religious life or to become a lay apostle is of far greater consequence than his learning Caesar's battle strategy against the Britons. Guidance is necessary in education if the pupil's *entire* personality is to grow, if he is to become what Pope Pius XI hoped, viz., "the supernatural man who thinks, judges and acts constantly and consistently in accordance with right reason illumined by the supernatural light of the example and teaching of Christ, . . . the finished man of character." [3]

[1] Francis J. Kerins, "No Priority for Guidance," *Catholic Educational Review*, LV (January, 1957), pp. 82–88.
[2] Philip L. Stack, *A National Study of the Guidance Services in Catholic Secondary Schools*. (Washington, D.C.: Catholic University of America Press, 1958), pp. 155–182.
[3] Pope Pius XI, *Christian Education of Youth*, trans. by National Catholic Welfare Conference. (Washington: NCWC, 1936), p. 36.

The school which neglects to foster a vigorous guidance program because it thinks that academic knowledge is sufficient to solve all the student's problems is directly causing him to shift for himself during the difficult adolescent years. The knowledge of virtue of itself does not make a pupil virtuous. Thus Hightower's classic study of 12,000 adolescents concluded that there was little or no relationship between the youths' knowledge of right and wrong and their actual cheating, lying, or altruism.[4] The adolescent pupil needs more than knowledge; he needs continuous guidance of all types.

Despite the necessity of a well-developed guidance program, there is a great deal of evidence which indicates that both public and Catholic high schools are quite deficient in guidance services. A 1958 survey by the American Personnel and Guidance Association showed that in that year there were 22,330 guidance counselors in public secondary schools, of which only 6,290 or 28 per cent were full time.[5] Froehlich's 1951 conclusion concerning the level of guidance counselors is similar to that of practically every investigation from 1930 to the present; viz., "Surveys of employed guidance workers have revealed the great disparity between recommended training and that actually possessed by the on-the-job counselors." [6] A study by Wendorf revealed that only 14 per cent of 727 Ohio high school guidance counselors hold state certification for that position.[7] This deplorable condition is undoubtedly true in other states and communities. One cause is that sometimes the post of guidance counselor is given by the principal as a reward or "plum" to a teacher who has proved his value and/or servility to the administration. Somewhat more encouraging is Goedeke's investigation which disclosed that 73 per cent of public school systems over 200,000 had full-time guidance counselors in their senior high schools.[8] However, in 1960 the ratio of public high school pupils to guidance counselors was still a high 600:1.[9] This ratio is being gradually reduced. Most teachers

[4] P. R. Hightower, *Biblical Information in Relation to Character and Conduct.* (Iowa City, Iowa: University of Iowa Press, 1930).

[5] Cited in Warren G. Findley, "Student Personnel Work: Elementary and Secondary," *Encyclopedia of Educational Research,* 3d ed. (New York: Macmillan, 1960), p. 1429.

[6] Clifford P. Froehlich, *Guidance Workers' Qualifications.* (Washington: U.S. Office of Education, 1951), p. 8.

[7] Robert A. Wendorf, "Qualifications of Guidance Counselors in Ohio High Schools," *Personnel and Guidance Journal,* XXXIV (May, 1956), pp. 569–571.

[8] M. Thomas Goedeke, *Operational and Supervisory Practices in Large City Guidance Programs,* unpublished doctoral dissertation, George Washington University, Washington, D.C., 1957.

[9] "News From the Field," *Catholic Educational Review,* LIX (February, 1961), p. 133.

have little or no guidance training. The guidance problem is compounded in those metropolitan high schools in which there are double and even triple sessions, because such schools are thereby transformed into educational factories where a close teacher-pupil relationship is difficult to achieve. The Conant Report emphasized that public high schools are very weak in their guidance services.

The guidance situation in Catholic high schools is even more serious. Fr. Stack's nationwide investigation plus his review of the pertinent research concluded that "the public high schools tend to provide more guidance programs and/or more guidance provisions than Catholic high schools." [10] Guidance is usually carried out in a haphazard rather than a systematic manner. His conclusions are substantiated in a study by Fr. Vernon of guidance services in representative high schools of a Midwestern archdiocese. This investigation showed that the pupil's parish priest, mother, and friends were his primary guidance counselors.[11] No data are available on the exact ratio of Catholic high school pupils to full-time, trained guidance counselors, but it is probably very high.

There are some indications that public and Catholic school educators are beginning to seriously attack this guidance problem. There is an increased awareness that guidance services must become professionalized. In 1952 several professional guidance groups merged into the American Personnel and Guidance Association, a society to which all guidance workers and guidance-minded teachers should belong. Alert specialists and teachers subscribe to its official publication, *The Personnel and Guidance Journal*. However, by far the most important stimulus to the improvement of guidance services was the National Defense Education Act. This act provides for Federal-state financial assistance, on a matching basis, to any community wishing to strengthen the guidance services of its public secondary schools. The act also gives very generous college tuition loan assistance to students or teachers preparing to engage in or actively engaged in guidance and counseling in a public secondary school. Most regrettably, the act does not extend this financial benefit to teachers in Catholic high schools. The act also furnishes Federal funds for the establishment of Guidance Institutes by approved universities, both Catholic and non-Catholic. Tuition and stipends for attendance at these institutes are paid by the government to teachers engaged in or preparing to engage in public secondary school counseling. However, institute students from Catholic high schools receive only free tuition (they are *not* given the stipend).

[10] Stack, *op. cit.*, p. 182.

[11] John E. Vernon, *Guidance Received by High School Students of the Archdiocese of Omaha on Five Major Problems of Their Lives*, unpublished master's thesis, Catholic University of America, Washington, D.C., 1960.

A study by Fr. Blee indicated that there is a growing interest in professionalized guidance and counseling on the part of alert Catholic secondary school educators.[12] Some Catholic educators like Cribbin go so far as to maintain that guidance is *the* primary function of the Catholic school.[13] In 1954 the Catholic Counselors Association was founded. Its official publication is *The Catholic Counselor*. In 1962 the National Catholic Guidance Conference was established. The purpose of the Conference is to promote in-service training in guidance techniques on the diocesan level through local Catholic Guidance Councils. It is the hope of the Conference that soon every diocese will form a Council. Zealous laymen wishing to devote their lives to the Catholic high school apostolate would do well to specialize in guidance and counseling, for the need is very great.

Much remains to be done. Most states still do not require teachers to take course work in guidance and counseling. The Educational Policies Commission of the NEA has formally recommended that all prospective teachers take at least one course in principles and techniques of guidance.[14] However, colleges and universities must begin to make their guidance programs more orderly. Findley's review of the research on the lack of uniformity in those colleges and universities which prepare guidance workers concluded that "the lack of uniformity reported by [the students] suggests confusion rather than a healthy individuality, and there appears to be a need for the development of a set of standards by which our counselor training programs can be evaluated." [15] The educational programs in Catholic colleges are not sufficiently stressing guidance, and certainly some Catholic graduate schools are lax in the matter of providing broad and deep guidance programs. Finally, Fr. Stack's study concluded that in the ten years following World War II "very few, if any significant increases in guidance procedures were noted in Catholic high schools." [16] The situation is still very grave.

Principles of Good Guidance

The following are some of the more important principles of good guidance, whether it be given by the teacher, the guidance counselor, or some other member of the school staff:

[12] Edward C. Blee, *A Study of Professional Characteristics of Counselors and Guidance Workers in a Selected Number of Catholic Secondary Schools,* unpublished master's thesis, Catholic University of America, Washington, D.C., 1960.

[13] James J. Cribbin, "Guidance: Primary Function of the Catholic School," *Catholic Educational Review,* LIV (November, 1956), p. 508.

[14] Education Policies Commission, National Educational Association, *Manpower and Education.* (Washington: NEA, 1956), p. 92.

[15] Findley, *loc. cit.*

[16] Stack, *op. cit.,* p. 182.

1. Guidance should at all times be a learning situation for the pupil. Pepinsky and Pepinsky have observed that guidance and counseling are social roles, and therefore the primary function of the guidance person or counselor is to facilitate the student's learning.[17]

2. Guidance should be developmental. It should not be conceived of as merely a salvage effort, an attempt to rescue and rehabilitate "discipline cases." Such a notion has led to the neglect of pupils with normal problems. As Mortensen and Schmuller have noted, guidance should be directed toward "the optimum development of *all* pupils." [18]

3. Guidance should be preventive; that is, it should help the student with his difficulties before they develop into problems.

4. Guidance should be flexible. It must be adapted to all types of pupils and all kinds of problems. Also, it must utilize all the various techniques, such as group guidance, counseling, and so forth.

5. Guidance should further exploration. Johnson, Busacker, and Bowman have stated that secondary school guidance should foster a wide range of exploratory activities because in this way the high school pupil can learn to appraise himself more accurately.[19] Adolescence is a time in which the exploratory thrust is very strong. Hence the pupil will explore no matter what, so the school should be on hand to guide these experiences, to integrate them, to give them meaning, to tether them to worthwhile values.

6. Guidance should be distributive in the sense that each member of the faculty and staff should have his particular guidance role. Guidance is not merely the job of the guidance specialist.

7. Guidance should be continuous. It should start as soon as the student has been definitely accepted by the secondary school and go on steadily throughout his academic career and beyond.

8. Guidance should be immediate. It should attempt to solve today's problems today. When Martha confronted Christ with the problem of her dead brother, He did not answer her plea by merely telling her that her brother would rise again in some remote escatological moment, but He solved her problem *instanter* by raising Lazarus from the grave.

9. Guidance should be permeated with values. (This principle shows that Catholic high schools are potentially a richer source of good guidance than are public schools.)

10. Guidance should be professional. Teachers and specialists should have had pre-service and in-service training in educational psychology, guidance, and counseling.

[17] Harold B. Pepinsky and Pauline Pepinsky, *Counseling Theory and Practice.* (New York: Ronald, 1954), p. 142.

[18] Donald G. Mortensen and Allen M. Schmuller, *Guidance in Today's Schools.* (New York: Wiley, 1959), p. 10.

[19] Mauritz Johnson, Jr., William E. Busacker, and Fred Bowman, *Junior High School Guidance.* (New York: Harper, 1961), pp. 138–156.

11. Guidance should be based on a personal relationship between the teacher (or specialist) and the student. Without such a relationship, guidance degenerates into a supermarket approach.

12. Guidance should always be consistent with respect for the pupil. Every student has dignity as a human being and as a child of God. Therefore guidance must avoid any attempts at placing the pupil into a preconceived mold; it should avoid any kind of teacher coercion.

13. Guidance should promote pupil self-direction. It should assist the student in making *his own* choices and decisions. Guidance should not be a process whereby the pupil will be gradually conditioned to accept the advice of the teacher or specialist. Nor should guidance be viewed as a system whose object is to provide the student with a pat, ready, predetermined answer. Rather, its goal is to work out together an intelligent solution to a problem.

14. Guidance should take into account the whole student, especially his emotions, attitudes, and intellectualizations. It should not solely be directed at his actions, since these are the effects, not the causes.

15. Guidance should provide for individual differences. Therefore both group guidance and counseling are necessary.

16. Guidance should be based on understanding. The teacher or guidance specialist must understand the pupils from the perspective of both an adult and an adolescent.

THE GUIDANCE PROGRAM

The guidance program is the concrete, organized group of guidance services and pupil personnel activities within a particular school and school system. A well-developed guidance program is indispensable if the goals of the school are to be realized. The program must be organized if it is to be anything other than a series of unrelated and hence ineffectual activities.

Organized school guidance was first developed at the beginning of this century in the Boston public schools by Frank Parsons. At about the same time, Eli Weaver of the Brooklyn public schools recommended that the post of guidance counselor be created. Both men conceived of school guidance as consisting solely of occupational guidance. With the advent of the mental hygiene movement in 1909, the concept of school guidance began to widen.

Today guidance services include the following: *the testing service,* in which the student takes those types of tests which are designed to furnish him with additional information about his interests, abilities, or personality structure, e.g., a vocational interest blank; *the records service,* in which pertinent information about the student is recorded by various school personnel for future reference, e.g., cumulative record folder; *the information service*, in which the student can obtain any special type of information he likes concerning some problem or need, e.g., a list of Secular Institutes with explanations of each Institute; *the group guidance service*, in which the individual sees and resolves both his own problems and group problems within a group context; *the counseling service*, in which the student discusses his problems with the teacher or specialist and in so doing devises a satisfactory plan of action leading to the solution of these problems; *the placement service*, in which the student is helped to attain his proper role in a particular situation, e.g., what courses to take, assistance in obtaining a certain type of job; *the follow-up service*, in which the student is offered continual assistance indefinitely after graduation.

There are six basic criteria of a good guidance program. First, there should be a clear and specific definition of the objectives of the program. Second, there should be a delineation of the various aspects of the service, e.g., counseling. Third, there should be a variety of specialized roles, e.g., guidance counselor, school psychologist. Fourth, the program should be organized. Fifth, the program should be geared not merely to solve a pressing problem of present urgency, but also to uncover and solve latent or incipient problems. Sixth, the program itself should be periodically evaluated to ensure that it is functioning properly and meeting new, emerging situations.

On the secondary school level, there is considerable improvement to be made in guidance programs. Dugan's survey of American public high school guidance services concluded that "thus far, the organization of a [school] guidance program has been too dependent upon an 'educated' guess." [20] Fr. Stack's investigation concluded that "guidance services in Catholic high schools were isolated and frequently did not constitute a program of guidance services." [21] Similarly there was little or no co-ordination under a school guidance director. On the school system level, most public school systems have a system-wide director of guidance. Fr. Drolet's study revealed that 64 per cent of diocesan superintendents favored the idea of having a diocesan director of guidance. However, his investigation showed that there were not many diocesan school systems which actually had a director. Fr. Drolet recommended that public and Catholic schools establish communicating liaisons between their own guidance director and the system director. [22]

[20] Willis E. Dugan, "The Organization and Administration of Guidance Services," *Review of Educational Research*, XXX (April, 1960), p. 107.

[21] Stack, *op. cit.*, p. 181.

[22] Howard V. Drolet, *A Study of the Services Facilitating Guidance Provided by the Diocesan Superintendent's Office of Education in the United States.* (Washington, D.C.: Catholic University of America Press, 1959), p. 82.

Personnel in the Guidance Program

The guidance program involves the concerted action of various members of the school and system staff. The most important of these are the teacher, the teacher-counselor, the guidance specialist, the school psychologist, the school social worker, and the child guidance clinician. The teacher and the teacher-counselors are guidance generalists; the counselor, the school psychologist, the school social worker, and the child guidance clinician are guidance specialists.

The Teacher. The classroom teacher is the heart of the school's guidance program. It is he who, better than anyone else, knows the broadest range of pupils as they react in a variety of situations. Therefore all guidance begins with the classroom teacher, and in those schools in which the guidance program is weak, ends with him. Myers has observed that teachers must understand that guidance is not of necessity formal; indeed much of it is informal.[23] All guidance does not take place in an interview situation. Discussions after class with students, field trips, homeroom activities, democratic methods of teaching, individual attention in class as well as interviews are some of the very many ways a teacher can offer effective guidance. Strang in her writings has urged teachers to be constantly alert for guidance opportunities.[24] Arbuckle has stated that the teacher should not refer a student to the guidance counselor at the first sign of a disturbance.[25] This is shifting responsibility. Rather, the teacher should work with such a pupil until it becomes evident that the pupil needs more specialized help than the teacher is competent to offer.

The Teacher–Counselor. The teacher-counselor is a person who officially combines teaching and counseling duties. In many high schools the teacher-counselor is called the "grade advisor." The chief advantage of the teacher-counselor is that by being a teacher he knows the pupils better than does the guidance counselor. The principal disadvantage is that, because the teacher is largely responsible for both giving marks and maintaining classroom discipline, many pupils might not openly confide in the teacher-counselor, e.g., a student who has guilt feelings arising from cheating on an examination in the teacher-counselor's own course. Nevertheless, the overwhelming majority of modern educators favor the position of teacher-counselor. Thus, for example, the Commis-

[23] Florence C. Myers, "I Wish Teachers Would . . . ," *NEA Journal,* XL (February, 1951), p. 99.

[24] See, for example, Ruth Strang, *The Role of the Teacher in Personnel Work,* 4th ed. (New York: Bureau of Publications, Teachers College, Columbia University, 1953), p. 114.

[25] Dugald S. Arbuckle, *Guidance and Counseling in the Classroom.* (Englewood Cliffs, N.J.: Allyn and Bacon, 1957), p. 113.

sion on the Education of Adolescents of the Association for Supervision and Curriculum Development has officially recommended that "each student should have one [faculty] staff member who guides him throughout his high school career." [26] Notwithstanding, there is some evidence that the teacher-counselor is not as effective as he should be. Thus Caravello reported on a study conducted with a group of adolescents all of whom had graduated from the same public high school one year prior to the study. The investigation showed that these pupils thought that the guidance counselor was of far more help to them than was the teacher-counselor. Those areas in which the teacher-counselor's assistance was weakest were help with personal problems and choice of post-high school employment.[27] Not infrequently teacher-counselors lack adequate professional training in psychology, guidance, and counseling. Sometimes the principal appoints a personal favorite to this position without regard to merit or ability.

The Guidance Counselor. The guidance counselor is a professionally trained and certified staff member whose position involves only guidance services, with no teaching load. A guidance counselor is required to take a certain specified minimum number of professional courses in psychology, guidance, and counseling before the state will grant him certification. However, knowledge of guidance theory and techniques alone do not make a person an effective guidance counselor. He must also have a pleasing personality, be *au courant* with the students' world, and be understanding.

The guidance counselor should provide the following minimal services: (1) interview and counsel the students concerning their problems and difficulties; (2) help to place each student in an appropriate school or occupational level; (3) conduct case conferences and similar guidance procedures; (4) follow up graduates and dropouts; (5) maintain a guidance file for every student; (6) direct the school's nonclassroom testing program; (7) place at the disposal of teachers pertinent professional literature such as guidance research and reviews; (8) assist teachers in developing and improving their techniques of group guidance and counseling; (9) hold guidance discussions with the staff at faculty meetings; (10) work with the faculty in promoting programs and activities which further mental health; (11) initiate cooperative parent-teacher-counselor conferences; (12) work with the administrators and teachers in evolving a guidance-oriented curriculum; (13) develop and direct a

[26] Commission on the Education of Adolescents, Association for Supervision and Curriculum Development, *The High School We Need* (Washington: ASCD, 1959), p. 13.

[27] Santo J. Caravello, "Effectiveness of High School Guidance Services," *Personnel and Guidance Journal,* XXXVI (January, 1958), pp. 323–325.

school research program; (*14*) serve as a liaison between the school and the system guidance staff.

The lack of a sufficient number of guidance counselors in public high schools has resulted in less than adequate guidance programs. Fr. Stack's nationwide study revealed that "the counseling programs in Catholic high schools appear to emphasize incidental counseling [by faculty members untrained in guidance] rather than regular counseling on the basis of definite case loads with trained counselors as counseling personnel." [28] The National Education Association has recommended as a minimum ratio 1 guidance counselor for every 250 students. [29] Wrenn, expressing the opinion of most educators, states that the guidance counselor should have pertinent professional training at the M.A. level and beyond. [30] Certainly the guidance counselor should be a member of professional societies, such as the Division of Counseling Psychology of the American Psychological Association and, of course, the American Personnel and Guidance Association.

The guidance and disciplinary functions of the school should not be fused in one person, the guidance counselor. This functional confluence nullifies any possible deep permissive relationship between the counselor and the student, and hence seriously cripples good guidance. Unfortunately some schools fail to grasp this. Hill's and Green's survey of guidance counselors in public schools showed that some of these persons thought that disciplinary responsibilities should be part of their function. [31] Fr. Stack's investigation disclosed that in nearly two-thirds of the Catholic high schools surveyed, the disciplinary and guidance functions were performed by the same person. [32] A study by Brother Philip Harris, O.S.F., of over one hundred Catholic high schools in New York State disclosed that in two-thirds of these schools the counseling services were given not by a guidance counselor or other specialist but by the school principal. [33]

Some educators seem to think that the panacea for all educational problems lies in sending the pupils to the guidance counselor. The guid-

[28] Stack, *op. cit.*, p. 161.

[29] Conant's recommendation on this point merely reiterated the NEA position.

[30] C. Gilbert Wrenn, "Status and Role of the School Counselor," *Personnel and Guidance Journal*, XXXVI (November, 1957), p. 176.

[31] George E. Hill and Donald A. Green, "The Selection, Preparation and Professionalization of Guidance and Personnel Workers," *Review of Educational Research*, XXX (April, 1960), p. 124.

[32] Stack, *op. cit.*, p. 165.

[33] Brother Philip Harris, O.S.F., "Organizing the Counseling Program," in Stafford, C.S.V. (ed.), *Counseling in the Secondary School*. (Washington, D.C.: Catholic University of America Press, 1960), p. 15.

ance counselor is not the miracle man in the school. The teacher is still the heart of the guidance program, and the counselor can work only from there. The teacher should develop a close professional relationship with the guidance counselor. He should visit the counselor's office as often as time permits. This practice will facilitate that type of teamwork crucial to an effective guidance program.

Priests are indispensable guidance counselors in a Catholic high school. Certainly this function is more consonant with the priestly vocation than administration or classroom teaching. The spiritual relationship which priests automatically have with their children in Christ places them in a uniquely favored guidance position. Unfortunately not all priests in Catholic high schools are trained in guidance procedures or counseling techniques. Sometimes they feel no need of this special knowledge since they may have yielded to the temptation of believing their power to absolve sins can be extrapolated to a perfect ability to guide and counsel the young. As a result they are prone to give little more than practical, common-sense advice or abstract principles derived from Scholastic manuals, both of which offer scant help to an adolescent with personal, social, or emotional problems.[34] However, some forward-looking priests are now beginning to specialize in guidance. In any event, Religious and lay teachers in Catholic high schools should cooperate to the fullest with the priest guidance counselor.

The School Psychologist. The school psychologist is a professionally trained individual who does advanced clinical work and performs other highly specialized guidance services in schools. The school psychologist normally has had a deeper level of professional training than the guidance counselor, particularly in clinical and/or counseling psychology, while the guidance counselor has had a broader professional background, e.g., sociological psychology principles of guidance, educational philosophy, and so forth. The school psychologist customarily works in many schools rather than only in one. Usually he is a referral person to whom are sent students whose psychological problems are too complex or disturbing for the guidance counselor. The recommended ratio is 1 school psychologist for every 1,000 pupils. No public or Catholic school system has anything approaching this ratio, although most public school systems do have school psychologists. In Nassau County (New York), which includes some of the country's most advanced public school systems as far as guidance facilities are concerned, there were employed in 1955, 65 full-time psychologists, 17 part-time psychologists, and 14 part-time

---

[34] For a more complete discussion of this whole paragraph, see George Hagmaier, C.S.P., and Robert W. Gleason, S.J., *Counselling the Catholic.* (New York: Sheed and Ward, 1959), pp. 31–50.

psychiatrists.[35] A few Catholic school systems are beginning to hire psychologists, since as Fr. Drolet's study pointed out, some diocesan superintendents are becoming aware of the value of employing trained psychologists.[36]

The School Social Worker. The school social worker is a professionally trained specialist who works directly with the pupil, parents, school, and specialized community agencies, coordinating their efforts in order to assist the pupil. He is employed by the school system rather than by an individual school and is customarily trained as a social worker rather than as a teacher. His coordination efforts are facilitated because he is operating outside the structure of a particular school. The pupils with whom he works are referred to him by the guidance counselor. Alert public school systems are beginning to hire school social workers in increasing numbers.[37]

The Child Guidance Clinician. A child guidance clinic is a formalized psychological setting in which emotionally disturbed children are diagnosed and treated with professional care. The students referred to the clinic have problems too severe for the guidance counselor to handle but not severe enough to require hospitalization. The clinician-pupil relationship is a long-term one and involves depth psychology, testing, case conferences, psychotherapy, and similar practices. Despite the importance of child guidance clinics, only about 25 per cent of all public schools had them in 1955, according to a study by Abrahamson and associates.[38] There are no data for Catholic school systems; however, alert dioceses do have some psychological services attached to the diocesan Catholic Charities or Catholic Youth Organization. Costello and Casriel have recommended the establishment of central mental hygiene clinics serving several high schools.[39] Thus there would be several such clinics in every school system.

Teamwork. An effective guidance program involves the coordination of guidance and pupil personnel services both within the school and within the system. The guidance services should certainly be integrated with the home, the church, and the specialized community

---

[35] T. Ernest Newland, "Psychological Services: Elementary and Secondary," *Encyclopedia of Educational Research,* 3d ed. (New York: Macmillan, 1960), p. 1069.

[36] Drolet, *op. cit.,* p. 84.

[37] See Mildred Sikkema, *School Social Work Practices in Ten Communities.* (New York: National Association of Social Workers, 1953).

[38] David Abrahamson and others, "Status of Mental Hygiene and Child Guidance Facilities in Public Schools in the United States," *Journal of Pediatrics,* XLVI (January, 1955), pp. 107–108.

[39] Mary Ellen Costello and Henry H. Casriel, "A Mental Hygiene Clinic in a High School," *School Review,* LXV (Summer, 1957), pp. 193–203.

agencies. As Riccio and Brother Ignatius Roach, F.S.C., have noted, "A student's success in any educational endeavor is definitely related to the manner in which non-classroom influentials reinforce or go counter to the principles, attitudes and ideals expressed in the classroom. The many social forces operating in the community from which the school draws its student body more than outweigh the relatively small social stimulus provided by the school on the total development of the individual student." [40] Therefore the teacher and all the guidance personnel should constantly make use of community resources and agencies in every aspect of the guidance program.[41]

Coordination is also facilitated by the formation of a guidance committee, composed of administrators, the guidance counselor (s), teachers, parents, and community leaders. Some alert public and Catholic schools have such a committee.[42] Stoops and Wahlquist further recommend that a follow-up committee of school and community people be established to advise the counselor so as to ensure that there are no gaps in the follow-up guidance of graduates.[43]

Guidance should be coordinated with every other aspect of the school's work. This synchronization should especially take place with the curriculum, for many a guidance program has been wrecked on curricular rocks. Certainly the curricular design should promote rather than impede guidance. The Core curriculum (see Chapter VI) of all curricular types best fosters guidance for several reasons. First, it is centered around problem areas, e.g., racial injustice in place of life-abstracted subject-matter lines such as history, art, religion. These problem areas mesh pupils' personal, intellectual, emotional, and social concerns with what the school feels the students should learn. The very curriculum itself thereby becomes deeply integrated with guidance. Second, it provides for large blocks of time for uninterrupted classwork instead of the relatively short segmented periods of forty-five and fifty minutes. This permits the teacher to get to know each pupil better, a requirement for effective guidance. Large blocks of time also mean that each teacher will not teach as many students as in a subject-centered design, a fact which also facilitates greater knowledge of the pupils.

[40] Anthony C. Riccio and Brother A. Ignatius Roach, F.S.C., "Influence of Social Factors on the Guidance Program," *Catholic Educational Review*, LIX (October, 1961), p. 448.

[41] See Edgar G. Johnston, Mildred Peters, and William Evraiff, *The Role of the Teacher in Guidance*. (Englewood Cliffs, N.J.: Prentice-Hall, 1959), pp. 228–234.

[42] Norbert Riegert, "One School's Approach to Guidance," *Catholic School Journal*, LXI (September, 1961), p. 86.

[43] Emery Stoops and Gunnar L. Wahlquist, *Principles and Practices in Guidance*. (New York: McGraw-Hill, 1958), p. 206.

Third, it fosters a more permissive classroom atmosphere. Teacher-pupil planning, committee work, class discussions, and other pedagogical devices promote a classroom climate generative of good guidance and sound mental health. Authoritarian classroom climates sometimes associated with the subject-centered design actually promote pupil problems. Fourth, guidance is one of the bases on which the whole concept of the Core design is built. It is not brought into the curriculum, as is the case in the better subject-centered classes; rather the Core curriculum itself flows from guidance wellsprings.[44]

Both the individual school and the school system as a whole should provide continuous in-service education for teachers to help improve their knowledge and use of guidance principles and practices. The school can devote faculty meetings to guidance. It can also arrange for special conferences, demonstration counseling interviews, and guidance films such as *Counseling: Its Tools and Technique,* or *Client-Centered Therapy.* The school system should offer special courses, institutes, workshops, and supervised practicums in guidance. Public and Catholic high school systems should work closely with the professors of guidance and secondary education at nonsectarian and Catholic colleges. Priests working in Catholic high schools should participate in annual symposia on pastoral psychology, such as the annual joint workshop carried on at the Menninger Foundation in Topeka among the Benedictines of Atcheson and the Jesuits of St. Mary's.[45]

To be effective a guidance program must receive enthusiastic support from the school administration. Only in this way can there be accomplished such necessary things as guidance-oriented scheduling, the acquisition of specialized guidance personnel, school guidance workshops and clinics, and stimulation of teachers toward guidance.[46] Nevertheless, as Roeber, Smith, and Erickson have observed, the success of the school's guidance program ultimately "depends on the state of readiness of the school staff to accept, contribute to and utilize it."[47] Hence the remainder of this chapter will concern itself almost exclusively with helping the teacher (rather than the counselor or other guidance specialists) to improve his knowledge of guidance principles and practices.

[44] See Janet A. Kelley, *Guidance and the Curriculum.* (Englewood Cliffs, N.J.: Prentice-Hall, 1955), pp. 88–110; also Roland C. Faunce and Nelson L. Bossing, *Developing the Core Curriculum,* 2d ed. (Englewood Cliffs, N.J.: Prentice-Hall, 1958), pp. 195–197.

[45] See Harold C. Bradley, S.J., "Workshop on Pastoral Theology," *American Ecclesiastical Review,* CXLVI (May, 1962), pp. 327–330.

[46] Walter F. Johnson, Buford Stefflre, and Roy A. Edelfelt, *Pupil Personnel and Guidance Services.* (New York: McGraw-Hill, 1961), pp. 113–122.

[47] Edward C. Roeber, Glenn E. Smith, and Clifford E. Erickson, *Organization and Administration of Guidance Services.* (New York: McGraw-Hill, 1955), pp. 26–27.

Methods of Securing Data

Guidance data of all types are extremely important for careful, comprehensive, and thorough guidance. As Recktenwald has observed, "Counseling with inadequate data can result in dangerous decisions." [48] Guidance data must be as complete as possible and also readily available to all school personnel. Fr. Stack's own investigation together with his survey of the pertinent research concluded that Catholic high schools were clearly superior to public high schools to the degree to which they made their guidance records available to all faculty members. [49] Traxler has commented that "the value of personnel records is almost directly proportional to their use by the classroom teacher." [50] The more these records are accessible, the more easily they can be used.

Willey and Andrew have identified two broad types of information needed for guidance records, namely, longitudinal information which provides a picture of the pupil over a long period of time and cross-sectional which furnishes a multisource account and analysis of the present state of the pupil. [51] However, it must be remembered that too much data or overdetailed records can actually hinder guidance.

Educators disagree on whether guidance information should be made available to parents. Those who advocate withholding this information argue that the parents will not be able to grasp the significance of the information or will use it for undesirable purposes, e.g., neighborhood boasting about their son's IQ. However, it would seem that guidance information should be made available to parents. The parent has the primary right in education, a concept held by every American community and by the Catholic Church. The school stands only *"in loco parentis,"* and hence in justice has normally no basis for withholding such information. Therefore both public and especially Catholic high schools should work closely with one another, each assisting the other as much as possible in the guidance of youth.

How can the teacher secure guidance data? The principal methods are the cumulative record, the anecdotal record, the trait rating scale, the case study, sociometry, the autobiography, the diary, the standardized test, the questionnaire, the information-gathering interview, the referral, the parent conference, and the case conference.

[48] Lester N. Recktenwald, *Guidance and Counseling.* (Washington, D.C.: Catholic University of America Press, 1953), p. 109.

[49] Stack, *op. cit.,* p. 158.

[50] Arthur E. Traxler, *Techniques of Guidance.* (New York: Harper, 1957), p. 185.

[51] Roy DeVerl Willey and Dean C. Andrew, *Modern Methods and Techniques in Guidance.* (New York: Harper, 1955), p. 60.

The Cumulative Record. The cumulative record is a record of a pupil's overall progress and growth as compiled progressively since his entrance into elementary school. In short, the cumulative record brings together in one place most of the information which the school possesses about a pupil. It is not basically a bookkeeping device; rather its purpose is to preserve in one compact form pertinent data which will assist the school in guiding and otherwise aiding the pupil. The cumulative record folder for each pupil is usually kept in the homeroom teacher's possession. The better schools have a duplicate in the guidance counselor's office. The cumulative record, despite its critical importance, is a fairly recent educational development, having been initially devised in 1928.[52] In today's schools, the first place a teacher normally goes to locate desired data about a student is the cumulative record folder.

The cumulative record should contain data about the pupil in all the following areas: (*1*) personal, e.g., date of birth, sex; (*2*) home and community situation, e.g., father's occupation, number of siblings; (*3*) health and physical growth; (*4*) test scores and ratings, e.g., intelligence quotient, reading level; (*5*) pupil's set of values; (*6*) aptitudes, e.g., music; (*7*) scholarship ratings, e.g., marks, rank in class; (*8*) participation in student activities, i.e., "extracurricular" events; (*9*) work experience; (*10*) absence information; (*11*) special achievements; (*12*) interests and hobbies; (*13*) vocational plans; (*14*) personal and social adjustment; (*15*) anecdotal records; (*16*) pertinent miscellaneous information.

In order that a cumulative record system may be maximally helpful to the teacher and guidance personnel, it should possess certain characteristics. It should be (*1*) based on the school's educational philosophy; (*2*) so constructed that it aids guidance and instruction in the most effective manner; (*3*) comprehensive, i.e., include more than the pupil's scholastic attainments; (*4*) cooperatively formulated by teachers, guidance specialists, and administrators; (*5*) longitudinal, i.e., continuous throughout the student's entire school career; (*6*) readily accessible to all the faculty and staff; (*7*) available to inquiring parents; (*8*) decentralized and centralized, i.e., one set in the homeroom teacher's possession, another in the guidance counselor's office; (*9*) well organized, e.g., nonrepetitive; (*10*) concentrated, i.e., compressed into consolidated form; (*11*) visible and legible; (*12*) easy to prepare, i.e., not requiring excessive clerical work by the teacher; (*13*) cooperatively filled in by the teacher and pupil in the appropriate places; (*14*) contain the key to its interpretation when necessary, e.g., meaning of scholastic marks;

---

[52] Joan Bollenbacher, "Student Records and Reports: Elementary and Secondary," *Encyclopedia of Educational Research,* 3d ed. (New York: Macmillan, 1960), p. 1439.

(15) admissible of easy and repeated handling, e.g., stiff cards rather than paper; (16) durable.

The Anecdotal Record. The anecdotal record is a series of short statements by the teacher or staff member recording objectively a series of incidents regarded as significant in the observed life of the pupil. Contrary to the apparent opinion of some teachers, a good anecdotal record is not easy to make out. To be both valid and effective, every anecdotal record should incorporate the following criteria: (1) be primarily used in helping to understand the pupil; (2) record only important events which are pertinent and significant to the development of the pupil; (3) comprise a representative sampling of pupil behavior; (4) contain accounts of desirable as well as undesirable pupil behavior, since it is supposed to be a history, not an indictment; (5) be imbedded in the social context in which it took place, e.g., a socially disruptive class; (6) remain fairly short; (7) in a form such that other teachers and schools will readily understand what was recorded; (8) be an objective, factual description of the specific activity of the student; (9) record the teacher's or other observer's interpretation separately.

The last two criteria are of capital importance, else the entire anecdotal record will be rendered invalid. Interpretation must never be admixed with account, because then the account no longer remains the account, but becomes instead the teacher's version of the account. Thus, for example, the actual fact of a student disagreeing with a teacher's explanation might be recorded by an autocratic teacher as "Johnny manifested a disrespect for authority as well as rudeness in his question," while a democratic teacher might write "Johnny displayed critical thinking in his question." The teacher's interpretation is important, to be sure, but a subsequent reader of the anecdotal record will want to know where the pupil's behavior ends and the teacher's interpretation begins. Some suggestions will be of assistance in making the anecdotal records objective. First, record only what happened, not the impression of what happened. Second, record only what was actually observed. Third, keep adjectives and adverbs at a minimum, as these tend to be interpretative. Fourth, avoid emotionally toned or "color" words.

The anecdotal record should be written on a specially printed or mimeographed form. This form should provide for the inclusion of the following minimal data: date of observation; name of student; place of observation; name of observer or recorder; specification of milieu; objective description of the pupil's behavior; interpretative comment.

When should the teacher fill in an anecdotal record form for a student? Obviously it is usually impossible to do so in the middle of a lesson even though the event to be recorded has just occurred. Traxler has suggested that during the class and immediately following the event to be recorded, the teacher simply jot down the name of the pupil with a brief associative phrase. At the conclusion of the school day or during his preparation period the teacher can then fill in the anecdotal record form, using the pupil's name and associative phrase as a memory aid.[53]

The Trait Rating Scale. The trait rating scale is a list of specific kinds of pupil behavior graduated into degrees. These degrees are usually on a five-point scale. Thus, for example, an item on pupil concentration would be subdivided: "(a) almost immediately distracted, (b) short attention span, (c) average concentration, (d) long attention span, (e) intense absorption in work." The teacher is asked to check the box next to the appropriate letter or, in the case of linear scale forms, to indicate with a vertical line the place on the scale which best characterizes the student. The principal advantage of the trait rating scale is that it can be completed quite easily and quickly. It has four main shortcomings. First, it is interpretative rather than factual, thus admitting of the rater's personal bias. Second, lack of training in using a trait rating scale causes some teachers to rate too high or too low. Third, a central tendency in scores is quite common; i.e., most raters give median scores chiefly because they possess insufficient information about the trait to be rated. This can be offset to some extent by providing a "no opinion" blank next to each trait. Fourth, the halo effect is quite prevalent; i.e., the teacher who knows certain traits of a pupil will tend to rate him similarly for all traits. Notwithstanding these limitations which cause low reliability, a trait rating scale, if properly used, can supply helpful guidance data.

The Case Study. The case study or case history is a detailed collection of all the various data, past and present, school-related and school-unrelated, about a particular pupil. It is far deeper and more extensive than the cumulative record. Its purpose is to assist the teacher and guidance specialists in analyzing the manifold aspects of a pupil's behavior, ascertain the fundamental causes, and synthesize the results so that a positive, remedial course of action will become apparent. It affords the teacher a thorough and scientific approach to a student's problems.[54]

Sociometry. Sociometry is a projective procedure which assesses the dynamic interpersonal relationship among members of a group. It is a valuable tool for acquiring guidance data because it identifies those pupils whose peer relationships are such that their personal development

---

[53] Arthur E. Traxler, *The Nature and Use of Anecdotal Records,* rev. ed. (New York: Educational Records Bureau, 1949), pp. 17–22.

[54] Charles E. Germane and Edith C. Germane, *Personnel Work in the High School.* (Morristown, N.J.: Silver Burdett, 1941), pp. 129–130.

is being helped or hindered. The vehicle for sociometry is the sociometric test. This is a simple device by which a group of students are requested to indicate in order of preference a voluntary choice of a specific number of companions for a given activity. Thus, for example, the test would ask each student to name three members of the class with whom he would like to spend an idle afternoon. Each student will naturally select those classmates whom he likes best. The results of the test are depicted in graphic form. On the form, called a sociogram, pupils are represented by numbered circles (boys) or triangles (girls), and an arrow connects the choosers and/or the chosen. The results are then tabulated so that the teacher can tell instantly how many pupils were chosen by their peers, and in what order of preference. Most sociograms reveal that some students will be chosen by almost everyone, while others will be selected by only a few or none. The former are called "stars," the latter "isolates." The teacher should not reveal the results of the sociometric test to the class.

There are several things a teacher can do to effectively utilize sociometric data for the furtherance of guidance activities. First, discover the isolates. These are normally the students with social problems. The teacher should attempt to find out why they are isolates. Later he can employ such guidance procedures as placing an isolate on a committee with a star. Second, ascertain the stars. These pupils can be helpful in the teacher's guidance efforts. Third, watch for reciprocal relationships. Find their causes and utilize the results for small-group guidance purposes. Fourth, look for in-groups or cliques (indicated by arrows arranged in triangular fashion). This will show different factions and will indicate which students to approach and not to approach in a joint effort to help someone from another clique.

Sociometric data must be implemented with additional information. Thus, for example, a sociogram identifies the isolates but does not reveal the specific differences among them. Each isolate is different and thus requires a different form of guidance. Gronlund has identified five distinct types of isolates, viz., the self-sufficient, the withdrawn, the aggressive, the cultural, and the emotionally disturbed.[55] Stars and the average pupils also vary widely within their respective groups.

The teacher should give sociometric tests at various intervals during the school year. This procedure will enable him to detect the patterns of pupil social growth and will thus provide him with a knowledgeable base upon which to initiate his social guidance activities.[56] Gronlund's

[55] Norman Gronlund, *Sociometry in the Classroom*. (New York: Harper, 1959), pp. 289–291.

[56] Mary L. Northway and Lindsay Weld, *Sociometric Testing*. (Toronto, Canada: University of Toronto Press, 1957), pp. 4–5.

review of the pertinent research concluded that classroom grouping made on the basis of prior sociometric tests not only improved the social adjustment of individual pupils, but also the social structure of the whole group.[57] Other types of sociometric devices such as "guess who" tests, friendship scales, and social distance scales should also be utilized. Sociometry has tremendous potential in the guidance program and should be used more extensively by public and Catholic high school teachers.

The Autobiography. The autobiography is the story of the pupil's life written by himself. Like sociometry, it is a projective device. Autobiographies may be either structured or unstructured. A structured autobiography requires the student to follow an organized outline, e.g., school history, home life, etc., and tends to be more like a questionnaire. An unstructured autobiography is one in which the pupil is merely instructed to write his life history. The unstructured autobiography is the more truly projective device and tends to reveal to a greater degree the personality and values of the student.

The teacher using the autobiography as a guidance technique should look for the following things in the pupil's account of himself: (1) General tone. Is the pupil apathetic, enthusiastic, imaginative, egotistic, sensitive? (2) Facts stressed. Which series of events consumes the most emphasis, e.g., happy experiences, play experiences, religious experiences? This furnishes an insight into what is important to the student. (3) Details omitted. What significant details should normally have been mentioned but were omitted, e.g., father's alcoholism, brother's death? (4) Facts distorted. Which events or details were reshaped, e.g., an unpopular boy who writes that he is enjoying a vibrant social life? (5) Values expressed. What does the pupil prize and hold dear, e.g., love of family, need to excel, desire to serve God and man? (6) Defense mechanisms. What problems is he attempting to bury, e.g., rationalization of a weak spiritual life?

The teacher should place some, but only a limited, stress on handwriting, neatness, and spelling as evinced in the autobiography. The internal manifestations are the important elements.

The Diary. The diary is a daily account of his life written by the student. Some adolescents keep a diary in which they reveal their innermost thoughts, absorptions, and interests. Diaries are especially popular with teen-age girls. A teacher who has a personal relationship of trust with the student can perhaps encourage the student to show him the diary. However, utmost caution and discretion must be exercised because this practice can easily degenerate into snooping, prying, and vain

[57] Gronlund, *op. cit.*, p. 16.

curiosity, particularly on the part of women teachers. Often it is wiser for the school to restrict diary perusal to the guidance specialists. In no instance should the teacher open the pupil's diary (or his letters, for that matter) without his consent. This is especially important in Catholic and other private boarding high schools.

The Standardized Test. The standardized test is one which has been composed by a group of experts and has been extensively pretested for a period of years on large groups of students. There are many standardized tests which are of great assistance in obtaining guidance data, e.g., the Minnesota Multiphasic Personality Inventory and the Mooney Problem Check List, High School Form.[58] Test results should not be regarded as isolated data but rather as related to the pupil's other in-school and life experiences. Considered in this way, the test results will gain in meaning and significance.[59] The administration and interpretation of these tests are customarily done by the guidance specialists; however, the teacher should keep apprised of the results. High schools should make more extensive use of guidance-directed standardized tests. Fr. Drolet's study concluded that "Catholic secondary schools lag far behind Catholic elementary schools in being participants in the uniform diocesan testing program." [60]

The Questionnaire. The questionnaire is a printed device which asks the pupil to indicate specific information which the school regards as important for the guidance of students, e.g., home study conditions, work experience, further educational plans. It is from the questionnaire that the school and the teacher receive their first guidance leads about the pupil. As a supplement to the regular school questionnaire, the teacher should ask the students to fill in additional information blanks which he himself has specially composed. A skillfully devised questionnaire can uncover many promising guidance leads.

The Information-gathering Interview. The information-gathering interview is a conference between pupil and teacher for the purpose of eliciting specific desired data from the pupil. This type of interview is especially helpful in obtaining data not asked for in the questionnaire or in getting a more complete picture of incomplete or fragmentary data, e.g., home conditions. The teacher should utilize the interview as a guidance procedure, and not as a vehicle to extract information from the student for curiosity's sake. Nor should the teacher turn the inter-

---

[58] For information on the various types of standardized tests available, see Oscar K. Buros (ed.), *The Fifth Mental Measurements Yearbook.* (Highland Park, N.J.: Gryphon, 1959).

[59] See Robert L. Thorndike and Elizabeth Hagen, *Measurement and Evaluation in Psychology and Education.* (New York: Wiley, 1955), p. 498.

[60] Drolet, *op. cit.*, p. 83.

view into an inquisition. The information-gathering interview should proceed according to the outline of the interview report, which lists spaces for responses to planned questions, e.g., "What precisely do you think is causing you difficulty in studying English?"

The Referral. The referral is the notification sent to a teacher or some other school person about a pupil who needs guidance or other special assistance. The referral helps to identify problems which might otherwise be unknown to the teacher. Referrals to the teacher may come from many sources, viz., guidance counselor, parent, community agency, or other pupils. These different people should be encouraged to make referrals to the teacher or guidance specialists. The importance of referrals should not be minimized. Studies have shown that quiet pupils have problems also, many of them serious.[61] Such students are frequently overlooked by the teacher because they seldom become overt misbehavior problems. A referral often is the first step in identifying and solving the problems of these students. Also, teachers should make referrals to the guidance counselor, using a specially printed form. These referrals should be objective statements and comments, not exaggerations of misconduct or problems. Hoyt and Laughary's investigation revealed that in Iowa secondary schools, guidance counselors were not adequately utilizing available referral sources.[62] This condition could probably be generalized validly to most American public and Catholic high schools.

The Parent Conference. The parent conference is an interview between the teacher and the pupil's father and/or mother. This conference is a very helpful guidance device because it provides the teacher with an insight into the pupil's problems otherwise impossible to attain. Who knows the pupil's background and personality better than do his parents? An NEA study showed that 99.2 per cent of all public school teachers surveyed thought that teacher-parent conferences were important guidance vehicles, but only 40 per cent of these teachers made use of this practice.[63] In Catholic high schools the percentage may be lower. To secure the greatest parental cooperation and help, the teacher should utilize effective guidance techniques in the very teacher-parent conference itself, as Sister M. Gabrieline, I.H.M., has advocated.[64] Some

[61] See John W. M. Rothney, *The High School Student.* (New York: Holt, 1953), pp. 177–243.

[62] Kenneth B. Hoyt and John W. Laughary, "Acquaintance with and Use of Referral Sources by Iowa Secondary School Counselors," *Personnel and Guidance Journal,* XXXVI (February, 1958), pp. 388–391.

[63] "Teachers View Public Relations," *NEA Research Bulletin,* XXXVII (April, 1959), pp. 35–40.

[64] Sister M. Gabrieline, I.H.M., "Techniques in Interviewing Parents," *Catholic School Journal,* LV (April, 1955), pp. 113–114.

of these conferences should definitely take place in the pupil's home. Often this tells more than words can.

The Case Conference. The case conference is a group meeting of teachers, guidance staff, parents, and members of pertinent community agencies to pool their information, share their insights, and collectively discuss the problems of one individual student. The case conference is a dynamic learning situation because each member of the group learns something additional, gains a new viewpoint of the particular student.[65] Thus one person's necessarily restricted view of the student broadens into a total picture of him, a picture which not only amplifies but often radically alters a prior personal judgment; e.g., the history teacher alleges that a certain boy is an overt misbehavior problem, while the art teacher says he is extremely creative, the guidance counselor states he is emotionally sensitive, the parent notes he has been working to augment the family income while the father is sick, and the boy's employer declares he is a very responsible worker. Margolin and Williamson have commented that despite the fact that the case conference has long been recognized as a sound guidance procedure, it has been used only to a limited extent in schools. This is regrettable for two reasons; first, because the school setting is perhaps the most fertile area for uncovering and treating pupil problems, and second, because it offers unlimited possibilities even when school personnel are untrained in guidance techniques.[66] Psychologists, psychiatrists, and social workers have been utilizing the case conference in their hospital and community work for a long time.

GROUP GUIDANCE

Group guidance is that given to a group of students rather than to an individual pupil personally. The pupil's psychosocial needs (see Chapter XII) make group guidance not only desirable but in fact necessary. Group guidance has a three-pronged objective. First, the group can attack some problem which either most of the members of the group or the group qua group face. Since it is a group problem, it should be pondered and solved by the group, not by some individual. Second, the group can act in concert to help a peer solve his problem. This procedure is beneficial both to the group and to the individual. It gives the group new understanding about and insights into the prob-

---

[65] See Strang, *op. cit.*, pp. 443–451; also Los Angeles County Community Coordinating Council, *Manual for Case Conference Committees.* (Los Angeles, Calif.: The Council, 1956).

[66] Reuben J. Margolin and Albert C. Williamson, *Case Conferences in Education.* (Boston: Humphries, 1961), p. 11.

lems of others and reinforces the principle of group responsibility toward the individual person. (The obvious relation of this principle to the operation of the Mystical Body heightens the importance of utilizing group guidance in a Catholic high school.) Also it helps the individual pupil, since it gives him concrete evidence that the group is friendly and wishes to help *him*. Man is a social animal and craves the help of his fellow men. The Alcoholics Anonymous have implemented this principle with celebrated effectiveness. Third, the teacher can dispense information of interest to the group; e.g., job opportunities could be shown in a film on religious vocations.

To be effective in group guidance, the teacher must understand adolescents and their world from within that world. The teacher must be related to that world. In the words of Sister Mary Xavier, O.S.U., the teacher "must project himself into the adolescent world." [67] Pope Pius XII observed that every teacher, especially every Catholic teacher must be "a child of his own era . . . not something apart from the life led in his own country today." [68] There are some non-Catholic as well as Catholic teachers, however, who hold the opposite opinion. Thus Sister M. Vernice, S.N.D., has contended that reading "frivolous stories in magazines" would open the mind of the Religious teacher "to the contamination of the world." [69] But good guidance is impossible unless the teacher knows and understands the adolescent and his world, however "contaminated" it might seem to appear. This knowledge and understanding cannot be gained unless the teacher experiences in some measure what the adolescent is experiencing. This is the great pedagogical teaching of the Incarnation, the total plunging into the milieu. Guidance should be Incarnational, never Jansenistic.

In group guidance, the pupils should be the ones who determine which problems are to be discussed. After all, guidance is supposed to help them with their actual problems, rather than with the problems the teacher *thinks* they have. A climate of free expression is absolutely essential in a group guidance situation. Unless the pupils sense a permissive atmosphere, they will not reveal either their problems or their feelings. Hence the teacher must studiously avoid all forms of autocracy and authoritarianism. Moreover, as Gordon has observed, the teacher must encourage expression by the pupils not only of positive

[67] Sister Mary Xavier, O.S.U., "Fostering Security of Youth through Guidance Programs," *Catholic Educational Review*, LVIII (January, 1960), p. 38.

[68] Pope Pius XII, *Address to the Second Congress of the Italian Union of Secondary School Teachers*, Sept. 4, 1949, in Yzermans (ed.), *The Unwearied Advocate*. (St. Cloud, Minn.: St. Cloud Bookstore, 1956), vol. II, p. 76.

[69] Sister M. Vernice, S.N.D., "The Sister in Service and Her Reading," *Catholic Educational Review*, LVII (May, 1959), p. 296.

attitudes and feelings, but negative ones as well.[70] This release of hostility not only makes for a climate of understanding, but serves as a cathartic prerequisite to positive responses and action. In group guidance, the teacher should not lordly give *all* the advice, but instead ask members of the group to help as much as possible. After all, group guidance should feature guidance by the group.

Koile has noted that some school officials think the chief value of group guidance is to provide a short cut to a good guidance program. "They erroneously believe that they are getting an inexpensive and easily administered counseling program or an effective substitute." [71] Such a view almost totally misunderstands the nature of group guidance and its place in the overall guidance program. Group guidance, to be effective, must be purposefully coordinated with individual guidance, i.e., counseling. Certainly group guidance can never replace counseling, nor should it be an excuse for the absence of a vigorous counseling program. Besides, most group guidance is far more effective in classes having a low teacher-pupil ratio. The high teacher-pupil ratio in some public and most Catholic high schools hinders group guidance activities.

Methods of Group Guidance

The teacher and the guidance counselor should make use of the various methods in their group guidance relationships with students. There are five major methods which can be used, depending on the circumstances and exigency: discussion, sociodrama, multiple counseling, group therapy, and brainstorming.

Discussion. The nature and techniques of discussion were treated in Chapter IX. In that chapter, research evidence was adduced to show that discussion has a significant effect in changing pupils' attitudes. Attitudinal change is one of the most important outcomes of group guidance. Discussion also contributes toward creating a healthy feeling tone in the class. It also deepens the pupils' knowledge and understanding of the problems affecting different persons. The teacher should not always serve as the discussion leader; often good group guidance is furthered by use of a pupil panel or symposium followed by an all-class discussion with the panelists or symposiasts. The cell technique developed by Catholic Action theorists features problem-centered discussion revolving around the threefold steps of observe, judge, act (see Chapter IX). All these methods assist the pupils in solving their own problems, in attaining a spirit of self-direction.

[70] Ira J. Gordon, *The Teacher as a Guidance Worker.* (New York: Harper, 1956), pp. 223–225.

[71] Earl A. Koile, "Group Guidance: A Fringe Activity," *School Review,* LXIII (December, 1955), p. 483.

Sociodrama. The nature and techniques of sociodrama or role playing were also discussed in Chapter IX. Sociodrama was originated primarily as a guidance device. Developed by Jacob L. Moreno, it is based on the momentous effect which a person's role or totality of roles in interpersonal relationships has on both his actual personality and his own self-concept.[72] A person achieves healthy social adjustment when he understands and evaluates his own role in relationship to others and their role in relationship to him. Sociodrama, as noted in Chapter IX, requires that the participant in the role-playing situation switch for the duration of the sociodrama from his normal societal role to a new interpersonal role and act in a manner befitting his new role. Thus, for example, a student who in reality is very intelligent and snickers at the slower pupil may, in guidance sociodrama, be asked to play the role of a slow pupil, while the role of a brighter pupil is given to someone else. Or a shy boy might be asked to assume the role of the captain of the football team in the locker room at halftime trying to encourage fainthearted teammates. The sociodrama is an extremely valuable group guidance vehicle which should be utilized more by teachers.

Multiple Counseling. Multiple counseling is a small-group guidance situation involving three to ten students who work together toward the solution of some common pressing problem. Some of the more important characteristics of multiple counseling, as given by Driver, one of the principal advocates of this technique, include: (*1*) limitation on the number of sessions, usually based on the nature of the problem; (*2*) organization of the group on the basis of a common problem or need; (*3*) concentration of attention on problems of personal and social adjustment; (*4*) establishment of an intimate, permissive group climate; (*5*) use of the eclectic method of counseling; (*6*) utilization of social techniques, especially role playing; (*7*) self-revelations of group members encouraged but not required; (*8*) initiation and undertaking of group projects; (*9*) supplementation by individual counseling; (*10*) evaluation of outcomes and results by the group.[73]

Caplan's investigation into the effects of multiple counseling on junior high school boys who had severe problems with school authorities concluded that as a result of this guidance technique their social behavior improved significantly and their personal conflicts lessened.[74]

[72] Jacob L. Moreno, *The Theatre of Spontaneity: An Introduction to Psychodrama.* (Beacon, N.Y.: Beacon House, 1947). This is not his first book on the subject, but it is probably one of his best.

[73] Helen I. Driver, *Multiple Counseling.* (Madison, Wis.: Monona, 1954), pp. 19–34.

[74] Stanley W. Caplan, "The Effect of Group Counseling on Junior High School Boys' Concepts of Themselves in School," *Journal of Counseling Psychology,* IV (Summer, 1957), pp. 124–128.

Multiple counseling has many guidance possibilities and should be utilized as often as possible. However, because of the skill required, teachers without extensive background in guidance and counseling should not undertake this technique.

Group Therapy. Group therapy is much like multiple counseling, but with certain differences. First, there is usually no limit on the number of sessions. Second, the primary emphasis is chiefly on deep-seated personal conflicts. Third, it employs the non-directive method of counseling. Fourth, it is used almost exclusively in serious mental cases. For the last reason, group therapy should be conducted only by the school psychologist or psychiatrist or in the child guidance clinic.

Brainstorming. Brainstorming is a group attempt to solve a well-defined problem by offering *any* solution which comes to mind, no matter how wild, unconventional, or abstruse. No group member is permitted to criticize these ideas whether from "practical" considerations or for any other reason. Rather, the participants are encouraged to build on the expressed ideas or to synthesize them. The technique of brainstorming was developed by Osborn to unleash creative ideas. An advertising executive, Osborn discovered that very often a person's ideas and feelings were repressed to a considerable extent by a group climate which always halted creative innovations and thoughts by interposing prudential considerations and critical appraisals.[75] Brainstorming has proved highly successful in business and industry, where it is used with great frequency, particularly in the upper echelons. Teachers, too, can utilize brainstorming with great success in a group guidance situation. Often the pupils' creative insights and keen imaginative probings hold the key to the solution of some otherwise insoluble problem.

Doing Group Guidance

Group guidance can be done in a variety of settings, each of which has its own distinct advantages. First, the special group guidance period is a formalized block of time which is supposed to be devoted exclusively to some aspect of group guidance. Forward-looking high schools provide for the inclusion of one or two group guidance periods in their weekly schedules. Because of pupil readiness brought about by the formal designation of a guidance period, the teacher can do much to help the students solve their problems. Guidance motion pictures like *The Eye of the Beholder* and *The Quiet One* can be shown and discussed. Second, the regular classroom provides many guidance opportunities for the alert teacher. Exploration can be made a part of any course, e.g., a social

[75] Alex F. Osborn, *Applied Imagination*, rev. ed. (New York: Scribner, 1957).

studies class can inquire into the power structure of the community.[76] The learnings in each course should be related by the teacher and his instructional methods to the pupils' lives and problems, thus deepening education by adding the guidance dimension. Third, the Core class is an ideal setting for guidance. As Chiara has stated, "A [basic] function of the Core class is to absorb many of the guidance and counseling services into its learning activities." [77] The inherent problem orientation of the Core, which meshes the pupils' concerns with those learnings the school wishes the pupils to attain, provides the optimum curricular vehicle for group guidance.[78] Fourth, the homeroom should be used for guidance. The homeroom teacher, because of his very function, gets to know his pupils much better than do most teachers and, therefore, is in an advantageous position to engage in effective group guidance work. Also, as Brother Philip Harris, O.S.F., has observed, pupils in a homeroom feel that they are not only individuals but members of a group. This sense of identification is of great assistance in furthering group guidance.[79] Fifth, the activities program easily lends itself to guidance. A dynamic teacher working with pupils on activities, such as sports, social life committees, and commencement, can constantly take advantage of the innumerable guidance openings which these activities present. Sixth, the assembly programs can be utilized for group guidance, primarily of the informational kind. Outside speakers should be enlisted, particularly to discuss occupational, educational, and social problems. Students can stage guidance-oriented assembly programs which will benefit both participants and audience. Seventh, special guidance groups such as are formed for multiple counseling sessions can be of invaluable assistance in helping pupils with their problems.

INDIVIDUAL GUIDANCE OR COUNSELING

Individual guidance is customarily called counseling. Counseling may be defined as the relationship between two persons in which one of

[76] Robert H. Knapp, *Practical Guidance Methods.* (New York: McGraw-Hill, 1953), pp. 71–72; Hubert H. Mills, "Curriculum and Guidance," in Douglass (ed.), *The High School Curriculum,* 2d ed. (New York: Ronald, 1956), pp. 327–343.

[77] Clara R. Chiara, "The Core Teacher's Major: Youth," *School Review,* LXIII (November, 1955), p. 424.

[78] See Lucille L. Lurry and Elsie J. Alberty, *Developing a High School Core Program.* (New York: Macmillan, 1957).

[79] Brother Philip Harris, O.S.F., "Using Homeroom for Guidance in Personality Development," *Catholic Educational Review,* LVII (February, 1959), pp. 97–105; also Wilson Little and A. L. Chapman, *Developmental Guidance in the Secondary School.* (New York: McGraw-Hill, 1953), pp. 296–320.

them attempts to assist the other in attaining for himself some particular form of happiness or adjustment to a life situation. This attempt may be directive, non-directive, or eclectic. Each teacher should be a counselor and should provide individual guidance services to the students. A teacher who neglects to counsel his students is seriously derelict in his duty. Hereafter in this chapter the teacher in his capacity as counselor will be referred to merely as "the counselor." Consequently this usage should not be confused with the term "guidance counselor" or simply "counselor" as it has been used previously in this chapter or, as it is found in the professional literature, meaning one type of guidance specialist. The pupil in the counseling situation will usually be called "the client" or "the counselee."

Recktenwald, a Catholic guidance expert, has stated that "the purpose of counseling is to make the counselee increasingly more able to guide himself." [80] It is not the aim of counseling therefore to provide the pupil with a set of predetermined answers or to render him even more docile and dependent on the teacher. Counseling is a mutual learning process, a growth experience for both the counselor and counselee. [81] The teacher must recognize this.

Counseling is not therapy. Bordin has contended that the difference between counseling and psychotherapy is more quantitative than qualitative, i.e., psychotherapy delves more deeply. [82] Therapy is the province of the school psychologist and psychiatrist; it should not be undertaken by the teacher.

Counseling may be short-term or long-term. Short-term counseling is that which perdures only for a few interviews and sometimes comprises only a single interview. This type of counseling is useful in those cases in which the client only wishes information or has a small problem which admits of a relatively simple, easy solution. Long-term counseling is that which lasts over a period of many interviews, and is employed chiefly in cases involving personal, social, and religious problems.

Several factors contribute to the success of a counselor's work. Strang has gone so far as to say that the counselor's reputation is probably the most important single factor. [83] Certainly few students will seek guidance assistance from a teacher who has a reputation throughout

[80] Recktenwald, *op. cit.*, p. 110.

[81] Jane Warters, *High School Personnel Work Today*. (New York: McGraw-Hill, 1956), p. 172.

[82] Edward S. Bordin, *Psychological Counseling*. (New York: Appleton-Century-Crofts, 1955), p. 14.

[83] Ruth Strang, *Counseling Technics in College and Secondary School*, rev. ed. (New York: Harper, 1949), p. 121.

the school for playing favorites or for being autocratic. The counselor must inspire confidence so that, as Sister Jeanne Francis, S.P., has remarked, the client will gain the courage to face his problems and make decisions for himself.[84] Confidence on the counselor's part is easily transferred by the student to his own thoughts and actions. The counselor should know and understand his clients, the adolescent pupils. What Bishop Temuco said to his Chilean priests applies directly to counselors, viz., "We are not doing enough. More than as disbursers of charity help, which is not sufficient, the working people want to see us defend their rights, fight for justice, and even more, share their privations and humiliations." [85] The counselor must be Incarnational, immerse himself totally in the students' world. This is especially important for Religious. The counselor should have a pleasing personality. He should have a clear perception of values, recognizing that some values are eternal while many others are dynamic, changing, and relative. A counselor should have achieved a sound psychological adjustment in his own life. He should possess a good knowledge of the principles and techniques of counseling. Some teachers seem to have reshaped the famous Cartesian axiom into their own maxim of "I exist, therefore I can counsel skillfully." Preservice training in counseling procedures should be augmented by continuous in-service work. Reading annotated transcripts of interviews, participating in counseling workshops, and attending appropriate graduate level courses are very helpful to the conscientious teacher.[86] The counselor should also develop human relations skills. Similarly he must remember that the pupil with a problem is coming into the interview with an intertwined combination of intellectualizations and emotionalizations. Hence he must react to the client not only with his intellect, but with his emotions as well. Finally, a deep sense of professional ethics should characterize the counselor. He must never reveal what was said to him in confidence, e.g., reporting to a teacher that a certain student told him that he was cheating, or disclosing to the administration the identity of a school thief who bared his guilt feelings in a counseling interview. In Catholic schools the counselor should recommend to this type of client that he see a sympathetic, knowledgeable priest.

[84] Sister Jeanne Francis, S.P., "Counseling: Prescription for Yesterday's Ills," *Catholic School Journal*, LXI (January, 1961), pp. 48–49.

[85] "Bishop Instructs Chilean Priests on Needed Reforms," *Catholic Transcript*, (Mar. 8, 1962), p. 1.

[86] Edgar L. Harden, "Stimulating Faculty Growth," in Erickson (ed.), *A Basic Text for Guidance Workers*. (Englewood Cliffs, N.J.: Prentice-Hall, 1947), pp. 400–412.

Counseling Theories

The method or technique which a counselor uses in the interview will be determined by the particular counseling theory to which he subscribes. A knowledge of the contrasting theories is, therefore, a prerequisite to effective counseling. There are three principal counseling theories, viz., directive, non-directive, and eclectic.

The Directive Theory. The directive theory of counseling is the oldest and most familiar of the three guidance approaches. It still has many advocates today, with E. G. Williamson being perhaps its most celebrated champion.

A. CHARACTERISTICS. Directive counseling is a formal process devised by the counselor whereby the client's problem is identified by the counselor and solved principally by him in the shortest possible amount of time. The interview is highly structured by the counselor. Emphasis is placed on counselor identification and solution of the client's problem, the assumption being that if the client could do either, he would not be seeking assistance; in fact he would have no problem. Directive counseling seeks to help the client to solve his problems eventually, but not now (this is what the counselor is supposed to do in order to help the client in his present weakened state). Directive counseling, as Williamson has repeatedly stated, is an information-giving process.

B. THEORETICAL BASES. There are at least seven distinct theoretical bases of directive counseling: (1) The client possesses neither the means nor the ability to identify and/or solve the problem for himself, else why does he need the counselor's assistance? (2) the counselor, therefore, should identify the client's problem and offer him a solution; (3) the counseling process should be conducted on an intellectual plane, such as giving information or advice, since this is what the client needs to solve his problem; (4) the counselor, by virtue of his professional training, knows the proper information and advice to offer the client; (5) the counselor must take much if not most of the responsibility for the client's decision making; (6) the counselor should carefully control the interview so that only ideas and data pertinent to the problem are discussed; (7) the counselor must have at his disposal as much data and as many records as possible relating to the client so that he will be familiar with the client and can be in a position to offer pertinent contextual advice.

C. PROCEDURES. There are six essential steps which a counselor must take in his total relationship with the client: (1) analysis of data concerning the student; (2) synthesis of data into a meaningful, total picture showing pupil strengths and weaknesses; (3) diagnosis of the client's problem on the basis of this analysis and synthesis; (4) prognosis or determination of the future course of the problem and possible methods for its solution; (5) interview with the client; (6) follow-up or evaluation to assist the pupil after the termination of the counseling situation.[87] The extent to which the directive approach is counselor-centered can be easily seen from the fact that it is not until the fifth step of the process that the counselor first encounters the client. Williamson has delineated five specific procedures used by the directive counselor during this interview step: first, establishing rapport; second, cultivating self-understanding; third, advising or planning a program of action; fourth, carrying out the plan; fifth, referring the student to another personnel worker for assistance if necessary.[88]

D. WEAKNESSES. The directive theory of counseling has the following weaknesses: (1) It tends to render the client passive in the interview and thereby to inhibit his learning, a process which demands pupil mental self-activity; (2) its highly structured approach tends to clamp the client in a closed-ended psychological vise, limiting the free expression and release of his ideas and attitudes; (3) its emphasis on information presentation by the counselor leaves little room for extended emotional discharge by the client; (4) it tends to weaken the client's self-direction while at the same time promoting overdependence on others for the solution of his problems; (5) it can easily degenerate into an autocratic situation where the counselor imposes his solution on the client; (6) it tends to minimize the client's psychological independence and integrity; (7) it encourages a situation in which the counselor has an overly facile solution all prepared to be dispensed like a pill to the client before the latter even comes in for the first interview; (8) it fails to recognize that solutions arrived at by the client are more lasting and are more easily transferred into action than those presented externally by the counselor.

The Non-directive Theory. The non-directive theory of counseling is quite modern and represents an outflowing from psychoanalytic theory and phenomenological psychology. Otto Rank may be considered its forerunner, and Carl R. Rogers its most important exponent.

A. CHARACTERISTICS. Non-directive counseling, sometimes called client-centered counseling, is an unstructured process whereby the client completely by and for himself gains insight into his problem and then solves it. The course and direction of the interview are totally

[87] E. G. Williamson and J. G. Darley, *Student Personnel Work.* (New York: McGraw-Hill, 1937), p. 168.

[88] E. G. Williamson, *Counseling Adolescents.* (New York: McGraw-Hill, 1950), p. 224.

determined by the client. Normally the entire counseling relationship lasts for a fairly long period of time. The basic principle underlying this theory is that only the client can gain significant and true insights into the nature of the problem, and only he can really solve it. Any advice by the counselor is ineffectual in the deepest sense. The client is helped not by the suggestions of the counselor, "but by the *actual experience* he undergoes, in terms of *feeling* and *willing. He* must be the central figure, not the counselor." [89] To facilitate this liberational experience, a completely permissive and free climate must pervade the counseling relationship so that thereby the client is encouraged to realize himself by himself. The counselor refrains from giving any advice, since the crux of the client's problem is not an inability to perceive the solution, but rather the necessity of his overcoming those emotional and attitudinal blocks which prevent him from seeing the solution. The counselor avoids any criticism or even comment on whatever attitudes, feelings, or ideas the client expresses, no matter how opposed they are to reality or to the counselor's own viewpoint. Rogers has maintained that every person has within him an urge, a powerful tendency, to self-direction and self-regulation and that the sole task of the counselor is to help the client liberate this urge.[90] The counseling process does not begin until the individual has a desire to be helped.

B. THEORETICAL BASES. There are at least seven distinct theoretical bases of non-directive counseling (paralleling the bases of the directive approach): (1) The client possesses within himself the sole means of identifying and solving his problem; (2) the counselor, therefore, should assist the client to utilize his self-directional force to solve his problem for himself; (3) the counseling process should be conducted chiefly on an emotional plane since it is a poor emotional or feeling-laden attitudinal adjustment which is blocking the client from insight into and solution of his problem; (4) the counselor does not know what advice to give because only the client really knows and experiences his own personal problem and conflicts; (5) only the client can assume full responsibility for himself and his decision making; (6) The counselor should in no way control the interview, so that the client will feel free to discuss permissively any feelings or attitudes he desires, no matter how abstruse or opposed to the counselor's beliefs; (7) records about the client are useless because the key to the solution of

[89] Charles A. Curran, *Counseling in Catholic Life and Education.* (New York: Macmillan, 1952), p. 46.

[90] Carl R. Rogers, "Lessons Learned in Counseling," in Dugan (ed.), *Counseling Points of View.* (Minneapolis: University of Minnesota Press, 1959), p. 25.

his problem lies in the present, immediate emotional blocking, not in the data of the past.[91]

C. PROCEDURES. There is only one step which the counselor takes in his total relationship with the client. That step is the interview. The analysis, synthesis, diagnosis, prognosis, and follow-up are all done by the student himself, the first four during the interview itself. However there are at least eleven stages through which the interviews pass, some of them successive, some of them linear throughout the entire process: (1) establishment of rapport so that a climate of security and permissiveness is created, an atmosphere conducive to the completely free expression of the client's feelings; (2) implied indication by the counselor that he does not possess all the answers or even *the* answer; (3) initial release and expression by the client of almost exclusively negative feelings, a process which might last for the first few interviews; (4) reflection of the client's feelings by the counselor through such comments as, "Then that is the way you feel about . . ."; (5) acceptance by the counselor of any expression of the client; (6) little or no talking by the counselor throughout all the interviews; (7) faint, initial expression by the client of positive feelings; (8) gradual development by the client of insights into the problem, based on intellectual and emotional values, goals, and attitudes; (9) gradual initiation of totally self-conceived and self-directed activities by the client; (10) evaluation of positive, lasting, constructive activities pursuant to the solution of the problem; (11) termination of the counseling interview by the client because his problem has been solved.

D. WEAKNESSES. The non-directive theory of counseling has the following weakness: (1) The lack of counselor advice deprives the pupil of the broadening guidance of a more mature, more learned, and more experienced person, thereby rendering the pupil a prisoner of his own personality and experiences; (2) sometimes the client does not probe to the root of the problem or uncover underlying disturbances; (3) the client frequently tends to take an overoptimistic and sanguine view of himself, a fact which hinders the development of realistic insights; (4) the client's evaluation of himself is accepted by the counselor at face value without reference to the objective data of the case; (5) clients who have very low mental endowment usually lack the ability to accurately diagnose their difficulties or propose intelligent solutions; (6) the counseling situation can easily break down in the case of those clients for whom verbal communication is very difficult; (7) clients with serious psychological or emotional problems often cannot assume

[91] See Carl R. Rogers, *Counseling and Psychotherapy*. (Boston: Houghton Mifflin, 1942); also his *Client-Centered Therapy*. (Boston: Houghton Mifflin, 1951).

full responsibility for themselves and their decisions, but need the assistance of someone stronger and well adjusted; (8) clients with weak personalities sometimes need strong encouragement at least in the beginning; (9) this theory tends to neglect some of the consequences of Original Sin, especially as pertains to the darkening of the intellect and weakening of the will; (10) this theory completely ignores the use of case history data, so that diagnosis in terms of the overall, long-term development of the client is neglected; (11) non-directive counseling is inoperable in many school situations in which the counseling relationship is perforce restricted to one or at best a very few interviews; (12) gaining insight often takes a very long time, even in those counseling relationships in which an unrestricted number of interviews is possible; (13) many guidance problems are not emotional, but are strictly informational (e.g., how to obtain a particular type of job), and hence not suited to the non-directive approach; (14) this theory maintains that counseling cannot begin until the client comes to the counselor for help, a condition which will cause many of the more acute adolescent problems to go untreated; (15) this theory fails to provide for adequate school or counselor follow-up.

In some Catholic circles there has been criticism of non-directive counseling. These criticisms, which have emanated chiefly from those without a background in psychology, have charged, first, that this theory denies Original Sin and, second, that a Catholic counselor can neither accept nor condone immoral goals or feelings of the counselee. The first indictment is weak because it overemphasizes Original Sin to the exclusion of the Redemption. Thus Fr. Byrne, relying heavily on the great German theologian Scheeben, has shown that some theologians state that man has remained essentially good even after the Fall, and hence carries within him the urge to goodness, thereby nullifying any conflict between Rogerian theory and Catholic doctrine vis-a-vis Original Sin.[92] With regard to the second charge, it must be remembered that keeping silence does not condone; rather keeping silence simply means that the counselor is not saying anything. This is the familiar theological principle, *qui tacit, tacit*. Summing up the recent research, Frs. Hagmaier, C.S.P., and Gleason, S.J., have concluded that "the imparting of information [even moral advice] is likely to be the least important and least effective of the counselor's techniques." [93] These two priests, who themselves lean strongly toward non-directivism, hold that the client should be aided by the counselor to uncover for

[92] John T. Byrne, "Rogers' Counseling Theory and the Nature of Man," *Catholic Educational Review*, LVIII (February, 1960), pp. 116–117.

[93] Hagmaier and Gleason, *op. cit.*, p. 32.

himself his deep-seated problem and work out the solution in his daily living. They contend that when the counselor gives advice, he deprives the client of the positive satisfaction of uncovering and solving the problem for himself. Paternalism is not guidance. Summing up this entire matter, Fr. Moynihan, S.J., has stated that there exists no necessary conflict between non-directivism and Catholicism.[94] Fr. Charles A. Curran, in his classic work uses a Rogerian foundation upon which to build a Catholic system of counseling.[95] In short, Catholic teachers should take to heart the words of Fr. Ward, C.S.C., "We [Catholics] must shift from the idea of saving good things to the idea of assimilating good things." [96]

The Eclectic Theory. The eclectic theory of counseling attempts to combine the best features of the directive and non-directive approaches. Its advocates maintain that both of these theoretical schools have developed guidance approaches which cannot be omitted in a successful counseling relationship, e.g., the emphasis on use of case histories, helpful advice, and follow-up by the directivists, and the stress on emotional release, permissive atmosphere, and self-direction by the non-directivists. Eclectic theorists maintain that "the exclusive use of one [counseling] method for all cases is contrary to the fundamental principle of clinical psychology, namely that the approach should be adapted to the individual, his needs, and the situation." [97] Between the extremes of the directive and non-directive approaches there is a continuum. The eclectic method does not consistently take any one specific place in this continuum but slides along, so to speak, as the needs of the individual client or the dynamic exigencies of the counseling situation warrant. With some clients, an eclectic counselor will be more non-directional than with others, and vice versa. During the interview itself, an eclectic will vary his approach according to the counselor-client interaction at the moment. Nordberg, a Catholic guidance expert, summed up the consolidational nature of the eclectic theory when he stated that eclecticism cautions the directivist to "lead, but lead gently" while it admonishes the non-directivist to "lead gently, but lead." [98] F. C. Thorne

[94] James F. Moynihan, S.J., "Pastoral Counseling," *Personnel and Guidance Journal*, XXXVI (January, 1958), p. 328.

[95] Charles A. Curran, *Counseling in Catholic Life and Education.* (New York: Macmillan, 1952).

[96] Leo R. Ward, C.S.C., *New Life in Catholic Schools.* (St. Louis: Herder, 1958), p. 159.

[97] Ruth Strang, *Counseling Technics in College and Secondary School, op. cit.,* p. 117.

[98] Robert B. Nordberg, "Counseling: Non-directive or Non-coercive," *Catholic Educational Review*, LVI (January, 1958), p. 42.

is perhaps the foremost exponent of the eclectic theory.[99] The classroom teacher who counsels his students should in the main use the eclectic approach. The directive approach can easily lead the teacher who is comparatively untrained in professional counseling into authoritarianism and autocracy in his relationship with clients. On the other hand, the non-directive technique is too difficult for anyone who lacks training in professional counseling. Also, the greater versatility and flexibility of eclectic counseling make it a more suitable technique in a school situation in which so many different types of students are involved.

The Counseling Interview

The interview is the actual conference between counselor and counselee. It is the customary form for individual guidance or counseling. The teacher in his role of counselor should never permit routinization to characterize his interviews. Even if he has been counseling for many years, he should nonetheless realize that each client presents him with a new and vast adventure in understanding, love, and cooperation with the Holy Spirit in the furtherance of the renewal of the face of the world. He should never become stale in his counseling apostolate. His attitude should be one of freshness, eagerness, permissiveness, and understanding, with no taint of autocracy or phariseeism. McDaniel has stated that "attitude is more important than technique, and will in general pervade and control techniques and proceedings." [100] This is not to minimize skill in counseling techniques, but rather to emphasize the counselor's attitude.

Preparation for the Interview. Prior to the interview, the counselor should examine as many records on the client as are available.[101] It is often wise to have these records readily accessible during the interview so that they may be immediately consulted if the need arises. The counselor should also make proper arrangements concerning the place of the interview. The interview should be conducted in a private place, preferably a separate room. If this is not available, an empty classroom will do. The room should be relatively free from any chance of interruption, such as telephone calls or people entering. The room should have a pleasant, informal atmosphere. A comfortable chair should be provided

[99] Frederick C. Thorne, *Principles of Personality Counseling.* (Brandon, Vt.: Journal of Clinical Psychology, 1959); see also Shirley A. Hamrin and Blanche B. Paulson, *Counseling Adolescents.* (Chicago: Science Research Associates, 1950), pp. 82–109.

[100] Henry B. McDaniel, *Guidance in the Modern School.* (New York: Holt, 1956), p. 146.

[101] E. G. Williamson, "Some Issues Underlying Counseling Theory and Practice," in Dugan (ed.), *Counseling Points of View, op. cit.,* p. 1.

for the client so that he may feel relaxed and at ease. The chair should be so arranged that the client is not facing the window or bright lights. There should be no desk or other furniture between the counselor and client because this might automatically create the impression of a superior-inferior relationship. Nor is it conducive to promoting a relaxed feeling on the part of the client.[102] It is also psychologically poor procedure to tell the student: "You will report to me this afternoon at 2:15 for an interview." The student will immediately conclude that he has done something wrong and will probably be worried all day about the impending interview. This will cause not only mental upset but a diminution in the quality of his classwork. It is better either to cooperatively make an appointment ahead of time with the client or to have the interview with him at the very time he is notified.

The Initial Interview. The initial interview should be devoted almost exclusively to the attainment of a good relationship with the client. Little or no effort should be made to work on the solution of the problem. Indeed it is not even necessary for the client to directly identify his problem or its suspected cause. Furthermore, as Cottle and Downie have written, "The counselor needs to use the first interview to find out how the client feels, not just to collect a series of related facts which can be fitted into a case history, or to give out specific information without knowing how it will be used by the client." [103] (All this, of course, assumes that the counseling relationship will last for at least several interviews.)

The following are some of the more important techniques which the counselor should employ during the initial interview:

1. Stand up and shake hands with the client when he enters the room or office for the interview, addressing him by name.

2. Display warmth, not professional frigidity.

3. Be at ease, else the client will not be at ease.

4. Begin with a warm-up period. The warm-up period may be either an extension of something the client said in his opening remarks of the interview, or it may be in the form of a counselor question about something he thinks interests the client, based on an examination of his cumulative record or case history.

5. Adjust both manner of speech and vocabulary to the client, e.g., to a boy from an underprivileged neighborhood, to a gifted girl interested in medicine.

[102] Clifford E. Erickson, *The Counseling Interview.* (Englewood Cliffs, N.J.: Prentice-Hall, 1950), pp. 52–54; Jane Waters, *Techniques of Counseling.* (New York: McGraw-Hill, 1954), pp. 310–311.

[103] Wm. C. Cottle and N. M. Downie, *Procedures and Preparation for Counseling.* (Englewood Cliffs, N.J.: Prentice-Hall, 1960), p. 73.

6. Evince by means of voice tone, facial expression, and demeanor a deep interest in the client and his problem. The client must never feel that he is "just another case" to the counselor.

7. Establish rapport. Rapport is a personal relationship between two people involving reciprocal confidence, understanding, and security. Rapport is not really a technique, but rather both concomitant and resultant of a giving over of one's personality to another. It cannot be turned on like a faucet; rather it develops. Unfortunately, as Strang has noted, "Rapport is too often thought of as a 'bag of tricks,' devices used at the beginning of an interview." [104] Fr. McIntyre, S.J., has correctly written that "the most important element in the counseling situation is establishing rapport." [105]

8. Conduct the interview in an unhurried manner.

9. Let the client do most of the talking.

10. Show understanding at all times; e.g., do not comment if the client comes late for the interview.

11. Empathize the problems of the client. Dymond defined empathy as "the imaginative transposing of oneself into the thinking, feeling and acting of another, and so structuring the world as he does." [106]

12. Reflect the client's feeling, e.g., by saying, "Then you feel you are almost forced into trouble by Miss Jones because she is too strict."

13. Accept the client's attitudes and feelings even if they are at variance with reality or morality. Later the client can be helped to correct his errors. The counselor can convey his acceptance by following the client's comments with a noncommittal "yes," "mm," or "I see."

14. Do not probe, but merely encourage the client to talk. Probing, if deemed necessary, can be done in subsequent interviews.

15. Watch out for unfavorable sex attitudes of the client toward the counselor. Some of the client's feelings toward sex may be transferred to the counselor; e.g. a boy who feels that women are hyperemotional and intellectually inferior may transfer his feelings to a woman counselor.

16. Determine cooperatively the length of future interviews. An interview with a time limit known by both counselor and client is usually more productive. The interview should last at least one-half hour. A fifteen-minute interview is too short—it tends to become a "bullet interview."

17. Makes a definite appointment for the next interview.

Succeeding Interviews. The succeeding interviews should be devoted to helping the client identify and solve his problem(s) with the assistance of the counselor. The client, not the counselor, should be

[104] Strang, *Counseling Technics in College and Secondary School, op. cit.*, p. 125.

[105] John P. McIntyre, S.J., "Counselor-Centered Acceptance," *Catholic Educational Review*, LVI (May, 1958), p. 299.

[106] Rosalind F. Dymond, "A Scale for the Measurement of Empathic Ability," *Journal of Consulting Psychology*, XIII (April, 1949), p. 127.

the primary agent and moving force in solving the problem. The counselor's role is to help the client progress in attaining increasingly deeper insights, for these will not only suggest the direction in which the problem will be solved, but will also tether the solution to a meaningful base. To solve his problem the client must make some definite selective decision, and as Fr. Curran has observed, "Every choice response always includes some definite action in conjunction with insight." [107] In the succeeding interviews, the counselor should continue to use relevant techniques employed in the first interview, e.g., empathy, acceptance, reflection of feeling, while discarding those procedures appropriate only to the first interview, e.g., extended warm-up.

The following are some of the more important techniques which the counselor should use during succeeding interviews:

1. Give the client undivided attention. Do not try simultaneously to complete the notes from the preceding interview or to work on some other business such as correcting homework papers.

2. Encourage the client to earnestly want to solve his problem. Counseling will be fruitless unless the client really wishes to solve his problem.

3. Promote an atmosphere of expectancy, i.e., a climate which causes the client to be confident of reaching a solution as a result of the interviews.

4. Be concerned not only with what the client is saying but also with how he is saying it.

5. Help the client to identify his problem. He knows something is wrong, but often not exactly what is wrong.

6. Adjust the counseling procedure to the client or to the exigencies of the moment, e.g., a directive approach for a client who wishes only occupational information, a non-directive or eclectic method for a client with a deep personal problem.

7. Think *with* rather than *for* the client.

8. Do not overtalk the client. Strang has stated that the greatest temptations for the teacher in the counseling role are "to talk when he should be listening, to be swift and authoritarian in his responses, to give advice, and to be content with immediate, superficial results." [108]

9. Ask general leads, e.g., "Tell me more about. . . ."

10. Use what Erickson has called "conversational hooks," i.e., questions or statements designed to get the client to relate the discussion to his problem or to some particular aspect of it.[109]

11. Pose open-ended questions to indicate to the client that the inner nature and full impact of his problem have not been grasped. This procedure will

[107] Charles A. Curran, *Personality Factors in Counseling.* (New York: Grune & Stratton, 1945), p. 67.
[108] Strang, *The Role of the Teacher in Personnel Work, op. cit.,* p. 241.
[109] Erickson, *op. cit.,* p. 73.

not only deepen the counselor's knowledge of the problem, but will demonstrate to the client that the counselor is not assuming an omniscient role.

12. Do not ask questions which suggest the answers.

13. Phrase the question so that it will not admit of a simple "yes" or "no" answer. The question should cause an extended client response, e.g., questions which begin with "why," or "what are your feelings about. . . ."

14. Do not cross-examine a client or otherwise subject him to an inquisition. This is very important, especially for teachers of an autocratic bent.

15. Probe cautiously, discreetly, and only when absolutely necessary.

16. Urge and persuade only in the most important and necessary matters, and even then exercise extreme caution.[110] The process goal is always to assist the client in wanting to do something precisely because *he,* not someone else, wishes to do it.

17. Utilize silence as a forcing device only with great circumspection.

18. Give encouragement to the client when he is in need of it, e.g., "I think you are coming along very well in . . . ."

19. Develop and stress only one major idea per interview.

20. Suggest to the client that he think through his insights verbally with the counselor.

21. Ask the client to make periodic summaries of what has occurred during the interview.

22. Restrict the length of the interview to the time limit decided in the first conference.

23. Ask the client near the close of the interview to formulate a plan of action or proposal for attack of his problem. This plan should be specific and achievable in terms of the client and his particular stage of development. It should not attempt to solve the problem in one grand stroke. The counselor should be careful lest all or even most of the recommendations emanate from him. Tyler has remarked that sometimes a client's "indecision with regard to a plan of action represents a general indecisiveness growing out of personal problems rather than doubts related to the specific issue."[111] In such a case the counselor's advice or recommendations are futile because the client must first be helped to eliminate the underlying problem. The degree to which the client has carried out his plan of action can serve as the beginning of the following interview.

24. Make a definite appointment for the next interview.[112]

Following Up the Interview. After the conclusion of each interview, the counselor should allow time to make some pertinent notes about

[110] Stanley S. Marzolf, *Psychological Diagnosis and Counseling in the Schools.* (New York: Holt, 1956), pp. 351–352.

[111] Leona E. Tyler, *The Work of the Counselor,* 2d ed. (New York: Appleton-Century-Crofts, 1961), p. 201. Italics omitted.

[112] Frank G. Davis and Pearle S. Norris, *Guidance Handbook for Teachers.* (New York: McGraw-Hill, 1949), p. 80.

what developed during the interview. These notes should be written on standardized forms and placed in the pupil's cumulative record folder. The notes should contain two separate sections, one for an objective account of exactly what occurred during the interview and the other for the counselor's interpretative remarks. There are several good reasons why the counselor should make notes of the interview. First, notes provide requisite information for the successful resumption of counseling in future interviews. Second, notes compiled over the course of time show the trend of pupil growth so that an overall, long-term picture emerges. Third, notes furnish the guidance specialist with necessary information and background material. It is probably better to make notes after the interview than during it, lest the client gain the impression that he is being inquisitioned. This could well lead to the lack of a truly permissive climate and thus seriously hinder rapport. Tyler, however, is of the opinion that it makes no difference when the notes are made.[113] For information-gathering interviews, it is preferable to make notes during the conference itself.

When the client has indicated that he has successfully solved his problem, the interviews should be terminated. However, the conscientious counselor should make a follow-up several months later. This follow-up should consist of an interview with the former client to ascertain whether the problem has been permanently solved. The counselor can also make pertinent but judicious inquiries of fellow teachers, parents, and the guidance specialists in an effort to determine how well the pupil has resolved his problem.

TYPES OF GUIDANCE

There are five principal types of guidance, viz., scholastic, vocational, personal, social, and religious. Every teacher should provide all these forms, although only in Catholic high schools can religious guidance be given in its fullness.

Scholastic Guidance

Scholastic guidance is that assistance which the school gives the pupil to help him solve his special academic problems and progress in his present school situation. It does not deal with encouraging a student to go to college or assisting him in the selection of an appropriate postsecondary school. Scholastic guidance consists in more than summoning a pupil for an interview, looking at his marks, commenting that he should work harder, and then calling in the next student. There are

[113] Tyler, op. cit., p. 74.

two stages of scholastic guidance, namely, preadmittance guidance and in-school guidance.

Preadmittance Guidance. Preadmittance guidance is that assistance which the school gives the prospective pupil concerning school life and academic matters. Preadmittance guidance not only is of great help to the prospective pupil in acquainting him with his new school environment, but it also enables the school to know the youth better, to ensure his proper placement in the appropriate class or other group, and to supplement the records of his elementary and/or junior high school career. Each school should publish a brochure listing its regulations, its curricular offerings, its specialized services, and the activities which it sponsors or with which it cooperates, e.g., dances, Young Christian Students affiliated sections. If possible, teachers and guidance counselor as well as administrators should interview the incoming students. Fr. Stack's nationwide study together with his review of the pertinent research led him to conclude that public high schools "provided pre-admittance interviews to a greater extent than did Catholic high schools." [114] However, Catholic high schools were not too remiss in this regard, for 66 per cent of them reported preadmittance interviews, a figure which indicates that this area is one of the brighter spots in Catholic high school guidance programs.

In-school Guidance. In-school guidance is that assistance in academic and school life matters which the pupil receives during his school career. A review of the pertinent research by Hoehn and Saltz showed that personal interviews between teachers and their students have resulted in significantly higher marks for the students, especially when the conferences related the pupil's scholastic adjustment and achievement to his personal interests and problems.[115] Moreover, an investigation conducted by Hoehn and Saltz confirmed what had been implicit in these studies, namely, that if a teacher has had little or no guidance training, the results of his interviews are usually negligible and sometimes even harmful to the pupil's scholastic achievement.[116] This can be illustrated by the case of a boy who tells the teacher in an early September interview, "I want to change my program for this year." A teacher trained in non-directivist technique might reply, "You're not happy with your present program?" whereas another teacher educated in directivist procedures might inquire, "To what do you wish to change?" However, a teacher untrained in counseling (or one with an auto-

---

[114] Stack, *op. cit.*, p. 155.

[115] Arthur J. Hoehn and Eli Saltz, "Effect of Teacher-Student Interviews on Classroom Achievement," *Journal of Educational Psychology,* XLVII (November, 1946), pp. 433–434.

[116] *Ibid.*, pp. 424–435.

cratic personality) might well reply, "You can't do that now because the deadline for making program changes has past." [117] The teacher as counselor must not only be concerned with institutional roles but also with the personal welfare of his client.

The teacher must help the pupil ascertain the cause of his scholastic problem. Why is he not performing well? Poor study or work habits? Lack of interest? Lack of ability? Inappropriate class placement? Excessive academic load? Emotional problems? Personality clash with the teacher? Poor teaching? Home problems? Physical illness? Laziness? Sometimes special abilities can actually give rise to scholastic as well as personal problems. Thus researchers from the University of Texas discovered that talented, creative junior high school youths were often misunderstood by their parents and rejected by their classmates. These researchers recommended counseling and home visitation by the teachers to stimulate increased school performance and personal adjustment.[118] Teachers in schools situated in low socioeconomic areas should make every effort to provide mature, reality-related scholastic guidance. Miller's review of the pertinent research concluded that there was a definite relationship between high school dropouts and socioeconomic status.[119]

Fr. Paul, O.S.F.S., has recommended that each high school student receive a duplicate copy of his scholastic record so that he can realistically appraise both his objective achievement and his achievement in relation to his ability. This record would include his IQ, reading score, aptitude scores, rank in class, and marks.[120] Such a procedure would serve as an intelligent basis for teacher-pupil counseling interviews and would assist the pupil in formulating more realistic vocational plans. However, every teacher should vigorously oppose any public posting of pupil marks, a practice detrimental to good guidance, to mature intellectual development, and to Christian spiritual life.

Fr. Stack's study concluded that "definite limitations were observed in the paucity of various [guidance] services offered in the Catholic high schools concerning the promotion of high scholastic achievement." [121] One probable reason for this is the failure on the part of a good many Catholic teachers and administrators to see intellectual work as a *directly* spiritual act. When a person thinks, he is

[117] Arnold Buchheimer and Sarah Balogh, *The Counseling Relationship.* (Chicago: Science Research Associates, 1961), p. 8.

[118] "Secondary Education Notes," *Catholic Educational Review,* LVIII (February, 1960), p. 126.

[119] Carroll H. Miller, *Foundations of Guidance.* (New York: Harper, 1961), pp. 183–194.

[120] Henry A. Paul, O.S.F.S., "Counseling and Student Use of the High School Record," *Catholic Educational Review,* LIX (September, 1961), pp. 376–381.

[121] Stack, *op. cit.,* p. 177.

participating in God's life because it is by exercising his intelligence that he is deeply fulfilling that Divine imagehood which makes his sharing in the Godhead unique among all earthly creatures. Then, too, there are some Catholic teachers who see in the intellectual life a source of danger. But as O'Dea has observed, the fact of risk is inseparable from the intellectual life, and indeed from a vibrant Christian life. Pupils should be engaged in an intellectual and hence spiritual quest, not in a search for a rule of safety.[122]

Vocational Guidance

Vocational guidance is that which assists the individual in his efforts to choose a life's work, to prepare himself for entrance into it, to enter it, and to make progress in it.[123] The three principal types of vocational guidance are occupational, further educational, and religiovocational.

Occupational Guidance. Occupational guidance is that assistance which the school gives the student in his search for suitable job placement or employment. Historically, it is the first type of vocational guidance which developed, and it is the kind which still receives the greatest attention in the literature and in public high schools. Occupational counseling is usually given by the guidance counselor. However, for many reasons a student will often seek counseling assistance from a teacher; e.g., a student might ask his chemistry teacher about job opportunities as a chemist in industry. In homerooms or other group guidance situations the teacher will frequently be asked to give occupational guidance.

Vocational psychologists such as Super and Roe have been responsible for a healthy change in occupational guidance emphasis from the concept of jobs as specific functions merely to be done to the humanistic approach of jobs as opportunities for self-realization and personal fulfillment.[124] Indeed Super conceives of occupational development as one aspect of individual development. He has translated the various life stages into vocational development steps which reorient a person's occupational outlook. Thus, for example, in high school a youth is exploring possible careers, while in the period between twenty-two and twenty-four years of age he is busy trying out his choice. Hence high

[122] Thomas F. O'Dea, *American Catholic Dilemma: An Inquiry into the Intellectual Life.* (New York: Sheed and Ward, 1958), p. 37.

[123] See Committee of the National Vocational Guidance Association, "The Principles and Practices of Educational and Vocational Guidance," *Occupations*, XV (May, 1937), p. 772.

[124] Donald E. Super, *The Psychology of Careers.* (New York: Harper, 1957); Anne Roe, *The Psychology of Occupations.* (New York: Wiley, 1956).

school occupational choices should not be regarded as definitive, and alternatives should be offered.

In his occupational counseling or guidance, the teacher should endeavor to help the student choose an occupation consonant with his personality. An investigation by Melton of the relation between personality and vocational interest in high school students disclosed that there exists a definitely measurable relationship between the two.[125] Therefore the teacher and, particularly, the guidance counselor should utilize standardized personality inventory tests throughout the pupil's high school years. A study by Sister Rosamund Murphy, O.P., of the relationship of high school students' stated choices to their subsequent careers revealed a considerable stability when the categories were grouped under Kuder classifications.[126] So, for example, a pupil who as a sophomore had decided on teaching as a probable career and by his senior year had changed his mind in favor of social work would in both instances be grouped under the same Kuder category of "personal-social" occupations.

High school students are greatly in need of occupational guidance. Kinnane's review of the pertinent research revealed that in their tentative occupational choices students aspire to careers higher than their abilities warrant and make choices based on the social and economic rewards of the occupation rather than on the suitability of the job to their personality and talents.[127] Hutson's review of the pertinent research concluded that high school students do not take into account their abilities when making a choice of a future occupation.[128] A study by Folsom and Sobolewski showed that high school students tended to make a high correlation between estimates of income of various occupations and ranking of their social status.[129] O'Dea has observed that Catholic students enter the lucrative professions of law, medicine, and politics in far greater percentages than they do intellectual careers, thus giving rise to speculation about the altruism and spirituality of the

[125] William R. Melton, Jr., "An Investigation of the Relationship between Personality and Vocational Interest," *Journal of Educational Psychology*, XLVII (March, 1956), p. 171.

[126] Sister Rosamund Murphy, O.P., *A Study of the Relationships of High School Students Stated Choices and Their Subsequent Careers*. (Washington, D.C.: Catholic University of America Press, 1957).

[127] John F. Kinnane, "Realism in Vocational Preference," in Stafford (ed.), *Counseling in the Secondary School, op. cit.,* p. 65.

[128] Percival W. Hutson, *The Guidance Function in Education*. (New York: Appleton-Century-Crofts, 1958), pp. 131-135.

[129] Willys W. Folsom and Edmund L. Sobolewski, "Income and Social Status of Occupations," *Personnel and Guidance Journal*, XXXVI (December, 1957), pp. 277-278.

pupils' motives and of the schools which helped to shape these motives.[130]

Occupational counseling of female high school students needs considerably more clarification and increased attention because a woman's occupational role in contemporary society is much more complex than that of a man. Super has identified seven distinct career patterns for women: stable homemaking career, conventional career, stable working career, double-track career, interrupted career; unstable career, multiple-trial career.[131]

The school should inaugurate "career conferences" in which representatives from various occupations come into the school and discuss with the students job opportunities in their particular lines of work. Froehlich has remarked that a survey of pupil interests should not be made the complete directional guide for career conferences, else it is likely that exclusive emphasis will be placed on the professions.[132] Tradesmen, craftsmen, merchants, mechanics, social service workers, and businessmen representative of community life should also participate. In Catholic high schools, intellectual and scholarly careers should be given special attention in view of the shortage of Catholics in these areas. Career conferences should broaden the pupils' occupational horizons and show them new vistas. Frank has suggested that the school mobilize the active cooperation of various community groups in sponsoring extended career conferences and actual practicums along the lines developed in the Career Conference Unlimited Program of the San Diego public school system.[133] Certainly the school should cooperate with the local representatives of the armed services so that in career conferences the male pupils will be apprised of the nature of their future military obligations and concomitant opportunities.[134]

Career conferences should be supplemented by career days on which the students are taken on escorted tours through a store, factory, or office. This not only provides a concrete image of the various occupations but also serves as an antidote to the excessively glowing pictures which some overeager industrial or corporate recruiters might have painted. Of course various subject-matter or problem-area teachers and homeroom teachers in particular should further implement career con-

---

[130] O'Dea, op. cit., p. 118.

[131] Super, op. cit., pp. 77–78.

[132] Clifford P. Froehlich, Guidance Services in Schools, 2d ed. (New York: McGraw-Hill, 1958), p. 152.

[133] Stanley D. Frank, Strengthening Vocational Guidance Programs in San Diego County, unpublished doctoral dissertation, Teachers College, Columbia University, New York, 1962.

[134] Carroll L. Shartle, Occupational Information, 3d ed. (Englewood Cliffs, N.J.: Prentice-Hall, 1959), pp. 300–329.

ferences and career days not only in the classrooms but by field trips, assignments, or collateral readings.[135]

The guidance counselor should maintain a reasonably complete file of career opportunities and occupational information. The United States Employment Service of the Department of Labor offers considerable occupational assistance. This Service also publishes the *Dictionary of Occupational Titles*, which lists and classifies over forty thousand different types of jobs. It is the most extensive compilation of occupational information available. The various state employment services are eager to assist schools in whatever way they can. Individual teachers should maintain occupational files and also liaisons with these services in the field of their specialty.

Fr. Stack's study pointed out that Catholic high schools could and should do much more in attempting to place students in jobs.[136] Fr. Drolet's investigation concluded that "occupational guidance programs do not appear to be receiving from the Diocesan Departments of Education much support or encouragement." [137] Perhaps the primary underlying cause of this is an absence of any developed theology of work in the Church. Catholics in general do not think of work as a divinely impregnated act, something which of itself joins the person to God. Rather it is conceived of as something which is done when one is not praying, or at best something which may be offered up to God, sanctified by a religious intention. Fr. Teilhard de Chardin, S.J., has observed that each labor, each work a person performs, *of itself* fulfills not only Christ's work, but Christ Himself, for by work a person returns Christ to Christ.[138] Until the Church develops a mature theology of work Catholic schools will never give to occupational guidance its commensurate importance and dimension.

A study by Mother M. Paul Kienzler, O.S.U., revealed that 87 per cent of the vocational motivations expressed by students in Catholic high schools were on the purely natural level. Supernatural motivation as regards careers decreased consistently from the freshman to the senior year.[139] This investigation highlights not only the need for a drastic upgrading of guidance in Catholic high schools but a serious reexamina-

---

[135] Robert Hoppock, *Group Guidance.* (New York: McGraw-Hill, 1949), pp. 56–59.

[136] Stack, *op. cit.*, p. 168.

[137] Drolet, *op. cit.*, p. 84.

[138] Pierre Teilhard de Chardin, S.J., *The Divine Milieu*, trans. by Wall. (New York: Harper, 1960), p. 31.

[139] Mother M. Paul Kienzler, O.S.U., *A Comparative Study of Vocational Motivation of Students in Catholic Secondary Schools,* unpublished master's thesis, Catholic University of America, Washington, D.C., 1958.

tion of the direction and thrust of the entire Catholic school program, from curricular design to teaching methods to deep pupil participation in the liturgy and Catholic Action.

Further Educational Guidance. Further educational guidance is that assistance which the school gives the student with respect to opportunities and placement in a postsecondary school. The most common of the schools is the four-year collegiate or university institution of higher learning. However, other types of postsecondary schools should not be neglected, such as community colleges, junior colleges, secondary school extensions, and specialized postsecondary institutions (e.g., secretarial, professional, industrial, or trade schools).

Any student possessing the requisite talent and aptitude should be assisted in every way toward further educational opportunities, especially in regard to colleges and universities. Annually many bright and even exceptionally bright youths discontinue their education after high school. It is one of the major tasks of a program of further educational guidance to remedy this lamentable situation. Science Research Associates have commented that, in particular, bright high school girls constitute a major source of untapped talent.[140] All too many of these adolescents terminate their education because of lack of funds, imminent marriage prospects, or sheer indifference—all of which could be largely counteracted by a strong program of further educational guidance.

The guidance counselor usually has charge of college selection procedures. Nevertheless, the teacher's role in further educational guidance is still considerable. Perhaps more than anyone else, he can do the most to arouse an interest and enthusiasm in students to continue their academic careers. Subject-matter or problem-area teachers are often asked for college guidance by the students in their classes. College and university professors are aware that many of their students, including some of the best, would not be in their classes were it not for the wise and promotional guidance these students received from their high school teachers. The entire high school staff, particularly of a Catholic institution, should at all times foster a school climate which places great value on the intellectual life—not an intellectual life whose sole purpose is to serve a pragmatic end, such as rebutting an atheist (the moralist position), or which is not deeply meshed with the rest of the student's actions or with life itself (the intellectualist position), but rather, one which sees truth, whole and entire, as one of man's highest values. Truth is not only a proper mental grasping of reality, but it is also a Person, Christ. Moreover, the Holy Spirit dwells in truth. Hence truth has for a Catholic a superadded abundance. Catholic teachers must therefore make

[140] "Secondary Education Notes," *op. cit.*, pp. 126–127.

every effort to help their students to prize truth, to spend a lifetime in search of its fullness.

Normally a good Catholic college or university is the best place for a Catholic high school graduate to continue his educational career. To facilitate entrance into Catholic colleges and universities, the Catholic College Admissions and Information Center was established in the early 1960s at Assumption College, Worcester, Massachusetts. This Center serves as a national clearinghouse for students seeking admission into Catholic colleges. It has on file academic transcripts of students and other pertinent data.

Teachers and guidance personnel should counsel students, especially the indigent, about scholarship opportunities. Scholarships generally come from three principal sources: the college itself; private organizations, such as churches, clubs, industry, foundations, and unions; the state, e.g., New York State Regents Scholarships. Scholarships from the first and third sources are usually awarded as a result of competitive examinations, the scores of which are contextually considered in the light of other data on the pupil's personnel record. Unfortunately, much of the machinery for granting scholarship aid is geared to reward pupils having an overdocile character, a photographic memory, and conformist ideas. These students not infrequently lack the creativity which is usually associated with youths possessing the opposite characteristics. Teachers and guidance specialists should identify those creative abilities which elude objective measurement and include this information on the records which will be sent to college scholarship or admissions officers or to the College Scholarship Service in Princeton, New Jersey. If a pupil fails to qualify for a scholarship, he should be urged to apply for a low-interest college-aid loan from the college itself, a local bank, or the Federal government. As much as 50 per cent of a National Defense Education Act loan may be canceled at the rate of 10 per cent per year up to five years if the borrower becomes a teacher in a public elementary or secondary school. Employment in a Catholic school will not serve to reduce the principal of the loan, an unfortunate lacuna in the law.

Teachers should arrange for their students to visit colleges either individually or in groups. Colleges are usually happy to cooperate in such a venture. A pupil's visit should occur during a normal collegiate day so that he may gain an accurate impression. The pupil should audit some courses to ascertain the quality and type of teaching. He should observe the class sizes, investigate the library facilities, inquire about the guidance and personnel services, look into dormitory and dining-hall conditions, find out the social life opportunities, and question the college students to determine their personal opinion of the institution.

The college catalog should be examined to detect the extent of academic inbreeding of the faculty. Inquiries should be made to ascertain to what extent most or all of the pupils are broadly representative of many states or geographical sections.

Public and Catholic secondary schools should offer advanced placement courses in their schools. Most forward-looking secular and Catholic colleges grant academic credit for such courses. But perhaps the most important thing a teacher should remember about further educational guidance is that in the present age it must begin in the early part of the pupil's high school career.

Religiovocational Guidance. Religiovocational guidance is that assistance which the school gives the student concerning the eventual attainment of his proper state in life. "State in life" is here considered from the religious perspective. Canon 107 says that there are only two states of life: the clerical and the lay. Religious are therefore either clerics or lay people, depending on whether or not they have received first tonsure.[141] (First tonsure is the initial canonical step which a seminarian takes in his path to the priesthood.) Religiovocational guidance should not be conceived narrowly as the exclusive assistance of pupils with a vocation to the clerical or Religious life. The lay state is also a vocation, and pupils should receive guidance to prepare to live this type of Divine calling in the most spiritual and holy manner. A life dedicated totally to Christ does not belong to the clergy or Religious alone. Everyone is called to consecrate his life to God, each in a different way, each with a special ministry. The purpose of religiovocational guidance, therefore, is to help each pupil glorify God according to God's will in his regard.

The statements of the recent Popes have indicated that it is the task of every Catholic to promote vocations to the clerical and Religious life. Obviously, public secondary schools cannot foster religious vocations; however, Catholic high schools can and should. Fr. Drolet's study concluded that guidance concerning religious vocations is being given special attention by diocesan departments of education.[142] In fact, this type of guidance is probably the one area to which Catholic high school programs and teachers are according sufficient attention.

While the Catholic high school teacher should actively foster vocations to the clerical or Religious life, he nevertheless must avoid using high pressure tactics. Fostering religious vocations is a noble form of guidance, but it should never be permitted to degenerate into the deliberate maneuvering of a student into the Religious life. A religious

---

[141] Besides Canon 107, see T. Lincoln Bouscaren, S.J., and Adam C. Ellis, S.J., *Canon Law*, 2d ed. (Milwaukee: Bruce, 1951), pp. 93–105.

[142] Drolet, *op. cit.*, p. 84.

vocation is a gift from God, not the exclusive fruit of the efforts of vocation recruiters. High pressure stratagems may lure a youth into the seminary or novitiate, but they will not keep him there. Indeed one Religious Congregation used such "hard sell" techniques during a "Vocation Week" that a number of non-Christians signed up to join the Congregation.[143]

All religiovocational guidance should inculcate in the students an awareness that *they* can and must create a new age for the Church. The twentieth century is a pivotal era in the Church's history, one which will give direction to the next two or three hundred years. It is the high school students of today who will shape the history.

Personal Guidance

Personal guidance is that assistance which the school gives the student to help him resolve his inner conflicts or his other personal maladjustments. Mackie and associates have noted that the school is the only professional community agency which reaches every child and youth. Furthermore, compulsory attendance laws require the school to maintain continual contact with the students. Hence the school constitutes a home-base institution for students with personal problems, even if they are referred to other people or agencies for additional help.[144]

A psychologically maladjusted person is one who does not behave in a manner consistent with his set of values or goals.[145] (This, of course, differs from social maladjustment.) In Rogerian terms, the greater the disharmony between a person's concept of self and his experience of self, the more he is maladjusted.[146] The two principal ways in which the individual can psychologically readjust are, first, to change his behavior so as to bring it into harmony with his values and goals, or second, to alter his values and goals because of a realization that they are unrealistic or otherwise defective.

DiVesta's review of the pertinent research concluded that pupils with an authoritarian attitude are characterized by poor personal adjustment, hostility, and rigidity. Such students were found to encounter greater difficulty in certain types of learning (especially with unstructured materials) than pupils possessing a more humanitarian at-

---

[143] "Too Many Vocations," *Brooklyn Tablet*, Feb. 17, 1962, p. 5.

[144] Romaine Mackie and associates, *Teachers of Children Who Are Socially and Emotionally Maladjusted*. (Washington: Department of Health, Education and Welfare, 1957), p. 1.

[145] Everett L. Shostrom and Lawrence M. Brammer, *The Dynamics of the Counseling Process*. (New York: McGraw-Hill, 1952), p. 10.

[146] Rogers, *Client-Centered Therapy, op. cit.*, p. 526.

titude.[147] A study by Symonds of happy and unhappy students disclosed that both groups were remarkably alike in their problems and interests; they differed in their personal adjustments to their problems, with the unhappy group making the poorer adjustments. Moreover, the unhappy students were more concerned with themselves and their interpersonal relationships, whereas the happy group were more interested in the affairs outside themselves. The unhappy group were more directly concerned with sex whereas the happy group were more interested in making themselves attractive in social life relationships. Also the happy group were more interested in a philosophy of life, ideals, and religion than were the unhappy group.[148] An investigation by Gaier of pupils with an anxiety personality revealed that the anxious student spends about half the classroom time thinking about himself rather than about the material being studied. He also spends considerable time musing about specific objects in the classroom, e.g., a classmate's clothing or the teacher's desk.[149]

Undue use of defense mechanisms is a common cause of personal problems. Thorpe has classified defense mechanisms into five groups, viz., those which lead to attempts to forget reality, distort reality, atone for reality, retreat from reality, attack reality.[150] All in all, a substantial number of pupils in high schools today have mental health problems of varying intensity. A few are emotionally disturbed to a serious degree. Teachers should be ever on the alert to detect pupils with personal problems and to give them proper guidance. In this connection it is well to recall Hutson's review of the pertinent research which indicates that the school itself is often a major factor in contributing to its pupils' maladjustment.[151] Some causes of maladjustment include a rigid curriculum not geared to the pupils' interests or needs, overemphasis on conformity, undue stress on marks resulting in frustration, autocratic teaching procedures, poor placement of pupils in a group, and athleticism. One investigation based on twenty years of prison work concluded that schools play a substantial role in the making of criminals.[152]

[147] Francis J. DiVesta, "Meaningful Learning: Motivational, Personality, Interpersonal and Social Variables," *Review of Educational Research*, XXXI (December, 1961), p. 515.

[148] Percival M. Symonds, "Happiness as Related to Problems and Interests," *Journal of Educational Psychology*, XXVIII (April, 1937), pp. 290–294.

[149] Eugene L. Gaier, "The Relationship between Selected Personality Variables and the Thinking of Students in Discussion Classes," *School Review*, LX (October, 1952), pp. 404–411.

[150] As interpreted by Mortensen and Schmuller, *op. cit.*, pp. 87–91.

[151] Hutson, *op. cit.*, pp. 100–106.

[152] Arthur C. Johnson, Jr., "Our Schools Make Criminals," *Journal of Criminal Law and Criminology*, XXXIII (November, 1942), pp. 310–315.

The school and the teacher should constantly strive to promote good mental health as the best preventive against personal problems. Guidance for incoming students should center around making them feel they "belong" to the whole high school community. Student initiations and "hazings" result more in personal problems than fun. The teacher should use a different approach in counseling boys and girls on personal problems. This is necessitated by the difference in effect which the physical changes of adolescence have on the boy's and girl's self-concepts.[153] Tyler has observed that because of lack of time, most personal guidance done in school will be "minimum change guidance," i.e., merely attempting to help the pupil successfully hurdle a particular problem rather than get at the root cause of the problem. She has proposed three steps to this type of guidance and counseling: (1) general exploration, in which the teacher as counselor freely establishes rapport and looks for clues; (2) clarification, in which the counselor helps the client put the problem into the contextual relation of his (the client's) value system—out of this clarification a plan of action develops; (3) reinforcement, in which the counselor lets his own words and actions strengthen and approve the pupil's actions.[154]

Personal guidance services should be markedly improved in both public and Catholic high schools. Fr. Stack's study concluded that teachers and counselors in Catholic high schools gave more attention to assisting pupils in choosing their courses than in helping them to deal with their personal problems.[155] A study by Sister Katherine Paul Gregory, R.S.M., of five basal sets of religion textbooks used in Catholic secondary schools concluded that in only one of these sets was there sufficient information given to the pupils on how they could solve their religioemotional problems.[156] One probable major cause for this neglect has been identified by Frs. Hagmaier, C.S.P., and Gleason, S.J., as a tendency of Catholic authors and preachers to overstate the preeminence of man's rational and volitional faculties as regulators of the emotions.[157] Allied to this is a seeming predilection for viewing man's intellect as somehow a separate substance, not inextricably enmeshed in the human body. Indeed, when the pure bared intellect is isolated from the flesh and the complex world which nourishes it, personal maladjustment and anxiety will be produced.

[153] See Rosalind Cassidy and Hilda Kozman, *Counseling Girls*. (New York: McGraw-Hill, 1947), pp. 97–193.

[154] Tyler, *op. cit.*, pp. 211–224.

[155] Stack, *op. cit.*, pp. 175–176.

[156] Sister Katherine Paul Gregory, R.S.M., *An Evaluation of the Treatment of Emotions in Five Basal Sets of Religion Texts for Catholic Secondary Schools,* unpublished master's thesis, Catholic University of America, Washington, D.C., 1962.

[157] Hagmaier and Gleason, *op. cit.*, p. 5.

Social Guidance

Social guidance is of two principal types: that which assists the pupil in achieving successful relationships with his peers and that which helps him attain satisfying relationships with members of the opposite sex. The latter type is more precisely termed "social life guidance."

Often a pupil's social maladjustment to his classroom peers is indicative of an even wider social maladjustment. Thus a study by Gronlund and Whitney revealed that a pupil's low social acceptability in the classroom, as measured by sociometric tests, correlated highly with low social acceptance by nonschool peers and neighborhood groups.[158] Since the degree of a student's social acceptance affects not only his personality but his learning also, the teacher should endeavor to provide him with social guidance. Much of this can be successfully accomplished in the classroom situation. Socialized classroom procedures such as discussion, committee work, cells, and role playing (treated in Chapter IX) will help the student learn how to work with his peers. Sometimes shyness, timidity, or overdocility prevent him from achieving satisfactory social relationships. In these cases the teacher, through the use of democratic socialized teaching methods, should encourage the pupils to think for themselves. Autocracy on the part of the teacher in the classroom, in group guidance, or in counseling will merely reinforce the pupil's social problem. In some instances a pupil has attained poor social adjustment because he is authoritarian, arrogant, or intolerant toward his peers. Gough, in his study of school intolerance discovered that in general the prejudiced pupils were markedly inferior both in intelligence and academic performance.[159] The teacher should strive to foster in such pupils an appreciation of the dignity of each person and of the value of everyone's contribution. He should also explore to ascertain whether such attitudes constitute a defense mechanism to mask feelings of inferiority or insecurity.

Lee has listed four purposes of social life guidance: fulfillment of an adolescent's personality, contribution toward personal-social adjustment, promotion of better interpersonal relationships, stimulation of a high *esprit de corps* among the student body.[160] Psychologically incomplete, a boy or girl needs to have social contact with members of the opposite sex to fill the natural void in his or her personality. Social

[158] Norman E. Gronlund and Algard P. Whitney, "Relation between Pupils' Social Acceptability in the Classroom, in the School and in the Neighborhood," *School Review*, LXIV (September, 1956), pp. 267–271.

[159] Harrison B. Gough, "Studies in School Intolerance," *Journal of School Psychology*, XXXIII (May, 1951), pp. 327–369.

[160] James Michael Lee, "Catholic Women's Colleges and Social Life," *Catholic Educational Review*, LIX (May, 1961), pp. 326–328.

life guidance should have a very special place in Catholic high schools, for there the importance of the family is stressed. Despite this fact, there seems to be some evidence which indicates that Catholic high schools are not providing sufficient social life opportunities. Thus Smith's study showed that Catholic college freshman girls, most of whom attended Catholic high schools, felt ill at ease at social affairs.[161] Social life opportunities are particularly important for high school girls planning to attend a Catholic college. Havemann and West's nationwide study disclosed that 48 per cent of the Catholic women college graduates were spinsters, compared with 31 per cent and 23 per cent of their Protestant and Jewish counterparts.[162] Providing social life opportunities should not be confused with having frequent teas. The school should sponsor at least one dance a week and should also increase the students' dating opportunities. Of course social life activities must be kept in balance and should not be so numerous as to interfere with the attainment of the other objectives of the school. Catholic teachers should not magnify out of proportion possible moral dangers of social life so that as a result the school's social life program becomes asphyxiated. All life involves danger, and those who would seek to eliminate danger cannot hope to live successfully much less fruitfully in this world.

Obviously it is easier to provide social life activities in coeducational high schools than in single-gender schools. Many Catholic high schools are of the latter type, because of the condemnation by Pope Pius XI of coeducational high schools, a proscription which was reinforced in 1958 in an instruction by the Sacred Congregation of Religious. (The instruction stated that coeducation in Catholic high schools is permissible only in localities in which the bishop deems it gravely necessary. In such instances the Sacred Congregation has listed specific precautions which must be taken, e.g., boys and girls must sit on opposite sides of the classroom and must enter the school at different times. Nor are Religious (religiosi) permitted to conduct such schools.)[163] Public and Catholic single-gender high schools should improve their social life guidance and maintain it at a high level. The importance of this was demonstrated in a study by Sister M. Assunta Highbaugh, O.S.B.,

[161] Mary Elinor Smith, *Problems of Freshman College Girls in Relation to Levels of Achievement,* unpublished master's thesis, Catholic University of America, 1950, Washington, D.C., p. 20.

[162] Ernest Havemann and Patricia West, *They Went to College.* (New York: Harcourt, Brace, 1952), pp. 55–56.

[163] Pope Pius XI, *Christian Education of Youth.* (Washington: NCWC, 1936), pp. 26–27; also S. C. de Religiosis, *"Instructio de juvenum utriusque sexus promiscua institutione,"* Acta Apostolicae Sedis, L (March, 1958), pp. 99–103.

which showed that a high percentage of dropouts from the Catholic single-gender high schools investigated gave as their reason a desire for coeducation.[164] Some Catholic dioceses have established coinstitutional high schools to resolve the problem and still be faithful to the commands of Pope Pius XI and the Sacred Congregation.

Social life guidance should also be accompanied by appropriate counseling, especially as pertains to healthy morality. The teacher should steer a middle course which will neither countenance promiscuity in the name of mental health nor promote Jansenism and prudery in the name of religion. Concerning the latter, Frs. Hagmaier, C.S.P., and Gleason, S.J., have remarked that "perhaps the greatest single shortcoming of the sexual attitudes [of Catholics] is the lack of down-to-earth, positive preparation for sexual maturity. For every sentence in Catholic literature which prepares the young person to enjoy and appreciate the sexual aspects of love, there are hundreds of sentences which define precisely and often unrealistically the threatening and dangerous aspects of man's sexual life." [165] Good social life counseling by an understanding and knowledgeable teacher can be very important to an adolescent.

Religious Guidance

Religious guidance is that assistance which the school gives to the pupil to help him know, love, and serve God better in this world so that he will be happy with Him in the next. While a public high school may constitutionally have a nondenominational moral and spiritual group guidance program, it may not legally establish religious group guidance. It would seem, however, that religious counseling would be within the legitimate rights of the public school teacher. Thus Williamson has maintained that counseling cannot be undertaken apart from the pupil's framework of values. He has stated that it is the task of the counselor to enable his counselees "how to understand more clearly their own value orientation and how to guide their behavior more rationally and more consistently in terms of the standards they have chosen." [166] If the pupil's basic value structure is religious, then effective counseling cannot be areligious. Of course only in a church-related school can religious guidance and counseling be carried on in a mature, developed, and integrated manner. Herein is a distinct advantage of the Catholic

[164] Sister M. Assunta Highbaugh, O.S.B., *A Study of the Cause of the Drop-outs in the Catholic Secondary Schools of Indianapolis, Indiana,* unpublished master's thesis, Catholic University of America, Washington, D.C., 1960.

[165] Hagmaier and Gleason, *op. cit.,* pp. 62–63.

[166] E. G. Williamson, "Value Orientation in Counseling," *Personnel and Guidance Journal,* XXXVI (April, 1958), p. 526.

high school. The priest-counselor should be the nerve center of the religious guidance program in the Catholic school. As always, the teacher still is the heart.

Fr. Moynihan, S.J., has observed that just as an overemphasis on skills and techniques has been the weakness of many non-Catholic pastoral counselors, the reverse has been true of clerical and Religious teachers and guidance workers. The counselor must be extremely understanding of his client's religious problems together with their related practical difficulties. While he "is not unconcerned with what the client may want to do, he may find it impractical and unwise from the point of view of effective counseling to use persuasion, let alone coercion." [167] Therefore, as Wrenn has observed, the counselor must "be prepared, by thought in advance, to deal with religious problems as permissively and as thoughtfully as he would any other emotion-laden experience of the client." [168] The teacher as religious counselor should help the pupil to live his religion better, rather than argue with the pupil about it or defend it.

Teachers who engage in religious guidance and counseling should have a clear, humane, and preferably profound concept of the nature of religion, morality, and the spiritual life. Fr. McLoughlin has written:

> There are some who are guiding and training youth who have two mistaken notions. The first is the sort of direction which aims at penance for the sake of penance, sacrifice for the sake of sacrifice, and drains all the joy out of the spiritual life by failing to identify the proper motive with all the exercises of self-denial. The second links the spiritual life and perfection in it with a meticulous performance of a series of devotions. There is lack of emphasis on why the act of devotion is performed and why the individual desires to perform it in the most precise manner. It would be wrong to pour individuals into a mold, even though the counselor knows that this mold has prepared others well for the fulfilment of their vocation.[169]

Of the first of these mistaken notions, Dom Stevens, O.S.B., has written: "Morality does not consist in abandoning one's own judgment and following blindly a predetermined set of rules without love or understanding. Christian behavior is more than following the voice of duty; it is more than mere avoidance of evil or serious sin. Rather it is an intelligent and mature pursuit of virtue in which the individual's prudent judgment must make real the goodness of aspirations and

---

[167] Moynihan, *op. cit.*, p. 330.

[168] C. Gilbert Wrenn, "Psychology, Religion and Values for the Counselor," in *ibid.*, p. 333.

[169] Michael J. McLoughlin, quoted in "Thoughts for Vocation Directors," *Catholic School Journal*, LXI (March, 1961), p. 28.

intentions." [170] Of the second mistaken notion, Pope Pius XII stated in an address to Catholic teachers:

> Even the exercises of piety must be kept in proper moderation, lest they become an almost intolerable burden and lead to disgust for spiritual things. Not rarely does one notice the deplorable effects of an excessive zeal in this respect. One has seen students, even from Catholic schools where moderation was not practiced and a regimen of spiritual exercises imposed that would be excessive even for young clerical students, return to their homes and neglect the most elementary duties of Christian life, such as attendance at Sunday Mass. [171]

Teachers who counsel youth with religious problems should be sympathetic rather than unfeeling, doctrinal rather than moralistic. Fr. Moynihan, S.J., has commented that the counselor should remember that "what may appear and is often labelled as an agnostic tendency in the adolescent may arise not from a dissatisfaction with religion per se, but with the manner in which it may have been presented." [172] Lawler has commented that students "seeking the bread of doctrine are handed the stone of apologetics, and no matter how valuable this latter may be in assaulting the strongholds of heresy, it is not very nourishing to a hungry soul." [173] Nor should religious counseling degenerate into giving the client a rigid set of rules the observance of which is supposed to solve his religious problems. Apropos of this, Fr. Greeley has noted that it is more important to guide the student concerning principles and ideals than to issue rules. [174] Nor should the teacher forget that morality is an inexact science. The borderline between good and evil might be clearly marked in the manuals of theology, but it becomes quite blurred in human actions. Thus Cardinal Leger has stated that "between the clear principles of morality and their final application, too many judgments of fact, too many technical considerations intervene to permit one always to arrive at certitude." [175] Indeed probably one of the greatest causes of a pupil's religious problems is his quest for moral exactness and certitude in his thoughts and acts.

The teacher as religious counselor should attempt to help the

[170] P. Gregory Stevens. O.S.B., "Current Trends in Moral Theology," *Catholic Educational Review*, LVIII (January, 1960), p. 8.

[171] Pope Pius XII, *"Nell'Accogliervi,"* in *The Pope Speaks*, III (Winter, 1956–1957), p. 255.

[172] Moynihan, *op. cit.*, p. 329.

[173] Justus George Lawler, *The Catholic Dimension in Higher Education.* (Westminster, Md.: Newman, 1958), p. 236.

[174] Andrew M. Greeley, *Strangers in the House.* (New York: Sheed and Ward, 1961), p. 141.

[175] Quoted in Benjamin L. Masse, S.J., "Is Government Doing Too Much?" *America*, CV (Aug. 26, 1961), p. 658.

student to develop an approach, an adjustment to reality which is at once healthy and Christlike. Some Jansenistically oriented teachers see the secular only as the object of ascetic exercises, something which was created in order to be avoided. The imposition of this view by teachers has all too often resulted in either rebellion against religion by the student or its opposite, the culmination in a diseased spirituality which the student feels is true religion. The first of these, rebellion, is exemplified in the life of Bertrand Russell whose early religious experience could be summed up by his favorite childhood hymn, "Weary of Earth and Laden with My Sin." [176] Small wonder that he became anti-God and antireligion. In contrast, a healthy, Christlike view was expressed by Fr. McCormick, S.J., who in his commentary on the *Summa Contra Gentiles* observed that "right knowledge of creatures is of high importance because right knowledge of God depends upon it." [177] One of the tasks of the teacher as counselor is to help the pupil to gain the right knowledge so that a healthy, mature love will develop therefrom. As Lee has observed, "Christ did not steel himself against the world or reject it; He blessed it and made it divine." [178] The teacher should use the kerygmatic approach in his religious counseling. This approach attempts to interweave doctrine with the love, joy, and beauty of Christ's message. Its core is the good news of salvation, and the Person of Christ is used as the chief illustration. Kerygma then is an approach, an attitude, not a formal counseling or pedagogical method.[179] As St. Francis de Sales said, a sad saint would be a sorry saint. The same applies to students.

The Catholic high school teacher can promote religious guidance by encouraging his students to read good spiritual books. Adolescents should be discouraged from reading overly sentimental, saccharine, exaggerated spiritual matter which characterizes a sizable portion of spiritual literature. Religious books and periodicals should present a vigorous and realistic view of spirituality. Not infrequently does defective religious literature serve to repel normal adolescents from cultivating a taste for spiritual things.

In Catholic high schools, religious guidance should be an outcome

[176] Bertrand Russell, *The Conquest of Happiness.* (New York: Liveright, 1930), p. 16.

[177] John F. McCormick, S.J., *St. Thomas and the Life of Learning.* (Milwaukee: Marquette University Press, 1942), p. 18.

[178] James Michael Lee, "Notes toward Lay Spirituality," *Review for Religious,* XXI (January, 1962), p. 45.

[179] See Johannes Hofinger, *The Art of Teaching Christian Doctrine.* (Notre Dame, Ind.: University of Notre Dame Press, 1957); Hofinger (ed.), *Teaching All Nations,* rev. by Howell. (St. Louis: Herder, 1961).

of Confession. The very nature of the sacrament is an intrinsically powerful guidance force. Thus Fr. Van der Veldt and Dr. Odenwald have commented that Confession not only removes sins but also tends to rid the penitent of guilt feelings and so contribute to his psychological security.[180] Confession is increasingly being regarded as a personal encounter with the all-loving, all-merciful God, replacing what Fr. Masure has described as "the auditing of accounts on the part of the sinner and an act of censure on the part of the director (please God these censures never turned into inquisitions)." [181] Besides the therapeutic effects of the sacrament itself, the concomitant religious counseling in the confessional serves a vital guidance function.

The annual retreat in a Catholic high school is an excellent group guidance vehicle. There are three suggestions which every school should heed concerning its annual retreat. First, it should occur early in the year to help students who have not received the sacraments during the summer counteract those morally dangerous friendships which may have been made during the vacation, to avoid inattention at conferences because of that preoccupation with studies which would occur if the retreat were held sometime later in the academic year, and to initiate the school year in an atmosphere of holiness. Second, it should be spread over a minimum of three days, else little will be accomplished. Third, the retreat master should be selectively chosen on the basis of solid piety, speaking ability, knowledge of adolescent psychology, teaching skills, and understanding of the teen-age world.

In the senior year moral and religious guidance and counseling should be given to all male students as part of the school's spiritual preinduction program to prepare them for their future tour of duty in the armed services. Barracks' morals are not conducive to leading a vigorous spiritual life. A special pregraduation retreat for seniors should constitute one phase of this program in Catholic high schools.[182]

Cribbin has observed that there are some Catholic high school students who after graduation leave the Faith partly for personal reasons and partly because of their resentment over certain aspects of their high school education. While such people are fortunately not numerous, they nevertheless do exist, and Cribbin has emphasized that Catholic educators should not delude themselves into thinking that they are

[180] James H. Van der Veldt, O.F.M., and Robert P. Odenwald, M.D., *Psychiatry and Catholicism*, 2d ed. (New York: McGraw-Hill, 1957), pp. 237–240.

[181] Eugène Masure, "Trends in Contemporary Spirituality in France," in Gautier (ed.), *Some Schools of Catholic Spirituality*. (New York: Desclée, 1959), p. 356.

[182] See Brother Bartholomew A. Clark, F.S.C., *Religious and Moral Pre-induction Programs in Catholic High Schools*. (Washington, D.C.: Catholic University of America Press, 1955).

all neurotic.[183] The high school should conduct periodic follow-up guidance not only with these extreme cases, but with all its former pupils. Fr. Stack's nationwide investigation plus his own review of the pertinent studies concluded that public and independent high schools "had at least three times as many follow-up provisions as the Catholic high schools." [184] Follow-up guidance is especially important in those Catholic high schools in which a high percentage of the graduates enter secular colleges or the business world. Of course, follow-up studies must be supplemented by other procedures. Rothney and Mooren's study discovered that the results and conclusions subsequently drawn from follow-up studies conducted by schools are representative of the whole only to the degree of their return. The reason for this is that the degree to which these follow-up inquiries are answered and returned is directly proportional to the successful adjustment of the students to post-school life. Incomplete returns, therefore, present an overly sanguine picture which the school should discount to the appropriate degree.[185] Teachers and guidance counselors should therefore utilize many follow-up devices. Four such techniques have been suggested by Humphreys and Traxler, viz., the questionnaire, the telephone call, the letter, and the interview.[186] The school should send biweekly or monthly mimeographed letters to all former students. These letters should serve primarily as a guidance vehicle, and in Catholic high schools should include a goodly amount of religious guidance. All too often the only follow-up letters the school sends out are appeals for funds.

CONCLUSION

Counseling and guidance in public and especially in Catholic high schools are very inadequate. They must be upgraded, drastically and soon. Improvement of the guidance procedures and the counseling system in public high schools was the very first specific recommendation Conant made in his famous report.[187] The address of Pope John XXIII to the Seventh Inter-American Congress on Catholic Education "called upon Catholic educators to consider very objectively whether the religious formation given in [Catholic] schools was producing the results

[183] James J. Cribbin, "Essentials and Incidentals in Guidance," *Catholic Educational Review*, LIX (December, 1961), p. 615.

[184] Stack, *op. cit.*, p. 170.

[185] John W. M. Rothney and Robert L. Mooren, "Sampling Problems in Follow-up Research," *Occupations*, XXX (May, 1952), pp. 573–578.

[186] J. Anthony Humphreys and Arthur E. Traxler, *Guidance Services*. (Chicago: Science Research Associates, 1954), pp. 217–221.

[187] James B. Conant, *The High School Today*. (New York: McGraw-Hill, 1959), pp. 44–46.

that he and the Church had a right to expect. The implication was that there is much room for improvement and his stirring message went on to specify some of the areas where improvement should be made." [188] As far as Catholic secondary schools in the United States are concerned, it would certainly seem that one of the principal areas for this needed improvement is in the quality and quantity of guidance and counseling.

Many Catholic educators are aware of this need to improve. In 1960, the National Catholic Educational Association officially stated that "adequate progress in guidance programs is *essential* to excellence in education." The Association also published a formal resolution to "encourage research and study in guidance by Catholic colleges and universities" and to "urge that regard be given to proper emphasis for professional guidance practices in [Catholic] schools." [189]

Hunter has written: "There are innumerable ways of insuring good guidance programs and adequately trained personnel for all our schools. The needs are great; the costs are not exorbitant; the returns are far beyond expectation." [190]

[188] Edward B. Rooney, S.J., "The Seventh Inter-American Congress on Catholic Education," *Bulletin of the National Catholic Educational Association*, LVI (May, 1960), p. 20.

[189] "Resolutions," *Bulletin of the National Catholic Educational Association*, LVII (August, 1960), p. 33. Italics supplied.

[190] Genevieve P. Hunter, "Action toward a Minimum Guidance Program," *Catholic High School Quarterly Bulletin*, XVI (January, 1959), p. 23.

CHAPTER XV DISCIPLINE

Nature and Purposes of Discipline

Discipline means various things to various teachers. Sheviakov and Redl have identified three different meanings commonly attributed to discipline: (1) the degree of "order" which a teacher has established in a classroom situation; (2) the methods and techniques which a teacher has employed to establish, maintain, and repair "order" in a classroom situation; (3) the type of punishment which a teacher uses.[1] In this chapter, discipline is conceived of as including all three meanings.

Discipline may be defined as that combination of all the constructive influences which the school exerts on the pupil in its efforts to guide him toward appropriate and acceptable behavior. Discipline is primarily a positive rather than a negative force. It is an amalgam of *all* the school's influences, not just the techniques of the teachers. Discipline is basically goal-oriented; it does not exist for itself. The goal toward which it is directed depends on the educational philosophy which at once undergirds and penetrates every school activity.

Discipline is of two types, external and internal. External discipline is that which is imposed on a pupil from without, e.g., by a teacher. Internal discipline is that which the student freely imposes on himself.

[1] George V. Sheviakov and Fritz Redl, *Discipline for Today's Children and Youth*, rev. by Richardson. (Washington: ASCD, NEA, 1956), pp. 2–4.

542

External discipline is often superficial. Its chief value is to serve as a temporary crutch until the pupil's will becomes sufficiently strong to exercise mastery over himself. Therefore external discipline should lessen as the semester progresses and give way to internal discipline.

There are three basic purposes of all discipline. First, it should develop in the student self-control and personal responsibility. It should lead to greater voluntary control, not an increase in surveillance techniques or a multiplication of reprisals. True discipline is self-control precisely because of the voluntary choice of the pupil to be so controlled. The student must be guided to the realization that he is never completely free, that he is at all times subject to the laws of his own being, of nature, of God, and of the common good. In order to attune his actions to the laws of these realities, self-control is necessary. Some modern educators have erroneously concluded that a person is completely free until this freedom violates someone else's rights.[2] This view shares the shortcomings of its parent philosophy, social utilitarianism, in that it ignores the primary and ever-present relevance of the natural law. Self-control helps to protect the pupil against those of his impulses which may be disordered. Public and Catholic schools alike recognize the vital importance of self-discipline. The Educational Policies Commission of the National Education Association has declared that a working democracy requires self-control, and that the school must "demonstrate that personal privilege is only one part of democracy." [3] Catholic schools possess a deeply ingrained tradition of love for and promotion of a healthy, Christlike spirit of asceticism and mortification. Indeed self-denial and the taking up of his cross are among the best ways a student can purge himself of the effects of Original Sin and grow in grace. All discipline, therefore, should lead first to self-discipline, then to self-guidance. The streams of discipline should flow into the river of guidance.

The second purpose of discipline is to help the pupil and the class to learn more effectively. Learning cannot take place amid chaos; discipline is necessary. When misbehavior occurs, it must be checked for the sake of the offender as well as the group. But if discipline is to promote learning, it must stress the rehabilitation of the offender, not just his punishment.

The third purpose of discipline is to help each student grow and develop as a person. Its function, therefore, is far deeper than keeping the pupil quiet so that the teacher's work will be rendered easier.

[2] See, for example, Curtis Paul Ramsey, "Classroom Discipline: A New Approach to Reality," *Peabody Journal of Education*, XXXIV (January, 1957), pp. 209–214.

[3] Educational Policies Commission of the National Education Association, *Learning the Ways of Democracy*. (Washington: NEA, 1940), p. 37.

Discipline must promote, not impede, mental hygiene. Moreover, constructive discipline will also stimulate virtue. It will help the student develop a correct conscience, one which is neither rigoristic nor lax. Also it will inculcate in him a habit of right action. This type of habit should be one of the most important goals of the school. Not only is it vital for everyday living, but also in times of crises when clear, deliberate thinking becomes difficult or impossible, and a person acts largely by habit. For Catholic teachers and Catholic high schools, discipline should be modeled after the manner in which Christ guided and led his *disciples*.

"The goal of discipline is to make it unnecessary." [4]

Discipline should never become an end in itself; it should be directed toward and productive of a goal. This goal should be consonant with the educational goals of each pupil as well as the class as a whole. The classic example of discipline for the sake of discipline is that of the dueling fraternities in German universities. There encounter with danger in controlled swordplay is conceived of as an exemplary way of promoting discipline for the sake of discipline. However, what usually results are wounds which scar the face rather than discipline which strengthens the will.

Self-control is almost always emphasized in education for character. But character cultivation arises from positive development as well as negative control. Indeed positive development is the more important, for it is this which fills up one's being; self-control only preserves it. Self-control must feed on positive elements, else it becomes empty formalism, as has happened so often in the past. Also, self-control can become so excessive as to dehumanize the pupil.

The teacher should carefully distinguish between occasional and habitual misbehavior. The fact that a pupil manifests excessive hostility one day does not necessarily imply that he is always unruly and unmanageable or that he constitutes a serious misbehavior problem. The teacher should also realize that while habitual pupil misbehavior has its unpleasant aspects, it also serves an important function in that it is a danger signal notifying him that there is something wrong with or disturbing in the pupil's personality and/or interpersonal relationships. Many of such serious defects go unnoticed in school when the pupil troubled with them is quiet or withdrawn rather than overtly hostile.

A study by Eaton, D'Amico, and Phillips concluded that school misbehavior problems can be classified either as violations of classroom

---

[4] Louis P. Thorpe, *The Psychology of Mental Health*, 2d ed. (New York: Ronald, 1960), p. 347.

work and behavior requirements or as violations of moral standards.[5] The teacher, particularly in a Catholic high school, should keep this distinction in mind. Failure to do so may lead to an undue magnification of the pupil's offense on the part of the teacher and unnecessary guilt feelings on the part of the pupil.

Despite its great value and importance, constructive discipline still does not seem to be properly understood or appreciated by some public and Catholic high school teachers and administrators. An NEA investigation of discipline in public schools disclosed two divergent types of discipline theories and practices: "Some schools conceive of discipline as being largely restrictive and negative . . . [while] other schools base discipline upon concepts of developmental psychology and regard discipline as a learning process by which the pupil is guided in the development of self-control and in the recognition of his responsibilities to himself and to his group, and underscores prevention as well as correction of misbehavior." [6] Henning's study of the opinion of public high school principals concerning the frequency of pupil misbehavior discovered that the following were the five offenses most commonly mentioned: congregating in lavatories and halls, running in corridors and stairs, misbehavior in class, wasting and damaging school property, and showing general rudeness and lack of consideration toward other students.[7] Oliva, commenting on Henning's findings, remarked that "principals are more interested in order and surface discipline than in causes of maladjustment." [8] Fr. Stack's nationwide study of guidance services in Catholic secondary schools concluded that "limitations were noted in the number of disciplinary services offered by Catholic high schools." [9] Some articles and books on discipline written by both Catholic and non-Catholic educators have concentrated on devices and techniques to help the teachers control and/or suppress their students rather than suggesting procedures to redirect pupil energy into worthwhile channels. Teachers should realize that what is needed are more firm and eager hands on the wheel, not a stronger foot on

[5] Merrill T. Eaton, Louis A. D'Amico, and Beeman N. Phillips, "Problem Behavior in School," *Journal of Educational Psychology*, XLVII (October, 1956), p. 355.

[6] "Discipline in the Public Schools," *NEA Research Bulletin*, XXXV (December, 1957), p. 153.

[7] Carol J. Henning, "Discipline: Are School Practices Changing?" *The Clearing House*, XXXIII (January, 1949), pp. 267–273.

[8] Peter F. Oliva, "High School Discipline in American Society," *Bulletin of the National Association of Secondary-School Principals*, XL (January, 1956), p. 17.

[9] Philip L. Stack, *A National Study of the Guidance Services in the Catholic Secondary Schools.* (Washington, D.C.: Catholic University of America Press, 1958), p. 164.

the brake. What the blind should have is not a watchdog to bite them when they go astray, but a seeing-eye dog to lead them to their destination.

The importance of constructive discipline can never be minimized. Thus Cronbach has written: "At the root of every teaching failure are disciplinary problems, but not the sort the phrase brings to mind. Discipline is a condition where the pupils are using their time in educationally desirable ways. The teacher who cannot establish this condition cannot teach." [10] Good discipline does not necessarily mean that everyone is completely silent except the teacher—indeed such pupil passivity might be a sign that nothing is being learned. Discipline (and orderliness) mean that degree of pupil attention and involvement which is appropriate to the specific learning activity engaged in. Committee work necessitates some noise. A role-playing situation will cause the focus of attention to shift from the teacher to the participants. Occasionally in a fruitful all-class discussion, some groups of pupils will become so interested in the topic that they begin to talk it over among themselves while the discussion between teacher and class is going on. A skillful teacher will recognize that this often does not constitute misbehavior, since by its very nature misbehavior is something which causes the pupil to cease engaging in a purposeful learning activity. Of course there are many situations in which complete pupil silence is necessary if learning is to take place.

ELEMENTS IN DISCIPLINE

The six chief elements in discipline are the student, the circumstance, the teacher, the classroom, the methodology, and the administration.

The Student Element

There are three basic internal factors which cause a student to behave or misbehave as he does, viz., his psychophysiological composition, his home and out-of-school environment, and the school itself.

Psychophysiological Composition. A pupil's temperament is an important factor in the conditioning of his behavior. Some students are by nature active, others passive. Some have psychological or emotional disturbances, e.g., excessive hostility feelings, while others have achieved adjusted personalities. Pupils vary in their degree of intelligence. Adolescence itself is a period of psychophysical exuberance and a striving

[10] Lee J. Cronbach, *Educational Psychology.* (New York: Harcourt, Brace, 1954), p. 482.

for independence. Sex differences are extremely important as behavior factors. Thus, for example, Fr. McCarthy, S.J., has observed that the ideals of girls are usually less broad and more restricted than those of boys because girls derive their ideals from the home and local life whereas boys tend to see the wider picture, the world view.[11] Allers has noted that girls possess a greater capacity for suffering than do boys.[12]

Unfortunately some teachers either ignore or are unaware of these psychophysiological differences in students. At least one study has shown that male students receive more teacher disapproval than do female students.[13] This disapproval is due to many factors, chief among them being the docility and meekness of girls and the overt expressiveness of boys. Instead of constructively channeling the energies of the boys, teachers seem more prone to repress them, causing undesirable educational and psychological consequences. Since girls appear to be less intellectually inclined and motivated than do boys, disciplinary guidance for girls should center more on the emotional than on the purely rational.[14] The zest should not be taken out of the exuberance and independent spirit of adolescence, but rather directed to educationally productive activities, such as sharing responsibility for classroom planning, initiating supplemental field trips, and the like. Pupils with very low intelligence or extreme emotional disturbances should be placed in special classes. The teacher should always remember that because of individual differences, the same "discipline techniques" will not work with equal effectiveness on all pupils.

Home and Out-of-school Environment. The nature and degree of the effect of the home and out-of-school environment on pupil personality and behavior were treated in Chapter V. Two additional studies will serve to reinforce what was stated there. An investigation by Wattenberg of boy and girl "repeaters" in police offenses concluded that a hostile or unfavorable home situation has a more deleterious effect on girls than on boys because boys can find an escape from the home to a large extent through sports or youth clubs whereas girls have no escape activities of comparable attraction.[15] However, it was noted that home conditions have a profound effect on the behavior of both boys and

[11] Raphael C. McCarthy, S.J., *Training the Adolescent.* (Milwaukee: Bruce, 1934), p. 162.

[12] Rudolf Allers, *The Psychology of Characters,* trans. by Strauss. (New York: Macmillan, 1931), p. 260.

[13] William J. Meyer and George G. Thompson, "Sex Differences in the Distribution of Teacher Approval and Disapproval in Sixth Grade Children," *Journal of Educational Psychology,* XLVII (November, 1956), pp. 385–394.

[14] Allers, *op. cit.,* pp. 261–266.

[15] William W. Wattenberg, "Differences between Girl and Boy 'Repeaters,'" *Journal of Educational Psychology,* XLVII (March, 1956), pp. 137–146.

girls, a fact which teachers have always known. A study by Ritholz concluded that Aristotle's concept of the psychological *tabula rasa* applies also to discipline; i.e., a child at birth does not naturally have an innate concept of *most* infractions of accepted behavior, but rather acquires this knowledge from his home and immediate neighborhood environment.[16] In dealing with a pupil who misbehaves, the teacher must always be cognizant of the powerful influence of the home and out-of-school environment.

School. Whenever two or more persons come together, as in a school, a social system begins to emerge. Individuals adopt expectations for one another, and members assume social roles. A social consciousness forms, and with it group motives, intentions, values, and judgments. Many pupils who by themselves are not misbehavior problems become so precisely because of the school group's interaction with them. If this interaction is an irritant or a thwart, the student will perpetrate misbehaviors in order to release the tensions caused by the situation. Thus, for example, a pupil who is rejected by his classmates might manifest overtly hostile behavior in order to gain their attention. On the other hand, a pupil with a psychological or emotional problem will encounter difficulty in a group situation such as the classroom. Dresher's investigation of normal and antisocial dropouts revealed a significant relationship between misbehavior and unsolved personal problems, moral and social deprivation, social inadequacy, and social disorganization.[17] The learning situation itself can also foster misbehavior, particularly if the pupils are required to engage in tasks which hold little interest or meaning for them. Paradoxically, even a good learning situation tends to promote misbehavior by causing tension in the pupils. Tension arises in a person from two causes, viz., caring about a goal and uncertainty as to the success in its attainment. Hence a good classroom learning situation automatically involves tension because if the educational goal is meaningful and purposeful, the pupil will care about it, and also he will not be sure until the very end that he has attained the product and process outcomes. A tense pupil will seek to relieve his tensions in a variety of ways. He may directly discharge them through overt acts: this is the customary misbehavior problem. Or he may withhold this type of release until later when he discharges his tensions on unrelated objects or places, e.g., on a smaller brother at home. A third possibility is that he might repress or "bottle up" his tensions, which is not healthy

[16] Sophie Ritholz, *Children's Behavior.* (New York: Bookman Associates, 1959), p. 84; see also, "Discipline: A Symposium," *NEA Journal,* XLVII (September, 1958), pp. 368–381.

[17] Richard H. Dresher, "Seeds of Delinquency," *Personnel and Guidance Journal,* XXXV (May, 1957), pp. 595–598.

psychologically, physiologically, or emotionally. Fourth, the pupil might release his tensions by working all the harder on the problem at hand, utilizing the extra energy brought on by his tensions as a learning lever. The skillful teacher will not permit a pupil's tensions to erupt into misbehavior, but will divert the energy into educationally worthwhile channels. This is constructive discipline.

The above point can be treated in another way. A study by Wattenberg of boys who ran away from home revealed "an interplay of several home and school factors leading up to the truancies."[18] Outstanding among these factors was the search for adventure and independence. Some questions naturally arise: Why was the classroom so lacking in adventure? Should it not have constituted a great adventure in search of the truth? Was the instruction so exclusively teacher-centered that it repressed the pupils' independence? In short, did the school materially contribute to the pupils' misbehavior?

Classroom discipline involves both the group and the individual pupil. Hence the teacher should not institute any disciplinary measure which, although benefiting the individual, would harm the group. Conversely the teacher should not institute any disciplinary measure which, although benefiting the group, would harm an individual.

Other Considerations about the Student. If aggression is the most commonly identified pupil misbehavior problem, it is also the most widely misunderstood. Actually every adolescent has a need for aggression because he requires an experience of satisfaction to compensate for the frustrations he receives while growing up. Some psychologists have further contended that aggressive behavior is related to a person's inner need for survival and for social mobility, both of which must be preserved if he is to live successfully in the modern world.[19] Hence the teacher should not regard pupil aggression as a sign of rebellion, but rather an expression of a psychosocial need which is stronger in some than in others. For an extremely aggressive youth, guidance clinics provide "release therapy" where he may discharge his hostility by throwing darts or breaking clay models. Once the anger is thus expelled and the frustration released, the youth often reverts to positive feelings about the person or object of his original aggression. This type of emotional bloodletting is valuable because it enables the pupil to release his aggression without any concomitant guilt feelings. When he encounters aggressive pupil behavior the teacher should not revert to instinct and attempt to repress it; rather he should sublimate it into

[18] William W. Wattenberg, "Boys Who Ran Away from Home," *Journal of Educational Psychology*, XLVII (October, 1956), p. 342.

[19] Elizabeth Geleerd, "The Beginnings of Aggressiveness in Children," *Child Study*, XXXIV (Fall, 1957), pp. 3–7.

worthwhile and acceptable activities, e.g., media which require bodily or mental expression, such as sports, the dance, painting, or puzzles. Catharsis is necessary for human development, and the pupil will seek release in one way or another. It remains for the teacher to properly channel it.

Torrence's studies indicate that the pupil who disrupts the class, disagrees with the teacher, interrupts class discussion, and manifests an extremely critical spirit may not be a future delinquent but rather a budding genius. All these characteristics have been found to be part of the personality matrix of many creative students.[20] Whether or not this type of student develops his creativity depends in large measure on how the teacher and the school deal with his creative thrusts. Insensitive teachers have all too often crushed the seeds of pupil creativity by rigid and sometimes harsh disciplinary measures. Of course a teacher should not go to the opposite extreme and bow to every whim or caprice of his pupils. Such overpermissiveness which was advocated by some ultra-progressive educators has been condemned by Pope Pius XI in his encyclical, *Christian Education of Youth*. On the other hand, the teacher should not merely issue prohibitions to block the expressions of pupils' needs or interests; he should provide effective, worthwhile substitutes. Thus, for example, when supermarkets found that requests to mothers not to place their small children in shopping carts went unheeded, they installed carts having special attachments where the tots could sit.

The teacher should not unduly stress conformity in the name of discipline. Indeed such an overemphasis actually can cause misbehavior, since it is an attempt to repress independence and initiative, both of which are vital to the human personality. Pope Pius XII in an address to teachers and pupils stated that "strict uniformity tends to stifle all personal initiative, . . . the unyielding urgency of regimentation sometimes fosters hypocrisy; . . . excessive severity ends by turning strong characters into rebels and weak ones into spineless automatons."[21] Speaking of Catholic religious superiors and teachers, Fr. Valensin commented that there is "an all-too-frequent tendency . . . to prefer run-of-the-mill conformists who lack radiance and vigor, to those dynamic personalities who, even though they be loyal and virtuous, tend to be unmanageable under authority that is uncertain about its rights and limitations."[22] Nor should a teacher regard any pupil who is not overly

---

[20] "Disruptive Child Seen as Creative," *The New York Times*, Apr. 11, 1962, p. 41.

[21] Pope Pius XII, *"Nell'Accogliervi,"* in *The Pope Speaks*, III (Winter, 1956–1957), p. 254.

[22] Quoted in Paul Hoffer, S.M., *Guide for Religious Administrators*, trans. by Rus. (Milwaukee: Bruce, 1959), p. 40.

docile or who disagrees with him as a misbehavior problem. Every pupil has a personal right to dissent, and no teacher should attempt to deprive him of this right.

Constructive discipline encourages healthy pupil independence and initiative; it does not repress them. The teacher therefore should not attempt to completely shield the pupil from the possibility of making mistakes. Free will is one of man's most precious natural gifts (indeed perhaps his most precious), and it should not be taken away from him except for a very grave reason. Besides, man learns a great deal from his mistakes, which explains to a great extent why theologians recognize that St. Augustine rather than St. Thomas is *"The* Doctor of Grace." As Fr. Greeley has stated: "Without freedom to make their own decisions—and their own mistakes—young people will never reach emotional maturity." [23]

At no time should the teacher ever attempt to take away the pupil's self-respect, even when he is being punished. Pope John XXIII in an address observed that every teacher *owes* his pupils the greatest reverence because they are entitled to it as human beings created in God's likeness.[24] The teacher should treat his pupils either as adolescents or as young adults, but never as children. In speaking to them, he should never say, "Now *children,* I want you to . . . ." Nor should he heap invective on them, indulge in name calling, or elaborate on their faults in public. The teacher should rarely if ever shout at a pupil. By shouting continually he will lose not only his effectiveness as a teacher but also the respect of the class. Besides, no teacher should shout at his brother or sister in Christ. In dealing with his pupils, the teacher should keep in mind the admonition of St. John Chrysostom: "No matter who are the men with whom you have to deal, you should speak to them courteously remembering that they are your brothers and that you are a sinner." [25]

The teacher should trust his pupils. This will breed confidence in their abilities and bring about an improvement in learning and a lessening of misbehavior. St. Ignatius recognized this when he said: "Men are rendered loyal by being believed loyal. It is far better to be deceived in some instances than to appear suspicious." [26] The author's personal experience in teaching "problem" adolescents in a large metropolitan secondary school was that never once did these "tough" youths ever betray his trust when he gave it to them, which he did frequently.

[23] Andrew M. Greeley, *Strangers in the House.* (New York: Sheed and Ward, 1961), p. 116.

[24] Pope John XXIII, *"La Vostra Presenza,"* in *The Pope Speaks,* VI (Spring, 1960), pp. 256–261.

[25] Quoted in Hoffer, *op. cit.,* p. 19.

[26] Quoted in *ibid.,* p. 12.

Constructive discipline is cooperative discipline. It is based on the principle that each pupil, as a person, has a right to participate in those plans and policies which directly affect him. To deny him this right constitutes dictatorship. Therefore it is a good policy to cooperatively establish classroom routines and regulations. This consumes considerably more time than the customary autocratic procedure, but in the long run it is far more effective in reducing misbehavior. The pupils not only know the principles underlying classroom regulations, but also will obey these rules better since they had a personal share in their formulation. Adolescents will accept responsibility if it is given to them; too often it is denied them, and then teachers wonder why pupils become irresponsible. A satisfactory way of sharing authority is for the class to elect monitors for various positions of importance in classroom routine and organization, e.g., cleaning chalkboards, checking attendance, collecting homework, and so forth. The monitor or student-assistant approach gives the pupils a sense of participation, a feeling that the classroom is theirs, not the teacher's alone. Often it is a rewarding policy to place known troublemakers in positions of responsibility. This act of trust has rehabilitated quite a few "problem" students.[27]

The Resistant Learner. The resistant learner, sometimes referred to as the "won't learner," is one who simply refuses to learn. These pupils, who represent only about 1 per cent of the total high school population, account for a disproportionately high percentage of vandalism, classroom disruption, and school crimes of all sorts. Educators like Roy and Hillson believe these youths should not be kept in school, for it is obvious that they cannot or will not profit from their school experience. These educators have observed that parents, labor unions, and certain civic organizations such as the National Child Labor Committee constitute the principal opposition to any proposal which would release these pupils from school before their sixteenth birthday. They contend that these very organizations would not tolerate at their own meetings behavior such as that perpetrated by the resistant learners in classrooms, nor would the members of these organizations encourage or even permit their own children to be seated next to or in the same room with resistant learners.[28] Certainly resistant learners cannot profit from ordinary classroom instruction, and so should be removed for their own sake and for the educational welfare of the other pupils. However, they should not be released completely from the school's care, thrown out on their own. These youths need help, perhaps more than do the normal

[27] Ruth Amsterdam, *Constructive Classroom Discipline and Practice.* (New York: Comet, 1957), pp. 56–58.

[28] "Panel VI: The Resistant Learner in Our High Schools," William Friedman, recorder, *High Points*, XXX (February, 1958), pp. 43–48.

adolescents. They should be placed either in special classes or in special schools and be given extra guidance opportunities. It should not be forgotten that some of America's most successful literary figures and businessmen were once resistant learners. There is no pupil who cannot be rehabilitated.

Juvenile Delinquency. Juvenile delinquency has increased at an alarming rate since World War II. This includes not only petty crimes but serious offenses as well. Car thefts by high school students are becoming more numerous. Narcotics "pushers" are inducing more and more teen-agers to become addicts, particularly in urban areas. Cutts and Moseley have observed that most prostitutes begin to "ply their trade" while still adolescents.[29] Many illegitimate children are born annually to American high school girls, and there are even more abortions. Alcoholism, distribution of pornographic literature, and vandalism are becoming more frequent. While it is true that these offenses exist only among a small percentage of high school students, they nevertheless do exist.

The teacher should be alert to detect any possible sign of incipient juvenile delinquency. Effective detection rests on two things. First, the teacher should carefully examine each pupil's cumulative record, looking for such items as a broken home, parental alcoholism, divorce, or personal past record of offenses. Second, the teacher should observe the person and behavior of each of his students. The value of this two-pronged effort was demonstrated in the Gluecks' classic study of juvenile delinquents. This investigation of carefully matched groups revealed that observant, alert, guidance-minded teachers can distinguish potential delinquents in at least five different ways: physically, in being essentially mesomorphic in constitution, e.g., muscular, solid; temperamentally, in being restless, energetic, impulsive, destructive; attitudinally, in being hostile, defiant, suspicious; psychologically, in preferring direct concrete expression to symbolism or abstraction; socioculturally in coming from homes of little understanding, affection, or stability.[30] Of course a pupil characterized by any or all of these qualities often does not develop into a delinquent. Fine's review of the pertinent research concluded that "almost 90 per cent of those traits which characterize a delinquent appear in children before they are eleven." [31] (The most important single factor was home conditions.) Fine's conclusion

[29] Norma E. Cutts and Nicholas Moseley, *Teaching the Disorderly Pupil.* (New York: Longmans, 1957), p. 113.

[30] Sheldon Glueck and Eleanor Glueck, *Unraveling Juvenile Delinquency.* (Cambridge, Mass.: Harvard University Press, 1950), pp. 281–282.

[31] Benjamin Fine, *1,000,000 Delinquents.* (Cleveland: World Publishing, 1955), p. 151.

highlights the importance of consulting the pupils' cumulative records.

An investigation by Kvaraceus would seem to indicate that pressures brought on the pupil by the school and classroom are a contributing cause of delinquency. He discovered that among the 761 delinquent boys and girls studied, there was a significant decrease in their delinquency rate during the summer months when school was not in session. His conclusion was that frustration and lack of educational success constituted the school's chief roles in fostering delinquency.[32] These findings are corroborated by Vedder's study which concluded that the school itself is full of predisposing stimuli which elicit aggression responses from maladjusted youth.[33] Since this is the case, the school as well as the teacher should exert especial effort to provide meaningful educational experiences to the potential delinquent. Serious curricular modifications should be made with regard to his program of studies. It is not "watering down the curriculum" if the potential delinquent learns remedial reading from a sports car magazine rather than in a class which is comparing the prose structure of Hazlitt and Lamb.

The potential delinquent should be encouraged to participate in such student activities as varsity athletics or social service programs. Unfortunately many schools have eligibility requirements in marks or conduct as prerequisites to participation in the activities program. This is regrettable, since it bars from these activities the very youths who could profit most from them. Indeed participation in these activities can serve as the first step in a rehabilitation program for potential delinquents. A teacher who has a class of troublemakers should not increase rigidity on that account, but rather be extraflexible. Previous calamitous encounters with rigidity may be one important reason why they are troublemakers. They can be helped by relaxing rigidity, thus removing a basic cause of their hostility. A teacher should never intimate to a student in any way that he thinks he is incorrigible, for this would prompt him either deliberately to act in such a way as to live up to the status role thus accorded him or to withdraw mentally from the situation, shutting himself up within the walls of his own personality. With chronic offenders the teacher should utilize group guidance techniques, arrange for counseling interviews, work with the guidance specialists and, if possible, with the home. These youths should be given tasks involving responsibility. Above all the teacher should try to act as a "big brother" to the potential delinquents. Some teachers seem to pay a great deal of attention to the good students and neglect or ignore those

---

[32] W. C. Kvaraceus, "Delinquency: A By-product of the School," *School and Society*, LIX (May 13, 1944), pp. 350–351.

[33] Clyde B. Vedder, *The Juvenile Offender*. (New York: Doubleday, 1954), p. 91.

who habitually misbehave. They appear to have forgotten that Christ left the ninety-nine good sheep to go after the one which was lost.

The teacher should avoid basing his conclusions on the surface manifestations of problem pupils. He must probe deeper to find the basic cause. Often a student's outward behavior masks the real difficulty; e.g., the youth who habitually tears up his textbook might be trying to conceal the fact that he is a poor reader. Merely punishing him for his offenses will not effect a cure for the basic problem.

The Circumstance Element

The influence of the home is perhaps the most important circumstance which causes a pupil to behave or misbehave as he does. A study by the NEA concluded that "the factors most frequently associated with misbehavior in school, in the opinion of classroom teachers, are related to irresponsible parents, unsatisfactory home conditions, and lack of supervision due to the mothers' working outside the home." [34] Studies of juvenile delinquents confirm this opinion.

The influence of the local milieu or neighborhood is also a prominent circumstance. Warner's classic study concluded that families in lower socioeconomic areas often hold different values from families in "upper class" neighborhoods; e.g., the former frequently think school attendance is a waste of time while the latter regard it as crucial to social and economic success.[35] Street fighting and boisterousness are considered signs of strength in underprivileged neighborhoods, but the same behaviors are considered manifestations of weakness, barbarity, and low intelligence in wealthy areas.

A team approach is perhaps the best method in dealing with misbehavior problems involving home and/or community. Conscious cooperation of the various teachers and guidance personnel will not only increase understanding, but also enable a unified program of remedial action to be undertaken. The homeroom teacher or guidance specialist should attempt to work with community agencies such as the Boys Club in order that this unified program may continue after school hours, on weekends, and during vacations. Catholic high schools should attempt to form a closer working relationship with the Catholic Youth Organization. Visits to the home are also of great help. Here cooperation between the school and social service agencies (in Catholic high schools with Catholic Charities) can further extend and make more comprehensive this unified program.

[34] "Discipline in the Public Schools," *NEA Research Bulletin*, XXXV (December, 1957), p. 155.

[35] W. Lloyd Warner and Paul S. Lunt, *The Social Life of a Modern Community*. (New Haven, Conn.: Yale University Press, 1941).

In some instances, other circumstances are of such a type that they seem to invite and provoke a pupil to misbehavior. Sister Mary Jutta, O.S.F., has given a good example of such a circumstance. "A basketball tournament is scheduled for 3:30 at the town hall. If dismissed punctually, the pupils of a certain school could reach the hall just in time for the game. Unforeseen circumstances force the teacher to keep his class overtime. Two boys who sit near the door slip out unnoticed." [36] What should the teacher do if he later detects that two boys were missing? What if these boys were players on one of the teams? Could the teacher possibly have prevented the unforeseen circumstance from arising? This example demonstrates that constructive discipline is more than a matter of following a few simple rules. Circumstances alter a situation and affect a pupil's behavior, often radically. Hence the teacher's understanding is so crucial to truly constructive discipline. Rules are helpful, but they are not enough.

The Teacher Element

A very important factor in promoting or reducing pupil misbehavior is the teacher himself. His personality can win over even the most recalcitrant student; on the other hand, it can actually cause a normal pupil to misbehave. A sense of humor is a great asset to a teacher in dealing with problem students, whereas a cold, rigid personality is a definite hindrance.

A study by Lewin concluded that pupils in autocratically conducted classrooms attempted to use hostile attention-getting mechanisms almost thirty times more than did students in a democratically conducted class.[37] An investigation by Kounin and Gump revealed that pupils who have punitive teachers "manifest more aggression in their misconducts, are more unsettled and conflicted about their misconduct in school, and are less concerned with learning and school-unique values" than pupils who have nonpunitive teachers.[38] These studies forcefully demonstrate that teacher authoritarianism is a primary cause of overt pupil misbehavior, on the one hand, or inferiority feelings and toadyism, on the other. Both constitute misbehavior problems. Perceptive Catholic writers are also aware of this fact. Thus Bishop Roberts,

[36] Sister Mary Jutta, O.S.F., *School Discipline and Character.* (Milwaukee: Bruce, 1930), pp. 255–256.

[37] Kurt Lewin, "Experiments in Social Space," *Harvard Educational Review,* IX (January, 1939), pp. 21–32.

[38] Jacob S. Kounin and Paul V. Gump, "The Comparative Influences of Punitive and Nonpunitive Teachers upon Children's Conceptions of Misconduct," *Journal of Educational Psychology,* LII (February, 1961), p. 49.

S.J., has observed that the tendency toward tyranny and arbitrariness in superiors which in turn breeds subserviency in inferiors is more to be feared than a so-called "spirit of rebellion" in these inferiors.[39] Fr. Hoffer, S.M., noted in this regard that "we can be sure that disobedience in a given situation, whether in a class or in a [religious] community, is more often attributable to the incompetence of the head than to a spirit of independence in a subordinate." [40]

There are at least three basic causes of teacher authoritarianism. The first is insecurity. A teacher who is insecure because of defective personality, knowledge, or pedagogical skill will resort to authoritarianism as a defense mechanism against feelings of inadequacy and against the possibility of being bested by his students. The second cause is low intelligence. Studies such as that of Kounin have concluded that the higher the intelligence, the less the rigidity.[41] The third cause is a mistaken concept of authority or an erroneous theory of human nature. Of the latter, Msgr. Johnson observed that autocracy or even despotism in the classroom cannot be justified on the basis of the teacher's belief in the doctrine of Original Sin. Such belief does not in any way give authorization to harsh regimentation or a rule of fear, nor does it demand that a pupil never speak unless spoken to by the teacher.[42] Of course a teacher may be secure, intelligent, and possess correct concepts of authority and human nature and still be autocratic.

The authoritarian teacher is primarily interested in maintaining a regimented orderliness in a class, while the democratic teacher is chiefly concerned with the growth of each individual within the context of a purposeful learning situation. The authoritarian teacher demands a discipline based on the unquestioning obedience of the pupil, while the democratic teacher seeks a discipline arising out of a desire of the pupils to learn in the most effective manner possible. The autocratic teacher has his leadership solely because of his status role; the democratic teacher has his because the pupils freely recognize him as their leader. What Brother Antoninus, O.P., has written about the religious superior applies with equal cogency to the democratic teacher: "In the ideal community, the superior is not an autocratic mastermind, but rather an umpire presiding over the creative efforts of the individual members as they engage in their projects in the fabric of the assumed collective

[39] Cited in Hoffer, op. cit., p. 47.

[40] Ibid., p. vi.

[41] Jacob S. Kounin, "Experimental Studies of Rigidity. I. The Measurement of Rigidity in Normal and Feeble-minded Persons," Character and Personality, IX (1941), pp. 251–273.

[42] George Johnson, "Progressive Education," Bulletin of the National Catholic Educational Association, XXXVII (August, 1940), p. 564.

goal." [43] Autocratic teaching is an affront to the dignity of the pupil, an affront to which pupils sometimes react by becoming misbehavior problems. Thus Two Sisters of Notre Dame wrote: "To compel submission of one human being to another by the low motive of natural fear is to degrade human nature: it constitutes tyranny." [44]

The teacher who wishes to promote constructive discipline should avoid autocratic, harsh, and even brutal classroom control, on the one extreme, and a weak, indulgent, and ineffectual control, on the other. The authority of the teacher is vital in the classroom. This authority should not be absolutist, neither should it be abdicated. A skillful teacher will share certain elements of his authority with his pupils. If some authority is delegated to the students, they can scarcely rebel against it, for to do so would be tantamount to rebellion against themselves.

While autocracy is still a problem in public schools, it seems to constitute a particularly acute difficulty for teachers in Catholic schools. Perhaps the chief cause of this is a mistaken identification of authoritarianism and authority. O'Dea has asked: "Does our Catholic teaching so combine authoritarianism and the verbal formula as to discourage active inquiry on the part of the student? Is such passivity in religious matters mistaken for faith?" [45] Some writers think that the root cause of this autocracy may be traced to the education and discipline received in seminaries and novitiates. A study of seminary education by Fr. Brooks, O.Praem., concluded:

A type of passive obedience is sometimes encouraged. The initiator of projects and the creative thinker may be viewed suspiciously as youths who are courting a spirit of independence which is irreconcilable with the spirit of obedience. The impression remains that the truly obedient subject is the one who waits for the Superior to initiate the action. But it is not the mind of the Church that obedience should serve as a cloak of respectability for inactivity; nor is it Her intention that subjects renounce all creativity and independent thought in the name of obedience. [46]

Fr. Fichter, S.J., has noted that some communities of Religious also have the same tendency to regard suspiciously those of its members who

[43] Brother Antoninus, O.P., "The Artist and Religious Life," *The American Benedictine Review*, XI (December, 1960), p. 232.

[44] Two Sisters of Notre Dame, *Aids to Will Training*. (New York: Pustet, 1943), p. 163.

[45] Thomas F. O'Dea, *American Catholic Dilemma: An Inquiry into the Intellectual Life*. (New York: © Sheed and Ward, 1958), p. 135.

[46] Robert M. Brooks, O.Praem., "The Former Major Seminarian," *Bulletin of the National Catholic Educational Association*, LVIII (August, 1961), p. 49.

are creative, initiate projects, or engage in independent thinking.[47] The answer to this problem is a rethinking of the nature of obedience. Obedience should provide a positive framework for the exercise of pupil initiative and independence; it should not serve exclusively as a negative barrier. Nor should obedience be construed as a forced conformity with all the ideas of the teacher or superior. Obedience should promote pupil activity rather than merely seek to preserve the *status quo*. Fr. Ferree, S.M., has stated: "Any Catholic school which at the present time aims to make 'good Christians' instead of 'active apostles' is just about four and a half centuries too late to be of any outstanding use to the Church, though it is, of course, still possible that it may be of some use to the individuals who happen to pass through its portals." [48]

Fostering constructive discipline becomes much easier when the pupils see the teacher as a person. In this way the pupils come to know him as a warm friend, not a cold, impersonal force. The teacher should always be friendly to his pupils, maintaining, of course, the proper distance. Although this distance should always exist, it should not be enormous.

Stouffer conducted an important investigation which compared the attitudes of secondary school teachers and mental hygienists on the relative seriousness of various forms of student misbehavior. The comparison revealed that overt objective behavior disorders were rated the more serious by the secondary school teachers, while inner subjective problems were considered the more serious by the mental hygienists. The misbehavior problems which the mental hygienists rated more serious than the teachers included withdrawal, fearfulness, shyness, tattling, and daydreaming. The misbehavior problems which the mental hygienists rated less serious than the teachers included impertinence, destroying school materials, tardiness, cheating, interrupting, and smoking. Thus the hygienists seem to have viewed the pupils' disorders in terms of the inner dynamics of their future personal development, whereas the teachers saw the misbehaviors in the light of good classroom order and their own authority. Stouffer concluded that teachers are more interested in external measurements of a pupil's behavior than in good mental hygiene.[49] Teachers therefore should avoid placing an ex-

[47] Joseph H. Fichter, S.J., "The Sociological Aspects of the Role of Authority in the Adaptation of the Religious Community for the Apostolate," in Haley, C.S.C. (ed.), *Proceedings of the 1958 Sisters' Institute of Spirituality*. (Notre Dame, Ind.: University of Notre Dame Press, 1958), p. 27.

[48] William Ferree, S.M., "The Population Explosion and Vocations to the Higher Life," *Bulletin of the National Catholic Educational Association, op. cit.*, p. 438.

[49] George A. W. Stouffer, "The Attitude of Secondary-School Teachers toward Certain Behavior Problems of Children," *School Review*, LXIV (November, 1956), pp. 358–362.

clusive premium on overt orderliness at the expense of their pupils' mental health and personal development. Kvaraceus' review of the pertinent research on the different attitudes of teachers and psychologists toward misbehavior problems confirmed Stouffer's findings; however, Kvaraceus observed that the post-World War II studies reveal that while there is still some difference in the attitudes of teachers and psychologists, nevertheless, those of the teachers are coming more into harmony with those of the psychologists.[50]

Hymes has commented that one of the teacher's major contributions in promoting constructive discipline is to confront the pupils with their misbehavior.[51] Often the students are unaware of the nature, seriousness, or possible consequences of their offenses. Once they themselves come to a realization of what they have done, they frequently repent and make amends. Individual counseling by the teacher can do much to bring about such an awareness. This is positive discipline and is superior to a curt public reproof.

In establishing a climate of constructive discipline, the teacher's conduct and demean on the first day of the new school year are very important. Particularly is this true for the new teachers in the school, because they have no established reputation upon which to rely. Quite frequently the pupils will "test out" a teacher on the first day of school to see how much they can get away with. Therefore it is imperative that on the very first day, and indeed for the first week, the teacher be friendly but firm. Once a proper teacher-pupil working relationship is formed, the disciplinary climate can become normal. The teacher should dress neatly and conservatively; this is especially important for female teachers who are young and pretty. It is a good practice to discuss misbehavior problems with one's colleagues, for very often they will have helpful suggestions. Some teachers, however, seem reluctant to discuss their misbehavior problems with their colleagues for fear they will be stigmatized as weak teachers, unable to cope with the classroom situation. Above all the teacher should not yield to the temptation of sending his misbehavior cases to the principal's office. To do so is a public abdication of authority and an admission to the class of weakness and ineffectuality. Each teacher should learn how to deal constructively with offenders, otherwise he should renounce the profession. Only in extreme cases and as a last resort should the principal be notified.

Discipline in the Catholic high school should be at all times Christlike. It should promote virtuous living and sanctity, not fear. In this

[50] William C. Kvaraceus, "Behavior Problems," *Encyclopedia of Educational Research*, 3d ed. (New York: Macmillan, 1960), p. 138.

[51] James L. Hymes, Jr., *Behavior and Misbehavior*. (Englewood Cliffs, N.J.: Prentice-Hall, 1955), p. 26.

regard a priest or Religious must be particularly careful in his disciplinary actions toward students. A fear of priests or Religious resulting from poor disciplinary practices can lead to unhealthy clerical-lay relations in later life. It is not uncommon for a pupil to be afraid of a priest, a brother, or a sister. This can easily cause in the mind of the student an identification of fear and punishment with religion. Priests and Religious in Catholic high schools should remember what St. Benedict wrote in the Prologue of his Rule: "We must, therefore, establish a school of the Lord's service, in the institution of which we hope to order nothing that is harsh or rigorous." And the comment of the Sacred Congregation of Religious about religious superiors can easily be extrapolated to clerical and Religious teachers and their effect on a student: "When a Religious abandons his vocation, the superior of the house is often more in need of God's mercy than the one who left it." [52]

The Classroom Element

The nature, type, size, condition, and management of the classroom have a definite effect on discipline. Kvaraceus' review of the pertinent research concluded that larger classes are more productive of juvenile delinquents than are smaller classes.[53] A questionnaire survey by Eaton and associates of over two hundred classroom teachers revealed that teachers thought that one of the chief causes of pupil misbehavior was large class size.[54]

The physical conditions of the classroom can do much to distract the pupils from the learning activities at hand and so act as causative elements of misbehavior. The teacher should therefore attempt to make the physical conditions of the classroom as attractive as possible. The lighting and illumination should be more than adequate, the temperature comfortable. The room should be well ventilated, for stuffy rooms lead to fatigue in intellectual tasks. The seating should be conducive to learning. Movable furniture is extremely helpful in this regard.

Classroom Management. Classroom management refers to the manner in which the daily classroom routine is organized and conducted. Prospective teachers fresh out of college come prepared to teach their content or problem area in a pedagogically proper manner. However, many of them are relatively uninformed about noninstructional duties and procedures of classroom management. As a result they may inad-

[52] Quoted in Hoffer, *op. cit.*, p. 47.

[53] William C. Kvaraceus, *Juvenile Delinquency.* (Washington: Department of Classroom Teachers, NEA, 1958), p. 4.

[54] Merill T. Eaton and associates, "Some Reactions of Classroom Teachers to Problem Behavior in Schools," *Educational Administration and Supervision,* XLIII (March, 1957), pp. 129–139.

vertently cause misbehavior problems. To remedy this situation, the following suggestions on the techniques of classroom management are offered:

1. All classroom rules and regulations should be reasonable and founded on rational ground.

2. There should be some definite seating arrangement, one which will make it possible for the teacher to see each student at every moment. In all-class discussions it is best to seat the pupils by size. When pupils are engaged in small-group work, they should be seated around tables. Classes with a small enrollment can have the seats arranged in rectangular or circular fashion.

3. All pupils should be in their places ready for work when the bell rings for the beginning of class.

4. Students should have all materials they might need during the class readily available on the desks. Borrowing of materials should be discouraged.

5. There should be a definite system for the collection of assignments and the distribution of corrected papers.

6. No pupil should be permitted to leave the room without permission.

7. Classroom interruptions should be kept at a minimum, e.g., notes to or from the office.

8. Janitorial duties performed by students, e.g., erasing chalkboards, opening windows, and the like should be routinized.

9. There should be an orderly procedure for dismissal when the bell rings signaling the end of class. This does not mean the pupils must file out silently two by two in kindergarten fashion.

10. Clerical work, e.g., filling in the roll book, should be done promptly, but preferably not during class time. Unfortunately some principals seem to regard clerical work as the teacher's most important function, so that in their schools teaching interferes with the regular work of the teacher.

11. To assist the substitute teacher, should the occasion for this arise, the names of student assistants and other relevant information, e.g., location of fire exits, should be posted in a prominent place in the classroom or on the teacher's desk.

The basic principle underlying effective classroom management is routine and definiteness tempered with appropriate flexibility.

The Methodology Element

One of the most important factors in discipline is the pedagogical skill of the teacher. Being a good teacher in itself reduces misbehavior problems. The following pedagogical suggestions will help the teacher promote constructive discipline and forestall misbehavior:

1. Plan each lesson carefully. Unplanned lessons move slowly and become dull to the pupils.

2. Utilize motivation at the beginning of the lesson and keep it high throughout.

3. Relate the problem or content under study to the pupils' interests and needs. A purposeful lesson will absorb their attention.

4. Provide continuous pupil participation throughout the entire lesson. Youths, particularly early adolescents, crave excitement in which they can be directly involved. A teacher who does not allow his students to participate in learning will soon find them participating in misbehavior. Mayer's nationwide study of American schools concluded that "there is one blanket statement which can be safely said about the world's schools: the teachers talk too much." [55]

5. Foster pupil creativity, originality, and initiative in every phase of the lesson.

6. Gear the work to the pupils' abilities. A teacher who makes work impossible for the pupils will soon have the pupils making life impossible for him.

7. Keep the classroom atmosphere informal; e.g., do not normally require a pupil to stand when reciting. Excessive formalism breeds rebellion.

8. Frequently change the type of classroom activity, from discussion to committee work to panels to cell meetings and so forth. This will keep the work at a lively, interesting pace. In committee work, the chairman is responsible for the discipline of his group.

9. Make sure that the pupils are constantly busy and at work. Idleness causes boredom and boredom generates misbehavior. If the teacher fails to keep his pupils busy, they will certainly keep him busy.

10. Direct questions to inattentive pupils.

The curricular design can help or hinder even the best teacher's methodology. A unified curriculum such as Core merges pupil interest and content into problem areas of personal and eternal concern to the students. Thus involvement in classwork is heightened and misbehavior lessened. When the pupils come into the classroom at the beginning of a large block period, they need not be assigned work because they are in a continuing phase of an overall problem. They already know what work must be done in the class to solve it. In a fragmented curricular design such as the subject-centered approach, every lesson is atomistic and only generally developmental. Pupil interest is subordinated to the covering of a specific amount of material designated in the syllabus. In such a design the teacher who wishes to maintain good discipline should, prior to the lesson, put some sort of introductory exercise on the chalkboard so that the pupils will have something to do when they enter the room.

[55] Martin Mayer, *The Schools.* (New York: Harper, 1961), p. 8.

The Administrative Element

The wholehearted cooperation of the administration is necessary if constructive discipline is to be fostered. There is some evidence that school administrators are not doing enough in this regard. Dresher's investigation of high school dropouts concluded that the school did not provide proper or even adequate guidance, curricular flexibility, or individualized instruction, particularly with respect to the misbehavior problems, despite the fact that these youths received failing marks, were frequently absent, did not participate very much in the activities program, failed to get along with their peers, and were consistently rated as poor school citizens by their teachers.[56] The administration should take the lead in developing a climate of constructive discipline throughout the entire school and should do all in its power to implement this climate through specific positive measures and services.

The establishment, maintenance, and revision of school-wide rules should be a cooperative enterprise involving administration, faculty, and students. This can be done by a committee composed of representatives of each group. A school in a democracy should be run democratically, otherwise it bears open testimony that it does not practice what it preaches. Some administrators like to talk about "our school family," but they become quite silent when it comes to the right of determination by the members of that family. The Student Council should have a definite voice in the management of the school; it should not be a sop thrown to the students to keep them quiet or amused. Some schools use student courts to deal with infractions of rules.

Schools, particularly Catholic high schools, should work toward the establishment of an honor system. In some areas this may be impossible, but there are many other places in which the students can profit from an honor system. Even in schools where the honor system is an established tradition, there are occasional breaches; however, despite these lapses, the system is advantageous because of the lessons it teaches in responsibility and personal dignity. An honor system, to be effective, must never be imposed on the pupils from without; if the students themselves do not desire it, then it will be ineffectual. Also before an honor system is introduced, much cooperative planning and subsequent refining have to take place.

TEACHER REACTIONS TO PUPIL MISBEHAVIOR

There are two principal ways in which a teacher can react to the misbehavior of a pupil; he may punish him, or he may treat him with kindness.

[56] Dresher, loc. cit.

Punishment

It was observed in Chapter XII that most educators hold punishment as greatly inferior to reward in promoting effective learning. Nevertheless, punishment is sometimes not only necessary but desirable. It serves to redirect misbehavior into acceptable channels. In this way, punishment may stimulate new worthwhile behavior which itself will be subsequently rewarded. The effects of this reward will be positive reinforcement. Therefore even though the effect of punishment is temporarily negative, it may under certain circumstances permit the positive and more permanent effects of reward to become operative.

There are some ultraprogressive educators who would flatly condemn the use of any and all punishment. While a permissive approach is valuable, it can be overdone. Democracy does not mean that the teacher should allow his pupils to indulge in whatever behavior they choose. On the other hand, there are some ultraconservative educators who seem to think the only alternative to an overly permissive approach is harsh, Hammurabilike punishment. They observe with great satisfaction that in the "traditional" schools of yesteryear the teachers did not spare the rod and spoil the child. These educators, however, seem to confuse tradition with the debris of the ages and humanitarian advances with laxist retrogressions. Then, too, there are those teachers who, in times of difficulty, revert to primitive methods of coping with problems, e.g., a teacher who slaps a pupil because he "talked out of turn." To be sure, harsh, repressive punishment is quicker and easier; however, both Christianity and democracy are committed to the slower but infinitely more salutary process of searching for causes and fostering pupil growth from within.

Punishment should never be used *by itself*, because it is a negative reinforcement. Rather, constructive discipline dictates that the teacher offer concomitantly with the punishment a positive alternative to the student so that the punishment will propel him to seek these positive realities more avidly than he otherwise would. Cutts and Moseley have remarked: "Punishment is at best a negative means of control. It is not a substitute for teaching a pupil *why* he should behave differently. And it is certainly not a substitute for finding and correcting the causes of misbehavior." [57] Nor should punishment be administered as an end in itself; instead it should be meted out only to reinforce in the pupil the concept that he should not repeat a certain wrong deed. Punishment should always be used to promote learning, not to serve as an end in itself. Even then its advantages are not clear. Hilgard and Russell have listed four objections to punishment as a motivation for learning:

[57] Cutts and Moseley, *op. cit.*, p. 28. Used by permission of David McKay Co., Inc.

(1) While punishment may alter behavior, the results of punishment are less predictable than the results of reward. Reward says: Repeat what you have done. Punishment says: Stop it! But the punishment does not tell what to do, and the result may simply be emotional upset; (2) The interpersonal aspects of the punishment situation are fraught with more hazards than those in reward. As a teacher or parent becomes emotionally upset, it is an easy matter to take out aggression on children through punishment. The children may be provocative, but the danger of injustice in punishment is great, and children are extremely sensitive about injustice . . . ; (3) The results of punishment are said to be less permanent as far as learning is concerned than the results of reward. The evidence to date comes largely from animal experiments but the possibility is a good one that the effects of punishment are primarily emotional, affecting performance rather than learning; (4) Punishment under some circumstances tends to fix the punished behavior rather than eliminate it.[58]

Some teachers think that one of the chief advantages of punishment is its usefulness as a deterrent. However, this alleged advantage may be legitimately questioned on a number of counts. Does not such punishment tend to make the end justify the means? Furthermore, this type of punishment is often injurious to the pupil's mental health. It creates a punitive class climate, one which is hardly conducive to optimum psychological development or creative learning. Deterrent punishment is associated with dictatorial societies, where, for example, one man will be whipped and lashed in the public square for stealing some food "to serve as a lesson for all." Often deterrent punishment does not serve its avowed purpose of redirecting behavior; rather it motivates the pupil or group to seek more ingenious devices to evade the rules. By the same token, there is no real positive educational or psychological value in administering superfluous punishment, the type whose purpose is "to make sure they keep in line." Surely modern civilization has passed beyond the Devil's Island stage of development.

Principles of Punishment. To be productive of educationally, psychologically, and morally worthwhile learning outcomes, the form of punishment administered should meet the following criteria:

1. Punishment should be used only as the last resort. Only when conferences, explanations, and divers guidance devices have failed should punishment be used.

2. Punishment should at all times be corrective, never of a punitive or deterrent type.

[58] Ernest R. Hilgard and David H. Russell, "Motivation in School Learning," *Learning and Instruction,* National Society for the Study of Education, Forty-Ninth Yearbook, Part I. (Chicago: University of Chicago Press, 1950), p. 49.

3. Punishment should be such that its process and product outcomes are desirable behavior, and hopefully desirable learning.

4. The form and type of punishment should be psychologically appropriate to the pupil.

5. The pupil should both know and accept the purpose of the punishment.

6. The pupil should realize that he is being punished.

7. Punishment should be true punishment, i.e., something unpleasant to the student. Thus, for example, detaining a pupil after school might not really be punishment, because in certain neighborhoods detention will gain for that pupil considerable peer prestige. Of course punishment can be true punishment yet not be harsh.

8. Punishment should be based more on the motive for the misbehavior than for the misdeed itself. Catholic theology has always recognized the primacy of the intention. A pupil may have done something wrong without knowing it was wrong. There is a difference between guilt and blame.

9. If punishment must be administered, the teacher should act firmly and decisively.

10. Once punishment has been opted by the teacher, he should punish the pupil as soon after the misbehavior as possible. Delaying punishment seriously weakens its effectiveness as a learning device, because the reinforcement is not immediate.

11. Punishment should be short and simple. Prolonged punishments either lose their effectiveness or seriously damage a pupil emotionally.

12. The punishment should be commensurate with the seriousness of the offense. In this regard it is inadvisable for the teacher to notice every minor behavior infraction. He must learn to develop the technique of feigning unawareness of very small offenses. Failure to do this can lead to mild teacher neurosis.

13. The punishment should normally be administered in such a way that it does not publicly embarrass or humiliate the pupil. Very occasionally public punishment is advantageous from the point of view of group pressure on the offender, but even in these rare instances great caution should be exercised.

14. While administering punishment, the teacher should not continually refer to the pupil's past offenses.

15. The punishment should always be just and administered fairly. Punishing a pupil unjustly or in an unfair manner will make the teacher permanently or at best temporarily a victim of an unfavorable group attitude.

16. The group should never be punished for the offenses of one individual. A teacher should not inflict reprisals on the entire class in order to force an undisclosed or covert culprit to reveal his identity. Such Nazi tactics are out of place in public and certainly in Catholic high schools.

17. Punishment should always be administered in a manner which manifests a conscious liking for and acceptance of the pupil being punished. A review

of the pertinent research by Jones concluded that punishment is most effective under these conditions.[59]

18. When punishment is necessary, the teacher should not threaten; he should act. Punishment in the present is more effective than a threat of future punishment. Similarly the teacher should not make threats which he cannot carry out. This will cause pupils to lose respect for the teacher's authority and his ability to punish in the manner he desires.

19. Punishment should never be administered in anger or in a spirit of rancor.

20. After the punishment has been administered, the teacher should "let bygones be bygones" and restore and resume a normal relationship with the pupil.

Punishment Devices. There are at least ten different devices which teachers currently use to punish pupils who misbehave.

A. REPROOF. Reproof is public verbal condemnation of another's unworthy actions. The review of the research in Chapter XII concluded that reproof is usually not so conducive to learning as is praise. Besides, constant scolding soon becomes ineffective. Nevertheless reproof, particularly if it assumes the form of constructive critical wit, can sometimes be a beneficial form of punishment. Fr. Damon Kelley, O.Carm., has defined critical wit as "the ability to express criticism or the expression of criticism which employs cleverly jocose words and appropriate voice tones, gestures and facial expressions. Critical wit is both an ability and an expression." [60] As identified by Fr. Kelley, there are three chief types of critical wit, viz., banter, ridicule, and derision. The last two should not be used by the teacher because they can cause psychological harm to the student and hence adversely affect his learning. They are also un-Christian modes of expression. Banter, however, can serve as a constructive vehicle for reproof, since the wit of what is said will cushion the sting of the content. Nevertheless, banter must be used skillfully, else the pupil will be ignorant of the jocular tone and take great offense.

B. FORCED APOLOGY. Forced apology may be either public, i.e., before the class, or private, i.e., to the teacher personally. In general, forced apology is a poor punishment device because it promotes hypocrisy in the pupil. An apology should be a sincere expression of regret, not an exercise in false pretense.

C. SENDING A NOTE TO THE PARENTS. This device is quite efficacious if handled properly. It punishes the pupil in that it brings his mis-

[59] Vernon Jones, "Character Education," *Encyclopedia of Educational Research,* 3d ed. (New York: Macmillan, 1960), p. 190.

[60] Damon Kelley, O.Carm., "The Use of Critical Wit in the Classroom," *Catholic Educational Review,* LVII (December, 1959), p. 599.

behavior to the attention of his parents, something which is distasteful to him. It is remedial in that it promotes a combined home-school program of corrective, constructive discipline. However, the teacher should not send notes home to the parents only when the pupil misbehaves; when he behaves well, the parents should also be informed. At the same time the teacher must remember that there are some parents who do not seem to care very much about the conduct of their offspring —this may be precisely why some pupils misbehave in the first place.

D. DEMERIT SYSTEM. A demerit system is one which assigns a weighted number of negative points or demerits for specified behavior infractions. When a pupil has accumulated more than a designated number of demerits, he is denied certain "privileges," e.g., participation in the student activities program. The demerit system was opposed as early as 1916 by Bagley on the grounds that it delays the administration of punishment and transforms the teacher into a bookkeeper of demerits.[61] Furthermore the demerit system approach tends to create a punitive classroom climate which discourages pupil initiative and creativity (for fear of getting a demerit). The teacher becomes a policeman who wields a demerit pencil for a nightstick.

E. DEPRIVATION OF PRIVILEGES. This device seeks to punish the pupil by removing some prized possession or activity. Deprivation of privileges as a punishment device should be used with great discretion because it can do more harm than good. Certainly there seems little justification for depriving a pupil of the chance to improve himself through participation in some learning activity, even though the school might think this activity is peripheral, e.g., a field trip or a sports event. To be sure, a pupil who has misbehaved often needs fruitful participation in the activity more than do other pupils. Deprivation of privileges often constitutes ineffectual motivation. McKown has cited six separate studies, all of which indicate that there is no evidence to support the assumption that participation in the school's activities program adversely affects school marks.[62]

F. LOWERING A MARK. This device consists in revising a pupil's mark in a downward direction as a punishment for misconduct. This practice can never be condoned because it invalidates the mark, rendering it of little worth and use. It is also a violation of the virtue of justice. As was noted in Chapter XIII, there should be a separate and distinct mark for a pupil's conduct, with appropriate subheadings.

G. ISOLATION. Isolation consists in removing a pupil from the group

---

[61] William C. Bagley, *School Discipline*. (New York: Macmillan, 1916), p. 206.
[62] Harry C. McKown, *Extra-Curricular Activities*, 3d ed. (New York: Macmillan, 1956), pp. 600–602.

in some manner. Isolation, properly used, may be a constructive punishment device. It may serve to extricate a pupil from disturbing or provocative influences, or it may remove a disruptive pupil from a purposeful group. However, isolation should be employed only with caution, because it can promote psychological disturbances in the pupil and lead to poor mental hygiene. Before isolating a pupil, the teacher should consult the guidance specialist and the school psychologist. Unfortunately, unforeseen exigencies sometimes make such consultations impossible.

H. DETENTION. Detention is a device whereby the pupil is required to remain after school hours. Detention may be a constructive technique if used properly. It should serve an educationally worthwhile purpose, such as remedial work or completion of extra homework which was assigned because of the misbehavior. However, even this has its limitations, because it may make learning synonymous with punishment in the mind of the pupil. In the detention period, the student should not be required merely to sit in his seat with his arms folded. This makes a mockery out of education and places the teacher in the position of consciously forcing the pupil to waste time. Fr. Stack's study indicates that some Catholic high schools still require a pupil to spend detention in writing over and over the particular school rule which he violated.[63] This practice is psychologically unsound, ridiculous, and unsuited to the mentality of the adolescent. Detention, to be effective, should not be used with great frequency.

I. CORPORAL PUNISHMENT. Virtually all educational theorists agree on the inadvisability of corporal punishment. It tends to be ineffective, to be an admission that might makes right, to set a poor example for the students, and to result in possible physical harm to the pupil. It upholds the supremacy of brute, naked force as the ultimate *raison d'être* for obedience. Sometimes corporal punishment can boomerang on the teacher, as when the adolescent offender is physically bigger and stronger than he. Cutts and Moseley, summing up the pertinent research concluded:

Where corporal punishment is regularly used (as in certain English schools and in some private schools) it is accepted as routine and is no more a deterrent than any other punishment. Students may feel left out if they are not sometimes whipped, and may even boast of the severity of a whipping and the skill of the master who gave it. Nor does corporal punishment seem to have a good effect when it is administered rarely, or as a last resort, or brutally.[64]

Only a very few states have enacted statutes prohibiting teacher-

[63] Stack, *op. cit.*, p. 75.
[64] Cutts and Moseley, *op. cit.*, p. 35. Used by permission of David McKay Co., Inc.

inflicted corporal punishment. However, almost all states have laws forbidding cruelty to children, and under these laws a teacher can be prosecuted for brutal or dangerous corporal punishment or that which was administered in an improper manner. Occasionally a pupil has brought suit against a teacher for having inflicted corporal punishment, but the courts have usually dismissed the charges on the grounds that the teacher stands *in loco parentis*. Most alert public and Catholic school systems have abandoned corporal punishment as an instrument of discipline. The various United States military services which have had many years of experience with all sorts of persons including some extremely tough individuals have a strict rule that no officer shall lay hands on an enlisted man. Most educational theorists contend that schools should follow suit.

Notwithstanding, it has been the experience of the author as a secondary school teacher, experience confirmed by the testimony of colleagues and other seasoned teachers from around the nation, that in an extremely few isolated instances corporal punishment may be beneficial. This is particularly true in so-called "blackboard jungle" schools in certain large metropolitan areas. The good teacher always starts with the pupil where he is, and some recalcitrant or recidivist pupils know and respect only the law of force. A poll of public school superintendents revealed that 72 per cent of them favored the use of corporal punishment as a corrective for misbehavior.[65] Hence there is an apparent difference of opinion between schoolmen in the field and the educational theorists.

Oliva has advised that the teacher heed the following suggestions in administering corporal punishment: (1) Make sure beyond all doubt that the pupil is guilty of a major offense. (2) Know the state laws regarding corporal punishment. (3) If possible, obtain parental consent first. (4) Give the punishment in private but with at least one adult witness. (5) Do not strike the face, ears, or head or any other sensitive part of the body. (6) Do not mete out punishment while in a rage or in a hyperemotionalized state. (7) Record the offense and punishment, and file it with the principal.[66] The NEA Research Department has suggested that corporal punishment be administered within statutory requirements, be suitable to the age, sex, and condition of the pupil, be commensurate with the crime, be justified by the behavior of the pupil, leave no permanent mark or injury, be corrective rather than

[65] "Most Superintendents Favor the Use of Corporal Punishment," *The Nation's Schools*, LVIII (July, 1956), pp. 57–58.

[66] Oliva, *op. cit.*, p. 83; see also Richard L. Loughlin, "Controlling the Class," *Bulletin of the National Association of Secondary-School Principals*, XLII (November, 1958), pp. 107–111.

malicious or vindictive, and be meted out in a teacher-pupil relationship.[67]

In general, however, the teacher should use intelligence rather than physical force in solving misbehavior problems.

J. SUSPENSION AND EXPULSION. Suspension is the official removal of a pupil from the entire school situation for a short, temporary period of time. Expulsion consists in an official permanent removal of a pupil. In public high schools extremely serious misbehavior is the principal reason for suspension or expulsion; in Catholic high schools expulsion may also be caused by consistently failing marks.[68] Sometimes suspension or expulsion fails to constitute true punishment because it provides the pupil with the opportunity to roam as he pleases, particularly if suspension or expulsion occurs in the late spring or early autumn. Suspension or expulsion should not be made in an arbitrary, autocratic manner by school authorities. Rather the pupil should be given an official hearing before a board of suspension and expulsion and be permitted ample opportunity to present his defense. The members of this board should be administrators and teachers of the school as well as representatives from the school system. If it is decided that the pupil should be expelled from the school, arrangements should be made for his transfer to another school or specialized institution. In any event the guidance specialists and community agencies should follow up the expellee. However, suspension and expulsion should not be viewed by the school as the ultimate disciplinary weapon. This title should be reserved for expert guidance, a process by which most, and perhaps all, suspendees and expellees can be salvaged. Suspension or expulsion is an admission by the school that it has ceased trying to help the pupil; it has given up; it has failed in its mission.

Rewards and Punishment. As was noted in Chapter XII, reward is generally (but not always) superior to punishment as a worthwhile motivational force. Even so, reward, like punishment, must be properly administered if it is to promote constructive discipline and learning. A reward should not be given to a pupil for his natural ability, but rather for his use of it. Thus a naturally reserved pupil should not be rewarded because he does not disrupt the class. Rewards for good behavior must be given judiciously, for contrary practice might not teach a pupil what is right conduct, but instead, the art of bargaining for a reward.[69]

[67] "Corporal Punishment," *NEA Research Bulletin*, XXXVI (October, 1958), p. 89.

[68] Stack, *op. cit.*, pp. 72–73.

[69] Othilda Krug and Helen L. Beck, *A Guide to Better Discipline.* (Chicago: Science Research Associates, 1954), p. 23.

Punishment and the Supernatural Dimension. Spiritually, man is living in the Christian era when love is supposed to rule. Practically, man is still in the Stone Age when force, suppression, and reprisal prevail. Stone Age punishment consists in an eye for an eye, a tooth for a tooth. Christ's message was that His followers should return good for evil. This great teaching of Christ, like all His doctrines, is eminently practical. Punishments have all too often bred hate, and force has generated even greater force. The peace agreements which the Americans made with West Germany and Japan after World War II, for the first time in history, did not punish the vanquished. These countries are now among our staunchest allies. Fr. Hoffer, S.M., has written that "obedience rendered only from a motive of fear is neither supernatural nor meritorious." [70] St. Francis de Sales commented that "gentleness makes men penitent whereas severity makes them hypocrites." [71] Punishment often operates according to Newton's Third Law: For every action there is an equal and opposite reaction.

The Catholic teacher about to administer punishment should recall the words of St. Thomas Aquinas, Patron of Schools: "In this life there is no punishment for punishment's sake. The time of the Last Judgment has not yet come. The value of human penalties is medicinal and in so far as they promote the public welfare and the cure of the offender." [72]

Kindness

A few pupils are chronic misbehavior problems. Many others act in an undesirable manner only once in a while. To some extent, obstinacy and willfulness are the prime causes of their actions. Yet at the very bottom there are psychological sources for these misdeeds. Therefore the key to constructive discipline ultimately lies not in punishment or condemnation but in understanding. Fr. Flanagan, founder of Boys Town took as his motto, "There is no such thing as a bad boy," to which may be added, "There is only an unhappy one."

In today's force-oriented world, it may seem natural to regard discipline as basically coercive. Such a conception is grounded in the crassest materialism. Its psychological foundations are just as weak, because kindness will win over a person whereas harshness tends to harden him in his undesirable actions. Sociologically considered, coercion does not act in the interests of optimal group relationships. Furthermore as St. Francis de Sales said: "A superior is appointed more for the

[70] Hoffer, *op. cit.*, p. 64.
[71] Quoted in *ibid.*, p. 75.
[72] St. Thomas Aquinas, *Summa Theologica*, IIa–IIae, q.68, a.1.

benefit of the weak than for that of the strong. If he must be good to the perfect, he must be exceptionally kind to the imperfect." [73] From a theological point of view, kindness which is rooted in charity remains one of the two great commandments.

The professional literature favoring more humane classroom discipline began in this century and gained great impetus in the 1920s and 1930s.[74] It has been increasing ever since. This same approach has gained considerable headway in Catholic writings, particularly since 1950. These developments have occurred primarily because in this century men are acquiring a more mature understanding of the deep psychological and emotional forces which affect every person. To this can be added the renewed Catholic awareness that charity is not merely an abstract virtue, but that it constitutes the fundamental basis for *every* act of daily living.

In dealing with misbehavior offenses, the teacher should at all times be sympathetic. But sympathy must never be confused with ultra-sentimentality. If a girl states that she was inattentive in class because she sat up all night with her sick mother, the teacher should first commiserate, then investigate. There are some pupils who attempt to excuse their misbehavior by inventing fanciful tales to deceive credulous teachers. Furthermore, chronic offenders, while receiving kindness, should not be excused from all schoolwork or given such extraordinary privileges that other pupils, particularly the waverers, deem it profitable to become "disciplinary cases" so that they too may share in the accruing rewards. True sympathy dictates that the teacher be kind and charitable. Charity is the rule always, but it must be a charity founded on knowledge.

The teacher in a Catholic high school can never separate kindness from its supernatural wellsprings. Therefore in exercising constructive, humane discipline, he should constantly appeal to the supernatural motivations of his pupils. He should remind the pupils that when they offend any of the members of Christ's Mystical Body by misbehavior, they offend Christ Himself. He should inculcate a love of true obedience within the pupils. They should be encouraged to follow Christ Who said: "Not My will, but Thine be done," Christ Who was "obedient unto death, even to death on a cross." "Therefore God has exalted Him," a testimony that the supernatural rewards for obedience are great. The teacher should make sure that the obedience he is inculcating is the virtue of loving humility, not the pseudo virtues of toadyism,

[73] Quoted in Hoffer, *op. cit.*, p. 19.
[74] See Pickens E. Harris, *Changing Conceptions of School Discipline.* (New York: Macmillan, 1928).

sycophantism, overdocility, and inactivity, all masking as virtue. The pupil should be encouraged to receive the sacraments frequently to nourish his motivations with supernatural strength. Indeed modern adolescents are in a better position to profit from sacramental reception than the youth of any previous age because of the modern Church laws urging frequent Communion and mitigating the laws of fast. Nor should the teacher ignore the spirit of sacrifice and the desire for heroism which characterize adolescence. The deep Christian concepts of suffering and spiritual victimhood should be discussed with the students. Suffering and spiritual victimhood should be goals for the lay person; they were not intended by Christ to be reserved only for Religious.

The Catholic teacher sometimes is himself the cause of pupil misbehavior because of defective spiritual notions. Some Catholic teachers seem to think, at least implicitly, that a lay person cannot be a good Christian and at the same time take joy in earthly pleasures. But as Fr. Breton, O.F.M., has written: "All creation is good. All creation is [man's] brother. It contains no hidden snares. It lifts him to God." [75] There are those Catholic teachers who seem to equate a girl's legitimate desire to look pretty and be socially attractive with a noxious spirit of vanity. Nor should the Catholic teacher fail to distinguish between the sin and the sinner. Charity dictates that he despise the offense but continue to love the offender.

In doubtful cases or in those instances in which the teacher wishes to choose the more efficacious course of truly constructive discipline, he should remember that he can never make a mistake using kindness and Divine charity.

ADDITIONAL PRACTICAL SUGGESTIONS

This chapter has thus far imbedded a great number of practical suggestions for constructive discipline in its treatment of the various topics presented. However there are some *additional* practical suggestions which did not readily lend themselves to a meaningful developmental inclusion within the framework of these topics. Nevertheless these suggestions are very helpful to a teacher wishing to promote constructive discipline; therefore they are listed below:

1. Suspend judgment until all the evidence on the case is in.

2. Keep objective. There should be no favorites, on the one hand, and no pupils whom the teacher is "out to get," on the other.

[75] Valentin Breton, O.F.M., "Franciscan Spirituality," in Gautier (ed.), *Some Schools of Spirituality,* trans. by Sullivan. (Paris: Desclée, 1959), p. 67.

3. Be consistent so that the pupils know what to expect. It is not good to be strict one day and lenient the next.

4. Learn the names of all the pupils in the class as soon as possible. The troublemakers should not be given the opportunity to seek refuge in anonymity.

5. Get the leader on your side.

6. Require the pupils to dress neatly. Sloppy or caste-oriented clothes can subconsciously cause misbehavior, e.g., jeans, shorts, or motorcycle jackets. However, the rules for dress should be reasonable, never prudish or overly stiff.

7. Anticipate trouble, problems, difficulties.

8. Be relaxed and natural. Tenseness reflects insecurity, and some pupils will capitalize on this.

9. Avoid making public issues of misbehavior. This eliminates the danger of an audience for the troublemaker. It is better for class control as well as for guidance to interview the offender after class.

10. Do not institute petty or overmeticulous rules or regulations.

11. Never give a pupil the impression that he has no chance of passing the course. Not only is this unjust and professionally unethical, but it will cause the pupil to misbehave and render discipline in his case impossible.

12. Before the lesson is started, make sure that every student is paying attention.

13. Speak distinctly, in a conversational tone and pitch. Never shout at the pupils. Shouting connotes autocracy and insecurity. It is also an indication that the teacher is losing control of the class.

14. Phrase commands positively rather than negatively.

15. When commands or directions are necessary, state them only once. Do not repeat them.

16. Make all directions as simple and as clear as possible. If the directions are complicated or opaque, the pupils will become confused and seek emotional release by misbehaving.

17. In an all-class discussion, keep the eyes fixed on the entire class rather than on one student.

18. Do not let a group of students crowd around the teacher's desk. This hampers a view of the rest of the class.

19. Do not interrupt the class to challenge latecomers. See them privately after class.

20. Do not become hyperemotionalized or otherwise lose control when confronted with a misbehavior problem, however serious.

21. Never make the offense personal; e.g., avoid saying, "You're bothering me," but rather state "You're interfering with the progress of the class."

22. Do not nag.

23. Explain the reasons for teacher-made prohibitions or regulations and permit subsequent discussion if possible. Rules should have rational bases and not be the result of an autocratic whim.

EPILOGUE TO DISCIPLINE

The sun and the wind argued between themselves which was the stronger. To settle the issue, it was agreed that each in turn would attempt to force a man who was walking along a city street to remove his overcoat. Mustering its harshest force, the wind blew, and blew, and blew, but the harder it blew, the more the man bundled his overcoat around himself. Then the sun tried. It shone clear and warm, and soon the man, seeing that it had become such a fine day, took off his overcoat, stretched his arms, smiled, and said to himself: "How wonderful is life."

"God is love," wrote St. John in his First Epistle.

The lessons are clear. The teacher who wishes to promote constructive discipline will attain far greater results by warmth and kindness than by harshness. Further, the teacher who wishes to follow in the footsteps of God can best do it by constantly showing his pupils love.

"Put your sword back into its place; for all those who take up the sword will perish by the sword." [76]

[76] Matt., XXVI. 52.

SELECTED REFERENCES
FOR FURTHER READING

CHAPTER I

Blum, Virgil C., S.J., *Freedom of Choice in Education.* (New York: Macmillan, 1958).

Brown, Elmer E., *The Making of Our Middle Schools.* (New York: Longmans, 1903).

Bunker, Frank Forest, *The Junior High School Movement: Its Beginnings.* (Washington: Roberts, 1935).

Burns, J. A., C.S.C., *The Principles, Origin and Establishment of the Catholic School Systems in the United States.* (New York: Benziger, 1912).

——— and Bernard J. Kohlbrenner, *A History of Catholic Education in the United States.* (New York: Benziger, 1937).

Butts, R. Freeman, *The American Tradition in Religion and Education.* (Boston: Beacon Press, 1950).

——— and Lawrence A. Cremin, *A History of Education in American Culture.* (New York: Holt, 1953).

Cubberley, Ellwood P., *Public Education in the United States.* (Boston: Houghton Mifflin, 1947).

———, *Readings in Public Education in the United States.* (Boston: Houghton Mifflin, 1934).

Curti, Merle, *The Growth of American Thought.* (New York: Harper, 1951).

———, *The Social Ideas of American Educators.* (Paterson, N.J.: Littlefield, Adams, 1959).

Educational Policies Commission, *Moral and Spiritual Values in the Public Schools.* (Washington: The Commission, 1951).

Edwards, Newton, and Herman G. Richey, *The School in the American Social Order.* (Boston: Houghton Mifflin, 1947).

Ellis, John Tracy, "The American Catholic and the Intellectual Life," *Thought,* XXX (Autumn, 1955), pp. 351–358.

Elsbree, Willard S., *The American Teacher.* (New York: American Book, 1939).

Honeywell, Roy J., *The Educational Work of Thomas Jefferson.* (Cambridge, Mass.: Harvard University Press, 1931).

Knight, Edgar W., *A Documentary History of Education in the South before 1860,* 3 vols. (Chapel Hill, N.C.: University of North Carolina Press, 1949–1952).

————, *Education in the United States,* 3d rev. ed. (Boston: Ginn, 1951).

———— and Clifton L. Hall, *Readings in American Educational History.* (New York: Appleton-Century-Crofts, 1951).

McCluskey, Neil, S.J., *Public Schools and Moral Education.* (New York: Columbia University Press, 1958).

McGucken, William J., S.J., *The Jesuits and Education.* (Milwaukee: Bruce, 1932).

Spurlock, Clark, *Education and the Supreme Court.* (Urbana, Ill.: University of Illinois Press, 1955).

Stokes, Anson Phelps, *Church and State in the United States,* 3 vols. (New York: Harper, 1950).

Walsh, James J., *Education and the Founding Fathers.* (New York: Fordham University Press, 1935).

Woody, Thomas, *A History of Women's Education in the United States.* (New York: Science Press, 1929).

CHAPTER II

Bestor, Arthur, *The Restoration of Learning.* (New York: Knopf, 1955)

Commission on the Reorganization of Secondary Education, *Cardinal Principles of Secondary Education,* Bulletin no. 35. (Washington: Government Printing Office, 1918).

Committee for the White House Conference on Education, *A Report to the President.* (Washington: Government Printing Office, 1956).

Committee on the Orientation of Secondary Education, Department of Secondary School Principals, *Issues in Secondary Education,* Bulletin no. 59. (Chicago: NEA, 1936).

Donlan, Thomas C., O.P., *Theology and Education.* (Dubuque, Iowa: Brown, 1952).

Educational Policies Commission, *Moral and Spiritual Values in the Public Schools.* (Washington: NEA, 1951).

————, *The Purposes of Education in American Democracy.* (Washington: NEA, 1938).

Harvard Committee, *General Education in a Free Society.* (Cambridge, Mass.: Harvard University Press, 1945).

Lynd, Albert, *Quackery in the Public Schools.* (New York: Grosset & Dunlap, 1953).

McCluskey, Neil G., S.J., *Catholic Viewpoint on Education.* (Garden City, N.Y.: Hanover House, 1959).

Maritain, Jacques, *Education at the Crossroads.* (New Haven, Conn.: Yale University Press, 1943).

————, "On Some Typical Aspects of Christian Education," in Fuller (ed.), *The Christian Idea of Education.* (New Haven, Conn.: Yale University Press, 1957), pp. 173–198.

National Society for the Study of Education, *Adapting the Secondary-School*

Program to the Needs of Youth, Fifty-Second Yearbook, Part I. (Chicago: University of Chicago Press, 1953).

————, *The Community School,* Fifty-Second Yearbook, Part II. (Chicago: University of Chicago Press, 1953).

O'Brien, Kevin J., C.Ss.R., *The Proximate Aim of Education.* (Milwaukee: Bruce, 1958).

O'Dea, Thomas F., *American Catholic Dilemma: An Inquiry into the Intellectual Life.* (New York: Sheed and Ward, 1958).

Pius XI, Pope, *Christian Education of Youth.* (Washington: NCWC, 1936).

Rickover, H. G., *Education and Freedom.* (New York: Dutton, 1960).

Smith, Mortimer, *The Diminished Mind: A Study of the Planned Mediocrity in Our Public Schools.* (Chicago: Regnery, 1954).

Smith, Vincent Edward, *The School Examined: Its Aim and Content.* (Milwaukee: Bruce, 1960).

"The Imperative Needs of Youth of Secondary-School Age," *Bulletin of the National Association of Secondary-School Principals,* CVL (March, 1947).

Ward, Leo R., C.S.C., *New Life in Catholic Schools.* (St. Louis: Herder, 1958).

Woodring, Paul, *A Fourth of a Nation.* (New York: McGraw-Hill, 1957).

CHAPTER III

Alexander, William M., and J. Galen Saylor, *Modern Secondary Education.* (New York: Rinehart, 1959).

Association for Supervision and Curriculum Development, *The High School We Need.* (Washington: NEA, 1959).

Conant, James B., *The American High School Today.* (New York: McGraw-Hill, 1959).

Gardner, John W., "National Goals in Education," The President's Commission on National Goals, *Goals for Americans.* (Englewood Cliffs, N.J.: Prentice-Hall, 1960), pp. 81-100.

Hovet, Kenneth, "What Are the High Schools Teaching?" *What Shall the High Schools Teach?* 1956 Yearbook, Association for Supervision and Curriculum Development. (Washington: ASCD, 1956), pp. 69-94.

Janet, Sister Mary, S.C., *Catholic Secondary Education: A National Survey.* (Washington: NCWC, 1949).

————, *Catholic Secondary Schools, U.S.A.* (Washington: NCWC, 1960).

Jenks, William F., C.Ss.R., *Function and Growth of the National Catholic Educational Association in the Field of Special Education.* (Washington, D.C.: Catholic University of America Press, 1961).

Keller, Franklin J., *The Comprehensive High School.* (New York: Harper, 1955).

Lee, James Michael, "A New Role for the High School," *Bulletin of the National Association of Secondary-School Principals,* XLIII (December, 1959), pp. 102–105.

————, "The Place of Science in the High School," *Catholic Educational Review*, LVII (May, 1959), pp. 302–307.

McKenna, Bernard H., "Greater Learning in Smaller Classes," *NEA Journal*, XLIV (October, 1957), pp. 437–438.

National Catholic Welfare Conference, Department of Education, *Summary of Catholic Education, 1955–1956*. (Washington: NCWC, 1958).

National Education Association, "How States Compare on School Support," *NEA Research Bulletin*, XXXIX (February, 1961), pp. 11–15.

————, "The Junior High School Today," *NEA Research Bulletin*, XXXIX (May, 1961), pp. 47–50.

Prosser, Charles A., and Thomas A. Quigley, *Vocational Education in a Democracy*. (Chicago: American Technical Society, 1950).

Scott, W. E., and W. C. Glenwright, "What Are Recent Developments in the Construction of New School Buildings?" *Bulletin of the National Association of Secondary-School Principals*, XLI (April, 1957), pp. 211–215.

Trump, J. Lloyd, and Dorsey Baynham, *Guide to Better Schools*. (Chicago: Rand McNally, 1961).

U.S. Office of Education, *Biennial Survey of Education, 1955–1956*. (Washington: Government Printing Office, 1959), chaps. 1–5.

————, *Small Schools Are Growing Larger*. (Washington: Government Printing Office, 1959).

CHAPTER IV

Adorno, T. W., *The Authoritarian Personality*. (New York: Harper, 1949).

Aquinas, St. Thomas, *De Veritate* (trans.) (Chicago: Regnery, 1952–1954).

————, *Summa Theologica*, trans. by Fathers of the English Dominican Province. (New York: Benziger, 1947–1948).

Bernard, Harold W., *Adolescent Development in American Culture*. (Tarrytown-on-Hudson, N.Y.: World, 1957).

Brennan, Robert E., O.P., *Thomistic Psychology*. (New York: Macmillan, 1941).

Butler, J. Donald, *Four Philosophies and Their Practice in Education and Religion*, rev. ed. (New York: Harper, 1957).

"Concepts," *Encyclopedia of Educational Research*, 3d ed. (New York: Macmillan, 1960), pp. 323–333.

Congar, Yves M. J., O.P., *Lay People in the Church*. (Westminster, Md.: Newman, 1956).

Cronbach, Lee J., *Educational Psychology*. (New York: Harcourt, Brace, 1954).

De Letter, P., S.J., "The Encounter with God," *Thought*, XXXVI (Spring, 1961), pp. 5–24.

Dewey, John, *How We Think*. (Boston, Heath, 1933).

Dowd, Sister Mary Amadeus, *Change in Moral Reasoning through the High School Years*. (Washington, D.C.: Catholic University of America Press, 1948).

Gesell, Arnold, et al., *Youth: The Years from Ten to Sixteen*. (New York: Harper, 1956).

Harmon, Francis L., *Principles of Psychology*, rev. ed. (Milwaukee: Bruce, 1951).

Hart, Charles A., *The Thomistic Concept of Mental Faculty*. (Washington, D.C.: Catholic University of America Press, 1930).

Hilgard, Ernest, *Theories of Learning*, 2d ed. (New York: Appleton-Century-Crofts, 1956).

Kelly, William A., *Educational Psychology*, 4th ed. (Milwaukee: Bruce, 1956).

Koffka, Kurt, *Principles of Gestalt Psychology*. (New York: Harcourt, Brace, 1935).

Kolesnik, Walter B., *Mental Discipline in Modern Education*. (Madison, Wis.: University of Wisconsin Press, 1958).

McCarthy, Raphael C., S.J., *Training the Adolescent*. (Milwaukee: Bruce, 1934).

Mouroux, Jean, *The Meaning of Man*. (New York: Sheed and Ward, 1948).

Mulrooney, Thomas W., "Curricular Provisions for Individual Differences," in McKeough (ed.), *The Curriculum of the Catholic Secondary School*. (Washington, D.C.: Catholic University of America Press, 1949), pp. 48–61.

National Society for the Study of Education, *Adolescence*, Fifty-Third Yearbook, Part I. (Chicago: University of Chicago Press, 1954).

———, *Modern Philosophies and Education*, Fifty-Fourth Yearbook, Part I. (Chicago: University of Chicago Press, 1955).

———, *The Psychology of Learning*, Forty-First Yearbook, Part II. (Chicago: University of Chicago Press, 1942).

Nordberg, Robert B., "The March to Holism: Where Are We?" *Catholic Educational Review*, LVIII (April, 1960), pp. 240–247.

Reutter, E. B., "The Sociology of Adolescence," *American Journal of Sociology*, XLIII (November, 1937), pp. 414–427.

Schneiders, Alexander A., *The Psychology of Adolescence*. (Milwaukee: Bruce, 1951).

Thorndike, Edward L., *Educational Psychology*. (New York: Bureau of Publications, Teachers College, Columbia University, 1913), vol. II.

CHAPTER V

Aquinas, St. Thomas, *Summa Theologica*, trans. by Fathers of the English Dominican Province. (New York: Benziger, 1947–1948).

Brennan, Robert E., O.P., *Thomistic Psychology*. (New York: Macmillan, 1941).

Dashiell, John F., *Fundamentals of General Psychology*, 3d ed. (Boston: Houghton Mifflin, 1949).

Doane, Donald C., *The Needs of Youth*. (New York: Bureau of Publications, Teachers College, Columbia University, 1942).

Donceel, J. F., S.J., *Philosophical Psychology*. (New York: Sheed and Ward, 1955).

Drees, Victor, O.F.M., *The Effects of Practice on Memory Performance*. (Washington: Catholic Education Press, 1941).

Ebbinghaus, Hermann, *Memory*, trans. by Ruegger and Bussenius. (New York: Teachers College, Columbia University, 1913).

Encyclopedia of Educational Research, 3d ed. (New York: Macmillan, 1960).

Garrett, Henry E., *General Psychology*. (New York: American Book, 1961).

Harmon, Francis L., *Principles of Psychology*, rev. ed. (Milwaukee: Bruce, 1951).

Havighurst, Robert J., *Developmental Tasks in Education*, 2d ed. (New York: Longmans, 1952).

Kelly, William A., *Educational Psychology*, 4th ed. (Milwaukee: Bruce, 1956).

Moore, Thomas Verner, O.S.B., "The Scholastic Theory of Perception," *The New Scholasticism*, VII (July, 1933), pp. 222–238.

Mullaly, Sister Columba, *The Retention and Recognition of Information*. (Washington, D.C.: Catholic University of America Press, 1952).

National Society for the Study of Education, *Adapting the Secondary School Program to the Needs of Youth*, Fifty-Second Yearbook, Part I. (Chicago: University of Chicago Press, 1953).

———, *Adolescence*. Fifty-Third Yearbook, Part I. (Chicago: University of Chicago Press, 1954).

———, *Intelligence: Its Nature and Nurture*, Thirty-Ninth Yearbook, Part I. (Chicago: University of Chicago Press, 1940).

——— *Learning and Instruction*, Forty-Ninth Yearbook, Part I. (Chicago: University of Chicago Press, 1950).

Parnes, S. J. (ed.), *Compendium No. 2 of Research on Creative Imagination*. (Buffalo: Creative Education Foundation, 1960).

Ryan, John Julian, *Beyond Humanism*. (New York: Sheed and Ward, 1950).

Schneiders, Alexander A., *The Psychology of Adolescence*. (Milwaukee: Bruce, 1951).

Spitzer, Herbert F., "Studies in Retention," *Journal of Educational Psychology*, XXX (December, 1939), pp. 641–656.

CHAPTER VI

Anderson, Vernon E., *Principles and Procedures of Curriculum Improvement*. (New York: Ronald, 1956).

Athill, Mother Emmanuel, C.S.A., *Teaching Liturgy in the Schools*. (Notre Dame, Ind.: Fides, 1958).

Bellack, Arno, "Selection and Organization of Curriculum Content: An Analysis," *What Shall the High Schools Teach?* Association for Supervision and Curriculum Development, 1956 Yearbook. (Washington: ASCD, 1956), pp. 97–126.

Benne, Kenneth D., and Bodizar Muntyan (eds.), *Human Relations and Curriculum Change.* (New York: Dryden, 1951).

Cremin, Lawrence, "The Curriculum Movement," in Alcorn and Linley (eds.), *Issues in Curriculum Development.* (Tarrytown-on-Hudson, N.Y.: World, 1959), pp. 3–16.

Douglass, Harl R. (ed.), *Education for Life Adjustment.* (New York: Ronald, 1950).

Faunce, Roland C., and Nelson L. Bossing, *Developing the Core Curriculum,* 2d ed. (Englewood Cliffs, N.J.: Prentice-Hall, 1958).

Flaum, Laurence S., *The Activity High School.* (New York: Harper, 1953).

Gruber, Frederick C., and Thomas B. Beatty, *Secondary School Activities.* (New York: McGraw-Hill, 1954).

Janet, Sister Mary, S.C. (ed.), *Building the Integrated Curriculum.* (Washington, D.C.: Catholic University of America Press, 1953).

———— (ed.), *The Christian Foundation Program in the Catholic Secondary Schools.* (Washington, D.C.: Catholic University of America Press, 1952).

Leonard, J. Paul, *Developing the Secondary School Curriculum,* rev. ed. (New York: Rinehart, 1953).

McKeough, Michael J., O.Praem. (ed), *The Curriculum of the Catholic Secondary School.* (Washington, D.C.: Catholic University of America Press, 1949).

McKown, Harry C., *Extra-Curricular Activities,* 3d ed. (New York: Macmillan, 1956).

Miller, Franklin A., James H. Moyer, and Robert B. Patrick, *Planning Student Activities.* (Englewood Cliffs, N.J.: Prentice-Hall, 1956).

Riley, Edward F., C.M., *Extracurricular Activities Programs in the Catholic High Schools.* (Washington, D.C.: Catholic University of America Press, 1954).

Romine, Stephen A., *Building the High School Curriculum.* (New York: Ronald, 1954).

Rugg, Harold (ed.), *Democracy and the Curriculum.* (New York: Appleton-Century, 1939).

Saylor, J. Galen, and William M. Alexander, *Curriculum Planning for Better Teaching and Learning.* (New York: Rinehart, 1954).

Smith, B. Othanel, William O. Stanley, and J. Harlan Shores, *Fundamentals of Curriculum Development,* rev. ed. (Tarrytown-on-Hudson, N.Y.: World, 1957).

Stratemeyer, Florence B., et al., *Developing a Curriculum for Modern Living,* rev. ed. (New York: Bureau of Publications, Teachers College, Columbia University, 1957).

Thompson, Nellie Zetta, *Your School Clubs.* (New York: Dutton, 1953).

CHAPTER VII

Aquinas, St. Thomas, *The Teacher*, trans. by West Baden. (Chicago: Gateway, Regnery, 1954).

Barzun, Jacques, *Teacher in America*. (Garden City, N.Y.: Anchor Books, Doubleday, 1955).

Bierberg, Rudolf P., C.PP.S., "Basis of Academic Freedom in Catholic Education," *Catholic Educational Review*, LIV (September, 1956), pp. 400–403.

Briggs, Paul W., "The Bay City Experiment," *The Journal of Teacher Education*, VIII (March, 1957), pp. 3–6.

Chandler, B. J., *Education and the Teacher*. (New York: Dodd, Mead, 1961).

Claire, Sister M., O.S.B., "A Program of Faculty Meetings," *Catholic School Journal*. LIX (June, 1959), pp. 39–41.

Delrey, Sister M., S.N.D., "Attitudes of Parents toward Lay Teachers," *Catholic Educational Review*, LIV (October, 1956), pp. 459–466.

Drobka, Frank, "The Teacher and the Integrated Curriculum," in Sister Mary Janet, S.C. (ed.), *Building the Integrated Curriculum*. (Washington, D.C.: Catholic University of America Press, 1953).

Fleege, Urban H., "Why Not Use Teacher's Aides?" *Catholic School Journal*, LIV (October, 1954), pp. 251–252.

Gilson, Etienne, "The Christian Teacher," in Pegis (ed.), *A Gilson Reader*. (Garden City, N.Y.: Image Books, Doubleday, 1957).

——, "The Eminence of Teaching," *McAuley Lecture, 1953*. (West Hartford, Conn.: St. Joseph College, 1954).

Hemeyer, Will, and Jean B. McGrew, "Big Ideas for Big Classes," *School Review*, LXVIII (Autumn, 1960), pp. 308–317.

Highet, Gilbert, *The Art of Teaching*. (New York: Vintage, 1954).

Lieberman, Myron, *Education as a Profession*. (Englewood Cliffs, N.J.: Prentice-Hall, 1956).

Long, Sister M. Brideen, "A Synthesis of Recent Research Studies on Predicting Teacher Efficiency," *Catholic Educational Review*, LV (April, 1957), pp. 217–230.

McDonald, Gerald E., "Some Starting Points in Reforming American Catholic Education," *Catholic Educational Review*, LVII (November, 1959), pp. 526–531.

MacIver, Robert M., *Academic Freedom in Our Time*. (New York: Columbia University Press, 1955).

Mayer, Mary Helen, *The Philosophy of Teaching of St. Thomas Aquinas*. (Milwaukee: Bruce, 1929).

National Society for the Study of Education, *In-Service Education*, Fifty-Sixth Yearbook, Part I. (Chicago: University of Chicago Press, 1957).

Pius XII, Pope, "Aims of an Italian Teachers Union," in *The Pope Speaks*, I (Second Quarter, 1954), pp. 11–15.

Riesman, David, "Thoughts on Teachers and Schools," *Anchor Review No. 1*. (Garden City, N.Y.: Anchor Books, Doubleday, 1955), pp. 27–60.

Ryans, David G., *Characteristics of Teachers*. (Washington: American Council on Education, 1960).

Vernice, Sister M., S.N.D., "The Sister in Service and Her Reading," *Catholic Educational Review*, LVII (May, 1959), pp. 289–301.

Wiles, Kimball, *Supervision for Better Schools*. (Englewood Cliffs, N.J.: Prentice-Hall, 1955).

CHAPTER VIII

Bennett, Robert A., "Unit Ideas for the New School Year," *The English Journal*, XLIX (September, 1960), pp. 400–408.

Besvinick, Sidney L., "An Effective Daily Lesson Plan," *The Clearing House*, XXXIV (March, 1960), pp. 431–433.

Bossing, Nelson L., *Teaching in Secondary Schools*, 3d ed. (Boston: Houghton Mifflin, 1952).

Giles, H. H., *Teacher-Pupil Planning*. (New York: Harper, 1941).

Hosmanek, John J., "Planning for Good Learning," *Bulletin of the National Association of Secondary-School Principals*, XLIII (December, 1959), pp. 28–30.

Joan, Sister M., O.P., and Sister M. Nona, O.P., *Guiding Growth in Christian Social Living*. (Washington, D.C.: Catholic University of America Press, 1944–1946), vols. 1–3.

Macomber, Freeman Glenn, *Teaching in the Modern Secondary School*. (New York: McGraw-Hill, 1942).

Mussio, John King, "The Catholic Teacher," *Bulletin of the National Catholic Educational Association*, LVI (August, 1959), pp. 207–215.

Oliver, Daniel W., "The Unit Concept in Social Studies: A Re-examination," *School Review*, LXVI (Summer, 1958), pp. 204–217.

Phinney, William L., "Producing Better Lesson Plans," *Bulletin of the National Association of Secondary-School Principals* (November, 1958), pp. 103–104.

Simpson, Ray H., *Improving Teaching-Learning Processes*. (New York: Longmans, 1953).

Wiles, Kimball, *Teaching for Better Schools*, 2d ed. (Englewood Cliffs, N.J.: Prentice-Hall, 1957).

Woodruff, Asahel D., *Basic Concepts of Teaching*. (San Francisco: Chandler, 1961).

CHAPTER IX

Anderl, Stephen, and Sister M. Ruth, F.S.P.A., *The Technique of the Catholic Action Cell*, 3d ed. (La Crosse, Wis.: St. Rose Convent, 1945).

Bloom, Benjamin S., "Thought Processes in Lectures and Discussions," *Journal of General Education*, VII (April, 1953), pp. 160–169.

Bossing, Nelson L., *Teaching in Secondary Schools*, 3d ed. (Boston: Houghton Mifflin, 1952).

Burton, William H., *The Guidance of Learning Activities*, 2d ed. (New York: Appleton-Century-Crofts, 1952).

Butler, Frank A., *The Improvement of Teaching in Secondary Schools*, 3d ed. (Chicago: University of Chicago Press, 1954).

Craig, Robert C., "Directed versus Independent Discovery of Established Relations," *Journal of Educational Psychology*, XLVII (April, 1956), pp. 223–234.

Crawford, Claude C., *How to Teach*. (Los Angeles: Southern California Book Depository, 1938).

Jacobs, Arthur J., *Role Playing as an Educational Method*, unpublished doctoral project, Teachers College, Columbia University, New York, 1951.

Junior Town Meeting League, *Teaching Controversial Issues*. (Middletown, Conn.: Junior Town Meeting League, 1948).

Keltner, John W., *Group Discussion Practices*. (New York: Longmans, 1957).

Kilpatrick, William Heard, "The Project Method," *Teachers College Record*, XIX (September, 1918), pp. 319–335.

Klein, Alan, *Role Playing in Leadership Training and Group Problem Solving*. (New York: Association Press, 1956).

Maaske, Roben J., "The Symposium Method of High-School Teaching," *School Review*, LVII (April, 1949), pp. 217–222.

Macomber, Freeman Glenn, *Teaching in the Modern Secondary School*. (New York: McGraw-Hill, 1942).

National Society for the Study of Education, *The Dynamics of Instructional Groups*, Fifty-Ninth Yearbook, Part II. (Chicago: University of Chicago Press, 1960).

Risk, Thomas M., *Principles and Practices of Teaching in Secondary Schools*, 3d ed. (New York: American Book, 1958).

Simpson, Ray H., *Improving Teaching–Learning Processes*. (New York: Longmans, 1953).

Smith, Edward W., Stanley W. Krouse, Jr., and Mark M. Atkinson, *The Educator's Encyclopedia*. (Englewood Cliffs, N.J.: Prentice-Hall, 1961).

Stovall, Thomas F., "Lecture vs. Discussion," *Phi Delta Kappan*, XXXIX (March, 1958), pp. 255–258.

Struck, F. Theodore, *Creative Teaching*. (New York: Wiley, 1938).

Thayer, Vivian T., *The Passing of the Recitation*. (Boston: Heath, 1928).

Wagner, Russell H., and Carroll C. Arnold, *Handbook of Group Discussion*. (Boston: Houghton Mifflin, 1950).

Wellington, C. Burleigh, and Jean Wellington, *Teaching for Critical Thinking*. (New York: McGraw-Hill, 1960).

Wiles, Kimball, *Teaching for Better Schools*, 2d ed. (Englewood Cliffs, N.J.: Prentice-Hall, 1959).

Wingo, G. Max, "Methods of Teaching," *Encyclopedia of Educational Research*, 3d ed. (New York: Macmillan, 1960), pp. 848–861.

Woodruff, Asahel D., *Basic Concepts of Teaching*. (San Francisco: Chandler, 1961).

Yoakam, Gerald Alan, *The Improvement of the Assignment*. (New York: Macmillan, 1932).

CHAPTER X

Armstrong, William H., *Study Is Hard Work*. (New York: Harper, 1956).

Brink, William C., *Directing Study Activities in Secondary Schools*. (Garden City, N.Y.: Doubleday, 1937).

Cole, Luella, *Students' Guide to Effective Study*, 4th ed. (New York: Rinehart, 1960).

Crawley, S. L., *Studying Effectively*. (Englewood Cliffs, N.J.: Prentice-Hall, 1945).

Cuff, Noel B., "Study Habits in Grades Four to Twelve," *Journal of Educational Psychology*. XXVIII (April, 1937), pp. 295–301.

Dudycha, George J., *Learn More with Less Effort*. (New York: Harper, 1957).

Frederick, Robert W., *How to Study Handbook*. (New York: Appleton-Century, 1938).

Lewis, Norman, *How to Read Better and Faster*, 3d ed. (New York: Crowell, 1958).

McMurry, F. M., *How to Study and Teaching How to Study*. (Boston: Houghton Mifflin, 1909).

Pear, T. H., *The Art of Study*. (New York: Dutton, 1931).

Robinson, Francis P., *Effective Study*. (New York: Harper, 1961).

Seward, S. S., *Note-Taking*. (Boston: Allyn and Bacon, 1910).

Strang, Ruth, *Guided Study and Homework*. (Washington: NEA, Department of Classroom Teachers, 1955).

———. "Homework and Guided Study," *Encyclopedia of Educational Research*, 3d ed. (New York: Macmillan, 1960), pp. 675–680.

Woodring, Maxine Nave, and Cecile White Flemming, *Directing Study of High School Pupils*. (New York: Bureau of Publications, Teachers College, Columbia University, 1935).

Wrightstone, J. Wayne, *How to Be a Better Student*. (Chicago: Science Research Associates, 1956).

CHAPTER XI

Allen, William H., "Audio-Visual Communication," *Encyclopedia of Educational Research*, 3d ed. (New York: Macmillan, 1960), pp. 115–137.

Bowers, Kenneth L., *The Opaque Projector*. (Austin, Tex.: University of Texas Press, 1960).

Brown, James W., Richard B. Lewis, and Fred F. Harcleroad, *A-V Instruction: Materials and Methods*. (New York: McGraw-Hill, 1959).

Clark, Ella Callista, "The Teaching Machine and Programmed Materials," *Catholic School Journal*, LXI (December, 1961), pp. 17–19.

Clausse, Roger, *Education by Radio*. (Paris: UNESCO, 1949).

Cronbach, Lee J. (ed.), *Text Materials in Modern Education*. (Urbana, Ill.: University of Illinois Press, 1955).

Cross, A. J. Foy, and Irene F. Cypher, *Audio-Visual Education*. (New York: Crowell, 1961).

Dale, Edgar, *Audio-Visual Methods in Teaching*, rev. ed. (New York: Holt, 1959).

Fund for the Advancement of Education, *Teaching by Television*. (New York: Ford Foundation, 1959).

Lumsdaine, A. A., and Robert Glaser (eds.), *Teaching Machines and Programmed Learning*. (Washington: Department of Audio-Visual Instruction, NEA, 1960).

Meeks, Martha F., *Models for Teaching*. (Austin, Tex.: University of Texas Press, 1956).

Mellenbruch, Julia, *The Tape Recorder in the Classroom*. (Austin, Tex.: University of Texas Press, 1959).

Pius XII, Pope, *"Miranda Prorsus"* in *The Pope Speaks*, IV (Winter, 1957–1958), pp. 319–346.

Sands, Lester B., *Audio-Visual Procedures in Teaching*. (New York: Ronald, 1956).

UNESCO, *Filmstrips: Use, Evaluation, Production*. (Paris: UNESCO, 1959).

Wittich, Walter Arno, and Charles Francis Schuller, *Audio-Visual Materials*. (New York: Harper, 1953).

CHAPTER XII

Bindra, Dalbir, *Motivation*. (New York: Ronald, 1959).

Buswell, Margaret M., "The Relationship between the Social Structure of the Classroom and the Academic Success of the Pupils," *Journal of Experimental Education*, XXII (September, 1953), pp. 37–52.

Current Theory and Research in Motivation. (Lincoln, Nebr.: University of Nebraska Press, annually since 1953).

Darley, John G., and Theda Hagenah, *Vocational Interest Measurement*. (Minneapolis, Minn.: University of Minnesota Press, 1955).

Dollard, J., et al., *Frustration and Aggression*. (New Haven, Conn.: Yale University Press, 1949).

Hoffer, Paul, S.M., *Guide for Religious Administrators*, trans. by Rus. (Milwaukee: Bruce, 1959).

Kausler, Donald H., "Aspiration Level as a Determinant of Performance," *Journal of Personality*, XXVII (September, 1959), pp. 346–351.

Lindzey, Gardner (ed.), *Assessment of Human Motives.* (New York: Rinehart, 1958).

Lynch, William, Jr., *An Approach to the Study of Motivational Problems in Education.* (Indianapolis, Ind.: University of Indiana Press, 1955).

McClelland, David C., et al., *The Achievement Motive.* (New York: Appleton-Century-Crofts, 1953).

Madsen, K. B., *Theories of Motivation,* 2d ed. (Cleveland, Ohio: Allen, 1961).

Marx, Melvin H., "Motivation," *Encyclopedia of Educational Research,* 3d ed. (New York: Macmillan, 1960), pp. 888–898.

Maslow, A. H., *Motivation and Personality.* (New York: Harper, 1954).

National Society for the Study of Education, *Learning and Instruction,* Forty-Ninth Yearbook, Part I. (Chicago: University of Chicago Press, 1950).

Page, Ellis Batten, "Teacher Comments and Student Performance: A Seventy-four Classroom Experiment in School Motivation," *Journal of Educational Psychology,* XLIX (August, 1958), pp. 173–181.

Phillips, Beeman N., and Louis D'Amico, "Effects of Cooperation and Competition on the Cohesiveness of Small Face-to-Face Groups," *Journal of Educational Psychology,* XLVII (February, 1956), pp. 65–70.

Reed, Howard B., Jr., "Anxiety: The Ambivalent Variable," *Harvard Educational Review,* XXX (Spring, 1960), pp. 141–153.

Ryan, F. J., and James S. Davie, "Social Acceptance, Academic Achievement, and Academic Aptitude among High School Students," *Journal of Educational Research,* LII (November, 1958), pp. 101–106.

Super, Donald E., "Interests," *Encyclopedia of Educational Research,* 3d ed. (New York: Macmillan, 1960), pp. 728–732.

Thorndike, E. L., *The Psychology of Wants, Interests and Attitudes.* (New York: Appleton-Century, 1935).

Witty, Paul, "A Study of Pupils' Interests, Grades 9, 10, 11, 12," *Education,* LXXXII (September–November, 1961), pp. 39–45, 100–110, 169–174.

CHAPTER XIII

Adams, Georgia S., and Theodore L. Torgerson, *Measurement and Evaluation for the Secondary School Teacher.* (New York: Dryden, 1956).

Ahmann, J. Stanley, and Marvin D. Glock, *Evaluating Pupil Growth.* (Englewood Cliffs, N.J.: Allyn and Bacon, 1959).

Baron, Denis, and Harold W. Bernard, *Evaluation Techniques for Classroom Teaching.* (New York: McGraw-Hill, 1958).

Bolmeier, E. C., "Principles Pertaining to Marking and Reporting Pupil Progress," *School Review,* LIX (January, 1951), pp. 15–24.

Bradfield, James M., and H. Stewart Moredock, *Measurement and Evaluation in Education.* (New York: Macmillan, 1957).

Buros, Oscar K. (ed.), *The Fifth Mental Measurements Yearbook.* (Highland Park, N.J.: Gryphon, 1959).

Corita, Sister M., B.V.M., "Report Cards Based on Christian Social Principles," *Catholic School Journal*, LIV (September, 1954), pp. 219–220.

Furst, Edward J., *Constructing Evaluation Instruments*. (New York: Longmans, 1958).

Greene, Harry A., Albert N. Jorgensen, and J. Raymond Gerberich, *Measurement and Evaluation in the Secondary School*. (New York: Longmans, 1954).

Lindquist, E. F. (ed.), *Educational Measurement*. (Washington: American Council on Education, 1951).

Micheels, William J., and M. Ray Karnes, *Measuring Educational Achievement*. (New York: McGraw-Hill, 1950).

National Society for the Study of Education, *The Measurement of Understanding*, Forty-Fifth Yearbook, Part I. (Chicago: University of Chicago Press, 1956).

Nunnally, Jum C., Jr., *Tests and Measurements*. (New York: McGraw-Hill, 1959).

Remmers, H. H., and N. L. Gage, *Measurement and Evaluation*, rev. ed. (New York: Harper, 1955).

Ross, C. C., and Julian C. Stanley, *Measurement in Today's Schools*, 3d ed. (Englewood Cliffs, N.J.: Prentice-Hall, 1954).

Rothney, John W. M., *Evaluating and Reporting Pupil Progress*. (Washington: NEA, Department of Classroom Teachers, 1955).

Schwartz, Alfred, and Stuart C. Tiedeman, *Evaluating Student Progress*. (New York: Longmans, 1957).

Strang, Ruth, *Reporting to Parents*. (New York: Bureau of Publications, Teachers College, Columbia University, 1947).

Thomas, R. Murray, *Judging Student Progress*, 2d ed. (New York: Longmans, 1960).

Thorndike, Robert L., and Elizabeth Hagen, *Measurement and Evaluation in Psychology and Education*. (New York: Wiley, 1955).

Travers, Robert M. W., *Educational Measurements*. (New York: Macmillan, 1955).

Wrightstone, J. Wayne, Joseph Justman, and Irving Robbins, *Evaluation in Modern Education*. (New York: American Book, 1956).

Wrinkle, William L., *Improving Marking and Reporting Practices*. (New York: Rinehart, 1947).

CHAPTER XIV

Arbuckle, Dugald S., *Guidance and Counseling in the Classroom*. (Englewood Cliffs, N.J.: Allyn and Bacon, 1957).

Bordin, Edward S., *Psychological Counseling*. (New York: Appleton-Century-Crofts, 1955).

Buchheimer, Arnold, and Sarah Balogh, *The Counseling Relationship*. (Chicago: Science Research Associates, 1961).

Curran, Charles A., *Counseling in Catholic Life and Education*. (New York: Macmillan, 1952).

Driver, Helen I., *Multiple Counseling*. (Madison, Wis.: Monona, 1954).

Drolet, Howard V., *A Study of the Services Facilitating Guidance Provided by the Diocesan Superintendent's Office of Education in the United States*. (Washington, D.C.: Catholic University of America Press, 1959).

Erickson, Clifford E., *The Counseling Interview*. (Englewood Cliffs, N.J.: Prentice-Hall, 1950).

Froehlich, Clifford P., *Guidance Services in Schools*, 2d ed. (New York: McGraw-Hill, 1958).

Gordon, Ira J., *The Teacher as a Guidance Worker*. (New York: Harper, 1956).

Greeley, Andrew M., *Strangers in the House*. (New York: Sheed and Ward, 1961).

Gronlund, Norman, *Sociometry in the Classroom*. (New York: Harper, 1959).

Hagmaier, George, C.S.P., and Robert Gleason, S.J., *Counseling the Catholic*. (New York: Sheed and Ward, 1959).

Harris, Brother Philip, O.S.F., "Using Homeroom for Guidance in Personality Development," *Catholic Educational Review*, LVII (February, 1959), pp. 97–105.

Hoppock, Robert, *Group Guidance*. (New York: McGraw-Hill, 1949).

Hutson, Percival W., *The Guidance Function in Education*. (New York: Appleton-Century-Crofts, 1958).

Johnson, Mauritz, William E. Busacker, and Fred Bowman, *Junior High School Guidance*. (New York: Harper, 1961).

Johnson, Walter F., Buford Stefflre, and Roy A. Edelfelt, *Pupil Personnel and Guidance Services*. (New York: McGraw-Hill, 1961).

Kelley, Janet A., *Guidance and the Curriculum*. (Englewood Cliffs, N.J.: Prentice-Hall, 1955).

Marzolf, Stanley S., *Psychological Diagnosis and Counseling in the Schools*. (New York: Holt, 1956).

Miller, Carroll H., *Foundations of Guidance*. (New York: Harper, 1961).

Moreno, Jacob L., *The Theatre of Spontaneity: An Introduction to Psychodrama*. (Beacon, N.Y.: Beacon House, 1947).

Mortensen, Donald G., and Allen M. Schmuller, *Guidance in Today's Schools*. (New York: Wiley, 1959).

Osborn, Alex F., *Applied Imagination*, rev. ed. (New York: Scribner, 1957).

Pepinsky, Harold B., and Pauline Pepinsky, *Counseling Theory and Practice*. (New York: Ronald, 1954).

Recktenwald, Lester N., *Guidance and Counseling*. (Washington, D.C.: Catholic University of America Press, 1953).

Roe, Anne, *The Psychology of Occupations*. (New York: Wiley, 1956).

Rogers, Carl R., *Client-Centered Therapy*. (Boston: Houghton Mifflin, 1951).

Stack, Philip L., *A National Study of the Guidance Services in Catholic Secondary Schools*. (Washington, D.C.: Catholic University of America Press, 1958).

Stafford, John W., C.S.V. (ed.), *Counseling in the Secondary School*. (Washington, D.C.: Catholic University of America Press, 1960).

Stoops, Emery, and Gunnar L. Wahlquist, *Principles and Practices in Guidance.* (New York: McGraw-Hill, 1958).

Strang, Ruth, *Counseling Technics in College and Secondary School,* rev. ed. (New York: Harper, 1949).

———, *The Role of the Teacher in Personnel Work,* 4th ed. (New York: Bureau of Publications, Teachers College, Columbia University, 1953).

Super, Donald E., *The Psychology of Careers.* (New York: Harper, 1957).

Thorne, Frederick C., *Principles of Personality Counseling.* (Brandon, Vt.: Journal of Clinical Psychology, 1959).

Traxler, Arthur E., *The Nature and Use of Anecdotal Records,* rev. ed. (New York: Educational Records Bureau, 1949).

———, *Techniques of Guidance.* (New York: Harper, 1957).

Tyler, Leona E., *The Work of the Counselor,* 2d ed. (New York: Appleton-Century-Crofts, 1961).

Van der Veldt, James H., O.F.M., and Robert P. Odenwald, *Psychiatry and Catholicism,* 2d ed. (New York: McGraw-Hill, 1957).

Warters, Jane, *High School Personnel Work Today.* (New York: McGraw-Hill, 1956).

Willey, Roy DeVerl, and Dean C. Andrew, *Modern Methods and Techniques in Guidance.* (New York: Harper, 1955).

Williamson, E. G., *Counseling Adolescents.* (New York: McGraw-Hill, 1950).

CHAPTER XV

Allers, Rudolf, *The Psychology of Character,* trans. by Strauss. (New York: Macmillan, 1931).

Amsterdam, Ruth, *Constructive Classroom Discipline and Practice.* (New York: Comet, 1957).

Cutts, Norma E., and Nicholas Moseley, *Teaching the Disorderly Pupil.* (New York: Longmans, 1957).

Glueck, Sheldon, and Eleanor Glueck, *Unraveling Juvenile Delinquency.* (Cambridge, Mass.: Harvard University Press, 1950).

Greeley, Andrew M., *Strangers in the House.* (New York: Sheed and Ward, 1961).

Hoffer, Paul, S.M., *Guide for Religious Administrators,* trans. by Rus. (Milwaukee: Bruce, 1959).

Hymes, James L., Jr., *Behavior and Misbehavior.* (Englewood Cliffs, N.J.: Prentice-Hall, 1955).

Jutta, Sister Mary, O.S.F., *School Discipline and Character.* (Milwaukee: Bruce, 1930).

Krug, Othilda, and Helen L. Beck, *A Guide to Better Discipline.* (Chicago: Science Research Associates, 1954).

Kvaraceus, William C., *Juvenile Delinquency.* (Washington: Department of Classroom Teachers, NEA, 1958).

Loughlin, Richard L., "Controlling the Class," *Bulletin of the National Association of Secondary-School Principals*, XLII (November, 1958), pp. 107–111.

McCarthy, Raphael C., S.J., *Training the Adolescent*. (Milwaukee: Bruce, 1934).

Oliva, Peter F., "High School Discipline in American Society," *Bulletin of the National Association of Secondary-School Principals*, XL (January, 1956), pp. 1–103.

Ritholz, Sophie, *Children's Behavior*. (New York: Bookman Associates, 1959).

Sheviakov, George V., and Fritz Redl, *Discipline for Today's Children and Youth*, rev. by Richardson. (Washington: ASCD, NEA, 1956).

Stack, Philip L., *A National Study of the Guidance Services in Catholic Secondary Schools*. (Washington, D.C.: Catholic University of America Press, 1958).

Vedder, Clyde B., *The Juvenile Offender*. (New York: Doubleday, 1954).

NAME INDEX

SUBJECT INDEX